Library of
Davidson College

THE AMERICAN NAVAL HERITAGE IN BRIEF

BY PAOLO E. COLETTA

University Press
of America™

359
C694a

Copyright © 1978 by

University Press of America, Inc.™

4710 Auth Place, S.E., Washington D.C. 20023

All rights reserved

Printed in the United States of America

ISBN: 0-8191-0390-4

Library of Congress Card Catalog Number: 78- 68813

To those who serve the U.S. Navy or wish to learn about its glorious heritage.

ACKNOWLEDGMENTS

Many friends have helped with this work. Constructive comments were provided by Dr. Gerald E. Wheeler, Dean, Social Sciences, San Jose State University. Although I have studied naval administration for twenty years, I hasten to acknowledge that I have edited essays written on various secretaries of the Navy, apologize if I have unconsciously mingled any one else's ideas with mine, and assume full responsibility for any errors in the text. These authors and their subjects are: Frank L. Owsley (Robert Smith, Paul Hamilton, William Jones); Edward Hall (B.W. Crowninshield, Smith Thompson, S.L. Southard); K. Jack Bauer (David Henshaw, Thomas Gilmer, John Y. Mason, George Bancroft, Dan A. Kimball, and Robert B. Anderson); Paul T. Heffron (W.H. Moody, Paul Morton, Charles J. Bonaparte, Victor Metcalf, and Truman Newberry); Roger Heller (Curtis D. Wilbur); Allison Saville (Claude Swanson and Charles Edison); George Lobdell (Frank Knox); Gerald E. Wheeler (Edwin Denby and Charles F. Adams); Joseph Zikmund (James V. Forrestal); Rear Admiral John W. Wadleigh, USN (Ret.) (Charles Thomas, Thomas S. Gates, William B. Franke); Captain Paul S. Schratz, USN (Ret.) (John Connally, Fred Korth, and Paul Nitze); and Captain Paul Ryan, USN (Ret.) (Paul R. Ignatius and John H. Chafee). Last, I must thank my wife Maria, son Bernarr, and daughter Paula Maria for their patience while I researched and wrote.

THE AMERICAN NAVAL HERITAGE IN BRIEF

CONTENTS

	Acknowledgments	ii
	Introduction	v
1.	Concepts and Definitions	1
2.	Seaborne Weapons Systems and Tactics: The European Heritage	6
3.	The Age of Expansion: Ships, Colonies, and Wars	26
4.	A Century of Wars, 1689-1763	34
5.	Two American Declarations of Independence .	52
6.	The War of the American Revolution	66
7.	A Chip on the European War Table, 1783-1815	74
8.	The U.S. Navy at Peace and War, 1815-1861 .	94
9.	Naval Power and the American Civil War, 1861-1865	116
10.	The Post-Civil War Denouement and the Rise of a New Navy, 1865-1898	138
11.	The Spanish-American War	150
12.	The U.S. Navy Comes of Age, 1898-1914 . . .	166
13.	Naval Power and World War I: Europe, 1914-1917	178
14.	The U.S. Navy in World War I, 1917-1919 . .	196
15.	Naval Disarmament and Rearmament, 1918-1941	218
16.	The Coming of World War II	250
17.	World War II in European Waters	258

18.	The U.S. Navy in World War II: Atlantic Theater	282
19.	World War II in the Pacific. Part I: From Pearl Harbor to Guadalcanal	304
20.	World War II in the Pacific. Part II: The Campaign against Rabaul	324
21.	World War II in the Pacific. Part III: The Dual Advance and the End of the Japanese Empire	344
22.	The Cold War and American Defense Organization, 1945-1950	380
23.	Korea and Continued Communist Containment, 1950-1961	402
24.	Kennedy, Johnson, and Sea Power in the Sixties	438
25.	The Challenge of the Soviet Navy	462
26.	Sea Power for the 1980s	486
	Bibliography	506
	Index	612

INTRODUCTION

A. BIBLIOGRAPHICAL AIDS. The objectives of this work are to briefly outline the American naval heritage and to provide a working bibliography. Because of the brevity of the work, references to many books and especially to periodical articles have been omitted.* Further bibliographical information can be found in

REF
Z6834
H5A4
 Albion, Robert G. Naval and Maritime History: An Annotated Bibliography, 4th ed. rev. and expanded (Mystic, Conn: Munson Institute of American Maritime History, 1972).

REF
Z1249
.M5G83
 Higham, Robin, ed. A Guide to the Sources of United States Military History (Hamden, Conn.: Archon Books, 1975).

REF
Z6835
.U5S6
 Smith, Myron J. The American Navy: A Bibliography, 5 vols. (Metuchen, N.J.: Scarecrow Press, 1973-1975).

REF
Z6207
.W8S57
 _____. World War II at Sea: A Bibliography on Sources in English, 3 vols. (Metuchen, N.J.: Scarecrow Press, 1976).

For articles, see among others:

Armed Forces Journal; Armed Forces Management; American Historical Review; American Neptune; Army, Navy, Air Force Journal; Army, Navy, Air Force Register; Army & Navy Chronicle; Army and Navy Journal; American Political Science Review; Air University Review; Aviation Week; Journal of American History; Mariner's Mirror (British); Military Affairs; Marine Corps Gazette; Military Review (British); Naval Aviation News; U.S. Naval Institute Proceedings; U.S. Naval War College Review.

---

* I have taken the liberty to shorten the names of some book publishing firms. Books without call numbers have been published so recently that the Library of Congress call numbers are unavailable.

For maps and battle diagrams, see:

        Martin, Gilbert. *First World War Atlas* (New York: Macmillan, 1973).

V63 .N55P67	Potter, E.B. and Chester W. Nimitz, eds. *Sea Power: A Naval History* (Englewood Cliffs, N.J.: Prentice-Hall, 1960).
G1038 .Y6	Young, Peter ed. *Atlas of the Second World War* (New York: Putnam, 1974).

For ships, see:

VA61 .B37	Bauer, Karl Jack. *Ships of the Navy, 1775-1969* (Troy, N.Y.: Rensselaer Polytechnic Institute, 1970). Vol. 1. *Combat Vessels*.
VA61 .A53	*Dictionary of American Fighting Ships*, 6 vols. (Washington: Naval History Division, 1959-).
VA61 .S47	Fahey, James Charles. *The Ships and Aircraft of the United States Fleet* (Various publishers, 1939-).
VA40 .F523	Jane, Frederick T. *Jane's Fighting Ships* (Various publishers, 1898-).

For chronology, see:

REF E182 .C73	Cooney, David. *Chronology of the U.S. Navy, 1776-1975* (New York: Franklin Watts, 1965).
V53 .N38	*Naval and Maritime Chronology* [from ten years of the *Naval Review* (Annapolis, Md.: Naval Institute Press, 1973).
REF Z1242 .N35	Nevins, Allan, James I. Robertson, Jr., and Bill I. Wiley, eds. *Civil War Books: A Critical Bibliography*, 2 vols. (Baton Rouge: Louisiana State University Press, 1967).
V23 .U546	USMC. *A Chronology of the U.S. Marine Corps* (Washington: HQ, USMC, 1965).
V10	*U.S. Naval Institute Proceedings*, the May issue entitled *Naval Review*: an annual since 1962.

D769   Williams, Mary H., comp. *Chronology, 1941-*
.A533 *1945* (Washington: OCMH, 1960).
v.8

For current American military posture statements, which supersede the annual reports of the Secretary of the Navy, Secretary of War, and annual and semi-annual reports of the Secretary of Defense, see:

> (Name of) Chairman of the Joint Chiefs of Staff, *United States Military Posture for FY ___* (Washington: CHINFO).
>
> *CNO Statement ... 20 July 1976*, and *CNO Report ... April 1977* (Washington: CHINFO).

For the naval profession, see:

VB259 Calvert, James. *The Naval Profession*, rev.
.C28   ed. (New York: McGraw-Hill, 1971).

UB210 Roskill, Stephen Wentworth. *The Art of Lead-*
.R6   *ership* (London: Collins, 1964).

B. THE INFLUENCE OF SEA POWER. Not an end in itself, sea power is one of the agencies used by countries in conducting their international relations. These methods include military power, economic warfare, diplomacy, and propaganda. Sea power may be defined more broadly than naval power, for it includes a host of elements such as a merchant marine, a population versed in seagoing skills, shipbuilding facilities, adequate harbors and yards, and a fishing fleet, as well as other factors. Nevertheless, the thrust of this study is directed primarily toward showing how navies have been used in the conduct of international relations to advance the national interest in peace and war. Particularly in time of war, the naval officer is called upon to exercise his professional knowledge and skill in supporting the national interest.

His gaining command of the sea, for example, may permit the transport of troops, launching of amphibious attacks, bombing of enemy targets, and logistic support of bases overseas. In time of peace, his major responsibilities include training for war, administering the service, advising civilian authorities in possible uses for naval power, and conducting research and development.

In the United States, civil authorities are legally responsible for the determination of grand strategy and national policy, such as whether the nation should support its interests by peaceful or belligerent means. The civilian authorities customarily make the decision on the advice of both civilian and military leaders. Civil authorities also allocate the logistic support for the method chosen. The naval officer then, at the highest level, advises on the proper strategy and at the lower levels implements the decision by undertaking appropriate tactics.

In ancient days this involved fighting ships under oars and sails; in the 19th century, steam ships; in modern times nuclear-powered ships. In ancient days the naval officer directed fighting with ships armed with rams and grappling devices; in the 19th century with long-range guns; in modern times with aircraft, missiles, torpedoes, and nuclear bombs.

C. CHRONOLOGY AND TOPICALITY. Page vii of the Preface of Potter and Nimitz, eds., <u>Sea Power</u>, states that the text "develops six main themes: (1) The influence of sea power upon history, (2) the reasoning behind strategic decisions; (3) the characteristics of successful leadership, (4) the evolution of naval weapons; (5) the evolution of naval tactics, and (6) the evolution of amphibious doctrine." These are excellent themes to develop throughout the sweep of naval history. However, to these should be added (7): The evolution of naval organization and administration.

Chronology runs forward; topics cut through time even if they are developed chronologically. To illustrate, take the last theme. There is no one particular place either in the text devoted entirely or even largely to the topic. It behooves the student to dig out material dealing with this topic and arrange it in logical order. For example, there was no American Secretary of the Navy until 1798. The first secretary, Benjamin Stoddert, established his own organization and followed what he considered good principles of administration. Changes came with the creation of the Board of Navy Commissioners in 1815, the adoption of the Bureau system in 1842 (expanded

during the Civil War and thereafter), the establishment
of the Office of the Chief of Naval Operations in
1915, the growth during World War II of the system
of the Joint Chiefs of Staff, and, last, changes in
naval organization and administration in keeping with
the National Security Act of 1947 as amended a number
of times.

D. WARS AND BATTLES. The following outline will serve
to study wars and battles:

    (1) The strategic situation prior to the battle;
    (2) Forces and leaders involved on both sides;
    (3) Tactics followed by both sides;
    (4) Tactical and strategic results of the battle.

In such extensive wars as the Anglo-Dutch Wars,
Seven Years' War, and War of the American Revolution,
battles may well be studied for their influence upon
the development of weapons and of tactics. The same
idea applies to modern wars, such as those involving
the United States and Spain, World War I, World War II,
Korea, and Southeast Asia. Compare, for example,
destroyer doctrine in World War I and World War II.

E. AMPHIBIOUS DOCTRINE. The success or failure of
an amphibious operation may be gauged by testing it
against the following items included in U.S. Marine
Corps amphibious doctrine:

1. Integral command
2. Thorough logistical and tactical planning
3. Effective reconnaissance
4. Realistic rehearsal
5. Combat unit loading
6. Balanced fleet fire support
7. Armored assault craft
8. Powerful ship to shore movement
9. Early commitment of reserves
10. Prompt and steady flow of supply across the beach
11. Aggressive exploitation.

F. CRITERIA FOR A LANDING AREA. Amphibious doctrine
sets out seven criteria for a landing area. As given
in the 1952 edition of USF-6, then the Navy's amphibious bible, these are:

1. Ability of naval forces to support the assault and

follow-up operations;

2. Shelter from unfavorable sea and weather;

3. Compatibility of the beaches and their approaches to the size, draft, maneuverability, and beaching characteristics of the assault ships and landing craft;

4. Offshore hydrography (i.e., water depths and bottom configuration);

5. The extent of minable water (any depth less than a hundred fathoms--600 feet--is considered minable, although currents also affect minability);

6. Conditions which may affect the enemy's ability to defeat mine-clearance efforts by the attacking force;

7. Facilities for unloading shipping; and how these may be improved.

U.S. Naval Academy
Annapolis, Md.
15 August 1977

Paolo E. Coletta

CHAPTER 1

I. CONCEPTS AND DEFINITIONS

Every nation has a domestic and a foreign policy. Democratic societies follow principles designed to bring the greatest happiness to the greatest number of its people; totalitarian regimes subordinate the standard of living of their peoples to the end that state power may be augmented. The degree to which a state achieves its foreign policy objectives is a partial measure of its power. A primary objective of all states is peace, obtained either by channeling the state's resources and energies into peaceful pursuits and an adequate defensive posture, or into diplomacy, or as a last resort to war. By diplomacy, a nation seeks to satisfy its desires by peaceful negotiation and to obtain advantages without arousing hostility. Nations may also use economic warfare and propaganda to seek their objectives. War is the forcible answering of problems that cannot be solved by peaceful means. Peace is the ultimate goal in both defensive and offensive war, albeit the one seeks to prevent conquest and the other to impose it.

National <u>military</u> policy may be envisaged as a frame of reference supported by a tripod composed of strategy, tactics, and logistics. The three legs are mutually supporting; national military objectives cannot be obtained without the cooperation of all three. Other conditions remaining equal, the limit to which a nation can exercise strength is determined by the availability of logistic support.

II. STRATEGY

Collins defines <u>Grand strategy</u> as "the art and science of employing national power under all circumstances to exert desired degrees and types of control over the opposition through threats, force, indirect pressures, diplomacy, subterfuge, and other imaginative means, thereby satisfying national security interests and objectives." In another instance he defines it simply as "the art and science of options" available to a nation for seeking its objectives. The great Helmuth von Moltke defined <u>strategy</u> as "the practical adaptation of the means placed at a general's disposal to the attainment of the object in view"; Liddell Hart as "the art of distributing and applying military means to fulfil the ends of policy."

More simply, <u>grand strategy</u> includes the determination at the highest state level of whether to seek the solution of policies by military force. If the answer is affirmative, decisions must then be made as to <u>when</u> and <u>where</u> to act (e.g., when operations should begin in what theaters and for what objectives). <u>Strategy</u> employed by civil or military leaders involves <u>where</u> to act in a theater, campaign, or battle and also involves objectives, communications lines, positions, how to achieve concentration, and whether to proceed by offensive or defensive measures.

A. OBJECTIVES IN WARFARE. Objectives may be physical, e.g., the destruction of an enemy vessel, but the purpose of the action should implement a larger objective, i.e., the destruction of the enemy naval vessel will reduce the enemy's sea power. Such destruction may be for the further purpose of cutting off the enemy's war-making potential, his sources of food and fuel; his communications; to demoralize the enemy; to force him from the theater of operations; or to make possible the occupation of his homeland. Each valid objective attained on the tactical level should aid in the attainment of the strategic objective of disarming the enemy morally, economically, or militarily, thereby lessening his will to resist and forcing him to abandon his intentions and submit to ours. Success will lead to the attainment of the prime objective, peace, and a more advantageous position in the post-war world. Failure of course will lead to loss of morale, perhaps of territory or population, lower one's credibility, and lessen prestige in the post-war world.

Wars are most often won on the land, with navies supporting ground forces by sea and/or air action. The naval strategist therefore seeks to select those objectives the attainment of which will contribute most to the main decision.

III. TACTICS

To Collins, tactics are "The detailed methods used to carry out strategic designs." They are the art of handling operational forces in battle. The <u>how</u> of war, they must respond rapidly to technological changes. A countermeasure must be devised for every enemy measure. Galleys fought in line abreast because their armament was forward and their exposed oars made their sides vulnerable. Sailing ships used column formation in order to unmask broadside fire. While turreted steamships still use the column formation, carriers employ a circular protective screen. With the advent of atomic weapons, survival has been sought in dispersion rather than in concentration.

Concentration-- defined as the economical handling of forces so as to bring overpowering strength at the right place at the right time--applies to tactics as well as to strategy. The alert commander will keep his forces close enough for mutual support, bring superior force against an inferior enemy force (or part of it), and prevent the enemy from employing concentration against his forces. In the end, pincers, enveloping movements, and "capping the T" tactics have concentration as their objective. Tactical concentration is superbly illustrated in Horatio Nelson's actions in the Battle of the Nile (1798) and at Trafalgar (1805), again by the Japanese while using split-forces in the battle of Tsushima. Using similar split-force tactics at the battles of Midway and Leyte Gulf, however, the Japanese failed to achieve concentration.

IV. LOGISTICS

Logistics is the science of providing, moving, and maintaining military forces, the means or the what of war. The implementation of both strategic and tactical decisions depends upon the provision of adequate logistic support.

Logistics is concerned with materiel, personnel, facilities, and services. For an operational force it generally includes supply; maintenance, repair, and salvage; medical services; personnel services; transportation; and construction. Part of the mission of a fleet is to control sea communications and maritime bases; thus a fleet may help determine what forces are available to either side by protecting its own bases and sea routes and destroying or denying the use of bases and sea routes to the enemy.

Galleys rarely operated far from shore. Sailing

ships were freed from intimate dependence on the land and developed great sea-keeping capacity. Steam again chained ships to bases and in part provoked the world contest for bases in the 19th century. In World War II, the U.S. Service Force freed combatant ships from dependence on the Zone of the Interior by building forward bases (complete facilities except for repairing extensive battle damage) and providing Mobile Logistic Support. The latter included Mobile Support Groups (services afloat and/or ashore, generally in a sheltered lagoon or bay, except for major repairs) and Underway Replenishment Groups (fast ships that supplied operational forces with vital items for limited periods by transfer-at-sea methods). Atomic propulsion has freed warships from dependence on bases for fuel supplies and has apparently limited the operational capacity of atom-powered ships to their food supplies and to the psychological stamina of their crews.

V. DISPUTING, SECURING, AND EXERCISING COMMAND OF THE SEA

Control of (command of) the sea is the prime objective of naval warfare. Three stages may mark the attainment of this objective--disputing command, securing command, and exercising command.

1. <u>Disputing Command</u>. Removal of the menace of the enemy fleet in early days was sometimes accomplished in a single action, e.g., the battles of Lepanto, 1571, Trafalgar, 1805, Manila Bay and Santiago de Cuba, 1898.

In modern warfare enemy submarines and air power may remain after surface forces have been destroyed. Raiding, blockading, mining, and commerce raiding are methods of disputing command of the sea where it is not already held, and may be the only methods afforded a weak naval power against a stronger one. A respectable "fleet in being" often acts as a powerful deterrent to aggression. Of course command may be secured and exercised in one or more areas while limited in others.

2. <u>Exercising Command</u>. A nation exercises command by defending its own seaborne commerce and supply, destroying the enemy's seaborne commerce and supply,

defending and supporting its own military forces transported by sea, and by destroying enemy military forces. In sum, the prime mission of a navy is to gain command of the sea and deny its use to the enemy. Secondary missions of a navy may include preparing the way for and conducting amphibious operations and giving strategic and tactical support to forces ashore.

The primary peacetime function of a navy is to prepare to fight <u>the next</u> war. A navy may also support national policies by shows of force.

CHAPTER 2

SEABORNE WEAPONS SYSTEMS AND TACTICS:
THE EUROPEAN HERITAGE

I. LONG SHIPS

A. EARLY GALLEYS. Long ships--galleys--were the capital ships of the navies of the Mediterranean and of certain northern peoples (e.g., of the Vikings and of Alfred of England). They had beautiful lines, with length about six times the measure of breadth. By the 5th century B.C., specialized versions included the bireme (two banks of oars) and the trireme (three banks of oars), each with three masts. Oars were used primarily in battle, sails for cruising or flight. Top rowing speed was about 8 knots per hour. A typical trireme of the 5th century B.C., was 150 feet long, carried 30 warriors and 170 rowers. Since the primary tactical objective of the galley commander was to pit soldier against soldier rather than ship against ship, grappling and boarding tactics prevailed. The <u>corvus</u> (first tested in 260 B.C.) and the <u>harpago</u> (first century B.C.) were devices to facilitate grappling. By the first century B.C., towers had been introduced fore and aft to provide platforms for archers, javelin throwers, and mechanical artillery. The largest Roman galleys carried four to ten banks of oars and towers several stories high. The ram made the long ship a ship-killer as well as a man killer, and fire power grew as the arquebus replaced the bow and arrow, the musket the arquebus, and cannon the musket.

B. GALLEON, GALLEASS, AND SHIPS OF THE LINE. A galleon was a large and clumsy vessel with three masts and three or four decks. It carried so much tophamper and was so overweighted that it could carry little canvas even in smooth waters and slight winds. A galleass was a heavy, sluggish vessel with a deck above the oarsmen on which as many as 30 guns were placed in broadside.

Since no practical method of determining longitude was developed until the 17th century and galleys could not survive in the long Atlantic swells, galley types were generally restricted to the Mediterranean where also, slave rowers were generally available.

Fine tactical weapons, they were strategically unsuitable: they were unproductive between wars, and they could not be used as cargo carriers. Although armed with guns and tremendously increased in size by the 16th century, galleys were now matched in power by the sailing ships.

Type and placement of weapons determined galley tactics. While galleys might cruise in column, they fought in line abreast, a formation that protected their vulnerable sides and presented the fighting part of the ship to the enemy. If the Battle of Lepanto, 1571, proved a draw between galley and galleon, the Battle of the Spanish Armada definitely proved the superiority of the sailing ship.

II. ROUND SHIP TO NAVAL VESSEL

A. THE ROUND SHIP. The kings of western Europe, frugal men who would not finance specially designed fighting ships, rented merchant ships for war service. The typical 14th century merchant ship was short, potbellied (average length was but twice the beam) and propelled by a single square sail of ample proportions. In contrast to the long ship, it was a fine strategic weapon but a poor tactical weapon. It rode well, was seaworthy, and possessed great sea endurance, but was so unmaneuverable that it could not be used in formation. Acting independently in battle, it used grappling and boarding tactics. The need for protection for the troops it transported led to the addition of "military works." An early refinement consisted of the erection of flimsy temporary towers (castles) fore and aft. These served as shelters and also provided height from which to hurl arrows, stones, hot pitch, and other weapons down upon the enemy. By the middle of the 15th century, forecastles and after- (or somer-) castles were regular features of the northern Round Ship. A cargo carrier in peace, a transport in time of war, the Round Ship gradually was developed into a new creature, a ship of the line. Refinements included using three, even four, rather than two masts and adding topmasts and courses and a spritsail under the bowsprit. Square rigged except for a lateen mizzen, and with high bows capable of standing up to high seas, the ship of the line could sail close to the wind and undertake long voyages. Sailing was also made easier, about the mid-15th century, by the provision of dependable clocks, sailing directions, and the magnetic compass, the latter followed by the compass rose. By about 1500, geographical globes and maritime charts were also available.

B. THE INFLUENCE OF THE GUN.

   1. <u>Adoption of the Muzzle-loader</u>. So long as guns were light and were used against personnel, they could readily be accommodated in strengthened and enlarged castles. The earliest cannon may have been used at Crecy, 1346. A small bore breech-loader was placed on an English ship in 1410. By 1485, castles were stout enough to support several guns. Henry VIII's revolutionary <u>Regent</u> carried 225 guns. These were man-killers rather than ship-killers. When experiments with various types of cannon resulted in the universal adoption of the heavy muzzle-loader, the trim of the ship was radically affected. Since the guns could not go "upstairs," they must go below.

   2. <u>Broadsides</u>. Parsimonious Henry VII of England rented ships as he needed them. Henry VIII, however, built a few specialized fighting ships. Typical of these first battleships was the <u>Henri Grace a Dieu</u> (<u>Great Harry</u>). The weight of muzzle-loaders drove Henry VIII's carpenters to adopt an Italian innovation and take the guns from the castles and put them along the sides of the ship, mostly in the waist; by cutting ports in the sides for the guns they introduced broadsides. Henceforth, round ships would be ship-destroyers as well as man-killers. A new sort of warfare had been devised, and the days of galleys and of grappling and boarding tactics were numbered.

C. NEW SHIP DESIGNS. England led the way in specialized warship design. Even in Henry VIII's day the high fore-and-after-castles were coming down and length of ship was increasing relative to beam. While lighter ships with low freeboard were built specifically as gun platforms, the standard English warship of 1550 was the flushdecked, low freeboard vessel of three or more beams length. Clinker-built gave way to carvel-built designs, with square rather than round sterns, and increased tumble-home permitted placing heavy ordnance nearer the center line.

Gun recoil was taken care of by lines and bolts to the heavy ships' sides. The forecastle, a prime target for the enemy, went first, the after-castle lingering on as the poop before it disappeared. Increased mobility was provided by increasing the length-beam ratio from three to one to six to one and by augmenting sails. Demand for even greater mobility led to the development of the galleass, a ship of the line that could be sailed or rowed. The British thus began with a round ship and developed a ship of the line. In contrast, the Spanish began with a galley and tried to add a broadside to it. The result, a hybrid also called a galleass, worked well against galleys but not against a ship of the line. The Round (Great) Ship that England abandoned, however, was retained by Spain for use in Atlantic waters.

III. SAILING SHIP CHARACTERISTICS

The problem of taking a ship anywhere, no matter what the direction of the wind, is solved by a combination of sail-plan and hull design that will make the wind propel the vessel towards and across as well as away from the wind. The sails of a windmill spin at right angles to the wind. Substitute the <u>bite</u> of the keel of a ship for the windmill and set the sails as nearly across the wind as possible and the ship will move forward <u>against</u> the wind. The best balance between sail and trim of a square rigger will result in a course to within four points (one point is about $11\frac{1}{2}°$) of the wind. Thus, if the wind is from the N, the ship will travel NE (port tack) or NW (starboard tack). <u>Tacking</u>, <u>beating</u>, and <u>reaching</u> all refer to the zigzag manner of sailing <u>against</u> the wind. The typical square rigger could sail about six points into the wind, the typical <u>fore-and-aft</u> rigged ship to within two points. <u>Wearing</u> is to put a ship across the wind keeping the wind behind the ship--running right off and coming up again with the wind on the other side.

IV. THE CLASSIFICATION OF SAILING SHIPS

A. RATES, NOMENCLATURE, AND RIGS.

1. <u>Rates</u>. Warships in the days of sail were designated by the number of guns they carried and

were divided into classes in accordance with the arrangement of their guns and the functions they performed. The major rates were:

    First Rate--a ship of 100 guns or more.
    Second Rate--a ship of 90 to 98 guns.
    Third Rate--a ship of 60 to 80 guns.
    Fourth Rate--a ship of 50 to 60 guns.
    Fifth Rate--a ship of 32 to 44 guns.
    Sixth Rate--a ship of 20 to 32 guns.

    2. <u>Nomenclature</u>. A 2,000 ton ship of the line, 16th to early 19th centuries, would crowd 1,000 officers and men and their gear aboard. It would contain seven levels but not seven decks.

<u>Deck</u>--an unbroken, permanent platform extending the full length of the ship.

<u>Platform deck</u>--partial deck above, between, or below a full deck.

<u>Quarterdeck</u>--the forward part of the aftercastle extended a variable distance from the stern.

<u>Poop</u>--a short, raised deck covering about the after third of the quarterdeck.

<u>Forecastle</u>--a short deck extending from the stem or slightly abaft the stem to a point about half way back toward the foremast.

<u>Orlop</u>--the lowest full deck. No ports or light. Astern, in the <u>After Cockpit</u>, messed the midshipmen and sublieutenants; it also served as a surgical operating room.

<u>Lower deck</u>--first true gun deck. It carried the heaviest (32 pdr.) guns. Its cross bulkheads were removable to facilitate fighting the guns. Here bunked and messed the bulk of the seamen, with 14 inches of space allowed per hammock! Livestock was housed forward.

<u>Middle deck</u>--carried the 24 pdr. guns. Aft were the wardroom and the side or stern galleries used by the lieutenants; forward was the galley (kitchen).

Main deck--home of the 18 pdrs. Aft were the admiral's stateroom and stern and quarter galleries. Amidships was the waist, between the gangways, with the quarterdeck forward, the poop aft, and the captain's stateroom below the poop.

Hold--space for ballast heavy stowage, fish locker, and spirits room. The magazines, always guarded by marines, were forward.

3. Rigs. The lateen sail of the Mediterranean and Indian Oceans and the lug sail of northern waters are examples of fore-and-aft rigs, in which the sail lies along the line of the keel. The Egyptians, Greeks, Phoenicians, and Romans used square sails. While the Romans also used a small headsail (spritsail) to help the ship go to windward, it was somehow lost and not rediscovered until the 15th century. The use of one mast was customary until the 14th century.

The most popular ship of the 16th century had three masts and was square-rigged, i.e., its sails ran crosswise. Beginning towards the bows, the masts were the foremast, mainmast, and mizzenmast. Sails were named after their masts. Thus the lower courses are foresail, mainsail, and mizzensail. If topmasts are added, the sails become fore-topsail, main-topsail, and mizzen-topsail. A third upper mast is called a top gallant mast, with sails named accordingly. A fourth upper mast is called the royal mast, with sails also named accordingly.

In the last quarter of the 18th century the full rigged ship appeared. This was a hybrid, square-rigged except for two fore-and-aft sails, a jib sail forward and an after mizzenmast with a lateen sail and a square topsail (spanker).

Most of the major types of sailing vessels were square-rigged. A ship had three masts, all square rigged. A vessel square-rigged on all masts but the last, which was fore-and-aft rigged, was a barque (bark). A brig was square-rigged on two masts. Barquantines and brigantines were square-rigged on the foremast only. A schooner was fore-and-aft rigged or partly square-rigged (topsail schooner). The Dutch pioneered in the use of the fore-and-aft rig.

On sailing ships, the <u>standing rigging</u> stands--it provides rigid support for the masts, while the <u>running rigging</u> runs--its function is to control the movement of sails and yards.

B. THE SHIP OF THE LINE.

    1. <u>Design</u>. Wooden warship design proceeded in a vicious circle of trying to get the best possible combination of strength, speed, and firepower. Technological weaknesses in guns made it necessary to use guns in large number. Too much weight caused wooden hulls to "hog," or sag at the ends, and also reduced speed. And more sails for more speed meant larger, stronger, and heavier ships with larger crews and greater cargo-carrying capacity. Hogging effectively limited wooden ships to a length of about 200 feet and to 2,500 tons burden. Two-deckers and three-deckers appeared in the first half of the 17th century, but no nation built a really good four-decker. By the end of the 18th century it was generally agreed that the 74-gun ship was the smallest vessel that could "lie in the line." The 74's were the most numerous and proved the most useful ships of the line.

    Oar tillers gave way to side rudders and the latter to rudders with tillers. Tillers were placed near the right side of the ship. Since the helmsman looked forward, the right side became the "steerboard" or starboard side of the ship. The whip staff of 1500 (a long staff extending through the decks from the helmsman on the main deck to the rudder) gave way to the wheel about 1700. Pitch and lead proved unsuitable for underwater protection, but by about 1750 copper was found quite acceptable. The British navy ordered copper for all ships in 1783.

    The French were the best ship designers, with the Dutch next, the Spanish third, and the British last. In the 18th century, a French 50 was considered equal to an English 74. The English learned much about design from French prizes taken in the first half of the 18th century. Although a School of Naval Architecture was established at Portsmouth in 1810, the English earned their great distinction in the design and construction of iron ships.

2. **A Typical 18th Century First Rate Ship**.
A first rate ship of the line had the following
dimensions: 2,290 tons (4,000 tons displacement);
gun deck, 190 feet; beam, 52 feet; draught, 21 feet;
and crew of 900 men. It would have 32 pounders on
the lower deck, 24 pdrs. on the middle deck, 18 pdrs.
on the upper deck, 12 pdrs. on the quarterdeck and
forecastle.

   3. **A Typical 18th Century 74**. A two-decker 74
of the 18th century had the following dimensions:
1,650 tons burden (2,000 tons displacement); main
deck, 170 feet; beam, 47 feet; draught, 18 feet; 650
men. Guns would include: 32 pdrs. on the lower deck,
18 pdrs. on the upper deck, and 9 pdrs, on the
quarterdeck and forecastle.

C. FRIGATES. "Frigate" traditionally meant any
ship-rigged single-decked man-of-war. Another dis-
tinguishing feature was its carrying of a secondary
battery on its quarterdeck. It was built for speed
and carried 28 to 30 guns. Too small to lie in the
line, its mobility made it useful in scouting,
patrolling, convoying, blockading, and "flag showing."

   After about 1750 frigates grew in size and in
firepower. During the Napoleonic period, 36 to 44
gun frigates were larger, better, and faster than
their predecessors and performed yeoman service.
France and Spain led in this development.

   The big United States frigates of 1797 were in
a class by themselves. The size of 74s, they had the
structural characteristics of frigates and could
outrun anything they could not outfight. They established an entirely new class of cruiser, one soon
standard in all navies. A somewhat earlier British
experiment with 64s designed to supplant the 74s
proved a dismal failure, and none were built after
the American Revolution.

D. SLOOPS-OF-WAR (Fr. *Corvette*). In the first half
of the 18th century a sloop was a single-decked,
two-masted man-of-war. In the second half of the
century the term was applied almost solely to the
ship-rigged single-deckers too small to have armed
quarterdecks. From a length of from 90 to 110 feet,
sloops, like frigates, grew in size and were more

heavily armed. By the 19th century few sloops had guns above decks, resulting in a completely flush deck. While the French led in sloop design, the Americans were close behind with the __Wasp__ class of 1813. Powerful, fast, clean ships, sloops were used for commerce raiding and privateer hunting.

E. MISCELLANEOUS. All navies contained brigs, schooners, and bomb ketches. __Brigs__ (square-rigged on two masts) and __schooners__ (fore-and-aft rigged on two masts) averaged 80-90 feet in length and were used mostly as privateer hunters and in the suppression of piracy, including the slave trade. __Bomb ketches__ were smaller (70-90 feet) and carried one or two large (10-15-inch) mortars for use against land fortifications. They were tactically limited because they had to moor for action, but their firepower proved invaluable in shore bombardment. __Gunboats__ (up to 70 feet, one gun up to an 18 pdr.) were designed to provide gunfire support in amphibious operations.

V. NAVAL WARFARE UNDER THE FIGHTING INSTRUCTIONS

Naval tactics prior to 1650 were almost identical with those used on land, but after 1650 such tactics proved unsuitable at sea. With broadsides, the direction of attack ceased to be the same as the line of advance, and operated at right angles to it. In consequence, long-range replaced melee tactics and line ahead replaced the line abreast formation. Directives were of course issued by commanders to their subordinates for action in battle. Those directives issued by supreme British naval authorities to commanders are known as __Fighting Instructions__. An early example of the latter are those issued by Sir Walter Raleigh in 1617, which reveal derivations from directives issued as early as 1578. In 1652 there first appeared the Articles of War, 39 in number, that laid the basis for modern ones.

A. THE DEVELOPMENT OF "LINE AHEAD" TACTICS. Probably the first book on "the science of movement by sail" was the two-volume __Naval Armada__ by an Italian, Pantero Pantera (1614). Although the Spanish Armada campaign shows the English groping toward a practical system of handling a fleet of ships of the line, the Early Stuart period was one of retrogression in this matter, leaving the discovery of how to handle ships in line ahead to the Generals-at-Sea of the First Dutch War, especially Robert Blake, George Monk, and Sir William Penn. In 1653 Blake issued a set of <u>Fighting Instructions</u> which proved a milestone in the evolution of naval tactics. Any formation but line ahead caused ships to mask each other's fire and to expose bows and sterns to raking fire from the enemy. More important, line ahead enabled a fleet to achieve unity of action and massing of fire. Therefore Article 3 established the <u>fleet line ahead</u> that was maintained until almost World War II. In consequence, armed merchant ships disappeared from battle lines.

After the Battle of the Gabbard (2-4 June 1655), the Dutch, who had been using divisions in line abreast, also adopted the line ahead. The British, however, had refined their tactics by adopting the close-hauled line. They set their sails back so as to sail as nearly against the wind as possible, making their ships more responsive to the helm and putting the entire line under better control.

The fleet line ahead was thoroughly established in the English Navy for the century following the Battle of Scheveningen (30 June 1653). Henceforth, too, those ships deemed fit to "lie in the line" were distinguished from smaller types by the designation ship-of-the-line (or <u>line of battle ships</u>, or <u>battleships</u>, or simply <u>ships</u>). Although some signal books, such as that of the Duke of York, were written (1673), no work on the science of naval evolutions appeared following Pantera until 1697, in the <u>Treatise of Naval Evolutions</u> written by the Jesuit Father Paul Haste, chaplain of the fleet of Louis XIV. Improvements appeared in the works of Morogues (1763), Salazar, d'Orvilliers, Nieul, Amblimont, and Chopart, the last published in 1839 when steamships were already plying the seas.

B. THE WINDWARD AND THE LEEWARD POSITIONS. The direction of the wind determined where a naval engagement would take place. Sailing ships could sail no closer than about $65°$ to the wind. Therefore the theater of action between ships could be no more than an area of $130°$ bisected by the wind, and no action was possible in the other sector of $230°$.

15

1. <u>The Weather Gage</u>. In battle the British sought the weather gage (position to windward of the enemy). The wind would drift gun-smoke into the enemy's eyes and float fireships into his battle formation. Ships heeled over by the wind could fire faster because their guns would recoil uphill and roll quickly back to battery. Enemy shots penetrating the hull at the water line were less dangerous because they would be above water when ships came about on the opposite tack. Moreover, the British sought the weather gage because it was the offensive gage. The windward fleet held the initiative and could attack at will. Once the fleet came down to the attack it could not readily disengage; therefore it was committed to reach a decision. England's ships were expendable, and her officers preferred the offensive.

2. <u>The Leeward Position</u>. Ships in the leeward position that were hit between wind and water would plunge these holes under water when they came about. In a brisk wind, however, ships to leeward enjoyed a gunnery advantage in that the ships to windward would be heeled over so far that they could not risk opening the lowest row of gunports on the engaged side and thus were deprived of the use of their heaviest guns. This position favored the <u>defensive</u>. Fleets to leeward could keep open their lines of retreat, and disabled ships could readily disengage. Moreover, since the attacker generally came down bows on, he could be met by broadside fire, and his rigging would be damaged and his mobility impaired before he reached close quarters.

The leeward gage was preferred by France and Spain. These had armies to support and did not consider their ships expendable. The French and Spanish fired on the British as they came down, firing at sails and rigging, and concentrating on the van, while the British fired at hulls. The French and Spanish suffered more casualties, but the French and Spanish found it relatively easy to fall off to leeward after having rendered their opponent powerless. The French and Spanish did not win victories, but they forced the British to return to base for repairs and meantime exercised local command of the sea.

Regardless of position, the Dutch sought close

quarters and fought with great determination. They were the only opponents who matched the British in aggressiveness.

C. THE FORMAL SCHOOL AND THE MELEE SCHOOL. The Second Anglo-Dutch War, 1665-1667, solidified the tactical ideas tried out in the First War. The <u>Fighting Instructions</u> of 1665, issued in the name of James, the Duke of York, added to Blake's the results of experiments tried in the battles of the Gabbard and of Scheveningen. The close-hauled line ahead was prescribed, at least for the leeward position, as was the hundred-yard interval between ships in column.

While the value of the line ahead formation was admitted by all, by 1665 there had arisen in the Royal Navy a dispute over <u>how far</u> the line should be maintained. Both "schools" believed in a line ahead <u>approach</u>, but they disagreed over what to do when in actual contact with the enemy. The battle raged for 40 years and was not actually settled until the last days of sailing ship warfare, during the Napoleonic period. Indeed, it was revived with the Battle of Jutland and with the early Pacific surface actions of World War II.

    1. <u>The Formalists</u>. Formalists wanted to keep the fleet line ahead throughout battle because they could thus achieve full impact, develop maximum firepower, and enable the commander to maintain complete control--he could, thus, exploit any advantage or extricate his fleet. Headed by the Duke of York and Sir William Penn, they also advocated the "conterminous line of battle." This meant that they would close-haul their ships in line ahead to windward and maneuver until their leading ship was exactly opposite the leading ship of the enemy. Remaining just outside of range, they would parallel the enemy, van to van, center to center, rear to rear. Upon signal, all ships would come down on the enemy. The worst position would be when the enemy stood at $90°$, for they could rake, but this was the price the Formalists were willing to pay for the weather gage and the conterminous line. Once more close-hauled, and within range of the enemy, action would commence. In general, ships to windward were not to break the enemy line or go chasing after single enemy units until the enemy fleet had been disabled. Formalism

suffered the disadvantage of sacrificing concentration by spreading force against equal force and making a battle simply a test of brute endurance.

    2. **The Meleeists**. Meleeists used the line head for **approach** but would let ships depart from the line in battle in order to exploit any advantage. The commander would lose control, and the decision would rest upon the initiative of subordinate commanders or individual captains. They would achieve concentration by **massing** superior force against an inferior part of the enemy's force and thus defeat him in detail. Led by George Monk (Duke of Albemarle) and Prince Rupert, the Meleeists sought to adapt land tactics to sea warfare. They advocated:

Massing -- decreasing the interval between ships so as to bring a preponderance of ships and firepower against *a part* of the enemy's line.

Doubling-- putting the enemy between two fires by shifting a part of one's fleet to the far side of the enemy line. This could be done about the van or rear of the enemy line.

Breaking-- going *through* the enemy's line rather than around it. Attacking ships had the advantage of firing double broadsides at the enemy while breaking through.

D. THE APOTHEOSIS OF FORMALISM. In the Battle of Lowestoft, 3 June 1665, with the Duke of York and Penn both present, the Dutch refused to cooperate with the Formalists. Unable to achieve a conterminous line, the Duke of York exploited a hole in the Dutch line and broke through. A year later, Meleeists massed on and broke the Dutch line but suffered greater losses than the Dutch. In the Battle of the Gunfleet, 22 June 1666, Albemarle massed on the Dutch but had his own line broken by the Dutch. Each school claimed victories denied by the other.

    The **Fighting Instructions** of 1672 directed the use of the conterminous line in reverse (van to rear, center to center, and rear to van) when fleets approached from opposite directions, and permitted the breaking of the line from leeward. In the Battle of the Texel (11 August 1673), the most important of the four naval engagements of the Third Anglo-Dutch War, Prince Rupert tried Melee tactics and got somewhat the worst of it.

In the Battle of Beachy Head, 3 June 1690, the Earl of Torrington used the fleet line ahead with Red (Dutch), White, and Blue squadrons from windward. He attempted to mass on the Comte de Tourville's rear with a rear strengthened at the expense of his center and van, which he did not wish to come down. But the Dutch, unfamiliar with his signals, went down. Tourville thereupon slowed them down by pounding their rigging, extended his van, doubled on the Dutch, and mangled them. Torrington saved himself by anchoring with sails set and letting Tourville go by. As a result, naval opinion shifted definitely in favor of Formalism. In keeping with the new attitude, Admiral Edward Russell's new <u>Fighting Instructions</u>, 1691, prescribed the conterminous line in all situations and forbade doubling on the van. Fearing that the enemy might concentrate on part of the English line while they concentrated on his, English tacticians concluded not to concentrate. Their purpose appears defensive, but their major objective was to keep control always in the hands of the commander, regardless of the fact that their system of signals was inadequate. While Russell's <u>Instructions</u> drew upon upon conclusions from the battles fought from the days of Blake through Beachy Head, they leaned heavily on the Formal side and proved a millstone about the neck of the British navy.

For the War of the Spanish Succession (1702-1713), Admiral George Rooke issued his own <u>Fighting Instructions</u> (1703). These are most important because in the long period of peace following the war they became the <u>Permanent Fighting Instructions</u> -- the law. As such they stultified British tactical progress for 90 years.

    1. <u>The Unfortunates</u>. Penalties applied to Admirals Thomas Mathews and John Byng illustrate the weight of Formalism on British tactics.

In the Battle of Toulon (11 February 1744) Thomas Mathews gave chase to a French-Spanish fleet that broke out of Toulon and headed for Brest. Disregarding the <u>Fighting Instructions</u>, he came down van to center, center to rear, rear to the empty sea. The British van and center were badly battered; only one prize was taken, and the rest of the enemy ships got away. Following an investigation and court martial, Mathews was cashiered. It was bruited about that Mathews was broken for having failed to follow the <u>Fighting Instructions</u>, with subsequent pernicious effect upon British tactics. Henceforth the conterminous line would be maintained inviolable except by the brashest officer.

John Byng was directed both to relieve Minorca, under French siege, and to protect Gibraltar. On the morning of 19 May 1756, he stood becalmed off Port Mahon, Minorca. When the Marquis de la Galissionere appeared to windward, Byng turned south to obtain the weather gage. Byng led the van division, Rear Admiral Temple West the rear division. The fleets approached on roughly reciprocal courses, with Byng to the south on an easterly course. Byng planned to reverse course and come down on Galissionere at a 45° angle, one which would permit the use of his broadsides. Unfortunately for him, this slanting or oblique approach was not clearly described in the <u>Fighting Instructions</u>, and his captains were completely confused. Moreover, Galissionere killed way in order to spoil Byng's strategem. Unable to clarify his intentions, Byng signalled to engage. Galissionere disengaged after heavily damaging West's division and while Byng's unharmed division was still outside of range. A council of war decided that repairs to ships and care of the numerous wounded forced a return to Gibraltar. While at Gibraltar, Minorca fell and Admiral Hawke came to supersede Byng and send him home for trial.

Byng cleared himself of the charge of cowardice but his peers convicted him of not having done his utmost to relieve Minorca and to protect the Mediterranean. On 14 March 1757, Byng faced a firing squad. English Admirals now viewed the <u>Fighting Instructions</u> more critically and ventured to make additions and corrections. With the death of Byng, Formalism began to wane.

    2. <u>Doctrine to Dogma</u>. Between 1692 and 1782

the English fleet did not win a clear-cut decision in
any engagement in which the enemy offered a regular
battle. The <u>Permanent Fighting Instructions</u> were
Admiralty Orders, hence had the force of <u>Standing
Orders</u>. Flag signals in use referred to little but
numbers in the <u>PFI</u>, thus denying a commander a voice
of his own. Thus Doctrine degenerated to Dogma.

VI. NATIONAL NAVIES

A national navy is defined as a sea force capable
of fighting as well as of engaging in peacetime
functions, that is permanent, and that is owned by
and paid for by a nation.

A. THE EARLY BRITISH NAVY. By definition, England
had the first true navy. Henry VII specialized in
trading ships but is considered the grandfather of
the British Navy. While Henry VIII used his navy
defensively, he created a fighting fleet of 85 sail
and a demand for permanence that was respected by his
successors. Elizabeth's use of her fleets to "take
trade" from her enemies led to that critical moment
in British life, the Spanish War, and to the first
modern naval struggle.

England emerged from the war with a toughened
maritime fighting force, skilled naval commanders,
a tradition of sea fighting, and a sense that its navy
had "national" implications. Howard's fleet had reduced the sea-worthiness of the Armada and destroyed
Spanish morale. The sea had done the rest. Nevertheless, the Golden Century of Spain ended, with
Spain   entering a period of decline not readily
apparent because of the resources sent her by her
European and overseas empires. Spain and England
fought until 1603 when James I of England brought
hostilities to an end and allied himself to Spain.

The decline of Spain aided the Dutch to win their
independence. Their formidable fleet soon enabled
the Dutch to take over most of the Portuguese commercial empire in the Indian Ocean, and their merchant
fleet rapidly acquired a prime position in Europe's
maritime carrying trade. The rise of the Dutch nation as a sea power, however, caused competition
with England and finally led to war.

B. THE BRITISH NAVY UNDER THE LATE TUDORS, CROMWELL, AND THE STUARTS. James' alliance with Spain and his refusal to issue letters of marque resulted in a great slump in both trade and in the navy. Without entering into the constitutional questions involved, Charles I's demand for "ship money" from the inland shires was the first national demand for a permanent and nation-paid-for navy. His Ship Money Fleet was the first nation-paid-for and nation-controlled fleet. Cromwell's was the first true national navy--a large, permanent, national, maritime fighting force paid for by Parliament, based on Navy Estimates, and controlled by the government.

The first "royal" national navy was that of Charles II. Albeit there was as yet no organized naval profession, no Admiralty, and no real administration, England's navy grew as England's trade increased. Since Charles himself could not pay for a fleet, the nation had to pay to have the navy protect the nation's trade. It was Charles who entitled the English fleet the "Royal" navy. Like Henry VIII, he gave the fleet his personal attention. He, Isaac Newton, and Christopher Wren all had their part in the building of the Greenwich Observatory. In his day, too, distinction was made in the duties of naval officers, "Articles of War" were issued for the government of the navy, and Fighting Instructions were issued to commanders to aid them in the conduct of battle at sea. Charles found in Samuel Pepys an admirable naval administrator.

VII. PEPYS, COLBERT, AND THE RISE OF NAVAL PROFESSIONALISM

Much has been written about wars and battles, little about organization (the structure for gathering men's minds to solve particular problems) and administration (management).

A. KEEPER OF THE KING'S SHIPS TO BOARD OF ADMIRALTY. In Britain, as early as the reign of King John in the 13th century, a Keeper (or Clerk) of the King's ships maintained those ships in time of peace and prepared them for war. Admirals were appointed for short periods or special cases, using largely hired merchant ships paid for by the King, or ships impressed from the merchants of the Cinque Ports and, in dire cases, of all merchants. As yet, sea warfare was soldier warfare. With the Tudors, Britain for the first time adopted a naval policy. The first Navigation Act, e.g., was passed in Henry VII's first Parliament. The Tudors also realized Britain's dependence upon Baltic countries for naval stores and, once England's oak forests were denuded, even for masts. While the Tudors placed British trade with the Mediterranean on a sound footing, John Cabot greatly extended British voyages in the Atlantic by discovering the Newfoundland fishing banks. These and other fisheries provided a reserve of skilled sailors.

By the end of the 17th century, the Keeper of the King's ships had become "Clerk of the Acts," or Secretary of a Board of Admiralty. The Board concentrated on material; aboard ship the emphasis was on the Seamanship Department, which included everything but ordnance. Dockyards, none permanent until the one at Portsmouth was built in 1496, employed men to build or repair ships as needed. The captain who fought his ship engaged in administrative duties while ashore, at least until his ship was placed in ordinary or sold and he returned to civil life. By about 1550, in addition to the Clerk of the Acts and the ranking admiral, the Board of Admiralty had a Lieutenant who took care of ordnance; a Treasurer who looked after finances; a Comptroller who checked the accounts of the Treasurer; and a Surveyor, or Inspector, of the shore establishment. The office of Lieutenant soon lapsed and became the chief administrative office and the Clerk of the Ships became the Clerk of the Acts. During his reign, Henry VIII issued his own <u>Fighting Instructions</u>. Soldiers finally disappeared from British ships in the days of James I (1603-1625), but not until the days of Cromwell, the Protector, did England acquire a truly national navy in which Parliament funded the fleet and provided articles for the government of the Navy.

The professional officer class owes its existence, and the Royal Navy its basic administrative regulations, to Samuel Pepys, who served as the Secretary of the Board of Admiralty from 1660 to 1673 and 1679 to 1682. In addition to preparing the agenda for the Board, he introduced record-keeping, established the maximum and minimum ages for aspirant officers, and put officers on full time service even though they were subject to a furlough (half pay) system when not needed. In addition he established a naval academy, qualification examinations for promotion, and a seniority system for retention in the service. Men who worked all year round thus became proficient and acquired a set of traditions and a strong esprit de corps and a very real sense of corporate unity. The last was enhanced, about 1750, by a distinctive uniform only naval officers could wear.

The energetic Cardinal Richelieu, who served King Louis XIV as Minister of Marine as well as in other ways, through purchases from the Dutch and French building had 40 ships and 10 fire ships in the English Channel in 1639. With him gone, the navy decayed until Jean Baptiste Colbert took office in 1661. A continental power, France found it difficult and expensive to follow both continental and amphibious strategies. Colbert concentrated on building a modern navy. He brought honesty to the financial service, increased taxes, made the tariff part of his mercantilistic plan, and stimulated industry and improved transportation. After 1669, as Minister of Marine, of the colonies, and of the King's buildings, he improved the arsenal at Toulon; created naval works at Rochefort; founded naval schools at Rochefort, Dieppe, and St. Malo; fortified the Channel ports; and created the naval base at Brest. He recruited annual classes of men who would serve 6 months at sea, used a half-pay system, gave bonuses for the building of ships, taxed imported ships, and prohibited Frenchmen from serving in foreign navies. In a "buy at home" campaign he stimulated the production of naval stores; by a timber conservation program he insured the provision of wood to the navy. Like Pepys, he obtained regular officers from the naval academies and stopped captains from trading on their own account. He employed scientists to work in hydrography, navigation, and ordnance. He gave allowances to the families of men at sea and free education for the children, and established a home for wounded and disabled sailors. His navy cleared pirates from the Mediterranean, escorted merchant convoys, and showed the flag both in the Mediterranean and the Atlantic. The "Father of the French Navy" died in 1683, before his fleet gave a smashing defeat to the combined English and Dutch fleets at Beachy Head in 1690.

CHAPTER 3

THE AGE OF EXPANSION: SHIPS, COLONIES, AND WARS

I. THE SEARCH FOR CATHAY

The search by Europeans for new routes to the Orient was in large part caused by Ottoman Turk restrictions upon trade between the Near East and Far East. The discovery of new lands while seeking "Cathay" was made possible by a number of factors: the rise of national states fronting the Atlantic; early versions of the corporate form of business enterprise (regulated or joint stock company) that permitted the accumulation of capital for trade or colonizing; acquisition of additional nautical knowledge; and the energy and daring of Columbus and various intrepid successors.

A. PORTUGAL AND SPAIN. Though small in territory and population, Portugal early acquired national unity and in the 14th century was the leading maritime power of Europe. To find a sea route to Asia, Prince Henry (1394-1460) founded a school of naval science, in 1419. When he died, Portuguese using speedy caravelles had charted the west coast of Africa almost to the Gulf of Guinea and colonized the Madeira, Azores, and Cape Verde Islands. After Vasco de Gama rounded the Cape of Good Hope and reached India (1497-1498), the Portuguese began a lucrative traffic with the East Indies. Large convoys of carracks in this trade soon supplanted Venice as the provider of Eastern goods. In 1519, moreover, Magellan, a Portuguese sailing for Spain, transited the strait that bears his name and reached the Moluccas. The sole surviving ship of his expedition was the first to circumnavigate the globe.

Although Columbus and Vespucci were Italians, they sailed for Spain, and the Genoese John Cabot sailed for England. Columbus's reaching the New World (1492) permitted Spain to colonize the West Indies. Soon thereafter "conquistadores" took Mexico (Hernando Cortez, 1521) and Peru (Francisco Pizarro, 1537). These were the forerunners of others who hispanized the Americas and brought Spain the wealth and power used to defeat the Turks (at Lepanto, 1571). That power increased after Spain annexed Portugal and her empire (1580).

B. BRITAIN BREAKS OUT. Until almost the end of the 15th century, England's overseas ventures centered about the Baltic, North Sea, and Newfoundland fisheries. Her navy was small, she lacked the skill in shipbuilding and navigation of the Portuguese and Spaniards, and her small ships fared badly in ocean seas. Located on the fringe of civilization, she was farther away from Asia than the Iberian nations. With little to sell except wool, she had less overseas trade than the Spaniards, Portuguese, and Dutch, and lacked the capital to support overseas expeditions. Moreover, she had to compete with powerful monopolies like the Hanseatic League, the Italian cities, and rising national states. Rather than being excited about the discovery of new lands, she concentrated at home upon grave religious and political problems and such foreign problems as Scotland and Ireland. A free trade policy established in the 14th century enabled a merchant class to achieve some political power, however, and the two Tudor Henry's provided stability in which commerce increased, capital accumulated, and business forms useful for overseas enterprises were devised. These circumstances enabled various "adventurer" and joint-stock companies to begin trade with Russia, other Baltic countries, and Mediterranean and African countries by about 1550. Henry VIII gave a great stimulus to his navy and Queen Elizabeth, after being convinced to abjure a continental policy, supported overseas enterprises as part of state policy. London and Plymouth soon eclipsed such ports of the West Country as Bristol and Southampton even if the Grenvilles and Raleighs led the fight against Spain.

The most important reason for the British reach for empire was the economic depression and loss of former markets in the mid-16th century. Men like William Hawkins began to trade with the Ivory Coast of Africa and with Brazil, and Wyndenham with Morocco. Others sought a Northeast passage across the top of Europe. They failed, but they started trade with Russia that involved exchanging woolen cloth for naval stores. Still others traded with Venice and her Eastern Mediterranean possessions. While the voyages of Drake, Cavendish, Wood, and others brought the English a rich trade with the East Indies, men who failed to find Northwest passage across the top of North America nevertheless took the first steps leading to trade and then to colonization. In 1562, John Hawkins began a triangular trade by selling African slaves in the West Indies and West Indian sugar, pearls, ginger and cowhides in Europe; Frobisher discovered the sound later called Hudson Strait (1576); John Davis charted the coasts of Greenland and Canada (1585-1587); and Sir Humphrey Gilbert was the first to try to plant a colony in North America (1583), only to be lost at sea. His half-brother, Sir Walter Raleigh, became the first Englishman to establish a colony, named Virginia, to the south (1585, 1587) even though all the settlers returned from the first attempts and the fate of the second remains a mystery.

Aiding British explorers and colonizers in the 16th and 17th centuries were the experience in seamanship and fighting learned from privateers, the intrusion of Englishmen into the Negro slave trade between Africa and New Spain, a great expansion of coastwise shipping of coal from Newcastle to London and nearby villages, a governmental campaign to obtain fish from the Newfoundland Banks to make up for the loss of the right to fish off Iceland, exploitation of whale fisheries off Greenland and Spitzbergen, a shipbuilding bounty, and the rise of a school of native nautical scientists that produced excellent instruments (such as the astrolabe and cross-staff and the improvement upon the latter known as the quadrant) and treatises in astronomy, geography, hydrography, mathematics, and navigation. Such aids to navigation as coastal marks, beacons, and buoys were in general use by 1565, and George Mercator's chart of the world appeared in 1569. Finally, unlike Spain, which rigidly controlled all colonial, trade, and navigation matters through the Casa de Contratacion at Seville, the British permitted individual initiative in educating navigators and training officers and seamen, and royalty occasionally participated in overseas ventures both legal and illegal.

II. THE END OF SPAIN'S GOLDEN CENTURY

Enriched by the gold of the New World and strengthened by the acquisition of Portugal, Spain tried to capture the Netherlands while France was weak and England remained at peace. English policy, however, was to oppose the holding by a strong power

of territory across the Channel, and enough troops
were sent over to enable the Dutch to avoid defeat.
By 1585, an undeclared war at sea began, with Drake
and others revealing the naval power of the British
by despoiling Spain's colonial cities and trade and
thus weakening her and causing the postponement of
the sailing of the Spanish Armada until 1588. The
English tactic of the "off-fight" and better ships,
gunnery, leadership, and seamanship, and harsh weather
resulted in the return of less than half the Spanish
ships and about a third of their crews. Spanish and
Catholic morale cascaded while that of England and
Protestantism multiplied. Protestantism and the
Dutch were saved; Papal and Spanish invincibility were
proved false. The golden century of Spain had ended.
The Dutch allied themselves to Britain and began a
rapid maritime, commercial, and colonial expansion.
The British also began to expand overseas. And the
victory of British ships of the line marked a new
era in naval warfare. Although the British fleet
was allowed to decay and privateering was forbidden
by royal order, national energies were devoted to
trade, exploration, and colonization after James I
made peace with Spain (1604).

III. FOR GOD, GOLD, AND GLORY

Spanish, Portuguese, and French colonies in the
New World were in some instances a century old before Britain founded her colonies.

Major stimuli for Spanish, Portuguese, and
French colonization were to acquire wealth, convert
the heathen, and obtain personal or dynastic glory.
Even though a Papal Bull divided the world between
Spain and Portugal (1494), France and Britain defied
it. In contrast to the British, who hugged the North
Atlantic littoral, Spain and France spread over so
much territory that they could not defend its frontiers. A French royal grant of territory between the
40th and 46th parallel (1603) laid the basis for a
later series of Anglo-French wars.

Spain, Portugal, and France kept a strong political, judicial, administrative, religious, social and
intellectual monopoly over every aspect of colonial
life, from which foreigners were excluded. Individual
enterprise was thus quite thoroughly stifled. As long

as the mercantilistic theory was followed, colonies were to exist solely for the benefit of the mother country.

Fish and furs rather than gold provided wealth for France. Relying upon Indians for their furs, the French allied with them and converted many to Catholicism. They also tried to build a string of forts between the St. Lawrence and the Mississippi, and to take the mouth of the latter from Spain. However, their failure to win over the Iriquois, who allied themselves first with the Dutch, then with the British, prevented the expansion of their empire in the north.

IV. DUTCH EXPANSION

Meanwhile the Dutch, who had been aided by England to obtain their independence from Spain (1648), branched out East and West. While the Dutch East India Company ousted Portugal from the East Indies, the Dutch West India Company (1621) took land in Brazil and in the West Indies and founded New Amsterdam on Manhattan Island (1624). From Manhattan the Dutch spread northward to Albany, eastward into Connecticut and onto Long Island, westward into the Jersies, and south into Delaware. Like the French, and Spaniards, however, they overextended themselves; they then gave preference to their eastern rather than their western ventures. Like the French and Spaniards, the Dutch monopolized the political life of colonists and in the patroon system tried to establish the feudal system in the New World. With a cosmopolitan population becoming increasingly English and the bankruptcy of the Dutch West India Company over its Brazilian venture, however, the Dutch colonies fell to Britain during the Anglo-Dutch wars.

V. BRITISH COLONIZING METHODS AND THEIR RESULTS

Britain's colonizing of the New World differed from that of Spain and France in that the British built permanent settlements whereas the Spanish and French were largely exploitative and concentrated on trade and profits. Although God, Gold, Glory were powerful stimuli, British royalty lacked funds to colonize, hence left the work to private (or corporate) hands. The British colonial economic monopoly was originally not too strict, and the colonists were left degrees of self-government and religious liberties unknown to French and Iberian settlers. Since social ideals carried by British colonists also differed greatly from those of the Latin peoples, they tended to serve themselves first and the king second.

A very important form used by the British for colonizing purposes was the joint-stock company, with the members of the company organizing as a self-governing body and expecting a share of the profits. But the "charter of privileges" extended to the company by the king included the precious privilege of self-government. An economic charter thus also permitted the exercise of government outside the kingdom.

The restoration of peace between England and Spain in 1604 and a number of other factors stimulated British colonization. Among these were a landed gentry skilled in self government; a virile middle class based on manufacturing, commerce, trade, and even privateering, and imbued with the Protestant Ethic; a body of soldiers and sailors available for peaceful pursuits; and the need of gainful employment by farmers driven out of agriculture by the Enclosure Acts. By the Poor Law of 1601, displaced farmers were made burdens on their parishes, and their number made it appear that England was overpopulated. Other factors included the accumulation of capital and the utility of the joint-stock form; the desire of Puritans and other dissenters to get way from the High Church Anglicanism of the Stuart kings; the royal encroachment upon the liberties of the people guaranteed by Parliament; the willingness of the Stuarts to let both Protestants and Catholics emigrate and yet enjoy the rights of Englishmen even if they were not represented in Parliament; the desire to spread the Gospel; pure adventurism; and enticing propaganda sent home by settlers.

After desperately hard early years, the British colonists prospered. Trade grew in farm produce, fish, furs, and timber products, even ships; with the Indians; and, especially in the south, in tobacco. The opportunity to own land outright was the greatest attraction to the greatest number, and ample land was at hand to support such social institutions as churches and schools. Local self government was permitted even

in royal colonies. New immigrants of various kinds
appeared to augment the labor force: indentured
servants, criminals, poor children, prisoners of war
(mainly Irish) and Negro slaves. Despite occasional
massacres of whites, the Indian menace was soon removed. With the passage of time, the private ownership of land and self-government created a hardier
people than those to the north or south who were
ruled by absolutism and lived in feudalism.

VI. COLONIES AS MAKEWEIGHTS IN THE BRITISH MERCANTILISTIC SYSTEM

As explained by Richard Haklyut, Thomas Mun,
and Sir Josiah Child, among others, mercantilism was
a policy to promote the interest of both the king and
the merchant. It was originally based upon the
bullion theory, i.e., that in the absence of colonial
sources of precious metals national wealth and power
could be increased by a favorable balance of trade.
Therefore precious metals could not be exported; trade
could flow only in British ships using British crewmen; aliens could not enter the British retail market
(indeed, as in the case of the Hanse, were expelled
in 1598); and merchants were authorized to organize,
even to monopolize, for foreign trade and colonizing
purposes. In this system, colonies were expected to
reduce the dependence of the mother country upon
foreigners by providing markets for finished goods,
sources of raw materials, havens for surplus population, and bases for defense or for raiding against an
enemy. The mercantile theory emphasized the idea of
the general balance of trade as against the balance
of a particular trade and of a self-sufficient empire,
with colonies to specialize in the commodities they
could best produce and so contribute to the welfare
of the whole. To this point colonies could be considered partners with the mother country. However,
the mother protected herself by regulations that prohibited competition. In case of conflict between
mother and child, the child would be sacrificed.
This system persisted until about 1776, until the
Physiocrats and Adam Smith applied the principles of
natural law to economics and at least suggested free
trade.

A. COLONIAL ADVANTAGES. Under mercantilism, colonies gained because they were protected from foreign competition, their shipping was protected by the British navy, they were stimulated to build ships and engage in allied industries, enjoyed a monopoly on producing for the English market, received subsidies for producing goods demanded in England, could trade in all markets opened by the British, and received drawbacks on their products that went through England to other colonies.

B. COLONIAL DISADVANTAGES. The colonies were restricted in the field of manufacturing and could not trade outside of the Empire. Because of an unfavorable trade, they lacked sufficient currency to engage in commerce. They paid duties to England, and the costs of manufactured goods and of freight and insurance were higher than they might pay elsewhere, say to the Dutch. As early revealed in the southern colonies, a surplus of a product meant a drop in its market price. The whole stifled colonial initiative. Examples of restrictions applied to favor producers in England are the Woolens Act, 1699, the manufacture of hats, 1732, and the manufacture of iron, 1750. Also, to protect British agriculture, certain enumerated articles at times had to go through England: sugar, tobacco, cotton, wool, indigo, dye woods, rice, molasses, naval stores, copper, and furs.

A saving factor was that the navigation acts that included these prohibitions were much evaded. Moreover, since the southern colonies had little industry, the restrictions applied mainly to the northern ones. Britain feared the growth of manufacturing above all else, for she realized that economic independence preceded political independence and that the demand for the one might lead to the other. However, since New England did not produce staple commodities and turned to manufacturing, as of wool, her ships must proceed to England empty to obtain cargoes. Hence the search for markets outside of England in order to obtain the wherewithal to pay for an unfavorable balance of trade. On the other hand, except for those paid for indigo, hemp, and flax, British bounties applied most to such northern products as naval stores, masts, and lumber.

CHAPTER 4

A CENTURY OF WARS 1689-1763

From 1689 to 1763, Britain and France fought four wars: War of the English Succession, 1689-1697; War of the Spanish Succession, 1702-1713; War of the Austrian Succession, 1739-1748; and the Seven Years' War, 1756-1763. Each of these wars in various degrees affected colonies as well as mother countries and also the conduct of naval warfare.

A. WAR OF THE ENGLISH SUCCESSION, 1689-1697. By 1689, due to Colbert and his successor and son, Colbert de Signelay, the France of Louis XIV had an extremely well administered navy comprised of 200 sails and 80 privateers. While Louvois created the most powerful army in Europe, the engineering skill of Vauban made France's fronters impregnable. Moreover, the number of colonists in America quadrupled.

Rather than making France a great maritime power, the Sun King chose to expand on the continent, including the left bank of the Rhine. In contrast, Britain sought maritime supremacy, depending upon profits from trade to subsidize allies on the continent. Alerted to French expansionism, William of Orange allied Holland with England, whose king, as William III, he became in 1688. When Louis XIV tried to seize the Spanish Netherlands, where Antwerp was "the dagger pointed at the heart of England," and to restore James II to the British throne, the allies resisted. Although French expeditions that landed in Ireland were defeated (especially important was the Battle of the Boyne, 1690), in 1690 Tourville defeated Torrington off Beachy Head. Henceforth Britain saw the value of keeping a fleet in being. When the French attempted to invade, in 1692, Barfleur defeated Tourville in the Channel and England was safe. The French thereafter resorted to commerce raiding, with Jean Bart being especially effective, but the French navy was held by the English, who deployed their ships about Brest in the Atlantic and Toulon in the Mediterranean. In the Treaty of Ryswick, 1697, Louis XIV agreed to the <u>status quo ante bellum</u> except for Strasbourg and recognized William as the English king.

B. WAR OF THE SPANISH SUCCESSION, 1702-1713. Charles II of Spain died childless but left heirs in France and Austria. His heritage passed to the grandson of Louis XIV, Philip of Anjou, who became King Philip V of Spain. Louis XIV exploited Spanish commerce; occupied Italy, the Rhineland, Spain, and the former Spanish Netherlands, thereby closing the Mediterranean trade to the British; forced Spain to give the Asiento (contract for supplying Negro slaves) to a French company; excluded British merchants from the Spanish West Indies; and proclaimed James II the King of England. With Flanders in French hands, Britain formed the Grand Alliance with Austria, Holland, Prussia, and various lesser states. John Churchill, Duke of Marlborough, drove the French from Flanders (1704), but Bavaria's joining Louis XIV stimulated the latter to attack Austria. The Alliance meanwhile kept strong defensive forces in the Channel and strong offensive squadrons in the Mediterranean. It also was strengthened by the adherence of the Duke of Savoy and of Portugal (1703). The British-Protuguese treaty remained a keystone in British policy for the next century, and the capture of Gibraltar (1704) gave the British a site for an excellent naval base. With the fleet of the Alliance guarding against enemy operations in the Mediterranean, Marlborough moved his army from the Rhine to the Danube to defeat Bavaria and succor Austria. The Battle of Blenheim (31 July 1704) saved Austria and Savoy and made possible the control of Bavaria. In 1706, while Marlborough's victory at Ramilies sped the retreat of the French from Flanders, Prince Eugene defeated the French Army in Italy and saved Savoy. Moreover, the capture of Minorca (1708) gave the British the fine harbor of Port Mahon from which to operate in the Mediterranean.

Colonial operations in this war grew largely out of demands for protection from colonial authorities. In 1710, an amphibious force under Captain George Martin, RN, and the colonial Colonel Francis Nicholson forced the French governor of Port Royal, the capital of Nova Scotia, to capitulate. The town was renamed Annapolis Royal (after Queen Anne). While another squadron destroyed settlements and shipping along the Newfoundland coast, a strong amphibious force failed to take Quebec (1711). British cruisers also protected colonial coasts, provided convoy escort, fought off privateers, and destroyed French seaborne trade.

Major terms of the Treaty of Utrecht (1713) were that France and Spain would never unite under the same crown; the Spanish Netherlands as well as Naples and Sardinia went to Austria, and Sicily to the Duke of Savoy; the fortifications at Dunkirk were dismantled; Britain retained Gibraltar and Minorca, thus remaining a Mediterranean power; Newfoundland and Nova Scotia (Acadia) went to Britain; Britain gained the Asiento and the right to have a single British ship trade annually with Spanish America; and Louis XIV abandoned James II and recognized the Protestant succession in England. While Britain increased her sea power during the war, that of Holland suffered so greatly that it never recovered.

C. THE WAR OF JENKINS' EAR AND OF THE AUSTRIAN SUCCESSION, 1739-1748. The Britain of Sir Robert Walpole and of the French Cardinal Fleury made pretence of remaining at peace while both strengthened their navies and merchant marines and the British especially forged ahead in industry. London succeeded Antwerp as the center of the world's commerce. Sir John Byng (the first admiral known to use "the chase" in battle) and an amphibious force relieved Sicily from a threat of Spanish occupation (1717-1720) and an Anglo-Dutch squadron helped Sweden against Denmark, Poland, and Russia, which threatened England's vital Baltic market of timber and naval stores (The Great Northern War). While Britain periodically sent squadrons to insure the free passage of her shipping in the Baltic, she also stimulated the production of American forest products, with the result that she was freed from dependence upon Swedish tar but not upon Baltic hemp and spars.

A capable fiscal reformer, Walpole kept England at peace for twenty-one years until trouble brewed between Spanish guardia-costas and British contraband traffic with Spanish America. One Jenkins had his ear cut off by a guardia-costas, and on 31 October 1739 Britain declared war on Spain ostensibly because of "the desire of the British mercantile interests for conquest and loot."

In November 1739, Vice Admiral Edward Vernon captured Porto Bello, on the Darien coast. The horrors of a subsequent amphibious operation against Cartagena have been told in Smollett, <u>Roderick Random</u>. In 1740-1741, Commodore George Anson circumnavigated the world while capturing Spanish prizes. Among those who served with him were Howe, Hyde Parker, Keppel, Saunders, and Saumarez, names to be met again. The war broadened into that of the War of the Austrian Succession when, over the issue of the Hapsburg inheritance, Britain, Austria, and Holland lined up against France, Prussia, and Spain. On the continent, Britain wished to keep the Rhine Delta out of unfriendly hands and to protect the Electorate of Hanover; on the sea, to prevent the expansion of French colonies in North America and India. Throughout, maritime and commercial rivalry was an important stimulus to action. As usual, the British navy defended Britain, escorted convoys and transported troops, and protected British sea lines of communications and assailed those of the enemy. Fortunately for Britain, the Franco-Spanish Family Compact, last renewed in 1743, did not entail close joint operations.

In an engagement off Toulon, beginning 22 February 1744, Admiral Thomas Mathews, commanding in the Mediterranean, began chasing swifter allied ships. Unable to get his line parallel to the enemy's, he left flying the signal for line and bore down on the enemy rear. Though a number of ships ahead and astern helped him, other captains did not, and few Spanish ships were taken or damaged before he retired. The engagement revealed the inflexibility of the <u>Fighting Instructions</u> and the lack of adequate signals. More important for morale, Mathews and his second in command, Vice Admiral Richard Lestock, were court martialed. Lestock was acquitted, but Mathews was found "guilty of divers notorious breaches of his duty" and cashiered--he had "not done his utmost" to destroy the enemy.

Without any declaration, France joined the war in 1743 and in 1745, under Marshall Saxe, overran Flanders and supported the exiled Stuart Prince Charles against the House of Hanover in a descent upon Scotland. However, English Jacobites declined to support Charles, who retired to Scotland after threatening London. When the Duc de Richelieu proposed to invade England with 15,000 troops, British squadrons in the Downs, in the newly-instituted Western Squadron based at Portsmouth, in the North Sea, and off Scotland intervened, and the French desisted and took to <u>guerre de course</u>.

Meanwhile Dupleix's plan to extend the French empire in India was contested by the British East India Company and sea power. Rear Admiral Edward Boscawen, with the largest squadron yet to appear in Eastern seas, arrived early in 1748 only to learn that peace had been restored.

Unlike the wars of the English and of the Spanish succession, which barely affected Britain's North American colonies, that of the Austrian Succession involved colonial military operations. As a defensive move, in 1745 British ships and colonial troops sought to capture the fortress at Louisbourg. This base on Cape Breton Island was the key to the St. Lawrence, thus to Canada. Its capture would prevent French assaults on British colonies and in turn protect Newfoundland, Nova Scotia, and the Newfoundland fisheries. While a naval squadron under Commodore Peter Warren blockaded Louisbourg and drove off French resupply ships, 4,000 New England troops, largely fishermen, invested the fortress on 17 June after a 6-weeks siege. A British attempt to seize Quebec failed, however.

Nevertheless, the British lack of a war strategy had enabled French overseas trade to continue and prosper. By 1747, however, with a strengthening of its Western Squadron, Britain was able both to defend the Channel and to operate offensively, as in preventing the sailing of French squadrons for America and India and in intercepting French trade. Off Cape Finisterre, in May 1747, Anson and Warren, using first the line and then chase, defeated de la Jonquiere. With Anson, a great teacher of tactics, at the Admiralty, and Hawke, who succeeded the ill Warren in command of the Western Squadron, French trade was seriously threatened. In the second battle of Finisterre, October 1748, using chase, Hawke defeated de l'Étanduèr and insured the capture of most of a large convoy and of almost 1,000 seamen. In 1749, with a refitted squadron, Hawke lay off Cadiz and a recovered Warren cruised in the Bay of Biscay in taking the war to Spain while Anson provided adequate escort of convoy for British shipping. In consequence, enemy shipping was barred from the seas while British trade flourished. But because French power on the continent remained supreme, the war ended in a stalemate. The Peace of Aix-la-Chapelle, April 1748, provided that Louisbourg would be restored to France in return for the Austrian Netherlands and Madras. Since nothing was said about the activities of the <u>guardia-costas</u> in South American waters, peace could not last long. Moreover, Britain's North American colonists were enraged because they had helped reduce Louisbourg, only to have it returned to France. Massachusetts alone spent ₤200,000, lost 7,000 men, and left large areas of land uncultivated during the campaign, yet she had not been consulted on peace terms. She naturally concluded that colonists were being used merely as pawns in the game of empire.

D. THE SEVEN YEARS' WAR, 1756-1763.

I. CAUSES OF THE WAR

The primary object of French colonial expansion in North America was wealth, in the form of gold or furs, whereas the British sought to establish homes. While only 65,000 Canadians controlled the area from Quebec to the Mississippi in 1750, 2,000,000 British subjects peopled the piedmont and coast from the Carolinas to Maine. In 1753, to guard their homeland, the French, under the aegis of the Marquis Duquesne, began to build a chain of fortifications from the Great Lakes to the Ohio, thence down the Mississippi to New Orleans. Fort Duquesne, at the apex, near present-day Pittsburgh, lay on land claimed both by Virginia and Pennsylvania. The repelling of the attempts of General Edward Braddock (1754) and of George Washington (1755) to oust the French from Fort Duquesne eventually led to the Seven Years' War, albeit contributary to the war was British-French rivalry over various West Indies islands and a French offensive to establish France in southern India. Earlier Anglo-French wars had begun in Europe and spread to the colonies. The Seven Years' War began in the colonies, spread to Europe, and became a worldwide war. The British North American colonists were all too eager to expel their northern enemies. They recalled that Louisbourg, captured by their blood in 1745 during King George's War (the colonial counterpart of the War of the Austrian Succession), had in the Treaty of Aix-la-Chapelle (Aachen) been exchanged for Madras, in far-off India. Moreover, the French and their Indian allies posed a bulwark to their westward expansion.

II. STRATEGIC CONSIDERATIONS

A. BRITISH.

1. <u>Newcastle's Plan</u>. Britain's Prime Minister, the Duke of Newcastle, although an experienced party manager, was wholly unfitted to conduct a war. He considered the safety of Hanover, the king's native state, before that of the colonies. Once he had negotiated for a Russian army, however, he released the Royal Navy to raid French sea communications. Sir Edward Hawke, for instance, seized the annual French convoy from the colonies, 300 ships, off Cape Finisterre, but in the absence of a British blockade three French squadrons got away to the West Indies or Canada. Also reaching Canada were the Marquis de Montcalm, his deputy, de Levis, and his aide, Bougainville. England's strategic situation was further improved when Frederick the Great, in order to finance his impedning war against Austria, allied Prussia with Britain (January, 1756).

2. <u>Pitt's Plan</u>. Newcastle hoped to defeat France on land and use the Royal Navy as defense against invasion. William Pitt, his Principal Secretary of State with authority to conduct the war, reversed the logic when he became Prime Minister. He would leave the continental war to subsidized allies, with occasional amphibious diversions, and conquer French America by sea power. Simply, Pitt would keep on the strategic defensive (hold) in Europe and on the strategic offensive (hit) in the colonies with Newcastle, First Lord of the Treasury, managing Parliament and providing Pitt unstinted logistic support. The French unwittingly cooperated by concentrating against Frederick, and Pitt placated public opinion by blockading the Toulon and Brest fleets and by occasionally sending frigate squadrons across to discourage the accumulation of invasion forces at French Channel ports. Divers "conjunct expeditions" (amphibious operations) were planned at his request in order to relieve the pressure on Frederick.

B. FRANCE. Louis, Duc de Belleisle, sought to avoid war on disadvantageous terms either in Europe or in the colonies. He would strike the hard blow that would produce a swift and acceptable peace--an invasion of England itself. He would force the English to split their fleet by capturing Minorca, combine the Brest and Rochefort squadrons, use 100,000 troops in amphibious assaults on three different English beaches, and support that expedition which gained a foothold. He thus gambled on the poor English army to compensate for his lack of command of the sea. But France's imperative need to bolster her land frontiers, the British Western Squadron, based at Portsmouth and Plymouth, and British blockading ships off Brest and Rochefort shattered Belleisle's dream. The pattern of war was set: France would fight on land, England on the seas. The only part of Belleisle's plan implemented was the capture of Minorca.

III. NAVAL OPERATIONS: EUROPE

A. THE BATTLE FOR MINORCA. Belatedly, in April 1756, Newcastle sent Sir John Byng to support the 2,800 troops at Port Mahon, Minorca. Byng's orders were vague: he was responsible not only for Minorca but for Gibraltar as well. He had no troops, no store vessels, no siege train. The French, meantime, dispatched from Toulon the Marquis de la Galissionere, with 150 transports carrying 16,000 troops of the Duc de Richelieu. Landing unopposed, Richelieu tried to get at Lieutenant General William Blakeney, the 84-year-old commander, in Fort St. Philip. Byng rushed to Minorca from Gibraltar with 13 ships. On 19 May, while becalmed off Port Mahon, Byng saw Galissionere on his windward side. Byng obtained the weather gage on the 20th, with Galissionere between him and Minorca. He detached one ship in order to be able to present his 12 to Galissionere's 12 in a conterminous line. When he came down, however, he came down obliquely, not bows on, confusing his captains. Galissionere then killed speed and spoiled his plan. Straightjacketed by the <u>Fighting Instructions</u> and plagued by accidents, Byng could not prevent the ships of one of his divisions from suffering heavy damage before Galissionere disengaged, lightly damaged. Deciding that he could not raise the siege of Port Mahon, with his ships in need of repairs and many men grievously wounded, Byng returned to Gibraltar. Blakeney surrendered on 28 June. While repairing at Gibraltar, Byng was succeeded and sent home for trial. He cleared himself of the charge of cowardice but was convicted of not having done his utmost to relieve Blakeney. After his execution, 14 March 1757, English admirals looked more critically at the Fighting Instructions and made corrections and additions. The death of Byng marked the beginning of the end of Formalism.

B. "CONJUNCT EXPEDITIONS."

    1. Rochefort, September 1757. The English attack on Rochefort, a major shipbuilding city and naval arsenal on the Bay of Biscay, was a failure from the start. There was no operation plan, and command relationships were not clear-cut. Captain Richard Howe captured the Isle of Aix, but a council of war concluded that a landing on the French coast was impossible. Chagrined, the troops returned home. Nevertheless, the expedition had diverted some ten French regiments from starting out for Germany, and Lieutenant Colonel James Wolfe learned some lessons that he later put to good use at Louisbourg and Quebec. Among these were the need of speed in attack, precise preplanning based on all available Intelligence, skillful direction of a well-conceived plan by "fit persons," and the willingness of a commander to lose a portion of his forces in order to obtain his objectives. In March 1758, with the Rochefort fleet on the point of sailing to the relief of Louisbourg, Hawke drove it ashore.

    2. Privateer Nests on the Normandy-Brittany Coasts.

    a. St. Malo, June 1758. Captain Richard Howe escorted the Duke of Marlborough and 13,000 regulars to St. Malo. After naval bombardment dispersed the defenders on shore, Marlborough's troops landed in Cancale Bay, eight miles east of St. Malo, whose governor blew up the causeway joining his fort to the shore a mile away. Marlborough's men retired in good order after burning more than a hundred raiders found in the port of St. Servan.

    b. Cherbourg, August 1758. Captain Howe escorted Lieutenant General Thomas Bligh in an attack upon strongly defended Cherbourg. Using specialized landing craft, Englishmen stormed ashore under an effective covering naval barrage. Cherbourg, defended only on its sea approaches, surrendered, had its fortifications and shipping destroyed, and was put out of the war. When Bligh's men got out of hand, looting and drinking, Howe embarked them to St. Malo.

  c. <u>St. Malo Again, September 1758</u>. Bligh was to complete the job begun by Marlborough, but he dawdled on the beach for three days before attacking, providing the Duc d'Auguillon ample time to prepare his defenses. When weather forced Howe to move his ships out of support range, Bligh gave up. As he was haphazardly reembarking his men, d'Auguillon attacked. Brilliant defensive action on the part of 1,400 of the Guards permitted Bligh to extricate his stragglers, but at the cost of almost every Guard lost or captured of the entire regiment. As a result, Pitt's conjunct expeditions fell into disrepute, but they had served Pitt's purpose by provoking the French to fleet action.

C. THE FRENCH COUNTERATTACK.

  1. <u>The Battle of Lagos, 18 August 1759</u>. In 1759, with the British army away on colonial conquests or on the continent supporting Frederick, only the Channel and the Royal Navy stood between France and the fulfillment of the revived Belleisle project of invasion. The Duc de Choiseul planned to land 50,000 men in Suffolk, another 10,000 in Scotland to confuse Pitt and perhaps form a second thrust on London, and also planned various other diversions. He would first secure command of the Channel by bringing the Toulon fleet to Brest.

  In the hope of frightening the English into recalling troops from distant enterprises, the French prepared ostentatiously for invasion in the Channel ports of Le Havre and Dunkirk. Their ruse failed. Recognizing the strategic mistake made by the French in splitting their fleet between the Atlantic and the Mediterranean, the British trusted Hawke to deal with the Brest squadron and Edward Boscawen to cope with Toulon.

Admiral Sabran de la Clue took advantage of a temporary absence by Boscawen and appeared off Gibraltar with 12 ships and three frigates on the night of 17-18 August. At sunrise de la Clue sighted eight sails and surmised they were those that had parted from him during the night. Upon discovering they were Boscawen's, de la Clue formed a tight line held to the speed of the slowest ship. Disregarding the niceties of the <u>Fighting Instructions</u>, Boscawen signalled "General Chase," thus releasing his fastest ships for attack. Although the attack was poorly executed, de la Clue was soon reduced to four ships against Boscawen's 14. Determined not to give up, de la Clue ran his <u>Ocean</u> aground in Lagos Bay so hard that her masts went by the board. The other three French ships soon surrendered. Without the Toulon fleet, France lost her chance to fight for control of the Channel and to invade England.

    2.   <u>The Battle of Quiberon Bay, 29 November 1759</u>. Choiseul abandoned his plan for a full-scale invasion of England but tried to implement the Scottish phase with the Brest fleet. Admiral Hubert Conflans sortied from Brest in a storm that drove his blockaders away, but Edward Hawke was soon on his trail. Surprised by Hawke on 29 November, when southwest of Belle Isle, on his way to capture a small British squadron in Quiberon Bay, Conflans had only time to draw his 21 ships in battle line; without a battle plan he sought only to escape. He underestimated Hawke's capacity for following him at the height of a vicious storm into the reef-strewn waters of Quiberon Bay. Hawke's van caught the French rear just as Conflans in the van entered the Bay. Knocking out one 74 and taking two prizes, Hawke anchored for the night, intent upon destroying Conflans come daylight. In the morning he found no French fleet. Seven French ships had slipped away to Rochefort, where they remained for the rest of the war. Seven more had lightened ship and entered the Villaine River, where they were stranded for a year. Finding himself alone, Conflans had deliberately crashed his ship on the rocks.

    France's navy was broken. England commanded the seas. While the Royal Navy could not stop every French raider that left port, it did provide security for English forces moving by sea, denied the same security to France, permitted more conjunct expeditions to be launched to relieve the pressure on Frederick, and enabled England to take her pick of the French overseas colonial empire.

IV. NAVAL OPERATIONS: THE COLONIAL WAR

A. THE CAPTURE OF LOUISBOURG, 1758. The French and their Indian allies enjoyed success in America in 1756 and 1757. In 1756 General Louis Montcalm captured Oswego, the British salient and prospective base of operations in the Great Lakes country. In 1757 he moved south from Montreal to capture Fort William Henry, on Lake George near the head of the Hudson. The British, meantime, planned to capture Louisbourg, thus unlocking the St. Lawrence and making possible attack by water on Montcalm's major base, Quebec.

1. The Opposing Forces. Louisbourg, on the east coast of Cape Broton Island, lay on a rugged promontory enclosing an excellent harbor. Opposed were Chevalier de Drucour with 3,800 troops, more than 200 cannon, and 3,000 seamen, and Lord Jeffrey Amherst, with 14,000 men and 150 guns. Edward "Old Dreadnought" Boscawen covered the transport fleet with 23 ships and 18 frigates, whereas the French had only five ships at Louisbourg. Pitt's desire to have Canada is reflected in his use of the most powerful and best planned conjunct expedition of the war to assault Louisbourg.

2. The Assault. Geography and hydrography posed grave problems for the English. Cliffs, shoals, and a prodigious swell faced the invaders. Rather than attack the town itself, the British landed in Gabarus Bay, on 8 June, with James Wolfe to the left, leading the main attack. When Boscawen's frigates lifted their covering barrage, the boats headed for the beach. Drucour fired early; the sea took a greater toll of boats and men than did his bullets. Wolfe's men found a toehold on the rocks, however, which Wolfe rapidly exploited. Reaching the plateau above, he charged. The French who were still alive sped away, with the British in pursuit until they came within range of cannon arcs of fire from Louisbourg. With British ships on blockade, Louisbourg could not be reinforced, and Amherst wisely substi-

tuted entrenchment and siege for gun and bayonet. Drucour surrendered on 27 July. The fall of Louisbourg unlocked the gate to the St. Lawrence and signified the beginning of the end of France in Canada.

B. THE QUEBEC CAMPAIGN, 1759.

1. *British Plans*. Wolfe had shown at Louisbourg that he was the man Pitt needed, and Amherst generously accepted a subordinate role in the campaign to capture Quebec. The British had a threefold plan to concentrate about Quebec by water: a) Wolfe and 8,500 men would ascend the St. Lawrence with a naval covering force strong enough to deal with either the Brest or Toulon fleet should either one evade blockade; b) Amherst and 12,000 men would seize Ticonderoga and Crown Point, on Lake Champlain, descend the Richelieu, meet Prideaux, by-pass Montreal, and descend the St. Lawrence to join Wolfe and assume command; c) John Prideaux and 5,000 men would capture Niagara and enter the St. Lawrence through Lake Ontario. Delays precluded Amherst's joining with Wolfe, but he performed the vital function of isolating Quebec by land while Admiral Charles Saunders isolated Quebec by sea.

Sea power gave Wolfe the mobility and additional fire power he needed to obtain victory. Saunders, with 23 ships and 13 frigates among the 177 ships, was to transport Wolfe to Quebec, guard his communications, and lend support to the Army as required. As at Louisbourg, geographical and hydrographical factors dominated military operations. With such superb navigators as Master James Cook aboard, however, and with their own surveys of the river, the English made their way along the St. Lawrence despite shoals and 20-foot tides.

The Wolfe-Saunders team cooperated perfectly while Montcalm and Governor de Vaudreuil failed to cooperate. The latter was ambitious, aspired to command, and conspired against Montcalm. Corruption in his administration weakened the fighting power of Montcalm's 14,000 men and 300 emplaced guns.

2. *French Defensive Measures*. Montcalm had obtained a copy of the British operation plan and had disposed his forces accordingly, relying upon his

Indian allies to halt Amherst and Prideaux while he repelled Wolfe. He stretched 11,000 men on the high banks of the river just below Quebec between the rivers Montmorency on his left and St. Charles on his right, and himself occupied a central position in Beauport. He also prepared fireships, blocked Quebec with a boom of chained logs, and put 1,000 seamen into his batteries.

    3. <u>Preliminary British Moves</u>. Seizing the undefended Isle of Orleans below Quebec (27 June), Wolfe had a good view of the Upper Town and Lower Town of Quebec, six miles distant. Beyond to his left stood the heights of Levis, to his right the roaring Montmorency. Above, Montcalm surveyed the beaches on which the British had planned to land. Accepting the disposition of Montcalm's forces, Wolfe gave Quebec some attention by taking the heights of Levis, whence he could fire into the town across the river.

    4. <u>The Fall of Quebec</u>. After a summer of planning and testing of Montcalm's defenses, Wolfe made his final move. On 12 September Saunders feinted with empty transports and noisy barrage at Beauport while Wolfe slipped ashore at Foulon. His men filed up the steep ascent and by dawn were 4,500 strong on the Plains of Abraham. Without waiting for all of his own units to join, Montcalm force marched from Beauport and attacked at once. In a battle that lasted less than an hour Wolfe and Montcalm lost their lives, Quebec fell, and Amherst was able to complete the conquest of Canada in security while the ships of Boscawen and Hawke guarded the St. Lawrence. All of French America except the two inconsequential islands of St. Pierre and Miquelon fell to Britain.

C. THE WEST INDIES. British trade with the West Indies in the 18th century was twice that with India and constituted a quarter of all British and a third of all French seaborne trade. Britain and France each employed 600 vulnerable merchant ships in the West Indies trade. Naval bases at Antigua, St. Christopher, and Barbados guarded Britain's prime possession, and France jealously guarded her rich islands of Guadeloupe, Martinique, Santo Domingo, and the Grenadines. Important strategic considerations in defending the West Indies included the easterly wind direction and the lack of good harbors except that of Castries in St. Lucia. Weather was a problem, and with the approach of the summer and autumn hurricanes warships as well as merchant ships departed the Antilles.

1. <u>French Strategy in the West Indies</u>. Lacking naval power, France loosed large numbers of licensed privateers against England's 2,000 ships in the West Indies as well as in the English Channel and in Indian waters. These took 500 ships in the West Indies alone during each of the first two years of the war. The fact that the French took more merchant prizes than the British merely reflects the great increase of British and diminution of French overseas trade during the war.

2. <u>British Strategy in the West Indies</u>. Pitt had three objectives for the West Indian campaign: a) to legitimatize the otherwise illegal trade between the British North American colonies and the West Indies; b) to crush the French privateers; and c) to establish British supremacy in all French holdings in the New World.

3. <u>British Spoliation of the French West Indies</u>. In January 1759, a strong British conjunct expeditionary force led by Commodore John Moore and Colonel John Barrington reached Barbados. Not far behind was Commodore M. de Bompart and a fleet of nine sails which had slipped by Hawke out of Brest. Moore and Barrington worked as a team. After rehearsal, they landed troops and captured Guadeloupe (surrendered 1 May 1759). Learning of Bompart, Moore took his 11 ships to Dominica to intercept him. Bompart slipped by, but, finding Barrington entrenched, sailed on to Santo Domingo. Conflans succeeded in bringing a convoy of 300 ships from Santo Domingo to France, but after the Battle of Quiberon Bay England leisurely reduced all the French islands in the West Indies except Santo Domingo and relegated privateering to a suicidal gamble. However, France's victories on the continent caused Britain to recede most of the islands in the Peace of Paris.

4. <u>The Capture of Havana</u>. Infuriated by Britain's violations of her neutrality and laws, Spain joined France in 1761. Long before Spain could bring

her 56 ships into action, Pitt had planned operations that would despoil her, as well as France, of her North American holdings. His primary objective was Havana, for which he collected a mighty conjunct expedition under Admiral George Pocock and the Earl of Albemarle.

Approaching Havana from the east in the spring of 1762, the British achieved surprise. Albemarle's landing of his troops near the city was a splendid example of the efficiency the British had acquired in amphibious operations. Two months of siege and the undermining of a wall of the Morro caused the fort and Havana to fall. The gold and goods of Havana paid for almost a year of Pitt's war.

D. OTHER BRITISH SUCCESSES.

1. <u>The Philippines</u>. As at Havana, the British achieved surprise in their attack on Manila, fountainhead of Spanish silver. Precise amphibious assault under cover of naval gunfire resulted in the fall of Manila in 12 days--and Spanish silver enabled Pitt to pay half a year's subsidies to his allies.

2. <u>India</u>. Because private companies had expended their resources in a decade of war for supremacy in India, the mother countries furnished naval squadrons and small bodies of troops. Thus Rear Admiral Charles Watson supported Robert Clive in a war against the natives that ended in the decisive Battle of Plassey, June 1757. With the provinces of Bengal, Orissa, and Bihar in its hands, the British East India Company won financial parity with the French in India. Clive then helped Watson win control of the sea by a combined attack that wrecked the French naval base at Chandernagor, forcing French naval vessels to operate from Mauritius, 2,100 miles away. Admiral George Pocock, Watson's successor, swept French seaborne communications lines and also battered the Comte d'Ache's squadron so badly in two engagements that it had to withdraw to Mauritius. Seaborne logistic support enabled the British to win additional victories. With the lifting of their siege of Madras, the French ended their last offensive in India. When d'Ache returned to give battle, Pocock inflicted damages that ended his capacity for further operations. D'Ache's abandonment of India

occurred in the epochal year 1759, the year of Quebec, Lagos Bay, Quiberon Bay, and Guadeloupe. In undisputed command of the seas, the British crushed the French Company's troops in the Battle of Wandiwash and made India British.

V. RESULTS AND LESSONS OF THE WAR

Frederick the Great dominated the continental aspects of the Seven Years' War, Pitt its global aspects. Pitt's strategy had caused his continental allies to lure France into wasteful campaigns across the Rhine while he established colonial supremacy and kept the Channel Fleet so strong that France dare not invade. Moreover, English overseas trade increased by a third during the war while that of France suffered grievously. Nevertheless, Pitt was ousted from power before the Treaty of Paris was written.

A. THE TREATY OF PARIS, 1763. In the Treaty, England ransomed Hanover and Frederick by granting generous terms. Belle Isle was exchanged for Minorca; Havana and Manila for Florida and a bit of Honduras; and Goree, off Dakar, for Hanover. Guadeloupe and Martinique were returned to France on the pledge that the fortifications at Dunkirk would be demolished. From the war England gained Canada, Florida, and all the area east of the Mississippi except New Orleans, several islands in the West Indies (Grenada, the Grenadines, St. Vincent, Dominica, and Tobago), a hold on Senegal, and confirmation of the possessions the British East India Company had acquired before 1763. French trade continued in an India that was under British political influence. Despite Pitt's protests, France was left with ample facilities to rebuild her shipping, her commerce, and her navy.

B. LESSONS OF THE WAR. In the field of tactics, the Seven Years' War started a trend in liberalizing the <u>Fighting Instructions</u>. Byng's blood paved the way for the gradual resumption of tactical initiative by British naval officers, as revealed in the <u>Additional Instructions</u> that were adopted. Unfortunately for Great Britain, those who led the various amphibious operations died without translating their experience into written doctrine, and the British would have to relearn the techniques of amphibious warfare again and again, at tragic cost. British naval administration was improved by the classification and building of ships according to their use for battle, scouting, and inshore work, and naval architecture was improved in consequence of studying French prizes. But the silent First Lord of the Admiralty, Admiral of the Fleet Lord George Anson, failed to leave behind any record of how he introduced and maintained tactical discipline in the wartime fleet. Moreover, since the French remained on the strategic defensive, they furnished no real fleet action in which tactics could be fully tested. Few other wars illustrate better the advantage of a defensive strategy such as that adopted by France. Soon after the Treaty was signed, the French rebuilt their naval establishment and sought revenge. Eschewing an invasion attempt against England, they were planning a descent upon Jamaica when the American Revolution erupted and gave them unexpected allies in the American colonists.

CHAPTER 5

TWO AMERICAN DECLARATIONS OF INDEPENDENCE

I. SALUTARY NEGLECT

Whether proprietary, corporate, or royal, the British North American colonies were quite neglected by an England immersed in political and religious programs until 1660, when Charles II sought to centralize them, fit them into a mercantilistic system, and extend them for defense against France and Spain. The Carolinas were founded to serve as a buffer between Virginia and Spanish Florida; Delaware, Pennsylvania, and New Jersey, with the Dutch colony at New Amsterdam added in 1664, filled in the central coastal area; and an abortive Dominion of New England was designed to provide defense against France. The mercantile system began with the Navigation Act of 1651 passed under Cromwell. This was amended in 1662, 1663 (the Staple Act) and 1672 Enforcement Act). The enforcement of these laws was entrusted to the Lords of Trade (1660), who were succeeded by the Board of Trade (after 1696).

While enjoying the benefits of these acts (e.g., protection by the Royal Navy, drawbacks on imported European goods, employment of American ships), New Englanders especially avoided them, as by trading with foreign West Indies islands. Various colonies also resisted political centralization following the Stuart Restoration (e.g., the Nathaniel Bacon rebellion against Sir William Berkeley, Virginia, 1676; the remaking of Maryland from a Catholic into a Protestant colony, 1689-1691; anti-Royalist and anti-Anglican activities that resulted in the annulment of Massachusetts' charter, 1684). Even more strenuous was colonial opposition to the Catholic King James II. John Locke's Of Civil Government, which supported the compact theory of government, became a colonial bible, and it was questioned whether either parliament or king could legislate for the empire. The royal colony was therefore preferred by English authorities as a way to gain additional control over colonial government. However, various proprietary colonies (Delaware, Maryland, Pennsylvania) and corporate colonies (Connecticut, Rhode Island) kept their original charters through the colonial period, while eight were royal. In the last, a crown-appointed governor followed instructions from home and could veto local legislation, yet he often was made compliant by his legislature's power of the purse. Meanwhile, as economic superseded religious objectives in English governments following 1689, colonists turned their anger against mercantilistic regulations.

In consequence of the Navigation Act of 1696, in 1697 a series of Vice Admiralty courts were established in America to enforce the navigation acts. Moreover, the Board of Trade would see to it that no colonial law contravened English law or policy. Appeal was possible, however, after royal disallowance. Among new regulations were those that forbade colonists to develop manufactures or to depreciate the value of money. Nevertheless, laxity of enforcement and the availability of free land enabled colonists to evade the laws and to some degree to establish manufactures.

II. COLONIAL CONDEMNATION TO CAPITALISTIC INFANCY

Colonial growth during the 18th century was rapid and expansive. The native birth rate and immigration multiplied the number of people by five, to about 2.5 million, in 1776. Not only did farmers reach out from tidewater to the Appalachians; pushing through gaps, traders and pioneers went west of the mountains. Some coastal towns became cities, while trade centers, forts, and settlements appeared in the piedmont, especially about the river fall line. Traders went toward the frontier first, then cattle drovers, pioneer settlers, and permanent farmers. With the last came the institutions of civilization. The rate of expansion differed. The best lands were taken up first, following the pacification of Indians. Land speculators enticed many individuals, whereas New Englanders preferred to establish new townships. Meanwhile colonial seaboard merchants, especially in New England's many ports and in New York, Philadelphia, Baltimore, and Charleston, invested in ships and trade. New England shippers brought southern staples to Europe and returned with British manufactures. Or they brought home West Indian molasses (mostly French and Spanish in violation of the Molasses Act), and made it into rum which they exchanged for African slaves they sold in the West Indies and the South. Or they carried the lumber, fish, grains, meats, and furs of the New England and Middle Colonies to Europe and returned with manufactured goods.

A. GROWTH OF A MERCHANT CLASS. As long as colonial manufacturing remained of the homespun kind, the colonial merchant was important as the exchanger of colonial and/or foreign commodities. Based mostly in New England, merchants also often operated as bankers and quickly dominated colonial society. Although Northern merchants frequently served English merchants on commission, they sailed their own cargoes and in addition provided the transportation needed by the South.

B. GROWTH OF MANUFACTURES. Ubiquitous saw mills and grist mills were the first American "factories," with rum and whiskey distilleries not far behind. In consequence of the mechanical ingenuity of New Englanders and the encouragement they gave to sheep raising, their section became self-sufficient in textile manufacturing by 1700. The <u>Blessing of the Bay</u>, built in Massachusetts in 1631, was the first American-built ship. By 1700, shipbuilding was a prime New England industry, with sales of ships being made to other colonies and to England and Europe as well. Moreover, the manufacturing of hardware items from bog-iron also first took place in New England. However, Massachusetts soon lost her supremacy in heavy iron manufacturing to Connecticut and then to Pennsylvania, the last also the home of the misnamed Kentucky rifle. By 1775, the colonies produced one-seventh of the world's pig and bar iron. Furthermore, shipbuilding skills were early transferred to house building and the manufacture of furniture. However, to prevent competition with English producers, the Woolens Act, 1699, prohibited the sale of colonial woolen textiles outside of the colony in which they were made; the Hat Act, 1732, forbade the manufcature or export of beaver fur hats; and the Iron Act, 1750, while encouraging the export to Britain of bar iron, prohibited the making of semi-finished or finished iron products.

    1. <u>A Note on British and American Timber and Shipbuilding</u>. Until the advent of the steam-driven iron ship, sea power depended basically upon the availability of ship timber and naval stores--keels,

knees, sternposts, masts, bowsprits, spars, yards, curved framing timbers, planking, ceiling, tar and pitch, rosin, turpentine, and hemp.

The number of oak trees between 15 and 18 inches in diameter (80 to 120 years old) growing near open water in England was limited and costly in part because England did not develop a national forest policy. English oak is durable and resilient, and trees grown in hedgerows often contain vital curved forms. Its tannic acid slows the sea worm, but it is subject to dry rot and corrodes iron. It took about 3,200 loads, of 50 cubic feet each, to build one ship of the line, and England would accept no substitute for oak until after 1700, when some use was made of Baltic oak for planking below the waterline but American live oak was rejected. Most desired from the American colonies were "single stick" masts. New England contained pines (Pinus sylvestris)--1 in 10,000--as large as 120 feet long and 40 inches in diameter. A chief rival was the Pinus apalustris, or "pitch pine" that grows in the South.

British dependence upon Baltic timber was evident long before the American colonies were established and helps to explain the concern to wrest trade in it from the Dutch through the navigation acts of 1651 and 1660 and to keep that trade open during wars even though Holland was a neutral. British timber policy in her American colonies has been characterized as a stimulus to revolution, and the shortage of timber hindered British efforts in the Dutch Wars, the War of the American Revolution, and the Wars of the French Revolution.

Timber, including masts, was one of the first items American colonists shipped to England. Sawmills followed the line of settlement and at least in New Hampshire and Maine, which offered poor alternatives in farming and fishing, became both the prime factor of economic life and the spur to new settlements. By 1652, a cargo of Maine masts began a supply that continued to the end of the colonial period. Such was the vital interest of the British navy in these masts, that, despite the higher costs of American over European transportation and labor, they on the one hand subsidized their production and on the other hand monopolized them. The royal Massachusetts charter of 1691, for example, forbade the cutting without license from the crown and under a penalty of Ł100 for every violation, of white pines "of the diameter of twenty-four inches and upwards at twelve inches from the ground." In 1711, the restriction was applied to all the colonies; in 1721, it was applied to <u>all</u> trees; and in 1729 the machinery for enforcement was perfected. Masts and naval stores were granted bounties which totaled Ł1.5 million between 1706 and 1776, but they were placed on the enumerated list, meaning that they could be sold only in England, where the Navy had first choice in acquiring them. Even though British enforcement of these acts was lax, the King's "Broad Arrow" created a tremendous amount of colonial hostility that ended only with the Revolution, when colonists cut off the mast supply.

Except during the Dutch Wars and the French war beginning in 1689, England did little to encourage colonial timbering. Although the Admiralty was averse to using colonial oak and particularly to the building of warships in the colonies, it ordered a warship from Massachusetts in 1694 and another in 1695, and four frigates from New England during the War of the Austrian Succession 1747. None of the frigates built proved worthy, however. Colonial timber nevertheless relieved the pressure on English oak for both naval and merchant ships, and the colonists built large numbers of merchant ships for themselves and for English, French, Portuguese, and Spanish merchants as well. In 1730, one-sixth of the English merchant fleet was built in America. In 1776, colonists were building a hundred ships a year, and their 2,343 ships accounted for a third of the entire British registry. Most of these, built in New England, displaced much less than one hundred tons; relatively few came from south of the Chesapeake. If colonial ships did not compare in quality with English-built ones, by 1776 shipbuilding was a well-established industry that provided a livelihood for many men from New England to the Chesapeake. Colonial ships that engaged in local, inter-colonial, West Indies, and European trade helped to equalize the unfavorable balance of colonial trade, and the loss of a major source of shipping greatly hindered the British during the War of the American Revolution.

III. THE MONEY SUPPLY

More important than any other English restriction upon the expansion of colonial capitalism was the control of the money supply. It should be recalled that mercantilism was based upon the bullion theory, which called for keeping money at home and adding to it by a favorable balance of foreign and colonial trade. Silver and gold with which to pay for their unfavorable trade balance with England came from a favorable colonial trade with Spain and Portugal and foreign West Indies islands.

Without sufficient currency, colonial trade proceeded by barter until Massachusetts minted a "pine tree shilling." By putting less silver into it than the English shilling, they hoped the British would refuse them. Britain disallowed their use on the ground that they were depreciated currency. When New York overvalued the Spanish dollar compared to its English value, England by law set the exchange value of money but let the colonists overvalue foreign coins by one-third. Given its growing population and more numerous and larger commercial and industrial ventures, colonists lacked fluid capital to carry on local commerce, amass the sums needed for expansion, or invest in bonds issued by their colonies in war years. War costs were therefore met by the issue of legal tender paper money to be paid for in a certain time out of taxes. The practice was so convenient that many colonies also issued paper money during years of peace. Inexperience with this medium soon led to trouble, however, and such money depreciated in value, with subsequent issues being inflationary and British creditors refusing to accept it in payment of debt. Badly bitten by the South Sea venture, in 1720 England forbade the issue of additional legal tender money. The result was a deflation that still further hindered the expansion of colonial capitalism. In general, farmer-debtors opposed merchant-creditors. In this instance, both classes favored the overthrow of British rule so that the one could enjoy an inflated currency and the other avoid competition from British creditors. With the overthrow of British rule, Americans only would exploit America's resources.

IV. LIBERTY OR EMPIRE

A. THREE COLONIAL WARS AND A GLOBAL WAR. The Anglo-

French wars beginning in 1689 were known in the colonies as King William's War, 1689-1697, Queen Anne's War, 1702-1713, and King George's War, 1745-1748. In each the colonist, who was a militiaman regardless of his trade, operated largely in defense of his frontiers. In the first, the New England frontier was defended against France but an expedition seized Port Royal, Nova Scotia, only to have it restored at the peace table. Both France and Spain threatened the colonies during Queen Anne's war, during which some skirmishing took place in Spanish Florida and British Charleston, and in the north Port Royal was taken again. In the Treaty of Utrecht, Britain gained the Hudson Bay country, Acadia, Newfoundland, and the <u>Asiento</u>, but Louis XIV built a great fortress at Louisbourg, a gun cocked against New England. In King George's War, while General Oglethorpe defended the southern border against Spain, New England troops seized Louisbourg (1745), only to have it exchanged for Madras at the end of the war. To the colonists it was quite clear that the recision of Port Royal and of Louisbourg meant the subjugation of their interests to those of the empire.

Unlike these three wars, the Seven Years' War began as the French and Indian War when British colonists who crossed the Appalachians found French forts in the Ohio Valley. Fighting that broke out at the forward edge of two expanding empires stimulated the Board of Trade to have colonial commissioners make a treaty with the Iriquois. Hence the holding of the Albany Congress, June 1754, the first attempt to achieve colonial unity. After the Congress failed to adopt Benjamin Franklin's Plan of Union only four colonies provided their quota of militiamen. In 1755, while leading two British regiments, General Edward Braddock was killed during an attack upon Fort Duquesne (Pittsburgh). George Washington, who was on his staff, then led a defensive holding operation. Although William Johnson defended the New York frontier, murderous French-incited Indian raids provoked the scattering of the French settlers at Nova Scotia.

The military and naval operations of the Seven Years' war having been covering (see chap. 4) interest centers upon the Peace of Paris, 1763, and its imperial and colonial implications. By the treaty, it may be recalled, Britain acquired Canada, all French claims in North America east of the Mississippi, and the Floridas, thus becoming the largest empire since Rome. However, in payment for her support, France was allowed to give Louisiana to Spain.

B. THE PROCLAMATION LINE OF 1763. Their physical security insured by the Treaty of 1763, colonists anticipated untrammeled economic expansion. They were soon caught between the King's Men, or Tories, who supported a greater role in government for King George III, who ascended the throne in 1760, and the Whigs, who championed parliamentary rule. More about this problem will be said below. More immediate was the British answer to the expectation held by the average colonist as well as traders and land speculators to strike it rich in the newly-won trans-Appalachian region--the Proclamation of 1763. With the French menace gone, British statesmen decided to prevent trouble with the Indians (Pontiac's Conspiracy occurred in 1763) and to garner profits from a fur trade with them. The Proclamation created governments for Quebec and East and West Florida with which the colonists had no quarrel. But it also stated that, excluding settlements already existing, no new settlement could be made west of a line drawn along the Appalachians. It thereby violated charters granted to several colonies and killed the hopes of fur traders, land speculators, and prospective settlers. The trade with the Indians, moreover, must be licensed. The British were fairly flexible in the enforcement of the Proclamation, as in permitting the control of the Indian trade to be vested in colonial superintendents who also permitted land companies to acquire some Indian lands near the Ohio and Kentucky rivers. To most colonists, however, the Indians rather than they were favored by the Proclamation.

C. TAXING THE COLONISTS. The British thought that the colonists should help pay off the large national debt incurred during the Seven Years' War and for the defense of the enlarged American empire, the latter costing about ₤500 million annually. Colonists replied that they were already paying high taxes to meet their expenditures during the war and that the British enjoyed a favorable balance of trade with them and also collected port duties from their trade. They had no great quarrel with taxes levied to support the mercantalistic system, in large part because they smuggled rather than paying them. When the

British revived the use of general warrants by which they could enforce the navigation acts, memories of John Otis defeated them. If, therefore, prohibition did not prohibit, perhaps the cutting of the tax on molasses from 6d to 3d per gallon would entice importers to pay it and hence increase the efficiency of the customs service. So thought George Grenville, Chancellor of the Exchequer, who pushed the Sugar Act through Parliament in 1764. But the colonists perceived that Grenville had introduced an obnoxious novelty, a tax to raise revenue rather than merely to regulate trade. In addition to that on sugar, he increased the tax on wine, coffee, and silk; stopped the payment of drawbacks on European goods shipped to the colonies from England, and took jurisdiction over smuggling cases from local courts and gave it to Admiralty courts. Despite colonial assertions that the English government lacked the power to impose "taxation without representation," Grenville proceeded with the Stamp Tax, 1765. All public, corporate, and legal documents, newspapers, pamphlets, advertising, and the like, must bear revenue stamps costing from a half penny to £1. The returns from such purely internal revenue taxes were to be applied to pay for colonial defense; cases arising under them would be heard by the Admiralty Courts. The old practice had been to request colonial governments to raise money; the new act dipped directly into the colonists' pockets. It also hit the most vocal elements in the population, such as lawyers, journalists, and merchants. Soon "Sons of Liberty" associations were formed to oppose the act; colonists refused to pay their British creditors; trade fell off in a boycott of British goods; and delegates from nine colonies who attended a Stamp Act Congress in October insisted that Parliament had violated their "natural rights" and that the act was therefore unconstitutional. To their saying that Parliament could not impose an internal tax upon them because they were not directly represented in Parliament, British officials answered that they were represented by means of "virtual representation," i.e., every man in Parliament represented every British interest. In its Declaratory Act of March 1766, Britain asserted its right to govern the colonies but, in part because of objections to it by British merchants, repealed the Stamp Act. Townshend resorted to laying import duties upon an enumerated list of English articles including lead, paint, paper, and tea in the name of regulating trade rather than raising revenue. He also reduced the power of colonial assemblies by arranging to pay royal officials from the proceeds of the new taxes, for the issue of writs of assistance, and for enforcement of the act by the Admiralty Courts. He thus subordinated colonial to imperial control. Other examples of imperial control were the suspension of the New York assembly when it refused to quarter soldiers and the dissolution of the Massachusetts, New York, and Virginia assemblies because they protested the acts. As over the Stamp Act, the colonists imposed a boycott on English goods, increased local production of the enumerated articles, and were so hard upon customs officials in Boston that two regiments of British soldiers were quartered there. On 5 March 1770 the "Boston Massacre" revealed the feelings of the people, and the soldiers were removed.

Upon becoming Prime Minister in 1770, Lord North repealed the taxes on the enumerated list except for a tax of 3d on a pound of tea, the latter to uphold the principle of imperial supremacy. Unsatisfied with what they perceived as a portent of the loss of self-government, "radicals" such as Samuel Adams and Patrick Henry sought to alert the common man to his predicament. Through clandestine Committees of Correspondence in their legislatures, by 1773 a continental organization had been formed which propagandized the rights of the colonists. In that year also the Tea Act stimulated revolutionary thoughts. If Lord North could bail out a corrupt and almost bankrupt East India Company through granting it a monopoly on its rotten tea, what could stop Britain from creating other monopolies and putting the colonial merchant out of business? While tea smugglers kept busy, colonists boycotted the use of tea, the Sons of Liberty so pressured tea purchasers that shiploads of it were returned home, and a group of "Mohawks" dumped tea cargoes from three ships into Boston Harbor. Similar "tea parties" were held in other ports. North thereupon determined upon punishing the colonies for their insubordination in keeping with King George's desire that the Americans be "mastered."

D. THE COERCIVE ACTS. To punish Boston's "Mohawks," Lord North obtained a bill that closed the port of Boston, effective 1 June 1774, until Boston paid for the tea and the customs duty on it. Riders sent out by Committees of Correspondence alerted colonists to the need to support Boston. In addition North obtained laws (May 1774) providing that 1) the upper Massachusetts house, elected by the lower, would henceforth be appointed by the King; 2) the royal governor could name and remove judges of the lower courts, and 3) town meetings could be called only by the governor. Moreover, the Administration of Justice Act provided for the trial of soldiers and officials in England rather than in the colony, and the Quartering act stated that soldiers must be sheltered in citizen's homes wherever they were needed to restore public order. To the colonists, these became "the Coercive" or "Intolerable" acts. In June came the Quebec Act. To make French Canadians happier with English rule, the act extended religious freedom to Catholics, permitted French legal and political institutions, and restricted land grants not only in Quebec but in the territory west of the Appalachians as far south as the Ohio River.

E. THE FIRST CONTINENTAL CONGRESS. All colonies except Georgia sent delegates to Philadelphia to confer during September and October to determine upon how the colonists could preserve their liberties from being obliterated by Britain. Among them were Samuel Adams, John Adams, Patrick Henry, and John Jay. The decision was to resist the Coercive Acts; boycott trade with Britain; decline the Joseph Galloway plan of a union in which a royally-appointed President General and a Grand Council selected by the colonial legislatures would govern the colonies; and to agree that Parliament could regulate external commerce but not transgress the rights of colonists as Englishmen. The import-export boycott would be enforced by a Continental Association acting through local committees. However, the door to conciliation was held open in a petition asking King George to stop colonial oppression. George, however, said the colonists must submit, approved the tea tax, and declared the New England governments rebellious. Those who sought liberty within the empire were thus left no alternative but complete submission, to be accomplished by force of arms if necessary. Lord North's "Conciliatory Resolve," which provided that no taxes would be levied on colonies that met Parliamentary requisitions, arrived on 20 April 1775--a day following the battles of Lexington and Concord.

F. THE SHOTS HEARD AROUND THE WORLD. While its citizens made life miserable for British soldiers quartered in Boston and the Continental Association enforced the economic boycott of Britain, militia companies were raised and military stores collected. The governor of Massachusetts, General Thomas Gage, intended to enforce the Coercive Acts by destroying a powder cache at Concord and arresting John Hancock and Sam Adams. Intelligence from Boston warned patriot leaders, and at Lexington British troops were faced by militiamen drawn up on the town green. With eight militiamen killed, the rest took to Indian-style fighting. At Concord, militia forces caused British troops to turn back without having destroyed the entire powder cache or arresting Adams and Hancock. On the return to Boston, the British had 200 men killed and wounded by colonial sharpshooters, then were besieged. In the other colonies, militiamen prepared for war and provided escorts for the delegates to the Second Continental Congress.

G. THE SECOND CONTINENTAL CONGRESS. Delegates sent to Philadelphia in May concerned themselves with providing an army and a leader for it, the leader chosen being Colonel George Washington, then forty-three years of age, but declining French aid. This done, Thomas Jefferson's facile pen touched up John Dickinson's "Declaration of the Causes and Necessity of Taking up Arms," which stated that the colonies did not seek to sunder their union with Britain but that they raised their armies "For the preservation of our liberties, being with one mind resolved to die free men rather than live slaves." This extralegal body then assumed the functions of government, as in issuing paper money with which to pay the Continental Army, but it also sent another petition to the king. Before it could reach England, however, Ethan Allan and the Green Mountain Boys captured the forts at Crown Point and Ticonderoga (May 1775), and colonists fighting with a spirit they had never shown when fighting for the king battled the British at Breed's and Bunker Hill (17 June 1775). They lost, but Washington soon appeared to begin welding an army together. King George not only declined to receive the petition but held the colonies to be in rebellion and ordered 30,000 British troops and German mercenaries to still the revolt.

Although Benedict Arnold and Richard Montgomery

failed to take Quebec during the dead of the winter of 1775, the Continental Congress agreed to accept surreptitious material aid from France, aid without which American independence could not have been won. The Continental Congress in December authorized a Navy and issued letters of marque and reprisal useful to the large merchant fleet. But as yet the colonists sought merely liberty within the empire, not independence.

V. TWO DECLARATIONS OF INDEPENDENCE

In a sense, Britain's forbidding Britons in December 1775 to trade and have contacts with American colonists could be taken by Americans as reflecting their independence. More important, in January 1776 Thomas Paine's <u>Common Sense</u> suggested obtaining colonial liberty without rather than within the empire. A skilled propagandist, he blamed the colonists' woes upon the "Royal Brute," George, who was violating "natural law," and urged the colonists to overthrow him and establish their own government on the basis of the law of nature. While various colonies established their own governments, the opening by Congress in April 1776 of American ports to trade to all but Britons may be looked upon as an economic proclamation of independence because it overthrew the mercantilistic system. On 4 July, political independence was also declared. But to achieve independence required six years of war.

CHAPTER 6

THE WAR OF THE AMERICAN REVOLUTION

I. AMERICAN NAVAL FORCES DURING THE REVOLUTION

During the American Revolution the Continental Congress called upon the various states to fill quotas for a regular army, navy, and marine corps. Since American colonial life was closely bound to the sea, many men were engaged in fishing, in waterborne transportation, or in the shipbuilding industry. Some had seen the world from American ships; some had fought as sailors in the war against France from 1756 to 1763. Decades of experience in self-defense should have provided the Congress with a superb navy. However, the states rarely met their quotas. Moreover, nearly every state had its own military and naval structure, and the large number of privateers preferred taking prizes to serving the government directly. The lack of an efficient naval arm proved one of the greatest of the American disadvantages during the war.

A. THE CONTINENTAL NAVY. A Continental Navy (November 1775) administered by a committee in which Robert Morris did most of the work, started with two sloops converted from merchantmen and reached a peak number of 53 vessels. British ships of the line numbered 131 in 1775 and 468 in 1783, while personnel increased from 18,000 in 1775 to 110,000 in 1783. Except for one squadron operation under Esek Hopkins, who raided Nassau (February 1776), Continental vessels served as commerce raiders until they were destroyed by the British. Among the daring captains who established the earliest traditions of the United States Navy were Nicholas Biddle, Lambert Wickes, Gustavus Conyngham, and John Paul Jones.

B. STATE NAVIES. Eleven State navies brought vitally needed supplies from overseas or tried to defend America's coast. The capturing of British ships in the Boston area by "Washington's Fleet" in order to obtain supplies of munitions illustrates Washington's knowledge of the value of naval forces. A prime example of wasted effort was the joint Massachusetts-

Continental Navy attack upon the British garrison in the Penobscot River area, Maine (August 1779).

C. PRIVATEERS. Letters of marque were issued by the Continental Congress to 1,697 vessels mounting 14,872 guns and manned by 58,400 men. The States also issued similar letters. Privateers put the British to the burden and cost of convoying their merchantmen and troop transports, seized British prizes valued at $18 million, and transferred great amounts of highly essential munitions and supplies to American hands. The British lost 2,980 merchant vessels to privateers during the war (excluding recaptures); the Americans lost 1,351, of which 216 were privateers. British commercial losses proved a powerful argument for ending the American war.

II. THEATERS OF OPERATION

Naval actions of the Revolutionary War started in American coastal waters and lakes but spread to the West Indies, Europe, and the Far East when France, Spain, and Holland joined against Great Britain. American naval efforts had little effect on the outcome of the war, but of broader significance was the renewed struggle between Britain and France for colonial domination.

III. BRITISH WEAKNESSES

British naval forces needed to command the seas and supply the forces landed in America were chiefly on paper. Of the 100 ships of the line in 1776, most rotted in reserve, where they had been placed at the close of the Seven Years' War. When Americans cut off the supply of masts, England turned to inferior Baltic fir, and many hulls rotted because of a shortage of English oak. Moreover, lacking a recruiting system, the British swelled out nucleus crews with volunteers and conscripts. In addition, British military and political leaders tended to underestimate their opponents, Parliament vied for power with George III in the management of the war, many naval officers resigned rather than fight the colonists, and few naval officers who remained on duty supported the king politically. With the outbreak of war, Britain lost about 2,000 American ships on the British register, or 400,000 tons, and their 18,000 men.

The king preferred the army to the navy and "economized" by building ships (64s) too weak to handle the large vessels of his European foes (74s). While having to operate in distant theaters of varied extent and nature, no Pitt could be found to direct strategy, and corruption at the Admiralty further weakened the Royal Navy. The support of operations in America alone required the greatest logistic effort until the cross-Channel invasion of the Continent in 1944. Having eschewed a naval war by blockade alone, the British had to meet the superior forces of France and Spain at sea while being hampered by the activities of the League of Armed Neutrality (1780). In Americans they found a rational spirit as dogged and determined as their own, and at sea they met a new and well-trained fleet the Duc de Choiseul had provided and merely awaited the day to obtain revenge for defeat in the Seven Years' War.

IV. MAJOR LAND AND NAVAL ACTIONS, 1776-1781

A. VALCOUR ISLAND, 11 October 1776. After Generals Richard Montgomery and Benedict Arnold failed to take Quebec (winter of 1775-1776), the British planned to invade New England from Quebec and launch a diversionary attack on the Carolinas while a force from Halifax took New York. Retiring along the Richelieu River into Lake Champlain, Arnold built a small fleet (15 ships) with which to meet the superior British force (30 ships) en route from Montreal. Defeated, Arnold won a strategic victory: General Guy Carleton's forces were so battered that he went into winter quarters, giving the Americans a year to strengthen their forces to meet Burgoyne.

Although the Carolinians hurled the British under General John Clinton and Rear Admiral Peter Parker back from Charleston (June 1776), Generals William Howe and Clinton took New York (August 1776).

B. SARATOGA, 7 October 1777. British strategy called for a junction of forces under General John Burgoyne from Montreal, Colonel Barry St. Leger from Oswego, and Howe from New York. They were to meet in Albany, cross to join Clinton in Rhode Island, and dismember New England from the rest of the country. Weakened by engagements with Generals Horatio Gates and Arnold in September, Burgoyne surrendered to Arnold at

Saratoga. The success of American arms led France (February 1778) to sign a Treaty of Amity and Commerce and a military alliance with the Continental Congress and throw herself upon Britain. When Spain followed suit, Britain's 72 ships faced 92 Allied ships.

C. BATTLE OF USHANT, 27 July 1778. An English force commanded by Admiral Augustus Keppel met Admiral d'Orvilliers 60 miles west of Ushant and took no prizes. A court martial that acquitted Keppel revealed that an admiral's professional judgment was considered superior to the formalized doctrines ossified in the British Fighting Instructions. The battle itself had no direct connection with the campaigns in North America.

D. D'ESTAING IN AMERICAN WATERS, 1778-1779. The mere fact that a French fleet entered American waters caused Clinton to evacuate Philadelphia for New York. Admiral Richard Howe, who transported Clinton's supplies, was bottled up in New York by Admiral Charles le Comte d'Estaing, but the "general-in-command-of-a-fleet" did not attack. Sailing on to the West Indies, d'Estaing captured Grenada and defended it against Vice Admiral John Byron, whom he crippled but failed to annihilate. Then, when sent to cooperate with the Americans against the British in Savannah, he sailed away and compelled the Americans to surrender. Yet d'Estaing had done more than raise false hopes in American breasts: 1) France had captured Dominica and Grenada and found her navy capable of overseas operations; 2) the Americans had gained because his presence had caused the evacuation of Philadelphia and Newport, loosening the grip of the British upon American merchant ships, and provided Washington with Intelligence for reaching a correct strategic decision at the climax of the war.

E. RODNEY'S MOONLIGHT BATTLE, 16 January 1780. The Spanish entered the war on 13 June 1779. Admiral George B. Rodney, ready for battle, with copper-bottomed ships, sighted Admiral Don Juan de Langara, who sought to interdict British resupply of Gibraltar. Rodney's speed enabled him to get between de Langara and Cadiz; he wrecked or captured all of de Langara's 11 ships.

F. CLASHES IN THE WEST INDIES, 1780-1781.

   1. **Rodney vs. de Guichen, April 1780.** In frustrating a French descent on Barbados, Rodney proposed to circumvent the French practice of firing high and dismasting their foes by massing two of his ships against one of the French, a direct contradiction of the "lines of equal strength" demanded by the Fighting Instructions. Unfortunately the signals in the Fighting Instructions could not serve Rodney's purpose, and his captains miscarried his plan for tactical concentration. As usual, the French saved themselves by firing high.

   2. **Hood and Rodney vs. de Grasse.** Rodney captured the rich island of St. Eustatius from the Dutch. His second in command, Admiral Sir Samuel Hood, sparred inconclusively with the Comte de Grasse (April 1781). Rodney saw de Grasse but did not engage him (June 1781), thus permitting him to proceed to Yorktown.

V. OPERATIONS IN EUROPEAN AND ASIATIC WATERS, 1781-1782

A. SPAIN REGAINS MINORCA. Major Spanish objectives throughout the war were Gibraltar and Minorca. A six-month Allied siege (August 1781-February 1782) regained Minorca for Spain and closed the Mediterranean to Britain.

B. HOWE RELIEVES GIBRALTAR. Gibraltar was continuously bombarded for 13 months while facing the largest Allied concentration of the war--ships, floating batteries, supporting vessels, and 40,000 troops serving 200 heavy guns--until resupplied by Howe (19 October 1782).

C. LESS IMPORTANT NAVAL ENGAGEMENTS, 1781-1782.

   1. **The Allied Fleet Fails to Attack Darby.** An Allied fleet under de Guichen and Admiral Don Luis de Cordoba operated in British waters for two months but failed to attack the British fleet under Admiral George Darby at Torbay (August, September 1781). Off Ushant, brushes between Kempenfelt and de Guichen (December 1781), and Howe and the Allied Fleet off Gibraltar (October 1782), proved unimportant.

2. *Parker vs. Zoutman*. The only operation involving the Dutch occurred when Vice Admiral Sir Hyde Parker attacked Admiral Zoutman (5 August 1781) and learned how tough the Dutch were. No political effects attended the four hour battle.

3. *Suffren*. Admiral Pierre Andre Suffren, dauntless, aggressive, and resourceful, supplied himself from captured stores and was making the Indian Ocean a French Lake when the war ended.

VI. THE YORKTOWN CAMPAIGN, 30 AUGUST-19 OCTOBER 1781

A. THE STRATEGIC SITUATION. Since Southern exports provided the Americans with revenues for war, the British captured Charleston (May 1780), let General Charles Cornwallis loose against the Carolinas and Virginia, and sought to cut communications between Generals Nathaniel Green and Washington by securing control of Chesapeake Bay. Cornwallis chose Yorktown as his base and waited for British naval forces. Washington, in New York, and Lieutenant General de Rochambeau, in Newport, marched to attack Cornwallis (rather than Clinton in New York), depending upon Admiral de Grasse to isolate Cornwallis from the sea. Hood, who had replaced Rodney, beat de Grasse to Chesapeake Bay and went on to join his superior, Admiral Thomas Graves, at New York. He would first smash the Comte de Barras' eight sails in Newport and then deal with de Grasse. De Grasse, meantime, anchored in the Chesapeake, besieged Cornwallis, reinforced Lafayette, and sent boats to aid Washington and Rochambeau reach Yorktown.

B. BATTLE OF THE VIRGINIA CAPES, 5 September 1781. De Grasse was unprepared for an attack, but Graves' inability to signal his intentions from the *Fighting Instructions* permitted the French to weigh anchor and get to sea. As they straggled out, Graves wanted Hood to close up and bear down on the enemy. By some mystique, Hood failed (or refused) to understand Graves' intent and remained out of the action altogether. For five days de Grasse lured Graves farther away from Yorktown, which Barras had meanwhile reached with the siege guns needed to beat Cornwallis. When de Grasse sped to join Barras, Graves, with 19 ships, could not attack 36 French vessels. He abandoned

Cornwallis, whose surrender on 19 October ended British hopes for victory in America.

C. RESULTS. The Yorktown campaign vividly illustrates how power can be exerted by controlling sea communications and furnishes additional proof of the inadequacy of the *Fighting Instructions*. The decision of Admiral de Grasse to bring his entire fleet into the Yorktown campaign made the American victory possible, and thus became the critical decision of the war.

VII. FINAL WEST INDIES OPERATIONS, 1782

A. HOOD vs. DEGRASSE. When de Grasse took St. Kitts, Hood enticed him to chase but slipped in behind him and took his anchorage (25-26 January), from which de Grasse could not dislodge him. French victory on the beach, however, caused Hood to leave (13 February). Joining Rodney, Hood planned to hunt down de Grasse.

B. BATTLE OF THE SAINTS, 12 April 1782. De Grasse, now with 36 ships, and the Spanish admiral, de Solano, 15 ships, were to cover an attack on Jamaica, England's richest Caribbean island. De Grasse's men and ships were worn out. Rodney had new or fresh ships mounting carronades fired according to new techniques devised by Sir Charles Douglas. De Grasse beat to windward through the Saints Passage, successfully withstood an attack by Hood's division, and finally, with the weather gage, faced Rodney. A sudden shift in the wind brought a British ship to windward of the French line. Disregarding the *Fighting Instructions*, Rodney broke the line and was followed by his captains. In the pursuit and melee that followed, Rodney took five prizes; more importantly, he had won command of the Caribbean for Britain.

VIII. CONCLUSIONS

The naval aspects of the Revolutionary War may best be studied as an illustration of what to avoid rather than what to do in war. Most important was that neither side saw the true objective: the destruction of the enemy's fighting fleet.

Corruptness and indifference reduced British naval power; British strategy involved expedient rather than necessary activity. It dispersed naval activity rather than concentrating it in the really vital areas; the failure to blockade Brest or Toulon permitted French ships to sail for America or the West Indies, and many small convoys with few escorts were easily taken. Political control destroyed initiative in the field, and command relationships in the American theater were not clear-cut. Yet the Royal Navy did a) through Sir Charles Douglas, raise gunnery from a trade to a science; b) improve its operations by adopting Kempenfelt's system of signals; and c) learn to countenance departures from the <u>Fighting Instructions</u>.

France rejected an opportunity to invade Britain by using her rejuvenated navy piecemeal instead of whole. Tenacious attachment to the tactical defensive reduced her admirals' effectiveness. Moreover, her Spanish ally could not agree upon suitable objectives: failing to support France in invading Britain, Spain dragged France into eccentric operations against Minorca, Gibraltar, and Jamaica. The war nearly drove France into bankruptcy.

American sea power contributed to victory over Britain by supplying indispensable munitions, gravely restricting British seaborne commerce, and providing direct naval cooperation and support to American military forces. Such American leaders as Washington, Madison, Robert Morris, and Jefferson learned at least two lessons from the war: 1) conclusive naval superiority some distance from shore was necessary to prevent disruption of coastwise commerce, enforce a blockade of seaports, and make invasion possible; 2) naval power was relative--so long as Europe remained divided, it could not send its full naval power against the United States. But, feeling safe in its continental insularity, the United States made the mistake, after 1783, of liquidating the Revolutionary Navy and remaining without either a Navy or a naval program.

CHAPTER 7

A CHIP ON THE EUROPEAN WAR TABLE, 1783-1815

I. FREEDOM WITHOUT STRENGTH

The Treaty of Paris, 1783, granted the American colonists independence, established their boundaries (Atlantic to the Mississippi, Florida to Canada), authorized them to use the North Atlantic fisheries, stated that no impediment would be placed to the collection of English debts in the former colonies, and recommended a cessation of persecution of Loyalists. Lack of American naval power permitted Britain to violate the terms of the Treaty of Paris of 1783, Spain to keep closed the lower Mississippi River, and the Barbary Powers to plunder American ships in the Mediterranean and hold their crews for ransom. Moreover, the United States could not win the respect of the great powers or secure favorable terms in their markets, protect its neutral trade in time of European war, or defend the homeland.

When 90 percent of American trade sought its prewar markets in Britain, in part because the British extended credit, the latter saw no need to write a regular trade treaty. Moreover, as a foreign nation the United States was closed out of British imperial markets. The British Navy no longer protected American ships, and British diplomats no longer supported American interests. The British rightfully complained that Americans failed to pay their prewar debts and continued to mistreat Loyalists. Americans in turn charged that the English did not pay for slaves they captured during the war, kept forts and posts within the northern American boundary, and refused to let Americans use the St. Lawrence River. With Spain, meanwhile, the United States argued over the correct northern boundary of Florida and Spain's closing of the Mississippi River to American trade. Trouble also loomed from depradations committed by the Barbary powers against American trade and, after 1793, the violation of American neutral rights by both camps of belligerents in the Wars of the French Revolution.

II. FROM ASSOCIATION TO NATIONHOOD

A. THE ARTICLES OF CONFEDERATION, 1781-1789. The Articles of Confederation provided for a league of friendship to handle primarily common defense matters. The state, not the central government, was sovereign; the latter was little more than a congress because it lacked separate executive and judicial systems. Though it had a War Department, men could not be drafted; though it had a Department of Finance, it could only requisition money from the states and not tax their people. It could borrow money, issue currency, and regulate coinage, weights, and measures, but it lacked the power to control commerce. Each state, regardless of size or population, had an equal vote; at least nine states must approve the exercise of an important power; and unanimity was required for amendments. There was no bill of rights.

The unique attribute that joined Americans was their collective ownership of a Western domain, which the Articles government ordered surveyed and for which it provided a territorial form of government as a transition step to statehood.

The most important factors responsible for scrapping the Articles in favor of a new Constitution were economic: large governmental debts and heavy taxes, postwar deflation, currency shortage, bickering between debtor and creditor (see Shays's Rebellion), lack of the British imperial market, and the closing of French and Spanish as well as British trade with the West Indies.

B. THE PHILADELPHIA CONVENTION AND THE NEW CONSTITUTION, 1787-1789. Largely conservative, the delegates at Philadelphia (1787) reached compromises that made a new Constitution possible. Articles directly affecting military matters included: 1) three branches of government, with the president as commander-in-chief of the armed forces and director of foreign relations; 2) Congress could lay and collect taxes in part to provide for the common defense and could borrow money; 3) Congress was empowered to define and punish piracies and felonies committed on the high seas, and offenses against the law of nations; 4) Congress was authorized to declare war, grant letters of marque and reprisal, and make rules concerning captures on land and water; 5) though it was restricted to appropriating money for the military forces for no more than two years, Congress had the power to raise and support armies and to provide and maintain a navy, make rules for the government of the land and naval forces, and also call forth the militia to repel invasions. The Senate must pass upon all military officers granted commissions or advanced in grade. Thus defense matters became national rather than state affairs under the new constitution.

C. FEDERALISTS AND REPUBLICANS DEBATE NAVAL POLICY, 1789-1801. In the elections of 1788, George Washington was elected president and John Adams vice president of a nation including about 4 million mostly rural persons. The original departments included State, Treasury, and War.

Support for a national navy came mainly from the states of the North Atlantic seaboard and the tidewater South. No naval actions occurred until the Barbary pirates violated American shipping and the Wars of the French Revolution forced the issue of defense of neutral rights. By this time naval policy was enmeshed in partisan politics.

1. The Republicans -- or followers of Thomas Jefferson, who were Francophiles, argued that the Department of War could superintend naval affairs until a navy was provided. They opposed a navy because it would be expensive, increase the national debt, expand presidential power, involve the United States in a war with Britain, lead to the creation of a standing Navy replete with aristocratic officers, delay development of the West, and create a bureaucracy. It would be "foolish and wicked," Jefferson said, to build a large navy, for no European enemy could send its entire fleet to America because of the weather and the need to defend the homeland. A small American fleet could thus take care of whatever was sent over. However, he desired sufficient naval force to chastise the Barbary pirates.

2. The Federalists -- or followers of Alexander Hamilton, who were Anglophiles, argued that a navy would support maritime interests. In the Mediterranean, e.g., a navy could protect American shipping, overawe the Barbary corsairs, reduce insurance rates,

and avoid the humiliation of paying tribute. A navy could also demand respect from France, which directed its warships and privateers to capture neutral ships supplying the enemies of the new republic. Federalists also argued that a navy had economic and political as well as military importance. Sea power played a part in winning independence and was needed for national defense. Protection must be provided Americans engaged in foreign trade, intercolonial commerce, whaling, and fishing, and also to defend cities lying along such exposed coasts or waterways as Chesapeake Bay, Delaware Bay, the Hudson River, and Lake Champlain. State navies used for static defense did more poorly than commerce raiders during the Revolution. During that war, naval superiority enabled the British to shift from one theater of war to another along the coast, wearing down American forces compelled to march overland. The Articles government had been powerless to back up its words with force. A navy was needed to get Britain to live up to the terms of the Treaty of Paris, punish or overawe the Barbary pirates, and defend its policy of neutrality in the War of the French Revolution. Hamilton and James Madison argued that a regular navy was an indispensable instrument of national policy in dealing with foreign nations. Such a navy could hold the balance of power in America and gain respect from Europe by threatening the West Indies. Specifically a navy could help the nation obtain access to foreign markets, the ocean carrying trade, the Atlantic fisheries, and free navigation of the Mississippi. Turning sectionalism to his account, Hamilton added that the Southern states could provide ship timbers and naval stores, the Middle States the iron, and the North the shipbuilders and skilled seamen.

The original stimulus for the building of an American navy thus came from the desire to chastise the Barbary pirates. The result was a compromise, however: a navy would be built but construction would stop if satisfactory terms were made with Algiers, Morocco having been quieted with an American payment of $10,000 in 1787. The vote was clearly sectional, with New England and the Middle Atlantic states favoring and the South Atlantic and frontier states opposed; Federalists for, Republicans against; coastal areas for, interior areas against.

That new ships would take years to provide was clear from the decision that they would be built of live oak and red cedar, which needed months of curing before they could be used. Moreover, they should be able to outrun anything they could not outfight, the words of Federalists being that they "should combine such qualities of strength, durability, swiftness of sailing, and force as to render them equal, if not superior [not merely to the Algerian corsairs, but] to any frigates belonging to any of the European powers." As designed by Joshua Humphreys, these frigates, such as the Constitution, were "a picture of beauty unsurpassed on the seven seas." But the Federalists proceeded to build ships not yet designed, out of timber not yet cut, in nonexistent shipyards, and with men not yet employed. Good politics came to the rescue in part in the announcement that one ship would be built at each of six seaports--Portsmouth, N.H., Boston, New York, Philadelphia, Baltimore, and Norfolk--in rented shipyards, and that supplies for their building would come from almost every state. The Federalists thereby involved as many states, companies, and individuals as possible.

Despite peace with Algiers in 1796, Federalists were able to overcome Republican opposition and called for the completion of at least three of the yet unfinished ships (Constitution and United States, and Constellation), for it was Federalist policy eventually to create a standing navy to protect the nation's interests.

III. THE UNITED STATES AS A NEUTRAL, 1793-1801

Caught between English Orders in Council and French decrees, American trade suffered.

The American Treaty Plan of 1776, which the French included in their Treaty of Amity and Commerce with the colonists in February 1778, held that contraband included only materials of war, "free ships made free goods," and that foodstuffs were not contraband. By an Order in Council dated 8 June 1793, Britain authorized the seizure and preemptive purchase of neutral foodstuffs bound for France; by a similar order dated 6 November it authorized the detention of ships serving French colonies. Therefore French private property on American ships could be taken, thereby violating the Plan of 1776. Moreover, England enforced the Rule of 1756--trade not open in peace could not be opened in time of war--and thus proscribed American trade with the French, Spanish and Dutch West Indies. Moreover, the French retaliated by seizing American ships that served England. In consequence, John Jay was sent to London to 1) adjust differences arising out of the Treaty of Paris of 1783; 2) obtain payment for British seizures; 3) get the British to open their West Indies to American trade; and 4) write a regular trade treaty. He was prohibited from reaching agreements that violated America's treaties with France. The treaty provided that the British would evacuate the Northwest posts and that various minor matters would be submitted for solution to arbitral commissions. Jay gave up on "free ships, free goods" by agreeing to British proclusive purchasing of cargoes destined for France and British seizure of French private property. Although Britain agreed to a trade treaty, its limitations upon American trade with her West Indies were so restrictive that the United States rejected them. In the Jay Treaty the United States agreed to British interpretations of the right of belligerents to interfere with neutral shipping. France regarded the treaty as a violation of the Franco-American treaties of 1778 and continued her depradations upon American commerce despite the American proclamation of neutrality (22 April 1793). With the help of President George Washington and Alexander Hamilton, Federalists overcame Republican opposition and won senatorial approval for Jay's treaty and thereby possibly averted an impending war. This treaty also had repercussions for Spain, which had allied herself with France against England and could not defend her American frontiers. In the Thomas Pinckney treaty, Spain granted the United States free navigation of the Mississippi and agreed to the 31st parallel as the northern boundary of Florida. With both Britain and Spain promising to control their Indians, the sovereignty of the United States was finally respected, only to be challenged by France. France captured 300 merchant ships by 1797. She then directed that all vessels carrying British goods be seized (January 1798). President Adams sought explanations and adjustment but was rebuffed (XYZ Affair, 1797). The Federalists then resorted to reprisals in an undeclared naval war in which American ships opposed only French armed vessels.

Because of continued French spoliations of American commerce, the Federalists decided to complete the building of the Humphrey frigates; build, purchase, and rent other ships; and establish a separate Navy Department that would keep the Navy upon a solid and permanent foundation. President John Adams's choice as first Secretary of the Navy was a Georgetown merchant, Benjamin Stoddert. Stoddert rushed the completion of the <u>Constitution</u> and the <u>President</u> and assembled more than 50 ships in various seaports. These ships protected America's coast, provided escorts for merchant ships, and won many victories against French merchantmen and even privateers. Stoddert's first annual report, 1798, also helped to establish Federalist naval policy by demanding a navy that would protect America's coast and defend seaborne commerce, thus demanding respect for America's neutral rights. That navy should consist of at least 12 74s, 12 frigates, and 20 to 30 smaller ships that would be built at home, thereby providing profit to American citizens and subsidizing American industry and making it independent of foreign supplies. He would also create a shore establishment to support the Navy, including shipyards, warehouses, and drydocks. Stoddert's recommendations tied all sections to support of the Navy, for a Navy would defend national interests. His recommendations for building ships of the line stemmed from his knowledge that frigates could not stand up to British ships. The six 74s authorized, however, could stand up to British and French ships, hit in the West Indies, and pit one nation against another that challenged American interests in a classic balance of power game. Congress obliged in 1799 by authorizing $1 million to build 6 74s, $200,000 for timber lands and timber, and $20,000 with which to build two drydocks. Stoddert went ahead and acquired new yard sites at Portsmouth, N.H., Boston, New York, Philadelphia, Washington, and Norfolk. Although Stoddert revised the code of naval regulations and built a naval hospital, Congress rejected his demands for the creation of the grades of admiral, vice admiral, and rear admiral, and for a naval reserve corps.

IV. THE UNDECLARED NAVAL WAR WITH FRANCE, 1798-1800

During the undeclared naval war with France, the

Adams administration doubled its expenditures, raised taxes, and augmented the national debt. Because the Navy was used against France, moreover, Jeffersonians vowed that once in power they would cut the Navy back.

A. OPERATIONS. Under President Adams, Humphreys's frigates were rushed to completion, a separate Navy Department was established, and the navy was augmented to 49 ships, including 3 frigates and 46 converted merchantmen. The navy operated in four squadrons in the strategically important West Indies during the Quasi-War. In the period 1798-1800, the British acted almost as allies and tutored the Americans in seamanship.

   1. Captain Thomas Truxtun was the outstanding American naval officer of the Quasi-War, revealing superb seamanship when his Constellation fought the Insurgente (9 February 1799), and Vengeance (1 February 1800). Moreover, Truxtun adapted British naval administration techniques to American use and established a system of discipline that created a body of skilled naval leaders.

   2. Abrogation of the French Alliance. At the outbreak of the wars of the French Revolution, the Franco-American military alliance of 1778 was still in force. Fortunately for the United States, her merchant fleet was of greater use to France than her puny navy, and France never called for the execution of the alliance. Washington accepted the advice of his Secretary of State, Jefferson, to follow a de facto policy of recognition with respect to the new French government. Jefferson also enforced the policy of neutrality in the Anglo-French war announced by Washington and agreed with Washington's policy that the United States should avoid permanent alliances with other nations.

During the undeclared war with France, Congress authorized the capture of armed French ships but not of French merchantmen and abrogated the French Alliance on the ground that France had violated it. American naval ships and privateers took more than 80 armed French ships, mostly in the West Indies, until an agreement was reached whereby the United States government assumed payment of the spoliation

claims against France, of some $20 million, and the
French Alliance was abrogated. This Convention of
1800 restored peace and included a commercial treaty.
Republican opposition to Adams's policies, and universal opposition to the Allien and Sedition Acts,
resulted in the election of the first Republican
president, Jefferson, in 1800.

V. JEFFERSON'S NAVAL PLANS, 1801-1809

Jefferson favored agriculture over commerce and
believed in economical government. Despite the repeal of the Excise Tax, which in 1794 sparked the
Whiskey Rebellion, Secretary of the Treasury Albert
Gallatin between 1801 and 1810 reduced customs duties
yet also reduced the national debt, greatly augmented by the Adams administration, by one third.
This result was achieved largely by cuts in defense
spending, hardly a logical recommendation when the
nation verged upon war, and was resisted, even if
ineffectually, by Republicans who lived along the
Atlantic seaboard, including Secretary of the Navy
Robert Smith, of Baltimore, who served from 27 July
1801 to 7 March 1809. Congress had the President
discharge all but a small nucleus of naval officers,
paid these only while they were on active service,
cut the Navy to six operating ships, and stopped the
building program and navy yard and drydock improvements. Could Jefferson have had his way, he would
have put all ships in a covered dock at Washington,
and said nothing about new construction. The Army,
needed for defense against Indians, remained untouched.

It may be recalled that the Peace of Amiens
brought merely a lull in the struggle against Napoleon
which resumed in May 1803 and continued to 1815. A
main task for Jefferson therefore was how to avoid
war. That Jefferson was flexible is revealed in his
purchase of Louisiana despite his constitutional
scruples and objection to large governmental expenditures. After failing to make Florida and then San
Domingo the key sugar isle in an American empire,
Napoleon decided to sell Louisiana. The closing of
the Mississippi by the Spanish Intendant irked the
United States. Why not take Louisiana over, sell it,
and gain both money and a friend who would support
him rather than the British?

Peace, the avoidance of heavy spending for a navy, and noninvolvement in foreign affairs were Jeffersonian tenets. Another example of Jefferson's flexibility was that he changed his tune when involved first with the Barbary Pirates and then with the belligerents in the Wars of the French Revolution.

Jefferson's military policy was based in part upon the fact that he governed men accustomed to the use of arms who would spontaneously rise to the nation's defense. His citizens, mostly farmers, demanded few services from government, resented taxation, applauded economy in government, and would extinguish the public debt. To seek to rival Britain on the sea was folly; ships were expensive, operated to the benefit largely of commercial and industrial interests, mostly Federalist, and in the end would be paid for by the nation's farmers. It appeared more logical to assume the small-navy view and resort to ships only for defense and for commerce raiding.

The Jefferson-Gallatin program opposed the building of ships of the line and relied instead upon passive coast defense. Four major elements would provide that defense: 1) fixed land batteries; 2) mobile land batteries; 3) floating naval batteries, and 4) gunboats positioned in all major harbors and waters (e.g., 50 between New York and Cape Cod, 40 along the Mississippi). Jefferson thought that 200 gunboats, costing about $3,000 each, would suffice. "It must be superfluous," he wrote Congress on 10 February 1807, "to observe that this species of naval armament is proposed merely for defensive operation; that it can have but little effect toward protecting our commerce in the open seas, even on our own coast; and still less can it become an excitement to engage in offensive maritime war, toward which it would furnish no means."

VI. JEFFERSONIAN RETRENCHMENT

During his last days in office, Stoddert acquired land for navy yards in order to establish a permanent shore establishment for the navy; revised the code of regulations governing the navy; recommended changing the law to allow the appointment of flag officers; and recommended the scrapping of all improvised ships, the retention of 13 large ships, and the construction

of sufficient ships to bring Navy strength to 12
ships of the line and 24 frigates. With the victory
of the Jeffersonians in the election of 1800, however, the expected change from a capital ship navy to
a mere coastal defense navy occurred. The administration authorized the retention of only 13 ships,
45 officers, and 150 midshipmen, and cut the naval
appropriations for construction.

   A veteran of the War of the Revolution trained
as a lawyer, Secretary of the Navy Robert Smith (27
July 1801-7 March 1809) lacked marine and naval experience. When he took office, his staff consisted
of an administrative division and an accountant's
office. As late as 1813, however, there were only 9
clerks in the former and 11 bookkeepers in the latter.
Smith was forced to make decisions on many matters in
which he lacked technical competence. Fortunately,
he leaned on the advice of Charles Goldsborough, who,
except for 2 years, served as Chief Clerk from 1798
to 1843. Nevertheless, his ineffectual leadership
permitted Secretary of the Treasury Albert Gallatin
to put the nation on a sound financial footing in
part by allowing the Navy to be regarded as an expensive and perhaps dispensable luxury. Soon the
Navy had only 6 ships in operation.

VII. HUMBLING THE BARBARY PIRATES

A. CAUSES OF THE BARBARY WARS. A satisfactory
treaty was made with Morocco (1786) and tribute kept
Algiers, Tripoli, and Tunis quiet until Algiers began capturing American ships in 1793. Jealous of
the tribute granted Tripoli and Tunis, Algiers demanded and received increased payments. When the
United States refused its inordinate demands, Tripoli
declared war (10 May 1801), and Morocco, Tunis, and
Algiers flared into new friction. Morocco swore
friendship when faced with a display of American naval
power (October 1803) and a show of force kept Tunis
friendly, but Tripoli held out until 10 June 1805.
These events stopped the Jeffersonian raid on the
navy, and Jefferson himself saw the need of sending
a punitive expedition to the Mediterranean.

B. NAVAL OPERATIONS IN THE MEDITERRANEAN. A squadron
of four ships commanded by Captain Richard Dale after
Captain Thomas Truxtun declined to serve replied to

the Bashaw's declaration of war. Without logistic support, Dale pondered the formidable fortifications of Tripoli for a year without doing anything about them. His blockade nevertheless angered Morocco, which declared war (1802).

1. "Preble's Boys." Captain Edward Preble was appointed to command the Mediterranean operations. He demanded the discipline of a regular service and possessed great physical and moral courage. "Preble's Boys" were soon a disciplined, fighting corps. While pacifying Morocco, Preble learned that William Bainbridge had run the Philadelphia on an unmarked shoal off Tripoli and lost his crew to the Bashaw. At night (16 February 1804), in the most spectacular feat of the war, LT Stephen Decatur, in a captured ketch, got alongside the Philadelphia and fired her, removing the stain upon American honor. While Preble's small squadron won no victories against an overpoweringly strong adversary, Preble is credited with solidly founding the United States naval officer corps.

2. Other Commanders. Neither Commodore Barron nor John Rodgers, Preble's successors, were able to improve the military situation. William Eaton, the American consul at Tunis, and American ships and Marines persuaded the Bashaw to abandon his demands for tribute. On 4 June 1805, for $60,000 the Bashaw restored peace, released Bainbridge and his crew, and promised not to molest Americans in the future as long as customary American "presents" were offered. The United States had succeeded in breaking the system of paying tribute and ransom. If these operations served as a training school for American sailors, they also convinced Jefferson of the value of gunboats, at least in shallow waters.

C. RESULTS. The Jeffersonians were forced to retreat from their niggardly policy and to double naval expenditures between 1802 and 1807. Defects in organization and administration were discovered in the Navy Department. On the other hand, Secretary Smith lent Paul Revere funds with which to manufacture copper sheathing for ships and the DuPont people funds for improving powder production methods. He also financed Robert Fulton's experiments with a torpedo that could be delivered by a harpoon gun and an anchored floating contact mine. Spectacular naval exploits and eventual success against the Barbary powers demonstrated how strength can compel respect. The Mediterranean undertakings illustrated both the difficulties of operating without close logistic support and the strategic advantages of seizing command of the home waters of the enemy. The U.S. Navy officers' corps was placed on a solid footing. Nevertheless, the Jeffersonians refused to learn the lessons of the Tripolitan war.

Then, rather than strengthening the Navy to resist the encroachments of the British and French upon American commerce, Jefferson tried to avoid war by keeping American ships off the seas as noted below, by an embargo that lasted from December 1807 to March 1809.

VIII. THE UNITED STATES AND THE WARS OF THE FRENCH REVOLUTION, 1801-1815

A. THE BROKEN VOYAGE. To evade the British rule of 1756, Americans brought cargoes from the West Indies to the United States, paid duties on them, then obtained a heavy "kick-back" when said cargoes were sent overseas. In the <u>Polly</u> case, 1801, the British Admiralty Courts upheld this "broken voyage." In 1805, however, in the <u>Essex</u> case, they condemned it, saying that only bona fide duty payments could "break" a voyage. While the British Navy seized American ships at sea, British ships also "hovered" off American ports in what amounted to a blockade. Britain also impressed seamen from American merchant ships and naval vessels (<u>Chesapeake-Leopard</u> affair, 22 June 1807).

B. BRITISH ORDERS IN COUNCIL AND FRENCH DECREES. On 21 November 1806, in his Berlin Decree, first of a series of edicts known collectively as the Continental System, Napoleon declared the British Isles blockaded, forbade all communication with them, authorized the seizure and confiscation of British ships and cargoes, and denied entrance to continental ports to neutral ships that visited England. The British struck back by barring all shipping from the coastal trade of France and her allies (7 January 1807), and permitted trade with the continent only to vessels that cleared British ports (11 November 1807). In his Milan Decree (17 December 1807), Napoleon directed that all ships searched by the British or obeying the Orders in Council were "denationalized" and subject to confiscation as British property. Neutral trade, mostly American, was thus crushed between British and French blows.

C. MADISON AND THE NAVY. President Madison, like Jefferson, neglected the Navy. Madison chose Paul Hamilton as his Secretary of the Navy. A veteran of the Revolutionary War and governor of South Carolina, he at least had military and executive experience, and he quickly tightened up naval finances, strengthened the antislave patrol along the southern Atlantic coast, kept naval surveillance over Caribbean pirates, and saw to it that a long-awaited naval hospital was built. Like Hamilton, he sponsored naval inventions, such as Fulton's spar torpedo and the construction of floating batteries and blockships. But when he suggested that offense was better strategy than inaction, that powerful, large, fast ships would be more economical than gunboats, and that these would provide a school for seamen and for scientific improvements, Congress replied by restricting American cruisers to American waters and seriously debated (1810) a proposal to reduce the Navy. The desire of the North Atlantic states to avoid a war that would destroy their commerce, and the War Hawks' vision of overland attacks on Canada and the Floridas played a part in keeping the Navy weak. The result was that 10 of the 18 seagoing ships available for war in 1812 had been built under Federalist auspices before 1801, and the Navy was woefully short of guns, powder, and personnel.

D. CONGRESS AND THE NAVY. In the Congressional debate over a proposal to build 10 new frigates (early 1812) representatives of the coast and commerce were pitted against those of the inland states and agrarian interests. Hazy conceptions of the meaning of command of the sea shadowed the remarks of even the best speakers. The majority remained wedded to Jefferson's gunboat policy; only a minority favored offensive action either by fleet against fleet or by cruisers and privateers against enemy merchantmen; few realized that command of the open sea is the best coast defense. The special session of Congress called to consider relations with Great Britain (July 1811) strengthened the Navy by authorizing the purchase of timber. During the three years of war the Navy merely doubled in size, with most new construction undertaken on the Great Lakes and at New York and Baltimore because New England opposed the war, and lacked even one drydock.

IX. THE WAR OF 1812

A. MARITIME CAUSES. The American decision to go to war with Britain was based in great part on the desire to stop Britain from impressing American seamen and violating American neutral rights on the seas. Almost 900 American ships and 6,000 men fell prey to the British between 1806 and 1812. Particularly galling were Britain's refusal to agree that a blockade could not be legal unless effective, her impressment from American naval quarterdecks (Baltimore affair, 1798, and Chesapeake affair 1807), her practice of hovering, and her stifling blockade.

B. NAVAL OPERATIONS AT SEA.

1. American Privateering Successes. Lacking ships,[1] organization, and a shore establishment, the U.S. Navy had recourse to commerce raiding upon British lifelines. Of the 1,344 British prizes taken by 526 American privateers, fully one-third were taken in the first ten months of the war. After much argument between captains who favored commerce raiding tactics and those who supported squadron operations, Captain John Rodgers proved the value of the latter. By showing himself off Britain, Rodgers put the British on the defensive, permitting American merchantmen to reach home ports unmolested. Soon Rodgers, Decatur, and Bainbridge had small squadrons patrolling the Atlantic. Their victories (12 out of 16 encounters) were won in part by the superior construction and armament of their ships and in part by their superior seamanship.

2. The British Regain Sea Control. In retaliation the British built or refitted ships that could vie with Humphreys-type American frigates. Mortified, they sloughed off carelessness and clamped a deadly blockade upon the American coasts. Blocked in port or taken at sea, the vessels of the United States gradually disappeared. Despite British superiority in the aggregate, the U.S. Navy had forced the British Navy to rearm all ships or remain outclassed ship for ship. British cutters and sloops

had a war of their own against fast American privateers that placed the Peninsular War in jeopardy and drove Britain to convoy her transports and merchantmen. Even escorts were not always safe, as illustrated by Captain Samuel Reid at Fayal. The loss of more than a thousand ships hurt the British and was a major cause in their desire for peace.

C. THE WAR ALONG THE NORTHERN BORDER.

1. <u>The Strategic Situation</u>. If the St. Lawrence is considered a tree trunk and the Great Lakes its branches, American strategy should have aimed at chopping as close to the roots as possible. But without a navy to cut Canadian communications at Montreal, the Americans struck overland. Erroneously deeming Lake Ontario the most important theater of operations, Captain Isaac Chauncey and Sir James Yeo built fleets. These sparred for position but accomplished little. Rather than taking Kingston, the logical objective, the Americans struck at York (Toronto), only incidentally improving the situation for them on Lake Erie.

2. <u>The Battle of Lake Erie</u>. On Lake Erie, however, with ships built from the forests nearby, Master Commandant Oliver Hazard Perry faced Robert Barclay, carronades to long guns, in the Battle of Lake Erie, 10 September 1813. Perry, the better seaman, used the weather gage to close Barclay. Trafalgar was refought; Perry, with almost twice Barclay's broadside weight, won a tactical and strategic victory.

Their position about Lake Erie having collapsed, the British abandoned the American northwest. Perry followed up his victory by transporting General Harrison's army across the Lake to attack the British; in the decisive Battle of the Thames, 5 October, he personally led a cavalry charge. Nevertheless, the British retained their hold on the Niagara Peninsula in Lake Ontario, thus blocking an attack on Montreal. Chauncey's obsession with watching Yeo's fleet in Kingston allowed the British to use the Lake. In sum, American preoccupation with western objectives left the British in control of the area north and west of Lake Ontario.

3. <u>Battle of Lake Champlain.</u> With Wellington

in Bordeaux, the British could spare troops for
America. In the spring of 1814, British troops took
a part of Maine. Hoping to present the area from
eastern Maine to Lake Champlain as territory to be
ceded to Britain at peace negotiations being conducted
at Ghent, Major General Sir George Prevost advanced
along the Richelieu River from Montreal to Platts-
burg, New York, the key to the Lake. As in Lake Erie,
the vessels that fought the battle were built on
nearby shores. Captain George Downie's crews were
mostly soldiers and militia, Master Commandant Thomas
Macdonough's of trained seamen. Macdonough chose to
fight from anchor, his inboard flank defended against
Prevost by Brigadier General Alexander Macomb.

On paper, the dispositions of Macdonough and
Downie resembled those in the Battle of the Nile,
with Downie, as Nelson, hoping to double on Macdonough's van. When Cumberland Head killed his wind,
however, Downie was caught by American carronades.
Macdonough had taken precaution to have spring lines
on his bow and stern anchors. When his starboard battery was shot away, he wound ship and presented his
undamaged port battery to the British, who surrendered. Macdonough's victory left the road to Montreal
open and helped win a favorable peace treaty for the
United States.

D. THE BRITISH INVASION. With Napoleon on his knees
in mid-1814, the British despatched more veterans to
America. In August, Major General Robert Ross and
5,000 troops escorted by Vice Admiral Sir Alexander
Cochran retaliated for the American raid on York by
raiding Washington. Captain Joshua Barney's 400
seamen and five 18-pounders checked Ross, giving
precious minutes to the American government to evacuate the city, part of which Ross burned. Jefferson's
gunboat navy had proved useless. Upon approaching
Baltimore, however, (September 1814), the British
found no weaknesses in the city's fortifications and
withdrew.

E. THE BATTLE OF NEW ORLEANS. A war that might have
been avoided ended with a battle fought after the
treaty of peace was signed. The U.S. Navy played an
important part in Andrew Jackson's defeat of Sir Edward Pakenham. Although the 14-gun <u>Carolina</u> was
destroyed in preliminary skirmishing, the 16-gun

Louisiana firmly anchored Jackson's right flank in the Mississippi.

X. RESULTS

A. THE TREATY OF GHENT.

    1. *Maritime Grievances.* The issue of impressment died with Waterloo, for Britain had no further need for American seamen, and the Peace of Ghent made no mention of the practice. Nor did it say anything about matters of neutral rights.

    2. *Territorial Disposition.* Nor did either country gain land, for the peace included restitution on the basis of *status quo ante bellum*. Although victorious in the field, Britain was glad to end a costly war that would hamper her should Napoleon escape from Elba and attempt to regain the continent.

B. THE WAR AND THE U.S. NAVY. The War of 1812 stimulated American naval development in various ways.

    1. *Construction.* The war stimulated naval construction. Jefferson's gunboats were sold, and almost a third of the wartime appropriations for the Navy went into new construction.

    2. *National Defense.* The war provoked discussion of the best methods of defense. Secretaries of the Navy William Jones (1813-1814) and Benjamin Crowninshield (1814-1818) recommended a capital ship navy supported by a systematic building program. Congress provided funds for strengthening the Navy for a six year period.

    3. *Disarmament.* The War threatened an Anglo-American naval race on the Great Lakes. The British soon agreed to the economical and mutually advantageous policy of disarmament for the Lakes (Rush-Bagot Agreement, 1817).

    4. *Personnel and Administration.* The position and influence of career naval officers was improved, with consequent amelioration in naval administration, particularly when three senior officers in 1815 were constituted a Board of Navy Commissioners to advise the Secretary of the Navy.

C. NAVAL LESSONS OF THE WAR.

1. **The Need for Defense**. In the War of 1812 the United States violated every known postulate of naval policy. It failed to produce the magic by which naval forces for an emergency can be procured quickly and easily.

2. **Weakness of Privateering**. The British convoy system killed the fallacy that cruisers and privateers could compel a strong maritime enemy to sue for peace. American hope that the British would be so busy protecting their commerce that their navy could not operate against the coast of the United States was dashed by an iron blockade.

3. **Fallacy of Gunboat Defense**. Also, British raids proved that gunboats and land defenses could not prevent attack from the sea. On the other hand, Britain's command of the sea and her blockade enabled the Royal Navy, by destroying American commerce, to paralyze the economic life and hence the military power of the United States.

4. **The Necessity for Command of the Sea**. The War taught the United States of the need for a capital ship navy which could meet the enemy at sea and by forestalling blockade and by convoying merchantmen keep trade flowing. It proved the tactical competence of American naval officers both in inland waters and on the high seas, earned the Navy a proud place in public opinion, and created the legend that the United States had once again defeated the world's greatest naval power. It demonstrated the soundness of building tactically superior warships; and it established the U.S. Navy as an important instrument in implementing American policy.

5. **The Need of Naval Administrative Reform**. Secretary William Jones served on a privateer during the War of the Revolution. A South Carolina and then Philadelphia merchant who traded with the Orient, he was also an inventor, having created a light lead case to enclose a measure of powder to serve guns of various sizes. With the British blockade tight, he answered demands for protection by dividing gunboats among various harbors and used floating batteries as well. He supported the creation of ships and of

amphibious forces on the Great Lakes and at Lake Champlain that made the victories of Perry and Macdonough possible, and sent naval ships and privateers to raid British commerce. It was he who supported Fulton's plan to build a steam battery. Launched on 29 October 1814, the <u>Fulton</u> appeared too late to serve in the war but well showed the possibilities of steam-powered warships.

With the destruction of Washington by the British imminent, Jones fired the Navy Yard but saved all naval records. More important in the long run was his recommending the use of gunboats only for harbor defense and the building of powerful ships of the line that would use standardized equipment, regularizing the mobilization of enlisted men, and establishing a naval academy. Most important was his reviving the suggestion originally made by Stoddert that a board of senior officers be created to advise the secretary and supervise matters assigned them--correspondence and reports, estimates, personnel management, and court martials--while civilians handled ordnance and transportation. He asked all captains to comment. These rejected the use of civilians and preferred corporate to individual responsibility. On 7 February 1815, Congress authorized a Board of Commissioners that would be completely subordinate to the secretary, thus retaining civil control, and set the number of officers at three. Naval administration would continue in this fashion until the bureau system was established in 1842.

CHAPTER 8

THE U.S. NAVY AT PEACE AND WAR, 1815-1861

I. NAVAL EMPLOYMENT, 1815-1861

With the end of the War of 1812, the U.S. Navy devoted itself to such peacetime pursuits as showing the flag, punitive expeditions, scientific research and developments, diplomatic missions, and regulating the slave trade. Offensive undertakings of the period included the chastising of the Barbary States and the War with Mexico.

II. THE END OF THE BARBARY PIRATES

A. AMERICAN OPERATIONS. Frequent interference with American trade in the Mediterranean by Algerian corsairs continued after 1807. The United States broke off diplomatic relations with Algiers in 1812, and in order to obtain a more explicit treaty declared war early in 1815. Commodore Stephen Decatur went to the Mediterranean (3 March-30 June 1815), found and destroyed several Algerian vessels, and after a show of force before Algiers obtained a satisfactory treaty including "most favored nation" privileges. Visits to Tunis and Tripoli resulted in indemnity for unfriendly acts committed during the War of 1812. In 1815 and 1816 American squadrons including the earliest ships of the line (74's) patroled the western Mediterranean. Finally Port Mahon, Minorca, was leased for a naval base to support a permanent American squadron in the Mediterranean.

B. INTERNATIONAL OPERATIONS. An international commission of the Congress of Vienna also determined to put an end to the lawless practices of the Barbary corsairs. When the Dey of Algiers rejected Britain's demand that the slavery of Christians be abolished, Admiral Viscount Exmouth, with British and Dutch ships, bombarded the city of Algiers, burned the Algerian fleet, silenced part of the shore fortifications, and forced his terms upon the Dey. Continued depredations by the corsairs led France to conquer Algeria in 1830. The Barbary nuisance was not finally eradicated, however, until steam driven merchant ships could outspeed Barbary vessels.

III. THE U.S. NAVY, 1815-1861

A. INTRODUCTION. Until 1815 the Secretary of the Navy and various clerks administered the Navy. On 5 February 1815, a three-man Board of Navy Commissioners was authorized to exercise authority over material and to advise the Secretary on all other matters. In 1842 a bureau system was adopted. Administration varied according to the political party in office and the seriousness of foreign threats to American security. The postwar reaction against naval expansion, the demilitarization of the Great Lakes, and the drop in economic activity following the War of 1812 caused less new construction, smaller annual appropriations for the Navy, the employment of small rather than large vessels, and reductions in naval personnel.

Overlooking the lessons of the War of 1812, American strategy still consisted mainly in providing coast defense by the use of fortifications, floating batteries, and ships distributed along the seaboard rather than a fleet that could stop the enemy far from the coast. Executive indifference or hostility, bureaucratic conservatism, and the older generation of officers resisted the trend toward steam vessels. The diplomatic crisis with Great Britain, 1837-1841, led to a great increase in official personnel, to the creation of the permanent Home Squadron, and to the appropriation in 1842 for the first ironclad warship authorized for any navy (Stevens Battery).

Congress ordered the sale of the Navy's gunboat flotilla (27 February 1815) and placed most large vessels in ordinary. Work on the seven 74's of the 1816 program was so slow that three of them were unfinished in 1861. In 1823 there were in operation three ships of more than 36 guns, 27 of 30 guns or less, 13 in ordinary, and 10 under construction (five 74's and five 44's). The trend toward larger ships culminated in the Pennsylvania, 120, the largest warship in the world when launched in 1837. In 1853, however, the United States did not have a single vessel capable of meeting successfully any first-class warship of a major European power.[1]

B. THE NAVY AND NATIONAL POLITICS. In general, the Whig party favored a strong Navy and the Democratic party opposed, although the last two presidents of the period (Pierce and Buchanan) strengthened the Navy. Manifest Destiny and slavery politics strongly affected naval developments.

1. <u>Territorial expansion</u> conditioned naval policy and development by strengthening the Navy to fight Mexico (1846-1848), to protect two ocean fronts after the war, and to prevent British expansion in Central and North America and in the Caribbean. It also led to a demand for an Isthmian canal under American control. The Congress did not build up the Navy until the outbreak of the Mexican War. Then, in addition to providing funds for four steam warships, it subsidized private shipping companies which would build steamers convertible to war use. The latter were poor substitutes for regular ships of war.

2. <u>Slavery politics</u>, in the years before the Mexican War, pushed naval affairs into the background or made it a pawn of sectional legislation. By 1861 the Southern desire for territorial expansion, the discovery of gold in California and Australia, increased European immigration, the Mexican War and the Crimean War, the boom in the Far Eastern trade, and the rapid increase of American industry and commerce contributed to an atmosphere favorable to naval development. With Franklin Pierce (1853-1857) the United States Navy was rejuvenated materially by the construction of six screw-driven steam frigates and five shallow draft screw-driven steam sloops of war (wood, 8-10 knots). Yet the U.S. Navy in 1861 was comparatively weak, its wooden walls no match for explosive shells, its steamers no match for those of Europe. Strategy still centered about the concepts of 1812 and prevented the building of a capital ship navy.

C. OPERATIONAL ORGANIZATION AND DUTIES. In this period the United States established various semipermanent squadrons: the Mediterranean (1815), the West Indies (1822, absorbed by the Home Squadron, 1841), the African (1853), the Brazil (1826), the Pacific (1817), and the East India (1817). These squadrons controlled the slave trade, combated piracy, and maintained the immunity of American ships to search from British vessels. The Navy also "showed the flag"; conducted voyages of exploration and scientific research (e.g., Lt. Charles Wilkes); aided vessels in distress; "chastised native insolence" (e.g., Captain John Downes at Quallah Battoo, Sumatra); opened up new markets abroad; assisted with diplomatic negotiations (Kearny in China, Perry in Japan); cooperated with the Army against the Seminole Indians in Florida; and acted as observers in foreign wars (Farragut witnessed the French shelling of Vera Cruz, 1838). The foremost function of the Navy was to defend and promote American maritime commerce. Since the ships of the various squadrons operated separately or in small groups, no real squadron or fleet organization existed.

IV. NAVAL ADMINISTRATION, 1815-1846

A. BENJAMIN F. CROWNINSHIELD, 1815-1818. Crowninshield, of the seafaring Massachusetts family, was the first secretary to have the aid of the Board of Commissioners, originally comprised of Commodore John Rodgers and Captains Isaac Hull and David Porter. Since Porter served until 1822 and Rodgers until 1837, and the terrible-tempered Charles Goldsborough until 1823, when he succeeded James Kirke Paulding as Board Secretary, continuity was well provided in the Board. The Board's first Secretary, Paulding, who served from 1815 to 1823, was then Navy agent in New York, 1823-1833, and thereafter became the Secretary of the Navy, again providing continuity.

Crowninshield's first task was to direct the transition of the Navy from war to peace; his second to deal with Algiers; his third to assert civilian supremacy over the Commissioners. By Presidential direction, the Board would procure stores, supplies, materials, and weapons, and design, repair and refit ships while the Secretary controlled ship movements and personnel and acted as the naval strategist. However, toward the end of his tenure Crowninshield became "irresolute and vacillating." He remained in Washington only when Congress was in session and let the chief clerk and the commissioners do most of the work. While he could not see the possibilities of steam-powered ships, he pushed experiments with cannon shells and deserved credit for the establishment of the first of the "distant stations," in the West Indies, Mediterranean, and eastern Pacific.

B. SMITH THOMPSON (1819-1823). Trained in the law, Thompson was absent from the Department almost as much as Crowninshield. He nevertheless had great interest in the education of midshipmen and was the first to direct that midshipmen be given examinations before being promoted to lieutenant—the first examinations ever used by the Navy. The Selection Board for 1820, incidentally, found David Glasgow Farragut deficient in seamanship! Thompson established a strong force in the West Indies to combat piracy, sent the first American ships on anti-slaver patrol off Western Africa, and also sent a ship to the East Indies. While he was in office, the first U.S. steamer to engage in warlike operations, the converted New York ferryboat <u>Seagull</u>, operated in the West Indies, but Thompson had no technological or scientific interests, and with his tour the U.S. Navy reached its post-War of 1812 nadir.

C. SAMUEL LEWIS SOUTHARD, 1823-1829. Only 36 years of age when appointed, Southard had gone through Princeton College in two years, read law, and gained admission to the bar. He also served as a state judge and U.S. Senator. Although he knew nothing of the sea, he was a better secretary than the other nine men who served between 1815 and 1842. His list of accomplishments was long: he pushed forward the construction of navy hospitals, adopted a naval criminal code, improved the naval officer rank structure, reorganized the Marine Corps; established a regular line of communication from Washington to the Pacific via Panama, increased the efficiency of the naval medical corps, started construction on the Navy's first two drydocks (at Charlestown and Norfolk), selected Pensacola as the site of the principal navy yard on the Gulf of Mexico, and introduced recruiting in inland areas. In addition he began surveying all the important harbors along the Atlantic coast; demanded the establishment of a naval academy that would educate both naval and Marine Corps officers, the latter as yet being obtained from West Point; spoke much about the need for a U.S. exploring expedition in the Pacific; and favored the adoption of steam-powered warships. His impact on the Navy is well shown by the increase of the number of ships from 35 to 52, of personnel from 3,400 to 5,600, and of annual operating costs from $2 million to $3 million. He thus reversed the downward swing of the Navy under Thompson and Crowninshield and furnished Andrew Jackson, who assumed the Presidency in 1829, a Navy that was an important adjunct to the government. Unheeded by Congress, however, was his call for higher ranks for officers, the establishment of a naval academy, and the sending out of an exploring expedition to the Pacific.

D. JOHN BRANCH, 1829-1831. A successful planter of North Carolina, Branch was trained in the law but never practiced it, and served in his state legislature, as Governor, and U.S. Senator before entering Andrew Jackson's cabinet. Busy with myriad internal affairs, Congress declined Jackson's recommendation to improve the Navy. Unfamiliar with naval affairs, Branch nevertheless instituted some reforms, as in revising the regulations for the government of the Navy, speeding up the construction of naval vessels, using Marines to apprehend thieves in the Navy's timber preserves, getting the President to dismiss naval officers who engaged in duels, suggesting that a bureau system might improve naval administration, and showing great interest in the building of steam batteries. Conversely, he showed little interest in sending an exploring expedition to the "South Seas." In the end, in his short service he accomplished little except to point out many shortcomings in the Navy Department that eventually were remedied.

E. LEVI WOODBURY, 1831-1834. Woodbury, of New Hampshire, graduated from Dartmouth College, followed the law and bench, and had a familiarity with naval affairs through serving on the Senate Committee on Naval Affairs from 1825 to 1831. Unfortunately, he assumed office just as President Jackson ordered cutbacks in the Navy, in consequence of which the Board of Navy Commissioners opposed introducing anything new either in ships or procedures. Except for providing safeguards during the flogging of seamen and hiring additional teachers to serve on several of the larger ships, his suggestions for reforms had already been voiced by Branch. Only two outstanding events marked his service: the obtainment of satisfaction by Commodore John Downes from Sumatra after natives plundered an American ship and took three lives, and the sending of Edmund Roberts to write the first treaties with such countries of the Far East as Siam and Muscat. Roberts failed to obtain a treaty with Cochin China and died before he could write one with Japan.

F. MAHLON DICKERSON, 1834-1838. Of impeccable political credentials and considerable wealth, Dickerson was nevertheless a poor secretary. Ill, and sixty-four years of age in 1834, he followed the lead of Commodore Rodgers, President of the Board of Navy Commissioners, rather than making his own decisions and providing the Navy with leadership. However, at the suggestion of his good friend Captain Matthew C. Perry, he authorized the building of the USS <u>Fulton</u>, a 700-ton steam-powered side wheeler armed with four 32-pounders. Although her range was extremely short, she initiated steam power into the Navy. Second, under the sponsorship of Samuel Southard, the former naval secretary now serving as chairman of the Senate Committee on Naval Affairs, Congress finally authorized what came to be known as the Charles Wilkes exploring expedition to the Pacific. With Dickerson ill, supervision of the expedition passed to the Secretary of War, Joel R. Poinsett, and Dickerson was no longer secretary when the expedition finally sailed, on 18 August 1838.

G. JAMES KIRKE PAULDING, 1838-1841. Martin Van Buren was elected President in 1836 on the understanding that he would continue the policies of his predecessor, Andrew Jackson. With respect to the Navy, this meant that he was not indifferent to its needs; he was friendly to it but had no great zeal for it. Moreover, he was swamped by financial troubles attendant the Panic of 1837 and tension along the northern border stimulated by a rebellion in Canada. In choosing Paulding as his naval secretary, Van Buren selected a man who had served as secretary of the Board of Navy Commissioners during much of the two terms of James Monroe, then as Naval Agent for New York until 1838. More of a literary man than statesman or administrator, Paulding nevertheless had many naval friends, particularly Commodore Rodgers, who for more than twenty years (1815 to 1837) dominated the board.

To administer a navy comprising about 50 ships and 10,000 officers and men and funded at about $5 million a year, Paulding had the use of nine clerks and a messenger, at an annual cost of less than $2,200, whereas the Board of Navy Commissioners expended about $12,000 annually for secretarial help and draftsmen yet complained that they needed at least three more clerks. The board members, moreover, held firmly to the belief that national security depended upon static coast defense and commerce raiding. While major navies abroad veered upon adopting iron ships, steam power, and Paixhans shells for their guns, they preferred ships whose design and ordnance differed little from those of the days of Rodney and Nelson. They were supported by Van Buren, Congress, and also Paulding. Of the latter it has been said that "He was not a warm friend to new fashions which threatened to overthrow naval traditions, denude the sea of romance and the sailing ships of their glory." He therefore planted himself across the path of progress toward "dirty and noise steamers." Favoring steam, however, were some oldsters like Matthew Calbraith Perry and Robert F. Stockton and such younger men as Matthew Fontaine Maury, Alexander Slidell Mackenzie, and John A. Dahlgren.

With the nation at peace, Paulding used the Navy to show the flag, protect Americans and their property overseas, and suppress the slave trade, with officers doubling as diplomats when necessary. Commodore Lawrence Kearny, for example, stood off China during the Opium War (1839-1842), and Paulding sent Wilkes his sailing orders for an expedition that would survey the Pacific Ocean. He also supported the creation of a Naval Academy, the training of apprentices on board operating ships, and the operation of as large a fleet as Congress would fund--a reversal of the policy of his two predecessors, who had sought to reduce its size. Although he opposed experiments with steam power and improved ordnance, five steamers were authorized during his term, and thanks to Matthew C. Perry an engineer corps was established. Perry, incidentally, also was instrumental in the adoption of optical lenses instead of reflectors in lighthouses and in proving the worth of shells over shot in an ordnance proving ground he established. Paulding called Perry and other steam advocates "iconoclasts," was horrified of steam-powered ships, which he called "fire breathing monsters," and would allay "the steam fever." He knew he could not stem progress, however. Therefore, "I am willing . . . to go with the wind, though I don't mean to carry full sail, and keep the steam enthusiasts quiet by warily administering to the humor of the times, but I will never consent to let our ships perish, and transform our Navy into a fleet of sea monsters." With respect to the organization of naval administration, he recommended the adoption of the bureau system, and in great part because of the war scare with Britain over the burning of the American ship *Caroline* in the Niagara River, 29 December 1837, he increased the number of officers and men and established the Home, or North Atlantic Squadron.

Paulding served the Navy in various capacities for 23 years. As naval secretary, however, he was too conservative to provide the leadership needed to help the Navy make the transition from wood to iron, sail to steam, shot to shell. Reforms on these matters had to be forced upon him by officers like M. C. Perry or by Congress.

H. GEORGE E. BADGER, 6 MAR.-11 SEPT. 1841. Badger served as naval secretary for so short a time that he failed to make an impression on his Navy or even sign an annual report. Much more important was Abel P. Upshur.

I. ABEL P. UPSHUR, 11 OCT. 1841-23 JULY 1843. A Virginia planter, lawyer, prosecuting attorney, judge, politican, and cabinet member, Upshur defended the past against the present in political affairs, as in espousing slavery and states' rights. The "Calhoun of Virginia" he might be. More important for the Navy, he counted a number of progressive young naval officers among his friends and entered his office saying that for the past 20 years the Navy had received from the government "Little more than a step-mother's care." He therefore set out to reform the Navy. Starting with his own office, he would then tackle ship construction, the navy yards, gunnery, personnel, naval justice, education, and science. He meant to overlook nothing.

First on Upshur's list of reforms was a rewriting of the rules for the government of the Navy, unrevised for 23 years. This accomplished, he replied to a resolution of the House of Representatives, dated 19 February 1838, that he report "a plan for the reorganization of this branch of the public service, adopting as the basis of his plan the division of the duties now performed by the Board of Navy Commissioners, and their assignment to separate Bureaux." The Committee of Naval Affairs furnished a bill to reorganize the Department by repealing the act establishing the Board of Navy Commissioners and creating six bureaus: Yards and Docks, Construction and Repair; Equipment, Provisions, and Stores; Ordnance; Hydrography; and Medicine and Surgery. The naval secretary could choose the chiefs of bureau, who would be responsible to him, and also create an office of the Judge Advocate General. Happy with most of the bill, Upshur saw, however, that it omitted the Bureau of Personnel he desired and wanted the Bureau of Equipment, Provisions, and Stores divided into two bureaus, one of Equipment, the other of Provisions and Stores. This last done, on 6 August 1841 the Senate joined Equipment with Construction and Repair and Ordnance with Hydrography. Upshur noted that Congress had joined bureaus that had no natural connections, but Congress paid no heed. However, the demise of the Board of Navy Commissioners meant that the naval secretary had no corporate board to advise him. He alone was the unifying factor in the Department. Moreover, because Congress did not specify a term of years of service for the bureau chiefs, some of them in the days following Upshur served for upwards of 25 years. At any rate, with nominations approved, the bureau system went into effect on 1 September 1842.

Congress had never fixed the number of officers and men in the Navy, the result being irregularity and inconsistency in numbers and promotions. At Upshur's request, Congress set the number of officers allowed in each grade. At his recommendation also, plans were drafted for regulating by law admission to a naval academy and providing that five years would pass before a graduate of such an institution would be entitled to examination for a warrant as "passed midshipman." Although he could not obtain the right to "select out" inefficient officers, Upshur sent the names of such men to the Senate, who would consider his message when time came for promotion.

"Trade is never secure, unless it can, at all times and in all places, appeal or support to the national flag; and it ought to feel that it is safe wherever that flag is displayed," said Upshur in calling for an increase in the size of the Navy. Although its trade was twice that of the United States, Britain maintained a navy eight times larger than that of the United States, and France, with only one-third the American merchant tonnage, had five times as many warships. Moreover, security against invasion by wooden ships had passed because of steam-powered ships and improvements in ordnance. Long before Mahan said it, he called for a fleet that could "meet the enemy upon the ocean, with men trained and disciplined for the contest." And whatever the number of ships Congress provided, they must match the quality of those of the leading naval powers. Unlike Paulding, he favored the building of steam-powered ships and would build experimental iron and screw ships in order that the U.S. Navy not fall behind the technology of Britain and France. Two paddle-wheel steamers authorized in 1839, the *Missouri* and *Mississippi*, had extremely limited range and aroused some merriment because they would lay their funnels on deck when using their sails. A third experimental ship, the *Union*, commissioned in 1843, never performed well. Captain Robert F. Stockton obtained Upshur's permission to place a submerged screw instead of paddle wheels in a full-rigged sloop-of-war displacing 954 tons. With the machinery going below the waterline, the ship would be fairly safe from shot and shell. With the help of John Ericsson, whom he enticed from England, the machinery of the *Princeton* was coupled directly to a 6-bladed screw. Thus was born the first screw-driven war vessel in the world, and also the first to burn anthracite coal. Meanwhile Upshur had four unarmored iron-hulled steamers built--the only ones of their kind built prior to the Civil War. The 570-ton side-wheeler *Michigan*, launched in Lake Erie in December 1843, was the first iron ship in the Navy. Because of the war scare with Britain, in 1842 Congress also authorized the building of the second "shot and shell proof" ironclad warship in the world if Fulton's "bullet-proof" boat authorized in 1814 was considered the first. Robert Livingston's "Stevens Battery," though worked on until 1854, was finally abandoned.

Despite much opposition, Upshur in 1842 obtained the largest funding for the Navy to date--$6,588,894-- and in addition created two scientific agencies that grew out of the old Depot of Charts and Instruments-- the Naval (or National) Observatory and the Hydrographic Office. Although he did not win authority to establish a naval academy, Congress authorized him to enlist engineers and establish an engineer corps.

Because of the growing number of Americans engaged in whaling, trade, and even agriculture, and because of atrocities committed by Mexico upon Americans and the endangering of American lives during a civil war in Peru, Upshur strongly recommended increasing the number of ships on the Pacific station and establishing a "post" on that coast to which American vessels could resort. "In addition to this, a naval depot at the

Sandwich [Hawaiian] islands would be of very great advantage." Also, in 1843, after Congress provided additional funds, Upshur sent instructions to Commodore Matthew C. Perry, who promptly obtained revenge for murdered Americans by killing a gigantic native chief, King Crack O, and destroying four towns before a treaty was concluded at Great Berribee, Africa, on 16 December 1843.

Two notorious events occurred during Upshur's tour: the <u>Somers</u> mutiny and Captain Thomas ap Catesby Jones' seizure of California. In September 1842, the <u>Somers</u>, Captain Alexander Slidell Mackenzie, sailed from New York to the Africa station. After investigating charges that a crewman, Philip Spencer, son of the Secretary of War, plotted to mutiny, murder the officers and younger apprentices, and sail the ship as a pirate and finding them true, Mackenzie approved the hanging of three men. Upshur convened a court of inquiry, which completely exonerated Mackenzie. A subsequent court martial of Mackenzie, held in 1843, upheld the verdict of the court of inquiry. Side effects of the affair were the disappearance of the apprentice system until 1864 and the giving of support to Upshur's contention that a school be established for naval officers.

Captain Thomas ap Catesby Jones, commanding the Pacific Squadron, was instructed to avoid giving offense either to the Mexicans or to the British in California. Upon learning that war between the United States and Mexico was probable, however, he rushed his squadron to forestall British occupation of California, which surrendered to him on 20 October 1842. Having alerted Jones to the possibility of war, Upshur recalled him but stated that he had acted without authority and jollied the matter along until Secretary of State Daniel Webster apologized in the name of the President to the Mexican minister in Washington and the affair blew over.

Meanwhile Commodore Lawrence Kearny suppressed the opium trade off the Chinese coast but also demanded redress of grievances visited upon Americans by Chinese during the Opium War. To present his demands, he was the first to sail an American warship into Chinese national waters, at Canton. By being tactful after the war ended, on 29 August 1842, he obtained for

American merchants "most favored nation" treatment, or the same commercial privileges China granted the British in the Treaty of Nanking. Kearny thus set the stage for President Tyler to send Caleb Cushing as the first American commissioner to China and for Matthew C. Perry to be sent to Japan a decade later.

Late in June 1843, Upshur succumbed to Tyler's pressure to succeed Webster as Secretary of State. As naval secretary, he should be remembered as having directed the Navy to take its first steps in the transition from sail to steam and from a principally defensive force to one able to project naval power overseas. He revised Navy Regulations, replaced the Board of Navy Commissioners with the bureau system, regularized officer promotion, and supported scientific advance in the Navy. In his time the first iron-hulled ship, the first screw-driven warship, and the first shell guns reached the fleet, and an engineer corps, a Naval Observatory, and a Hydrographic Office were established. The Navy was left much improved because of his twenty-one months of service. Tragically, he was killed on 28 February 1844 by the explosion of a gun named the Peacemaker during a cruise on the Potomac of the recently completed Princeton.

J. DAVID HENSHAW, 24 JULY 1843-18 FEB. 1844, and THOMAS GILMER. Tyler's choice of Henshaw, a Massachusetts Democrat, to succeed Upshur, was most probably motivated by his desire to win the presidential nomination in 1844. A wholesale druggist who branched out into banking, railroads and politics, Henshaw served in his state's senate and also as Collector of the Port of Boston under President Jackson until he became naval secretary under a recess appointment on 24 July 1843.

Like Upshur, Henshaw would increase the number of ships in the active fleet and was interested enough in science to recommend the establishment of a laboratory at the Washington Navy Yard to test not only naval purchases but ordnance materials. He favored Professor William Chauvenet's plan to give a two-year course in liberal arts and technical subjects to midshipmen assigned to the Naval Asylum, in Philadelphia--only to be blocked by a cut in naval funds and the feeling that midshipmen could not be spared for two years. When the Senate defeated his regular nomination, he turned his office over to Representative Thomas W.

Gilmer, a close friend and adviser to President Tyler, who was easily confirmed by the Senate on 19 February 1844. On the twenty-eighth, however, he was killed, with Upshur and others, by the explosion of the <u>Peacemaker</u> on the <u>Princeton</u>. After Commodore Lewis Warrington, the senior naval officer in Washington, served <u>ad interim</u> for almost a month, the office was filled by John Y. Mason, who eventually earned the distinction of being the only naval secretary to serve two nonconsecutive terms.

K.   JOHN Y. MASON. I.   26 MARCH 1844-10 MARCH 1845. Virginia-born and trained in the law, Mason served in the Virginia legislature from 1823 to 1831 and as judge of the superior Court in 1829 and 1830, when he was elected to Congress and in seven years became head of the naval affairs committee. In 1837 he was appointed a judge of the Federal District court for the Eastern District of Virginia. When named by President Tyler to be naval secretary, he transferred from the judicial to the executive branch "with great reluctance." One of his first acts was to witness Samuel Colt explode mines by electricity. There, as he fought off the usual congressional attempts to lower the Navy's funding, in the naval appropriations act for fiscal year 1845 Congress took away from the President the authority to set the size of the Navy and the pay of officers and limited the number of enlisted men to 7,500. This limit, barely enough to man the crews of ships on distant stations, resulted in the withdrawal of ships of the line and reductions in all ships' crews until the law was abandoned in 1857. On the other hand, the adoption of the British and French method of reducing the number of calibers of guns mounted resulted in an entirely new American ordnance system. Between 1845 and 1847, six models of 32-pounders and two of the 8-inch shell guns replaced the older complex of 32-pounders, 32-pound carronades, 42-pounders, 42-pound carronades, and many other guns. In 1847, at the Washington Navy Yard, Lieutenant John A. Dahlgren fitted sights and established range scales for all the new "standard guns." By 1848, he also devised a boat howitzer as the first "Dahlgren gun" and saw it adopted as the navy's standard design.

Important too was the "Wind and Current Chart of the North Atlantic" that resulted from the work of Lieutenant Matthew Fontaine Maury at the newly-completed

Depot of Charts and Instruments (also adapted for use
as a naval observatory), and succeeding volumes on
celestial observations. And, finding the Engineer-
in-Chief of the Navy, Gilbert L. Thompson, inefficient,
Mason removed him and replaced him with the Navy's
first real engineer, Charles H. Haswell, who quickly
ranked all engineers by order of merit. His attempt to
have Congress split Equipment off from Construction and
Repair, however, failed, and success in the matter had
to await the reorganization of 1862. By a general order
dated 26 February 1846, Mason for the first time defined
the relationships of line and engineering officers and
set down the duties of the latter.

Mason formally submitted his resignation on 3
March 1849 to the outgoing Tyler but remained in the
cabinet as President Polk's Attorney General.

L. GEORGE BANCROFT, 11 MARCH 1845-9 SEPTEMBER 1946.
Bancroft, confirmed by the Senate on 10 March 1849,
was an historian and Massachusetts Democratic leader
who was surprised to be named naval secretary when he
sought a diplomatic post in Europe in order to continue his historical work. Following President Polk's
injunction to raise the standards and morale of the Navy,
he began by revamping its educational and promotion
systems, slowed only by the need to arrange for Commodore James Biddle to proceed to China with a ratifica-
tion copy of the Treaty of Wanghia and then, as it
turned out, make an unsuccessful attempt to open Japan.
His recommendation of promotion by merit was killed by
the Senate.

In consequence of the United States' annexation
of Texas, war with Mexico appeared quite probable.
Bancroft therefore ordered Commodore David Conner to
Veracruz, diverted Commodore Stockton's Mediterranean
Squadron to Texas, and directed Commodore John D. Sloat
to concentrate the Pacific Squadron in Mexican waters.
On 28 May 1845, after Mexico broke diplomatic relations, preparatory orders for a move into Texas were
issued to General Zachary Taylor. Were war to break
out, Conner was told on 30 August, he was to blockade
the east coast of Mexico and seize Juan de Ulloa Castle
at Tampico. However, Mexico proved to be conciliatory,
and Conner withdrew his squadron on 23 October and
Sloat scattered his vessels at Mazatlan along the
Pacific coast. Were war to ensue, however, Sloat was

to capture San Francisco and such other Mexican ports as he could. Meanwhile, the Marine Captain Archibald Gillespie was to prepare California for subversion.

Bancroft made his only great contribution to the Navy with the founding of the Naval School at Annapolis, following largely the educational plans used by William Chauvenet at the Naval Asylum at Philadelphia.

Early attempts to found a naval academy were opposed because it would be expensive, might create a military class that would monopolize all high Navy positions, and give the President another instrument for patronage. Moreover, it was argued, the merchant service could provide officers in emergencies and enough officers for the peacetime Navy. Unemployed officers would therefore be unable to lobby for new construction and for the employment of more vessels in time of peace.

Until 1845 experience at sea had been the normal method of training apprentice officers; larger ships even carried civilian teachers. When tours at schools in Norfolk or Philadelphia between cruises failed to improve an unsatisfactory situation, the Matthew C. Perry plan of sending a number of apprentices to sea in small ships was tried. As already noted, on one of these, the Somers, Philip Spencer, son of the Secretary of War, and two others were hanged for inciting to mutiny. The incident demonstrated the need for a naval academy comparable to the military academy at West Point. For advice, Bancroft turned to a board comprised of Commodores George C. Read, Thomas ap Catesby Jones, and Matthew C. Perry and Captains Elie A. F. Lavallette and Isaac Mayo. The board approved his choice of site, Annapolis, a curriculum calling for two years at the school, three at sea, and one on a practice ship, and of Commanders Franklin Buchanan, William W. McKean, and Samuel F. DuPont to start the school. After Bancroft got Secretary of War William L. Marcy to transfer Fort Severn at Annapolis to the Navy (15 August), he ordered midshipmen not attached to ships and a staff headed by Buchanan to gather there in October. By the beginning of 1846 some 56 students were on board and the school got under way.

V. THE MEXICAN WAR

A. CAUSES. Mexico had threatened war ever since the annexation of Texas by the United States (February 1845) and broke off diplomatic relations in March 1846. Disputes over the boundary between Texas and Mexico; the halting by Mexico of payment of adjudged damages to American nationals; and American desire to acquire California led the United States to send John Slidell to Mexico City to seek adjustments (December 1845). His rebuff caused President Polk to send General Zachary Taylor and his command into territory in dispute between the United States and Mexico (January 1846). Blood was first spilled in the area in dispute between the Nueces River and the Rio Grande, (25 April 1846), and the United States declared war (13 May 1846). That same day, Congress authorized the President to complete all naval vessels building and to purchase or charter and arm and equip merchant ships for war use. Most ships acquired were of shallow draft, thus well suited to operate in the Gulf of Mexico as Conner's "Mosquito fleet."

B. NAVAL OPERATIONS.

1. On the Gulf Coast. Although Conner's allotted two-year tour was ending and his health was poor, the administration wanted an experienced man to handle Mexican matters and was pleased when he did not request his relief, M. C. Perry, to assume command until 1847. Following the outbreak of war, Conner's Home Squadron gave General Taylor active support by convoying supply ships, protecting bases, and transporting troops. Upon orders from Bancroft, Conner clamped a tight blockade on the Mexican coast and maintained it until he was relieved. In order to operate his steam vessels effectively, he established a coaling base in Anton Lizardo, south of Vera Cruz. He had to close Tampico, Tuxpan, Vera Cruz, Alvarado, and Tabasco. Perry led a successful expedition against Tabasco (October 1846) and the whole squadron took Tampico without a fight. At the time Taylor took Vera Cruz (March 1847), Perry relieved Conner. Perry took Alvarado and Tuxpan and retook Tabasco. Thereafter the maintenance of the blockade was routine. These operations revealed the need of small naval craft as well as capital ships and of a landing and occupation force that would cooperate with the Navy in operations against shore establishments.

Conner's meticulous planning for the taking of
Vera Cruz, then the most powerful fortress in the
Western Hemisphere, set new standards for future American amphibious operations. Each of the 10,000 soldiers
on the transports knew in which boat to embark and
with which wave his would go ashore. Naval gunfire
support was also provided. This was the first large
scale amphibious landing in U.S. military history.
Perry aided Scott by furnishing him with naval gun
crews and some heavy naval guns for use as siege artillery, and 300 marines marched with Scott to Mexico
City. They fought at Chapultepec and, when the city
fell, were chosen to mount guard in the "halls of
Montezuma."

  2. <u>In California</u>. Upon the declaration of war,
Bancroft ordered the Pacific Squadron (sailing vessels
because the United States had no coaling bases on the
Pacific coast) northward from its base in Peru to
blockade the Pacific coast of Mexico and to seize San
Francisco Bay. Captain John C. Fremont, USA, established the independent Republic of California (4 July
1846) and joined forces with Commodore John D. Sloat,
who took Monterey, San Francisco and Sonoma, and declared California annexed. Joining Commodore Robert
F. Stockton, who relieved Sloat, Fremont aided in the
capture of Los Angeles and in holding California
against a Mexican-Californian revolt. The absence of
clear-cut channels of command and doubts regarding
relative rank of the American military leaders--Stockton, Fremont and Kearny--created much confusion and
uncertainty and led to the court martial of Fremont.

    VI. THE IRREPRESSIBLE CONFLICT:
      FROM BANCROFT TO WELLES

  American naval affairs for about two decades preceding the Civil War rested with mostly Southern men
both in the administration and in Congress. In the
latter Stephen R. Mallory, of Florida--later Secretary
of the Confederate Navy--played a large part including
a term as chairman of the Senate Committee on Naval
Affairs. In the former, most secretaries were lawyers or
literary men lacking technical knowledge of the service
they administered. Isaac Toucey, of Connecticut, was
a southern sympathizer like the president he served,
James Buchanan, as noted below.

Because the eight secretaries between Bancroft and Welles[1] made little impact upon the Navy, it may be better to relate what was accomplished in the Navy as a whole rather than to discuss each man separately.

Thomas Y. Mason, in a second term lasting from 10 September 1846 to 7 March 1849, with the end of the Mexican War, supervised the return of the Navy to peacetime pursuits. Building during his term were four war steamers which turned out to be the highly successful Powhatan, Susquehanna, Saranac, and San Jacinto. That naval activity was becoming normalized, however, is revealed in Mason's granting permission to Lieutenant William F. Lynch to map the Dead Sea and the River Jordan (1848), to revive the East India Squadron and, following the submission of the Treaty of Guadalupe Hidalgo to the Senate in February 1848, to make preparations to withdraw American forces from Mexico. If he failed in any way it was in not recommending an increase in the Navy as a result of the acquisition of California.

Reaction against the Badger-Upshur policy of naval expansion and the end of the Mexican War resulted in cutting naval appropriations from about $9 million in FY 1848 to $6 million in FY 1849. The figure rose slowly until 1853, when the costs of building a steam navy and improving the navy yards had to be met. The $14 million of FY 1859, however, fell to $3 million in FY 1860.

The transition from sail to steam is revealed by the decline in the number of sailing ships from 59 to 44 between 1843 and 1860 and the addition of 38 steamers between 1835 and 1860. As yet, however, steam engines were used almost exclusively for auxiliary purposes. The Mississippi, e.g., displaced 1,693 tons and her 498 HP engines gave her a speed of 9.5 knots. Meanwhile attempts to standardize naval ordnance with 32-pounder guns and guns using 8-inch shells failed in part because by 1854 new 9-, 10-, and 11-inch Dahlgren guns were being placed in the newest steam frigates.

More progress was made in the navy yards than in ship construction. New yards were established at Mare Island, 30 miles north of San Francisco, and at Vicksburg; sites in Texas became available after Texas was annexed to the Union; and Pensacola was much improved. By the time of the Civil War, almost all the yards could build or repair steamships. Dry docks came more slowly, with large stone ones built at Boston, New York, and Norfolk, and sectional docks provided for Mare Island, Portsmouth, Philadelphia, and Pensacola.

Improvements in ordnance in this period are connected largely with John A. Dahlgren, who began improving ordnance at the Washington Navy Yard in 1847. In 1848 he established an experimental battery and gunnery ranges on the east branch of the Potomac and soon produced not only guns up to 11-inches but improved small guns, invented a navy howitzer, and manufactured rifled cannon.

Steam ships and improved ordnance called for better educated officers and men. The founding of the Naval Academy in 1845 was a great step forward. To further regulate the discipline of officers, however, dueling by them was made subject to court martial proceedings (1857) and even the giving of or accepting of a challenge was forbidden (1862). To insure that officers and certain ratings were qualified for appointment and promotion, entrance and promotion examinations were administered for engineers, naval constructors, boatswains, gunners, carpenters, and sailmakers. To train apprentices, the system used between 1837 and 1843 was revived in 1857, i.e., using a practice ship on a six month's cruise to teach boys between 14 and 18 years of age how to fight a ship. However, it was still the custom to ship a crew for three years and then to discharge them at the end of that time. That ample room existed not only in improving the habitability of ships but in the spiritual and moral welfare of sailors was the burden of Richard Henry Dana's <u>Two Years Before the Mast</u>. Largely because of Dana but also because of strong humanitarian sentiment arising especially in the North for freedom from war and liquor, freedom for women and slaves, and improvement in the lot of sailors, the blind, the ill, the insane, and the downtrodden, flogging was abolished (1850) and the rum ration was stopped (1861)--both measures passing against the voluble objections of the great majority of naval officers and even by some of the men.

Attempts of staff officers (surgeons, pursers, engineers, chaplains, and professors of mathematics) to obtain line titles rather than retain "assimilated" ranks failed, as did all attempts to obtain higher naval ranks. All Congress would agree to (1857) was that the commander of a squadron could be a "flag officer," a captain with more than 20 years' service could fly a square flag at the fore (equal to vice admiral), and a captain of less than 20 years could fly a square flag at the mizzen (equal to rear admiral). Moreover, the refusal of Congress to provide for a retired or reserve list meant that old men in the upper ranks clogged the promotion pipe line. (In the 1850s, a lieutenant when promoted to commander would be 53 years old, and a commander promoted to captain, 74 years old.) In practice, the secretaries of the Navy either gave shore duty or leave-of-absence pay to those who were incapacitated, yet a personnel board of 1855 headed by Commodores Shubrick, Perry, and McCauley found 210 of the 690 officers including 198 passed midshipmen incapacitated and recommended their ouster or furlough. President Pierce's adoption of the report caused a great stir and stimulated memorials from various state legislatures as well as from Representatives and Senators. As a result, Pierce directed that those hurt could have their cases reexamined--and 56 of them were restored by 1859.

Naval science made great strides in this period. Witness the names of Lieutenants Charles Wilkes, James M. Gilliss, and Matthew Fontaine Maury, the first memorable because of his expedition to the Pacific (1838-1842), the last two because of their work in the Depot of Charts and Instruments, later separated into the Naval Observatory and the Hydrographic Office. In 1849, a new Nautical Almanac Office began compiling an American ephemeris. Other hardy souls explored the Amazon and surveyed the Uruguay, Paraguay, and Argentine rivers while Commander W. F. Lynch explored the west coast of Africa (1852-1853) and Lieutenant O. H. Berryman proved that a cable could be laid between the United States and Europe. Last, various naval officers doubled as diplomats. Most important of these was Commodore Matthew C. Perry, who "opened" Japan (1853-1854).

The slavery issue subsided for only a short time following the passage of the Compromise of 1850. The nation was busy developing industrially, extending its continental frontiers, and spawning a rail and water communications network. The second process, however, stimulated angry passions when the Kansas-Nebraska bill proposed to repeal the Missouri Compromise and the Southern demand that slavery follow the flag was opposed by the North. Attempts by some Northerners to enforce the Fugitive Slave Law further fanned the flames of sectionalism; in 1854 the antislave Republican Party was organized. Civil War in Kansas followed and John Brown committed the "Pottawatomi massacre." The Democrat, James Buchanan, who defeated the Republican, John C. Fremont, for the presidency in 1856, wished to avert civil war by being friendly to the South. He was helped by the decision in the Dred Scott case (1857), which in essence said that slavery followed the flag. The slavery issue was forever kept before the public, as by the Lincoln-Douglas debates (1858) and John Brown's raid on Harper's Ferry (1859). By the time Lincoln won the presidency, various southern states verged upon seceding.

If Buchanan temporarized and sought compromise with the South, his Secretary of the Navy, Isaac Toucey, was one of the most pronounced Southern sympathizers in his cabinet. If he did not, as often alleged, send ships overseas so that they could not be used quickly against the South, he did administer the Navy as though everything was normal. He permitted the squadrons on distant stations to operate as usual; did nothing to improve naval defenses; kept repair work at its customary pace; and did nothing but seek a truce when a naval officer in the pay of the U.S. government headed troops which on orders of the Governor of Florida seized the Pensacola navy yard. Moreover, he meekly accepted the resignations of 68 naval officers from seceded states. On 2 March 1861, when the House resolved to investigate his conduct, it was already too late, for he left office on the sixth. A month later shots were fired at Fort Sumter.

CHAPTER 9

NAVAL POWER AND THE AMERICAN
CIVIL WAR, 1861-1865

I. CAUSES OF THE WAR AND OPENING EVENTS

A. CAUSES. The Civil War resulted from a multiplicity of causes, not from the slavery issue alone. The more important factors in bringing on the Civil War were: economic hostility between the North and South; the slavery issue; the problem of which section would dominate the American government; the constitutional issue of the right of a state to secede; and inability of either section to promote peace due to basic cultural antipathies. The precipitating incident of the war was the seizure of federal property by the southern state governments.

B. ACTIVITIES PRECEDING THE OUTBREAK OF WAR. Southern war preparations began following the election of Abraham Lincoln in November 1860. The states of the deep South began strengthening their state militias by organizing new regiments, buying arms abroad and from northern factories, and even purchasing munitions from federal arsenals in the South. With the secession of individual states from the Union, beginning with South Carolina on 17 December 1860, federal forts and arsenals within the seceding states were taken over. In Georgia, Fort Pulaski was seized; in Florida, Forts Marion and Clinch were seized; and federal troops were forced to withdraw from Fort Barrancas guarding Pensacola Bay. Alabama took possession of Fort Morgan, and Louisiana captured Forts Jackson and St. Philip guarding the Mississippi River approaches to New Orleans from the south. The seizure of these forts and arsenals gave the seceded states a good store of arms and munitions for the commencement of war.

C. GIDEON WELLES. Lincoln chose Gideon Welles as his naval secretary because he had experience as a civilian chief of the Bureau of Provisions and Clothing, 1846-1849, had helped him with the presidential nomination, advised that stern measures be taken if necessary to keep the South in the Union, and seemed to be just the man to "assist him in a responsible station in a period of some difficulty."

Welles faced a host of difficulties, among them the question of loyalty, obtaining expert helpers in the Department, and what to do about Sumter. When he took office, sixty-eight Southern sympathizers had already left the officer corps. To stem the flow, he appointed Captain Silas Stringham his detail officer with responsibility of assuring that only loyal officers served the Union. As his right bower, he chose the former naval officer Gustavus Vasa Fox to serve as Assistant Secretary and as his left bower William Faxon, who served him as the business manager of his <u>Hartford</u> (Conn.) <u>Press</u>. Fox served virtually as a civilian Chief of Naval Operations and dealt with such professional matters as operational planning, correspondence with squadron commanders, fleet movements, and the blockade, while Faxon served as Chief of Staff. Although Lieutenant General Winfield Scott said the Army could not relieve Sumter, Welles thought it could and should be resupplied by a fleet of tugs but would hold off lest such action drive Virginia and the Border States to secede. Fort Pickens, however, should be retaken.

D. THE FALL OF FORT SUMTER, APRIL 1861. Once South Carolina left the Union in December 1860 the federal forts guarding the harbor of Charleston were endangered. Major Robert Anderson moved his troops from Fort Moultrie to Fort Sumter the day after Christmas, 1860, to forestall their being taken by surprise.

    1. <u>Reinforcement Attempts</u>. On 9 January 1861, the <u>Star of the West</u> tried to bring supplies to the Sumter garrison but was driven off by the forts in South Carolina hands. In the third week in March, Lincoln ordered that a resupply expedition be prepared following a plan drafted by Fox. This called for relieving Sumter but for sending the most powerful unit in the force, the <u>Powhatan</u>, to Pickens instead. Upon learning that Secretary of State William H. Seward had caused Lincoln to impinge upon his naval prerogatives, Welles faced the President and won his point--he must administer the Navy. Bereft of the <u>Powhatan</u>, the Fox expedition drew fire at Charleston and placed the responsibility of starting hostilities upon the South.

    2. <u>Bombardment and Surrender</u>. In the early morning of 12 April 1861 a bombardment of Sumter

commenced under the direction of General P.G.T. Beauregard. After suffering considerable material damage but few casualties, Major Anderson surrendered his command of the fort on 14 April. The Civil War had begun.

E. LOSS OF THE NORFOLK NAVY YARD, APRIL 1861. Hoping that Virginia would remain in the Union, Lincoln restrained Welles' desire to reinforce the navy yard at Norfolk, the largest and best equipped of all the Navy's yards. The loss of Fort Sumter was less serious than the loss of the yard at Norfolk because of the supplies and equipment involved, including tons of powder and over 700 naval cannon, many of the latest Dahlgren design. Commodore C. S. McCauley had been ordered to evacuate the ships and equipment at the yard, but age and infirmities prevented rapid action on his part. Following the fall of Sumter, Welles took a great risk and sent the naval and Marine defenders of Washington to Norfolk--in vain.

1. The Merrimack. Worried also that the U.S.S. Merrimack, then being repaired, would fall into Confederate hands, Welles sent Engineer-in-Chief B. F. Isherwood to Norfolk to expedite matters and Commodore Hiram Paulding to relieve McCauley with orders to destroy the Norfolk yard and its equipment were evacuation necessary.

2. Loss of the Yard. With capture likely at any moment Commodore Paulding ordered the burning of the Norfolk yard and the destruction of its shops, drydock, and the incomplete Merrimack. Unfortunately for the North, Virginia seceded and Confederate forces arrived in time to save a great deal of the ordnance and to prevent the destruction of the drydock. The Merrimack's burning was incomplete and the vessel was raised. Moreover, Confederates blockaded the lower Potomac and thus cut off Washington's access to the sea.

II. NAVAL STRATEGIES IMPOSED ON THE
NORTH AND THE SOUTH

In general the strategies of the North and the South were determined by the simple fact that the North had a navy and the South did not.

A. UNION STRATEGY. The North possessed a navy at the beginning of the war, and proceeded to increase its size by over 100 ships during the first six months of the war and more joining the fleet every day. The principal task of its navy was to exercise "command of the sea." This it did in several ways.

1. <u>Blockade</u>. In order to implement the "Anaconda Policy" of General Scott, Lincoln on 19 April 1861 announced his intention of setting a blockade on the Atlantic and Gulf Coasts. The purpose of the blockade was to prevent the Confederacy from obtaining foreign supplies in exchange for exports, principally cotton. In setting the blockade, the Union gave <u>de facto</u> recognition of Confederate belligerency and paved the way for a similar recognition on the part of the European nations. With Great Britain leading the way, the larger nations of Europe declared themselves neutral, recognized Southern belligerency, and said they would respect the blockade. The greatest task of the Union navy in connection with the blockade was to make it "effective." For the purpose, the Chief of the Bureau of Construction, Equipment, and Repair, John Lenthall, designed conservative but sturdy, heavily-armed, screw-driven, wooden frigates. Forthcoming were 23 shallow draft gunboats designed to intercept blockade runners and a new class of light draft gunboats for close-in blockade duty--the famous double-enders. Moreover, upon learning that Stephen Mallory, the Confederate Secretary of the Navy, intended to build ironclads, which could destroy the Union blockaders, Welles established an ironclad board and asked Congress for $1.5 million to build 3 experimental vessels. Following approval on 4 August 1861, Welles set his board to work. Fortunately a member ran across John Ericsson, who offered a plan of "a floating battery absolutely impregnable to the heaviest shot and shell." Thus Welles obtained the idea of the "cheesebox on a raft," the famous <u>Monitor</u>. Because Mallory was converting the <u>Merrimack</u> to an ironclad, Welles told Ericsson to go to work. The keel of the <u>Monitor</u> was laid on 25 October 1861. She was launched on 30 January 1862, turned over to the Navy on 19 February, and commissioned on 4 March. Five days later she engaged the <u>Merrimack</u>, as related below.

2. <u>Amphibious Operations</u>. With the experience of Mexican War operations and conclusions drawn from observation of the Crimean War, the Navy Department was able to act with the Army in amphibious operations

119

against many Confederate bastions. The Navy supplied transports, support fire, landing boats, and shore parties in expeditions beginning at Hatteras Inlet in August 1861 and continuing through the war until the fall of Fort Fisher in early 1865. In view of its naval preponderance, the Union operations were seldom in serious jeopardy from Confederate forces afloat.

 3. <u>River Warfare</u>. Along with its operations at sea and against the Atlantic and Gulf Seaboard, the federal naval forces operated extensively in support of army operations on Chesapeake Bay, the James and York Rivers of Virginia, the Potomac, Mississippi, Ohio, Tennessee, Cumberland and Red Rivers, to name only the principal waterways where naval activities occurred. The Navy's tasks were many-sided and included operations against enemy gunboats, reduction of forts and batteries along the rivers, convoy and transport of troops, and raids against enemy lines of communication. Until October 1862, the naval forces operating on the rivers were under Army command; after that date the vessels came under the operational control of the Navy Department.

B. CONFEDERATE STRATEGY. In view of the overall Union strategy, the Southern naval forces had the rigorous task of disputing the Northern command of the sea. This problem was approached in several ways.

 1. <u>Attempts to Raise the Blockade</u>. Most Confederate naval effort went into attempts to raise the blockade. The use of privateers and cruisers was designed to draw Union ships away from blockade duty, to run supplies through the blockade, and thus show European nations that the blockade was not truly "effective."

 2. <u>Economic Warfare against the North</u>. Privateers and raiders (cruisers) were also used to convince the Northern shippers that the war was too costly and thus weaken the Union will to win. However, the South suffered from a lack of vessels with which to break the blockade.

 3. <u>Defensive Naval Operations</u>. In the principal seaports and along the rivers Confederate ironclads, gunboats, and steamships operated in defense of shore installations. Again because of weakness in numbers,

the Southern vessels failed in their principal mission of frustrating Union naval attacks.

    4. <u>Attempts to Enlist Foreign Assistance</u>. See IV-A.

C. NAVAL FORCES AT THE OPENING OF THE WAR.

    1. <u>Union Strength</u>. The most important factor affecting Union naval strength in 1861 was not the number of ships afloat but the potential strength of the Union navy once the North decided to turn its industrial might toward shipbuilding. In April 1861 there were about 90 ships on the Navy's list, with a mere 42 in commission. By December 1861 the federal navy had some 264 vessels in commission with more building. For river and harbor work the North built some 74 ironclads during the war.

    2. <u>Confederate Strength</u>. Because the large percentage of American commerce had been in Northern hands before the war, the South entered the war with few ships or trained seamen. A small number of the Union naval officers resigned to aid the Confederate cause. Of those who resigned the best known were perhaps Captain Franklin Buchanan and Captain Raphael Semmes. To overcome the problem of replacing lost vessels, the South turned increasingly toward such special devices as mines, spar torpedoes, and submersible craft to attack blockade ships and make its own defenses more effective.

III. UNION NAVAL OPERATIONS AT SEA

In view of the basic Union strategy of strangling the South economically, the Northern naval effort at sea was concentrated on the blockade and on operations to make that blockade more effective.

A. UNION OPERATIONS TO STRENGTHEN THE BLOCKADE. With 3,550 miles of coastline to blockade, and few ships available to do the job, it was imperative that the Union Navy obtain naval operating bases close to the principal ports under blockade. Any base taken had to be defensible from the land side.

    1. <u>Hatteras Inlet, August 1861</u>. In August 1861 an attack was launched by Flag Officer (equivalent to

Major General in the Army) S. H. Stringham with seven ships against Forts Clark and Hatteras guarding the Hatteras Inlet. Major General B. F. Butler provided 860 troops for the operation, and it was completely successful. The base itself proved worthless due to shifting channels and dangerous shoals. Although the operation was the first amphibious assault of the war, Welles could not get Stringham to clear the undefended sounds south of Hatteras and replaced him with Louis M. Goldsborough.

    2. <u>Port Royal, November 1861</u>. Captain S. F. DuPont on 7 November 1861 led a large expedition consisting of 11 naval vessels, 36 transports, and 13,000 men under Brigadier General T. W. Sherman against Port Royal. With the troops unable to engage because of bad weather, in the completely successful attack Captain DuPont demonstrated convincingly the capabilities of naval gunfire against masonry forts and proved that wooden ships could take part in such engagements. Situated between Charleston and Savannah, Port Royal facilitated naval operations to the south.

    3. <u>Minor Coastal Operations</u>. In time the Union navy, with army forces for assault work, was able to recapture most of the principal forts and harbors along the Atlantic and Gulf coasts. In early 1862 Albemarle Sound was brought under control by operations against Roanoke Island, Elizabeth City, and Newbern. Amelia Island, Jacksonville, St. Augustine, Norfolk, and Pensacola gradually fell to Union forces. By mid-1864 the South had control of little more than Mobile, Savannah, and the Atlantic coast between Charleston and Wilmington.

B. THE CAPTURE OF NEW ORLEANS, APRIL 1862. As the major port in the Confederacy, New Orleans early became a target of Union naval planning. Control of New Orleans would cut off the deep South from the Gulf by way of the Mississippi, close a major port of exit and entry for blockade runners, and affect adversely the South's chances for full diplomatic recognition abroad.

    1. <u>Planning the Operation</u>. Captain David G. Farragut was given orders on 20 January 1862 to prepare for an assault against New Orleans. Sixty years old at the time, physically active but near sighted, and passed over three times for squadron command, he

was chosen strictly on the basis of seniority. His forces available would consist of 17 steam vessels, 21 mortar boats under the command of Commander David D. Porter, and 13,000 army troops commanded by Major General B. F. Butler. Ship Island on the Gulf Coast had been seized the previous September and was used as a base of operations by Farragut. The operation required that Farragut take a fleet of unarmored vessels past two forts 90 miles below New Orleans at Plaquemine Bend in the river.

Confederate defenses consisted of the two forts at Plaquemine Bend: Fort Jackson on the south bank and Fort St. Philip on the north, both under the command of General Jackson K. Duncan. There were also a dozen unarmored gunboats in the river, plus the ironclad <u>Manassas</u> and the unfinished ironclads <u>Louisiana</u> and <u>Mississippi</u>. The Southern naval forces were commanded by Commodore John K. Mitchell, CSN.

    2. <u>Passing the Forts</u>. Beginning on 18 April Porter's mortar boats began their softening up operations against the forts. On the night of 20 April the <u>Itasca</u> and <u>Pinola</u> broke the defensive boom stretched across the river. On the night of 24 April Farragut's squadron engaged the forts, passed them, and later destroyed Commodore Mitchell's river force. Farragut lost none of his ships; casualties were remarkably light on both sides.

    3. <u>Capture of the City</u>. Once the forts had been run, New Orleans lay helpless under the guns of Farragut's forces. The Union navy entered the city on 25 April and General Butler formally occupied it on 1 May 1862.

C. THE MOBILE BAY CAMPAIGN, AUGUST 1864. After the fall of Vicksburg (4 July 1863), and with the initiation of the Atlanta campaign by Major General W. T. Sherman in the spring of 1864, the time was ripe for naval operations against Mobile. This was the last important Confederate stronghold on the Gulf Coast and a major base for supply of the deep South.

    1. <u>Confederate Defenses</u>. The Confederate defenses of Mobile Bay were not inconsiderable. Fort Morgan guarded the eastern entrance to the Bay; Dauphin Island at the entrance to the Bay had Fort Gaines on

its eastern extremity facing Fort Morgan, making a forced entrance extremely hazardous. To the west of Dauphin Island was a lesser channel commanded by Fort Powell. The entrance was further protected by underwater obstructions and torpedoes (mines). Inside the bay there were three gunboats and the new ironclad, Tennessee.

    2. <u>Farragut Forces an Entrance, 5 August 1864</u>. In view of previous experience, Admiral Farragut lashed his 14 wooden vessels together, in pairs, and had them pass the forts in column with his four ironclads to starboard. The ironclads engaged Fort Morgan heavily, thus weakening the concentration on the wooden vessels, among them Farragut's <u>Hartford</u>. During the passage into the bay the monitor <u>Tecumseh</u> was sunk by a mine, throwing the steamers <u>Brooklyn</u> and <u>Octarora</u> into confusion. To keep his column moving Farragut took the rest of the fleet around the <u>Brooklyn</u> and over the torpedoes. Fortunately, long immersion had fouled the firing devices and there were no explosions. Once inside the bay Farragut's fleet made short work of the gunboats and forced the surrender of the <u>Tennessee</u> (Admiral Franklin Buchanan).

    3. <u>Closing the Port</u>. Forts Powell and Gaines were destroyed and Fort Morgan surrendered. Mobile Bay was useless as a Southern port, but the city did not surrender until 12 April 1865.

    The Mobile Bay attack, like the New Orleans campaign, was a monument to the daring of Admiral Farragut. The lesson was again demonstrated that heavily gunned masonry forts could be passed successfully by wooden ships provided there was enough gunfire available to render the shore-based fire inaccurate. As at New Orleans the maximum utility was not obtained from the ironclad vessels available to the Confederates.

D. AMPHIBIOUS OPERATIONS AGAINST CHARLESTON AND FORT FISHER. The ports of New Orleans and Mobile were closed by naval operations which rendered their defenses useless, but the same technique could not be used against Charleston nor against Fort Fisher, the latter guarding the approach to Wilmington, North Carolina.

    1. <u>Operations against Charleston, 1863-1864</u>. In

the spring of 1863 DuPont was given charge of operations against the port of Charleston. Two years of war had given the South ample opportunity to perfect the defenses afforded by three masonry forts, Sumter, Moultrie, and Pinckney. There were earthwork-sandbag batteries in profusion, the most important being Fort Wagner, and the usual underwater protection. Within Charleston harbor were two formidable ironclads, the <u>Palmetto State</u> and the <u>Chicora</u>. Unimpressed by the capabilities of monitors, DuPont warned Fox that failure impended. Overruled, and overruled again when he asked for troops to capture some of the forts and thus reduce the volume of fire on his ships, on 7 April 1863 he sent nine ironclads led by the monitor <u>Weehawken</u> against the forts. He pitted 32 guns against nearly 200 of the enemy's. After several hours of heavy shooting the fleet retired. It was evident that the forts could not be razed or taken, and with 7 of nine monitors damaged, one in a sinking condition, DuPont dared not try again. In mid-July 1863 DuPont was relieved by Rear Admiral John A. Dahlgren, who decided to take the harbor by siege. By mid-August Fort Wagner had been invested and its guns turned against Fort Sumter. Continuous bombardment could not force the evacuation of Sumter and an amphibious assault against the fort failed miserably in the night of 8 September 1863.

Charleston finally fell, 18 February 1865, because its defenders fled before the approach of General Sherman from Savannah. Naval power did not reduce the port of Charleston, but the usefulness of the port had already been limited by the cordon of Union blockade vessels that patrolled the coast in ever-increasing numbers after 1862.

    2. <u>The Fort Fisher Campaigns, 1864-1865</u>. Fort Fisher commanded the approaches to the port of Wilmington, and by mid-1864 Wilmington was the principal port for foreign supplies to the Confederacy. A combined force with Rear Admiral David D. Porter commanding the ships and Major General B. F. Butler commanding 3,000 troops was organized to assault Fort Fisher in December 1864. On 22 December the <u>Louisiana</u>, with 150 tons of black powder aboard, was exploded against the Fort with little damage to the Fort. On Christmas day the troops were landed after Porter's fleet had silenced the batteries. The next day General Butler re-embarked his troops, saying that the batteries were still intact and his force too weak to capture the

Fort. Butler was subsequently relieved of his command.

On 13 January 1865 a second landing was made with Brigadier General A. H. Terry commanding 8,500 troops. Porter's monitors kept the forts under fire to hold down casualties to the amphibious landing. On the 14th Porter's force of some 50 ships shot up the batteries. On the 15th a force of 1,600 sailors and 400 marines from the fleet made a frontal assault on the fort while Terry's troops assaulted from the rear. The naval landing force suffered heavy casualties, but with the aid of well-directed fleet gunfire Terry's forces were able to take Fort Fisher.

3. <u>Lessons Learned</u>. The night assault on Fort Sumter and the fiasco in December against Fort Fisher showed the pressing need for a unified command for conducting amphibious operations. The admirable work done by Porter's vessels in supporting the amphibious wave and later covering the assaulting party ashore definitely proved the value of naval gunfire in shore operations. Once Wilmington was cut off the South was "hermetically sealed" and the blockade became 100 percent efficient, suggesting perhaps that control of the ports is the only sure way of making a blockade truly "effective."

IV. CONFEDERATE OPERATIONS AGAINST THE BLOCKADE

Union strategy at sea was to make the blockade as effective as possible. Confederate strategy was simply to do everything it could to raise or weaken the blockade, for once the blockade was proved ineffective, foreign intervention and recognition of the Confederacy would follow.

A. KING COTTON DIPLOMACY. The goal of Confederate diplomacy during the Civil War was to obtain full diplomatic recognition, and to attain this goal the South concentrated most heavily on Great Britain. President Jefferson Davis and his secretaries of state realized that other nations, like France and Spain, would follow the British lead in the matter of recognition. They further realized that recognition would make bond sales in foreign markets easier, and would probably result in British insistence on the right to trade with the South unless the North could make the blockade more effective. The South hoped that Union intransigeance on the matter of blockade would result in conflict with the British. In any case, the Confederates believed they could not lose. They had the utmost confidence that British industries could be starved for cotton very shortly and that Britain would have to fight for cotton or close its textile mills.

    1. The "TRENT Affair." In the fall of 1861 President Davis sent James M. Mason and John Slidell abroad to obtain recognition for the South. On 8 November 1861 the British mail-packet Trent was stopped by the San Jacinto, Captain Charles Wilkes, and the two Confederate envoys were removed. Great Britain and the United States moved to the verge of war but Secretary of State W. H. Seward recognized the impropriety of Wilkes' act--Wilkes should have taken the ship itself--and released the two men. Once in Europe, neither Mason in England nor Slidell in France was able to obtain recognition for the South.

    2. Failure of Cotton Diplomacy. The Southern diplomatic failure can be blamed on three things: a) the Confederates did not obtain the military supremacy in the field that would convince other nations that they could maintain their independence; b) the quality of Confederate diplomats sent abroad was far below that of their Union counterparts, and they suffered by comparison especially in results; and c) to stake their diplomacy on cotton was in itself a grave error, for the British were able to get by without the Southern staple.

B.   PRIVATEERS AND RAIDERS.

    1. Privateers. President Davis advertised that letters of marque would be issued by the South on 17 April 1861, two days before President Abraham Lincoln announced the Union blockade of the South from South Carolina to Texas. Perhaps with the lessons of history before him, Davis envisioned Northern shipping being laid to waste by a swarm of private warships in the fashion of the Revolutionary War or the War of 1812. He had few takers, about 30 letters of marque being issued in all; and by 1862 privateers were unimportant. The lack of interest in privateering was the combined result of high risk, low profit, few courts outside of

the Confederacy where prizes could be judged, and the international outlawry of privateering in the Treaty of Paris of 1856.

2. <u>Commerce Raiders</u>. Confederate commerce raiders were considerably more effective in weakening the Union blockade than were the privateers. Beginning with the <u>Sumter</u> under Captain Semmes (1861), Confederate raiders operated against Union shipping for four years and in practically every sea on the globe. Captain James D. Bullock and James H. North went to England in 1861 to purchase vessels for raiding purposes, and under their direction the very effective <u>Florida</u>, <u>Alabama</u>, and <u>Shenandoah</u> were launched against Union commerce.

Of all the raiders the <u>Alabama</u> was probably the most effective, destroying some 71 vessels between September 1862 and June 1864. On 19 June 1864, the <u>Alabama</u> was engaged by the <u>Kearsarge</u> off Cherbourg, France, and destroyed. The <u>Shenandoah</u> operated around the world, and in its cruising dealt the North Pacific whaling industry a mortal blow. To stop the depredations of the raiders, the North was forced to keep ships for their pursuit at the ratio of about ten to one. Beside weakening the blockade, the raiders hurt Northern shipping by forcing up insurance rates and by the positive destruction of hundreds of vessels.

C. THE USE OF IRONCLADS. As noted earlier, in May 1861, Confederate Secretary of the Navy Stephen R. Mallory noted that the South needed some ironclad vessels and was of the opinion that such vessels could easily destroy the blockade by sinking the blockading vessels with impunity. In response to his order came the raising and reconstructing of the <u>Merrimack</u>, renamed the <u>Virginia</u>. The North was a bit slower to see the need of ironclads but in September 1861 an "Ironclad Board" appointed by Secretary of the Navy Gideon Welles recommended that contracts be let for three experimental sea-going ironclads. The Board's recommendation spawned the <u>New Ironsides</u>, <u>Galena</u>, and <u>Monitor</u>.

1. <u>The Battle of Hampton Roads, March 1862</u>. Major General George B. McClellan's invasion of the Yorktown peninsula was undertaken with the assurance of the Navy Department that it could control the

waters around the peninsula. On 8 March 1862 the <u>Virginia</u>, Commander Franklin Buchanan, sailed from Norfolk against the Union fleet in Hampton Roads. The <u>Cumberland</u> was rammed and sunk; the <u>Congress</u>, in trying to escape, grounded and was destroyed by gunfire. The <u>Virginia</u>, though heavily hit, suffered little damage and retired.

Late on 8 March the <u>Monitor</u>, Lieutenant John L. Worden, arrived by sea from New York. The next day, when the <u>Virginia</u> emerged to finish off the Union vessels in the Roads, she was fought to a standstill by the <u>Monitor</u>. Both vessels withdrew for a period of watchful waiting. From this point neither side could risk its vessel because of the terrible loss that would accompany failure, but the North gained by having its blockade remain intact.

2. <u>Other Southern Ironclads</u>. Other ironclads built at various Southern ports for use in destroying the blockade failed to accomplish their primary missions. In late 1863 the <u>Atlanta</u> sailed from Savannah but was quickly forced to surrender to the more heavily armed monitor <u>Weehawken</u>. The <u>Albemarle</u> was built to attack Union naval forces off the North Carolina coast but was destroyed by a daring raid led by Lieutenant W. B. Cushing.

Submarine and semisubmersible craft developed by Southern engineers failed to seriously disrupt the blockade. After drowning five crews, the submarine <u>Hunley</u> attacked the blockade vessel <u>Housatanic</u> off Charleston harbor and sank it. The <u>Hunley</u> and its sixth crew were also lost.

D. BLOCKADE RUNNERS. Besides trying to weaken the blockade by attacks upon it, or by drawing off vessels to pursue raiders, the South took definite measures to evade the blockade by the use of blockade runners. In the course of the war well over a thousand vessels were seized or detained by the Union when trying to slip through the blockade, but in time there was developed a group of specially built vessels that could be depended on to run the blockade successfully. By January 1865 some 84 vessels of great speed, shallow draft, and low silhouette had been built for this dangerous trade.

In the end these blockade runners, though they

supplied the South with munitions and vital necessities, worked more harm than good. By bringing luxury and scarce non-strategic items in and exchanging them for gold the blockade runners drained the South's money supply, heightened the inflation, and weakened the moral fibre of the people. The capacity of the individual vessel was too low to meet the needs of the South, and the trouble taken to evade the blockade was rather firm evidence of the blockade's "effectiveness" rather than contrariwise.

V. NAVAL OPERATIONS ON INLAND WATERS

Naval activity during the Civil War did not consist of blockade and counter-blockade alone. On the rivers, especially those flowing through the South, fighting took place throughout the war. The rivers were important as lines of communication for the South, and into the South. Control of the rivers, particularly the Ohio, Tennessee, Cumberland, Mississippi, and Red Rivers, meant control of the food supplies and raw materials in the areas drained by them. The North was determined to deny those resources to the Confederacy. Moreover, control of the rivers allowed Union generals to transport large bodies of men into the South, and on some occasions to evacuate troops after defeat. Finally, river control generally meant control of railroads crossing those rivers. Thus, river control could be as effective as large scale cavalry raids against enemy lines of communication.

A. GRAND STRATEGY IN THE WEST. Very early in the Civil War Union generals like Winfield Scott and George B. McClellan recognized the need to acquire control of the Mississippi River. With the river in Union hands that part of the Confederacy east of the Mississippi would be an island surrounded by Union seapower. This was a part of General Scott's "Anaconda Policy." Securing control of the Mississippi was more easily said than done, for the states south of the Ohio and east of the Mississippi had either seceded or were undecided in their loyalty, Tennessee and Kentucky being the most important of the latter group.

    1. <u>Disposition of Forces</u>. Because of the indecision of Kentucky, both the North and the South respected its neutrality until September, 1861. On

September 3rd, Confederate General Leonidas H. Polk occupied Columbus, Kentucky, a railhead and port on the Mississippi River; and on September 5th, Brigadier General U.S. Grant occupied Paducah, Kentucky, at the confluence of the Tennessee and Ohio Rivers. Major General Don Carlos Buell, USA, in the meantime had occupied Louisville, Kentucky, and used it as a base of operations for an army of 45,000 men. As a result of these moves Kentucky remained in Union hands, but General Albert Sidney Johnston, CSA, established a line of defense for the upper South running from Columbus to Bowling Green, Kentucky, and on to the Cumberland Gap and manned by some 45,000 men. Opposing Johnston was Department of the West Commander, Major General Henry W. Halleck, with troops at St. Louis, Grant in Paducah, and General Buell at Louisville, acting independently of Halleck. On the Mississippi River there had been constructed a fleet of gunboats now commanded by Flag Officer Andrew Hull Foote, USN, but under the operational command of Halleck.

2. <u>General Johnston's Problem</u>. For General A. S. Johnston the situation was critical. He was outnumbered by the combined forces of Halleck and Buell and recognized that a concentrated move against either Columbus or Bowling Green would breach his line of defense and force a general retreat to the line between Memphis, Corinth, and Chattanooga, Tennessee. Acting in Johnston's favor was considerable pressure by President Lincoln on General Buell to move into east Tennessee and take advantage of Unionist sympathy in the area. In the end, however, wretched Confederate leadership was more damaging than the failure of the Union generals to mass their forces for a concerted effort at any point in Johnston's line.

B. CAMPAIGNS IN THE UPPER MISSISSIPPI VALLEY. In addition to ferrying and convoying troops during campaigns of 1862 in the upper South, Union gunboats attacked strongly fortified river positions.

1. <u>The Capture of Forts Henry and Donelson, January-February, 1862</u>. In an attempt to flank the Confederates out of their positions at Columbus and Bowling Green, General Grant began an operation of "strategic penetration" by driving against Fort Henry on the Tennessee and then Fort Donelson on the Cumberland. On 6 February 1862, Flag Officer Foote with

seven gunboats forced the surrender of Fort Henry after a two hour bombardment. Landing parties destroyed the railroad between Columbus and Bowling Green, and the gunboats proceeded upriver as far as Muscle Shoals, Alabama. It was an all-Navy affair that signalized a change from a purely defensive to an offensive war in the West. Following a good deal of bickering the Army agreed to let the Navy control riverine warfare.

A week later Foote's gunboats were on the Cumberland, where they assisted Grant by ferrying 5,000 troops and by taking Fort Donelson under fire. The gunboats suffered considerable damage but performed a great tactical job by closing the river to Confederate escape. In both campaigns the work of the gunboats foreshadowed their future efforts. They would often convoy and ferry troops, provide mobile artillery fire to forces ashore, engage forts and batteries, and make tactical surprise possible by rapid movement of troops.

2. <u>Island No. 10</u>. The fall of Forts Henry and Donelson forced Johnston's troops to evacuate Bowling Green and to fall back to Murfreesboro, some 60 miles south of Nashville. The troops under Polk at Columbus also retreated down the Mississippi, where some 6,000 of them were captured when Brigadier General John Pope, USA, captured Island No. 10. The capture of this island was made possible when gunboats <u>Carondolet</u> and <u>Pittsburg</u> ran past its batteries and thus allowed Pope to cross from New Madrid, Missouri, to invest the island.

3. <u>The Battle of Shiloh, 6-7 April 1862</u>. Once the Columbus-Bowling Green line was sundered, Union troops were slowly massed for a drive against the Confederate second line of defense, which followed the railroad from Memphis through Corinth to Chattanooga. With the important railroad junction there as his goal, General Halleck moved to Pittsburg Landing on the Tennessee River. Here, near the Shiloh Meeting House, the Confederate forces launched an attack on 6 April 1862. The Union forces were almost driven into the Tennessee on the first day until artillery from the river gunboats confused and to some extent demoralized the Confederates. The arrival of Buell's 20,000 troops on the second day saved the situation.

The Union lost considerable face, but more importantly the South lost General Albert S. Johnston. Though poorly aimed and undirected, the gunfire from the river boats had helped the North out of a difficult situation; and the fortuitous arrival of Buell's troops, by the Union-controlled Tennessee River, saved the campaign.

4. The Move on Memphis, May-June 1862. Following the Confederate repulse at Shiloh the Union army under General Halleck took Corinth late in May 1862. The Confederate position at Fort Pillow on the Mississippi River, now outflanked, was abandoned on 4 June. Union river gunboats and ironclads skirmished on numerous occasions with the Confederate river fleet, the last great battle taking place before Memphis on 6 June. The Union flotilla under Captain Charles Davis won the day and Memphis, now under the guns of the Union fleet, was forced to surrender. In late June Captain Davis took his gunboats south to Vicksburg and met the salt-water fleet of Admiral David G. Farragut, which had recently run the Vicksburg batteries. Though not absolutely controlling the river south of Vicksburg, the Union river fleet was able to move its armored vessels with relative freedom.

C. CLOSING THE RIVERS: VICKSBURG AND PORT HUDSON. The fall of Memphis and New Orleans left the Confederates in control of that portion of the Mississippi River between Vicksburg and Port Hudson, Louisiana. Between these two points the Red River emptied into the Father of Waters, and the Red became an important line of communication to Shrevesport and into Texas. From Shrevesport to Vicksburg traffic would move by water, and from Vicksburg foodstuffs and munitions from Mexico and Texas could be moved by rail to the east. As the Atlantic and Gulf blockade tightened through 1862, the cities of Vicksburg and Port Hudson assumed increasingly greater importance.

In July 1862 the Union river fleet under Commodore Davis tested the batteries at Vicksburg and found them stronger than before. In the same month the Confederate ironclad gunboat <u>Arkansas</u> steamed down the Yazoo River and put the weaker Union gunboats to flight. The time had obviously come when Farragut had to remove his steamers from the Vicksburg area, and he retreated below Baton Rouge. The South was able to fortify Port Hudson even more strongly as a result.

1. **Winter Campaigning Against Vicksburg, 1862-1863.** In November and December 1862 Major General Grant with Major General William T. Sherman and the river flotilla under Porter moved against Vicksburg. In trying to move by rail from Memphis, Grant had his lines of communication so badly disrupted he had to retreat. Sherman was defeated at the battle of Chickasaw Bluffs on 29 December; and Porter was helpless on the water with no army capable of dislodging the Vicksburg defenders. Following the failure of Grant and Sherman, Major General John A. McLernand took Porter and Sherman up the Arkansas River to capture Arkansas Post. The victory was sterile militarily but good for Northern morale.

After Chickasaw Bluffs the Union forces under Grant tried several different ways of either getting east of Vicksburg or north of it. All failed. Porter's river force was almost lost on two occasions while trying to flank Haynes' Bluff and Vicksburg by operating through swamps and bayous to the north and northeast of the city. An attempt to dig a canal across the great loop in the Mississippi at Vicksburg also failed.

2. **The Capture of Vicksburg, April-July 1863.** With all attempts to take Vicksburg from the north or from the river frustrated, Grant's only hope of success was to move his army past Vicksburg and surprise the city's defenders by an attack from the south. To accomplish this Grant moved part of his troops overland on the west side of the river, and Porter ran his gunboats and transports past the Vicksburg batteries. To mask the true design, General Sherman made a realistic feint at Haynes' Bluff. Finding Grand Gulf too well fortified for a landing, the troops went on down to Bruinsburg and disembarked. The river flotilla during this movement helped considerably by directing harassing fire on the batteries at Vicksburg, Grand Gulf, and Bruinsburg.

Once ashore at Bruinsburg, Grant outmaneuvered the forces of Generals John C. Pemberton and Joseph E. Johnson, finally laying siege to Vicksburg. Porter with his mortar boats helped with the siege, and on 4 July 1863 the bastion fell.

3. **The Fall of Port Hudson, July 1863.** At Port Hudson, Major General Nathaniel P. Banks and Admiral

Farragut conducted a siege operation similar to that of Grant. With the fall of Vicksburg, the garrison at Port Hudson was forced to capitulate (8 July 1863). The Mississippi was now under Union control its entire length.

D. THE RED RIVER CAMPAIGN OF 1864. Once victory was achieved on the Mississippi, Grant wanted to move on Mobile, but as on other occasions the army was divided and redistributed, making a large scale campaign virtually impossible. In the winter of 1863-64 General Banks planned a campaign up the Red River with Shreveport as its goal, and in March 1864 the operation began. Brigadier General A. J. Smith with 10,000 men supported by Porter's gunboats moved on Alexandria and took it. A supporting force from Arkansas failed to arrive and Banks was checked at Pleasant Hill, halfway to Shrevesport.

The retreat from Pleasant Hill to Alexandria almost turned into a disaster when Porter found the water too shallow to permit his boats to pass the city. Army Lieutenant Colonel Joseph Bailey built a series of dams that raised the river level sufficiently to float the gunboats over the rapids and saved Porter's fleet. No further campaigning was necessary on the Red River.

E. THE RESULTS OF THE RIVER OPERATIONS. River operations by the Union armies and Navy obtained the desired results for the grand strategy of the war. The Confederacy was split lengthwise by the federal seizure of the Mississippi, and the heart of the South was endangered by Union operations on the Tennessee and Cumberland rivers. The fall of Chattanooga and the consequent disruption of Confederate internal transportation was in large part made possible by Union control of the Cumberland River. The work of the Navy at Vicksburg hardly needs repetition.

The tactical use of river control for siege, bombardment, bridge destruction, and transportation of troops is worth noting. The powerful mobile artillery that assisted Grant at Belmont and Pittsburg Landing and McClellan's troops at Malvern Hill saved the day on several occasions and helped make future joint operations possible. There were, of course, clashes in the personalities at times, but offsetting the Butler-Porter quarrels can be found the wonderful cooperation of Grant and Foote that augured well for future river operations.

CHAPTER 10

THE POST-CIVIL WAR DENOUEMENT AND THE
RISE OF A NEW NAVY, 1865-1898

I. POSTWAR DEMOBILIZATION

The Civil War over, Secretary of the Navy Gideon Welles during his second term (1865-1869) dispensed with an assistant secretary and rapidly demobilized the greatest navy in the world. In 1865 there were 700 ships displacing 500,000 tons and carrying 5,000 guns. In 1870, there were 200 ships displacing 200,000 tons and carrying 1,300 guns. In 1873, the fleet, which ranked seventh in the world, mustered 63 wooden steamers, 48 ironclads (monitors), 29 sailing ships, and 25 tugs and yard craft. Most of the ships in active commission were scattered on "distant stations": North Atlantic-10; European-5; Asiatic-9; South Atlantic-3; North Pacific-4; South Pacific-3; and four unassigned. There were 1,892 officers and 7,500 enlisted men on active duty, with most of the officers employed in the 8 navy yards and other agencies of the shore establishment; the Naval Academy had 64 officers, 19 civilian professors, 193 midshipmen, and 16 cadet engineers. With rapid personnel demobilization, wartime Academy graduates rose quickly in grade until 1868. However, the commissioning of a number of wartime reservists at the end of the war and continued output from the Naval Academy so swelled the ranks that a "hump" continued for the next 20 years.

To administer the postwar Navy there was the office of the secretary of the navy and 8 bureaus, with 17 civilians aiding the secretary and from 1 to 5 officers and 4 to 10 civilians in each bureau, the Bureau of Provisions and Clothing, with 5 officers and 10 civilians, being the largest.

While the major European naval powers forged ahead with new ironclads and weapons, the U.S. Navy returned to sail power and ended its wartime research and development programs. The line officers who commanded ships saw engineers as little more than grease monkeys. In part because communications were slow, fleet commanders initiated their own tactical exercises. When ships gathered off Key West in 1874 in consequence of the <u>Virginius</u> affair, the officers were unprepared to

fight. Their ships were armed with smoothbore guns
that required close quarters, and fleet speed was but
4.5 knots. With ships scattered in small squadrons,
fleet concentration was impossible and fleet commanders could not engage in tactical or personnel training
by squadron.

II. THE NAVY AS A BACKWATER INSTITUTION

The U.S. Navy ranked low in administration, congressional, and public esteem for a number of reasons.
The Civil War over, to prepare for another war was
unthinkable. The generation following the war engaged
in solving such problems as reconstruction, paying off
the huge national debt, filling out the nation's
"natural" boundaries, building a transcontinental railroad net, creating mining and cattle empires, and
building an industrial plant capable of satisfying
national needs. Except for such minor overseas ventures as acquiring the islands of Midway and Wake and
part of Samoa, purchasing Alaska, and writing a reci-
procity treaty with Hawaii, the nation looked inward
rather than outward.

Uninterested in the Navy, the administration and
Congress declined to appropriate funds for new construction or to replace absolescent ships, and, as
noted below, various secretaries of the Navy returned
to the old-time policy of playing politics with the navy
yards. Nor did Congress fund the fruits of wartime
technological advances. For economy reasons, ship
captains were to use sails racher than coal. Dismissed
were John Lentnall, the longtime Chief of the Bureau
of Construction and Repair who designed the wooden
Union blockade ships. Out too went Benjamin F. Isherwood, Chief Engineer from 1861 to 1869. The pistons
of his engines worked athwartships rather than fore
and aft. He provided a new boiler 40 percent more
efficient and less expensive new than merely the scrap
value of an old one, and also the theory needed for
compound steam engines. His experimental sloop of
war, the <u>Wampanoag</u>, contained a highly-powered steam
engine in a finely designed hull. She made 16.6 knots
on her trials and at one point made 17.7 knots, thereby
setting a new record for both naval and merchant ships.
But a trial board headed by Rear Admiral L. M. Goldsborough disapproved of her because she burned coal.
Similar economy posited the building of wooden ships,

of single-cylinder engines, and of short-range smoothbores rather than ironclads, compound engines, and the rifles being adopted by Europe's navies. Indeed, the British ironclad Devastation, 1873, abandoned sails altogether a quarter-century before the Americans did with the cruiser Charleston.

Despite such progressive naval thinkers as Stephen B. Luce and Alfred Thayer Mahan, who saw the mission of the fleet to be the destruction of an enemy fleet far from America's coast, prevalent strategic thought centered about coastal defense and, in time of war, engaging in commerce raiding. With the American merchant marine wrecked during the Civil War and its failure to revive thereafter, many questioned the need of a seagoing navy at all. The mission of the fleet thus remained primarily to show the flag. For this purpose, sailing ships provided great seakeeping qualities at low cost. There were many foreign areas where the United States had no coaling stations or other naval facilities. Furthermore, in time of war, American ships could not obtain coal overseas. Between the end of the Civil War and 1873, Congress authorized the building of only four wooden cruisers, 3 monitors, and one iron-hulled cruiser, the Trenton. When completed in 1879, the last, rigged as a full brig, although the most powerful ship in the Navy (13 8-inch converted rifles and 2 Gatling guns) was no match for European cruisers let alone battleships.

The return to wood and sail, while cheap, had a number of evil side effects: 1) to obtain full canvas rigs, guns had to be positioned out of their way; 2) both hulls and propellers were designed to provide best speed under sail, and 3) space required for extra spars and canvas resulted in reducing that for boilers and engines.

III. NAVAL ADMINISTRATION, 1869-1885

A. THE DARK YEARS: BORIE, ROBESON, THOMPSON. During the short term as secretary of the navy of Adolph Borie (Mar.-June 1869), the eight years of George M. Robeson, (1869-1877), and four years of Richard W. Thompson (1877-1881), the Navy continued weak in part because the Admiral of the Navy, David D. Porter, at least until 1871, advised the use of sail rather than steam. Moreover Robeson, who preferred lobbying to serving the Navy, used the Navy yards to furnish employment to Republican friends in exchange for votes and wasted funds in reconditioning useless hulks rather than building new ships.

In 1871, Porter, as Chief of the Board of Inspections, alerted Robeson to the Navy's poor status: it ranked 8th among the naval powers, had only 29 serviceable warships, and contained so many foreign enlisted men that training or even communications aboard ship was difficult. Although Robeson replied that 3,000 miles of ocean protected the nation against Europe, the <u>Virginius</u> affair revealed the deficiencies of the navy, and the War of the Pacific (Chile vs Peru and Bolivia), showed that Chilean cruisers were better than any ships of the American Navy. When Chief Engineer James W. King returned in 1876 from a visit to Europe, he reported Europe far ahead, especially in the matter of compound engines.

Secretary Thompson was so obsessed with private business that he failed to keep in touch with the Navy. He was unimpressed when Porter told him in 1878 that the United States ranked 12th as a world naval power. Moreover, he was so obtuse that he accepted the chairmanship of de Lesseps' Panama Canal Co. at a time when President R. B. Hayes supported the Monroe Doctrine and tried to get the French out of Panama.

B. THE LIGHT BEGINS TO DAWN: WILLIAM HENRY HUNT, (7 Mar. 1881-16 Apr. 1882). By 1880, Republicans in power favored an expansionist foreign policy and saw the utility of a navy. They preferred to spend a Treasury surplus for warships than lower the tariff and so upset their business compatriots. They also listened to those who urged the rebuilding of the merchant marine so that it could capture some overseas trade and of the need of a navy to protect it. Hunt, whose son was a naval lieutenant, was personally interested in the Navy. Without congressional authorization, he created an advisory board to tell him what the Navy needed and started a drive to promote new construction. Following the death of President Garfield, he passed the report of his advisory committee to President Chester A. Arthur, who told Congress that "Every condition of national safety, economy, and honor demands a thorough rehabilitation of the Navy." Admiral John Rodgers, chosen to head a statutory board of 15 officers, was charged with recommending the size of the fleet and the characteristics of new construction. Although the board wanted an 8-year building program to provide more than 125 ships, they recommended 18 unarmored steel cruisers, 20 wooden cruisers, 10 torpedo boats, and 5 rams. Although the United States had not yet produced ship steel and steel cost 20 percent more than iron, it was much stronger yet more buoyant and resistant to fouling than iron and weighed less than wood. Other nations had both warships and passenger ships made of steel.

The types of ships recommended revealed continued attachment to defensive strategy--monitors for coast defense, cruisers for commerce raiding--but in the interest of economy the cruisers were to be unarmored, hence expendable. After the House Naval Affairs Committee reduced the Rodgers board recommendations to 6 cruisers and 1 ram, Congress in August 1882 authorized the building of only two steel cruisers but failed to fund them. However, the same act created a second statutory board, under Commodore Robert W. Shufeldt. Early in 1883, Congress cut the recommendation of 4 steel cruisers and a despatch boat by one cruiser and funded the first ships of the New Navy-- the <u>Atlanta</u>, <u>Boston</u>, <u>Chicago</u>, and <u>Dolphin</u> (ABCDs).

C. CHANDLER AND WHITNEY. For reasons not connected with the Navy, Hunt was exiled as minister to Russia. Notorious as a politico and lobbyist, his successor, William E. Chandler, did not improve his image by contracting with John Roach, whom he had earlier served as a lobbyist with Congress and who in turn contributed to his campaigns, to build all the ABCDs. Roach faced a real challenge in building ships of steel plate never before rolled in the United States. Moreover, the forging of 6- and 8-inch guns had never been attempted, and compound engines were to be found in very few American warships. Chandler may be called the "father of the New Navy" not only because he supported the building of the ABCDs and was responsible for contracting for their construction but because he was the first secretary to send naval attachés abroad and in addition was the "father" of the Naval War College.

If the material condition of the Navy was bad from 1865 until the ABCDs began operating, three events ushered in an intellectual naval renaissance. The U.S.

Naval Institute, founded in 1873, provided a forum for discussion for naval officers. Papers first read at Annapolis and then in Institute chapters in other cities were soon published in the Proceedings, thereby reaching Congress and the public at large. The Office of Naval Intelligence (ONI), established by Hunt, enabled Chandler to assign naval attachés abroad. The first of these, French Ensor Chadwick, was ordered to the American Legation at London late in 1882. Largely at the behest of Stephen B. Luce, Richard Wainwright, and Caspar F. Goodrich, Chandler approved the establishment of a Naval War College, at Newport, Rhode Island. There beginning in 1884, Captain Alfred T. Mahan, Professor James R. Soley, and Lieutenant Tasker H. Bliss, USA, began teaching the science of war to naval officers. Mahan later published the lectures he prepared for the college in his seminal work The Influence of Sea Power Upon History (1890).

Whitney (1885-1889), summoned to Washington by Democratic President Grover Cleveland to "clean up the Navy Department," tried to stop the Republican spoils systems in the navy yards; increased the accountability of property custodians and tightened the disbursing system; cleaned out old inventory amassed in naval depots; advertised for public bids on basic forgings for ships and guns that would be built in the navy yards, thus stimulating the steel industry; and reorganized the department into three main branches: personnel, material, supply. He also got Congress to limit expenditures on repairing wooden ships to 20 (rather than 30) percent of their original cost. So critical was he of the ABCDs that he took them from Roach, sending the latter into bankruptcy and hastening his death, and had them completed in navy yards, thereby extending their completion by several years. By the time the ABCs were commissioned (in 1889, 1887, and 1886, respectively), their European counterparts had forged far ahead. The ABCs were "protected" cruisers, but their armor covered only their machinery spaces. They were full rigged (10,400 square feet of canvas for the Atlanta and Boston, 14,800 for the Chicago), and had their main battery of 5-, 6-, and 8-inch guns mounted en echelon. The largest cruiser, the Chicago, displaced 4,500 tons and had a speed of 17 knots. The ABCs could thus neither defeat a counterpart nor run away from him. But some of Whitney's follow-on ships among the thirty he added to the

fleet were larger and more powerful. The <u>Newark</u> class
(<u>Newark</u> and <u>San Francisco</u>, authorized in 1885, 1887),
displaced 4,083 tons, were armored, and could make
19.5 knots. The <u>Charleston</u> (1885) displaced 3,730
tons, had a speed of 18.5 knots, and was the first
modern ship to utterly dispense with canvas. The
<u>Baltimore</u> (1886) was built from designs Chadwick acquired in England. She displaced 4,413 tons and had a
speed of 20 knots. The <u>Philadelphia</u> (1887) had almost
parallel characteristics, whereas the <u>Olympia</u> (1888)
which displaced 5,586 tons, was so well built that she
served for 40 years. Authorized in 1886 were two
heavily armored cruisers, the <u>Maine</u> and <u>Texas</u>. These
displaced 6,000 tons, had a speed of 18.5 knots, and
had the heaviest guns in the fleet--10-inch rifles.
After being launched, both were known as second-class
battleships. Meanwhile the armored cruiser <u>New York</u>
(1888) was given a displacement of 8,150 tons and
speed of 21 knots.

D. BENJAMIN F. TRACY: AN HONEST SPOILSMAN, 1889-1893.
A wounded veteran of the Union Army, Tracy practiced
law with the firm of Tracy, Boardman, and Platt but
renounced the political methods of Thomas Collier
Platt, a leader in the New York State Republican party.
The outstanding aspect of his career as Secretary of
the Navy was his use of strategic thought to govern
his shipbuilding program rather than the reverse of
letting ship types determine strategy. Where Whitney
only tried to do so, this honest spoilsman solidly
introduced the merit system into the navy yards and
refused to use his department to reward congressmen
or political or personal friends. He gave the Bureau
of Navigation the full direction over ship movements
and personnel detail and put supply and accounts more
completely under the Bureau of Supply and Accounts.
Whereas Whitney suffered the Naval War College to exist
while many conservative officers would close it, Tracy
used it to provide the advanced education naval officers needed to fight the battleships he would build.
As taught by Mahan, he came to believe that correct
strategy was that the control of the sea depended upon
a permanent force of capital ships under unified command that could defeat an enemy fleet far at sea and
that such a fleet should be kept in peacetime to protect overseas naval bases and the merchant fleet.
Strategic considerations thus replaced tradition as
the primary ingredient of policy making, ship building,

professional naval education, and administrative reorganization.

Tracy had to obtain the obedience and loyalty of eight technically proficient bureau chiefs who had excellent contacts with the congressional naval committees. From England, naval attaché Chadwick told him that "no such example of defective administrative organization exists in any civilized country as that . . . in ours. . . . Our system is no system." For the past six years, the Navy had produced one ship a year "because each one of the petty departments, which have erected themselves into semi-independence of control, is unwilling to merge itself in the great whole, whereby alone we can have a service." Whether Chadwick's letter influenced Tracy is unknown, but General Order No. 372, dated 25 June 1889, formed the chiefs of the five building bureaus into a Board on Construction that must cooperate in building ships and therefore free Tracy from their parochial disputes.

1. *The Squadron of Evolution, 1889-1891.* Late in 1889, Tracy directed Rear Admiral John Grimes Walker, longtime Chief of the Bureau of Navigation, to form a squadron of evolution comprised of the Atlanta, Boston, and Chicago and the new gunboat Yorktown. The last was commanded by Commander Chadwick, lately returned from London. The mission of the squadron was to test at sea the strategic and tactical principles studied at the Naval War College, determine doctrine for the first modern American steel ships, and report any deficiencies in them. Another objective Tracy had was to let the American people and also foreigners see what kind of ships the United States could build.

While making passage from Boston to Lisbon, the squadron got caught by a storm. While the cruisers stayed together, Chadwick "got lost" primarily because his tiller broke. Only his seamanship, strength, stamina, and ingenuity saved ship and crew. Chadwick's report to Walker, passed on to the Bureau of Construction, eventually resulted in strengthening the tillers of new gunboats. Sent home early, Chadwick personally reported to Tracy on other aspects of the squadron's tour, including tests of drill books issued by the department, ship equipment, and intelligence gathered on foreign ports. Subsequent calls by the ships of the squadron of evolution in numerous American ports helped endear the Navy to the public, which Tracy further insured by naming battleships after states and cruisers after cities. Having undertaken tactical evolutions as an integrated force under an independent unified command, the squadron of evolution became the nucleus of a permanent American fleet.

    2. <u>Building Battleships</u>. Upon taking office, Tracy had a fleet that ranked 12th among the world's naval powers (the United States had 39 ships built or building, Britain 367). He decided that the United States must build armored battleships which could defend the coast by destroying an enemy fleet of capital ships at sea and also threaten an enemy's coast. Expenditures for such a fleet would not only provide defense but stimulate both business and labor. Could he have his way, Tracy would have two fleets, one with 2 battleships in the Atlantic and one with 8 in the Pacific. To provide a balanced fleet, he would also build adequate numbers of cruisers and torpedo boats. With President Benjamin Harrison and Secretary of State James G. Blaine favoring a more spirited foreign policy, Tracy suggested acquiring overseas naval bases and also establishing a naval reserve. Fortunately, the administration had many friends in Congress, particularly in the naval affairs committees, on both the Democratic and Republican side. As sponsored by Senator Eugene Hale, of Maine, the second ranking member of the naval affairs committee, the naval building program introduced on 5 December 1889 called for 8 battleships, 2 armored cruisers, 3 cruisers, and 5 torpedo boats. Meanwhile a secret naval policy board established by Tracy called for an expenditure of $28,550,000 for ships displacing a total of 497,000 tons and making the U.S. Navy rank second only to Britain's. The leaking of the report incensed parsimonious, noninterventionist, and pacifist groups. The result was that Congress authorized three "sea-going coastal battleships" that pleased noninterventionists because of their range, limited to 4,500 miles, and slow speed. However, their other characteristics were excellent: displacement of more than 10,000 tons, length of 320 feet, speed of 16 knots, ample armor, main battery of 4 13-inch and 4 8-inch rifles, and secondary battery of rapid fire guns and 4 torpedo tubes. To please as many sections of the country as possible, they were named the <u>Oregon</u>, <u>Indiana</u>, and <u>Massachusetts</u>. They were the most powerful ships yet

built in America and capable of defending American waters. To help Tracy administer his growing navy, the position of assistant secretary of the navy was revived--and filled by James R. Soley. In 1892, finally, came real-battleships when Congress declined to specify fuel capacity or cruising range. Forthcoming in 1897 would be the Iowa (11,410 tons, 17 knots speed, main armament of 12-, 8-, and 4-inch guns). Tracy's new armored and regular cruisers were also larger and faster: Brooklyn (1892), 9,215 tons; Columbia and Minneapolis (1890-1891), 7,350 tons, with speed of 21 knots and enough bunkerage space to sail from New York to San Francisco. If not as numerous as the ships provided under Whitney, Tracy's ships were larger and had greater firepower.

E. DEMOCRATIC INTERLUDE: HILARY A. HERBERT, 1893-1897. Because of the severe depression beginning in 1893 and public debate over the money question and the tariff, the second Cleveland administration, largely noninterventionist, originally added little to the fleet. Both Secretary Herbert and his assistant secretary, William G. McAdoo, had served in Congress, and Herbert had been chairman of the House Naval Affairs Committee. Four small ships were authorized in 1894, and interest was revealed in improving the shore establishment because it could not service the large ships coming off the line. Herbert supported the Naval War College and began to use it not only as an educational institution but as a naval planning agency. Its war games, for example, would be tried out at sea by the North Atlantic Squadron. By the end of 1895, however, a desire to use shipbuilding as a relief works program to alleviate the depression, the rise of Japan as a major naval power in consequence of her defeat of China, and the dispute with Britain over the Venezuela boundary caused Cleveland to call for three new 10,000 battleships and 12 torpedo boats. The battleships Kearsarge and Kentucky, authorized in 1895, would displace 11,520 tons, carry four 13-inch guns in main battery, and have a speed of 16 knots. Controversial was the design of the Chief of the Bureau of Ordnance, William T. Sampson, for 8-inch guns superimposed over 13-inch guns in turrets forward and aft and the sacrifice of speed to protection and coal capacity. The Alabama, Illinois, and Wisconsin, authorized in 1896, were quite similar to the Kearsarge class. Because the Kearsarge- and Illinois-class ships were not commissioned until 1900 and 1901, the most powerful battleship with which the United States fought the Spanish-American War was the _Iowa_ and the largest cruisers the _Brooklyn_ and _New York_. It should be noted however, that in the six years between the authorization of the _Texas_ and _Iowa_ the displacement of American battleships almost doubled and that whereas the _Texas_ carried 2 12-inch and 6 6-inch guns the _Iowa_ carried 4 12-inch, 8 8-inch, and 6 4-inch guns in main battery.

F. THE "NERVES" OF THE NEW NAVY. Of the Academy class of 1874, Bradley Allen Fiske was the greatest inventive genius of the Navy of his generation, perhaps in the history of the Navy. Among other things he invented a telescope sight for guns; electric range, direction, and position finders; electric systems for hoisting powder, shells, and ashes; and electric turret-turning mechanism. In 1896 the Western Electric Co. began producing his stadimeter. Also to his credit were the electrical helm angle indicator, engine order telegraph, and a speed indicator log. Other conditions remaining equal, a ship fitted with Fiske's internal communications systems would enable her captain to destroy an enemy ship. Rather than being controlled by events, the American captain could use Fiske's apparatus to steer, give orders to the engine and rudder, and obtain the range at which to set his guns for firing on target.

Fiske had supplied the gunnery and ordnance equipment to the _Atlanta_, then to the _Brooklyn_. He had suggested that central electrical power stations be supplied ships. As Chief of the Bureau of Equipment from 1893 to 1897, French Ensor Chadwick ensured that such power plants were acquired and installed, with the result that, even if smaller, less powerful, and slower than their European counterparts, in electrical equipment American ships were as good as any produced anywhere in the world.

CHAPTER 11

THE SPANISH-AMERICAN WAR

I. DIPLOMACY

Under the leadership of General Martinez Campos, a ten-year Cuban revolt against Spain ended early in 1878. For the next 20 years American diplomacy with respect to Cuba centered upon commerce. Saddled by Spain with paying the costs of the civil war, about $400 million, and denied political or economic freedom, the Cubans revolted again beginning February 1895. Stimulating the revolt was the general economic depression that began in 1893 and the special blow dealt by the Wilson-Gorman tariff, which ended a reciprocity agreement and taxed Cuban sugar but let Hawaiian sugar in free. As usual, Americans were sympathetic to peoples seeking independence. Their sympathy was fanned by such yellow journals as Hearst's and Pulitzer's. They also wanted to help Cubans naturalized in the United States who were arrested by Spanish authorities.

A. GENERAL CAMPOS. Returned to Cuba as governor-general with full power and unlimited credit, Campos sought to defeat the Cuban <u>insurrectos</u> led by Maximo Gomez. Gomez used guerrilla tactics and a scorched earth policy against Spaniards. He also blackmailed Americans, who had between $40 million and $50 million invested in the island, if they wished their property to escape the torch. Moreover, Cubans studying in the United States or there for other purposes established juntas in New York and elsewhere to propagandize their cause and engaged in gun-running, especially from Florida. They thereby put the United States to the trouble and expense of enforcing its neutrality laws along 5,470 miles of coast between New York and the Mexican border. While Spain, with 67 ships of all classes in Cuban waters stopped but 5 filibustering ships in three years, the United States stopped 33.

B. GENERAL WEYLER AND "PATIENT ENDURANCE." A new phase in the struggle came early in 1896, when General Valeriano Weyler succeeded Campos and established concentration camps in which many loyal Cubans, deprived of adequate food, shelter, clothing, and medicines, died. Hence his nickname of "the butcher." His inhumanity provoked congressional resolutions calling for President Cleveland to recognize Cuban belligerency, to declare Cuba independent and to annex it, and that Spain free Cuba. Included was notice of the damage done to American property and the great cost of enforcing the neutrality laws. Opposed to such resolutions were primarily businessmen who feared hindrance to returning prosperity, inflation caused by war spending, and possible attack on U.S. shipping by Spain. Although congressional resolutions in no way bound the President, Secretary of State Richard Olney on 4 April 1896 told Spain of the desire of the United States for Spain's "prompt and permanent pacification" of Cuba by means of liberal reforms that would cause the insurgents to lay down their arms. The Queen Regent replied that reforms in Cuba would be instituted after the revolt ended and rejected an offer of the United States to act as mediator. In his last annual message, of 7 December 1896, Cleveland noted that Spain failed to pacify Cuba and that the United States was not only losing investments made there but that the annual trade with Cuba of $103 million in 1893 had dropped to $18 million in 1897 and that the insurrection involved the United States in "other ways both vexatious and costly." His government had shown "great restraint and patient endurance" toward Spain. Were Spain not to grant Cuba autonomy, that "patient endurance" could not last, and the United States might have to help Spain end the conflict. Our obligation to Spain would be superseded by "higher obligations" that would secure American interests and "the blessings of peace" for Cubans as well. While Cleveland refused to acknowledge the many congressional resolutions demanding a free Cuba even if this objective could be secured only through the use of American arms, such resolutions nevertheless stimulated the insurgents to hold out not just for reforms but for independence.

C. ENTER McKINLEY. Cleveland resisted the popular clamor for intervention against Spain in behalf of Cuba. His successor, William McKinley, was much more inclined to yield to it, especially since the clamor was raised against Weyler's _reconcentrado_ policy, which in a year killed nearly 200,000 people. Moved by humanitarianism, McKinley signed a bill on 24 May 1897 appropriating $50,000 for relief supplies to be dispensed by the Red Cross. More important, he stated that "if Spain did not end the horrors in Cuba the

United States would help Spain with her good offices; the United States could no longer remain a disinterested spectator."

D. ENTER SAGASTA. With the assassination of Cánovas del Castillo, of the Conservative party (8 Aug.), Práxedes Mateo Sagasta, of the Liberal party, took over as prime minister. He had to win over the Queen Regent and public opinion to a policy of granting reforms and autonomy while still making a show of force in Cuba and upholding <u>pundonor</u> (saving the face). On 18 September, U.S. minister Stewart L. Woodford asked Sagasta to assure the United States by 1 November that it would settle the Cuban problem. Otherwise "the United States must consider itself free to take such steps as its government should deem necessary to procure this result, with due regard to our own interests and the general tranquillity."

On 23 October, Woodford was told that Cuba would be granted autonomy but that Spain would retain "immutable sovereignty." Meanwhile the United States should stop aiding the rebels. As earnest of its plan, Spain recalled Weyler. His successor, General Blanco, immediately began to relieve the suffering of the <u>reconcentrados</u>, but Gomez continued his burning and pillaging. On 25 November, the Queen Regent gave Cubans the rights of peninsular Spaniards but said she must obtain the consent of the Cortes (parliament) prior to granting a limited sort of autonomy. The last was rejected by the insurgents bent on independence. In his annual message, of 6 December, however, McKinley called the <u>recontentrado</u> policy "extermination," declined to agree with Spain that the United States had not fully performed her international duties, and indicated that he had considered such alternatives as recognizing Cuban belligerency, recognizing Cuban independence, and intervening on humanitarian grounds as a neutral to end the war "by imposing a rational compromise." "I speak not of forcible annexation," he added, "for that cannot be thought of. That by our code of morality would be criminal aggression." He did, however, give the Sagasta ministry time to fulfill its promises toward Cuba. If it did not do so, the United States must intervene and would win approval from "the civilized world."

E. DE LOME AND THE <u>MAINE</u>. On 12 January 1898, Consul

General Fitzhugh Lee, at Havana, reported that mobs led by Spanish officers were attacking the offices of newspapers that advocated Cuban autonomy. With quiet restored, he nevertheless advised that "if Americans and their interests are in danger ships must be sent."

For two years, out of deference to Spanish sensitiveness, the North Atlantic Squadron held its winter exercises off Newport rather than in the sunny Bay of Florida. Its return to more congenial surroundings, Washington insured Spain, had nothing to do with Cuba. With discussions by Woodford concerning a new commercial treaty with Spain proceeding well, McKinley determined to send the battleship Maine from Key West to Havana "as a mark of friendship" and of "international courtesy." Spain in turn sent one of its ships to call at American ports.

On 9 February, Hearst's New York Journal published a private letter written by the Spanish minister, Dupuy de Lome, and stolen from the mails, which among other things said that American press criticism of Weyler "shows what McKinley is, weak and a bidder for the admiration of the crowd, besides being a would-be politician (politcastro) who tries to leave a door open behind himself while keeping on good terms with the jingoes of his party." Even more damaging was his suggestion that Spain send a prominent man who under cover of helping with commercial arrangements could propagandize "among the senators and others in opposition to the Junta and to try and win over the refugees." De Lome resigned but Spain was very slow in apologizing for his statements. While the letter created a public sensation, the fact that it was private and also purloined reduced its stimulus for war. The sinking of the Maine, however, was another matter.

The Maine had been in Havana harbor for three weeks when on the night of 15 February she exploded with the loss of 260 lives. Spanish officials of all grades sent condolences. Rear Admiral Montgomery Sicard, commanding the North Atlantic Squadron, appointed a court of inquiry headed by Captain William T. Sampson. For one week, the members stayed by the Maine while divers went down. For the next two weeks they interviewed survivors who had been taken to Key West. They spent the last week near the wreck. After

23 days, the Sampson board concluded that the ship had been sunk by an _external_ agent that had detonated the magazines. A simultaneous inquiry by Spaniards decided that she had been destroyed by an _internal_ explosion. Her captain, Charles D. Sigsbee, had told Secretary of the Navy John D. Long that "public opinion should be suspended until further report," and McKinley saw it his duty to "learn the truth and endeavor, if possible, to fix the responsibility." He kept the report secret for a week, hoping thereby to bring Spain to terms while cooling American ardor for war.

On 27 March, McKinley in an ultimatum listed terms for ending the war in Cuba. Spain would announce an armistice until 1 October while negotiations went on through his good offices. There would be an immediate end of the _reconcentrado_ policy and relief for the sufferers to be supplied by the United States. If peace terms could not be agreed upon by 1 October, McKinley would mediate between Spain and Cuba. If Spain agreed to these terms, McKinley would ask the insurgents to consent to them. On 31 March, Spain offered to arbitrate the question of the _Maine_, lifted the reconcentration order, and accepted American relief supplies. But peace would be decided by a parliament to meet in Cuba in May, and an armistice would be granted only if the insurgents requested one, which Spain knew they would not do. On the next day, when a newspaper leaked the report of the American naval court of inquiry on the _Maine_, Spain stood condemned by American public opinion, in Congress, and even more in the Democratic and Populist than in the Republican press. The unfavorable Spanish reply of 31 March further stimulated bellicosity.

For a year, McKinley had tried to avoid war while pressuring Spain to restore peace in Cuba. On 9 April, Spain conceded that McKinley could serve as mediator, and McKinley was aware of strong pressures on him to avoid war applied especially by Speaker Thomas B. Reed, Vice President Garrett A. Hobart, and a majority of his cabinet. On 4 April he nonetheless prepared to tell Congress that it must find a solution to the Cuban problem. Advised that more time was needed to get Americans out of Cuba and that the ambassadors of the leading European powers wished to speak with him, he postponed sending his message. The ambassadors spoke for Spain, who sought to ally Europe against the

United States. When Britain refused to go along and the Pope declined to mediate, Spain's cause was lost. On 9 April, when Spain granted the insurgents an armistice, it seemed that the road for mediation lay open, but McKinley sent his war message to Congress (11 April) and did not stress this latest Spanish concession. McKinley's grounds for war were: 1) to end the war in the name of humanity for the Cubans; 2) provide Americans protection of person and property in Cuba; 3) redress the injury to American trade and business, and 4) "and this is of the utmost importance . . . the present condition of affairs in Cuba is a constant menace to our peace and entails upon this Government an enormous expense." Since Spain conceded every American demand except independence for Cuba, McKinley was severely criticized by those who thought he should have avoided war and that peace could have come to Cuba through negotiation. On the other hand, both the insurgents and McKinley had demanded Cuban independence, which Spain would not grant. By 16 April, Congress had resolved that 1) "the people of Cuba are, and of right out to be, free and independent"; 2) Spain should remove her government and military forces from Cuba; 3) the President could use his armed forces to enforce this demand; 4) the United States had no intention of annexing the island (Teller Amendment), whose government would be left to its nationals, but the insurgent government was not recognized by the United States.

Upon receiving notification of this action, the Spanish minister returned home and Spain broke diplomatic relations. On 21 April McKinley announced a blockade of portions of the Cuban coast; on the 24th Spain declared war; on the 25th Congress declared war retroactive to 21 April, in order to cover the blockade retroactively. So began "the splendid little war."

F. SOCIAL PSYCHOLOGY. Richard Hofstadter has offered the thesis that the 1890s was a decade of "psychic crisis." During the great depression, political leaders sought a war to take attention off burning domestic issues. Second, the United States had not had a war since 1865, and every generation must have its own war. Third, businessmen saw that they could expand in the Caribbean and the Far East if Spain was defeated. Last, especially Democrats and Populists were motivated by humanitarian feelings towards the Cubans to demand war with Spain.

II. AMERICAN WAR PREPARATIONS

In the absence of Secretary Long during the summer of 1897, Assistant Secretary Theodore Roosevelt did all he could to prepare the Navy for war. Familiar with war plans prepared in the Office of Naval Intelligence, he knew that Spain had naval forces in the Philippines that must be destroyed if war came and had a hand in the selection of a "fighter," George Dewey, to command the Asiatic Squadron. Moreover, on 9 May Congress responded to McKinley's request and passed a $50 million appropriation "for the national defense and for each and every purpose connected therewith, to be expended by the President." Most likely, since he abhorred war, McKinley sought to jolt Spain into negotiating. On 17 March, Senator Redfield Proctor, one not given to histrionics, reported on a tour of Cuba and convinced many Americans including businessmen of the need of intervention.

To advise him, Long obtained the assistance of a Naval War (or Strategy) Board comprised of Sicard, the retired Alfred Thayer Mahan, and the Chief of the Bureau of Navigation, Arent S. Crowninshield. To answer demands from residents of coastal cities for protection, Long violated the principle of concentration. He established a Flying Squadron under Commodore Winfield Scott Schley at Norfolk, sent a Northern Patrol Squadron commanded by Commodore John A. Howell to cruise northward of Delaware Bay; and kept the bulk of the North Atlantic Squadron at Key West (where Sampson succeeded Sicard) to provide coastal defense and also cover Cuba. By placing Schley, senior to Sampson, under Sampson's command, Long made another error that eventually had serious repercussions. On 22 April, Sampson made passage toward Havana, notifying neutral ships on the way that a blockade was established. On the 24th, Dewey was directed to "capture or destroy" the Spanish squadron in the Philippines.

III. MILITARY OPERATIONS

A. THE PHILIPPINE CAMPAIGN

1. <u>Naval Forces Involved</u>. With prompt decision and bold vigor, Dewey sailed from Mirs Bay, China, 27 April, to attack the Spanish in the Philippines. He had seven combat vessels: four cruisers (<u>Olympia</u>,

Baltimore, Boston, Raleigh), two gunboats (Petrel, Concord), and one revenue cutter (McCulloch), a total of 20,000 tons and 100 guns, half of them larger than 4-inch. His closest base was 7,000 miles away. Rear Admiral Don Patricio Montojo, with only one modern vessel (3,500 tons, six 6.2-inch guns) and several small vessels, decided to fight at anchor under the lee of shore batteries rather than at sea.

  2. Battle of Manila Bay, 1 May 1898. Entering Manila Bay through channels Dewey did not believe the Spanish knew how to mine, Dewey found Montojo off Cavite. Using the elliptical course pattern of DuPont at Port Royal, he annihilated Montojo's collection of marine antiquities at a cost of only seven Americans wounded. Lieutenant Bradley A. Fiske, on a platform 40 feet up the mast of the Petrel, used his invention, the stadimeter, in what was the first modern instance of range finding for naval gunfire. Dewey also acquired the Spanish supply and repair facilities in the Manila Bay area, cut the cable to Hong Kong, and protected the Philippines against outside interference (five German warships came to Manila Bay) while American troops were transported to Manila from San Francisco.

B. SEIZURE OF GUAM. En route, the Charleston effected the bloodless conquest of Guam. Token Spanish resistance to a combined Army-Navy bombardment on 13 August prefaced the capitulation of Manila.

C. THE CARIBBEAN CAMPAIGN

  1. Establishment of the Cuban Blockade. Secretary of the Navy Long disapproved of Sampson's plan for an amphibious assault on Havana because the Army was not ready and because he deemed it unwise to risk the fleet before Havana while Cervera was free to strike. Sampson "guessed" that Cervera would have to put in at San Juan (P.R.) for coal, and, seeking decisive naval action, took part of his blockading forces from Cuba 1,000 miles away to San Juan (12 May). Mahan condemned this as an "eccentric movement," for he believed Cuba the true strategic center. After using his heavy ship to tow monitors and destroyers to San Juan, Sampson bombarded the harbor fortifications with little damage to them but the loss of one man on the cruiser New York. He missed Cervera but reemphasized the weakness

of ships against forts and the evil of including monitors with speedier ships. Cervera outguessed Sampson by arriving at Santiago via Martinique and Curacao (19 May). Sampson left San Juan for Key West (18 May) and ordered Schley to look for Cervera in Cienfuegos and Santiago. Obsessed with fear of a coal shortage, Schley preferred to coal than to blockade Cervera. He "retrogressed" for 27 hours and finally reached Santiago in the evening of 28 May. There he established an ineffective distant blockade and only perfunctorily fired upon the Morro forts and Spanish ships nearby. Sampson arrived on 1 June, assumed over-all-command, and established a tight semicircular blockade about the mouth of the Santiago channel, which he illuminated at night with searchlights.

    2. The Battle of Santiago, 3 July 1898. With the seizing of Guantánamo Bay by bluejackets and Marines led by Bowman H. McCalla (10-17 June), Sampson had a forward naval operating base within forty miles of Santiago. His fleet, however, could not clear the mine fields from Santiago's narrow, winding channel because of nearby shore batteries. To bottle up Cervera, Naval Constructor Richmond P. Hobson attempted to sink a collier athwart the channel. Spanish fire damaged her rudder and she sank in a position that proved no obstacle to navigation. Sampson then called upon the Army to take Santiago from the rear and drive Cervera out.

    a. Army Operations in Cuba. Brigadier General William R. Shafter's orders authorized him either to take Santiago and cover minesweeping operations or to aid Sampson to destroy Cervera. With Navy escort, an expeditionary force of 17,000 men from Tampa including Roosevelt's Rough Riders landed at Daiquiri, 18 miles east of Santiago, instead of attacking the weakened forts of Santiago under the cover of naval guns. Ignoring the harbor entrance forts, Shafter plunged inland toward Santiago itself, five miles from the sea. Entrenched after the fighting at San Juan Hill and El Caney, Shafter asked Sampson to force his way into the harbor in order to distract the Spanish!

    b. Destruction of the Spanish Squadron. On 3 July, Cervera, ordered out by the governor of Cuba, took his chance while Sampson, in the New York, proceeded to confer with Shafter and the Massachusetts was coaling at Guantanamo and all American ships were preparing for Sunday inspection and religious services. Sampson's signal, "Disregard the movement of the commander-in-chief," merely meant that he had left his blockade station and not relinquished or transferred command to Schley, second in command. When Cervera came out of the harbor, Sampson, five miles away, rejoined at best speed but arrived too late to participate in the battle except for firing at the destroyer Furor.

As Cervera's leading ship, the Infanta Maria Teresa, cleared the channel, Schley assumed she would either ram or fire torpedoes. He turned the Brooklyn hard to starboard, forcing the Texas to back down to avoid collision, and made a full "loop" that opened distance to about 1,500 yards before he steered westward parallel to the Spanish ships. Bending on full steam, the three American battleships (Indiana, Iowa, Oregon), and heavy cruiser Brooklyn destroyed all the Spanish ships in a running battle covering about 50 miles and lasting four hours. Schley claimed honor for the victory, then apologized to Sampson for having done so, yet professional and public opinion so divided over who had been in command that a foundation was laid for the long-lived Sampson-Schley controversy.

With the U.S. Navy's objective of destroying Cervera's fleet accomplished, Shafter asked Sampson to cooperate with the Army against Santiago City by forcing his way into the harbor. Sampson declined because the channel was partly blocked by the Reina Mercedes, which the Spaniards sank, strong shore batteries remained intact, and electric mine fields lay in the channel. When Shafter was backed by the War Department, the issue was presented to McKinley, who ordered Shafter and Sampson to confer and plan a joint attack on the city. Secretary Long, however, directed Sampson not to risk the loss of heavy ships in the channel; rather they should bombard the forts while Shafter seized them. Sampson sent Captain French E. Chadwick, commanding the New York and also serving as his chief of staff, to confer with Shafter (6 July) and tell him that bluejackets and Marines would take the Socopa Battery, west of the channel, while Shafter's men took the Morro, to the east, thereby making minesweeping of the channel possible. Chadwick also wrote surrender terms for the Spaniards that Shafter approved.

Unwilling to lose men in assaulting the forts, Shafter asked Sampson to shell them and also the city of Santiago. Sampson shelled Santiago for a number of days but would not take his heavy ships into the mined channel. With the Spanish surrender impending, Sampson sent Chadwick to represent him at a meeting with Shafter, who mistook the Spaniard's willingness to "capitulate" for their surrender. While Sampson prepared to provide cover for Major General Nelson A. Miles's expedition to Puerto Rico, Shafter denied Sampson the right to sign the terms of capitulation and tried to seize all Spanish shipping in the harbor. On 17 July, when the Spanish flag was hauled down from the Morro, Sampson arranged to sweep the channel and defied Shafter and seized the Spanish ships in the harbor, with his right to do so finally upheld by the Supreme Court.

D. PEACE WITH PROBLEMS. On 12 August, through the French minister to the United States, Jules Cambon, a protocol of peace was signed in Washington. The fighting was over, but two controversies mushroomed out of the Santiago campaign.

    1. The Sampson-Schley Controversy. Although junior to Schley, Sampson commanded the Atlantic fleet. Sampson was modest and disdained publicity; Schley, vivacious and flamboyant, courted the press. The controversy was less of their making than a contest by professional, political, and newspaper partisans to find a hero for the Caribbean campaign such as Dewey had been at Manila Bay. Schley had vacillated in seeking Cervera in May, established a poor blockade and proved unaggressive at Santiago before Sampson joined up, and turned the Brooklyn away from the Maria Teresa. Upon completing his loop, however, he had performed brilliantly. The question whether Sampson was in command during the battle may be answered by asking who would have been held responsible if the squadron had been defeated.

    2. The Sampson-Shafter Controversy. Shafter complained that Sampson did not force the Santiago channel whereas Sampson would not hazard his ships in mined waters. Rather than assaulting the entrance forts, Shafter assaulted the city. He also denied Sampson the right to sign the Spanish surrender terms even though Sampson had been his naval counterpart

in a combined operation. Clearly the Army was unprepared for war, lacked equipment and training for amphibious warfare, and seemed to compete for glory with the Navy rather than killing Spaniards.

IV. NEGOTIATING FOR PEACE

Often described as a man of "intellectual poverty and moral weakness," McKinley was nevertheless more responsible than anyone else for the character of the peace treaty and therefore for America's acquisition of empire.

By the time Spain asked the United States to end the fighting (18 July), the United States had taken Guam, landed troops on Puerto Rico, and kept control over Manila Bay. Spain would negotiate only over Cuba, which could go free or be annexed by the United States, and would compensate the United States for the other Spanish territories it occupied. McKinley found his cabinet divided over whether to take all the Philippine islands or only obtain a naval base there. He disregarded the fact that Emilio Aguinaldo had proclaimed an independent Filipino republic and that the American people were also divided over whether to take the Philippines. On 30 July, he announced his peace terms: 1) Cuba to go free; 2) Spain's cession of Puerto Rico and an island in the Marianas in lieu of pecuniary indemnity; 3) American occupation of the city, bay, and harbor of Manila pending the conclusion of a treaty that would determine the control, disposition, and government of the Philippines. When Cambon noted that a war beginning in the name of humanity was ending with demands for Spanish territory, he was told that the United States knew of no war in which the victor had not sought indemnification by the loser. All McKinley would negotiate was the Philippine question. Paris was chosen as the site for the peace conference.

As McKinley put it, "While we are conducting a war and until its conclusion we must keep all we get; when the war is over, we must keep what we want." By postponing the making of an immediate decision on the Philippines, he gained time to determine how much of the Philippines he wanted. Among others he asked for information, Admiral Dewey noted that Luzon was the most important island. However, when the peace protocol was signed at Washington 1430 on 12 August, it was 1730 on Friday, 13 August, on the Philippines. The United States thus could not claim the Philippines on the basis of military conquest. Although Spain tried to keep full control over the islands and crush the Filipino insurgents, McKinley correctly assumed military control on the ground that the military occupant was responsible for the protection of life and property. Therefore the United States rather than Spain would deal with the insurgents, who received short shrift and quickly concluded that they had fought with the United States against Spain for independence but instead would be subjected to a new conqueror.

McKinley appointed military men to both the Puerto Rican and Cuban commissions. Spain removed her troops therefrom on 20 September 1898 and 1 January 1899, respectively. Eugenio Montero Rios headed the Spanish delegation to Paris. Noting that the Senate to be elected in November 1898 would contain a Republican majority of eight, McKinley did not worry about senatorial approval for the treaty. He chose Cushman K. Davis, chairman of the Senate Foreign Relations Committee, Whitelaw Reid, Senator William P. Fry, and Secretary of State William R. Day, Republicans, and Senator George Gray, the sole Democrat, as his commissioners. Four Republicans could easily outvote Gray and by demanding the Philippines guarantee the United States naval and commercial supremacy in the Pacific.

Montero Rios would try to save the Philippines for Spain, saddle Cuba's $400 million debt upon the United States, and prolong negotiations with the hope that the November elections would return a Democratic president friendly to Spain. Mollified by the statement that possible monetary compensation would be made for the Philippines, Rios gave up on the Cuban debt question, and on 26 October McKinley decided to acquire all the Philippines, thereby denying the Filipinos freedom and becoming their master, and offered Spain $20 million for "any legitimate debt for internal improvements or other pacific purposes." Spain's hope for a Democratic president was dashed with the Republican victories in the elections of November, and on 10 December the treaty was signed. Rather than sell the Caroline Island to the United States, however, Spain sold them to Germany.

V. RATIFYING THE TREATY

In one of the most heated debates in the annals of American history, expansionists favored acquiring the Philippines on the bases of dollars, duty, and destiny, i.e., of economic and strategic advantages and religion. Antiexpansionists argued that the annexation of unwilling peoples violated the Declaration of Independence and the Constitution and that a republic could have no subjects. The Philippines would be costly to defend, and the United States needed no more land. However, the titular head of the Democratic Party, William Jennings Bryan, sought approval of the treaty on the ground that with Spain out of the Philippines the United States could grant the Filipinos their independence. Although his efforts probably convinced few senators, the Filipino insurrection that began on 4 February 1899 drew all factions together in support of the national interest and the treaty passed by a vote of 57 to 27, one more than the necessary two-thirds. The treaty was approved in Spain on 19 March; with the exchange of ratifications on 11 April the war ended.

VI. STRATEGIC AND TACTICAL RESULTS OF THE WAR

A. STRATEGIC. Faithful to the Teller Amendment, the United States freed Cuba (only to obtain a protectorate over it in 1901) and acquired Puerto Rico, Guam, and the Philippines. The United States now upheld the Monroe Doctrine, which included a noninterventionist policy toward Europe, but intruded itself into the Far East. It appeared revolutionary that the United States had acquired noncontinguous lands that could not become states and whose people could not become citizens, and whose possession involved the United States in world politics. It took three years, and an army of 70,000 Americans, with naval support, before the Filipino insurrection was subdued in 1901. Acquisition of the Philippines failed to augment American trade in the Far East, and so long as the Philippines remained undefended they remained hostages to Japan.

Before the war, the strategic frontiers of the United States paralleled its east and west coasts and in addition Alaska, Wake, Midway, and Samoa. With the end of the war, those frontiers extended 1,500 miles to Puerto Rico in the Caribbean and included strategic base sites in Cuba and Puerto Rico for guarding the approaches to an isthmian canal, and from the west coast to Hawaii (annexed by congressional joint resolution on 7 July 1898), Guam, the Philippines, and Samoa.

B. TACTICAL. The cruise of the <u>Oregon</u> from Bremerton to Key West showed the need for an isthmian canal. While the success of the American fleet aroused popular interest and stimulated the creation of a new dreadnought navy, the war revealed shortcomings in doctrine and gunnery:

   1. <u>Doctrine</u>. McKinley acted as his own commander-in-chief. While the Naval War Board provided strategic advice to the Secretary of the Navy, the need of a permanent board to provide such advice, determine naval policy, write war plans, and decide upon ship characteristics led to the creation of the General Board of the Navy by administrative fiat on 13 March 1900. Problems attendant army and naval cooperation at Manila and especially at Santiago, and the Sampson-Schley controversy, pointed to the need of unified command in all operations. Caribbean operations, for which logistic support came most from Key West, pointed to the value of fleet train, or underway logistic force. Landings made in the Philippines and also in Cuba showed the need for improved amphibious doctrine. Promise of improvement came with the creation of an Army War College, creation of an Army general staff, and of a Joint Army and Navy Board (1903).

   2. <u>Gunnery</u>. With the American naval gunnery score at Manila about $2\frac{1}{2}$ percent and that at the Battle of Santiago about 3 percent, improvement in gunnery material and practice was quite evident. Although Fiske used his stadimeter during the Battle of Manila Bay, the Navy was exceedingly slow in adopting his system of continuous aim firing.

   3. <u>Naval bases</u>. With the acquisition of Guantánamo Bay, San Juan, Guam, and the Philippines, the U.S. Navy had to operate along extremely long lines. To enable its ships to operate in both oceans, the cruising range of ships must be increased and a network of logistic support and repair facilities must be built.

CHAPTER 12

THE UNITED STATES NAVY COMES
OF AGE, 1898-1914

I. INTRODUCTION

    Rising German and Japanese naval power gave the United States food for thought. Lessons learned from the Spanish-American War; problems posed by the Caribbean and Pacific empire created by the war; the leadership of a president versed in naval strategy and aware of how naval power can help implement foreign policies; and the patriotic self-interest of various economic and professional groups stimulated the creation of the strongest navy in the Western Hemisphere. The adoption of a large number of technological innovations and inventions by the U. S. Navy resulted in the building of ships as efficient as those of any navy. Moreover, Mahan and his disciples finally succeeded in getting adopted a naval strategy fitting the needs and aspirations of the American people and a long-term policy best defined as "a navy second to none but Britain's," although there were some who demanded a navy "second to none."

II. THE UNITED STATES NAVY, 1898-1914

    A careful evaluation of the lessons of the Spanish-American war validated Mahan's first principles. The war also revealed various needs--of educating the American public in naval strategy, of bases to extend the radius of fleet action, of ships with enlarged cruising range, of an efficient logistics force, and of improved gunnery.

A. NATIONAL EXPANSION AND THE NAVY. Colonial expansion attending the war made a large navy imperative lest American supremacy in the Caribbean, the future isthmian canal zone and its approaches, and the Philippines be challenged or lost; and the feeling persisted that a nation now a world power must also be a naval power in order to implement its world-wide foreign policies.

    1. "Big Navy" Advocates. Certain private American interests, especially shippers, exporters, shipbuilders, and steel companies, and the Navy League of

the United States favored a large Navy. In addition, President Roosevelt was a firm believer in Mahan's tenets and left a big-navy legacy to his successor, Taft. Their Congresses, in general agreement on basic naval strategy, finally jettisoned the passive defense-commerce raiding policy for one involving a fleet capable of defeating an enemy fleet at sea. American public opinion came to demand "a navy second to none but Britain's."

  2. <u>Fleet Concentration Policy</u>. In this period of naval growth the United States and Great Britain followed a policy of concentration, Britain in home waters and the United States in the Atlantic. Fear of rising German naval power and perhaps a desire to mollify a similarly growing Japanese navy led the British to enter the Japanese Alliance, 1902, return home their ships in the Far East, and leave Japan responsible for maintaining security in the Western Pacific. The result put exceptional difficulties in the way of an American naval advance across the Pacific, but the return home of the British West Indies Squadron in 1904-1905 made the Caribbean an American lake. In 1907, there were 15 American battleships in the Atlantic and only four American armored cruisers in the Pacific.

B. SHIPBUILDING DEVELOPMENTS. For a decade after 1903, annual naval expenditures were more than double those of 1900 and almost seven times more than those of 1890. Almost two capital ships per year were laid down. Strong emphasis was placed on a battleship navy, with the result that the United States Navy in 1914 was strong in battleships but deficient, compared with the navies of the major powers, in cruisers, destroyers, aircraft, lighter-than-air craft, and submarines.

  1. <u>Battle Cruisers</u>. As the dreadnought rendered earlier battleships absolescent, so the battle cruiser rendered the armored cruiser absolescent, for the battle cruiser could outrun battleships and was designed as a "cruiser killer." Britain and Germany built battle cruisers, but the United States preferred the more heavily armored battleships.

  2. <u>Battleships</u>. The cost, size, and power of American battleships increased steadily throughout this

period. A first-line battleship of 1903 cost five and a third millions, the battleship of the 1907 program cost eight and a quarter millions, and the battleship of 1914 cost 15-20 millions. The battleship of 1900 was 400 feet long and displaced about 10,500 tons; and that of 1914 was 600 feet long and displaced 31,300 tons. In 1914, the United States had, built or building, 17 "first line" battleships (those less than 10 years old). While the United States had reached second rank in battleships and cruisers by 1907, she had been displaced in total naval tonnage by Germany and by France in 1914. However, the United States Navy always remained ahead of the German navy in firepower.

C. DOCTRINE. By 1910, the tactical use of destroyers as screens for capital ships had become doctrine for all navies. Destroyers proved valuable adjuncts to the scouting line, and by 1914 the destroyer was engaged in antisubmarine warfare.

By 1910 all navies had adopted the submarine as a fleet type for both fleet operations and inshore defense. Until 1914, however, few navies recognized the potential use of the submarine against merchant ships.

Cruisers were delegated the triple role of warding off torpedo attacks in the battle line, long range scouting, and commerce raiding. However, only capital ships had been equipped with fire control apparatus by 1914. As early as the 1880s Bradley A. Fiske dreamed of producing a continuous aim firing system. Providing telescopes for the guns was his first step. When his electric range finder did not work well, he used optical range finders and position finders to obtain target information. This information, digested with interior ballistic data in a gunnery plotting room below deck, was transmitted to the gun captains. Since the latter all used the same settings and the guns were fired together by the fire control officer, continuous aim battery firing was made possible. The provision of tall basket (cage) masts on battleships following the return of the Great White Fleet in 1909 enabled fire control officers to be located very high in the ship. Elmer Sperry's gyroscope was put to gunnery uses by 1911. By 1914, Sperry and Fiske patented a continuous aim battery firing system. Fiske also invented "check fire," with Sperry providing the gyroscopes to keep the prisms truly horizontal. In addition Fiske invented a turret range finder. This finder merely had its telescopes protruding from the turret and turned with it; it could be used for local fire control if the continuous aim battery firing system were shot away or damaged.

The airplane is an American invention. Within seven years of the first successful flight, American naval officers had landed and taken off from ships, revealing the feasibility of the carrier. The seaplane, catapult, and torpedo plane were developed. Germany took an early lead in the development and military use of rigid airships and of blimps.

Educational doctrine and naval administration were improved in all navies. The U. S. Navy Department was reorganized (1909) into four major divisions: fleet operations, material, inspection, and personnel. Used by Secretary of the Navy George Meyer (1909-1913), it was gradually phased out by his successor, Josephus Daniels, who feared that it would become a general staff and endanger civil control of the Navy. The great increase in the size of navies and in the complexity of ships led to the establishment of specialized "fleet schools" and placed particular stress upon the training of officers. While foreign navies kept their complements nearly full, the United States Navy, with a comparable number of vessels, ran its ships with only 50-75 percent of its authorized complement, thereby losing the opportunity for training more officers. A naval reserve system still lay in the future.

D. FUNCTIONS. During the period 1898-1914, the United States Navy was used as never before as an adjunct to the diplomacy of the "big stick," "dollar diplomacy," and "watchful waiting." In addition to keeping ships on its overseas stations, protecting the new Caribbean and Pacific possessions from potential enemies, and obtaining bases from which to undertake world-wide operations, it supported three American foreign policies in particular--the acquisition of an isthmian canal zone and the maintenance of the Monroe Doctrine and the Open Door.

1. <u>The Panama Canal</u>. American interest in an

isthmian canal, of long standing, was heightened by the dramatic dash of the Oregon in 1898. The acquisition of Hawaii and the Philippines dictated either the building of a canal or the maintenance of a two-ocean navy. Anglo-American friendship paid off in the form of the second Hay-Pauncefote Treaty, 1901, which permitted the United States alone to build, fortify, and operate an isthmian canal. In support of Roosevelt's urge "to make the dirt fly" the U.S. Navy helped Panama become independent of Colombia by interposing the Nashville between Colombia and Panama so that the troops of the former could not land on the isthmus. The Hay-Bunau-Varilla Treaty of 1903 that followed the Panamanian revolution leased the Panama Canal Zone to the United States.

2. The Caribbean. Theodore Roosevelt extended the pristine principles of the Monroe Doctrine, which were designed to keep Europe out of the Western Hemisphere, by policing the Caribbean and chastising those nations that disturbed the peace and thereby invited foreign intervention and challenged the security of the Panama Canal. The Platt Amendment was made part of the Cuban Constitution (1901) and gave the United States the right to intervene in Cuba and to establish naval bases thereon. From time to time, U.S. Marines landed and restored order in Cuba, Haiti, Santo Domingo, and Nicaragua. The U.S. Navy responded to the major Latin American threat to peace by seizing Vera Cruz, Mexico, in 1914.

3. The Far East. The U.S. Navy supported the U.S. Army's subjugation of the Filipinos (1899-1902) by providing gunfire support, ferrying troops and supplies, landing troops, and establishing blockades.

During the Boxer Rebellion (1900-1901), seamen from the U.S.S. Newark, Captain Bowman H. McCalla, augmented the legation guards at Tientsin, and 2,500 naval personnel joined the international expedition which finally crushed the rebellion.

Roosevelt was well aware of the confidence that the Japanese had acquired as a result of their victory over Russia in 1904-1905. As a variety of incidents generated a war scare in 1906-07, Roosevelt ordered American ships to concentrate in home waters mainly to learn how rapidly the United States Fleet could

prepare for war. He calmed the Japanese with the
Gentlemen's Agreement (1907-1908), and provided the
Japanese with an object lesson in American naval power
and efficiency and the American fleet with invaluable
experience by sending the fleet around the world (1907-
1909). Despite the fact that the cruise revealed the
need for developed bases and coaling stations in the
Pacific, the development of Pearl Harbor as a major
naval base and of Olangapo in the Philippines as a
secondary base did not begin until 1909.

A realist, Roosevelt agreed with Japan to a
hands-off policy in Korea in return for hands-off in
the Philippines (Taft-Katsura Agreement, 1905) and to
a mutual defense of the status quo in the Pacific
(Root-Takahira Agreement, 1908).

In 1904, when a native chieftain captured and
held for ransom a naturalized American citizen,
Roosevelt ordered Rear Admiral French Ensor Chadwick,
commanding the South Atlantic Squadron, who had reached
the Canary Islands on a world cruise, to Tangier. To
Tangier also came British and Italian warships and the
American Mediterranean squadron. With Chadwick acting
in a diplomatic role, the crisis soon blew over. More
important was the Moroccan crisis of 1905, which
threatened to engage Europe in a general war. In
consequence, Roosevelt sent a delegation to the Algeciras Conference, 1906. By demanding the open door in
Morocco, the Kaiser challenged British and particularly French control there. The open door was agreed
upon. Germany then greatly irked the British by sending a gunboat, the Panther, 1911, to visit Agadir, an
Atlantic port of Morocco. Were Germany to obtain
Agadir and also a Mediterranean base, she could sit
astride two of Britain's major maritime lifelines.
In the end, Germany agreed to accept French territory
in Africa in exchange for giving up the open door in
Morocco. The crisis ended, but Anglo-German tension,
stimulated moreover by an armaments race, did not.

III. TECHNOLOGICAL DEVELOPMENTS

A. THE DREADNOUGHT. The British Dreadnought, 1906,
was an "all big gun" ship. Earlier battleships had
carried main batteries of four 12 or 13-inch guns, an
intermediate battery of 6 to 8-inch rifles, and a
secondary battery of quick-firing guns. The Dread-

nought carried ten 12-inch guns and an anti-torpedo battery of 12-pounders. It could fire six big guns ahead or eight broadside. Main battery fire power was $2\frac{1}{2}$ times greater than that of earlier ships. It was larger (17,900 tons); 490 by 82 feet long, with a $26\frac{1}{2}$ foot loaded draft; carried more armor (11 inches on belt and over turrets and barbettes); clocked 21.5 knots on its trials; and was the most expensive British ship yet built. All major navies were forced to shift to dreadnought construction. The British Queen Elizabeths of 1914 carried 15-inch guns. The newest American battleships carried 14-inch guns, and were represented by the Texas and New York authorized in 1910.

B. REPRESENTATIVE DEVELOPMENTS IN OTHER AREAS. The battle cruiser displaced 17,250 tons, was 530 by $78\frac{1}{2}$ feet long with a 26 foot draft, clocked 26 knots, and carried a battleship's armament.

The Holland-type submarine of 1900 was 54 feet long, displaced 74 tons, had a single screw, and was driven on the surface by a gasoline engine and under water by batteries and an electric motor. It had a single, fixed torpedo tube. Like a modern submarine it had a double hull, with ballast tanks exterior to the inner hull, hydroplanes, periscope, and a conning tower. Its surface speed was seven knots. Submerged, it could make seven knots for a short period, or cruise for 50 miles at slow speed. It could dive to 28 feet in eight seconds. Bradley A. Fiske and Frank M. Leavitt increased torpedo range by providing superheated steam and turbine propulsion. Fiske increased accuracy by the use of gyrocompasses and also invented a magnetic exploder for torpedoes. In addition he patented a torpedo plane in 1912, long before the Navy could see utility in it. The gyrocompass (1908) and the diesel engine added to safety and cruising range. By 1914, the newest submarines displaced 500 to 800 tons.

Technical experts like Brittain, McLean, Scott, Chapin, Sims, and Fiske took advantage of improved gun steel, smokeless powder, better mounted and balanced guns, new targets, and fire control directors to increase the firing range of the largest guns from 6,000 yards in 1898 to 20,000 yards in 1914. Sims cut the firing time of a 12-inch gun from five minutes to 38 seconds and increased target hits from 40% in 1903 to 78% in 1907. Between 1898 and 1914 the speed of firing 6-inch guns increased 800%.

By 1914 airplanes had been tested for reconnaissance purposes under battle conditions (by the United States at Vera Cruz, 1914) and proved valuable as scouts, spotters, reconnaissance patrol craft. Still to come was the use of aircraft to drop bombs and torpedoes.

The radio was operational equipment in the British and American navies soon after 1900.

Other improvements of the period included better armor, oil burning boilers, new and improved electrical and hydraulic gear, better ship ventilation, and increased refrigerated space. Ordnance proving grounds and other shorebased establishments grew in number, and various fleet schools were founded for the training of enlisted and officer personnel.

IV. NAVAL ADMINISTRATION

A perennial problem during this period was to reorganize the Navy Department so that it could administer the operating forces and the shore establishment more efficiently. The first of Roosevelt's 6 naval secretaries, John D. Long, objected to the creation of a general naval staff because he feared it would endanger the liberties of the people. The success of the Naval War (Strategy) Board that served him during the Spanish American War nevertheless caused him to establish the General Board of the Navy, in March 1900, but to grant its members only advisory authority. Moreover, any secretary could abolish the board.

Long's successor, William H. Moody, was a Massachusetts lawyer who had served six years in Congress. He took office on 16 March 1902 and served until 30 June 1904. Well aware of the need to expand the number of ships and men in the navy of an America newly become an empire, he was able to explain these needs to the excellent contacts he had in Congress. By delegating routine duties, he also obtained time to discuss naval matters with the President and with the bureau chiefs. He relied heavily upon Henry C. Taylor, Chief of the Bureau of Navigation, who like George Dewey, president of the General Board, Stephen B. Luce, French Ensor Chadwick, Bradley A. Fiske, William F. Fullam, William S. Sims, Yates Stirling, and various other officers sincerely desired a general naval staff.

With Roosevelt anxious to build the navy from fifth rank to one second only to that of Britain, Moody asked the General Board to formulate a long-range naval program. On 17 October 1903, Dewey proposed building 48 battleships by 1920 and sufficient lesser ships to provide a balanced fleet. As increasingly larger battleships were built in his day, Moody was able to win from Congress the officers and men to man them, although he helped too by reducing the number of officers on shore duty.

Unlike Long, Moody realized that the purpose of a general staff was not to usurp civilian control but to keep the secretary informed of the strengths, strategies, and objectives of other nations so that strategic American plans could be drafted. Backed by Roosevelt, in April 1904 he proposed to Congress that he be authorized to be served by 7 officers freed of administrative concerns. One of these would be called the Military Advisor. Were his plan adopted, this group, which he called a General Board, would be granted a statutory basis and the secretary would have an excellent advisory and planning board. Congress disagreed, in part because the plan was opposed by the Assistant Secretary of the Navy, Charles H. Darling, and by the bureau chiefs, the latter fearing the loss of influence and power. Matters therefore remained as they were, with Congress believing that the Naval War College, the General Board, and the Office of Naval Intelligence could keep a secretary suffiently informed.

When Roosevelt appointed Moody his attorney general, he chose Paul Morton as his successor. It was a poor choice, and Morton served less than a year, from 1 July 1904 to 30 June 1905. A son of that rugged individualist J. Sterling Morton, secretary of agriculture in Cleveland's second term, Paul Morton was equally a self-made businessman who at the age of 51 years was the second vice president of the Atchison, Topeka, and Santa Fe Railroad and thus in charge of all its freight traffic. With the assistant secretary taking care of the industrial end of the Navy, his objective should have been to improve the military efficiency of the service. Despite continued calls for a general naval staff, which might improve military efficiency, Morton paid lip service to administrative reform and Roosevelt declined to push the issue particularly because it was opposed by Eugene Hale, chairman of the Senate Naval Affairs Committee.

Morton served Roosevelt well in the presidential campaign of 1904 and in demanding a larger Navy and larger battleships before Congress, in which he was respected for his great energy, dedication to his work, and evident business capacity. However, because his railroad violated anti-rebate laws, Roosevelt asked Moody to investigate. Although Morton was not personally involved in the illegal practice, he realized that he had become a political liability to Roosevelt and resigned.

On 1 July 1905 there entered into the naval secretaryship a man with a famous name, Charles Joseph Bonaparte, a descendant of Napoleon's youngest brother. Rich, well educated, and trained in the law, he took mostly cases that involved the civil rights of Negroes and of poor people and also was a leading light in civil service reform. One story has it that he would leave Baltimore on the 11 o'clock train, eat his lunch from a silver lunchbox, and leave Washington on the 1300 train for Baltimore. At any rate, he understood that he would serve only until Moody retired and he would become the attorney general. His administrative method was simple: since his workers could not fire him, he would fire them if they did not measure up. Moreover, he disliked congressmen, who in turn disliked him.

Bonaparte lacked technical expertise but like Roosevelt wanted a large navy and large battleships, especially after Britain startled the world with the <u>Dreadnought</u> in December 1905. At his recommendation, Congress authorized the 20,000-ton <u>Delaware</u>, which was even heavier than the <u>Dreadnought</u>. Happy with the work of the General Board, he did not support the creation of a general naval staff even though he thought the bureau system meant friction and delay. However, he asked his assistant secretary, Truman Newberry, to head a board and report a departmental reorganization plan. Knowing that the chiefs opposed a general staff, the board made no recommendations on the subject.

Bonaparte thereupon suggested dividing the work into four parts, one to be supervised by the secretary, one by the assistant, and two by flag officers. All naval material matters would be placed under one flag officer, and operations and personnel under the other, and the secretary and his assistant would divide the supervision of the civil agencies in the department. Although Congress did not agree, he laid the seeds for the aide system created by Secretary Meyer late in 1909.

Bonaparte understood that Roosevelt was his own naval secretary and generally followed the advice of the bureau chiefs on operational matters. His service ended on 16 December 1906 when Roosevelt made him his attorney general.

Bonaparte was succeeded by another lawyer, Victor H. Metcalf, who had served on the Naval Affairs Committee during his three terms in the House and also as Secretary of Commerce and Labor. Whether he influenced Roosevelt to send the Great White Fleet around the world is not clear, but the voyage occurred during his tenure, and he was pleased with the training it provided the men, the technical deficiencies it disclosed, the good will it earned, the power it demonstrated especially to Japan, and the handle it provided the administration in asking for more battleships.

In January 1908, while the Great White Fleet was on its voyage, a former naval lieutenant, fine marine artist, and American editor of Jane's Fighting Ships named Henry Reuterdahl published an article entitled "The Needs of the Navy" in McClure's Magazine. Reuterdahl undoubtedly obtained his ammunition from Sims, the Director of Target Practice, and also spoke for such other reformers, or "insurgents," as Fiske, Ridley McLean, and Albert L. Key. His savage critique of the many shortcomings in the Navy forced Senator Hale to investigate his charges, but he did nothing about them. A major problem was that ships were designed by staff officers who refused to accept advice from the line officers who fought them. Roosevelt called a conference of both line and staff officers at Newport, Rhode Island, in July 1908, to consider the characteristics of the four battleships building. With staff greatly outnumbering line officers at the conference, it was decided that the ships were too far advanced to make changes in them. However, Roosevelt saw to it that the deficiencies noted by the insurgents were corrected in follow-on construction and that a board of line officers would have an input into their design.

Metcalf would not change the bureau system and vigorously opposed a general naval staff. Conservative but competent, he was pleased that the American Navy by the end of his service, 30 November 1908, was second only to that of Britain.

Roosevelt's last naval secretary, Truman H. Newberry, served for only three months, from 1 December 1908 to 5 March 1909. A graduate of the Sheffield Scientific School of Yale University, he had wide experience in the railroad, steel, and automobile businesses which stood him in good stead with respect to the industrial side of the Navy. He had military experience too, for he had formed the Michigan naval militia and fought in the Spanish American War, and then served as the assistant secretary under Bonaparte and Metcalf. His plan for reorganizing the Navy called for enlarging the General Board by admitting representatives from the bureaus into it, thus providing for better cooperation. The plan was opposed as too radical by conservatives and too conservative by the insurgents, whereupon Roosevelt in his annual message of 8 December 1908 came out flatly for a general naval staff. To push for this objective he held a conference at the White House of former secretaries and active and also retired officers--only to learn that the group preferred Newberry's plan. Displeased, on 27 January 1909 Roosevelt asked Moody to head a commission consisting of 8 civilians and officers to report to him on naval reorganization. This so-called Moody-Mahan commission provided a set of general principles involved in naval organization and also for an improved version of the Bonaparte plan. The members would divide the Navy Department into five parts: the secretary; a first division headed by the assistant secretary (BuY&D, Busanda, and BuMed; a second division headed by a Chief of the Division of Naval Operations, who would be the secretary's principle military adviser; and divisions of personnel, material, and inspections. With Roosevelt ready to leave office, Congress about to adjourn, and Newberry and the bureau chiefs opposed to what they saw as a general naval staff, the commission's reports died on the Hill.

CHAPTER 13

NAVAL POWER AND WORLD WAR I:
EUROPE, 1914-1917

I. INTRODUCTION

World War I is considered the first global as well as total war because the alliance system and the entry of the United States into the war brought every major nation into the conflict. In the course of the conflict international law as such was more honored in the breach than in the observance, as in attacks on neutrals, reprisals against civilian populations, and the use of unrestricted submarine warfare and poison gas. The nations fighting for continued existence used total resources in prosecuting the war; and science and technology developed terrifying weapons of war in ever increasing numbers as time progressed. To make the picture complete nearly every family in the combatant countries in Europe suffered a casualty.

A. UNDERLYING CAUSES. Among the causes of World War I were:

1. nationalism, including the aspiration for nationhood and additional territory by such peoples as the Bulgars and Serbs; and ultra-nationalistic hatreds and desire for revenge, particularly the French hope of revenge for 1870 and the regaining of Alsace-Lorraine;

2. imperialism, or economic and territorial expansion, especially that of Germany after 1879 where it clashed with French and British interests; and

3. an elaborate alliance system that divided Europe into two camps, the Central Powers (Germany, Austria-Hungary, and Italy) and the Triple Entente (Britain, France, and Russia -- hereafter referred to as the Allies). The development and support of the alliances required an increase of armaments in all countries, and engendered suspicions and fears among the competing nations.

B. IMMEDIATE CAUSES. On 28 June 1914, at Sarajevo,

a Serbian murdered Archduke Franz Ferdinand, heir to the Austro-Hungarian throne. Austria demanded punishment of the guilty, compensation, and the right to police Serbian territory. Serbia refused the policing power, mobilized, and looked for support from Russia. Austria mobilized and looked for support from Germany. Austria declared war on Serbia on 28 July; Germany declared war on Russia, 1 August, on France, 3 August, and on Belgium, 4 August. Great Britain, allied to France and Russia, and horrified by the German "rape of Belgium," declared war on Germany on 4 August. Two days later the United States declared its neutrality. For the next two and a half years, Americans watched as the titanic conflict raged but, as shown in the next chapter, did not learn too many lessons from it.

II. THE STRUGGLE FOR COMMAND OF THE SEA

A. STRATEGIC CONSIDERATIONS.

1. *Interior and Exterior Lines.* World War I matched the world's greatest land power against the world's greatest sea power, providing a severe test of Mahan's doctrines of sea power. In a large sense, the Central Powers enjoyed the interior lines of position and Great Britain the exterior lines of position. Allied weaknesses including inadequate communications and lack of a unified command, and the breakdown of Russia prevented the application of sufficient pressure to realize an effective pincers operation against the Central Powers.

2. *Geography.* The geography of the British Isles and the coast of Northern Europe dictated grand naval strategy and favored Britain. Britain's Home Fleet, based at Scapa Flow, Cromarty, and Rosyth, stood ready to challenge German submarines heading for Britain's western approaches, the North Sea, or the Channel and to prevent the sortie of German surface units from either their North Sea or Baltic ports. Britain had a second, predreadnought, fleet in the Channel, and based her destroyers and submarines on Harwich. On the other hand, the Kiel Canal enhanced the mobility of the German fleet; mines and submarines protected the North Sea coasts; and the Baltic remained a closed German sea.

3. *Naval Strategy.* For differing reasons, both the British and Germans adopted a cautious naval

strategy. Since Britain must keep her sea routes open, destroy enemy commerce raiders and merchant shipping, keep the High Seas Fleet bottled up, and blockade Germany she had more to lose than to gain by a decisive naval engagement. Moreover, German technological superiority discounted Allied numerical advantage -- the British outnumbered the Germans in battleships, battle cruisers, and cruisers; the Germans had the larger number of destroyers and submarines; the British were superior to the Germans in naval strength in the outer seas. The German navy was subordinated to the army and was kept at hand as a bargaining counter in the diplomatic settlement of what the Germans believed would be a very short war.

4. <u>Escape of the GOEBEN and BRESLAU</u>. The escape of these two German cruisers from the Adriatic to Constantinople in early August 1914 provides an excellent illustration of the political and diplomatic effects that may result from naval activity. In consequence in part of the issue by the British Admiralty of orders containing inconsistent objectives, to its naval commanders in the Mediterranean, the latter failed to stop the cruisers. When Turkey "bought" the cruisers, her pro-German policy stood revealed. When she used them to bombard Russian Black Sea ports, the war was established on the Eastern Front.

B. GERMAN COMMERCE RAIDERS.

1. <u>In the Outer Seas</u>. At the outbreak of the war, Germany had eight cruisers on foreign stations: two were in the Mediterranean, several were in the Atlantic, and a squadron was in the Pacific, based on Tsingtao. Their objective was to cut the shipping lanes vital to Britain. However, radio made continued raiding operations almost impossible. Moreover, the British greatly outnumbered the Germans in surface forces and in replacement capability, and the Germans lacked accessible fixed bases.

Two ships, the <u>Emden</u> and the <u>Karlsruhe</u>, sank two thirds of all British ships lost during this period, accounting for 145,000 tons. Four other German cruisers accounted for the sinking of about 65,000 tons before they were destroyed or interned in neutral ports.

2. <u>The Battles of Coronel, 1 November 1914, and of the Falkland Islands, 8 December 1914</u>. When Japan

declared war, Admiral Count Graf von Spee left Tsingtao on a cruise along the western coast of South America. To protect their imports from South America, the British ordered Rear Admiral Christopher Cradock to seek out and destroy the German cruisers. While the German and British cruisers possessed about equal speed, the Germans had five ships to the British four because the slow battleship Canopus was 250 miles south at the time of the battle. Moreover, the Germans had larger guns, were superior marksmen, had director systems, and managed to silhouette the British against the setting sun. Also, the British could not use their 6-inch guns, which were placed low, in the rough sea. In less than two hours, von Spee destroyed the Good Hope and the Monmouth. The Glasgow and Otranto escaped. Von Spee won a tactical victory but gained little strategically. He was low on ammunition, which he could obtain only in Germany. Goods from eastern South America continued to flow to Britain. As a result of the battle, the British quickly installed directors on their cruisers and ordered Admiral Sir Doveton Sturdee with two battle cruisers to the Falklands, where von Spee was next expected. The Canopus and Sturdee arrived shortly before von Spee.

Von Spee began his attack on Port Stanley with two mistakes: he divided his force and started so late in the morning that he lost the advantage of surprise. Upon being discovered, he beat a hasty retreat. However, the advantage of speed lay with Sturdee, whose battle cruisers followed just outside of the Germans' range and with deliberate fire of their 12-inch guns sank the Gneisenau and Scharnhorst. Lighter British cruisers sank the Nurnberg, the Leipzig, and three German colliers. The Dresden escaped but was sunk in March 1915.

3. Results of German Commerce Raiding. Germany found cruiser commerce raiding not worth the cost of ships or men. They learned, however, of the need for using radio for reception only and of the need for scout planes for commerce raiders. While their cruisers operated, they succeeded in diverting scores of Allied warships from other important assignments and in disorganizing Allied sailing schedules.

C. THE STRUGGLE FOR THE NORTH SEA.

1. The Action in Heligoland Bight, 28 August

<u>1914</u>. As early as 5 August 1915, a German minelayer was off the Suffolk coast. She was chased and sunk by gunfire near the Scheldt, and on the return home the British <u>Amphion</u> struck at least one mine, possibly two, and sank. The British had almost completed sweeping the German mines when the first real naval clash occurred on 28 August, near Heligoland. The Germans established a regular patrol pattern in the North Sea. Late in the afternoon, cruisers would escort destroyers to sea and at daylight would escort them back home. Commodore Roger Keyes planned to take the German destroyer patrols by surprise. He would use submarines to lure the Germans west of Heligoland, when British surface vessels would sweep down from the north and up from the south, turn toward England, and trap them. Submarines off the Ems would watch for German reinforcements. The suspicious Germans, meanwhile, prepared a similar trap with 19 destroyers and 7 cruisers, with the German Battle Cruiser Squadron with steam up at the Jade Roads, only 60 miles away. The British sank three German cruisers before retiring just as the German Battle Cruisers Squadron approached.

The speed and firepower of the British battle cruisers were tested and found good. The British successfully accomplished the first combined operation of surface ships and submarines but still had much to learn about communications. The Germans failed to concentrate, feeding their cruisers forward piecemeal. The Germans now increased patrol activity in the North Sea, augmented the number of mine fields therein, and kept their battle cruisers and battleships in Schilling Roads, which was unaffected by the tide. Moreover, no more German sorties would be made without the Kaiser's personal approval.

    2. <u>The Dogger Bank Action, 24 January 1915</u>. On 23 January Vice Admiral Franz Hipper, scouting the Dogger Bank with a battle cruiser force, ran into Admiral Sir David Beatty's superior battle cruiser force. Beatty's battle cruisers were faster than Hipper's, and they had 13.5-inch guns while Hipper's had 11- and 12-inch guns. Hipper's vessels were better armored and enjoyed superior fire control apparatus and shells than Beatty's. Hipper lost the <u>Blucher</u> and almost 1,000 men, and the <u>Seydlitz</u> was badly damaged. The British lost a chance of greater victory, however, because of poor communications and

poor armor. They saw the need for better operational training in command and communications. Their weak turret tops were easily penetrated by plunging fire, and lack of flame-proof scuttles between handling rooms and magazines invited terrific explosions. Remedial steps had to be taken. In the engineering sense, the British battle cruisers had proved superb, and the British hastened to strengthen their armor. The Germans were justifiably proud of their water-tight integrity, which they further improved; they also increased the magazine spaces and strengthened the topside armor of their battle cruisers. Hipper also recommended that only fast ships operate with the battle cruisers in the future.

Britain's tactical victories in the North Sea in 1915 increased Germany's caution in using surface forces in the area and caused Germany to keep its capital ships in port until the spring of 1916.

D. THE BATTLE OF JUTLAND, 31 May-1 June 1916.

1. Strategic Considerations. On 18 January 1916, the aggressive Vice Admiral Reinhard Scheer succeeded to the command of the High Seas Fleet. Three weeks later the Kaiser sanctioned offensive operations by the navy, which had been tied to its bases since the Dogger Bank action. Naval action to break the British blockade and humble Britain would proceed as the German assault against Verdun gathered force. By destroying portions of the Grand Fleet, Scheer would be able to bring it to parity with his own and permit him to assault Britain's vital sea lanes. His defeat would not greatly worsen the strategic position of his fleet. Admiral Sir John Jellicoe, however, had little to gain and much to lose by risking a fleet action. As Winston Churchill said, he was the only man who could lose the war in an afternoon. His Grand Fleet must be preserved in order to maintain the blockade on Germany and repel threats to the sea lanes upon which British life and military effort depended. He would engage in a fleet action only if he knew he would win, and he would avoid action rather than be lured over minefields or drawn into a U-boat trap.

2. The Battle Cruiser Action. Jellicoe put to sea on the evening of 30 May and headed Southeast. Beatty, from Rosyth, was to sweep eastward to $56°40'N$,

long, 5°E. If he did not sight Scheer at that point, he was to turn North to join Jellicoe. Scheer left the Jade about midnight on the 30th, his battle line following 50 miles behind Hipper's Scouting Group.

At 1415 on 31 May, Beatty turned North according to plan. As he did so, one of his light cruisers sighted two of Hipper's advance scouts. Beatty turned SSE to get between Hipper and his bases. Hipper immediately turned about to draw Beatty into the jaws of the advancing High Seas Fleet. The opening action (1548) favored Hipper because Beatty was silhouetted against a clear sky. In the first 37 minutes of action Beatty had 2 battle cruisers sunk and a third damaged. When Admiral Evan-Thomas' 4 battleships closed in, however, the action favored Beatty, and 4 of the 5 German battle cruisers were hit heavily. Hipper turned away (1623) to the East before a determined British torpedo attack and broke off the action. At 1633 the British sighted Scheer.

At 1643 Beatty turned North to lure Scheer into Jellicoe's clutches. Evan-Thomas covered his retreat and scored heavily on Hipper's cruisers and the van battleships of Scheer's force.

3. Jellicoe's Advance South. At 1545, upon receiving Beatty's contact report, Jellicoe turned his 24 battleships South and planned to place himself between Scheer and his bases by day, maneuver to retain this position at night, and resume action the next morning if necessary. Partly because of lack of adequate communications, Jellicoe kept his battleships under his immediate control rather than sanction independent squadron operations.

4. The Main Fleet Action (1740-2100). At 1815 Jellicoe deployed to port in order to cross Scheer's "T" and get between him and his bases. He could have closed and made the action decisive, but he did not. The Germans, meanwhile, must break through his line in order to get home. Hipper punched into Jellicoe's van, losing the Lutzow but sinking the Invincible (1831) before he turned SE to avoid being capped. Scheer, to avoid being capped, ordered a 180° turn in succession (1835) to course SW and simultaneously launched a torpedo attack from which Jellicoe turned. When Jellicoe finally turned South, Scheer was 12 miles

to the SW. However, after steering W for 20 minutes, Scheer ordered another 180° turn and headed in single column straight for Jellicoe's line and into the heaviest cannonade ever fired at sea. To extricate himself, he ordered the third 180° turn by his fleet and turned West but sent his destroyers in a three wave attack against Jellicoe's battleships. Jellicoe again turned his battleships away from the torpedoes. Fifteen minutes later he turned back toward Scheer, who had turned South.

    5. The Night Action (2117-0210). Jellicoe correctly rejected a night action between fleets because he feared torpedoes, knew of the difficulty of distinguishing between friend and foe in the dark, and would not trust to luck when by standing on his course South he would remain between Scheer and his bases. Dawn would come at 0300, when he could resume daylight action. At 2100 he placed his destroyer flotillas to his rear and failed to inform them of his fleet disposition or to give them battle orders.

    Scheer, with only five hours of darkness remaining, chose the simplest solution -- a break through Jellicoe's line and run home via Horn Reefs. He reached the center of the British formation at 1145. The last contact, a destroyer skirmish, was made at 0210 and ended the last great surface action fought mostly by daylight, the culminating engagement of fleets without planes, of bodies without arms.

    6. The Significance of Jutland. In the strategic sense Jutland was of little importance. Lacking the strength to win, Scheer escaped with honor. The British retained their close blockade of Germany and their control of the North Sea. But with a ratio of fleet strength of 8 British to 5 German, the British had lost in a ratio of 8 to 5. To a nation schooled in the Nelsonian tradition, Jellicoe's fear of torpedoes, mines, and submarines appeared excessive, and his lack of aggressiveness proved a shock. The German High Seas Fleet remained, if only as a fleet-in-being. Therefore, the Grand Fleet must remain concentrated, and 100 destroyers that screened it could not be released for anti-submarine warfare and convoy escort in the Atlantic. By not winning a decisive victory, Jellicoe missed the opportunity of giving a decisive blow to German morale, of being able to give the British Army more naval support, and of entering the

Baltic, where the British could have relieved the
Russians by attacking the North German coast, and also
have taken aggressive action against German surface
forces and U-boat bases.

    a. <u>Material Results</u>. Conclusions reached by
Jellicoe's post-battle committees of investigation
resulted in: 1) the redesign of the British armor-
piercing shell and the adoption of a less sensitive
bursting charge, so that the shell would pass through
armor and then explode; 2) the working of additional
armor onto the turret tops and protective decks of all
the capital ships of the Grand Fleet; and 3) the addition of fire screens, baffles, and flameproof scuttles
to minimize the danger of flashbacks
from turret to magazine. Some officers concluded that
the new fast battleships made the battle cruiser obsolete.

    b. <u>Doctrinal Reforms</u>. The large number of ves-
sels used in a fleet engagement made it extremely
difficult in 1916 for one commander to supervise all
of the fleet action, and he therefore lost flexibility.
In order to achieve concentration, battle lines were
kept taut and independent squadron action was kept to
the minimum. All orders on movement and distribution
of fire emanated from the flagship, denying initiative
except to avoid torpedo attack.

    When Beatty assumed command of the Grand Fleet in
November 1916, he: 1) revised destroyer doctrine to
provide for immediate attack and maximum torpedo fire;
2) revised light cruiser force organization by providing a single commander who was made responsible for
adequate contact reports; 3) revised the Battle Orders,
including the provision that ships would turn toward,
not away from, torpedoes; and 4) replaced the Battle
Orders with Battle Instructions which permitted a
fleet commander to exercise more initiative in battle.

    III. ALLIED NAVAL ACTION AGAINST THE DARDANELLES

    By the end of 1914, the Western Front had become
a stalemate and Russia was closed to trade by the Germans in the Baltic and on the Eastern Front and by the
Turks to the South.

A. STRATEGIC CONSIDERATIONS. The question of how to

use military force to obtain the best strategic results fell to the province of the British War Council. **This** consisted at the time of Prime Minister Herbert Asquith, Field Marshall Lord Horatio Kitchener, also Minister for War, and the First Lord of the Admiralty, Winston Churchill. The First Sea Lord of the Admiralty was Admiral of the Fleet John Fisher. By siding with either Churchill or Fisher, Kitchener could determine military policy. Both Kitchener and Fisher focused attention on the Western Front. Fisher would center naval operations about the Kiel Canal and use amphibious operations along the North Sea and later in the Baltic behind Berlin. Both Churchill and Kitchener frowned on Fisher's northern amphibious projects, and Churchill soon dreamed of a purely naval ship action against the Dardanelles, erroneously believing that naval gunfire alone could reduce its shore fortifications.

B. NAVAL PLANS AND CONTROVERSIES.

    1. <u>Fisher's Plan</u>. In reply to Russia's request for relief from Turkish pressure in the Caucasus, Kitchener promised a show of force in the Aegean and committed himself to a purely naval operation against Turkey. Fisher's plan involved landing 75,000 men on the outer shores of the Dardanelles preparatory to the transiting of the Strait by surface vessels, the combat-unit loading of troops in England, and an assault immediately upon reaching the Dardanelles--in sum an amphibious operation which must begin promptly and have a single commander.

    2. <u>Churchill's Plan</u>. Churchill instead planned to reduce the Dardanelles by naval gunfire alone and was supported by Vice Admiral S. H. Carden, British naval commander in the Aegean. Given a month and unlimited ammunition, Carden would reduce the Dardanelles with 18 heavy ships, 16 destroyers, and minesweepers. He would: 1) destroy all forts at the Dardanelles entrance; 2) sweep mine fields to the Narrows and reduce the forts protecting the fields; 3) reduce the defenses at the Narrows; 4) clear mine fields in and above the Narrows, reduce the forts in the area, and enter the Sea of Marmora. The plan contained no provision for taking or occupying Constantinople or for dealing with mobile artillery.

The War Council approved of Steps 1 and 2 of Carden's plan. Further action would be taken <u>only</u> if conditions inside the Straits justified the cost.

   3. <u>Strengthening the Straits</u>. During the two months the British spent in reaching their decision, General Otto Liman von Sanders, head of the German military mission to Turkey, personally supervised the strengthening of Constantinople and of the Bosporous. While he trained mobile infantry-artillery teams, Admiral Guido von Usedom laid mine fields in the Dardanelles and erected forts to protect them.

C. THE FAILURE OF THE NAVAL ASSAULT.

   1. <u>Preliminaries</u>. Commodore Roger Keyes, sent in February to be Carden's Chief of Staff, agreed with Carden that conquest of the Dardanelles depended upon controlling the Narrows, that heavy ships could not proceed until the mine fields were swept, and that the defenses on Kilid Bahr plateau must be reduced before sweeping could be accomplished.

   2. <u>Attacks on the Outer Forts</u>. Between 19 February and 4 March, Carden's battleships and smaller units failed to reduce the forts protecting the entrance to the Dardanelles. Attempts to send small demolition parties ashore to destroy the defensive artillery met with no success, and by 4 March Carden was convinced that naval gunfire alone could not reduce the defenses of the Straits. He suggested an attack on the Gallipoli peninsula from the land side, thus approaching the defenders at Kilid Bahr from their unprotected rear. Churchill countered by suggesting a landing from inside the Straits, but Carden realized that Turkish artillery from the mainland and the peninsula would make this a very risky venture.

   3. <u>The Sweep to the Narrows, 1-23 March</u>. About 12 miles in from Cape Helles the Dardanelles narrows to a small defile protected by forts at Kilid Bahr on the Gallipoli Peninsula and Chanak on the Turkish mainland. Carden's battleships harassed these positions by indirect battleship gunfire across the peninsula and by direct fire from ships inside the Strait, yet mobile Turkish artillery drove away lighter vessels attempting to sweep mines laid in the Straits. On 18 March the British fleet, now commanded by Vice Admiral

John de Robeck, made a determined effort to clear the Narrows by sending 6 battleships to bombard the forts. Of 4 old French battleships that joined, 2 were sunk by mines. Minesweepers were so severely handled by artillery fire that de Robeck finally ordered a general withdrawal. In executing the withdrawal the British battleships *Irresistible* and *Ocean* struck mines and sank. De Robeck decided that the Narrows could not be forced until the forts on the Kilid Bahr plateau had been taken by an assault from the land side. Churchill and General Kitchener finally concurred.

D. THE GALLIPOLI CAMPAIGN, APRIL 1915-JANUARY 1916. The army-centered amphibious operation that followed: 1) modified former Allied strategy of concentrating wholly on the Western Front, 2) shifted from a naval action against the Dardanelles to an amphibious attack across Gallipoli, and 3) created a new logistics problem in the Aegean. Success depended in great part upon logistic feasibility.

   1. *Logistics*. In 1915 Britain lacked both an amphibious force and modern amphibious doctrine. General Ian Hamilton had no staff to draft plans, his men were untrained, and his ships were not combat-unit loaded. Therefore, instead of attacking immediately, he sent the transports to Alexandria for unloading and reloading. In a month the transports were ready, but Hamilton had not had time for staff organization, staff planning, or tactical rehearsal. Von Sanders, meanwhile, used his month of grace to dispose his 45,000 troops about the beaches upon which Hamilton would most likely land.

   2. *The Landings, 25 April 1915*. Hamilton divided his 50,000 men into two columns for a converging attack on Kilid Bahr from the north and west.

   His landing plans were good. However, officers inexperienced in large-scale amphibious assault were left to make many on-the-spot decisions. Moreover, the secretive Hamilton issued few instructions besides those for the landings, leaving men ashore without orders on how to proceed. The result was that they failed to exploit the landings made on five Helles beaches. Indeed, casualties as high as 70% were suffered by the landing parties. In the three successful landings, the commanders dug in but failed to exploit their advantages because they had no orders to advance. Hamilton's refusal to commit reserves at a beach within easy reach of Kilid Bahr was the last costly blunder. By sunset on the 26th von Sanders had gathered his troops into an entrenched line. A stalemate of trench warfare continued to the end of December in the Helles sector, and Hamilton's attempt to exploit his hold on Suvla Bay in August petered out in a series of errors.

3. <u>Failure and Withdrawal</u>. Naval gunfire support by heavy ships continued until late May, when a single submarine drove them off, leaving only destroyers to support the troops ashore. Breakdowns in communications entailed additional failures or tragedies. Meanwhile the fleet adequately and often gallantly provided logistic support, including the building of artificial harbors at two beaches, and British submarines hazarded the perils of the Straits to invade the Sea of Marmora, sink ships, shoot up trains, even sink vessels moored in Constantinople. In December 1915, Kitchener ordered a withdrawal. With staff officers now experienced in amphibious cooperation, the withdrawal (19-20 December 1915 and 8-9 January 1916) was planned soundly and executed skillfully.

4. <u>Results</u>. In 1916, in part because Russia refused to aid in the attack on Gallipoli and in part because Bulgaria joined the Central Powers, Turkey was strong enough to resist an Allied threat from the Aegean. Germany gained on the Western Front in exact degree to the Allied strength sent to Gallipoli, and the British expended their fleet and men while the Germans husbanded theirs for Jutland. In May 1915, as a result of Gallipoli, Fisher resigned, a Cabinet shuffle whirled Churchill out of the Admiralty, and the British began to pay more attention to sound strategic and logistic planning. Gallipoli deterred the development of British amphibious doctrine but provided lessons drawn upon by Germany, Japan, and the United States; the development of American amphibious doctrine owes much to lessons drawn from Gallipoli. As for Russia, the Straits remained closed and she was quite effectively cut off from supplies which the Allies might have furnished her.

IV. SUBMARINE WARFARE

In the long run, the most serious naval effort of

the Germans was their submarine offensive against the Allied merchant marine. In four years, U-boats sank 11,000,000 tons of Allied or neutral shipping, caused 85% of the losses suffered by the British merchant marine, and sank five battleships, eight cruisers, and seven destroyers of the Royal Navy.

A. ATLANTIC OPERATIONS.

1. German Use of the Submarine. In 1914 the Germans did not realize the potentiality of the submarine as a commerce raider. While they obtained bases in Flanders, they lacked the bases in Norway and western France they were to possess in World War II. Moreover, to operate on England's western approaches, U-boats had to run the gauntlet of the Dover Patrol in the Channel or take the costly detour around Scotland and then evade the Tenth British Cruiser Squadron patrolling between Scotland and Iceland. Generally accepted rules of international law made the use of submarines against merchantmen and liners appear inhuman to neutrals, and Germany wished to respect the law. However, in three years she was driven to unrestricted submarine warfare as the only instrument that could break the British blockade.

2. Operations in 1914. In 1914 Germany operated 18 submarines in the North Sea from bases in Heligoland, Emden, and the island of Burkum. (The typical U-boat displaced 900 tons submerged, had a normal cruising speed of 5 knots and an emergency speed of 10, had 4 torpedo tubes, and could carry 6 to 10 mines.) These submarines forced the British Grand Fleet to evacuate Scapa Flow while its net and boom defenses were strengthened, sank 8 British warships, and forced the British to undertake a vast anti-submarine research and development program and work their shipyards around the clock. British naval and merchant tonnage of 31 December was half a million tons greater than that of 1 January -- but the Germans had 49 new submarines on order.

3. The First German Submarine Campaign, February-September 1915. With the Western Front stalemated, the Germans considered using the submarine against British merchant shipping at the strategic center, England's home waters. On 4 February 1915 Admiral Hugo von Pohl, the Chief of the Naval Staff, announced a "submarine blockade" of Great Britain

and Ireland to become effective on 20 February. Admiral Alfred von Tirpitz denounced the plan as inviting American intervention and suggested that only a limited blockade of the Thames Estuary be maintained until the Flanders bases were operational, when a general blockade could be instituted. His suggestions were disregarded. American objections to violations of freedom of the seas and of neutral rights provoked the retort that Germany might cancel the blockade if the United States persuaded Britain to live up to the Declaration of London. The United States knew that Britain would not blunt her blockade, her most potent weapon. The German submarines that took station in the North Sea and English Channel on 20 February were now joined by the Flanders Submarine Flotilla that operated from new operational bases established at the ports of Ostend and Zeebrugge and accounted for almost one fourth of all German submarine sinkings. The sinking of the unarmed liner Lusitania, 7 May 1915, was a bad mistake. Germany made a purely legal defense of the sinking but lost face in the world's public opinion and forged another link in the chain of events that would lead the United States to intervene two years later. American reaction to the sinking of the Arabic (British, three American lives lost) caused Germany to re-evaluate her submarine campaign and to promise that unresisting liners would henceforth not be sunk without adequate warning. The promise was maintained until March 1916.

During 1915 the British blockade was made more effective by Britain's waging of unrestricted economic warfare, including the rewriting of the contraband regulations to suit herself, restricting the imports of the Scandinavian countries to prewar quotas, mining the North Sea, and issuing a "black list" against all foreign firms that traded with Germany. Britain also made limited progress in anti-submarine warfare (ASW), and in "razzle-dazzle" painting and camouflage of ships. The Dover Patrol and auxiliary patrols visited and searched passing merchantmen and defended the Channel seaway, particularly from Folkestone to Boulogne, while minesweepers kept the danger from German mines to a minimum. Experiments were being conducted on an operational hydrophone, mine-bearing nets were installed in the Dover area, and production of the hydrostatically fused depth charge was begun. These measures drove the larger German submarines to use the North Sea route. In addition, the British used Q-ships, submarine against submarine, and ordered their surface ships to ram the U-boats.

The year 1915 was fought to a draw on the seas. Britain replaced almost all her tonnage sunk but her blockade did not as yet seriously pinch Germany. Germany finished the year with 68 U-boats operable and a construction-to-loss ratio of five to one.

4. <u>Operations in 1916</u>. A German estimate of the situation early in 1916 permitted unrestricted submarine warfare in certain limited areas but not in a general campaign. Henceforth armed merchantmen would be treated as cruisers in an "extended" submarine campaign to begin 1 March. Tirpitz, who favored full use of German seapower, resigned. The sinking of the French <u>Sussex</u> (injuries to three Americans) immediately drew a threat of the breaking of diplomatic relations from the United States unless international law were adhered to, with the result that German submarines in western waters were recalled for duty with other fleet units for use only against enemy naval units. From May to September 1916, German submarines existed merely as part of a fleet-in-being. They were, however, used as scouts and for widespread minelaying operations. While the U-boat caused a reduction of 5 percent in the Allied merchant fleet in 1916 and British construction ran behind losses, British developments in hydrophone detection and depth charge attacks were becoming quite effective. The use of paravanes by warships and the arming of merchant ships drove the submarine below the surface and to recourse to the torpedo rather than to surface fire. Meantime Britain's economic warfare drove Germany to do without various strategic materials or to develop substitutes for them. Poor harvests also helped account for a serious decline in the German standard of living by the end of 1916. This situation, joined to pessimism in the German army, provoked a demand for unrestricted submarine warfare in high circles. Until February 1915 three British merchant ships had been sunk for every German submarine: by the end of 1916 the ratio was 15 to 1. The German High Command therefore took the calculated risk of using the submarine to win the war before American power could make itself felt. An estimate made by Admiral Hennings von Holtzendorf, Admiralty Staff, 22 December 1916, concluded that unrestricted submarine warfare would drive Britain out

of the war in the five months from February through
June 1917. It proved to be a bad estimate.

CHAPTER 14

THE U.S. NAVY IN WORLD WAR I, 1917-1919

I. AMERICAN UNPREPAREDNESS FOR WAR, 1914-1917

A. PRESIDENT WILSON AND THE NAVY. The unpreparedness of the United States for war stemmed from many factors. President Wilson took office during an economic recession. Spending for the Navy would not only hamper economic recovery but, after the war in Europe began, would appear unneutral. Moreover, his great interest lay in fulfilling the promises of his campaign slogan, The New Freedom. Uninterested in military matters, he thought military men should speak only when spoken to, thus blocking military input into the determination of foreign policy. His keeping of the bulk of the fleet in Mexican waters from 1913 to 1915 adversely affected morale, maintenance, and fleet training.

B. JOSEPHUS DANIELS AND THE NAVY. Daniels, a newspaperman who knew nothing about the Navy, saw officers as aristocratic tyrants. He would democratize the service by reducing their power and uplifting and dignifying the enlisted men. To fulfill his desire to "make the Navy a great university, with college extensions afloat and ashore," he established an academic department in every ship and at every station in which first term enlistees and volunteers would obtain both academic and practical instruction. He also relaxed discipline somewhat, made shipboard life more habitable, as by providing mechanical laundries, and obtained congressional authorization for enlisted men to compete for admission to the Naval Academy. To put officers on a par with the men, denied liquor since 1899, he discontinued the officer's wine mess. On the other hand, he obtained congressional authorization for a Naval Militia that could be federalized in time of war (16 Feb. 1914) and a Naval Reserve (3 Mar. 1915), and for additional chaplains.

Saying that a general naval staff would "Prussianize" the Navy and endanger civil liberty, Daniels let wither the Aide system he inherited and instead relied for advice upon favored bureau chiefs. He allowed the General Board to continue drafting war plans but directed that it must not violate neutrality by planning for war against a European belligerent, and he opposed the creation of a council of national defense and Navy-sponsored research and development. While the General Board could suggest ship characteristics, he would decide the number of ships to be built. Moreover, believing the naval shipbuilding program should be what the nation could afford rather than what the Navy needed, he halved the Board's recommendations. Although U.S. naval aviation ranked 14th in the world in 1913--14 aviators and 4 flying boats--he did not ask for meaningful appropriations for naval air until after the war in Europe began and then for much less than the service wanted because he would not have it appear that he was preparing for war.

Daniels denied the suggestions of his Aide for Operations, Bradley A. Fiske, made late in 1914, that he obtain legislative sanction for the aide system, approve an administrative plan whereby the bureaus could prepare for war, ask Congress for about 20,000 additional men to bring ships to full war complement, adopt a general staff, and augment naval aviation. Meeting secretly with five other officers and Representative Richmond Pearson Hobson, Fiske prepared a bill calling for an Office of Chief of Naval Operations to include 15 officers to write war plans. Whereas the Fiske-Hobson bill gave the CNO "general direction" over the Navy, Daniels got the Senate to retain civil control and to drop the 15 assistants. Fiske, however, obtained the assistants and thus was responsible for the creation of the office that directed the Navy throughout the war and eventually won praise from Daniels himself. Fiske also obtained approval to hold realistic war games sponsored by the Department rather than by fleet commanders. Although Fiske had a year to serve before retiring, Daniels rusticated him at the Naval War College and chose Captain William S. Benson, who had no interest or training in strategy, to be the first CNO.

From March 1913 to July 1915, then, Daniels impressed the Navy with his ideas on democracy, education, prohibition, parsimony, and humanitarianism and supported President Wilson's desire for peace and keeping armaments on an even keel. After the Great War began and Wilson announced American neutrality, he supported that neutrality at the cost of appearing unpatriotic to those who demanded additional defense if not intervention in the war. He insured that no

unneutral radio messages were transmitted from the
United States, directed that no active or retired
naval officer comment publicly on the war, and sought
an increase in the American merchant marine and submarines.

II. TOO LITTLE AND TOO LATE

On 18 February 1915, Germany began unrestricted
submarine warfare in the waters around Great Britain.
On 28 March, when an American traveling in an unarmed
British passenger liner died as a result of U-boat
action, the Wilson administration had to determine a
policy on U-boat warfare. The need for such a policy
was greatly heightened when the American tanker
Gulflight was torpedoed and particularly when 124
Americans were among those who lost their lives on
the Lusitania (7 May). Believing that Wilson's holding of Germany to "strict accountability" for her
U-boat actions would lead to war, Secretary of State
William Jennings Bryan resigned, in June. Meanwhile,
a first step was taken toward preparedness in the
naval act approved 3 March. If shipbuilding estimates
remained close to those for fiscal year 1914, the act
created the office of chief of naval operations, an
advisory committee on aeronautics and a naval reserve;
authorized a number of admirals and vice admirals;
and provided for a 32 percent increase in the number
of naval constructors. A second step came on 13 July
when Thomas A. Edison agreed to head a Navy Civilian
Consulting Board to advise the Department on problems
of steam engineering, ordnance, construction, and
particularly antisubmarine warfare. A third was the
taking of an inventory by this Board of the preparedness of the nation's industrial facilities for war.
A fourth was the Council of National Defense approved
on 29 August 1916, for it was its responsibility to
coordinate industry and resources "for the national
security and welfare." One of the boards created by
the council was the General Munitions Board, known as
the War Industries Board in 1917, whose function was
to coordinate procurement by the armed services. The
Overman Act, approved 20 May 1918, finally authorized
the War and Navy departments to requisition and withhold materials.

On 21 July 1915, Wilson directed the secretaries
of War and Navy to draft an "adequate national defense

program" for presentation to Congress in November. Daniels asked the General Board for advice. The Board recommended a navy "equal to the most powerful maintained by any other nation in the world" and called for a 6-year building program to cost $1.6 billion that would give the United States 48 dreadnoughts, or parity with Great Britain. Daniels cut the time to 5 years during which he would spend $100 million annually on new construction, with the total cost approaching $1 billion. With stress placed upon building battleships, battle cruisers, scout cruisers, destroyers, and fleet and coastal submarines, it is clear that the program was designed to achieve parity with Britain, not to produce ship types needed for an antisubmarine war.

Although Wilson campaigned from New York to St. Louis for the plan and Daniels said the U. S. Navy ranked fourth in the world, Congress would not budge. Republicans who wanted an even larger navy built in a shorter time battled Democrats who alleged that preparedness was being demanded only by shipbuilders, big industrialists, the armor-plate monopoly, and big-navy imperialists. In the end, the program was cut to three years, with work on 56 of the 156 ships authorized to begin immediately, and an increase was authorized in the number of enlisted men from 54,000 to 74,700, which number the President in an emergency could raise to 87,000. The naval act approved 29 August 1916 also gave the chief of naval operations 15 assistants to write war plans, authorized government armor-making and projectile plants and a naval experiment laboratory, and earmarked $3 million for naval aviation. To obtain officers for new construction, Congress increased the brigade at the Naval Academy from 900 in 1916 to 1,200 in 1917, reduced the course from four to three years, and graduated the class of 1917 one year early.

The naval act of 29 August 1916 called for more powerful and faster ships than any afloat. Four of the battleships displaced 32,000 tons and carried 8 16-inch guns in main battery. Three others were to displace 42,000 tons and carry 12 16-inch guns. Four of the battle cruisers were to displace 34,800 tons, carry 10 14-inch guns, and were 5 knots faster than British or German battle cruisers.

III. THE UNITED STATES ENTERS THE WAR, 6 APRIL 1917

Following the torpedoing of the <u>Sussex</u>, 24 March 1916, Germany stopped attacking unresisting Allied merchant ships. On 9 January 1917, however, the Kaiser ordered unrestricted submarine warfare to begin 1 February, meaning that neutral as well as belligerent merchant ships would be sunk in zones about Great Britain, France, Italy, and the Eastern Mediterranean. The United States, moreover, could send only one passenger ship a week to Britain provided she carried no contraband and had three vertical red and white stripes painted on her hull. Wilson thereupon directed Secretary of State Robert Lansing to prepare a note breaking diplomatic relations with Germany. Although some cabinet members advised declaring war, Wilson, hoping to devise a policy that would prevent either belligerent camp from winning the war, merely broke relations with Germany. However, on 4 February he directed the military departments to prepare plans for full mobilization, and on the 19th he directed all Navy bureau chiefs to report on the status of their forces. Congress acted, too. It increased appropriations for the services and empowered the President to commandeer shipyards and munitions factories in the event of war or national emergency. In addition, Daniels made joint plans with the Army for the air defense of the Atlantic and Gulf coasts.

Because of the U-boat menace, American merchant and passenger ships hugged their harbors. Demands arose that they be armed and escorted so they could sail overseas. Wilson approved of furnishing such ships with guns but not with armed guard crews. The British did not use convoy, he was told, because they thought dispersion in independent sailing preferable, and Daniels among others advised him that the use of convoy would lead to war with Germany. On 26 February, Wilson asked Congress for authority to arm merchant ships. So authorized, he directed Daniels to put guns and gun crews on merchant ships. Armed guards could shoot at submarines that came within torpedo range in the war zones but were not permitted to seek them out or to attack them anywhere else. On 18 March, news came that three American ships had been torpedoed by U-boats. Wilson thereupon decided to go to war rather than continue an armed neutrality. Aiding him in reaching this decision were the machinations of German and Austrian secret agents, and diplomats, the publication of the Zimmermann Note (1 March 1917), and the outbreak of the Russian Revolution. On 20 March, he called Congress into session for 2 April and directed that the Navy be built up to full personnel strength; on the 24th he recalled American diplomatic and consular officials from Belgium, announced voluntary censorship regulations, and asked Daniels to establish confidential liaison immediately with Great Britain. Daniels put all commercial radio stations under naval control, established censorship policies, stopped work on battle cruisers and put all workers instead on building destroyers and small craft, and called Rear Admiral William S. Sims, president of the Naval War College, to Washington. On 6 April, after Wilson approved a joint congressional resolution calling for war against Germany (war was not declared against Austria until 7 December) Daniels ordered the fleet to mobilize.

On 6 April 1917, the U.S. Navy was unprepared for war. There was no adequate war plan; no arrangement had been made to cooperate with the British to obtain overseas bases or to provide transports; only one third of the Navy's vessels were materially fit and only 10 percent were adequately manned; and the United States was woefully short of ASW ship types. When the United States entered the war, Allied defensive resources were taxed to the utmost by the unrestricted U-boat campaign. With the German High Seas Fleet immobilized, American battleships were not needed in Europe. But the United States had concentrated on building capital ships instead of antisubmarine ships and weapons. Democrats campaigning on Wilson's having kept the nation out of the war could not be expected to sanction warlike activity pointed at a particular belligerent as long as the nation remained neutral. Daniels, incidentally, consistently refused to the eve of American entry into the war either to admit the possibility of American entry or to place the Navy in readiness for war.

IV. AMERICAN NAVAL CONTRIBUTIONS TO THE WAR EFFORT

The 2 million Americans sent to France contributed to the Allies that margin of strength needed to defeat Germany. These troops, and productive American factories, won the war, for neither air power nor science, with the possible exceptions of the development of an effective underwater sound detector, a direction finder (radio compass), and an antenna mine played a vital role. Deserving of great credit was Rear Admiral Albert Gleaves's Cruiser and Transport Service and the U.S. Shipping Board, which produced Liberty Ships in large numbers. Even if American naval preparations were poor, they met the emergency and played an important part in saving the Allies. However, the battleship squadron sent to operate with the British Grand Fleet never fired a shot at the German High Seas Fleet. Moreover, no special study had been given to ways to combat submarines. The General Board's war plans envisaged not submarine warfare but a surface fleet engagement in the Western Atlantic, most likely in the Caribbean. Nor did Great Britain have plans for utilizing American naval power, even though since the winter of 1916 it had been expected that the United States would enter the war. Daniels's decision to keep working on the capital ships, but not under "forced draught," was a compromise which provided the United States with sufficient naval power to protect its postwar interests. With work stopped on capital ships, the construction of both antisubmarine craft and merchant ships was pushed.

Daniels had new naval headquarters built in Washington and concerned himself with industrial production and with both defensive and offensive operations. He established a Coastal Patrol to defend harbors and scrutinize all ships entering or leaving them. He supervised the largest shipbuilding program in history and planned for the operation and logistic support of ever larger fleets and of a new naval air program. He coordinated American with Allied programs, enrolled and trained men to serve as armed guard crews, and repaired and made operative certain interned enemy ships taken over by the United States. He gave highest construction priority to antisubmarine craft, first to wooden 110-foot submarine chasers, then to 35-knot "flushdeck" destroyers, then to minesweepers, seagoing tugs, and patrol boats. Significantly, five times more was spent during the war for submarines and antisubmarine ships than for capital ships. But the vast preponderance of ships authorized during 1917 and 1918 were not completed until after the war. For example, 257 of the 273 destroyers authorized were built between

1918 and 1922. Thus, when the war was over, taking account of the ships building, the United States had the largest fleet in the world.

Although increases in naval air in 1917 alone showed an increase in material of 1,400 percent, in personnel training of 3,000 percent, and of stations and training schools of 3,200 percent, only a dribble of this effort reached overseas. Mostly because of the lack of spare parts for American aircraft, American pilots used French and occasionally British fighters.

V. AMERICAN COOPERATION WITH THE ALLIES

A. THE ATLANTIC. While Daniels created a naval transport service to carry American troops to Europe, he talked with British, French, Italian, and, eventually, Japanese and Russian missions that came to the United States. It was agreed as early as 12 April 1917 that the U.S. Navy would guard the Eastern and Gulf coasts of the United States and the Atlantic coasts of South America, thereby releasing British and French cruiser squadrons that had borne the duty since 1914. Meanwhile, the British had asked that an American admiral be sent over to share his navy's "plans and inquiries" with them. Daniels gave Sims oral and then written instructions for his mission in England. He was to keep the Department fully posted on conditions abroad and advise how the naval service could best cooperate with the Allied navies in case the United States entered the war. He was also told that President Wilson was "decidedly of the opinion that ships should be convoyed." Moreover, Benson, who knew that Sims had been born in Canada and had been admonished by President Taft for Anglophile statements made in 1910, told him, "Don't let the British pull the wool over your eyes. It is none of our business pulling their chestnuts out of the fire. We would as soon fight the British as the Germans."

Distance and poor communications made Sims's cooperation with the Navy Department difficult. On the other hand, the administration failed to spell out its policies clearly, gave him an anomalous place in the Navy's organizational structure, and also failed to provide him with specific duties. Benson said he was merely "a transmitter of information" who was subordinate not only to him but to Henry Mayo, Commander-in-Chief of the Atlantic Fleet. Daniels saw him as an assistant to Benson, a liaison officer representing the Department on duties given him by himself and Benson. On his part, Sims found Daniels agonizingly slow in reaching important decisions and Benson, who lacked Naval War College training, unaware of the true status of the war effort he was directing. The situation improved after June 1917 when William Veazie Pratt, Benson's assistant, acted as liaison between Benson and Sims.

On 10 April 1917, Sims called upon the First Sea Lord, Sir John Jellicoe, who told him that he saw no solution to the U-boat problem. British estimates made in the spring of 1917 predicted British defeat by November unless the U-boat could be conquered. By the end of April 1917, 6.5 million of the 32 million tons of Allied merchant shipping had been sunk. Evasive routing and patrol of focal areas had proved ineffective, and experiments in convoying were just beginning. Older heads at the Admiralty opposed convoying because convoys consumed time, their speed being that of the slowing ships; overtaxed harbor facilities at arrival and departure times; called for sailing skills beyond those of merchant ship captains; and required escorts which could not be spared from the offensive duties in which they were engaged. Unvoiced arguments included the unwillingness of the Admiralty to release the destroyers that defended the large ships of the Grand Fleet and protected Britain from German coastal raids and even from possible invasion.

On 11 April, the British and French asked Daniels for destroyers to patrol their Atlantic coasts. Daniels had only 51 destroyers. Of these, 16 in full commission were with the Atlantic Fleet resting securely behind mine nets in Chesapeake Bay, the rest having reduced complements or engaged in neutrality patrol in various parts of the world. How many of these should he or could he send over? On 14 April, Sims asked for a "maximum number of destroyers, accompanied by small anti-submarine craft," for merchant tonnage, and for auxiliaries and bases to service them. He also warned that Germany would send U-boats to the East coast of the United States in order to divert attention from the strategic center, the waters about the

British Isles. Failing to convince Jellicoe to adopt convoys, he had better luck with Prime Minister David Lloyd George, who got the Admiralty to agree, on 30 April.

While the Navy Department considered placing a mine barrier across the North and Adriatic Seas, President Wilson on 17 April announced his decision--"Let the destroyers go to the other side." Within a week, 6 destroyers sailed for England, and soon 3 more, all ordered to operate under Sims, who was promised additional destroyers and also destroyer tenders, trawlers, mine craft, and tugs. Not until 1 August, however, did the United States have 37 destroyers, 2 destroyer tenders, and 8 yachts in European waters, causing Sims to believe he lacked cooperation from the Department. On 4 May, the day the first destroyers reached England, Wilson directed that all merchant shipping be convoyed and agreed to adopt routes established by the British. Not until November, however, was Sims given a staff adequate to supervise the operations of 375 ships of all classes, about 5,000 officers and 70,000 men, and 45 bases, including those at Brest, Gibraltar, Inverness and Invergordon, Queenstown, in the Azores, and in Malta.

The first American contribution to the naval war was thus the sending of destroyers and numerous submarine chasers for patrol and convoy escort duties. So successful was the convoy system that not a single troopship or American soldier or marine out of more than 2 million men was lost on the eastward passage to Europe; only 3 empty vessels went down on the westward voyage. Monthly shipping losses were halved for each remaining month of the war after November 1917.

U-boat losses jumped from 25 in 1916 to 66 in 1917, and new construction barely replaced losses. The highwater mark for sinking of Allied tonnage came in the first six months of 1917, and the next highest mark in the second six months. The convoy system, improved depth charges and hydrophones, the arming of merchantmen, and extensive coverage by airplanes and airships brought the U-boats under control in 1918. Three fourths of the U-boats destroyed were sunk in 1917 and 1918, with depth charges and mines claiming about half of the victims. The United States accounted for four kills, the Royal Navy for the remainder. The value of the submarine as a submarine killer was proved, especially by the British "R" boat; and the development of the American antenna mine cut the number of mines needed for a field from 4 to 1. The most extensive mine field in history, in the North Sea between the Orkneys and Norway, claimed various victims and quite effectively closed the North Sea route to the Atlantic.

To keep troops from leaving the United States, Germany sent five U-boats to the American coast between May and October 1918. These laid mines between Chesapeake Bay and New York. German mines and submarines accounted for 110,000 tons of American merchant shipping; the <u>San Diego</u> hit a mine and sank off Long Island, 10 July 1918.

The American destroyers that reached Queenstown, Ireland, on 4 May 1917, were soon followed by large numbers of submarine chasers and eventually by Battleship Division Nine, Rear Admiral Hugh Rodman, which operated as the Sixth Battle Squadron of the British Home Fleet, and a secondary squadron of three additional battleships. Major naval and air bases were developed in France, England, and Ireland. A fleet of small craft based on Gibraltar and manned by Naval Reservists escorted 600 convoys without loss in the final 15 months of the war. Ponta Delgada, Azores, was an operating base for submarine chasers and patrol aircraft.

The U.S. Navy raced against time to get troops to Europe and alter the balance before Germany could win the war. The British carried a few thousand more of the AEF than did American ships, with the United States, however, providing most of the escort. While the AEF tipped the balance in favor of the Allies, American seamen and marines also played a part. Marines saw action in some of the fiercest fighting of the war. Seamen manned naval batteries mounted on railroad cars and fired German railroad yards, bridges, and ammunition dumps, and disrupted German communications. The United States also furnished the antenna mine and planted 80% of the mines used in the North Sea Mine Barrage. The U.S. Navy's principal contribution to the war effort was its escorting and supplying of American ground forces. Nevertheless, American naval forces in European waters in 1918 (375 warships and 81,000 men) were greater than the entire prewar strength of the United States Navy. American "C-tubes" and "K-tubes" perfected British and French experiments and resulted in the production of hydrophones capable of picking up ship engine sounds at 20 miles, helping to reduce the U-boat menace.

B. THE MEDITERRANEAN. When Italy entered the war, Germany sent 9 coastal U-boats and 4 minelayers to join the seven Austrian submarines in the Mediterranean. By the end of 1915 more than 100 Allied merchant ships were sent to the bottom. A net barrier across the Strait of Otranto proved less effective than the one at Dover. The Mediterranean was the single bright spot for Germany in the naval war in late 1917: with the loss of only 2 submarines to Q ships she sent almost 100,000 tons to the bottom. The situation began to change late in 1917, when Britain assumed responsibility for administering a unified Mediterranean naval command, and Americans joined Allied convoy escorts. By October the Suez-Mediterranean route was clear for Allied shipping. Despite Allied surface patrols, mine fields, and attacks on German submarines and the Austro-German base at Durazzo, Albania, German submarines sank 5 million tons of Allied shipping in the Mediterranean during the war at the cost of only 17 boats. At the end of the war, the remaining 14 U-boats in the Mediterranean safely reached the Atlantic.

C. SIMS AND THE ALLIED NAVAL COUNCIL. Sims played an important if often forgotten role in the Allied Naval Council with respect to Allied cooperation with Italy, which remained neutral for ten months and then joined the Allies in 1915. Italy's objectives were to obtain more territory from the Allies than that promised her by the Central Powers in return for her neutrality and to insure that no other power challenged her hegemony in the Mediterranean. Both objectives seemed assured when the Treaty of London, 26 April 1916, spelled out territorial concessions and stated that France and Great Britain would help Italy until the Austrian fleet was destroyed or until the end of the war. On 14 May 1915 Admiral Count Paolo Thaon Revel, Commander-in-Chief of the Italian Navy and also the equivalent of the American Secretary of the Navy, sent his ships to their stations; on the 24th, Italy entered the war.

Italy understood that Britain and France would take care of the Atlantic and the Mediterranean, leaving the Adriatic to Italy. Except for Venice and Brindisi, however, the entire Italian Adriatic coast lacks natural shelters and anchorages and even adequate artificial ports. Moreover, its communications lines and industrial plants along these beaches can easily be bombarded from the sea. Austria, in contrast, had major naval bases at Pola, Sebbennico, and Cattaro, numerous islands parallel to the coast to offer protection to coastal towns, and many channels that permitted Austrian ships to sortie, strike, and retire to safety. The strategic offensive thus lay with Austria. When Britain failed to provide Italy with sufficient ships or the right kind of ships and France demanded supreme command over any operation in which her ships participated, Italy assumed that her allies were supporting their own rather than her interests.

An Associated Power rather than an Ally, the United States was completely free to enter whatever military arrangements she liked and even to make peace separately on her own terms. Italy played no important part in Wilson's decision for war or, for that matter, was hardly consulted until September 1917, when the Allied Naval Council was established. Even then, although the United States sent ships to Britain and France beginning in May 1917, she did not send ships to the Mediterranean until 7 December, when she finally declared war on Austria.

To concert plans for defeating the U-boat in the Mediterranean, Lloyd George called an Interallied Naval Conference at London in January 1917. As an ally, Italy called for ships to carry badly needed steel, coal, wheat, and ammunition, and small naval ships to escort them. Compared with the Atlantic, the Mediterranean appeared a backwater to the British and French, and they wondered why Italy did not undertake offensive operations. Italy replied that because the British and French failed to supply the ships they promised and so make the Italian Navy superior to the Austrian, Italy could undertake only defensive measures. Four months passed before the United States entered the war, however, and five more until the Allied Naval Council was created, the latter to serve as a coordinating link between the Allied admiralties and provide the cooperation needed to defeat a common enemy. Although Wilson refused to recognize the Treaty of London, he saw that arrangements must be made for the coordinated use of materials the United States provided the Allies. In August 1917, therefore, he sent Mayo and Sims to an Allied conference that discussed means of overcoming U-boats. Not yet in the war, Italian delegates spoke privately to Mayo. Mayo promised to send destroyers but was convinced that the Allies stressed their own objectives much more than common ones. Yet the conference defined the grand naval Allied strategy. The United States would provide mines for the North Sea Mine Barrage, ships for ASW, cruisers for escort of convoy in the Atlantic, and a battleship squadron to operate with the British Grand Fleet. With respect to Italy, the conferees discussed adopting the convoy system in the Mediterranean, increasing coal and merchant ship tonnage for her, laying a mine barrage at Otranto Strait and providing ships to patrol it, taking offensive steps against submarine bases in the Adriatic, and increasing supply flow from the United States to Italy.

Few actual results followed. Although the anti-submarine war improved, Italy was defeated at Caporetto (October), Russia deserted the war, and Germany shifted 40 divisions to the Western Front. Britain and France questioned whether the United States, fearing postwar commercial rivalry, was providing all merchant shipping possible, and Britain and France refused to provide Italy with the destroyers Italy said she needed to hold the Germans and Austrians. Lloyd George thereupon demanded increased Allied cooperation. On 5 November 1917, the Supreme War Council began to coordinate the political-military operations of the western coalition. Late in November appeared the Allied Naval Council (Britain, France, Italy, Japan, and the United States) to supervise the general conduct of the naval war. The fact that no supreme naval commander was selected measures the reluctance of the nations involved to truly merge their resources and subordinate their national objectives. Sims nevertheless saw his work on this council as the most important he performed in 1918. As a result, colliers, tankers, machine guns, steel plates, cannons, and patrol boats and subchasers were provided Italy by the United States, with consequent great improvement in Mediterranean convoy operation.

The most important agenda item discussed by the Allied Naval Council was antisubmarine warfare, with the Adriatic question a close second. The British and French saw Italy as stalling, to merely contain the Austrians and then, the war ended, acquire their territory at the head of the Adriatic and on the Dalmatian coast. One can imagine the distress of the Italians when Wilson and Lloyd George early in 1918 said they would not honor the territorial provisions of the Treaty of London and Wilson, in his Fourteen Points, said that Italy's frontiers would be settled on the principle of self-determination. Unless they gained the Trentino, Trieste, and the eastern shore of the Adriatic, Italy retorted, she would consider herself defeated in the war. De Revel, meanwhile, refused to undertake offensive operations in the Adriatic lest he lose ships and pointed out that though he was responsible for both the Adriatic and Tyrhennian seas his resources were scarce. The British and Americans sneered at his defensive mentality and looked askance at Italy's placing politics before naval operations. To stimulate Revel to undertake offensive steps, Sims promised ships, equipment, and an admiral to conduct such steps. Revel refused, saying that the Adriatic was an Italian matter, he was unwilling to assume untoward risks, and an Italian must command operations. Sims launched into Revel but gave up when it became evident that all the Italians would agree to was the building of the Otranto Mine Barrage and that their prime goal was to save their ships so that they would be superior to the Austrians at the end of the war. Although the problem was referred to the Supreme War Council, Revel counseled Premier V. E. Orlando to agree to a supreme allied naval commander for the Mediterranean but not for "Italy's Adriatic." The British and French cooperated with the Americans. The Italians did not cooperate with the British and French. No better example can be found of how the personal jealousies, political susceptibilities, and national prejudices and interests of the Allied civil and military leaders made naval cooperation impossible. With great daring, Italians drove torpedo boats over booms and in disregard of harbor defenses sank two Austrian battleships sitting in their harbors. The only operation fully agreed upon by the Allies for the Adriatic, the Otranto mine barrage, was not completed in time to affect the outcome of the war. By concentrating upon obtaining favorable political and economic objectives, Italy failed to agree to Allied naval policies. Nevertheless, Revel provided the naval terms for Austria to be included in the peace treaties: Austria was to surrender her navy, reduce her fortifications on the Dalmatian coast, and restore to Italy territory she occupied since the war began and accept new frontiers that satisfied Italy's demands for security.

VI. POLITICS, POLITICS--AMERICAN STYLE

A. THE U.S. NAVY AS A DIPLOMATIC MAKEWEIGHT. While Sims concentrated on the war effort and declined to consider political matters, on 4 July 1917 Daniels forwarded him a directive governing the American naval war effort. The U.S. Navy would heartily cooperate with the Allies in meeting the submarine threat and also in "any future situation." Subject only to the needs of home defense, the Navy would cooperate in Allied offensive measures, as by sending abroad all the antisubmarine craft it could spare from home needs, but it would not send over its fleet or any division thereof. Believing Sims to be an Anglophile, Wilson and Daniels hesitated to send him the forces he demanded until political arrangements were made with the Allies that protected the interests of the United States. To further such political arrangements, in October Wilson sent Colonel E. M. House, accompanied by a group including Benson and General Tasker H. Bliss, USA, to confer with the Allies, who were about to hold an Inter-Allied Conference in Paris to plan their campaigns for 1918. Wilson cautioned Benson: "All possible cooperation but we must be free," and Daniels perceived in the diverging interests of the Allies meat for fighting among themselves once the war was over. Moreover, Wilson sent only a military representative, Bliss, to attend the monthly meetings held in Paris by the Supreme War Council established by the Allies. Last, Wilson and Daniels refused to let American naval officers accept honors from the Allies. A special case was that of Sims, who the British Admiralty invited to attend their meetings even if he could not speak or vote. To the suggestion Daniels applied "An emphatic NO."

One British-American disagreement was over the laying of a mine barrage across the North Sea, a venture the British said was impractical if not impossible.

Wilson, however, demanded aggressive anti-U-boat action and through Daniels and Benson arranged with the British to lay the field. The French naval war effort was so poor, moreover, that Americans must patrol their coast, make harbor improvements, and prepare landing and other facilities for landing troops.

Sims and Daniels meanwhile disagreed on the employment of ships overseas. When Daniels ordered him to escort troopships and merchant ships going to Britain and France, Sims said that he must suspend patrol and escort duties in the Western Approaches, U-boat happy hunting grounds. Furthermore he preferred to protect merchant ships rather than troopships, saying that the Allies needed supplies more than men. Instead of removing him from command or severely reprimanding him, Daniels peremptorily reminded him that his "paramount" duty was to protect troopships, the control of which Washington viewed as much from a sense of professional pride as out of political considerations. Sims's judgment that U-boats would concentrate on merchant ships proving correct, the troopships reached Europe unscathed. During the summer of 1918 the United States landed seven soldiers and their equipment in Europe every minute of every day and night. Yet Daniels hesitated to visit Europe during 1918 because Sims and the British persistently called upon him for destroyers he could not deliver. Before he went over, furthermore, he suggested to the House Naval Affairs Committee a three-year postwar naval building program similar to that of 1916. He would not build as much, he hurriedly added, if "adequate" peace terms were reached. Indeed, with the war almost ended, he planned to cut back naval aviation and return shipping to private control. However, with Britain unwilling to give up the freedom of the seas and the French avid for reparations from Germany, he could use a new building program as a bluff to bludgeon these Allies to meet American demands including the creation of a League of Nations. Point was given the bluff when Congress on 22 May 1918 authorized $1.5 billion to complete the building program of 1916.

Nothing but praise for Daniels emanated from the House Naval Affairs Committee, some of whose members visited the European war zone, during the war. With the war over, however, it appeared paradoxical that President Wilson demanded world peace on one hand and the largest navy in the world on the other. Anticipating peacekeeping by the League of Nations, Congress limited the number of men in the Navy to 225,000, which effectively reduced the number of ships and aircraft the Navy could operate; cut in half the naval appropriations Daniels demanded; and said it would discontinue building on the 1916 program if the United States became a member of a world organization competent to maintain peace and to make competitive armaments unnecessary.

With the bulk of the German fleet surrendered, then scuttled, the British Navy was almost as great as the combined navies of the rest of the world. If the United States completed her 1916 program, however, she would be supreme, and Wilson, supported by Daniels and Benson, threatened to resort to competitive building if the British would not agree to parity. If Daniels and Benson saw the 1919 building program as vitally necessary, Wilson used it only as a bargaining weapon at the Peace Conference. On the ground that the other powers had stopped building and that the pending treaty of Versailles included a League of Nations, Wilson reversed himself and dropped his support for the 1919 program. Meanwhile the Republican Congress, more interested in economy than naval efficiency, reduced the statutory limit to 120,000 enlisted men, not enough to enable the Navy to carry out its functions, and Daniels's demands for a Navy equal to Britain's got nowhere. Indeed, in the press he became the American Tirpitz.

B. WASHING DIRTY NAVY LINEN IN PUBLIC. Congressional investigations conducted in 1917 and 1918 into naval activities in Haiti and Santo Domingo, the work of the naval bureaus, of the antisubmarine campaign, the Marine Corps, and the shipbuilding program resulted in praise for Daniels. When wartime commanders submitted lists of officers and men to be given the Distinguished Service Medal, Medal of Honor, and Navy Cross, Daniels submitted them to a Board of Awards. But he changed the recommendations of the board by dropping some men and adding others and greatly increasing the number of enlisted men to get awards. In consequence, both Mayo and Sims declined the DSMs awarded them, some journals charged that Daniels robbed naval heroes and gave the awards to his friends, and Senator Frederick Hale was assigned by the Senate Naval Affairs Committee to look into the charges. During hearings, Daniels alleged that Sims was overwhelmingly ambitious and lacked loyalty by putting the British before the American cause. Asked about the matter, on 17 January 1919 Sims offered a long letter written to Daniels on the seventh entitled "Certain Naval Lessons of the War" and leaked to the press. Hale was then charged with investigating Sims's citing of wartime errors made in policy, tactics, strategy, and administration. For the first six months of the war, at least, he said, the Navy was unprepared and slow to act. There were three major questions: 1) was the Navy prepared for war; 2) was the Navy in good material condition to fight a war; and 3) did the Department enter the war with well considered policies and plans?

The evidence on the first point was that personnel had been short in number and untrained for war. On the second point, it was disclosed that the United States did not have a single submarine ready for war in 1917; the battleships in reserve were unready; the destroyers were not in the best state of preparedness, partially because of their shortage of men; the fleet was unbalanced because it lacked battle cruisers, scout cruisers, light cruisers, and fleet submarines; and the scouting and screening ships were scattered about the world rather than mobilized with the fleet. On the third point, Sims was proved incorrect to a degree. A base plan providing for the organization of fleets, bases, communications, logistics, and the like, was available, but it was founded on the assumption that the Navy would meet an enemy fleet somewhere in the Atlantic. Did the plan apply to the war itself? Benson said it made no difference because the United States followed Allied plans. Yet the Department had made no effort to follow Allied plans. Nor did it provide a specific antisubmarine plan. Nor, added Sims, did it provide him with policies to follow until 4 July 1917. His conclusion was that because of these deficiencies the Navy had delayed victory for four months and had cost the Allied cause 2,500,000 tons of shipping, 500,000 lives, and $15,500,000.

The hearings established that there was room for improvement in the Department but failed to prove that its shortcomings stemmed from its administration. In 1921, a majority report signed by three Republicans confirmed most of Sims's contentions while two minority reports written by Democrats rejected his arguments.

Sims had failed to drive Daniels out of the Department—if that really was his objective—and also failed to obtain a devoutedly desired reform, a general naval staff.

C. IMMEDIATE POSTWAR OPERATIONS. Between the Armistice and the signing of the Treaty of Versailles, the U.S. Navy: a) furnished vessels for Allied forces at Archangel and Vladivostok; b) returned home most of the AEF in nine and a half months; c) removed the North Sea Mine Barrage; d) helped supervise the enforcement of Allied terms with respect to the naval disarmament of the Central Powers; e) disposed of surplus naval facilities and supplies in Europe; f) scrapped all clearly obsolete warships except the historic Oregon; g) furnished Benson as the American naval representative to the Paris Peace Conference; h) furnished transportation, food, and medical supplies for various relief activities in Europe; and i) protected American lives and property in various European trouble-spots.

D. NAVAL LESSONS OF THE WAR. Testing of naval theories, organization, and technology in the war resulted in certain important deductions:

1. Naval policy must always be closely correlated with foreign policy;
2. The public, the Navy, and the administration must cooperate in order to provide the kind of Navy needed to implement stated foreign policy;
3. "Naval preparedness" includes a shore establishment, provision for logistic support, efficient organization, and adequate numbers of personnel in addition to mere ships;
4. The rapid development of the submarine, mine, and aircraft rendered close blockade of enemy ports practically impossible, modified the capability of surface forces, and made changes in fleet organization, ship design, and tactics inevitable;
5. Advocates of the submarine and of air power sparked controversy over the future value of the capital ship;
6. The war immensely strengthened the military power of Japan and left the Philippines a hostage to fortune.

VII. THE PEACE SETTLEMENTS

A. NAVAL PROVISIONS OF THE GERMAN ARMISTICE. The armistice provided that Germany must surrender 10 battleships, 6 battle cruisers, 6 light cruisers, 50 modern destroyers, and all of her submarines. On 21 November 1918, the German dreadnought line entered Scapa Flow. One hundred fourteen of the 158 German submarines had surrendered at Harwich by 1 January 1919.

B. NAVAL PROVISIONS OF THE TREATY OF VERSAILLES.

    1. The peacetime German navy was to consist of no more than 6 predreadnoughts, 6 light cruisers, 12 destroyers, and 12 torpedo boats.

    2. Germany would have no submarines or military aircraft.

    3. Heligoland and a belt 30 miles wide on the right bank of the Rhine were to be demilitarized.

    4. The Kiel Canal was opened to the warships and merchant ships of all nations; German rivers were internationalized.

    5. In addition to paying the costs of the war, Germany was to hand over to the Allies most of her merchant fleet, a quarter of her fishing fleet, and build 200,000 tons of shipping for the victors annually for five years.

    6. Germany must surrender her last effective naval units, from battleships to torpedo boats, and break up all construction under way.

C. THE SINKING OF THE GERMAN FLEET IN SCAPA FLOW, 21 June 1919. On signal from the <u>Emden</u>, the captain of every German ship at Scapa Flow ordered the seacocks opened. Ten battleships, 17 cruisers, 50 destroyers, and 102 submarines, for a total of 500,000 tons, went to the bottom in protest against the Treaty of Versailles. Only four of the vessels were ever salvaged. For all practical purposes, the German navy ceased to exist. As punishment, practically everything Germany had left afloat had to be turned over to the Allies. Allied quarrels over the divisions of spoils were averted. Only the United States was now in a position to challenge Britain as the mistress of the seas.

CHAPTER 15

NAVAL DISARMAMENT AND REARMAMENT,
1918-1941

Mention has already been made (Chapter 14), of the Republican desire to discredit the Wilson administration's wartime accomplishments for purely political purposes and, in keeping with traditional Republican philosophy, to cut defense costs. Republicans also desired to return to Congress many powers that Wilson had exercised as commander-in-chief of the wartime effort.

I. POSTWAR NAVAL COMPETITION, 1918-1921

The Armistice of 11 November 1918 and the peace conference at Versailles did not end naval construction among the allied and associated powers. The principal naval powers, Great Britain, United States, and Japan, had heavy naval construction programs underway which sheer administrative momentum carried into 1919. It was clearly evident that the United States upon the completion of its great 1916 building program would possess a navy second to none.

A. NAVAL BUILDING PROGRAMS.

1. <u>The United States</u>. By 1 January 1919 the United States had a capital ship navy consisting of 16 dreadnought-type battleships afloat, 13 battleships building or authorized, and six battle cruisers authorized and soon to be laid down. Sixteen of the 19 vessels authorized incorporated improvements based on experience gained at the Battle of Jutland.

2. <u>Great Britain</u>. The British had 33 dreadnought-type battleships and 9 battle cruisers in service, and just 4 capital ships building. The latter were post-Jutland type in design.

3. <u>Japan</u>. In Japan the building programs were necessarily more modest; yet in 1920 a long range bill passed the Diet projecting a fleet of 8 battleships and 8 battle cruisers to be built by 1927. With their older battleships and battle cruisers the Imperial navy would have 25 capital ships in service by 1927, and all would have been built after 1913.

218

B. NAVAL CONSTRUCTION AND THE LEAGUE OF NATIONS.

   1. *New American Building Programs, 1918-1919.* In the summer of 1918 the U.S. Navy General Board proposed another great building program to include 12 battleships and 16 battle cruisers. With war's end this program was reduced to 10 battleships and 6 battle cruisers, duplicating to a large extent the 1916 bill. This program was introduced in Congress in December 1918 and remained before that body until May 1919. If accepted and built, the resultant navy would have been the greatest in the world.

   2. *The 1918 Program and President Wilson.* This great 1918 program was presented to Congress with President Wilson's consent. It appears to have had two objectives: forcing the British to accept the League of Nations, the American concept of neutral rights within the League Covenant, and British-American naval equality; and attempting to present the American tax-payer with the alternative of a great naval construction program or collective security within the League.

   3. *The Results of Wilson's Efforts.* With British acceptance of the League and a guarded admission of the American right to naval equality, President Wilson withdrew his support from the 1918 program in May of 1919. Construction continued on ships authorized in 1916; between 1918 and 1921 work was begun on the rest of the capital ships of the 1916 authorization. Despite Wilson's efforts, the United States refused to sign the Treaty of Versailles or to join the League of Nations. On the other hand, Navy Department attempts to introduce further construction authorization bills met with heavy resistance in Congress. The United States would neither join the League nor accept any great new naval construction programs.

C. GROWING PRESSURE FOR A DISARMAMENT CONFERENCE. In view of continued spending on naval armaments, pressure built up in all countries for an international conference to halt armaments rivalries. This pressure was abetted by a developing hostility among the three great naval powers, Britain, America, and Japan.

   1. *International Tensions.* The obvious American challenge to British naval and merchant marine supremacy

did little to improve Anglo-American relations. Distrust within naval circles was communicated to the public through the "big-navy" press in both countries, and the perennial Irish problem further agitated many Americans. In addition, the American government was genuinely concerned about the continuance of the Anglo-Japanese Alliance. In the Pacific, American-Japanese relations had been strained to the breaking point since 1915. Distrust of Japanese ambitions in Asia had led the United States to interpose itself on the side of China on numerous occasions. A growing anti-Japanese spirit in the western states, a mistrust of Japanese promises concerning its newly acquired Pacific mandate, and a positive concern for American Pacific possessions showed clearly a need for an international clearing of the air.

2. <u>Popular Concern</u>. In all countries there was a strong desire to ease the tax burdens necessary to support heavy naval construction programs. In the United States, positive resistance to naval expansion manifested itself in slashed naval budgets and drastic cuts in allowed personnel. In Japan there was fear in some circles of revolt and a turn toward socialism were the fiscal burden not lightened.

3. <u>Senate Pressure</u>. In December 1920 Senator William Borah gave expression to the growing desire for a halt in the naval armaments race by introducing a joint resolution directing the President to call an international conference on disarmament. Though Borah's resolution never got beyond the hearing stage, reports on the hearings popularized the idea of a great disarmament conference. With a new Congress (the 67th) and a new administration Borah reintroduced his resolution and again received widespread popular support. The new administration, although cool to the idea at first, eventually extended invitations to the conference on 16 August 1921.

II. THE WASHINGTON CONFERENCE FOR LIMITATION OF ARMAMENT, 12 NOVEMBER 1921-4 FEBRUARY 1922

The Conference that met at Washington was originally called to deal with the problem of armaments rivalry and its limitation. However, pressure in the United States, China, and the British dominions forced the Conference to add political problems in the Pacific to the agenda.

A. AGENDA AND DELEGATES. The Conference and its problems were handled by an extremely capable group of diplomats aided by hosts of technical assistants and political advisers. The United States delegation was headed by Secretary of State Charles Evans Hughes; with him as co-delegates were Elihu Root, the Senate Foreign Relations Committee Chairman, Henry Cabot Lodge, and the ranking Democratic member of the Senate Foreign Relations Committee, Oscar W. Underwood. Naval officers acted as technical advisers to the four delegates, but control of the delegation was firmly in civilian hands. The British delegation was nominally headed by Prime Minister Lloyd George, but former First Lord of the Admiralty Arthur Balfour controlled the Empire's representatives. Prince Tokugawa of Japan was the titular head of the Japanese group, but Admiral Baron Tomasaburo Kato was in full charge. Admiral Kato was the only naval officer among the accredited delegates, but he was considered to represent the civilian element in Japan.

B. FAR EASTERN PROBLEMS AND THEIR SETTLEMENTS.

1. **Basic United States Far Eastern Policy to World War I.** Previous to World War I the United States' interest in the Far East consisted of maintaining the Open Door and protecting the "territorial integrity" of China, and of defending the Philippine Islands. The American Navy was never completely adequate to implement this Far Eastern policy; but the likelihood of a serious challenge (Japan was in a position to dispute the United States) was never allowed to control naval planning. American naval attention, to a large degree, was riveted to the Atlantic and Germany.

2. **Changes After the World War.** The Japanese defeat of Germany on the Shantung Peninsula, the serving of the "21 Demands" on China, the acquisition of a mandate over former German islands in the northern Pacific, and participation in the Siberian intervention, served notice to all that Japan was now a powerful and ambitious military power in the Far East. The wartime and post-war naval programs of the Japanese brought that nation to the third rank.

Possession of a mandate over the Caroline, Gilbert, Marshall, and Mariana Islands left Japan in a position to dispute any American advance to relieve the Philippines. The terms of the mandate forbade the militarization of the Japanese-held Pacific islands, but few Americans were willing to rely on the mandate terms, particularly when the United States was not a League member.

3. <u>Broadening the Conference Agenda</u>. Many Americans and Englishmen hoped that Japan could be checked by diplomacy. Canada, Australia, and New Zealand were vitally concerned about the potential mischief that the Anglo-Japanese Alliance could cause were the United States and Japan to go to war. The Japanese were cool if not positively hostile to any move to include "problems of the Pacific" in the Conference agenda, but they failed to prevail. Although not a naval power, China was a victim of Japanese opportunism and worked avidly to have its case presented before the Conference. The Chinese wanted Japan out of China, and they knew that those powers interested in the Open Door were basically in sympathy with their position.

4. <u>The Four Power Treaty, 13 December 1921</u>. A key log in the jam of Far Eastern problems was the Anglo-Japanese Alliance, last renewed in 1911. The Four Power Treaty (United States, Great Britain, Japan and France) broke the "jam" by substituting a ten year multilateral agreement to respect one another's insular possessions in the Pacific and to consult were trouble to arise. The Alliance was specifically cancelled. For the United States, this guaranteed Philippine security and made Article XIX of the Five Power Treaty less offensive (see below).

5. <u>The Nine Power Treaty, 6 February 1922</u>. With the naval effectiveness of the United States severely curbed in the Five Power Treaty (see C-2), the Open Door policy was written into the Nine Power Treaty. The signatory powers (United States, Belgium, British Empire, China, France, Italy, Japan, the Netherlands, and Portugal) agreed to respect the territorial and administrative integrity of China, to adhere to the Open Door policy, and to meet for peaceful discussion in the event problems arose. This treaty, and the above-mentioned Four Power Treaty, wrote into international law a defense for American Far Eastern

interests. From the viewpoint of the diplomat and politician there was little reason now for not reducing American naval strength if the other nations were also willing to reduce theirs.

C. NAVAL LIMITATION AT THE CONFERENCE. While the knotty problems of the Far East were being unraveled, the great powers were at work on the reduction of naval armaments as well.

    1. <u>Secretary Hughes' Demarche</u>. At the opening of the Conference, American Secretary of State Hughes laid out a full program of naval reduction for all to consider. Based on ships built or building, he called for a 10-year holiday in capital ship construction and a radical paring down of those fleets already in existence until there was a tonnage ratio of 5-5-3-1.75-1.75 for the United States, Great Britain, Japan, France, and Italy, respectively. Since no other program was advanced, the American plan became the point of departure for the conference.

    2. <u>The Five Power Naval Treaty, 6 February 1922</u>. Twelve weeks of intense discussion and compromise saw the adoption of the Five Power Treaty. This embodied, in part:

    a. Capital ship tonnage for the United States and the British Empire would be 525,000 tons standard displacement, for Japan 315,000 tons, for Italy and France 175,000 tons. For 10 years, with specified exceptions, no capital ships were to be laid down.
    b. Capital ships (battleships and battle cruisers) were limited to a maximum of 35,000 tons per unit, and could carry no gun with a caliber exceeding 16 inches.
    c. Aircraft carrier tonnage for the United States and the British Empire would be 135,000 tons, for Japan 81,000 tons, for Italy and France 60,000 tons. Carriers were limited to a maximum of 27,000 tons per unit, except that any nation could build two carriers of 33,000 tons displacement apiece, provided the total allowed tonnage was not exceeded.
    d. No naval vessels exceeding 10,000 tons could be built unless as carriers or capital ships, and no vessel except a capital ship could

carry a gun larger than eight-inch caliber. (This made a cruiser limit of 10,000 tons displacement and eight-inch caliber guns.)
  e. With the exception of Hawaii, Alaska (Aleutians excluded), and the Panama Canal area, America's Pacific islands were to remain militarily in the status quo. Similar "non-fortification" provisions applied to the British (Hong Kong excepted), and Japanese (home islands excepted) possessions as well. This was the famous "Article XIX" of the Treaty.
  f. The Treaty was to remain in effect until 31 December 1936 but could be renounced with two years' notice.

D. THE UNITED STATES NAVY UNDER THE TREATY. The acceptance of the Washington Conference treaties by the U.S. Senate ushered in a dismal period for the American Navy. The paper guarantees of American Far Eastern interests led many legislators to believe that there was little need for even the small Navy remaining after the Conference, and this belief was reflected in parsimonious naval budgets and consistent hesitancy to authorize further increases in the naval establishment.

Throughout the 1920s and 1930s, many active and retired naval and naval reserve officers argued against pacifists and the administration, to no avail.

  1. The Unbalanced Fleet. In 1922, although rich in capital ships, destroyers, and submarines, the American Navy was woefully weak in cruisers. The British and Japanese navies far exceeded the United States in cruisers, both in quantity and quality. Despite this weakness Congress refused to authorize any new cruisers until 1924, and by 1927 only two of these were laid down. The result was that the U.S. Navy had to limp along with 10 modern light cruisers (Omaha class) and fill in with the pre-war cruisers that were distinctly inferior to their foreign counterparts in speed and weight of gunfire.

  2. Personnel Problems. With the 1916 program Omaha cruisers joining the fleet, aviation developments, and battleship modernization making each unit more complicated and requiring more men, and a large number of destroyers remaining in service, Congress began to

cut heavily into naval personnel. Enlisted allowances were slashed and appointments to the Naval Academy were reduced. By 1922 the Navy had to decommission vessels because of personnel shortages, and with each passing year the situation became more critical, particularly as aviation personnel demands became more pressing.

3. **Limitation of Naval Operations**. Lack of funds severely limited the operations of the Navy as well as its size. War games and training exercises after the Conference were radically curbed due to lack of funds for fuel, and fleet exercises in the early 1920s were limited to the Caribbean. This shortage of appropriations, plus the undeveloped nature of advanced bases at Guam and the Philippines, made large scale operations west of Hawaii impractical.

4. **The Navy and the Far East**. Heightened international tension in the Far East in the decade following the Washington Conference created a need for increased American naval power. The Four and Nine Power Treaties did not "freeze" the Far East, and with the passing of years such affairs as the Japanese exclusion act in the United States (1924), the unification of China (1927), and the movement into Manchuria of the Japanese (1931) showed that the United States needed naval power in eastern Asia to protect its nationals and their interests. Although there was little desire to reduce American commitments by either abandoning the Open Door in China or granting the Filipinos their independence, demand in Congress still continued for further naval limitation.

III. FURTHER ATTEMPTS AT NAVAL LIMITATION, 1922-1931

The Washington Conference treaties neither eased tensions in the Far East nor halted naval construction throughout the world. The rivalry in capital ship construction was superseded by a great building race in minor combatant vessels, mainly cruisers. By 1931 naval rivalry in all combatant vessel categories was controlled by treaty, but Japan's move into Manchuria and increased pressure on China clearly foretold the collapse of the naval limitation system.

A. NAVAL COMPETITION AFTER 1922.

   1. <u>Cruiser Construction Rivalry</u>. With a cruiser size limit of 10,000 tons and 8-inch guns set in the Five Power Treaty of 1922, the signatory powers moved to this maximum in most of the cruisers authorized or laid down after 1922. In the United States the Congress <u>authorized</u> 8 10,000 ton cruisers in 1924, but only after the Japanese had <u>laid down</u> 6 and the British 5. By 1927 America had begun construction on 2 of these heavier cruisers, whereas the Japanese had started 10 and the British 14. It was clearly evident in naval circles that the U.S. Navy was in third place in terms of possessing a well-balanced fleet, but it was realized that any great spate of cruiser construction in America would evoke more keel-layings in other countries.

   2. <u>Naval Limitations Attempts by the League, 1925-1931</u>. In December 1925 the League of Nations set up a Preparatory Commission to study problems of limiting naval and land armaments. For six years the major powers grappled with questions of quantitative and qualitative naval disarmament. They had arrived at few conclusions by the time the long expected League Disarmament Conference opened in February 1932. However, the efforts of the Preparatory Commission were not entirely wasted, for their studies were used at both the abortive Geneva Naval Conference in the summer of 1927 and the more fruitful London Naval Conference of 1930.

B. THE GENEVA NAVAL CONFERENCE, JUNE-AUGUST 1927. Because of evident slowness in coming to grips with naval limitation in the Preparatory Commission, President Calvin Coolidge in February 1927 extended invitations to the great naval powers to meet at Geneva in June. Great Britain and Japan accepted, but Italy refused to attend. With the Italian refusal the French also rejected the invitation to reduce or limit their navy; however, both countries were willing to send official observers. Unlike the Washington Conference, naval officers rather than leading statesmen acted as delegates and technical advisers. The United States sent Ambassador Hugh Gibson and Rear Admiral Hilary J. Jones as delegates.

   1. <u>Conference Problems Hindering Agreement</u>. The Geneva Conference was doomed from the day it opened.

The United States hoped to limit cruiser construction, possibly to the point where further American construction would be unnecessary, and sought a cruiser tonnage maximum of 400,000 tons. The British insisted that they needed 70 cruisers and were less concerned about total cruiser tonnage. Both the United States and Great Britain were agreed that there could be no further tampering with the 5-5-3 ratio and that there could be no additional limitations on naval bases. The Japanese never had to take a stand because of the clash of interests between the United States and Great Britain.

    2. <u>Reasons for the Conference's Failure</u>. There was no careful exploration of the British and American positions before the Conference, and failure was the result. The United States insisted on building heavy 10,000 ton 8-inch gun cruisers. This meant a total tonnage in excess of 400,000 tons in order to match the British demand for 70 cruiser units. Being unwilling to allow the British more cruisers than the United States, and knowing Congress would not appropriate for more than 400,000 tons of cruisers, the Americans allowed the Conference to fail. Successful naval disarmament depended upon the reduction by the British in the number of cruisers they required. The public on both sides of the Atlantic oversimplified the whole situation and decided that the Conference had failed "because the admirals were on top, rather than on tap."

C. THE LONDON NAVAL CONFERENCE, JANUARY-APRIL 1930. The failure at Geneva resulted in reopening the cruiser building race. In December 1927 a 71 ship bill was presented to Congress, but final action in February 1929 saw only 15 cruisers and 1 aircraft carrier authorized. Six cruisers from the 1924 bill were laid down in 1928. In Great Britain no larger cruisers were authorized or laid down, but in Japan, France, and Italy at least two new cruisers were laid down in each country. In all countries by 1929 there was heavy pressure to hold down future naval authorizations, especially with the expense of replacing older battleships looming.

    1. <u>Calling the Conference</u>. In the summer of 1929 Ambassador Charles G. Dawes began a series of discussions with British officials with the goal of reducing the areas of difference between the naval

points of view in America and Great Britain. These talks were capped in October 1929 by a visit of Prime Minister Ramsay MacDonald to America. President Hoover and MacDonald were able to arrive at naval agreements in all categories of vessels except the 10,000-ton cruisers, and here they were only 3 ships apart. The U.S. Navy believed it needed 21 cruisers, the British felt they could allow only 18. At this point the British issued invitations to a naval conference at London for January 1930. The five principal naval powers accepted. All nations sent large delegations headed by important civilian and naval figures but clearly dominated by the civilian side. The American delegation, seven strong, was headed by Secretary of State Henry L. Stimson and included Secretary of the Navy Charles Francis Adams.

2. <u>Negotiations in London</u>. From its opening, the London Naval Conference revealed a unanimity of views between the British and American delegations. The principle of absolute parity between the British and American navies had been agreed upon, and the major problem appeared to be holding the Japanese demand for a higher ratio (they wanted 5-5-3.5) in check, particularly as it applied to the heavy 10,000 ton 8-inch gun cruisers. Again, as at Geneva in 1927, neither Britain nor the United States would countenance further limitations in the fortification of their Pacific possessions. This was important because Singapore was rapidly becoming the most important British naval base in the Far East, and the United States was turning Pearl Harbor into its greatest naval bastion.

3. <u>The London Naval Treaty</u>. The London Treaty limited virtually all classes of naval vessels not already limited in the 1922 Washington Treaty. The number of battleships was further reduced, with the United States rendering unfit 3 (<u>Florida</u>, <u>Utah</u>, and <u>Wyoming</u>), the British 5 and the Japanese 1. Cruisers were divided into light cruisers (carrying guns less than 6.1 inch calibers) and heavy cruisers (carrying guns more than 6.0 inch), and both classes were limited. In ratios the Japanese received their increase to 70 percent (5-5-3.5), but the Japanese were limited to 60 percent of British or American allowed tonnage in heavy cruisers. Submarines and destroyers were also limited in the treaty.

Because neither France nor Italy would be bound

by the treaty sections limiting the tonnages of cruisers, submarines, and destroyers, Article 21 was inserted in the treaty. This allowed any nation signing the treaty to depart from limitations were it menaced by a non-signatory power. If this departure were to occur, then the remaining signatory powers could also increase their naval strength. This was the famous "escalator clause."

IV. THE COLLAPSE OF NAVAL LIMITATION, 1931-1941

The refusal of France and Italy to sign the heart of the London Treaty, and the inability of England and America to bring about a naval *rapprochement* between the two continental powers did not augur well for the future. The situation was further complicated by Japanese aggression in the Far East and the reluctance of the major powers to resist that development. The failure of the World Disarmament Conference in 1933, and the subsequent collapse of naval limitation by treaty in 1936, reopened the armaments race and helped to start the world on the road to World War II.

A. THE MANCHURIAN INCIDENT AND NAVAL LIMITATION. The Japanese conquest of Manchuria, beginning 18 September 1931, destroyed the stability of the Far East created at the Washington Conference. The Four Power Treaty had been violated, and it was assumed that the Nine Power Treaty would soon be worthless. The United States took the position in January 1932 that all of the Washington treaties were closely related; thus, the Five Power Treaty was also endangered. Clearly defiant of American and world opinion, the Japanese showed every intention of remaining in Manchuria. The American answer was to begin the construction of heavy cruisers and the "rounding out" of the fleet.

B. THE LEAGUE DISARMAMENT CONFERENCE, 1932-1934. The long-awaited world disarmament conference opened under a cloud at Geneva on 2 February 1932. Tension was high between the United States and Japan, France and Italy were unable to agree on a naval balance in the Mediterranean, nationalism was becoming more pronounced in Germany, and all countries were struggling in the grip of a worldwide depression.

1. *Hoover's Suggestion*. In June President Hoover won the sympathy of the world's taxpayers by

suggesting that all naval and military establishments be reduced one-third. This suggestion from the Quaker President was given very little consideration by the principal naval powers.

2. <u>Japan and Germany Withdraw</u>. In the spring of 1933 Japan announced her intention to withdraw from the London treaty at its expiration. Two months later, following the Lytton Commission report, the Japanese published their decision to withdraw from the League. The Conference virtually collapsed on 14 October 1933, when Germany withdrew, and the new Nazi government stated that Germany would leave the League.

C. THE LONDON NAVAL CONFERENCE, 1935-1936. Both the Washington Five Power Treaty and the London Naval Treaty of 1930 called for a conference in 1935 to reconsider naval limitation. The League disarmament conference failure, the naval building programs since legislated, and Japan's declared intention to withdraw from the Washington treaties all increased the pressure for a conference that promised success.

1. <u>Statements of Position</u>. The Japanese forced the Conference from the day of its opening (9 December 1935) to consider their demand for "a common upper limit," that is, the end of the ratio system. In this they had the sympathies of France and Italy. When denied their basic request, the Japanese withdrew on 15 January 1936. From the viewpoint of the United States it was then impractical to limit further the quantity of its naval tonnage were the Japanese to remain unrestricted.

2. <u>The London Treaty, 25 March 1936</u>. Despite the Japanese withdrawal, the United States, Great Britain, and France signed a treaty that limited the types and characteristics of vessels that could be constructed, but imposed no total tonnage limitation on any nation. Guns on capital ships were limited to 14 inches, carrier tonnage was reduced to a maximum of 23,000 tons per unit, and the signers agreed to a 6-year building holiday for cruisers in excess of 8,000 tons. It was further agreed to exchange all significant information on new construction.

3. <u>The Treaty's Failure</u>. As in the London Treaty of 1930, there was an "escalator clause"

230

allowing the signatory powers to ignore certain treaty provisions if their national security were endangered by a non-signatory nation. The Japanese refused to accept the 14-inch gun limit of the treaty when approached by the United States and Great Britain, and they also refused to exchange information relating to their construction programs. Although duly ratified by the signatories, the treaty was completely ineffective.

    4. <u>The United States and Great Britain</u>. A significant by-product of the naval limitation movement between 1927 and 1936 was the gradual improvement of Anglo-American relations. With the failure of the Geneva Naval Conference of 1927, the spirit of animosity between the two great English-speaking nations reached its greatest intensity. By 1929, particularly after Ramsay MacDonald took office in England and Hoover was inaugurated, there was a steady improvement in cooperation. This working relationship continued through the early 1930s and remained intact with the signing of the rather emasculated London Naval Treaty of 1936. In part this great <u>rapprochement</u> between England and America was the result of natural cultural influences; but equally important was the fact that both nations distrusted Japanese intentions in the Far East and found naval cooperation a necessary result of this uneasiness. In the Far East the British and American fleet commanders found the Dutch equally willing to think in terms of informal cooperation and support. Again Japanese pressure was the catalytic agent causing the non-Asiatic powers to work together.

    V.   AMERICAN NAVAL DEVELOPMENTS, 1922-1941

    The years 1922-1941 may conveniently be divided into two periods separated by the Manchurian Crisis of 1931-1932. In the earlier period there were few combat additions to the Navy, and the decade was therefore spent in training, development of new tactics and doctrines, and the creation of new naval weapons. In this first period naval aviation was born, and carrier and squadron uses were studied. After 1931, with Japanese-American relations becoming yearly more unstable, new naval units and types were added to the fleet in ever increasing numbers. In December 1936 the quantitative limitation of national navies was ended, and as noted above, qualitative limitation under the second London Naval Treaty meant very little.

A. NAVAL AVIATION. Following the World War, and in the light of British experience, the U.S. Navy developed an interest in taking aviation to sea. The collier <u>Jupiter</u> was converted into an experimental aircraft carrier and launched as the <u>Langley</u> in March 1922. Between 1922 and late 1927, when the <u>Saratoga</u> and <u>Lexington</u> were commissioned, the <u>Langley</u> served as an experimental vessel. Aircraft types, arresting gear, handling methods, and launching and recovery techniques were closely studied. By 1927 the handling of aircraft at sea had been developed to a fine art, but the use of aircraft in squadrons and groups, and the technical and strategic use of aircraft carriers needed further study.

1. <u>The Morrow Board</u>. After years of controversy over the role of naval aviation, the merits of a United Air Service, and the mission of Army aviation, all highlighted by the spectacular 1921 aerial bombing tests against naval vessels, President Coolidge in 1925 appointed a board headed by Dwight Morrow to study the place of aviation in civil and military affairs. The board separated civil from military aviation. Although it recommended granting Air Corps status to the Army Air Services, it also recommended establishing a Bureau of Air Commerce in the Department of Commerce. By legislation of 1926, the demands of the Air Corps for autonomy within the Army were answered, yet the Corps remained under strict civilian control. At the same time a national policy for civil air transportation could be implemented. The board also agreed that there was a need for aviation in the fleet. Following the Morrow Board report was the 1926 five-year naval aircraft procurement bill, and the organization of an efficient Naval Air Reserve program. The 1,000 planes called for in the 1926 program were designed to equip the new giant carriers once these were placed in full commission.

2. <u>The Carrier Task Force Concept</u>. During the early trial years most naval officers believed that carriers would act as fleet scouts. Aircraft were placed aboard cruisers and battleships for scouting purposes, and it was assumed widely that the carriers would act to defend the fleet against shorebased and

carrier aircraft of the enemy, and in some instances launch attacks against enemy forces. In the Caribbean maneuvers after 1925, and in the Pacific Ocean maneuvers of 1928-1929, it was shown that carrier aircraft could surprise defenders at shore installations. In the latter maneuvers, and more dramatically in the 1934-1935 exercises in the Hawaiian area, it was shown that carriers could operate independently with fast cruisers for screens and could strike effectively against enemy shore bases and fleet units. By the mid-1930s the fast carrier task force concept was beginning to take shape.

B. SHIP CONSTRUCTION. As noted above, following the Washington Conference of 1922 the Navy was extremely weak in combatant auxiliaries; and in capital ships there was little development due to various treaty strictures against building. Yet the interwar years saw many new types join the fleet, and many old vessels modernized.

    1. <u>Cruiser Developments</u>. Between 1922 and 1931 the cruiser additions to the fleet consisted of finishing the 10 <u>Omaha</u> class light cruisers (7,500 tons, 6-inch guns), laying down the 8 1924 heavy cruisers (10,000 tons, 8-inch guns), and commencing construction on the 1929 heavy cruisers. The London Naval Treaty created a new "treaty cruiser" displacing 10,000 tons but carrying 6-inch guns. Beginning with the <u>Phoenix</u> in March 1935, 6 London Treaty cruisers were constructed from the 15 authorized in 1929. The other 9 cruisers, commencing with the <u>Portland</u> in February 1929, were 10,000 ton 8-inch gun vessels. The London Treaty light cruisers proved to be excellent fleet units with heavy firepower, well-armored, and of great cruising radius. The heavy cruisers of the 1924 and 1929 bills were lightly armored, a bit unstable in some types, but possessing the necessary large steaming radius.

    Under the provisions of the National Industrial Recovery Act, the President ordered on 16 June 1933, 1 heavy, 3 light cruisers, and 2 aircraft carriers. With 19 cruisers authorized, the Vinson-Trammel Act of May 1934 ordered no others, but did formally recommend that the President have cruisers built to bring the Navy to full treaty strength.

Later naval acts, following the outbreak of war in the Far East, authorized percentage increases for the Navy. The Vinson Act of May 1938 increased naval tonnage by 23 percent, and the Vinson-Walsh "Two-Ocean Navy" Act of July 1940 increased the Navy another 70 percent.

2. <u>Capital Ships</u>. From February 1922 until Navy Day 1937 no battleships were laid down by the United States. In 1930 the 18 battleships were reduced to 15 by the London Treaty. Although no new ships were authorized until the Vinson-Trammel Act, those needing it were modernized by conversion to oil burning, modifications in superstructure, additions of anti-aircraft batteries, bulges, modern fire-control apparatus, and increases in gun ranges by modifications on the elevation mechanisms.

On 27 October 1937 the <u>North Carolina</u> was laid down. This and battleships that followed were nine or more knots faster than the <u>West Virginia</u> which joined the fleet in December 1923. The new battleships were better armed and armored and carried better fire control gear. On 14 June 1940, with the fall of France in mind, Congress authorized an increase of the battleship fleet of 21 vessels. The next month the Vinson-Walsh bill cleared the way legislatively for the great new battleship fleet that emerged during World War II.

3. <u>Aircraft Carriers</u>. The inter-war years were ones of trial and experimentation with aircraft carriers. By 1928, with the <u>Saratoga</u> and <u>Lexington</u> in the fleet, the Navy had decided that it preferred smaller carriers. With a treaty allowance of 135,000 tons the Navy would be allowed a maximum of three more units were it to build carriers over 20,000 tons. Carriers under 10,000 tons were considered but rejected; therefore, the <u>Ranger</u>, of 14,500 tons, was authorized in the 1929 naval act. The NIRA naval authorization of June 1933 resulted in the <u>Enterprise</u> and <u>Yorktown</u>, both displacing 19,900 tons. In 1934 the <u>Wasp</u> was authorized at 14,700 tons, thereby using up the allowed tonnage of the Washington Five Power Treaty. The last carrier of the <u>Enterprise</u>-<u>Wasp</u> class was the <u>Hornet</u>, and this class was followed in 1940 with the authorization of the giant <u>Essex</u> type carriers displacing 27,000 tons by design, but far

exceeding this when completed.

What is obvious is that the Navy preferred small carriers only when bound by the treaties or fiscal limitations of Congress. Once assured that ample funds were available, the Navy turned to the larger carrier. This type not only had the steaming endurance and speed of the Enterprise-class carriers, but it could carry a substantially larger number of aircraft.

C. MARINE CORPS AMPHIBIOUS OPERATIONS. World War I convinced a number of officers of the need for developing amphibious doctrines and techniques as well as materials. Rather than follow the British pattern of "combined operations," or Navy or Army-centered amphibious operations of the Mexican and Civil Wars, Americans conceived a Navy-centered amphibious force commanded by an admiral, with the commander of specially trained naval infantry, or marines, fully responsible for the tactical employment of the force.

1. Marine Corps Expeditionary Forces. Beginning in 1894 Marines were ordered aboard naval vessels as a form of naval infantry, and in 1921 a formal organization, called the Advanced Base Force, was established. This Advanced Base Force consisted of a reinforced Marine regiment, and until 1921 performed the many police duties called for in the Caribbean and Far East. With the logistical experience of the World War behind them, and equipped with weapons that made assault operations feasible, Marine Corps planners began to think in terms of using the Corps for advanced base seizures as well as for defense in islands already occupied. In 1921 the Marine Corps Expeditionary Force was set up at Quantico, Virginia, and in 1922 a Pacific Coast force was billeted at San Diego.

2. Operations with the Control Force. Between 1921 and 1933 the Navy and Marine Corps worked on war plans for operations in the Pacific. These plans envisioned assaults against fortified islands held by the Japanese. The details of such actions were worked out in the year by year operations of the Navy's Control Force in the Caribbean and Marine Corps activities in China. Here landing operations were practiced, and in situations like the Nicaraguan campaigns the Marines

learned new infantry techniques. By late 1933 the Expeditionary Force was conceded to be a permanent necessity for the Navy. The larger, division size, Fleet Marine Force was organized with assault, rather than defense, its principal mission. Fleet exercises after 1934 showed the soundness of the new Marine Corps Tentative Manual for Landing Operations. As these fleet maneuvers became more complicated, the need for specialized landing craft became more pressing. In 1939 the first specially designed assault craft by Andrew Higgins was used, and the ground was laid for the spectacular Marine conquests of World War II.

VI. NAVAL ADMINISTRATION, 1921-1941

Of the five secretaries of the Navy between 1921 and 1941, Edwin C. Denby, Curtis D. Wilbur, and Charles F. Adams served Republican presidents Harding, Coolidge, and Hoover, and Claude A. Swanson and Charles Edison held office under President Franklin D. Roosevelt.

A. DENBY. Trained in the law, Denby served as a gunner's mate during the Spanish-American War and from 1901 to 1911 represented the First Michigan District in Congress. By pulling strings in 1917, he became a private in the Marine Corps and rose rapidly to the grade of major during the war. While manufacturing automobiles, he campaigned for Warren Harding, who selected him as his naval secretary because he needed Republican strength in the important industrial state of Michigan.

Denby was advised largely by naval officers who had fought World War I, including Robert E. Coontz, the CNO, and obtained particularly wise counsel from his assistant secretary, Theodore Roosevelt, Jr., a colonel who had fought in France during the war.

Denby started out by saying that he wanted a Navy "equal to any other" and supported current shipbuilding programs, but Congress thought otherwise. Many of the ships of the 1916 building program still on the ways would never be completed because the naval building race between the United States, Great Britain, and Japan led to the Washington Disarmament Conference. As already noted, the decisions made at that conference were made by civil, not naval representatives.

Most naval officers felt that naval reductions, even if they granted parity with Britain's navy, still left the U.S. Navy qualitatively inferior and too weak to uphold American interests in the Far East. Denby's prime task was to try to keep his navy up to treaty strength. That objective included not only building warships but auxiliaries, such as cruisers, submarines, carriers, and logistic support ships to "round out" and balance the fleet. Congress instead reduced the Navy still further by cutting the numbers of officers and men, which were 32,209 and 494,358 on 1 December 1918, to 6,163, and 100,000, respectively, on 1 January 1922. That fiend for economy, Thomas S. Butler, Chairman of the House Naval Affairs Committee, recommended 4,500 officers and 86,000 men for fiscal year 1923 even though the larger postwar capital ships and the naval aviation program required many more men. For the rest of the 1920s this anomaly existed: with larger ships and more aircraft, the number of men was still further reduced. Normal attrition kept the officer corps almost in balance, but despite the need for more officers, Congress cut the size of Naval Academy classes by reducing the number of congressional appointees from 5 to 3--which meant that the Academy operated at 60 percent of capacity.

Denby's department suffered grievously because Presidents Harding and Coolidge directed cuts in government spending and the directors of the new Bureau of the Budget (1921), not the naval secretary, set the limit to the naval budget for Congress. That limit was about half of what Denby said he needed, and the total was reduced from $44 million for fiscal year 1921 to $22 million in fiscal year 1925. Lacking funds, he had to defer ship maintenance and overhaul and see at least the older ships deteriorate and morale sink. While a General Board paper, "United States Naval Policy," dated 29 March 1922, called for "A Navy Second to None," the Navy was unequal to Britain's in many ways and with respect to its merchant marine as well. However, Congress not only refused funds to modernize the older battleships, it so pared naval costs that fleet steaming was severely curtailed, with consequent deterioration of personnel training. The only success Denby had was in getting Congress to fund the modernization of the 4 oldest battleships--the _Florida_, _Utah_, _Arkansas_, and _Wyoming_--for Congress declined his insistent demand that it provide 16 badly needed heavy cruisers (10,000 tons, 8-inch guns). The Bureau of the Budget approved the building of 8 such cruisers on condition that Congress fund them and that no money be spent to begin construction until 1 July 1925 at the earliest. While Congress funded the operation of 102 destroyers, each manned at 90 percent of complement, it provided for only 3 "V"-class submarines, prototypes of the fleet submarines that operated so successfully during World War II.

The greatest expansion that occurred in the Navy of the 1920s was in naval air, with Denby defending his service from the attacks upon it by General "Billy" Mitchell and also opposing his demand for a united air service. Meanwhile a powerful naval lobby led by Captain William A. Moffett resulted in the creation of a Bureau of Aeronautics (12 July 1921) of which Moffett was appointed chief with the rank of rear admiral (25 July 1921). Until his tragic death in the crash of the dirigible Akron in 1933, Moffett pushed the idea that naval aviation was a vital adjunct of the operating fleets and that "it must go to sea on the back of the fleet." While the fleet collier Jupiter was converted to an aircraft carrier on which the Navy could establish air doctrine, Denby had plans drawn for converting two battle cruiser hulls for the 33,000-ton carriers Lexington and Saratoga, placing aircraft on battleships and cruisers, and experimenting with the lighter-than-air rigid dirigibles Shenandoah (American), ZR-2 (British), and Los Angeles (German).

Denby made a lasting impact only with his reorganization of the fleet and war planning. As arranged on 6 December 1922, the Atlantic Fleet was abolished. A Scouting Force (cruisers) and Control Force (light defense ships) would operate in the Atlantic and the Battle Force (major task force) in the Pacific. A Base Force provided training and logistic support. Above the commanders of the forces in the Atlantic was a Commander-in-Chief, United States Fleet (CINCUS). Operating quite independently were the Asiatic Fleet, Naval Forces Europe, Special Service Squadron, and Naval Transportation Service. Because the Pacific Fleet contained 12 of the most modern battleships, and was destined to receive the Lexington and Saratoga, the term "Battle Force" was most appropriate for it. With the Washington Conference ended, largely at Assistant Secretary Roosevelt's behest the colored war plans were revised and greater attention was given to Plan Orange, for war against Japan, now the most likely potential enemy. The plan was kept current by six modifications to it made between 1924 and 1928.

Unfortunately, Denby early in his tenure agreed to transfer the Navy's oil reserves to the Interior Department. The story of the peculations of Secretary Albert B. Fall is well known. Though questioned about the transfer by the Senate, no taint or corruption could be laid to Denby, but political pressure was such that the Senate asked President Coolidge to demand his resignation. By letter of 17 February 1924, Denby told Coolidge he would resign effective 10 March.

B. WILBUR. In place of Denby, Coolidge wanted a "clean" man, especially one who would bolster the Republican party in the election of 1924. It may well be that his request for information about Ray Lyman Wilbur, President of Stanford University, resulted in data on his brother, Curtis D., a Naval Academy graduate (1888) who had resigned from the Navy to enter the law and was serving as Chief Justice of the State of California. In any event, Curtis "answered the call" and was approved by the Senate on 18 March. He would be aided by Assistant Secretary Roosevelt, who stayed on until 30 September, and then by Theodore D. Robinson (11 November 1924 to 4 March 1929). Although Wilbur objected to having an assistant secretary of the navy for aviation, such a post was created in July 1926. To it Coolidge appointed Edward P. Warner, a professor at M.I.T. A specialist in aeronautics and aerodynamics, Warner worked closely with Moffett.

Concluding from inspection tours that the material condition of the fleet was unsatisfactory and that funding for the shore establishment was inadequate, Wilbur in September 1924 appointed a board headed by Admiral Edward E. Eberle to recommend general naval policy for the next ten years. In a preliminary report made in December, the board recommended the modernization of six older battleships, speeding the construction of the <u>Lexington</u> and <u>Saratoga</u>, and continuing experiments with dirigibles. In its final report, of 17 January 1925, the board called in addition for a 3-year building program incorporating lessons learned from the bombing of the battleship <u>Washington</u>, the building of 8 10,000-ton cruisers, and the provision of an "adequate" aircraft program.

Getting money in peacetime from an administration and a Congress devoted to economy, tax reduction especially for big business, and disarmament, proved very difficult. No more than Denby could Wilbur support the General Board's policy statement of March 1922 that the Navy should be "second to none," build the Navy up to treaty strength, or compete with Great Britain and Japan, which were engaged in a building race in ship classes not covered by the naval disarmament treaty of 1922. Nevertheless, in the summer of 1924 Thomas S. Butler, Chairman of the House Naval Affairs Committee, called for the building of 8 10,000-ton cruisers and of 6 river gunboats and the modernization of the 6 oldest battleships. It passed Congress, but with an amendment that permitted the President to suspend all or part of it if another naval disarmament conference was held.

Because the various naval forces were evolving different procedures yet would have to concentrate in time of war, Wilbur abolished the Control Force to free its ships for other duties and established type commands within each force to provide maintenance and common training (1930-1931). Early in 1932, because of the Japanese invasion of Manchuria, he sent the Scouting Force to join the Battle Force in the Pacific, thereby leaving only a Training Squadron in the Atlantic. The latter was not reinforced until July 1937, when it was renamed the Training Detachment.

Obtaining funding for the Butler bill was another matter, and as late as 1926 3 of the 8 cruisers remained unfunded, with the administration hoping that the naval conference to be held at Geneva would make them unnecessary. Revolts against the administration in both the House and Senate sent a funding bill into conference. At the same time the Geneva conference proposed extending the Washington Treaty limitations of 5-5-3 to auxiliaries. When the conference failed to reach agreement on cruisers, Congress overrode Coolidge and funded the 3 cruisers. Coolidge, angry about Geneva, called for building 10 additional

10,000-ton cruisers, and Wilbur advised building the fleet up to parity. The General Board suggested a 5-year building program to provide 5 battleships, 5 aircraft carriers, 25 cruisers, 9 destroyer leaders, 28 destroyers, and 35 submarines between 1929 and 1933. Wilbur cut the number of ships to 71, still not enough to bring the Navy to parity but providing ample ammunition to antinavy and pacifist elements. In February 1928, Wilbur cut 10 cruisers, 4 carriers, and all destroyer leaders and submarines from the "71 bill." Although the House approved the "15 cruiser bill," the Senate dawdled until 5 February 1929. Coolidge signed it on the 13th, only three weeks before Herbert Hoover was inaugurated as President. Funding was provided, however, for only one cruiser.

Clearly favoring naval air power, Wilbur testified before Congress in opposition to Mitchell's demands for a united air service and was pleased with the recommendations of the Morrow board and especially happy with the adoption by Congress on 24 June 1926, of Moffett's Five Year Plan, which called for an operating armada of 1,000 planes and 3 lighter-than-air ships. Beginning in 1925, Wilbur had aeronautics taught at the Naval Academy and directed that every junior officer qualify as a naval observer or naval aviator, and in 1926 he made up for the lack of officer aviators by training enlisted men as pilots. In an unprecedented step, he gave Moffett a second and then a third term as Chief of the Bureau of Aeronautics, and in Captain Joseph M. Reeves he found the man to develop tactical doctrine for air combat at sea. Among the officers Reeves taught were Ernest J. King and Marc A. Mitscher. Furthermore, Wilbur reached an agreement with the Army whereby the Marine Corps would be trained especially to conduct landing operations. For the purpose, the Corps set forth its amphibious doctrine in a seminal <u>Landing Manual</u>. On the other hand, Wilbur had trouble with Rear Admiral Thomas P. Magruder, who charged that there were too many bases and that navy yard administration was poor, and with the retired Bradley A. Fiske, who sued him for infringement of his 1912 patent on a torpedo plane. Magruder was eased out, and in 1931, finally, a federal court turned Fiske down on the ground that he had never provided a working model of a torpedo plane.

Wilbur never overcame congressional miserliness with respect to personnel. Although 3,000 men were needed for each of the new carriers in addition to their air crews and surface ships operated at between 90 and 95 percent of complement, Congress reduced his personnel quota to 86,000 men. With officer separations and resignations running 4.7 percent compared with a prewar 3.5 percent, in 1925 he appointed a board to advise ways of obtaining especially aviation personnel. The Naval Reserve Officers Training Corps and the financial pinch came to his rescue. The first NROTC programs were initiated at George Washington University and at St. John's College, Annapolis, Md., in the fall of 1924. The popular program soon enrolled over 1,000 men and by 1926 was expanded to colleges and universities in the East, West, and South. By 1927, Wilbur had the 5,500 officers allowed by law. Similar efforts by naval reservists recalled to active duty for recruiting purposes brought the enlisted ranks up to their legal limit even if an annual loss of 22 percent of the men meant deficiencies in specialist ratings.

C. ADAMS. Although Wilbur would have stayed on, President Hoover replaced him with the rich businessman and avid yachtsman Charles Francis Adams, a direct descendant of two presidents. As the assistant secretary, Hoover selected another yachtsman, the New Orleans shipbuilder and capable administrator Ernest Lee Jahncke. When Warner decided to return to M.I.T., he was succeeded as assistant secretary for air by David S. Ingalls, a naval aviator in World War I who was trained in the law and had served in Congress.

Adams's unenviable task was to administer the Navy during its postwar nadir. He faced the same problems Denby and Wilbur had failed to solve: a navy not second to none or built up to treaty strength; how to maintain the fleet's operational readiness in time of aggravated financial depression; continued questions relating to disarmament limitation; and the financial and foreign policies of Hoover.

Hoover had greatly increased America's export trade as Secretary of Commerce. Would he demand a navy capable of supporting that trade and the merchant marine? It soon became clear that he was interested in limiting if not in reducing the navies of the entire world. Stunned by the $1 billion it would cost to round out the fleet between 1932 and 1944, he decided that he could afford a navy to defend America's shores but not one to support American interests overseas. During a call by Prime Minister J. Ramsay MacDonald in October 1929, plans were made to hold a naval conference beginning January 1930 in London, with Hoover willing to solve the cruiser question by having fewer cruisers than the British and giving notice of his intent by suspending work on 3 out of the 5 heavy cruisers under construction. Hoover thus made the plans which Adams must explain to the service. If palatable to Hoover, the London treaty was a disaster to most naval personnel, who in addition were dismayed when Hoover would not build the navy up to even the reduced limits provided in the treaty. Except for agreeing to modernize 3 battleships, Hoover asked Adams to cut spending and turn back appropriated funds, and when Adams supported a bill introduced by Carl Vinson in January 1932 that would build the navy to treaty strength he lost a great deal of credibility with Hoover.

Hoover and the State Department, not naval men, set American goals for the League of Nations World Disarmament Conference that convened early in 1932, that goal being only enough defense to thwart an enemy invasion. To insure compliance from the naval officer corps, he directed Adams to muzzle it. With Japan in Manchuria and Hitler ranting about changing the limitations placed upon Germany in the Treaty of Versailles, the conference got nowhere. Neither did Hoover's attempt to revitalize it by calling for a one-third reduction in all navies.

Though he wished to build up the Navy so that it could support American interests, Adams simply could not bring Hoover to his point of view. During his term, however, 8 cruisers of the 1924 program were commissioned, and 7 of the 15 cruisers of the 1929 program were laid down and 2 were commissioned, and a few destroyers and submarines were begun. This modicum was the result of financial stringency and Hoover's giving higher priority to limitation than to construction.

On 1 April 1931, a reorganization of the fleet took effect. It provided for a Battle Force in the Pacific, with subordinate battleship, cruiser, destroyer, mine, and air commands; a Scouting Force in the Atlantic with similar subdivisions; a Submarine Force; and a Base (Logistic) Force.

As under Denby and Wilbur, so under Adams material deteriorated, personnel was short, especially in the aviation field, and various ships were sent to the breaker's yard. One bright spot caused by the depression was the increase of re-enlistments, from 72.8 percent in 1929 to 93.3 percent in 1933 and the enlisting of academically better qualified men.

Like Denby and Wilbur, Adams opposed a department of defense and a unified air service, and when he left office the Navy had probably the best naval air program in the world, one nurtured well by Ingalls and Moffett. When Ingalls left in June 1932 to run for the governorship of Ohio, he was not replaced on the ground of economy. There would not be another secretary of the navy for air until President Franklin D. Roosevelt named to the post another World War I naval aviator, Artemus L. Gates.

D. SWANSON. Swanson, who served as naval secretary from 4 March 1933 to 7 July 1939, was trained in the law. Elected to Congress in 1892, he served six terms before becoming Governor of Virginia and then going on to the Senate in 1913. In 1914, when he was 52 years of age, he became a member of the House Naval Affairs Committee and was soon chairman of that committee and of the Foreign Relations Committee as well. By 1933, when he became Secretary of the Navy, his experience particularly qualified him for the post. However, he was almost 71 years of age and too ill much of the time to tend to his duties. As the assistant secretary of the navy Roosevelt chose Henry Latrobe Roosevelt, who had fought in World War I, left the Marine Corps as a lieutenant colonel, then engaged in business, and was a good administrator. When he died, early in 1936, he was succeeded by Charles Edison, who served until 1 January 1940. As already noted, Roosevelt also resuscitated the post of assistant secretary of the navy for air, which went to Artemus L. Gates.

While in the Senate, Swanson had had close contacts with Assistant Secretary of the Navy Franklin D. Roosevelt and Secretary of the Navy Josephus

Daniels and supported "a navy second to none." During the 1920s he and such senators as Hiram Johnson and David I. Walsh and House members Frederick Britten and Nicholas Longworth continued to dream of a navy second to none and of course opposed the numerous disarmament conferences of the 1920s and early 1930s. The election of Roosevelt as President gave them their chance to rebuild the Navy, with Roosevelt being in effect his own Secretary of the Navy but Swanson helping through his excellent contacts with longtime friends in both congressional naval committees. Especially important in the Senate was Chairman Park Trammel, who gave way to Walsh in 1937. In the House, naval affairs were directed by a Georgia fireball named Carl Vinson. Similar excellent relations existed between Swanson and the naval appropriations committees.

As it existed in 1933, the Navy could not carry out its primary wartime missions. For example, with Japan's navy built up to 95 percent of treaty allowance and the American Navy only up to 65 percent, Japanese equalled American power. Roosevelt stated that the Navy would be built to treaty limits and hurried to mend its deficiencies. On 24 March 1933, the CNO, Admiral William Veazie Pratt, proposed an 8-year, $1 billion program to provide 119 combatant ships and 420 aircraft, not including ships authorized, on the ways, or built as replacements. Fiscal year 1934 provided a beginning with 2 carriers, 4 light cruisers, 4 destroyer leaders, 16 destroyers, 4 submarines, and 2 gunboats, their cost defrayed by $238 million of NIRA money. Noticeable was the fact that new battleships must wait and that 85 percent of new construction was allotted to private shipyards. The funding of the last heavy cruiser allowed by treaty came in 1934, when Congress also passed the Vinson-Trammel Act, which "authorized construction of vessels and aircraft to bring the Navy to the prescribed treaty strength, and to replace ships as they become overage." Funding for 2 1,850-ton destroyer leaders, 24 1,500-ton destroyers, and 12 submarines came in 1935. In that year also, because Great Britain announced the construction of her King George V-class replacement battleships, Swanson ordered design plans for the North Carolina-class battleships. In 1936 came funding for the third carrier permitted by treaty, the Wasp, and also 2 light cruisers, 15 destroyers, and 6 submarines. The year 1936 also saw the abrogation of all the naval treaties. In consequence of P.L. 528, dated 17 May 1938, which authorized a 20 percent increase in tonnage, Congress funded 8 destroyers and 4 submarines in 1938 and 2 battleships, 2 cruisers, 8 destroyers, and 6 submarines in 1939 and set a limit on the number of aircraft at 3000. The regular appropriation bills for fiscal year 1940 and 1941 added 4 battleships, 4 cruisers, 16 destroyers, and 6 submarines. In sum, while Swanson held office--he died in July 1939--the number of combatant ships increased from 155 to 235. In 1940 came the "Two Ocean Navy" bill that provided a 70 percent increase in the Navy and included the primary ship types that fought World War II: the *Iowa*-class battleships, *Alaska*-class battle cruisers, *Fletcher*-class destroyers, and the 1,500-ton fleet type submarines, with a new fleet train being built for good measure and personnel increases almost enough to match--the last thanks to Vinson. By 1938, there were 96,500 men; by 1939, 102,500; by 1940, 107,550. Beyond obtaining a 20 percent increase in the number of officers, Swanson got Congress to increase each congressman's Naval Academy appointees from 3 to 4, retain lieutenant commanders and lieutenants passed over in 1936, increase the corps to 11,000, and establish a Naval Reserve. He also instituted a Naval Reserve Aviation Cadet program. In little more than five years, then, personnel were available for combatant ships to operate at 85 percent of normal complement.

Roosevelt kept Swanson out of war planning but ordered a revision of the Orange Plan in 1935 so that by 1939 it became an offensive rather than a defensive plan. Realistically, the line was drawn from the Aleutians through Hawaii to Panama, with the Philippines written off, no plans for island-hopping across the Pacific, and no buildup of Guam because Congress refused to provide the $65 million needed. With respect to attempts by naval officers like CNO William H. Standley to extend military control over the Navy, however, Swanson stood with Roosevelt and vetoed plans by which a general naval staff would be created and the CNO would be given control over the bureaus.

Some errors were made. The Marine Corps did not grow while Swanson served; nor were amphibious landing craft devised even though the prototype for the LCVP appeared in 1936 in the Higgins-built Eureka LCP(L). And Roosevelt erred in building the Alaska-class battle cruisers and in preferring antisubmarine patrol to convoying. If little was done to provide shipborne radar and effective torpedoes, great progress was made with the F4U and F4F carrier fighters and fleet submarines. With Roosevelt as commander-in-chief, Swanson as second in command, and Vinson third, the Navy came a long way between 1933 and 1940.

E. EDISON. After Henry Roosevelt died, Roosevelt chose Charles Edison, the son of Thomas A. Edison, to succeed him, saying that Edison was an excellent businessman familiar with government methods and, "best of all, is wholeheartedly devoted to our cause." Edison took office on 18 January 1937, and served for three years, sharing with the CNO, Admiral William D. Leahy, and the Chief of the Bureau of Ordnance, Rear Admiral William R. Furlong, the duties of acting secretary when Swanson was ill. Edison's primary duties concerned management of the navy yards, public works, labor, and personnel administration. However, in 1938, he was made Coordinator of Shipbuilding in order to bring together the "activities of all bureaus and officers involved in shipbuilding." In this matter, he did well and greatly improved the shipbuilding program. Following Swanson's death, Roosevelt chose him as his naval secretary and thus in position to direct the construction of the U.S. Navy to a "Navy second to none" during a period of increasing tension in foreign affairs.

While Edison supervised the enormous increment in naval strength, most of the Atlantic Squadron became engaged in supporting the Neutrality Patrol Roosevelt established on 6 September 1939. Edison faithfully executed Roosevelt's order to carry out the unneutral act of routinely patrolling international waters from Newfoundland to Cape Horn and observing, tracking, and reporting belligerent ships. When the embargo on arms and munitions expired, in November 1939, Roosevelt directed Edison to bolster the Neutrality Patrol by an additional forty destroyers, a step which perhaps Edison should have recommended. In any event, Roosevelt sounded out Colonel Frank Knox, the prominent Republican newspaper publisher, to replace Edison even while the latter took the truly important step of sponsoring a bill to integrate the Bureaus of Engineering and of Construction and Repair into a new Bureau of Ships. With the aid of the Chief of the Bureau of Navigation, Chester W. Nimitz, and of Rear Admiral Samuel M. Robinson, Chief of the Bureau of Engineering, he got the bill through. He also gained Roosevelt's permission to graduate the senior class at the Naval Academy a semester early in order to provide officers for new construction.

Hitler rather than Roosevelt moved Edison out. With most of France in German hands, on 20 June 1940, Roosevelt announced that Henry L. Stimson would relieve Harry Woodring as Secretary of War and Knox would replace Edison. For the year that he served, Edison performed many of Swanson's duties, brought great knowledge of engineering and technology into his administrative work, reorganized the bureau structure, and augmented the fleet. But he could not build the fleet fast enough to suit Roosevelt.

CHAPTER 16

THE COMING OF WORLD WAR II

I. THE YEARS AFTER VERSAILLES

A. THE REALIGNMENT OF THE POWERS AFTER 1919. World War I destroyed the prewar balance of power in Europe. Germany was prostrate and disarmed for the indefinite future; the Hapsburg Empire was divided into a weak Austria and weaker Hungary; Turkey was dismembered; Russia was in the throes of a civil war. England, France, and Italy, although victorious, were relatively poor and virtually bankrupt. In contrast Japan, which had limited her war effort almost exclusively to the Pacific area, was stronger. The United States, despite colossal expenditures and terrific effort, suffered no severe casualties from the war. Indeed, it emerged as a creditor rather than debtor nation and with its industrial economy diversified and intensified by its war effort.

B. THE RISE OF THE DICTATORSHIPS. "Injustices" in the Treaty of Versailles and sufferings induced by the Great Depression have been suggested as two reasons why millions followed the leaders of the totalitarian states. Millions more were attracted by the grandiose dreams of empire held by Hitler, Mussolini, and the Japanese leaders of the so-called "have not" nations. The failure of the democracies to punish Japan's invasion of Manchuria in 1931 was followed by naked aggression when Italy conquered Ethiopia in 1935-1936. After this the world assessed the League of Nations and the collective security system as impotent. Hitler thereupon denounced the Treaty of Versailles, began to rearm Germany, marched into the "permanently demilitarized" Rhineland, and with Mussolini intervened on the side of the rebels in the Spanish Civil War (1936-1939). In 1938 Hitler boldly united Austria to Germany and demanded that Czechoslovakia cede to Germany the German-speaking Sudetenland. At a conference in Munich, September 1938, between Hitler, Mussolini, Chamberlain, and Daladier, France dishonored her military alliance with Czechoslovakia, bargained away the Czech's freedom in return for a promise of no future aggression by Hitler, and alienated Russia. The "peace in our time" augured by Chamberlain lasted but a year.

C. THE FAILURE OF COLLECTIVE SECURITY, 1919-1939.
Joint international action was the watchword of the
post-World War I world. The Treaty of Versailles had
disarmed Germany, and the League of Nations would
handle threats to world peace. Germany was admitted
to this League in 1926 and Russia, suspect to both the
democratic and fascist states, in 1933. The League
successfully handled most international crises between
1919 and 1931, and international harmony marked the
reaching of agreements in the fields of war debts and
reparations, in disarmament, and in the writing of
treaties of conciliation and commerce. However, man's
hope that another war could be avoided began to fade
when pressure was applied by the "have not" nations
upon the "have" nations. Britain, France, and the
United States, satisfied with the status quo, failed
to take concerted action, to rearm, or to undertake
aggressive diplomacy, thereby emboldening the totalitarian states to increase their demands and launch
dynamic diplomatic offensives. The United States, by
rejecting global responsibilities, building high tariff
walls that provoked retaliation and stimulated nationalism, and by withdrawing from the Far East, was
partly responsible for the coming of World War II.
The breakdown of arms limitations also favored the
aggressor nations.

II. THE OUTBREAK OF THE WAR IN EUROPE

A. AGGRESSION AND NONAGGRESSION. At first it appeared that Hitler accepted the advice of the geopolitician Karl Haushofer and others to avoid a two-front war. In March 1939, he conquered the rest of
Czechoslovakia and Mussolini overran Albania, and in
May, Hitler and Mussolini signed a ten-year military
alliance known as the Rome-Berlin Axis. After insuring himself against a two-front war by negotiating
the Moscow-Berlin Nonaggression Pact (August 1939),
Hitler invaded Poland on 1 September. Hitler's invasion of Poland marked the beginning of the war in
Europe, for Britain and France declared war on Germany
on 3 September.

B. "THE PHONY WAR." Not wishing at the time to face
a real war with Britain and France, Hitler was pleased
merely to consolidate his grasp on Poland during the
winter of 1939-1940. He even accepted the Russian
occupation of the eastern half of Poland (28 September

1939), for he wished to keep the war localized while he built up his navy for a push west in 1944 or 1945. His refraining from aggressive tactics during the winter of 1939-1940, and his instructions that the Hague Convention be respected in the war at sea, and Britain's loss of only six men killed in action out of the 100,000 men committed on the continent during the first five months of the war provoked comments about the "Phony War," "Twilight War," "Sitzkrieg," and "Great Bore War."

C. EXTENSION OF THE CONFLICT. In the spring of 1940, however, Hitler launched "blitzkrieg" attacks that swallowed Denmark and Norway in April, the Netherlands and Belgium in May, and France in June, the latter shortly after Mussolini entered the war (10 June). Moreover, the European war had been joined to the Sino-Japanese conflict by the Axis connections, and nations at peace wondered about the precise limits of Axis ambitions. Axis expansion on the land involved warfare at sea, and the anti-Axis nations were driven to cooperate in the economic sphere, for none was self-sufficient. The war spread, too, because some of the countries involved, like Britain, France, and the Netherlands, possessed widespread empires located in all the continents. Finally, the war was an ideological war between "two worlds," one democratic, one fascist, and a total war because the entire civilian as well as the military power of the nations involved was thrown into the conflict.

III. THE UNITED STATES ANSWERS HITLER

A. THE GRAND STRATEGY OF THE DEMOCRACIES. Both the British and French had developed a defense complex. Britain anticipated a purely defensive war in Europe while naval blockade ultimately exhausted Germany, overlooking the fact that naval blockade may not be effective against a self-sufficient land power served by adequate internal lines of communications and that her worldwide naval bases, fueling stations, and seaborne commerce might not remain unmolested. The French had planned to attack only in answer to an attack halted by the Maginot Line; their armored forces were weak and their government was neither technically nor psychologically prepared for aggressive war. Many Americans also visualized World War II as another World War I: the Maginot Line would hold;

Allied sea power would blockade Germany; an Allied land offensive would then wipe out the weakened Wehrmacht; and the United States need not intervene.

B. NEUTRALITY LEGISLATION, 1935-1939. The United States had shunned involvement in the European collective security system. Moreover, while Americans disapproved of Hitler's pogroms, there were vociferous isolationist groups that opposed American commitments that might lead to war and helped create a demand for neutrality. Interventionists, almost from the beginning, wanted to aid the Allies "short of war."

The United States had entered World War I in great part to preserve the freedom of the seas. The neutrality legislation of the period 1935-1939 surrendered this freedom. When the president proclaimed the existence of war, it would be unlawful to sell or transport munitions to the belligerents and for Americans to sail on the ships of belligerents. Loans to belligerents were also prohibited, and the neutrality laws were made to cover both civil and international wars. In 1937 these restrictions were relaxed to the extent that belligerents might purchase certain commodities if they would pay for them and haul them away ("cash and carry"), thus favoring the nations that controlled the seas. However, the president was still prohibited from discriminating against an aggressor. In 1939, when the cash and carry clause expired, American ships were free to sail through European combat zones. In the interest of helping the Democracies, President Franklin D. Roosevelt asked Congress to repeal the arms embargo but to insulate the United States from war by granting him the authority to prohibit American ships from sailing into designated danger zones. The compromise reached after long and acrimonious debate lifted the arms embargo (but retained cash and carry) and authorized the establishment of danger zones.

C. STRENGTHENING THE AMERICAS. Between 1933 and 1941, various Pan American conferences aligned the 21 American Republics against the European dictator states. These Republics went on record as opposed to armed intervention, to the intervention by one state in the internal or external affairs of another, and they agreed to refuse recognition of territorial gains made by force (1933). They also agreed to consult

with one another when peace was threatened and to adopt
a common attitude toward international war outside of
the Americas. Moreover, the United States invited all
American states to cooperate in enforcing the Monroe
Doctrine against non-American violators (1936). A
more militant defensive step was taken in 1939, when
a Hemispheric Safety Belt from 300 to 1,000 miles wide
south of Canada was established; within this the European belligerents were to refrain from naval action.
A truly cooperative enforcement of the Monroe Doctrine
was devised in 1940 by the provision that territory of
European Powers in danger of falling into unfriendly
hands might be taken over and administered jointly
by the American Republics pending its final disposition.

D. AID TO THE DEMOCRACIES SHORT OF WAR. Citing
international law to justify its actions, the United
States aided the Allies by:

    1. freezing the credits of those countries
overrun by the Axis Powers and releasing those of
nations fighting the Axis (e.g., Russia);
    2. devising a "trade-in" scheme whereby obsolescent airplanes could be sold by the manufacturers
to the Allies and similar schemes for the transfer
of artillery, rifles, and ammunition;
    3. relaxing border regulations between the
United States and Canada in order to speed military
aid and permit British flyers to train in the United
States, and permitting Allied ships to be repaired in
American shipyards;
    4. trading 50 obsolete destroyers to Great
Britain in exchange for the right to establish bases
in various British possessions from Newfoundland to
British Guiana;
    5. Lend Lease;
    6. taking over and using all freign ships immobilized in United States ports;
    7. blacklisting Axis-connected firms in Latin
America, with which Americans were not to do business;
    8. taking over the defense of Iceland and Greenland;
    9. agreeing with a belligerent (Britain) on the
war and postwar aims of the Democracies (Atlantic
Charter);
    10. escorting convoys carrying goods destined for
the European democracies and Russia;

11. ordering sunk all Axis submarines operating within American defensive areas;
12. arming American merchant ships;
13. repealing the Neutrality Act of 1939 (13 November 1941) in order that American goods might reach the democracies wherever needed;
14. refusing to recognize territorial changes made by force and protesting the violation of treaty obligations; and
15. placing an embargo on the export to Axis countries of strategic materials needed for the defense of the United States and of the Democracies.

E. WAR EXCEPT FOR SHOOTING. With even isolationists convinced the United States must prepare for an attack now deemed probable, the United States in 1940 appropriated $13 billion for the American armed services, including a "two-ocean" navy, adopted peacetime conscription for the first time in its history, mobilized its industry, and re-elected Roosevelt over Wendell Willkie as the better qualified man to direct the destinies of the nation in those critical times. Hitler's attack on Russia, 22 June 1941, sent Russian forces reeling backwards during the summer and fall of 1941. While another nation had been added to the anti-Axis bloc, the democracies, including the United States, were placed in the embarrassing position of explaining their partnership with totalitarian Russia.

Heavy losses of freighters carrying Lend Lease goods to the European democracies and to Russia almost provoked the United States into a shooting war with Hitler. American submarines were ordered to report U-boats to the British but not to fire upon them until the USS <u>Greer</u> was attacked, 4 September 1941. A Congress enraged by the sinking of the <u>Reuben James</u>, in October ordered the arming of merchant ships and the repeal of all neutrality laws that barred them from war zones. The blow that brought the United States into the war, however, fell not in the North Atlantic but in the Pacific--at Pearl Harbor.

IV. JAPANESE-AMERICAN RELATIONS, 1931-1941

A. AMERICAN NON-RECOGNITION POLICY. Basing its objections on the Open Door, Kellogg-Briand Pact, and Nine Power Treaty, the United States objected to the Japanese occupation of Manchuria in 1931, refused to recognize the puppet state of Manchukuo, and promised to cooperate with the League of Nations if sanctions were imposed upon Japan.

Stronger representations were made in 1937 when Japan invaded North China and when Japanese flyers bombed and sank the river gunboat USS Panay (12 December 1937). China was aided by the United States' refusal to invoke the neutrality laws, extension of credits, insistence that Japan live up to treaty obligations, and refusal to renew the commercial treaty with Japan of 1911 when it expired in 1940.

B. JAPAN EYES THE SOUTHERN RESOURCES AREA. The German-Japanese Anti-Comintern Pact of 1936, joined by Italy in 1937, and the Rome-Berlin-Tokyo Axis of 27 September 1940, were designed to guarantee that Russia would not interfere with the expansionist plans of either Germany or Japan, although the Russo-German non-aggression pact of August 1939 gave the Japanese food for thought. However, the Japanese thrust into China had bogged down, with consequent strain upon Japan's resources. Somehow China must be isolated from external aid. A break came when the fall of Holland and France orphaned the Netherlands East Indies and Indo-China and spread the British navy thin. The great resources of the East Indies were now within Japan's grasp. Pressure applied to the Vichy Government resulted in the military occupation by Japan of northern Indo-China, a step closer to Singapore, but until the resources of the East Indies were obtained, Japan must continue to purchase various strategic materials from the United States. Sales of aircraft and aviation gasoline continued until July 1940, of iron and steel until the fall of 1940, and of oil until July 1941. If, thought the Administration, the United States sold oil to Japan, Japan would not strike at the East Indies. Thus the United States furnished the materials for the aggression it wished to prevent. On 17 October 1941, Japanese premier Fumamaro Konoye gave way to General Hideki Tojo, who was more pro-Axis in his attitude. Tojo shortly thereafter declared that the influence of Great Britain and of the United States must be eliminated from the Far East.

In 1940 and 1941 the United States requested and received from Japan a declaration that the status quo in the Far East would be respected. Japan's violation of this declaration, in particular its moving into northern Indo-China, led to drawn-out diplomatic discussions. In November, 1941, Japan sent a special envoy, Saburo Kurusu, to aid its Ambassador, Admiral Nomura, and to stall for time in negotiating with Secretary of State Cordell Hull while the Japanese Navy prepared to strike. On 26 November 1941, the United States maintained that Japan should give up her ill-gotten gains in China and Indo-China, deal only with the Chungking (Chiang Kai-shek) government in China, and reject treaty commitments like the Rome-Berlin-Tokyo Pact. Intent upon the creation of its Greater Eastern Asia Co-Prosperity Sphere, the Japanese rejected the American propositions.

C. PEARL HARBOR. The United States possessed the priceless advantage of having broken the Japanese diplomatic code and knew that the Japanese were preparing to strike, but no one knew exactly where. On 27 November, the United States Navy Department sent a "war warning" to Pearl Harbor, Manila, and Panama. An earlier warning had indicated that the Japanese might strike "in any direction," including Malaya, Borneo, or the Philippines; but the warning of 26 November suggested only the possibilities of a strike to the south. By 6 December, Washington knew that a strike impended. At 1:00 P.M., 7 December (8:00 A.M. Hawaiian time) while the Japanese diplomats prepared to exchange notes with Secretary Hull, Japanese forces struck at Pearl Harbor as well as at Guam, Wake, the Philippines, Hong Kong, and Malaya. The United States replied to the attack by declaring war on 8 December, whereupon Japan's allies, Germany and Italy, declared war on the United States. The United States declared war on Germany and Italy on 11 December.

CHAPTER 17

WORLD WAR II IN EUROPEAN WATERS

INTRODUCTION. For more than two years, the United States remained a neutral during World War II. During that time every conceivable form of naval warfare was used offensively by Germany and, after 10 June 1941, Italy: commerce raiding, submarine, air, and amphibious warfare. Conversely, the Allies hunted down raiders and U-boats and used air warfare largely defensively. Early in July 1940, after France capitulated to Hitler (22 June), Britain launched her first offensive operation, paradoxically, against French naval units at Mers-el-Kebir (Oran) to insure that they would not be joined to the German navy. The first combined operation of the war, against Dakar by British and Free French forces, was a disaster, but then so were the hopes for Operation Sea Lion, a German amphibious invasion of Britain. By the end of 1941, the British accounted for all German commerce raiders that were at sea but fought an uphill battle against the U-boat in the Atlantic and German-Italian attempts to cut the British Mediterranean lifeline. Although Hitler took Norway and Crete, Mussolini could not take Malta even with German help and Hitler had to support him in order to subjugate Greece. The United States, meanwhile, changed from a neutral position to one of benevolent neutrality and helped the Allies in many ways "short of war."

THE ALLIES ON THE DEFENSIVE, 1939-1941

At sea, World War II opened with the torpedoing of the British liner <u>Athenia</u>, 3 September 1939, the day England and France declared war on Germany. The six years of conflict in the Atlantic (1939-1945) resulted in few naval battles the caliber of Jutland (1916) or Leyte Gulf (1944); rather the Atlantic war was a struggle concerned principally with attacks against, and the protection of, Allied convoys. The principal protagonists were the submarines and those seeking to eliminate them. Naval activity, on the other hand, was more conventional. Fleets opposed one another, but through policy and chance the Allied naval forces never came to grips with major Axis concentrations in any naval "Gotterdamerung." Indeed, convoying, support of amphibious operations, and shore bombardments composed the daily routine of the rival navies. Naval attrition, slow as it was in both the Atlantic and Mediterranean, worked to the advantage of the Allies; and in the end Axis inability to replace units lost was the final reason for their failure at sea.

I. NATIONAL STRATEGIES AT THE OUTBREAK OF WAR

A. THE GERMAN POSITION. In September 1939 the German nation faced a military problem similar to that of August 1914--how does a land power defeat a sea power; and how should that land power utilize its numerically inferior navy?

1. <u>German Naval Strength</u>. Having been limited by the Versailles Treaty until repudiating it in 1935, Nazi Germany had not built up a Navy at all comparable to that of the British except in submarines. In 1939 the German Navy consisted of these major units: four old battleships, two modern battleships building (<u>Bismarck</u> and <u>Tirpitz</u>), two battle cruisers (<u>Scharnhorst</u> and <u>Gneisenau</u>), three pocket battleships (<u>Graf Spee</u>, <u>Admiral Scheer</u>, <u>Deutschland</u>), four heavy cruisers built or building, six light cruisers built or building, 34 destroyers, and 57 submarines.

2. <u>Nazi Naval Strategy</u>. With the limited naval strength available, the German Naval War Staff planned to use its fleet for these general tasks: attacks on enemy shipping by the surface and undersea units; blockade of the British and French coasts; exercise of local command of the sea through the support of amphibious operations and the provision of naval artillery support to army movements ashore; and as a "Fleet-in-being" to menace the British Navy. It was assumed that the German concentration of heavy surface units in the North Sea, or in the Baltic, would force the English to keep the main portion of their fleet in home waters. Such a British concentration would require the withdrawal of units from convoy and commerce protection duties, thus leaving British and Allied shipping subject to raids by cruisers, armed raiders, submarines, and shorebased bombers.

Except for the delusions associated with the aborted amphibious assault against the British Isles in 1940 (Operation Sea Lion), the Germans devoted their principal naval efforts to the destruction of English commerce in order to bring the British to terms by starving their industries, population, and military forces. This could be accomplished only by sinking British tonnage faster than it could be replaced.

B. ALLIED NAVAL STRATEGY. From the opening of hostilities the naval strategy of the British and French forces was essentially to counter German naval operations. The British Navy and the Dominion units had to keep communications open to the British Isles, the nerve center of the Empire's war on the Nazis. With French aid the British also had to protect the flow of supplies to the continent, prevent German sorties in strength into the Atlantic, drive the German merchant marine from the seas, and carefully regulate neutral shipping to the Germans and their allies.

The Mediterranean was of particular importance to the Allied cause. For the English, free use of the Mediterranean from Suez to Gibraltar meant thousands of miles saved on shipments to and from the Far East, and thus better utilization of a merchant marine being rapidly decimated by German submarines. From North Africa the French drew badly needed troops and supplies. At the outbreak of war Britain assumed responsibility for the eastern Mediterranean basin, and France, with units based on Toulon, Marseilles, Oran, and Algiers, for the defense of the western Mediterranean.

1. <u>British Naval Forces and Dispositions</u>. In September 1939 the British Empire had these major naval units at its disposal: 12 battleships plus five building, three battle cruisers, six aircraft carriers and six building, 25 heavy cruisers, plus nine building, 32 light cruisers with 10 building, six anti-aircraft cruisers, 183 destroyers, and 57 submarines. This navy was distributed around the world, though the larger units were based on the British Isles. In home waters were concentrated nine capital ships, four aircraft carriers, and roughly one-third of the cruisers, destroyers, and submarines. British forces in the Mediterranean made up the next largest concentration of Allied sea power. The defeat of France in June 1940 and Italy's entry into the war required significant changes in the disposition of British units throughout the world.

2. **The French Navy**. In view of its equally widespread responsibilities, the French Navy, like that of the British, was distributed around the world at the outbreak of war. The Navy, commanded by Admiral Jean Francois Darlan, consisted of seven battleships plus two building, one aircraft carrier, 19 heavy and light cruisers, 72 destroyers, and 78 submarines. In numbers of units the French Navy was larger than the German, but in quality and firepower the difference was less noticeable. Once war had begun, the French were given the primary responsibility for control of the Mediterranean west of Corsica and Sardinia. The French also agreed to form a "force de raid" consisting of the two battle cruisers Dunkerque and Strasbourg, the aircraft carrier Bearn, three cruisers, and ten destroyers. This task group, operating out of Brest, was to destroy enemy raiders in the eastern Atlantic. Because of its size, the addition of the French Navy to the German fleet would have cast considerable doubt on the British Navy's ability to maintain sea supremacy in its home waters. For that reason the French promised informally that they would never allow the Germans to use their vessels.

C. THE NEUTRALS. In September 1939 four major nations remained uncommitted to the struggle.

1. **The United States**. Although the United States declared itself neutral, it changed from neutrality to benevolent neutrality toward Britain and her allies, and finally to the status of a non-belligerent rendering full aid to the Allied cause.

2. **Italy**. Mussolini's Fascist regime, formally a non-belligerent in September 1939, openly aided the Nazi cause. By their "Pact of Steel" of March 1939, Mussolini and Hitler had given the world notice that Italy could hardly remain outside the current struggle for any length of time. However, French use of the western Mediterranean was unchallenged as long as Italy remained a non-belligerent.

3. **Japan**. For a year the Japanese remained technically neutral. On 27 September 1940, in the Tri-Partite Pact, Japan, Italy, and Germany aligned themselves in a defensive treaty aimed primarily at the United States from the German viewpoint, and Russia and the United States from the Japanese point of view.

Because of known Japanese sympathy for the Nazi cause, the Japanese Navy posed a defense problem that provoked the British to keep a fairly large number of cruisers and smaller units in the Far East.

   4. <u>The Soviet Union</u>. The German-Soviet non-aggression pact of 24 August 1939 gave Hitler the green light for his drive against Poland and gave the Soviets almost two years to prepare for the inevitable struggle with the ubiquitous Nazis. With his eastern borders secure, and the Baltic in friendly Soviet hands, Hitler could concentrate on his land campaign in the West and the destruction of British commerce. Once western Europe was mastered, with the exception of the stubborn British, the power of the German <u>blitzkrieg</u> was turned on the Russians in June 1941. Russia then changed from a neutral to a co-belligerent of those seeking the defeat of the Third Reich.

II.   THE WAR AND BRITISH TRADE

   The task of the German Navy in World War II was by definition a simple one: destroy the British merchant marine and all neutral carriers supplying the British Isles. For the English the tasks were equally simple: through exercise of command of the sea deny its use to German surface ships, and limit the losses to British commerce by a vigorous prosecution of anti-submarine warfare.

A. BRITISH TRADE AND ITS PROTECTION. In 1939 the British merchant marine and ships under British registry consisted of approximately 3,000 dry cargo ships and tankers, and about 1,000 coasting vessels, totaling 21 million tons. On any one day an average of 2,500 ships under British registry were at sea. These ships provided the life blood of Great Britain--food, raw materials, and transportation for British manufacturers. Once war began, this merchant marine transported war materials, weapons, munitions, the ever-vital petroleum products, and troops. The defense of so many vessels operating across the seven seas posed a formidable challenge for Anglo-French sea power.

   1. <u>Measures Taken for the Protection and Control of Trade</u>. As noted before, the largest concentrations of the British fleet were in home waters and in the eastern Mediterranean. Smaller groups were located

around the world for trade protection and countermeasures against surface and sub-surface raiders. Neutral trade was subjected to inspection and control at certain contraband control bases near the entrance to the North Sea and Mediterranean. A long range blockade was maintained by setting up inspection stations at Haifa, Malta, and Aden, in order to inspect Axis-designated goods that might move by way of the Black Sea or the Red Sea. Though not completely effective, the British blockade managed to seize some 300,000 tons of contraband during the first six weeks of the war.

2. Convoys and Arming of Merchantmen. British merchantmen were gathered into convoys from the day the war began. Because of critical shortages in escort vessels, merchant convoys could be escorted only a few hundred miles west of the British Isles. By April 1941, 19° W. longitude was the close escort limit for westward moving convoys, and 53° W. was the limit for eastbound groups. The British concentrated their escorts in the southern and western approaches to the United Kingdom, for until 1941 this was found to be the practical limit for heavy submarine attacks by the Germans. With the extension of the American neutrality patrol to Iceland in July 1941, American convoys were escorted to the British approach zones, and British convoys were given a measure of security by the presence of American escorts at sea.

The British made plans for arming merchant vessels before the war began. In September 1939 about 3,000 ocean-going ships needed anti-submarine and anti-aircraft ordnance. By March 1941 a total of approximately 4,500 British and Allied vessels had been equipped with guns of some type. A larger problem never adequately solved was that of training gun crews for the armament provided.

3. Air Support and Trade Protection. Until the sinking of the Courageous in September, 1939 the British had planned to have their carriers take an active role in convoy and anti-submarine operations. With the loss of such an important unit, plans were changed; until the advent of the escort carrier, British fleet carriers operated only in task forces or with exceptionally high priority convoys. Air defense of trade and aerial anti-submarine duties were allocated to the Royal Air

Force Coastal Command and to the guns of the convoys and their escorts. The R.A.F. Fighter Command, which took responsibility for coastal trade protection, for several years was hampered by an inadequate shore-based fighter director system.

B. AMERICAN "AID SHORT OF WAR." Directly and indirectly the United States and its Latin American neighbors rendered valuable aid to Great Britain and her allies in their struggle to preserve their merchant marine from Nazi depredations.

    1. <u>Neutrality Patrol</u>. To warn submarine marauders away from American shores and present direct evidence that the United States was prepared to defend the Western Hemisphere, a Neutrality Patrol was created from the Atlantic Squadron on 5 September 1939, with patrol limits roughly 200 miles offshore in an area stretching from the Grand Banks south through the Antilles to Trinidad.

    2. <u>Pan-American Declarations</u>. In October 1939 an Inter-American conference meeting at Panama declared an area from 300 to 1,000 miles wide adjacent to the coasts of North and South America closed to hostile activity by both the Axis and Allied powers. Finally, with the fall of France in June 1940, the Pan American nations resolved that "orphaned" Western Hemisphere colonies of defeated European powers would not be allowed to pass under Axis control.

    3. <u>Destroyer-Naval Base Deal</u>. Desperate for escort vessels due to increased submarine activity in the Atlantic, and having full responsibility for supply lines in the Mediterranean, the British needed more tangible aid than declarations. In September 1940 President Roosevelt agreed to exchange "moth-balled" World War I vintage "four piper" destroyers for badly needed naval bases in the Western Hemisphere. By April 1941 the British had received 50 destroyers and 10 "Lake Class" Coast Guard cutters, and the United States had obtained sites for a string of naval bases from Argentia, Newfoundland, to Trinidad.

    4. <u>Lend-Lease Act</u>. As the American nation became more clearly aware that England could not be allowed to fall, "aid short of war" was increased at the risk of becoming a co-belligerent. In March 1941

the American Congress passed the Lend-Lease Act, allowing American industries to supply the Allied war machine with weapons and munitions to the limit of American industrial capacity. Once Russia was attacked in June 1941, aid was supplied the Soviets under lend-lease agreements.

III. GERMAN OFFENSIVE MEASURES, 1939-1941

Once war began, the German Navy operated along the strategic lines already noted. While a major portion of the British Navy waited in home waters for a sortie by major enemy naval units, German submarines, surface raiders, aircraft, and smaller type vessels began their vigorous campaign against British shipping. In the period September 1939 to January 1942 the British Empire, its allies, and neutrals lost 9,075,591 tons of merchant shipping (2,580 vessels). Almost 50% of the tonnage sunk fell victim to the U-boat, with aerial attack and mines accounting for approximately 25%, and raiders sinking about 10%. Attacks by warship raiders accounted for a mere 42 sinkings of 360,146 tons in the first 30 months of the war.

A. SURFACE ACTIONS, 1939-1940. Because Britain kept heavy naval concentrations in home waters and defended these with mines and the R.A.F., Germany launched its Norwegian campaign in the spring of 1940 in order to obtain Atlantic ports. The defeat of France in June 1940 added Bay of Biscay harbors, yards, and submarine pens to German sea power. The fall of France, however, did not add the French Navy to that of the Germans.

1. <u>The Cruises of the DEUTSCHLAND and GRAF SPEE</u>. While the pocket battleships <u>Deutschland</u> sank but two ships in the North Atlantic before it was recalled to Kiel (1 November 1939), the <u>Graf Spee</u> raided in the South Atlantic and Indian Oceans from September to December 1939, sinking 9 ships totaling 50,000 tons. To deal with these raiders, the British and French organized 8 hunting squadrons comprised of cruisers and destroyers to operate in the Atlantic and Indian oceans. On 13 December 1939, Force G, Commodore Sir Henry Harwood (2 heavy cruisers, 2 light cruisers), intercepted the <u>Graf Spee</u> in the approaches to the River Plate. The battle appeared lost for Harwood, but Captain Hans Langsdorff broke off and headed for Montevideo at best speed. Forced to leave Montevideo

after a 72-hour respite, and believing himself outnumbered, he ordered the Graf Spee scuttled (17 December). Shortly thereafter he committed suicide.

2. The SCHARNHORST and GNEISENAU. On 21 November 1939 Vice Admiral Marschall took the battle cruisers Scharnhorst and Gneisenau to raid convoys in the North Atlantic. In the Iceland-Faeroes Channel the armed merchant cruiser Rawalpindi was sighted and sunk by the Scharnhorst, but not before she had radioed the location of the raiders. Marschall withdrew to the East and eventually returned to Wilhelmshaven Roads on 27 November. In engaging the Scharnhorst the British merchant cruiser allowed the convoy it was escorting to escape. No further attacks on commerce were attempted by German surface warships until late 1940.

3. The Norwegian Campaign, April-June 1940. Norway posed a strategic problem to both the Germans and the British. As a source of industrial raw materials, particularly iron ore, it was essential to the Germans that Norway remain neutral or come under their control. After several German vessels had used neutral Norwegian coastal waters to exit from the Baltic, it became essential to the British to close these protected waters with mines even at the price of Norwegian neutrality. In March 1940 the British prepared an expeditionary force to help the Norwegians defend their land in the event the Germans chose to attack, and in early April the British Navy began sowing mines in Norwegian coastal waters. Coincident with the British operations, the Germans launched an invasion of Denmark and Norway.

a. The German Attack. German naval forces were divided into six groups in support of landings, from north to south at Narvik, Trondheim, Bergen, Egersund, Kristiansand, and Oslo early in April. Surprise was achieved, and Norway fell to the Germans and to Norwegian traitors. Once in Norway the Germans rapidly converted airfields into Luftwaffe bases for defense of coastal shipping and assaults on British sea power.

b. Naval Actions. The Norwegians and their English allies put up a spirited resistance to the Nazis, inflicting heavy naval casualties that the Germans could ill afford. They lost the heavy cruiser Blucher and light cruisers Konigsberg and Karlsruhe. The Gneisenau and heavy cruiser Hipper were badly damaged, and ten destroyers were lost in a battle in Narvik Harbor.

  c. **Loss of Norway**. British attempts to support the Norwegians and drive the Germans out failed by 1 June. The British supply lines to Narvik were lengthy and risky, and German pressure in the South of Norway was overwhelming. Besides, the Nazi juggernaught had crushed the French, and Britain's complete attention was directed toward extracting her troops from the continent. In the final sea battle of the Norway campaign the Scharnhorst, Gneisenau, and Hipper attempted to break up the British evacuation of Narvik. The German force sank the carrier Glorious, but destroyer and submarine torpedoes took the battle cruisers Scharnhorst and Gneisenau out of service for almost six months.

  d. **Results**. The Norwegian campaign cost the Germans heavily. The cruisers Konigsberg, Karlsruhe, and Blucher were irreplaceable. The damage to the Lutzow, Gneisenau, and Scharnhorst was sufficient to remove them from active service for another six months, just when the British were reeling from their defeat on the continent. Yet the withdrawal of the British from Norway and the absolute dominance achieved there by the Germans provide rather conclusive evidence that sea supremacy must be accompanied by air superiority before the dominant sea power can launch and sustain a successful invasion.

B. NEUTRALIZING THE FRENCH FLEET, 1940. The opening of the Danish and Norwegian campaigns in early April 1940 marked the change from the "Phony War" to the Blitzkrieg again.

  1. **The Dunkirk Evacuation**. On 10 May, Hitler turned his armies against the French and English; by month's end the Franco-British forces were pressed against the Channel at Dunkirk. On 26 May the British high command put "Operation Dynamo" into motion, hoping to remove at least 45,000 troops from the continent. By 4 June, the amazing number of 338,226 had been rescued by practically every vessel afloat in southern England. This feat was accomplished because the British combined local sea command with temporary air

superiority in the vicinity of Dunkirk.

2. **The French Collapse.** On 10 June 1940 Italy joined forces with the Nazis and attacked the French, who surrendered to the Germans on 22 June. German occupation of the Atlantic and Channel ports of France created a strategic problem of the first magnitude for the British. German submarine and surface raiders were now 1,500 miles closer to the important Southern Approaches to the English Channel; German submarines could spend more time on station; and the danger to Allied merchant shipping from German bombing attacks was increased. Of even graver significance was the possible capture and use of the French Fleet by the Germans, though this could not be done within the terms of the French surrender. Were the French and Italian fleets to combine with the German surface units, British sea supremacy would be seriously jeopardized. Finally, the cessation of French naval operations in the western Mediterranean forfeited control of this area to the Italian Navy.

3. **British Attacks on the French Navy.** To preclude German use of French naval units the British Cabinet decided to neutralize or destroy the principal units in the French Navy. On 28 June 1940 Vice Admiral Sir James F. Somerville formed Force H at Gibraltar with the mission of controlling the western basin of the Mediterranean. This force included 2 battleships, a battle cruiser, an aircraft carrier, 2 light cruisers, and 4 destroyers. On 3 July Admiral Somerville tried to induce Admiral Marcel Gensoul to fight on with the British, demilitarize his units at Mers-el-Kebir (Oran) or in a British port, or to sink them. Gensoul refused and Somerville attacked. The battleship <u>Bretagne</u> was sunk and the battleship <u>Provence</u> and battle cruiser <u>Dunkerque</u> were beached; the battle cruiser <u>Strasbourg</u> and five destroyers escaped to Toulon. At Alexandria, Admiral Sir Andrew B. Cunningham convinced Vice Admiral R. E. Godfroy that his cruiser squadron should be demilitarized and interned. At Dakar the new battleship <u>Richelieu</u> was immobilized by damage suffered from carrier aircraft attacks; and at Casablanca the unfinished battleship <u>Jean Bart</u> was kept under surveillance.

French blood shed at Mers-el-Kebir hampered relations between Britain and France for several years after 1940. The neutralization of the French Navy had been accomplished, and several major units (two battleships, four cruisers, eight destroyers) had been enlisted on the British side as Free French contributions to the defeat of the Germans. The destruction of French sea power in the western Mediterranean left the British alone facing the Italian Navy and Air Force.

4. <u>Dakar: Operation "Menace."</u> In September 1940, an attempt was made to capture Dakar in order to make the southern convoy routes more secure.

Operation "Menace," as the Dakar operation was appropriately called, beautifully illustrated everything that could go wrong in this, the first Allied combined operation of the war. It was launched by Winston Churchill against the advice of his military leaders, and Charles de Gaulle grossly overestimated the amount of support his Free French movement had in Africa. Planning was poor; men were untrained; there were no special armored landing craft; there was no special communications ship. Strategic intelligence was faulty; security for the operation, nil; communications, bad. British commanders sailed in one ship, de Gaulle in another. Fog prohibited the use of British carrier-borne aircraft while Vichy French air, naval, and coastal defenses proved stronger than expected. If Anglo-French relations did not deteriorate, British prestige dropped in the United States, and Churchill gave an early example of using military forces for political aims. However, Germany was unable to use Dakar as an effective base against the British, and early in 1941 the British built the first LST (landing ship, tank).

C. OPERATION SEA LION, 1940. Once France was overrun, Hitler ordered an invasion of England for 28 September 1940. Realizing that command of the air was absolutely necessary, Marshall Hermann Goering was ordered to launch his <u>Luftwaffe</u> against the English beginning 5 August. The mere 25 British home defense squadrons exacted such heavy tolls of the <u>Luftwaffe</u> that Admiral Erich Raeder declared, two weeks before the invasion date, that British air power would make an invasion suicidal. On 17 September "Operation Sea Lion" was postponed indefinitely, and on 13 February 1942 it was finally abandoned.

Neither Admiral Raeder nor Hitler were completely

sure the operation was practical. The Army chiefs, with little experience in amphibious operations, were overly sanguine, while Marshall Goering believed the defeat of the R.A.F. would probably bring surrender and actually make the operation unnecessary. At the British Admiralty offices, once the R.A.F. showed its staying power, there was confidence in the traditional role that sea power had played through the years. Lacking command of the air, the German invasion would have failed.

D. RAIDER ACTIONS, 1940-1941. Continuing the policy of sending German cruisers to harass commerce in order to weaken the antisubmarine protection given convoys, the pocket battleship Scheer, the cruiser Hipper, the battle cruisers Scharnhorst and Gneisenau, and the battleship Bismarck were sent to sea between October 1940 and May 1941.

1. Cruiser Raiding. Operating in the Atlantic and Indian Oceans the Scheer sank 16 vessels (99,059 tons) during the period 23 October 1940-1 April 1941. In two sorties the Hipper sank nine vessels (40,000 tons). For two months the battle cruisers Scharnhorst and Gneisenau ravaged commerce in the mid-Atlantic, sinking or capturing 22 vessels (115,622 tons). These raids proved the inadequacy of the British patrols and forced the further dispersal of major fleet units for convoy and escort duty. Yet the presence of such battleships as the Malaya and Ramilles with convoys tended to limit the losses inflicted by the raiding cruisers.

2. The Cruise of the BISMARCK, May 1941. In view of the slight likelihood that a full fleet sortie would be attempted by the Germans, the British fleet was dispersed rather widely, with major units concentrated at Scapa Flow under Admiral Sir John Tovey, and at Gibraltar under Vice Admiral Somerville. Once word was received that the Bismarck and a heavy cruiser (Prince Eugen) were at sea, Admiral Tovey covered Iceland Strait with 2 new battleships and the carrier Victorious. To the Denmark Straits were sent the heavy cruisers Suffolk and Norfolk, the battle cruiser Hood (flag), and the new battleship Prince of Wales. Somerville and his Force H were also alerted for action.

a. The loss of the HOOD. In the early morning

of the 24th, Rear Admiral L.E. Holland, the commander of the one British task force, intercepted the Bismarck with the Hood and the Prince of Wales. Maneuvering the two ships together in close order formation, Admiral Holland approached from an after-bearing, losing the use of the after turrets of both his ships. An error in identification concentrated fire on the Prince Eugen at first, and before the Hood could change to the Bismarck she had blown up and sunk.

    b. The Destruction of the BISMARCK. Later on the 24th the Bismarck turned on the shadowing Suffolk, permitting the Prince Eugen to escape south for a fueling rendezvous. A few hours later the Bismarck escaped from the shadowing force and began steaming for Brest. For a day and a half she was unreported, but in the morning of the 26th a Coastal Command flying boat sighted her. Admiral Somerville's force (Ark Royal and Renown) was in the best position to intercept but too weak for a surface engagement. Swordfish aircraft from the Ark Royal torpedoed the Bismarck, jamming her rudder and making surface interception possible. Captain Philip Vian and five destroyers meanwhile had made the interception and harassed the Bismarck through the night of the 26th. By morning of the 27th Admiral Tovey arrived with the King George V and Rodney; by 1015 he had reduced the Bismarck to a shambles. Unable to sink her by gunfire at pointblank range, the cruiser Dorsetshire gave her the coup de grace with three torpedoes.

    3. The End of Warship Surface Raiding. The loss of the Bismarck and the lack of results by the Prince Eugen, plus the disabled condition of the Scharnhorst and Gneisenau, left the Germans in no condition to resume surface raiding immediately. Hitler was now convinced that surface ships were useless in such roles and restricted their movements to safe waters or to missions with no risk involved. Full reliance for victory was now placed on the U-boat and the Luftwaffe.

E. THE UNDERSEA WAR, 1939-1941. Germany possibly could have won the war at sea by the end of 1941 had two conditions been met: that Germany had stressed submarine construction in the years 1937 to 1939, and that the German high command from the first day of hostilities had emphasized "tonnage warfare," i.e., the sinking of British and Allied surface shipping wherever found. German surface warfare was never a genuine threat to the Allies--the submarine was.

   1. *German Conflict of Policies*. Until January 1943 the German Navy was commanded by Grand Admiral Raeder and the submarine forces by Admiral Karl Doenitz. Reflecting Hitler's and his own strategic concepts, Admiral Raeder emphasized the development and use of his surface navy in the first years of the war, and used the submarines for support of fleet operations and invasion campaigns. As a result the underseas fleet did not grow at the rate desired by Doenitz and was unable to bring its full strength against enemy merchant shipping. Compounding Doenitz' problem was the fact that Marshal Goering was unwilling to support submarine operations with his air force, preferring to bring the British to their knees through air power alone. It was only after Raeder's fleet proved impotent and Goering's *Luftwaffe* was shot from the sky that the Navy was turned over to Doenitz. By then, January 1943, it was too late.

   2. *German Submarine Operations, 1939-1941*. In the years 1939-1941 some 4,779,068 tons of Allied merchant shipping totalling 1,017 vessels were lost to direct submarine attack at the cost of 66 German and 38 Italian submarines. Another 1,003,428 tons (391 ships) were sunk by mines laid mostly by U-boats. Beginning the war with 57 submarines, the German Navy showed no gain in units by September 1940, having commissioned 28 vessels and lost the same number. With about 35% of its vessels actually on station at any time in the first year of the war, the 453 ships (1,895,704 tons) destroyed is rather grim evidence of U-boat effectiveness. The fall of France in June 1940 allowed Doenitz to shift operations to the French coast, raise his percentage of boats operating, and increase their time on station. The bloody harvest of 1940-1941 showed the operational menace the submarines created in the Southern and Western Approaches of the British Isles.

   3. *German Tactics and Difficulties*. German submarine operations were hampered throughout the war by the limited operational intelligence available to the submarine commanders. During the first year, submarines operated singly against enemy convoys in the approaches to the United Kingdom. As heavier surface and air

escort was provided the convoys in the Approaches, submarines were driven to operate farther to the West and South; evasive routing then made interception more difficult for the Germans. In the fall of 1940 Doenitz organized picket lines of submarines: once a contact was made all subs were directed by radio from headquarters to a point of interception. This was the beginning of "Wolf Pack" operations. Cooperation by Goering, and the use of long range planes to locate convoys, would have helped Doenitz considerably, but such cooperation seldom materialized.

Superior sound ranging gear (Asdic) allowed the British to cope with the submarines with some degree of success, but this eventually drove the German commanders to emphasize night surface attacks into the heart of convoys. Superior radar equipment was found to be the answer to this, but the early years saw heavy losses at the hands of daring U-boat skippers. Eventually, airborne radar was to prove the most effective of all instruments used in hunting submarines.

The United States played a significant part in these first years of the war. The Neutrality Patrol established at the outbreak of hostilities prevented German commanders from operating at the shipping route vortices in the western Atlantic. American destroyers turned over to the British proved a godsend to replace the badly mauled and lost escort craft after the Dunkirk evacuation.

IV. THE MEDITERRANEAN THEATER, 1939-1941

The British have always been concerned about the Mediterranean Sea, saying, "Who holds the Mediterranean holds the world." Until the fall of France and the Italian entry into the war (June 1940), British domination of the exits from the Mediterranean and use of the Sea as a highway to the East remained unchallenged. The shift of Italy from non-belligerency to active participation, and the loss of the French Navy as an ally, forced the British to fight for control of the Mediterranean. This fight was constantly complicated by the threat of a German invasion of the United Kingdom.

A. THE ITALIAN POSITION. The Italians were strong in position and bases but strikingly unprepared for war at the time they turned on France.

1. <u>The Italian Navy</u>. In June 1940 the Italian Navy possessed four 23,000-ton pre-World War I dreadnoughts that had been modernized, two 35,000 ton battleships recently completed, and two more under construction. In operation were seven heavy 10,000-ton 8-inch gun cruisers, twelve light cruisers mounting 6-inch guns, about 60 destroyers, and approximately 121 submarines. In combatant auxiliaries (cruisers, destroyers, submarines) the Italians at all times during the first two years of the war outnumbered the British forces in the Mediterranean. Adding strength to the defensive ability of the Italian Navy were the <u>mezzi navali d'assalto</u>, or assault machines. These consisted of pocket submarines, piloted torpedoes, explosive-laden motor boats, and towed mines. Considerable damage was caused throughout the war by the assault craft, the most spectacular being the mining of battleships <u>Valiant</u> and <u>Queen Elizabeth</u> on the night of 19-20 December 1941.

Italy is admirably located to control the central Mediterranean. With naval bases and airfields at Cagliari in Sardinia; Palermo and Messina in Sicily; Pantelleria in the Sicilian Channel; at Spezia, Naples, Taranto, and Brindisi on the Italian mainland; and on the North African shores at Tripoli and Benghazi, the Italians were in a position to interdict British lines of communication through sea, air, and undersea attack.

2. <u>Italian Weaknesses</u>. The principal Italian weaknesses lay in the country's poverty in natural resources and absence of a strong industrial complex. Lacking significant deposits of coal, iron, and oil, and having no rubber, Italy's industries were hard put to build up a military machine or sustain a war effort. British control of non-Mediterranean sea routes denied essential raw materials to the Italians, and Germany was not in a position to feed two war machines simultaneously. The loss of approximately one-third of the Italian merchant marine due to internment at the time war was declared was a costly and completely avoidable mistake.

3. <u>Italian Naval Strategy</u>. In view of Italy's low industrial capacity and lack of petroleum products, the Italian Navy chose to fight on the defensive.

From their admirable location at the Mediterranean "waist" the Italians were in a position to interdict British convoys and make raids in force whenever targets presented themselves. Because their military aviation was an independent service, the Italian Navy did not have adequate air coverage in its operations. It was constantly at a disadvantage when meeting smaller but carrier-escorted British naval forces. With government concern over possible losses outweighing interest in destruction of enemy concentrations, Italian fleet commanders could hardly exhibit the daring and aggressive spirit that brings victory at sea.

B. THE BRITISH POSITION. From September 1939 until June 1940 the British shared responsibility with the French for the control of the Mediterranean. For both countries free use of the Sea was crucial: oil for both fleets came from the eastern Mediterranean; the use of the direct route, rather than the Cape of Good Hope route, saved 8,500 miles between London and Alexandria; French North Africa was a source of fighting men for France's armies, and the French Navy had the task of convoy protection. Finally, as later discussions with the Americans were to point up, British strategic thinking had always envisioned a return to the continent and attacks on "Fortress Europe" by way of Mediterranean ports.

1. <u>Alexandria, Gibraltar, and Malta</u>. Fortunately for the British, the Egyptian Treaty of August 1936 was honored, as was the Anglo-Turkish Agreement of May 1939, and the eastern end of the Mediterranean remained substantially in their control. Defense of this area became the principal naval task of Admiral Sir Andrew B. Cunningham, whose Mediterranean Fleet was based on Alexandria. France's defeat caused the British Admiralty to form Force H as a "detached squadron" based on Gibraltar. This squadron had the double task of disputing Italian attempts to control the western Mediterranean and standing by to engage any major German surface concentrations that broke out into the Atlantic. At the Mediterranean waist the British retained Malta throughout the war. They used the island effectively to attack Italian convoys by air and as a base for escort operations to protect Alexandria- or Gibraltar-bound convoys. Possibly the greatest Italian and German error in their Mediterranean operations was their failure to seize Malta during 1940.

2. **British Advantages.** Though not readily apparent, the British in the Mediterranean had two significant advantages in their operations against the Italians. Lacking numbers, the British force commanders substituted aggressiveness, for major surface units could be provided more readily by the British than the Italians. While fighting for their Mediterranean lifeline the British also had the advantage of relatively secure interior lines of communication. Gibraltar and Alexandria could be supplied from the sea by way of the Cape with a minimum of interference; and aircraft for the eastern Mediterranean were flown across Africa from Tokoradi on the Gold Coast, by way of the Lake Chad region, to Alexandria.

3. **British Strategy.** British strategy from 1939 had the goal of keeping the sea passage open from Gibraltar to the Suez. It was early determined that Malta would be held at all costs to dispute Italian control of the central Mediterranean. Naval forces at Alexandria and Gibraltar were organized and used to protect Mediterranean convoys, attack Italian naval forces when success was possible, and provide support to British ground forces when operating in North Africa, Greece, and Crete. In North Africa, British armies pushed westward against the Italians to knock out bases in Libya, and they moved eastward against Italian forces in Eritrea, Ethiopia, and Italian Somaliland. To support their Mediterranean strategy British planners moved badly needed divisions from the United Kingdom to the Near East. Of immeasurable advantage to the British was American sympathy for their cause, as revealed through loans, sales, and lend-lease.

C. NAVAL ACTION IN THE MEDITERRANEAN--1940. From June of 1940 until March 1941 naval activity in the Mediterranean was indecisive, but on the whole the Italians were the losers. In some half dozen battles and raids the Italians suffered the loss of four cruisers and incurred major damage to or loss of four battleships. The British lost only two cruisers, although the carrier _Illustrious_ was badly damaged. A major change came in the spring of 1941, when the Germans began operations in the Mediterranean.

1. Actions Off Calabria and Cape Spada, July 1940. In early July 1940, Admiral Inigo Campioni took two battleships, six heavy and 12 light cruisers, and

24 destroyers, and sought to break up British convoys attempting to support or evacuate Malta. On 9 July, off Calabria (the toe of the Italian peninsula), he made contact with the British Mediterranean Fleet from Alexandria under Admiral Cunningham. The British force consisted of three battleships, five light cruisers, a handful of destroyers, and the carrier Eagle. After a brief exchange of gunfire the Italians retreated. Ten days later (19 July), two Italian light cruisers operating near Cape Spada at the western tip of Crete blundered onto a destroyer squadron escorted by the light cruiser HMAS Sydney. The Italians retreated, losing the cruiser Calleoni.

Both actions pointed up the Italian reluctance to engage British forces unless the latter were distinctly inferior. Lack of Italian naval aviation hampered search and denied important information to the fleet at sea. Attacks by Italian bombers on Campioni's fleet in the Calabria action further emphasized the trouble the Italian Navy and Air Force were having with coordination under battle conditions.

2. The British Attack on Taranto. On the night of 11-12 November 1940, a detachment of the Mediterranean Fleet consisting of the carrier Illustrious and support ships launched an air attack against the Italian fleet at the Taranto naval base. In two strikes, torpedo planes left the new battleship Littorio holed and listing and the battleships Cavour and Duilio resting on the bottom. Minor damage was also inflicted on a cruiser and destroyer. As a result of the Taranto raid the Italians used Spezia and Naples for their remaining battleships until their harbor defenses were reorganized. From the British viewpoint the attack was most significant, for it shifted the balance of naval power decidedly in favor of Cunningham's Mediterranean Fleet.

3. Action off Cape Spartivento, 27 November 1940. Two weeks after the Taranto raid the Italians had their opportunity to even the score. British forces from Gibraltar and Alexandria were converging west of Sicily. Campioni, with two battleships, six heavy cruisers, and 14 destroyers, was superior to either British force. However, poor reconnaissance plus an understandable caution caused the Italians to miss the opportunity of engaging either force separately.

D. THE GERMAN INTERVENTION, 1941-1942. Italian ineptness at sea was matched by that of army commanders on land. After overextending supply lines in Libya and failing to bring the Albanian and Greek campaigns to a successful conclusion, Mussolini was forced to accept German aid. From the first Stuka bombing attacks in January 1941 until General Erwin Rommel's armies were stopped before Alexandria, the British control of Egypt and the eastern Mediterranean hung in the balance.

1. Germany Enters the Mediterranean.

a. Italian Troubles. With Suez as his goal, Mussolini poured Italian forces into North Africa during the summer of 1940; by September Marshal Rudolfo Graziani stood inside Egypt at Sidi Barani. Here the Italian advance was blocked until General Archibald Wavell began his counterattack in December. By early February 1941 the Cyrenaica bulge was again in British hands, and British armies were at El Agheila. After launching an invasion of Greece on 28 October 1940, the Italians found themselves unable to conclude the campaign. Greek stubbornness supported by British aid, particularly aircraft, kept the Hellenic armies in the field. To counter the Italian move in Greece the British occupied Crete, establishing a fueling base on Suda Bay for British naval forces.

b. Reasons for Intervening. Impatient with the Italians, eager to pursue the old German drang nach osten, and planning ahead for the invasion of Russia, Hitler decided to intervene on behalf of the Italians. The German Air Fleet was thrown into southern Italy, Sicily, and North Africa to help the Italians master the central Mediterranean. Rumania joined the Axis and was occupied in November 1940. Under similar circumstances Bulgaria was taken over on 1 March 1941. On 6 April German armies and air forces smashed into Yugoslavia and Greece. Paralleling these Balkan moves, the Italian Army in Libya, strengthened by General Rommel's armor, began a second move across the Libyan desert. By 14 April 1941 Tobruk was invested and the Italo-German army was in Egypt.

c. The X Air Fleet Attacks. The full impact of German aerial support was felt by the British in early January 1941. On 10 January an Alexandria to Malta convoy was attacked by the Germans. Pressing their dive bombing attacks with skill and courage, the German pilots badly damaged the carrier Illustrious and the cruiser Southampton. The Southampton had to be sunk, but two weeks later the patched up Illustrious managed to escape to Alexandria. Operating from the Dodecanese Islands, the Luftwaffe sowed so many mines in the Suez Canal that the British had to close it for a time.

2. Battle of Cape Matapan, 28-29 March 1941.

a. British and Italian Dispositions. Inspired by their own successes, the Germans pressed the Italians to send their fleet to sea and attack the weakened British, who were pouring troops into Greece. Reluctantly, Admiral Angelo Iachino organized a raiding force to sweep to the north and south of Crete. To the north would go five cruisers and six destroyers commanded by Vice Admiral Carlo Cattaneo. The southern group, commanded by Admiral Iachino, consisted of the battleship Vittorio Veneto (flag), three heavy cruisers, and eight destroyers. Due either to unusual prescience or very accurate intelligence, Admiral Cunningham sortied at the same time (27 March) with three battleships, Warspite (flag), Barham, and Valiant, the carrier Formidable, and nine destroyers. At Piraeus, Vice Admiral H.D. Pridham-Wippel was ordered to rendezvous south of Crete with four cruisers and four destroyers.

b. The Battle. The Italian naval command had ordered the northern raiding force (Admiral Cattaneo) to rejoin the main body on the 28th. That morning Admiral Pridham-Wippel's cruisers contacted Admiral Iachino's cruisers and retreated toward Cunningham's force. Fearing a trap, the pursuing Italian heavy cruisers turned and joined the main body, now steaming toward home. Air strikes were launched from the Formidable throughout the day with no significant results until sunset, when the heavy cruiser Pola was torpedoed and stopped. Thinking the British battleships were four hours away, Admiral Iachino ordered the heavy cruisers Zara and Fiume to stand by the Pola. Needless to say, the Formidable's torpedo planes made Cunningham's smashing success possible. Radar on the British ships and the absence of it on the Italian vessels enabled the British to sink three Italian cruisers at night.

E. THE BRITISH BELEAGUERED--1941. Except for the victory at Cape Matapan, 1941 cheered the British little. Year's end found a bright ray in the raising of the siege at Tobruk and the entry of the United States as a fighting ally against the Germans, but Malta was under full attack and Rommel was yet to commence his great 1942 advance across the Libyan deserts.

   1. Withdrawal from Greece, April 1941. The first week in March 1941 the British began the movement of some 58,000 troops into Greece to help stiffen the Greek resistance to an expected German attack. When the attack came a month later the Germans could not be stopped. Their Panzer divisions and 800 planes of the IV Air Fleet overwhelmed the British and Greek armies. On 21 April the Greek king gave his permission for a British evacuation. British local control of the sea as a result of the Battle of Cape Matapan prevented any Italian interference with the evacuation.

   2. Abandonment of Crete, May 1941. Once in Greece the German high command laid plans to take Crete. Lying 60 miles from the Greek mainland, the island and its airfields could prove a serious menace unless in German hands. Finding that assault from the sea was too costly, even though they dominated the air above it, the Germans invaded Crete from the air on 20 May. The airfields on the North Cretan periphery were readily taken, and on 26 May the British were again faced with an evacuation. The saving of some 17,000 troops cost the British two cruisers and four destroyers and major damage to two battleships, the carrier Formidable, three cruisers, and a destroyer.

   3. Malta and North Africa. The defense of Malta, at the time considered by some as an extravagant waste of men and equipment, was directly related to the whole British effort in the Near East. Once Greece and Crete were in German hands it appeared to the British that a gigantic pincer operation was closing in on Suez, the southern prong being the Italo-German effort in North Africa. Malta was in a key position to dispute logistic support of the Axis' African armies. To increase the effectiveness of Malta, Force K was formed of two cruisers and two destroyers; it commenced operations from Malta in October 1941. In November two more cruisers and a pair of destroyers were added. During the time the Force operated, as high as 77% of the

supplies destined for North Africa was sunk.

The cost of sustaining Malta was high. The carrier *Ark Royal* was lost in November 1941 after flying off planes to strengthen the island. On 19 December one cruiser was lost and two cruisers were severely damaged when Force K steamed into a minefield while attacking the port of Tripoli. Yet throughout 1941 and into 1942, despite round-the-clock bombing of General Kesselring's II Air Fleet, Malta held out, and ships operating from the island continued to deny gasoline and oil to Rommel's Afrika Corps. When the "Desert Fox" was finally stopped, 60 miles from Alexandria at El Alamein, in June 1942, the ships and planes at Malta were as responsible for stopping the Germans as the embattled British Eighth Army. Italy and Germany lost one plane for each of the 1,400 Maltese killed.

V. THE SITUATION IN JANUARY 1942

By the end of 1941 there was some brightening in the skies from the British viewpoint as far as the war in Europe was concerned: technical developments had temporarily checked the German submarines in the Western Approaches; Malta was holding out; supplies were being denied to Rommel; and the Italians continued to be timid at sea. The Mediterranean Fleet at Alexandria had lost the *Barham* to submarine attack (25 November 1941), and the *Queen Elizabeth* and *Valiant* were bottomed in Alexandria harbor by a daring Italian attack with piloted torpedoes, but the new *King George V* class was being completed, and there was no pressing need for capital ships at Alexandria at the time. America's entry into the war provided ships, men, and dollars. Darkening the scene, however, was the Japanese sweep in the Far East and the German drive into Russia.

CHAPTER 18

THE U.S. NAVY IN WORLD WAR II: ATLANTIC THEATER

INTRODUCTION

From the German viewpoint the Japanese attack at Pearl Harbor was ill-advised, for the Nazis had their hands full fighting a great land campaign against the Russians and an undersea war against the British that promised to become more difficult once America made her naval power felt in the Atlantic. Indeed, America's entry into the war guaranteed eventual victory for Britain and her allies. The large questions were whether America's industrial machine could be geared for total war in time to prevent England's collapse and whether the American people and their Latin American allies would understand that victories would not come until sufficient war materials were produced. The Germans and the Japanese believed Americans "soft" and unwilling to bear those deprivations necessary in total war; nor did they believe that Latin America as a whole would follow American leadership.

I. AMERICA ENTERS THE WAR

The declarations of war between the United States and Germany were merely formalities, for both countries had been at war for almost a year. American military leaders had been cooperating with the British since August 1940, and American naval vessels had been escorting American vessels loaded with military contraband for the British since June 1941.

A. PRE-WAR AMERICAN NAVAL ACTIVITIES. As noted in the previous chapter (Section II-B) the United States, in concert with its Latin American neighbors, moved gradually from a position of neutrality to one of aiding the British "short of war." After 1939, United States Navy vessels entered the war zones in the traditional role of protecting American neutral commerce.

1. <u>Joint Planning with the British</u>. Once Europe went to war, American military planners were concerned whether Britain could hold out and with what the role of the United States would be if it were forced to go to war. In August 1940 the Assistant Chief of Naval Operations, Rear Admiral Robert L. Ghormley, was sent

to Britain for informal "exploratory discussions." He reported that the British could hold out against the Luftwaffe's worst. On the basis of his report the President, Secretaries of War and Navy, and the military service chiefs agreed in November 1940 that should the United States go to war, even in both oceans, the principal effort should be directed toward the defeat of Germany. In late January 1941 the British sent over their top military men to talk with their American opposite numbers. On 27 March 1941 a paper known as "ABC-1 Staff Agreement" summarized the conclusions on Anglo-American-Canadian cooperation reached by the military leaders. "Beat Hitler first" became the guiding principle for all American planning until April 1945.

    2. Convoy Duty, 1941. The "ABC-1 Agreement" also provided that the U.S. Navy would begin escorting convoys bound for the United Kingdom as soon as practicable. On 1 April a Support Force was organized from the recently constituted Atlantic Fleet and in June the U.S. Navy assumed responsibility for escorting convoys from North American to Iceland. To prevent German establishment of air bases or weather stations in Greenland, the United States in May 1941 occupied the island; and in July it relieved the British of the duty of occupying Iceland.

    The United States was as short of escort vessels as the British. By July, however, American shipyards were beginning to mass produce diesel-engined destroyer escorts (DE's). Operations in waters infested with German submarines led inevitably to a series of incidents: on 4 September the destroyer Greer was unsuccessfully attacked; on 16 October the destroyer Kearny was torpedoed and badly damaged, and on 31 October the destroyer Reuben James was torpedoed and sunk. Following the Reuben James attack, Congress changed the American neutrality laws to permit the defensive arming of American merchantmen.

B. THE UNITED STATES IN THE BATTLE OF THE ATLANTIC, 1941-1943. Following the attack at Pearl Harbor the United States declared war on Japan and a few days later on Germany. As a co-belligerent in the Atlantic war, the United States soon found its merchantmen under heavy attack off its own coasts.

1. U-Boats off the Atlantic Seaboard. With the transmission of the code word "Paukenschlag," Admiral Doenitz launched his undersea fleet against American coastal traffic along the Atlantic seaboard. Beginning on 12 January 1942, German submarines in six months' sank 100 vessels in the Eastern Sea Frontier area (Maine to Florida) at a loss of just six craft. As coastal convoying began, the Nazis moved farther south and concentrated their efforts in the Gulf of Mexico and Caribbean areas. In the month of May 1942 some 73 vessels were sunk in the Gulf and Caribbean, and in June the total reached 69. With tanker ("milch cows") submarines able to refuel his U-boats at sea, Doenitz was able to shift his vessels from areas of intense antisubmarine operations to less dangerous waters and yet keep a maximum number of submarines on station. Reflecting this mobility is the fact that only 11 submarines were lost to American attack in the second six months of 1942. The only bright spot in this picture was that trans-Atlantic convoys suffered fewer losses than usual during this period of emphasis on the American East Coast.

2. American Efforts to Counter the U-Boat.

a. Administrative Changes. In March 1942 Admiral Ernest J. King, previously Commander-in-Chief Atlantic Fleet, and currently heading the United States Fleet, relieved Admiral Harold R. Stark as Chief of Naval Operations (CNO) and combined the offices of COMINCH and CNO. Sea Frontier commands were organized for the prosecution of antisubmarine warfare (ASW), and the naval districts became purely administrative commands. From March 1942 until May 1943 the Sea Frontier commands were to direct ASW operations. In May 1943 the Tenth Fleet was organized as an operational command to direct ASW in the Atlantic.

b. Operational Difficulties. As would be expected, American antisubmarine operations were hampered during the first year of the war by lack of materiel, inexperience, absence of an effective ASW doctrine, and dispersion of effort. Due to transfers of vessels and equipment to the British and Russians, and the slowness of American naval planners to request ships smaller than standard destroyers, the United States was caught at the beginning of the war with few vessels suitable for ASW work. From British experience it was known that aircraft were excellent ASW weapons, but disagreement between the Navy and Army Air Corps prevented the most efficient use of shore-based patrol bombers. In the late summer of 1942 the Army turned over a large number of its aircraft to naval aviation for ASW uses; however, control of air ASW was not turned over to the Navy until late 1943. The establishment of Sea Frontier commands helped unify ASW doctrine within a command, but there were tremendous differences in doctrine on the North Atlantic convoy routes, Eastern seaboard, and the Caribbean, not to mention differences between the American and British approach to fighting submarines. The establishment of the Tenth Fleet helped solve this in 1943, though differences continued to exist between Atlantic and Pacific Ocean practices. The problem of lack of experience was taken care of by the German U-boat commanders.

    c. **The Weapons of ASW**. With British experience and American ingenuity great strides were made in developing ASW weapons and techniques. Depth charges were improved both in lethal range and sinking speed, and guns for firing depth charges were improved. To get lethal charges on a submerged target before sound contact was lost, "ahead thrown" weapons ("hedgehogs" and "mousetraps") were mounted on ASW vessels. Progress with underwater location devices and in the use of such equipment made submarine destruction a precise science. Radar, both surface and airborne, was radically developed in the course of the war to the point that U-boats were no longer safe if surfaced at night in a fog.

    By 1943 the delivery of destroyer escorts and other ASW vessels began in such numbers that all merchant vessels at sea could count on having surface escorts. Establishment of air bases throughout the Atlantic and along the North and South American coasts extended the air coverage afforded convoys and ships sailing independently. Submarines that violated radio silence could be located with improved high frequency direction finder equipment (H/F-D/F), and planes sent to the transmission point in a matter of minutes. The expanded use of escort type carriers (CVE's) finally made it possible to take aviation to sea for extended ASW operations. Development of "hunter-killer" techniques between surface ships, and between pairs of aircraft, accounted for the steep curve of U-boat sinkings after the spring of 1943.

II. ANGLO-AMERICAN COOPERATION IN THE MEDITERRANEAN

In view of the high-level strategic decision to give the war against Germany priority, the United States spent the opening year of the war recouping from the disaster at Pearl Harbor, organizing the antisubmarine war, preparing for offensive operations in Europe, and moving from the "defensive" to the "offensive-defensive" in the South Pacific with the launching of the assault in the Solomons. By the beginning of 1943 American troops had come to grips with Axis forces in North Africa, and by the end of the year the Mediterranean was again completely safe for Allied use.

A. THE NORTH AFRICAN CAMPAIGN, 1942-1943. To relieve pressure on Russia and bolster American and Allied self-confidence at home, the Allied leaders wanted to re-enter the continent as soon as possible. At the insistence of President Roosevelt the American Joint Chiefs of Staff pressured the British for a full-scale invasion of Europe in 1942 (Operation "Bolero"), and planned an alternative diversionary attack ("Sledgehammer") to help the Russians, if the situation warranted it, in September 1942. The British felt that the time was not propitious for a cross-channel invasion and proposed landings in northern Norway ("Jupiter") or North Africa ("Gymnast"). After several months of discussions the Combined Chiefs of Staff (British and American service heads) on 25 July 1942, recommended a campaign in North Africa. The goals of the campaign (Operation "Torch") were to crush the Italo-German armies in North Africa, thus relieving the Allies of transportation dangers in the Mediterranean, and to weaken German pressure on the Soviet Union, thereby serving as the oft-demanded "second front."

   1. Trafficking with Vichy: "Temporary Expediency." Vichy France, neutral but dominated by Hitler's puppet, Marshal Philippe Petain, was recognized by President Roosevelt not as a matter of "appeasement" but in order to have a listening post in the center of the French empire to acquire intelligence for military operations. Were recognition withheld, all American diplomatic and consular officials must return home. While Admiral William D. Leahy kept his ears open in Vichy, Robert Murphy, a career foreign officer, became Roosevelt's personal representative in North Africa and also

became Eisenhower's political adviser on African questions. Murphy, well acquainted with Admiral Jean Darlan, Minister of Marine, and General Maxime Weygand, Minister of National Defense, knew that Darlan would never let his fleet fall into German hands and that Weygand was anti-German. The latter, moreover, had 125,000 combat-trained regulars and 200,000 reservists in North Africa. In the Weygand-Murphy Accord, December 1940, the United States promised Vichy financial aid and was permitted to reestablish its consulate at Dakar, Vichy's major African naval base. A month after Hitler attacked Russia, Roosevelt offered fighter planes to the French in North Africa, and the British promised logistical support also.

Eisenhower could land in North Africa in such force as to overcome Vichyite opposition or convince the Vichyites to cooperate with him. Murphy established a fifth column among Frenchmen friendly to the United States and also converted Darlan, now second in command to Petain, who happened to be in Algiers visiting a sick son. Thus the "Darlan deal" was made: Darlan would order the French to cooperate in return for a guarantee of French sovereignty in North Africa and his becoming High Commissioner there.

2. **Plan of Operations**. With 8 November 1942, as D-Day, three simultaneous attacks were planned for the Casablanca, Oran, and Algiers areas. Lieutenant General Dwight D. Eisenhower was named Supreme Commander of the Allied Expeditionary Force. Under him Admiral Sir Andrew B. Cunningham, RN, commanded all naval forces. Staging in the United States, a Western Naval Task Force (TF 34) under Rear Admiral H. K. Hewitt, USN, and made up of a support fleet and 35,000 troops commanded by Major General George S. Patton, had as its target Casablanca, in French Morocco. A Central Task Force with 39,000 American troops was to attack Oran, on the Algerian Mediterranean coast; and farther to the east 49,000 American and 23,000 British troops were to descend on the port of Algiers. Vice Admiral James F. Somerville's Force H was to provide naval support for the Oran and Algiers operations. Once French Morocco was captured the expeditionary force was to start east into Tunisia, with capture of the key ports at the Mediterranean waist, Tunis and Bizerta, as its goal. In driving east it was expected that the Italo-German armies would be trapped between Eisen-

hower's invaders and the advancing British Eighth Army under General Sir Bernard L. Montgomery.

3. **The Invasions, 8-11 November 1942.** In choosing French Morocco and Algeria to invade, the Allies hoped for an early defection by the Vichy forces and of the attachment of Vichy France's fleet and armies to the Allied cause. Though the French Navy originally resisted the amphibious assaults, the Army did not, and on 11 November all French forces, at the command of Admiral Jean F. Darlan, ceased fire.

   a. <u>Casablanca</u>. The attack on Casablanca consisted of three separate landings; at Safi to the south, Fedhala close by, and Mehdia to the north. Due to rough surf, inexperience, and communications problems, the landings were accomplished most inexpertly; the one at Safi was the best handled. At Casablanca, naval resistance from the battleship <u>Jean Bart</u> and other units was smothered by shells from the American battleship <u>Massachusetts</u>, carrier aircraft strikes from the <u>Ranger</u>, and pin-point gunfire from American cruisers and destroyers. The landing at Mehdia, with Port Lyautey as an immediate target, was the most difficult, but the French surrender of 11 November solved all problems.

   b. <u>Oran</u>. Knowing that the French Navy would never forget the British attack on Oran (July 1940), American troops made the landings at Oran behind British naval support. Assaults were made east and west of the city and resistance was quickly overcome. Two coast guard cutters, <u>Walney</u> and <u>Hartland</u>, were sunk trying to take troops directly into the harbor at Oran.

   c. <u>Algiers</u>. The Eastern Task Force, covered by British gunfire, made landings east and west of the port of Algiers. As at Oran the city was captured without great difficulty, but two destroyers were badly damaged (<u>Broke</u> later sank) trying to enter the harbor to capture the port.

4. <u>The German Defeat in Africa.</u> Following the North African landings the Nazis occupied Vichy France. The Navy at Toulon was scuttled to prevent its falling into German hands. The three invasion forces quickly joined and began their drive eastward. Though reinforced by air, Rommel's troops were caught between

Eisenhower's and Montgomery's armies and finally surrendered in mid-May 1943. North Africa was again in Allied hands, 250,000 prisoners were taken, and the major threat to Suez was eased.

B. THE SICILIAN CAMPAIGN, JULY-AUGUST 1943. In January 1943, President Roosevelt and Prime Minister Churchill met in Casablanca with their service chiefs. Agreement was reached upon strategy for the coming year and upon "unconditional surrender" terms. British reluctance to begin "Bolero" in 1943 was evident, and it was decided to invade Sicily as an alternative (Operation "Husky"). The expected results of "Husky" were to further relieve the Russians by forcing German attention toward Italy and Sicily; knock Italy out of the war and perhaps get Turkey in; and completely free the Mediterranean for Allied use.

1. <u>Plan of Operations</u>. D-Day was to be 10 July 1943. General Eisenhower was named Supreme Commander, Admiral of the Fleet Cunningham controlled all naval forces, and Air Chief Marshal A. W. Tedder commanded all aviation. Landings were to be made on the southern shores of Sicily by the American Seventh Army (Lt. Gen. Patton) covered by Vice Admiral Hewitt's Western Naval Task Force, and on the southeastern coast by the British Eighth Army (Montgomery) supported by the Eastern Naval Task Force under Vice Admiral Sir Bertram Ramsay, RN. The goal in Sicily was to drive toward Catania and Messina, thus seizing the island and trapping its 350,000 defenders. Unfortunately for the whole operation, air cover was not used most efficiently. The Army Air Corps and the R.A.F. preferred to direct their own squadrons rather than put tactical control in the hands of the assault forces. Moreover, although the Navy wished to attack at daylight so that gunners and coxswains could see the beaches they were assaulting, the Army had its way with an attack while it was still dark.

2. <u>The Assault, 10 July 1943</u>. The American landings, at three points, were preceded by heavy naval bombardment. Throughout the whole ship-to-shore phase, and even during the early break-out period, naval gunfire with pinpoint accuracy was used to break up counterattacks and blast away enemy emplacements. In general the landings were remarkably well executed; the light (5 percent) casualties bear this out.

3. <u>Sicily Secured</u>. On 17 August Army troops entered Messina and brought the Sicilian campaign to a close. Italian morale was badly shaken by the loss of Sicily and by the failure of the Italian Navy to come out and fight. Mussolini was deposed by the King on 25 July and a Fascist Republic was organized under Marshal Pietro Badoglio. The Germans managed to save about 45,000 of their troops, and over 60,000 Italians escaped. Though effective in their amphibious operations, the Anglo-American naval forces were most inept in allowing such a large Italo-German group to cross the Straits of Messina.

C. THE INVASION OF ITALY, 1943-1945. At the Quebec ("Trident") Conference of August 1943, Roosevelt, Churchill, and the Combined Chiefs decided to exploit the conquest of Sicily by invading Italy. It was agreed that only troops from the Mediterranean theater would be used and that this "limited operation" would in no way interfere with the projected cross-channel attack set for 1 May 1944. By an invasion of Italy (Operation "Avalanche") it was hoped that the Italians would finally surrender, since they were already negotiating. It was also expected that such an attack would pin down more German divisions, make airbases available for bombing the Balkans and Germany, and reduce further the danger to Mediterranean communications. General Eisenhower was continued as the Supreme Commander until relieved by British General Sir Henry Maitland-Wilson in late December 1943.

1. <u>The Assault at Salerno, 9 September 1943</u>. Following a British landing on 3 September at Calabria, the Italian government surrendered. Resistance continued by the Germans until the spring of 1945. On 9 September British and American (General Mark Clark's Fifth Army) armies were landed in the Gulf of Salerno. Air strikes and naval bombardment prepared the way, but heavy resistance was met from the water's edge. The surrender of the Italian Navy on 11 September relieved the assault forces of a major concern, but German resistance was greater than predicted. In the face of overwhelming naval gunfire from the battleships <u>Valiant</u> and <u>Warspite</u>, and finding it necessary to regroup to meet the British Eighth Army coming north from Calabria, General Albert Kesselring withdrew from the Salerno sector. Naples fell on 1 October, but a stalemate developed when the Germans dug in at the Volturno River, north of Naples.

2. <u>Anzio, January-May 1944</u>. To break the stalemate at the Volturno River, a landing up the Italian coast at Anzio was planned for 22 January 1944. Through careful deception, tactical surprise was achieved by the naval force under Rear Admiral Frank J. Lowry, USN. The Anzio beachhead soon became a trap even though the landing was made unopposed. Beyond the range of naval artillery, and commanding local ridges, six Nazi divisions were able to keep the Allied forces pinned down. By 25 May the Fifth and Eighth Armies managed to push north far enough to rescue the Anzio force, and on 4 June Rome was entered. Moving ever northward against the Germans, the Allied armies, now joined by the Italians, eventually drove the Nazis to surrender in the spring of 1945.

III. THE INVASION OF WESTERN EUROPE, 1944-1945

The invasion of western Europe was the focus of Allied planning virtually from the day the United States declared war on Germany. Before the American entry, military leaders in the United States agreed with their British counterparts that Germany rather than Japan was the principal enemy. From the spring of 1942, President Roosevelt pressed for the commencement of "Operation Roundup"--the invasion of Europe and the defeat of Germany. Finally, with Allied control of the Mediterranean and Atlantic sea lanes assured, the British were ready for the cross-channel thrust into "Fortress Europe."

A. VICTORY IN THE ATLANTIC.

1. <u>The U-Boat Defeated</u>. Though the winter of 1942-1943 found the German undersea fleet sinking Allied cargoes in prodigious numbers, the cause was almost lost for the Germans. As noted above (I-A), the spring of 1943 found the Allied naval effort against the submarine beginning to pay dividends. Merchantmen losses fell steadily in the North Atlantic, and American shipyards by mass production methods turned out replacements far in excess of losses. Aviation and improved radar equipment held the submarine down. In the Bay of Biscay, submarine sinkings mounted steeply as U-boats were detected on passage into the Atlantic. In May 1943, Doenitz finally had to call the submarines in until new ways were devised to improve their defenses. Better dual-purpose anti-aircraft guns gave

the U-boat a chance to fight it out with attacking aircraft, but it was too easy to reinforce the aircraft. Passage to the Atlantic in groups provided greater firepower against planes, but the planes merely attacked in squadron strength.

In September 1943 the submarines tried to defeat the convoys and their escorts with acoustic torpedoes, but towed noisemakers ("foxers") ruined the torpedoes' effectiveness. In 1944 the submarine fleet was equipped with "snorkels" to allow low speed underwater use of the diesel engines. Though able to get into the Atlantic by making the total passage submerged, the underwater speed of the U-boat was far too slow to permit attacks on convoys with continuous success. Aircraft also proved able to locate submarines at snorkel depth. Finally, in late 1944 and 1945, Doenitz and the German Navy pinned their hopes on the type XXI and XXIII submarines. Capable of high speeds while submerged, these U-boats would be able to attack, escape, and attack again. However, air bombing of the parts factories, assembly plants, and shipyards so slowed the delivery of the new boats that only one got to sea before the surrender in May 1945.

The Allied victory over the U-boat was a victory of scientific developments, massive merchant shipbuilding programs, and highly skilled use of ASW weapons by the Allied navies.

2. The Scharnhorst and Tirpitz. With his submarines running into ever greater trouble, Grand Admiral Doenitz decided to send the battle cruiser Scharnhorst on a sortie against North Atlantic shipping destined for Russia. Departing its Norwegian base on Christmas eve 1943, the Scharnhorst was intercepted by three British cruisers. After a brief engagement, the German retreated eastward and was met by a task force under Admiral Sir Bruce Fraser consisting of the battleship Duke of York, the heavy cruiser Jamaica, and accompanying destroyers. In a high speed chase the Scharnhorst was disabled by gunfire and then sunk by torpedoes.

Once the Bismarck was destroyed, the battleship Tirpitz still remained a threat to Allied shipping in the North Atlantic that required the British to keep powerful squadrons ready. After a brief sortie in

1943, the <u>Tirpitz</u> was hidden in Norway's Alten Fjord. On 22 September 1943 two British midget submarines managed to get to the <u>Tirpitz</u> and damage her. After being repaired she became the target of numerous carrier strikes, but none was able to sink her. With the Russians pressing in during 1944, the <u>Tirpitz</u> was moved farther south to the Tromso Fjord. While free of Russian capture and carrier strikes, she could be reached by long-range bombers. Finally, on 12 November 1944, two squadrons of British Lancasters dropping 12,000-pound bombs sank her at her moorings.

B. PLANNING OPERATION OVERLORD. At the "Trident" Conference of August 1943 in Quebec a tentative date for the invasion of France was set for 1 May 1944. At the Teheran Conference in December 1943 the date was made firm.

    1. <u>Leadership</u>. Though the British had thought to direct the invasion in its earliest planning, the fact that American troops would be more numerous called for an American Supreme Commander. President Roosevelt nominated General Eisenhower, who as Supreme Commander took over planning in January 1944. General Sir Bernard L. Montgomery was to command the invasion armies, Admiral Sir Bertram H. Ramsay, RN, all naval forces, and Air Chief Marshal Sir Trafford Leigh-Mallory all air cover. American naval forces were directed by Rear Admiral Allan G. Kirk, USN.

    2. <u>Plan of Attack</u>. President Roosevelt directed the Supreme Commander to invade the continent and bring the Germans to surrender. Unlike the Italian invasion, or any previous operations, the goal of "Overlord" was unlimited--the defeat of Nazi Germany. British plans made over a period of years proved helpful, and the invasion date was set for 5 June 1944, with the blow to fall on the Normandy beaches of France near the Cotentin Peninsula. Three airborne divisions would be dropped the night before D-Day, and five divisions would make the assault on five beaches: Utah and Omaha beaches (U.S.) and Gold, Juno, and Sword beaches (British). To conceal the point of attack, the French coast from Calais to Cherbourg was bombed steadily and communications from the interior were disrupted.

    In earlier planning it was assumed that a simultaneous attack would be made in the Toulon-Marseilles area ("Anvil"), but the lack of landing craft made this impossible. Instead "Operation Dragoon" was to be launched at division strength on 15 August.

    3. **Naval Plans**. The success of the invasion depended upon the navies. Under Admiral Ramsay, five task forces were organized to transport troops to the beaches and protect them en route. The Western (American) Task Force under Rear Admiral Kirk was composed of assault forces "U" (Rear Admiral D.P. Moon, USN) and "O" (Rear Admiral J.L. Hall, USN). Naval gunfire support was provided force "U" by Rear Admiral M.L. Deyo with the battleship Nevada, five cruisers, destroyers, and the British monitor Erebus. Fire support for force "O" was commanded by Rear Admiral C.F. Bryant, USN, with the battleships Arkansas and Texas, three cruisers, and destroyers. The Eastern (British) Task Force, commanded by Rear Admiral Sir Philip Vian, RN, was similarly organized and was backed by the heavy guns of the battleships Warspite, Nelson, Rodney, and Ramilles and the monitor Roberts. Besides transporting the troops and providing gunfire support, the naval force had to defend the operation against surface and sub-surface interference by the German Navy, sweep mines, provide anti-aircraft fire, bring supplies and reinforcements, and evacuate the inevitable casualties.

C. THE NORMANDY INVASION, 6 JUNE 1944. The tactical surprise achieved in the initial assault held down casualties. Because no major seaport was the initial target, the Germans were surprised by the choice of invasion site. The poor weather before D-Day caused a relaxation of German vigilance, although considerable effort was made to deceive the Germans through feints, naval bombardments, and bombing raids in the Calais-Boulogne area. The naval forces fulfilled their assigned role effectively; naval gunfire turned many desperate situations into local victories for Allied forces. At Omaha Beach the American landing met a hurricane of fire, but naval gunfire and sheer personal courage secured the lodgement by the early afternoon of D-Day.

    1. **Logistics**. Because the attack was not launched against a port, the invading forces had to bring their own. Two floating piers ("Mulberries A and B") were towed to the invasion sites and moored. They provided wharfage for transports and cargo vessels where none existed. "Mulberry A" at Omaha Beach was usable by 17

June but was destroyed by a gale a few days later. "Mulberry B," at the British beaches, then provided pier space for both groups until the ports of Caen and Cherbourg were available. Oil was pumped ashore through pipelines from tankers, and later through cross-channel lines. The amazing number of 300,000 men and 50,000 vehicles, and 100,000 tons of supplies were landed in the first six days; and within a month 1,000,000 troops had landed in France.

    2. **Extending the Foothold.** From their beachhead the Allied armies moved inland. Cherbourg and its badly damaged harbor was taken on 26 June, Caen fell 8 July, and Paris was captured 25 August. The American Third Army drove south and west toward the German naval bases at Brest, Lorient, and St. Nazaire while the British and Canadian forces started up the Channel coast toward Antwerp. After an amphibious assault on Walcheren cleared the water to Antwerp, the city fell to the Allies on 4 September 1944.

D. OPERATION DRAGOON, 15 AUGUST 1944. With the date for the Normandy invasion set, planning proceeded for the invasion of the Toulon-Marseilles area.

    1. **Plans.** British General Maitland-Wilson was appointed Supreme Commander for "Dragoon," with naval forces at sea being commanded by Vice Admiral H.K. Hewitt, USN. The assault, aimed at the area between Cannes and Marseilles on the French Riviera, was to be made by elements of three infantry divisions and an airborne division. Later ten reinforced divisions were to be fed in, bringing the total to 450,000 troops. Once ashore at St. Maxime, St. Tropez, and St. Raphel, Toulon and Marseilles were to be captured; then a drive north up the Rhone River valley was to begin.

    2. **The Landings.** The assault was made on three beaches. Naval gunfire support was excellent, and tactical air strikes were provided from the seven escort carriers in Admiral Hewitt's force. Toulon was finally captured on 28 August, and Marseilles fell the same day. Driving north from Marseilles, Major General Alexander M. Patch's Seventh Army made contact with advance units from General Patton's Third Army near Dijon. Southwestern France was now in Allied hands.

IV. THE GERMAN COLLAPSE

A. DEATH OF THE GERMAN NAVY. With the successful completion of "Dragoon" the last major naval operation in European waters had been consummated. Naval forces were used to transport armies across the Rhine River, but this was essentially a side-show. The German Navy in the Baltic delivered fire support for their retreating countrymen as the Russians drove toward the Gulf of Riga and Danzig, and in the end the old battleship Schleswig-Holstein, and pocket battleships Scheer and Lutzow (Deutchland) were sunk while engaging the Russians.

B. WHY THE AXIS FAILED. In assessing the causes of the Italo-German failure in World War II several points seem worth mentioning:

1. Essentially Germany and Italy lacked the resources and industrial ability to challenge an Anglo-American coalition. Compounding their problem was the mistake of turning on Russia in June 1941.

2. From the naval viewpoint German-Italian strategy had many shortcomings. Because of limited replacement ability, both nations husbanded their surface forces until increased Allied naval strength made their use suicidal. Early Italian audacity in the Mediterranean might have broken the British hold. More extensive sorties by German surface naval forces could have spread Allied convoy defenses so thin that the submarine could have been even more effective in the years 1939-1941.

3. Effective use of German and Italian forces was hampered by intra-service and inter-service rivalries. Failure to turn the undersea fleet to full tonnage warfare until 1943 undoubtedly hurt the Nazi cause. Submarine effectiveness could have been improved considerably, particularly in the years 1939-1941, had Marshal Goering been willing to put his Luftwaffe to naval uses. Rivalry between the Italian Air Force and Navy denied the fleet necessary aviation at sea.

4. Time proved that Malta was the "linch pin" of the Mediterranean theater. Had the Germans or Italians taken the island in 1940, Rommel's North

African campaign would not have suffered as it did. Some strategists feel that Hitler could have driven through Spain and taken Gibraltar as well as Malta, and that he should have tried the operation through Spain at the time of the Sicilian campaign.

5. In terms of grand strategy Hitler failed to pursue specific goals until achieved. Professing a horror of war on several fronts, he nevertheless fought on several fronts, until German commitments far exceeded resources.

V. ADMINISTRATION OF THE NAVY IN WORLD WAR II*

A. FRANK KNOX, 11 JULY 1940-28 APRIL 1944. Knox, born 1 January 1874, served with Theodore Roosevelt's Rough Riders, turned to journalism, then fought in France during World War I and retired from the Army as a colonel of field artillery. For many years he was the general manager of the Hearst newspaper chain; in 1931 he acquired the Chicago Daily News, of decided Republican tendencies. Although he lost a bid for the top spot, he was Alfred Landon's running mate in 1936--and suffered ignominious defeat at the hand of Franklin Roosevelt's forces. A severe critic of the domestic policies of the New Deal, he nevertheless supported its foreign policies and with the outbreak of war in Europe in 1939 called for increasing particularly America's naval arm. As Secretary of the Navy starting 11 July 1940, he had to answer his own challenge.

Roosevelt invited both Knox and Henry L. Stimson to join his cabinet in order to make it bipartisan. At confirmation hearings, Knox said that he wanted a Navy second to none. While he would not send troops to Europe, he would aid the Allies "short of war" including the use of convoys if necessary. After his confirmation, the sixty-six year-old former soldier appeared to his naval colleagues to be in good health, sometimes too quick to reach decisions, and always able to express his ideas with choice profanity. In August, Knox severed his relations with his newspaper.

Already experienced as a business manager, Knox concentrated on making policy decisions and supervising

* This topic is arbitrarily placed here because of the greater length of the next chapter.

the work of immediate subordinates. He lacked technical competence to judge many matters involved in a Navy that included 2,000 operating ships and 1,750 aircraft; numerous bases, yards, and other installations spread from Puerto Rico in the Atlantic to the Philippines in the Pacific; and 318,800 people, about half of them in uniform. In June 1940, Congress expanded the Navy by 10 percent. Eight days after he entered office, Congress provided for a "Two Ocean Navy" including 1,325,000 tons of new construction, 15,000 naval aircraft, and 100,000 tons of auxiliaries. Procurement thus became one of his greatest responsibilities. This responsibility was eased first by the Naval Reorganization Act of 20 June 1940, which merged the bureaus of Construction and Repair and of Steam Engineering into a Bureau of Ships and also provided for an Under Secretary, and second by authority granted on 28 June 1940 to dispense with competitive bidding and to grant advance payments of up to 30 percent on defense contracts.

When Knox took office, his staff of 7 civilians and 7 naval officers was insufficient to supervise the growth of the Navy. Of great help to him were his naval aide, Captain Morton L. Deyo, and Major John H. Dillon, USMC, his administrative assistant who had already served Secretaries Claude Swanson and Charles Edison. The fact that Lewis Compton, the Assistant Secretary, stayed on until relieved by Ralph Bard in February 1941 eased the transition for Knox, and his choice of James Forrestal, a New York investment banker, as the Navy's first Under Secretary brought him a good manager to handle industrial mobilization and procurement problems. At Forrestal's suggestion, Knox agreed to have Artemus L. Gates serve in the revived post of Assistant Secretary of the Navy for Air. Among Knox's fourteen special assistants was a young lawyer named Adlai Stevenson, who from 1941 to 1943 acted as his legal counsel but also as traveling companion, speech writer, and personal representative at many conferences. With Admiral Harold R. "Betty" Stark, the CNO, as with various other bureau chiefs including Rear Admiral Samuel M. Robinson, BuShips, Admiral William R. Furlong, BuOrd, and Rear Admiral Ben Moreel, BuY&D, he moved from cordiality to friendship. To shift the load of routine matters from administrators to clerks, Knox obtained an increase in the number of clerks and typists and hired the management consulting firm of Booz, Allen, Hamilton, and Fry, to undertake the first of four management studies of naval administration, with such studies to continue under an Office of Management Engineer, and also a study of management in the Secretary's Office. In consequence of the latter, Knox divided his office into the SO (Secretary's Office) and EXOS, the Executive Office of the Secretary that contained workers responsible to him or to his civilian deputies but did not belong to any other naval agency. By the time of Pearl Harbor, SO had grown to 25 civilians and 9 officers and EXOS gained a Statistical Division, Procurement Legal Division, Office of Public Relations (which Knox took away from the Office of Naval Intelligence), Coordinator of Research and Development, and an Administrative Office, the last replacing the Office of Chief Clerk established in 1798. On 30 January 1942, Knox also established the Office of Procurement and Material, which Forrestal headed. Meanwhile at the suggestion of the British Ambassador to the United States, Knox carried to a cabinet meeting the idea that 50 American destroyers be exchanged for various British bases on or along the east coast of the Atlantic.

As a result of the Lend Lease law, signed on 11 March 1941, which he supported before Congress, Knox could have damaged British warships repaired in American yards and fill British orders for aircraft and weapons. He supervised the seizure of German, Italian, and Danish ships interned in American ports and helped draft plans for extending American protection over Greenland. After Hitler invaded Russia, on 22 June 1941, he angered isolationists and noninterventionists by publicly asserting that it was time to clear Germans from the Atlantic. After Roosevelt sent a brigade of Marines to relieve the British garrison on Iceland, he again importuned Roosevelt to use convoys and privately cheered when the President secretly finally did so, on 19 July. Following an attack by a U-boat upon the destroyer <u>Greer</u> near Iceland on 4 September, Roosevelt gave his "shoot on sight order" and the public knew that convoys were being used. The danger involved was drummed home when a German torpedo severely damaged the destroyer <u>Kearney</u> on 17 October, a U-boat sank the destroyer <u>Reuben James</u> two weeks later off Iceland, and various merchant ships were also sunk.

From an inspection trip to Hawaii and subsequent events Knox knew that the Commander-in-Chief Pacific

Fleet, Admiral James O. Richardson, not only disagreed with Roosevelt's keeping the fleet at Pearl Harbor (he wanted it returned to the West Coast where it could be better protected) and with the manner in which decisions that affected the Navy were reached in Washington. Knox knew more than Richardson did about what the Japanese were doing because he was on the very limited distribution list of the Japanese diplomatic messages being decrypted by Operation Magic, and when Richardson again complained to Roosevelt, Roosevelt relieved him as CINCUS. Richardson had nevertheless alerted the administration to startling weaknesses in the defenses of Hawaii, for which the Army was primarily responsible, weaknesses that Knox believed might provoke the Japanese to launch a surprise attack upon Pearl Harbor. When the Chief of Staff of the Army, George Marshall, and others told Roosevelt that Hawaii was "impregnable," Knox kept quiet. The "war warning" sent to Army and Navy commanders in the Pacific on 27 November 1941 made an impact upon Admiral Thomas C. Hart, commanding the Asiatic Fleet, in the Philippines, but not upon Admiral Husband E. Kimmel at Pearl Harbor who, incidentally, was not receiving Magic despatches. Soon after reading the decoded fourteen-part Japanese message that ended diplomatic negotiations with Japan and stating in his first annual report that "the United States Navy is second to none," Knox was in his office with Stark and Richmond Kelly Turner, chief of the War Plans Division, when a messenger brought a despatch from Pearl reading "Air Raid Pearl Harbor, This is no drill."

"My God," Knox said to Stark. "This can't be true. It must mean the Philippines!"

"No sir," replied Stark. "This is Pearl." When Knox informed Roosevelt by telephone, he may have noted surprise but also relief in the President's voice. Knox flew to Pearl to assess damage and offered recommendations for repairs or survey to Roosevelt on 14 December. On the 17th Supreme Court Justice Owen J. Roberts agreed to chair the first Pearl Harbor investigation. Meanwhile Knox relieved Kimmel and ordered Admiral Chester W. Nimitz as his relief. When Roosevelt moved the post of CINCUS from Hawaii to Washington and gave the billet to Admiral Ernest J. King, Knox was happy to have a man nearby who he knew would change the defensive attitude of the Navy to an offensive one. When it proved difficult for CINCUS and the CNO, Stark, to cooperate, Knox asked the General Board for advice and with Roosevelt decided to have King fill both positions. With King installed, on 21 March 1942 Stark was sent to London to command United States naval forces in Europe.

Because King rather than Knox directed naval operations, King drew closer to Roosevelt and Knox often was not even informed about impending operations. However, as a firm believer in civilian control of the military he stoutly resisted King's frequent attempts to diminish civilian influence in the Navy, as in seeking to get procurement, which Knox had moved from the CNO's office to EXOS, back under military control. Forrestal complained to Knox, Knox to Roosevelt, and Roosevelt vetoed King's plan to reorganize the Navy so that he would have control over material. King nevertheless created an Assistant Chief of Naval Operations (Personnel) and an Assistant Chief of Naval Operations (Material), thus cutting Forrestal out. With Knox present, Roosevelt voiced his displeasure to King, who withdrew his plan. When King tried again a year later, Roosevelt for a second time vetoed reorganizing the Navy in time of war, but did not adopt Knox's suggestion that King be sent to direct the war in the Pacific.

Early in 1944, following several strenuous trips to visit many naval installations and war fronts, the old Rough Rider began to weaken. On 22 April he suffered a mild heart attack; on the 24th, a severe one. Despite the ministrations of the famed heart specialist Dr. Paul Dudley White, he died on the 28th and was buried in Arlington National Cemetery. To the Navy he had given good leadership, effective public relations, and improved management. Most important, he had been able to get the Navy's civil and military heads to work together in prosecuting a successful war.

B. JAMES FORRESTAL, 19 MAY 1944-17 SEPTEMBER 1947. Having served for four years as Under Secretary and being in the good graces of both Congress and the public, Forrestal, nominated on 9 May 1944, won unanimous senatorial confirmation. His excellent work in procurement had helped create a mighty Navy. Now he must keep the momentum of production and of operations going and help Roosevelt (and then Truman) decide upon how to defeat and then treat postwar Germany and Japan, including the decision whether to use atomic bombs on Japan (which he opposed using unless Japan was given prior warning).

The war over, Forrestal ruled a Navy in process of demobilization. Argue as he might, he could not get President Truman to maintain an adequate defense that would deter another war even when he pointed to Soviet intransigence in many matters. For naval defense he suggested a Navy of 400 major combatant ships and 8,000 aircraft and the use of mobile carrier forces and of Marines. Rather than the $5.1 billion he wanted for the Navy in FY 1947, he got $4.1 billion. In consequence, at the end of 1946 the Navy included only 319 major combatant ships, 1,461 aircraft, and .5 million persons. Forrestal nevertheless defrayed the expense of having an American fleet patrol the Mediterranean.

As COMINCH, King was directly responsible to the President; as CNO, he was responsible to the Secretary of the Navy. Not only were lines of responsibility muddled but, as already noted, King tried to bring material from Forrestal's old office into the office of the CNO. Like Knox determined to support civilian authority over the military, Forrestal nevertheless let King wear his two hats until the war ended. Meanwhile he created both an office of Comptroller and an Organizational Top Policy Group, the latter to decide upon differences between civilian and professional leaders and also to plan the Navy's program with respect to postwar defense reorganizational plans. The war was barely over when Forrestal asked Thomas Gates to study the department's structure. In consequence of the "Gates report," on 23 September 1945 the shore establishment was reorganized. Subsequently Forrestal separated "consumer logistics" from "producer logistics" and placed the former in military, the latter in civilian hands, and also created an Office of Naval Material and revised the Office of the CNO into the now familiar Deputy Chiefs system, starting with five: Op-01, Personnel; Op-02, Administration; Op-03, Operations; Op-04, Logistics; and Op-05, Navy Air. Moreover, the CNO was made responsible to both the President and the naval Secretary, and much more attention was given to Naval Air and to submarine warfare than had formerly been the case.[1]

CHAPTER 19

WORLD WAR II IN THE PACIFIC

PART I. JAPANESE EXPANSION: PEARL
HARBOR TO GUADALCANAL

I. THE JAPANESE NAVAL PLANNING ORGANIZATION

Japanese Imperial Headquarters, formed in November 1937, had as its nucleus the Army and Navy general staffs. Although the Emperor was the titular head of the headquarters, in effect the army and navy ministers dominated the government. However, the Army and Navy operated independently. If disagreement developed between the commanders in chief of the Army and Navy, stalemate and inaction resulted. Naval Planning was accomplished in the First Section of the Navy Department; Logistics plans in the Second Department; Naval Intelligence was provided by the Third; Communications in the Fourth; and Radio Intelligence by a special section. Naval operational plans emanated either from Imperial Headquarters or from the First Department of the Naval General Staff. Important plans were discussed first at Headquarters and approved by the Army before the Navy could proceed with them.

II. PEARL HARBOR

A. JAPANESE DECISIONS AND PLANS. Admiral Isoroku Yamamoto, Commander in Chief of the Japanese Combined Fleet, suggested an attack on Pearl Harbor as early as January 1941. Plans were made by September, but the decision to go to war against the United States was not reached until 1 December. The attack on Pearl Harbor was decided upon the next day. The Japanese believed their strike timely, for the Germans were threatening Egypt on the North African front, Hitler's hordes were also before Moscow, the United States was committed to the defense of the Atlantic Community before the defense of the Pacific, and they might be able to seize and consolidate their hold upon Southeast Asia before the United States could act.

B. THE STRIKE. Since 1939 the United States had divided its fleet fairly evenly between the Atlantic and Pacific Oceans. On 7 December 1941, there were

86 warships at anchor in Pearl Harbor--8 battleships, 9 cruisers, 20 destroyers, 5 submarines and various auxiliaries--about a third of the striking power of the U.S. Navy and about two thirds of the major warships the United States had in the Pacific. Fortunately for the United States, no carriers were at Pearl Harbor. However, security measures in Hawaii proved slack, and the Japanese attacked with total surprise, on a Sunday, and effectively carried out their well conceived plan.

Six carriers with their support forces, Vice Admiral Chuichi Nagumo, left the Kurile Islands on 26 November and steered between Midway and the Aleutians in order to avoid detection. At 0530 7 December (Hawaiian time), from a position 239 miles north of Oahu, Nagumo launched 183 planes for his first attack wave. Wheeler Field, Hickam Field, the naval stations at Kaneohe and Bellows Field, and the Marine Air Base were hit hard. The first aerial torpedoes and bombs fell on the principal targets, the battleships moored at Ford Island, at 0755. The second wave, of 171 fighters and bombers, struck shortly after 0830, the third at 0915. Altogether, 19 warships were hit. Five battleships were sunk and three others damaged. Three destroyers, a minelayer, and a target ship were also sunk, and three cruisers, a seaplane tender, and a repair ship were damaged. At least 177 planes were destroyed as many more damaged; while casualties numbered almost 5,000, two thirds of them killed. The Japanese lost fewer than 50 planes in action and in crash landings. With few planes left on Oahu and an inadequate search plan, the Americans permitted the Japanese to escape undetected.

C. RESULTS. In less than two hours the Japanese attack so altered the balance of sea power in the Pacific that the United States was forced to assume an anxious defensive. Yet the attack has been called a "strategic imbecility." The old battleships sunk were too slow to accompany the new fast carriers. The Japanese had neglected to destroy oil storage tanks and the repair facilities on Oahu, and the American mainland with its tremendous industrial resources was untouched. More important, no carriers had been present. Most important, the attack united the American people in a vigorous prosecution of a war forced upon them.

III. GUAM AND WAKE

Guam, practically defenseless and flanked by Japanese bases to the north and south, was overwhelmed in two days, surrendering on 10 December. Wake's defenses, while weak, were better than Guam's. Indeed, the 12 Wildcat fighters and 450 Marines led by Major James P.S. Devereux, USMC, caused a Japanese invasion force to retire. Meantime Admiral Husband Kimmel, at Pearl Harbor, ordered Rear Admiral Frank Jack Fletcher to bring relief forces to Wake. But turmoil attendant the relief of Kimmel and Fletcher's slow-down to fuel en route caused the recall of the expedition when it was within 600 miles of the island. On 23 December, the Marines surrendered to an overpowering Japanese force.

IV. THE AMERICAN STRATEGY OF RETREAT AND HOLD

Japan had built up to 81 percent of American naval strength by 1941. But the United States had to divide its fleet between two oceans and had lost a good share of its naval strength at Pearl Harbor. Moreover, Japan had and the United States had not developed its Pacific islands. Therefore Japan commanded vast reaches of the Pacific early in World War II.

Committed to humbling Germany first, the United States went on the defensive in the Pacific until it could create sufficient power to shift to the offensive. Meanwhile it could dispute command of the sea by undertaking suicide missions (e.g., the ABDA forces), cutting Japanese communications (with submarines), and raiding enemy bases (with carrier forces). Once information of enemy plans for advance were obtained and American strength sufficed, the United States would seize command of the Pacific.

A. THE STRATEGY OF RETREAT. In mid-December, Admiral Chester W. Nimitz relieved Admiral Kimmel as Commander in Chief Pacific Fleet. Soon he was also Commander in Chief Pacific Ocean Areas, with responsibility for the entire Pacific except General Douglas MacArthur's South West Pacific Area.

Often it would appear that these two commands were more interested in fighting each other than the enemy. "To go between them was like passing from one autonomous feudal kingdom to another, crossing a frontier bristling with mutual antipathies and suspicions."

On 30 December, Admiral Ernest J. King, Commander in Chief United States Fleet and Chief of Naval Operations, instructed Nimitz to 1) cover and hold the Hawaii-Midway line and maintain communications with the west coast; and 2) maintain communications between the west coast and Australia by covering and holding the Hawaii-Samoa line, the latter to be extended to the Fiji Islands as early as practicable.

B. THE ALLIED RETREAT. The small American naval force in the Far East under Admiral Thomas C. Hart was to fall back from the Philippines upon the Malay Barrier when war broke out. When Japanese land-based planes from Formosa destroyed most of the U.S. Army planes on Luzon, Hart left for Australia, leaving MacArthur to delay the Japanese advance southward from Lingayen Gulf by holding out in Bataan and Corregidor. As the Japanese sped from Luzon onto Jolo and Borneo, they also thrust from Indo-China into Malaya. Two pincers, one along Malaya, the other along the west coast of Borneo, closed upon Sumatra and the rich island of Java. The British attempt to stop the Japanese advance toward Singapore cost them the battleship <u>Renown</u> and the battle cruiser <u>Prince of Wales</u> (10 December). By 19 December the Japanese had reached the Straits of Malacca. In less than two weeks, by a series of amphibious landings that met little resistance by sea or air, the Japanese were ready to spring upon the East Indies.

C. JAPAN SEIZES THE SOUTHERN RESOURCES AREA.

1. <u>The ABDA Forces</u>. British General Archibald Wavell, in command of the American, British, Dutch, and Australian (ABDA) forces in the East Indies, gave command of the naval forces therein to Admiral Hart. Difficulties of language and dissimilarity of strategic objectives precluded effective cooperation. Only one successful operation, a raid against a Japanese invasion force off Balikpapan (23 February 1942) marked the entire East Indies campaign. Japanese control of the air prevented Allied reconnaissance and left every Allied move open to Japanese view. With inferior strength, the ABDA forces could not take advantage of their interior line of position and were crushed

between the two arms of the Japanese pincers. A force under Dutch Rear Admiral Karel Doorman was repulsed when it sought action off Balikpapan (24 January), in Madoera Strait (4 February), off Banka Island (13-14 February), and in Badoeng Strait (19-20 February).

In mid-February Admiral Hart was relieved by Dutch Vice Admiral Conrad Helfrich, who was left with little but hope, for the Japanese took Timor (16 February), raided and left Darwin, Australia, useless as a naval base (19 February), and thus cut the Allied link between the East Indies and Australia. By 25 February the Japanese were poised for the assault on Java.

2. <u>Battle of the Java Sea, 27-28 February 1942</u>. On 25 February, Rear Admiral Jisaburo Ozawa, with transports, was at the Anambas Islands; Rear Admiral Shoji Nishimura, with transports and a covering force was in Makassar Strait; a small Japanese force occupied Bawean Island as an advanced observation base; and a carrier force was to the south of Java. Of two vessels bearing aircraft speeding to Helfrich from Freemantle, Australia, one, the <u>Langley</u>, was sunk, and the other, the freighter <u>Seafarer</u>, reached Tjilitjap too late.

From Surabaya, on 27 February, Doorman led his five cruisers and nine destroyers to battle. Caught between two Japanese forces, he fought his way toward the Japanese transports until he was forced to retire, with heavy losses. ABDA survivors were now divided between Surabaya and Jakarta. Of Doorman's Striking Force, only four American destroyers escaped, by slipping through Bali Strait.

3. <u>The Fall of Java</u>. By 9 March the Japanese were in complete possession of Java. The ABDA forces had been expended to gain a little time, performing magnificently against overwhelming odds. Theirs was the last defensive Allied action. The Japanese had come up against the line the United States was determined to hold, and the United States meant to strike back.

V. EARLY AMERICAN STRIKES IN THE PACIFIC: HOLD AND HIT

General Douglas MacArthur reached Darwin on 27 March and took command of the South West Pacific Area, for which the United States had already assumed responsibility. MacArthur would hold while United States submarines and carriers would strike at the most advanced Japanese position, the Gilbert Islands (taken December 1941) and Rabaul, New Britain (taken January 1942), in order to prevent a Japanese thrust against Samoa.

A. AMERICAN CARRIER RAIDS, January-February 1942. In January 1942, a *Yorktown* force, Vice Admiral Frank J. Fletcher, and *Enterprise* force, Vice Admiral William F. Halsey, Jr., prepared at Pearl Harbor to neutralize the Marshalls and Gilberts. Bad weather and a paucity of targets made the raid (1 February) only a modest success. A *Lexington* group, Vice Admiral Wilson Brown, that sought to strike Rabaul in order to prevent a Japanese attack on New Caledonia and the New Hebrides ran into Japanese bombers when within 350 miles of Rabaul and was forced back (20 February). Halsey's raid against Wake and Marcus islands (24 February and 4 March) found few targets. A Brown raid against Japanese recently landed at Lae and Salamaua, northern New Guinea, sank or damaged several ships but did not deter the troops already ashore.

B. THE JAPANESE STRIKE TOWARD INDIA. The British, meanwhile, alerted against a possible Japanese strike against India and Ceylon, gathered strong forces in Ceylon. Nagumo's carrier force raided Colombo (5 April) and Trincomalee (9 April) while Kurita's heavy surface force entered the Bay of Bengal, sinking between them four British warships and 135,000 tons of merchant shipping. The British never saw either Japanese force, but R.A.F. planes from Ceylon took such a heavy toll of Nagumo's planes and pilots that Japan could provide only two heavy carriers for the Battle of the Coral Sea in June.

C. DOOLITTLE HITS TOKYO. The most daring in the series of American carrier raids was the Halsey-Doolittle raid on Tokyo on 18 April. The 16 B-25s that took off from the *Hornet* when 650 miles off Japan hit Tokyo with little physical effect but with eventually important strategic results.

Even if they did not damage the enemy materially, these raids helped dispell the gloom engendered by Pearl Harbor and showed that the United States was fighting back. One plane narrowly missed a plane the Emperor was flying in, and Yamamoto swore revenge. Yamamoto, born in 1884, was 58 years old in 1942. He had fought in the Battle of Tsushima, studied at Harvard, knew American ways, and especially was aware of America's industrial might and that it was now or never--Japan had to have a quick, decisive victory before the United States got its productive capacity into high gear.

VI. THE JAPANESE OVEREXTENDED THEMSELVES: BATTLE OF THE CORAL SEA

A. JAPANESE EXPANSIONIST PLANS. The Japanese had conquered the Philippines, Netherlands East Indies, Burma, and Malaya in about half the time anticipated, with only a few thousand casualties, and with the loss of no naval vessel larger than a destroyer. Rather than consolidating their new empire within a defensive perimeter, they decided to exploit their advantage and extend their control in the Pacific in three steps: 1) take Port Moresby, in southeastern New Guinea, and Tulagi in the lower Solomons in order to secure the Empire in the southeast and prepare the way for an advance farther to the southeast; 2) occupy Midway and the Aleutians in order to extend Japanese defenses in the Central Pacific and force an engagement with the U.S. Fleet; 3) seize New Caledonia, Fiji, and Samoa in order to cut communications between the United States and Australia. The Halsey-Doolittle raid, by making the Japanese conscious of the lack of defenses to the east of the home islands, stimulated them to seek such defenses in Midway and the western Aleutians. Step 1 led to the Battle of the Coral Sea and Step 2 to the Battle of Midway, while Step 3 brought U.S. Marines to Guadalcanal.

B. PLANNING STEP ONE--PORT MORESBY AND TULAGI. Port Moresby would provide for the security of New Guinea and a base to neutralize Allied airfields on Australia. Tulagi would cover the flank of the Port Moresby operation and act as an advance seaplane base for a later descent upon Ocean and Nauru islands, which contained phosphates essential to Japanese agriculture, and then upon Fiji.

1. <u>Japanese Forces</u>. Because of the rugged Owen Stanley mountains, it was easier for the Japanese to go from Lae-Salamaua to Port Moresby by sea via the Jomard Passage to the east than overland. The Port Moresby forces included a large Landing Force for Port Moresby and a smaller one for Tulagi; a Support Force to support both landings; and a light carrier Covering Force to cover the Tulagi landing and then escort the Port Moresby Landing Force through Jomard Passage and also cover the landing. In addition, six submarines and land-based aircraft would scout in the Coral Sea and report any contacts with American forces to a heavy carrier Striking Force working out of Truk. Such division of forces and multiplicity of objectives is typical of Japanese strategy during most of the war. Some concentration in this operation was provided, however, by a unified command; all forces would be directed by Vice Admiral Shigeyoshi Inouye, Commander Fourth Fleet.

2. <u>American Forces</u>. The Battle of the Coral Sea occurred in MacArthur's South West Pacific Area, but the naval forces remained under Nimitz' control. Land-based aircraft and naval forces were therefore uncoordinated. Although the United States had broken the Japanese naval code and possessed the advantage of accurate and detailed intelligence of Japanese plans, only two carrier forces were available to meet the Japanese threat to Port Moresby. Already in the South West Pacific Area was Rear Admiral Frank J. Fletcher's <u>Yorktown</u> force, soon joined by Rear Admiral Aubrey Fitch's <u>Lexington</u> force from Pearl Harbor, the USS <u>Chicago</u> from Noumea, and HMAS <u>Australia</u> and <u>Hobart</u>, Rear Admiral J.C. Crace, RN, from Australia. The April raid on Tokyo kept the <u>Hornet</u> and <u>Enterprise</u> from joining in time for the battle. Nimitz left Fletcher free to decide when and where to operate.

C. THE BATTLE OF THE CORAL SEA.

1. <u>The Raid on Tulagi, 4 May 1942</u>. The two American carrier forces, under Fletcher, joined in the southeastern Coral Sea on 1 May but fueled separately. Out of visual contact with the <u>Lexington</u> group on 3 May, when he learned of the Japanese occupation of Tulagi, Fletcher decided to strike with his <u>Yorktown</u> group alone rather than summon the <u>Lexington</u> by breaking radio silence. His 141 planes consisted

of Grumman F4F Wildcat fighters and obsolescent Douglas SBD-III Dauntless dive bombers and Douglas TBD-1 Devastator torpedo-bombers. Fletcher's attack continued through 4 May, with great expenditure of ammunition, meager results, and ample illustration of the decline of efficiency under battle conditions and the lack of effective air strike coordination. Fletcher withdrew during the night and on 5 May rejoined the Lexington group, fueled, and at night closed Port Moresby. The Japanese Striking Force (carriers) meanwhile, rounded the southern end of the Solomons and on 6 May entered the Coral Sea.

2. <u>Action off Misima: Loss of the NEOSHO and SIMS</u>, <u>7 May</u>. After launching his morning search flight, Fletcher detached Admiral Crace's cruiser-destroyer force to prevent the Japanese from passing through Jomard Passage. By doing so, he weakened his screen and reduced his antiaircraft protection. The erroneous report of carriers to the northwest caused Fletcher to send his planes against what was actually a cruiser-destroyer force. Fortunately, a new contact report placed a carrier force only 35 miles from the original contact--the strike had to veer only slightly to attack the <u>Shoho</u> (Covering) Force. Thirteen bombs and seven torpedoes soon sent the little <u>Shoho</u> down. Fletcher wisely refrained from launching a second strike while the Japanese made a series of fantastic errors.

Reports reached Inouye of three carrier forces-- one was actually Fletcher's, the second Crace's cruiser-destroyer group, and the third the tanker <u>Neosho</u> escorted by the destroyer <u>Sims</u>. Land-based planes from Rabaul ineffectually attacked Crace, but Hara's large carriers (Striking Force) sent a full strike against the <u>Neosho</u> and <u>Sims</u>, eventually sinking both. The sinking of the <u>Shoho</u> finally disclosed to Hara that Fletcher was to the west, close to the Port Moresby Landing Force. His late evening searches actually passed over Fletcher without seeing him. The opposing forces were within a hundred miles of each other, but both Fletcher and Hara decided to avoid a night action.

3. <u>The Battle, 8 May</u>. The two forces found each other almost simultaneously: at 0815 they were 175 miles apart. Each force contained two carriers, each had an almost equal number of planes, some 120, but experience favored the Japanese. The battle consisted

mostly of simultaneous air strikes. Yorktown pilots found the Shokaku at about 1030. She avoided torpedo attacks but took two bombs. Lexington pilots never found the Zuikaku, which was hidden by clouds, but hit the Shokaku with three bombs which set her afire forward so that she could not launch aircraft. Able to maintain 30 knots but unable to use her flight deck, the Shokaku departed for Truk. Hara had launched 90 planes including 18 torpedo bombers, 33 bombers, and 18 fighters. Bad American fighter direction permitted them to come in unopposed to within 20 miles. The Yorktown evaded two torpedo attacks before she received several bomb near misses and one direct hit forward that did no serious damage. The resulting fires were brought under control; there was no reduction in fighting efficiency. The Lexington, however, took two torpedo hits to port and two direct bomb hits. She took a 6 degree list to port, but this was corrected by shifting oil, and her speed remained above 24 knots.

It appeared that Fletcher had won. The Lexington had been slowed, but the Shokaku had been put out of action. Fletcher could still put 49 planes into the air; Hara had only nine fit for operations. However, at 1247 an explosion of gasoline vapors from ruptured lines shook the Lexington. Frequent explosions followed. At 1956, a torpedo from an American destroyer sent her burning hulk down. The Americans still had much to learn about damage control and fighting fires.

Japanese pilots reported both American carriers sunk, and Hara so reported to his superiors. Nevertheless, feeling insecure with regard to land-based aircraft, Inouye postponed the Port Moresby invasion. Admiral Yamamoto countermanded Inouyes' withdrawal of the Striking Force and directed it to annihilate the remaining American forces. Takagi searched south and east for Fletcher, who, on Nimitz's order, had already retreated beyond reach.

4. Results. The Battle of the Coral Sea was the first carrier battle of the war and the first battle in history in which opposing ships never came within sight of each other. Tactically it was a Japanese success. The United States had lost the 33,000 ton Lexington, the Neosho, and the Sims. The Japanese lost the 12,000 ton Shoho and a destroyer and small craft at Tulagi.

Strategically, however, the Americans had won. For the first time since the war began, Japanese expansion had been checked. The Port Moresby force had not reached its objective, and Step 1 of Japan's expansion plan had been foiled. Some of the sting was taken away from the fall of Corregidor, 6 May, and the damage to the Shokaku and the need for reforming the carriers' air groups kept both large carriers out of the battle of Midway. There began the heavy attrition of Japanese land-based and carrier-based aircraft and pilots that progressively lessened Japan's military power. And the saving of Port Moresby provided a base wherefrom the Allies could begin an advance through New Guinea.

D. THE BATTLE OF MIDWAY

1. **Enter Raymond Spruance.** Step 1 of the Japanese strategic plan was to seize the Southern Resources Area and acquire forward defensive positions in the lower Solomons and at New Guinea. Even before the Japanese learned of the failure of Step 1 in the Battle of the Coral Sea, they activated Step 2--the seizure of Midway Island in June in keeping with plans made early in May. Their Intelligence was bad. They thought they had sunk both the Lexington and Yorktown and did not believe that Halsey's Hornet and Enterprise force, in the South Pacific, could intervene against them in time.

Following the launching of Doolittle's planes against Tokyo, Nimitz ordered Halsey from Pearl Harbor to support Fletcher, but on 7 May Halsey was still 1,000 miles away when the Battle of the Coral Sea was fought. He then interposed his force between the Japanese and New Caledonia, but the Japanese retreated from the Coral Sea to Rabaul. Under great stress and operating in fierce heat and humidity, Halsey developed an itchy skin disease that exacerbated his renowned ill temper. When he returned to Pearl Harbor, Nimitz ordered him to a hospital. Earlier, Halsey had written Nimitz: "Admiral Raymond Spruance has consistently displayed outstanding ability combined with excellent judgment and quiet courage. I consider him fully and superbly qualified to take command of a force comprising mixed types and to conduct protracted independent operations in the combat theater in wartime." Rather than choosing another aviator to relieve Halsey, Nimitz selected Spruance to command Task Group 16, using Halsey's staff. Senior to Spruance would be Fletcher, with Task Force 17, just returned from the Southern Pacific and needing to have the <u>Yorktown</u> repaired.

Of the Academy class of 1907, Spruance tried to do everything better than anyone else but did it in a quiet, retiring, almost shy way that attracted no attention. He served in battleships, obtained graduate instruction in electricity and engineering, and commanded destroyers and destroyer divisions, meanwhile reading widely especially in government and international relations. After refining his strategic thought at the Naval War College and serving in ONI and as executive officer of a battleship, he returned to the Naval War College to serve as head of the Correspondence Course Department, and then as head of the Tactics Section of the Department of Operations. After serving as Commander of the Tenth Naval District --changed to Caribbean Sea Frontier in 1941--he was billeted as Commander Cruiser Division Five, Pacific Fleet, USS <u>Northampton</u>, flag, at Pearl Harbor. He accompanied Halsey when the <u>Enterprise</u> delivered planes to reinforce Wake and barely missed being at Pearl Harbor when the Japanese struck. For several months he then was in Halsey's company when the latter hit the Marshalls, Wake, and Marcus, and launched Doolittle's planes against Japan. While not a pilot, he had a great respect for the capabilities of fast carriers. Would this student of the art of war do well at war itself?

2. <u>Japanese Plans</u>. On 3 June, a day before the attack on Midway,* and partly as a diversion, a carrier force would strike the Aleutians and landings would be made on Adak, Attu, and Kiska. On 4 June a large carrier force would approach Midway from the northwest, destroy its planes, and soften it up. On 5 June, occupation forces approaching from the southwest would take Midway, convert it into a Japanese base, and rename it "Glorious Month of June." When the United States fleet appeared either to defend or retake Midway, Japanese submarines placed in its path would

---

* Midway is an atoll composed of two islands, Eastern and Sand.

provide early warning and perhaps inflict some damage.
The Japanese carrier force would then attack the Americans and might get between them and Pearl Harbor, when
the heavy surface ships of the Main Body would come
from the northwest to close the pincers for the kill.
To Yamamoto, the principal value of Midway, aside
from using it as an invaluable advanced and warning
base, was to draw Nimitz out. Yamamoto knew that he
must annihilate the U.S. Fleet in 1942 or lose the
war. Had he taken his 8 carriers (400 aircraft), 11
battleships, 13 heavy cruisers, 11 light cruisers,
and more than 60 destroyers directly to Midway and
forced the Americans to give battle, no doubt he would
have won. However, although he was the great architect of Japanese carrier warfare, he hoped to destroy
the American fleet with heavy guns. Moreover, as in
the Japanese plan for Step 1, he had a dual objective,
multiplicity of forces, and a tactical dream of pincers movements and envelopment.

    Midway operations were played out on a table top
on Yamamoto's ship, the <u>Yamato</u>, for four days ending
1 May. In the game, the Red Team (U.S. Fleet) caught
Blue (Nagumo's carriers) while their planes were off
bombing Midway. Under the rules, 9 hits were scored,
the <u>Akagi</u> and <u>Kaga</u> sunk. The chief of staff hastily
reversed the umpire: six hits were erased; the <u>Akagi</u>
was refloated; and mimeograph machines began rolling
out the operation order.

3. <u>Japanese Forces</u>. Admiral Osoroku Yamamoto, Commander Combined Fleet, was in overall command of six
different Forces (fleets or air fleets). Vice Admiral
Moshiro Hosogaya's Northern Force, destined for the
Aleutians, included supply, screen, and support groups,
Rear Admiral Kakuji Kakuta's Second Striking Force,
and occupation groups for Adak-Attu and Kiska. Vice
Admiral Chuichi Nagumo's First Carrier Striking Force
(heavy carriers) would operate in the Central Pacific.
The <u>Akagi</u> was a 30,000-ton carrier, the <u>Kaga</u> even more
powerful. While the <u>Hiryu</u> and <u>Soryu</u> were listed at
10,000 tons by the old London treaty, they actually
displaced 18,000 tons. To the south and west of
Nagumo was Yamamoto's Main Force (including the 64,000
ton, 18"-gun <u>Yamato</u> as flagship). On 3 June the Main
Force detached its Guard Force (Vice Admiral Shiro
Takasu) of four battleships and two cruisers to operate

as the Aleutian Support Group; it was to be ready to
support either the Aleutians or Midway strike. Vice
Admiral Nobutake Kondo's Midway Invasion Force, with
its Main Body, included a Carrier Group, Close Support
Group, Supply Group, Screen, and Minesweeper Group,
as well as a Transport Group. As usual, a submarine
force scouted ahead, with two patrol lines designed
to cover Pearl Harbor. One group of four boats was
to lie about 500 miles west of Oahu; a second, of seven
boats, was to lie athwart the Pearl Harbor-Midway route.
These boats were to be on station by 1 June.

4. American Forces.

    a. Midway Forces. Because the United States was
decoding and reading Japanese messages, its knowledge
of Japanese plans was remarkably complete. Nimitz
knew Yamamoto's intentions, targets, and time table.
The relative paucity of American forces--3 carriers
[230 aircraft], 13 cruisers, 13 destroyers--however,
caused Nimitz to have to decide whether to let the
Aleutians go by default or to reinforce them at the
expense of the Central Pacific. He did send a small
surface force north but reserved the carriers for
Midway. Midway, too small to support sufficient
forces to repel a large-scale attack, was strengthened in every possible way. Midway proved a tactical
asset to the United States because it could accommodate more planes than a carrier, could not be sunk,
and had radar.

    b. Naval Forces. The Hornet-Enterprise force
raced from the South Pacific and arrived at Pearl
Harbor on 26 May. With a screen of five large and
one light cruiser and nine destroyers, Spruance left
Pearl Harbor on 28 May. By compressing three months'
work into three days, it was possible for the Yorktown to put to sea, on 30 May. Fletcher, the senior,
took command when the two forces joined northeast of
Midway on 2 June, and operated in separate dispositions but within supporting distance and generally
within sight of each other. Nimitz, at Pearl Harbor,
retained overall command. The three carriers and
their escorts were all the United States could assem-
ble at the time except for 19 submarines stationed to
cover the western approaches of Midway. Nimitz' orders
for the naval forces were: "You will be governed by the

principle of calculated risk, which you shall interpret to mean the avoidance of exposure of your force to attack by superior enemy forces without the prospect of inflicting, as a result of such exposure, greater damage on the enemy."

5. Japan Obtains Two Aleutian Bases

    a. **American Defense Measures.** Since Admiral Robert A. Theobald believed the Japanese meant to draw him out to the western Aleutians while they struck at the Dutch Harbor-Cold Bay area, he concentrated his force for the defense of the latter and never saw the enemy. The principal bases for his land-based aircraft (range 400 miles) were at Kodiak, Cold Bay, and Umnak. He positioned submarines and picket boats both south of Dutch Harbor and in the Bering Sea.

    b. **Japanese Operations.** Kakuta's two light carriers eluded all of Theobald's forces, struck at Dutch Harbor on the night of 2-3 June, and retired to the southwest, where Theobald failed to find them. Unable because of bad weather to reach Adak, Kakuta on 4 June struck again at Dutch Harbor; he also discovered the secret American air base at Otter Point, Unalaska. Considering it too risky to land only 350 miles from Otter Point, Hosogaya cancelled the landing on Adak. On 6 June, however, Japanese troops took Kiska and on the 7th took Attu.

6. The Japanese Attack Against Midway

    a. **3 June--First Contacts.** Midway contained about 150 aircraft, from B-17s and Catalinas to antique Buffaloes and 6 Grumman TBR Avengers that were beginning to replace the Douglas Devastator. On 1 and 2 June, carrier- and Midway-based planes swept 800 miles to the north and northwest but failed to see the Japanese. The first contact, made on the morning of 3 June, placed the enemy 500 miles to the southwest of Midway. A B-17 group attacked this occupation force but made no hits. A second contact revealed another force 700 miles to the southwest. Since these were taken to be the occupation forces proceeding from the Marianas and the main attack was expected from the northwest, the American carriers closed to 200 miles northeast of Midway and waited for dawn. B-17s and torpedo-rigged

PBYs attacked the transports throughout the night and managed to torpedo one oiler.

   b. 4 June--The Attack at Midway.

      1. Nagumo Strikes. The Japanese carriers, approaching Midway from the northwest under a frontal area, launched at 0430 when they were 240 miles away. They sent off 36 torpedo bombers (Kates), 36 dive bombers (Vals), and 36 fighters (Zekes) and prepared another 108 planes on deck, putting torpedoes on level bombers in case American ships were located. A contact report at 0507 placed Nagumo 40 miles southeast of his true position. All Midway planes took off against the carriers while the Japanese planes approached. Meeting Zekes 30 miles out, the 27 Marine fighters knocked down about a third of them, but only a dozen severely battered Marine fighters returned. Meantime everything above ground on Midway was damaged except the runways, which the Japanese intended to use.

      2. Midway Strikes Back. The B-26s and TBFs that reached Nagumo's carriers scored no hits, and most of them were shot down. Of the second strike, flown by pilots fresh from flight school, only half returned; it inflicted no damage. A flight of B-17s at 20,000 feet escaped damage and inflicted none, and a second Marine group had little success. In about three hours the Japanese had smashed Midway; without damage to any of their vessels they had accounted for half of Midway's planes. Then the American carriers entered the battle.

      3. The American Carriers Enter the Battle

         a. Spruance's Tactics. At first contact, Fletcher headed for Nagumo and ordered an attack. In determining his launching time, Spruance had to make one of the crucial decisions of the day. In carrier warfare, even more than usual in war, the side that strikes first reaps great advantages. To strike after the planes of the first wave returned and were on deck, unarmed and without fuel, was tempting, but this consideration was secondary to striking the enemy carriers before they could launch a strike at his own. He could not be sure that his task force had not been observed, and only two Japanese carriers had been reported to him while he believed they had five or six. His torpedo plane range, moreover, was only 175 miles. Last, his directive told him to attack only when the enemy carriers were "definitely located." He had originally decided to launch at 0900, when the distance had closed to 100 miles, using his entire air power. Believing that he could catch Nagumo with his planes just returning from Midway, he launched when he was 155 miles out. After his dive bombers had orbited above for an hour waiting for the launching of the torpedo planes, he told the bombers to go--thereby making it impossible to present a coordinated bomb-torpedo attack. Because the contact report on Nagumo's position was erroneous, furthermore, his torpedo planes were low on fuel when they finally found him. When it was suggested that they return for fuel, Spruance interposed a veto and ordered an attack lest surprise be lost.

    b. <u>Nagumo's Dilemma</u>. Nagumo had sent only half of his planes against Midway; the rest were armed with torpedoes for use against surface ships. When another strike against Midway was deemed necessary and his search planes revealed no American carriers, he issued the fateful order to his second wave to remove torpedoes and reload with bombs. Thirteen minutes later one of his search planes reported the American force 200 miles to the Northeast. Nagumo turned toward his enemy and ordered those planes still carrying torpedoes to retain them. He was prevented from launching immediately, however, because he was under air attack, his force was in turmoil because the submarine <u>Nautilus</u> had fired torpedoes toward one of his battleships, and the returning first strike had to be recovered. By the time he was ready to launch, American planes were upon him. Experienced Zeke pilots easily shot down almost all of the torpedo planes.

    c. <u>Destruction of the First Carrier Striking Force</u>. Preoccupied with the low-flying torpedo planes, however, the Japanese forgot to look up and permitted an <u>Enterprise</u> dive bomber strike to close in. The carriers <u>Akagi</u> and <u>Kaga</u> were set afire while <u>Yorktown</u> bombers hit the <u>Soryu</u> also, starting fires. Four hits on the <u>Hiryu</u> later in the day accounted for the last Japanese carrier. All four Japanese carriers were destroyed. In 191 sorties, carrier-based dive bombers had made 32 hits, 15 of them vital in the destruction of the four Japanese carriers and Mikuma and damaging the Mogami and the destroyer Arashio. In contrast, the 62 sorties made by the Seventh Air Force B-17s based on Midway made no hits whatsoever.

d. The Yorktown is Stopped. At 1000 and at 1100, before she was hit, the Hiryu sent two waves to attack the sole American carrier yet reported. Effective Combat Air Patrol (CAP) kept all but eight of the 18 bombers from reaching the Yorktown. Three bombs hit, one down the smokestack, but repairs were rapidly made and speed was maintained at 20 knots when the second wave came in. Two torpedoes hit portside amidships, and the carrier listed 26 degrees to port and stopped. After the crew was removed, a destroyer stood by.

7. Withdrawal and Pursuit

a. Night Counsels.

1. Japanese Decisions. Despite the loss of his carriers, Yamamoto decided to proceed with his operation. He ordered Kondo to join with his Main Body of the Invasion Force and prepare for a night surface engagement. By midnight, however, he had to face facts. He had lost four fast carriers and their 250 planes. He had not learned until 1300 that there were three American carriers. These, reduced to two, were now on a northeasterly course, with little likelihood of their being forced into a surface action. Indeed, were he to continue eastward he would be within range of their air strikes by dawn. Therefore he cancelled the Midway operation and withdrew to the west.

2. The American Situation. That the air action of the day had decided the Battle of Midway was not yet apparent to the Americans. They had lost the Yorktown and their plane losses had been heavy; few planes remained on Midway, and at 0130, 5 June, a submarine began to shell the island as though in preparation for a landing. After abandoning the Yorktown (later sunk on 7 June), Fletcher shifted to the cruiser Astoria and turned tactical command over to Spruance, who would now have to make the important decisions.

b. 5 June--The Pursuit. Spruance rejected a night

encounter and wished to be in position in the morning of 5 June either to attack retreating enemy forces or to break up a landing attack on Midway. Had he continued westward he would have been caught between Kondo, coming north, and Yamamoto, coming south. But he wisely turned east at midnight. At 0930 on 5 June he was 50 miles north of Midway, with major Japanese units 200 miles to the northwest. At 1125 he turned northwest for a stern chase. At about 0200 the submarine <u>Tambor</u> had caused the heavy cruisers <u>Mogami</u> and <u>Mikuma</u> to maneuver evasively, collide, and trail oil. Strikes from Midway increased the damage to the <u>Mikuma</u>. However, no other important Japanese forces were sighted by Spruance's search planes during the pursuit of 5 June.

  c. <u>6 June--Last Contacts</u>. Early on 6 June, Spruance's planes sank the <u>Mikuma</u> and knocked the <u>Mogami</u> out of the war for two years. By evening Spruance's pilots and crews were exhausted. Most of his destroyers had retired to fuel, and Wake Island was only 400 miles ahead (bombers could reach 600 miles). Therefore Spruance turned east to his first fueling rendezvous since 31 May. Yamamoto, meanwhile, had sent a strong surface force against Spruance which would have caught him had he not turned east when he did. On 7 June Yamamoto attempted to decoy Spruance into approaching aircraft and submarine traps near Wake, but Spruance spurned the bait. When he proceeded north on 11 June toward a second Yamamoto trap, Nimitz got suspicious and recalled him to Pearl Harbor.

8. <u>Results of Midway</u>

  a. <u>For the Japanese</u>. Midway was a contest of air power, one in which the Japanese never had the chance to use their superiority in surface ships. For the Japanese it was the first major defeat since the 16th century. Sunk were four carriers and one heavy cruiser; downed or sunk with their carriers were 253 planes; lost were 3,500 men, including 100 first-line pilots. The Japanese concealed their defeat from responsible officials as well as from their public, but they could not hide the fact that the tide had turned, that the United States could now take the offensive at will. Mistakes made by the Japanese included: 1) their multiplicity of scattered forces, which made cooperation and mutual support impossible; 2) their failure to achieve surprise; 3) their pursuit of divided objectives; 4) inadequate screening of their carriers; 5) the lateness of the positioning of their submarines between Pearl Harbor and Midway; and 6) the strategic blunder of depending on the enemy to make mistakes. Nevertheless, the Japanese still had their Fleet, minus its carriers, and they had occupied Attu and Kiska--temporarily.

    b. **For the United States**. Through prompt and intelligent exploitation of knowledge of Japanese plans the United States achieved surprise. Spruance's tactical decisions were sound, his performance superb. Although the Americans revealed a more professional touch than at the Coral Sea, they could have done better: their naval air scouting and communications could have been better; more damage could have been inflicted had Yamamoto's retreat been learned earlier; better damage control might have saved the Yorktown; the performance of carrier-based planes and of American torpedoes paled in comparison with the Japanese; and their land-based aircraft proved disappointing. In addition to the Yorktown, the United States lost one destroyer, 150 planes, and 307 men. American planes and pilots were expendable, however, and the Japanese pilots were certainly not. Having won a strategic victory to rank with Salamis, Lepanto, and Trafalgar, the United States could replace its strategy of the offensive-defensive with that of the aggressive defensive.

CHAPTER 20

WORLD WAR II IN THE PACIFIC:
THE CAMPAIGN AGAINST RABAUL

I. STRATEGIC PLANNING FOR THE RABAUL CAMPAIGN

A. JAPANESE PLANS. The Japanese had drawn one defense line from the Kuriles through the Malay Archipelago and westward to Burma, another in the southeast through the Solomons, with Rabaul, New Britain, the nerve center and major base. From the latter they planned to cut the United States-Australia line by extending into the Fiji Islands, New Caledonia, Port Moresby, and Guadalcanal. The Battle of the Coral Sea spoiled their plan for Port Moresby, the Battle of Midway their plan to extend northeastward except for Attu and Kiska. They therefore went on the defensive temporarily. They cancelled the order for the invasion of New Caledonia, the Fijis, and Samoa and determined to strengthen their defensive perimeter. A cruiser-destroyer force was sent to the Bismarcks, and air strength was increased in New Guinea, the Bismarcks, and the Upper Solomons. Their navy having failed, their army would now strike from northern Papua at Port Moresby across the Owen Stanley Mountains. To cover the flank of this operation and to provide an advance base for later moves southeast, a seaplane base would be established at Tulagi and an airfield constructed on Guadalcanal.

B. AMERICAN PLANS. The results of Midway permitted the Americans to plan to block Japanese expansion by an offensive-defensive move. Admiral King's intelligent guess was that the Japanese would spring next from Rabaul. In order to counter moves from Rabaul against the United States-Australia supply line and to provide a springboard for an Allied drive through the Solomons and the Bismarcks, King ordered a base built on Efate, New Hebrides, and established a new South Pacific Force and Area under Vice Admiral Robert L. Ghormley. Ghormley immediately ordered the construction of another New Hebrides base at Espiritu Santo.

General MacArthur, meanwhile, suggested the capture of Rabaul by a series of swift attacks along New Guinea and up the Solomons. To avoid building airfields for Army Air Force bombers, he wanted Nimitz's carriers to cover his flanks. King and Nimitz did not see carriers as expendable; they would not provide them as targets for land-based air and submarines in the confined waters of the Solomons. Nor would they tie these mobile strategic forces to MacArthur's troops. King's proposal of a step by step plan was approved instead (2 July 1942). Operation Watchtower, under the strategic command of Nimitz, called for the occupation of the Santa Cruz Islands, Tulagi, and of adjacent areas (Phase I). Then strategic command would pass to MacArthur, who would coordinate a naval move up the Solomons with an army thrust on Papua against Salamaua and Lae (Phase II). The pincers would then close on Rabaul (Phase III).

II. THE OCCUPATION AND HOLDING OF GUADALCANAL

A. HENDERSON FIELD TAKEN. Admiral Ghormley would exercise strategic control of Operation Watchtower; Admiral Fletcher had tactical command of the Expeditionary (carrier) Force; Rear Admiral Richmond Kelly Turner would command the Amphibious Force; and Major General Alexander A. Vandegrift would command the 1st Marine Division, which would make the assault. Discovery of the Japanese airstrip on Guadalcanal forced the inclusion of that island in the operation, to which only a month was devoted for planning and training. D-day was set for 7 August, with the Guadalcanal airstrip the major strategic objective. The Japanese landing on Buna late in July pleased the Americans because it revealed the Japanese intent upon Papua rather than upon the Solomons.

Ghormley remained at Noumea. He never saw his fleet or discussed plans with his top commanders, and Fletcher caused consternation by stating that he would not support the operation beyond the fourth day. On 7 August, the Marines landed on Lunga Point, Guadalcanal, while Fletcher's carriers stayed south of the island. By the evening of 8 August the future Henderson Field was taken; but the commitment of reserves to take the Tulagi-Tananbogo-Gavutu area precluded the execution of plans for the Santa Cruz Islands phase of the operation.

The Japanese quickly sent air attacks against Turner and Fletcher. While these were repulsed with small American losses, they slowed the unloading of the transports. Turner decided to stay on for two more days until he learned that Fletcher was eager to withdraw and that a Japanese surface force was heading down "the Slot" through the major Solomons. He decided to pull out on 9 August. He was discussing withdrawal with Vandegrift and British Rear Admiral V.A.C. Crutchley when the Japanese entered "Ironbottom Sound" for the first of many naval battles in the Guadalcanal area, the Battle of Savo Island.

B. BATTLE OF SAVO ISLAND, 9 AUGUST 1942.

1. *The Japanese Achieve Surprise.* Admiral Gunichi Mikawa came down the Slot with five heavy and two light cruisers and a destroyer. At about 0100 he passed through the passage between Cape Esperance and Savo Island and entered the Sound. The Allied forces were divided into a North Force, patrolling between Florida Island and Savo, a South Force, patrolling between Savo and Guadalcanal, and an East Force, guarding the eastern end of the Sound. Picket destroyer <u>Blue</u>, west of Savo, failed to see Mikawa. Since warnings from other ships either failed to reach Turner or were neglected by the force commanders, Mikawa achieved complete surprise. Steering first toward the South force, he blew the bow off the <u>Chicago</u> and sank the <u>Canberra</u>. Splitting into two divisions, he turned North. Using intelligence provided by observation planes he had launched earlier, he caught the North force between his columns, searchlights on, guns blazing. All three American heavy cruisers, the <u>Vincennes</u>, <u>Astoria</u>, and <u>Quincy</u>, were soon afire and sinking. At 0220 Mikawa ordered withdrawal, smashing the destroyer <u>Ralph Talbot</u> on his way out.

2. *Results.* Mikawa had not reached his objective, Turner's transports, but he had sunk four American cruisers and killed a thousand Americans. He withdrew because he wished to be out of carrier aircraft range by dawn, all his torpedoes were expended, and an American shell had destroyed the chart house on his flagship. He had done well and would not tempt fate a second time. The Americans were defeated because their ships had not been in the proper condition of readiness to meet a sudden night attack; failed to realize the implications of enemy planes sighted before Mikawa's attack; depended too much on the destroyer pickets' radar; had poor reconnaissance and communications; and were tired and confused. Moreover, Fletcher's early withdrawal precluded the use of planes in the battle.

C. BATTLE OF THE EASTERN SOLOMONS, 22-25 AUGUST 1942.

   1. *Japanese Plans to Recapture Guadalcanal.*
With the arrival of F4Fs and SBDs on Henderson Field, the tide began to turn in favor of the Allies. The Japanese drive to recapture Guadalcanal precipitated six sea battles and three important land battles. The Japanese failed because of bad strategy, bad tactics, and faulty Intelligence. At first they lacked sufficient troops for an immediate attack. Nor would they commit their fleet in an engagement with the Allied Fleet in the Coral Sea. They planned to put men ashore and recapture the airfield, send carrier planes to win local control over the air, and then move the fleet in to assume command of the waters around Guadalcanal--a topsy-turvy procedure. Moreover, they concentrated on Papua until Guadalcanal was too strong to retake, and their land and sea tactics proved so inflexible that the Allies were able to predict their moves and achieve surprise themselves.

   2. *The Japanese Attack.* From Rabaul came Rear Admiral Raizo Tanaka with an Occupation Force of 1,500 men. As a Support Force, Vice Admiral Nobutake Kondo proceeded from Truk with two large screening units, one including the large carriers *Shokaku* and *Zuikaku*, the other the light carrier *Ryujo*, to guard Guadalcanal. On 23 August, just as Tanaka and Kondo reached the edge of an overcast that concealed their advance, Fletcher sent the *Wasp* to fuel and took station 100 miles east of Guadalcanal with the *Enterprise* and *Saratoga*. On 24 August, in clear weather, Tanaka was 250 miles north of Guadalcanal and Kondo 40 miles to his east. Far ahead was the light carrier *Ryujo*, which was to send all her planes to neutralize Henderson Field and remain as a defenseless decoy for Fletcher while the *Shokaku* and *Zuikaku* attacked him. Fletcher took the bait and sank the *Ryujo*, but he wisely retained an outsized CAP for his two carriers. Learning of the large Japanese carriers, and hoping to divide the enemy, Fletcher separated his carriers. His CAP got most of Kondo's planes, although three got through and slowed the *Enterprise* to 24 knots. Meanwhile his planes missed the Japanese carriers and hit a seaplane carrier instead. Kondo retired but "Tenacious Tanaka" kept boring in until Henderson bombers and B-17s from Espiritu Santo drove him off. Although hampered by poor radio discipline on the part of his fighter pilots and by insufficient radio channels to permit effective

fighter direction, Fletcher lost only 17 planes from all causes, but he had won the battle only because the Japanese had been more timid than he. The two big carriers he left afloat gave plenty of trouble later. So did the Japanese failure to follow the advice of a participant in the battle that "Gradual reinforcement of landing forces by small units, subjects all of the troops involved to the danger of being destroyed piecemeal. Every effort must be made to use large units all at once."

D. BATTLE OF CAPE ESPERANCE, 11-12 OCTOBER 1942.

    1. The "Tokyo Express." Darting into Ironbottom Sound by night, the "Tokyo Express" would land small detachments of troops, lob shells at Henderson Field, and be out of reach of American bombers by dawn. The Japanese controlled the Sound by night, the Allies by day. Japanese submarines fared well against Allied ships guarding the line of communications between Guadalcanal and Espiritu Santo. The Saratoga took a torpedo from a Japanese submarine on 31 August; two weeks later two submarines torpedoed the Wasp, North Carolina, and the destroyer O'Brien; and on 20 October the heavy cruiser Chester was damaged. The Saratoga was repaired in three months, and the North Carolina was repaired, but the Wasp and O'Brien had to be abandoned, leaving the Hornet and Washington to guard the whole Pacific. At this time the Japanese, stopped by MacArthur when only 32 miles from Port Moresby, decided to give up their Papuan objective and concentrate on Guadalcanal. When the Tokyo Express ran at full speed and threatened to outnumber the Americans on Guadalcanal, a Hornet-Washington force paved the way for a resupply convoy guarded by a cruiser-destroyer force under Rear Admiral Norman Scott.

    2. Scott's Night Action at Cape Esperance. On the night of 11 October Scott, south of Savo Island, capped the T of three cruisers and two destroyers coming down the Slot to cover a landing group. A Japanese cruiser and destroyer were sunk, and another cruiser was set ablaze, but one of the three American destroyers caught between the two forces was sunk and one was damaged. When the Boise used her searchlight to find a target she was knocked out of action. The American victory was accidental.

E. BATTLE OF THE SANTA CRUZ ISLANDS, 26 OCTOBER 1942.

1. *Japanese Prepare for Battle*. Despite the lack of special landing craft, the Tokyo Express built up Japanese forces on Guadalcanal to a peak of 29,000 men by mid-October. Confident that Henderson Field would now be taken, Kondo came down from Truk to within 300 miles of Guadalcanal with the largest force seen since Midway: five carriers, five battleships, 14 cruisers, and 44 destroyers. American morale was lifted with the replacement of the unaggressive Ghormley by Halsey. Saying "Jesus Christ and General Jackson! This is the hottest potato they ever handed me," Halsey (18 October) promised Vandegrift full support.

Halsey had two carriers, two battleships, 9 cruisers, and 24 destroyers. He ordered the *Washington* force to stop the Tokyo Express and sent Kinkaid to relieve Fletcher. Kinkaid took station northeast of Guadalcanal with the *Hornet* and *Enterprise*. When the Marines stopped the Japanese onslaught on Henderson Field, 20-25 October, Kondo took his forces north, within striking range of Kinkaid's carriers, which were off the Santa Cruz Islands. Halsey, from Noumea, ordered Kinkaid to attack.

2. *The American Attack*. Early on the 26th, *Enterprise* search planes put two bombs on the deck of the light carrier *Zuiho*. Kondo, who had launched earlier, found the *Hornet* separated from the *Enterprise*. Concentrating on the former, he knocked it out of action while American planes simultaneously crippled the heavy cruiser *Chikuma* and damaged the *Shokaku*, putting the latter out of the war for nine months. A second attack by Kondo put three bombs onto the *Enterprise*, and a third attack damaged two other ships. Kinkaid withdrew to the southeast. Repeated air attacks on the *Hornet*, now without fighter cover, resulted in forcing her abandonment.

3. *Results*. Kinkaid's tactical defeat proved a strategic victory. He had lost 74 planes and Kondo 100, aggravating the Japanese pilot replacement program. Japanese carriers never again appeared in support of the Solomons campaign, and the Americans finally learned to keep their carriers together within a strong screen, improve their fighter direction, and keep them out of confined waters. The Marines, meanwhile, by repelling the assault of 20-26 October, wiped

out the last serious troop threat to Henderson Field.

F. THE NAVAL BATTLES OF GUADALCANAL, 12-15 NOVEMBER 1942. While the Tokyo Express ran again at high speed, Admiral Tanaka prepared to bring a 13,500 troop reinforcement down from the Shortlands with a battleship-cruiser group in support and Kondo's carriers to provide air cover from the north. Kondo, however, was ordered to avoid a naval engagement. Stripping his island garrisons, Halsey sent all the reinforcements he could find to Guadalcanal, and by order of President Roosevelt all possible ships and planes flocked to the South Pacific. Halsey ordered Kinkaid not to take the Enterprise north of Guadalcanal. Both Yamamoto and Halsey were determined to secure Guadalcanal in November.

1. The First Battle. Kinkaid was still two days' journey from Guadalcanal when Turner learned that Kondo was sending a battleship-cruiser force under Vice Admiral Hiroaki Abe to bombard Guadalcanal while Tanaka raced down from the Shortlands. Turner sent Rear Admiral Daniel J. Callaghan, with five cruisers and eight destroyers, against Abe's two battleships, one cruiser, and 14 destroyers.

Callaghan entered Ironbottom Sound from the east on Friday, 13 November. He had no battle plan, did not provide for scouting ahead, and made poor use of radar. When he spotted Abe, who entered from the west, he turned north, perhaps seeking to cross the "T". His leading destroyers, however, spied Abe's destroyer scouts, swung out of line, and threw the van into disorder. In the melee which ensued, the most desperate sea fight since Jutland, ships fired on friend and foe. Abe lost two destroyers and the battleship Hiei. Callaghan and Scott were killed; four American destroyers and the cruiser Atlanta were lost; a cruiser and a destroyer were rendered unnavigable; and the Juneau was torpedoed and sunk while retiring. Nevertheless, the American objective was achieved, for Abe retired and Tanaka's Occupation Force returned to base.

2. The Second Battle. But the Japanese were not through. On 14 November, Tanaka once more approached Guadalcanal, with Mikawa (4 heavy and 2 light cruisers, and 6 destroyers) in support and Kondo (2 carriers, 2 battleships, one heavy cruiser) operating at extreme range to the north. Despite the loss of seven of his

transports during the forenoon, Tanaka kept on with his
remaining four and his eleven destroyers. While Mikawa
was blasting Henderson Field in the early hours of 14
November, Rear Admiral Willis A. Lee was steaming north
with the Washington-South Dakota force detached from
the Enterprise group. Mikawa lost one cruiser and had
three cruisers and a destroyer crippled by air strikes
as he retired. That night, Kondo's bombardment group
attacked Lee south of Savo Island, sinking two destroyers and damaging two more. The Washington and South
Dakota were separated by a power failure on the latter.
Lee, an expert in radar-controlled gunfire, used the
Washington to knock out the battleship Kirishima and a
destroyer and to protect his damaged ships. Kondo
gave up, but Tanaka persisted until he had beached his
four shattered transports on Guadalcanal, where they
were destroyed. Japan's last attempt to reconquer
Guadalcanal had failed. Henceforth Yamamoto risked
no capital ships in the defense of the Solomons. The
South Dakota had to return to the United States for
repairs but Turner's reinforcement group reached Guadalcanal while Tanaka's was lost. Henceforth the United
States took the offensive and the Japanese the defensive in the Solomons. Churchill chose this moment,
when MacArthur landed near Buna, the Allies invaded
North Africa, and Guadalcanal appeared secure, as "the
end of the beginning."

G. THE BATTLE OF TASSAFARONGA, 30 NOVEMBER 1942.

    1. Kinkaid's Tactics. Halsey now assigned Kin-
kaid's new cruiser-destroyer force the task of stopping Tanaka's Tokyo Express. Kinkaid provoked a
reformation in tactics. His battle plan for night
action called for a) the use of float planes for early
warning and parachute flare illumination; b) a full-
speed destroyer attack in which ships would turn away
outboard after firing torpedoes at the enemy's flanks;
and c) cruiser fire from an optimum 12,000 yards to
commence when the torpedoes hit or it was evident that
the enemy was alerted. Kinkaid, detached, left Rear
Admiral Carleton Wright to execute his plan.

    2. The Battle. On the night of 30 November,
Admiral Tanaka again entered Ironbottom Sound from
the west with eight destroyers. Wright entered via
the eastern channel and was proceeding west, unaware
of Tanaka because a calm precluded the use of float

planes. When he spotted Tanaka, Wright turned to parallel his course but failed to send his destroyers out. Tanaka sped along the coast of Guadalcanal on opposite course, then reversed course and split into divisions, each of which fired torpedoes at the extended American track. Four of the five American cruisers were hit, and one went down. The Japanese used superior optical equipment and were so well trained in night tactics that none fired a gun except the <u>Takanami</u>, which was sunk. American fire had been most inaccurate; destroyers had been tied to the cruisers; cruisers had been tied in column instead of maneuvering independently to avoid torpedoes; and star shells failed to operate. This defeat caused the Americans to restudy night tactics and to adopt Kinkaid's plan as standard practice. Good American damage control saved three cruisers.

H.   ENTER ARLEIGH BURKE.   Burke, (USNA, 1923), was no "slash"; he admittedly had to study hard to avoid bilging, and for a Class A offense while a first classman he lost so many numbers it took him thirty years to regain them.   By 1943 he had 20 years of service and a Master's Degree in Engineering, but he was stuck as inspector of the antiaircraft and broadside mounts manufactured at the Naval Gun Factory, in Washington, rather than commanding a destroyer, in which he excelled.   His superior in the Bureau of Ordnance simply would not let him go.   Befriended by a secretary, he received orders as the commodore of Destroyer Division 43, soon to gather in the South Pacific.   By the time he reached the Solomons, in February 1943, six naval battles had been fought.   In the battle of Tassafaronga, particularly, the Japanese had performed brilliantly with their "long lance" Model 93 torpedo, which could run true up to 11 miles at almost 50 knots and up to 22 miles at 36 knots, and carried a 1,000-lb. payload, or twice that of the American Mark XV.   After studying numerous battle reports, Burke recommended to his superiors as doctrine for his four destroyers that "When contact with an enemy force is made destroyers in the van should initiate a coordinated torpedo attack WITHOUT ORDERS."   Relying upon the competence of his captains, he would trust their initiative while retaining full responsibility for their operations.   Listening carefully was Rear Admiral Aaron S. "Tip" Merrill, commander TF 68, with whom he first operated and from whom he in turn learned much that was useful to him as "ComDesSlot," i.e., in charge of destroyers seeking to wreck the Tokyo Express in The Slot. Promoted to captain and to commodore of Destroyer Squadron 43, with Merrill having a large hand in the matter, Burke would show his mettle at the Battle of Empress Augusta Bay and at the Battle of Cape St. George. Among Burke's captains was DeWitt Clinton Ellis "Ham" Hamberger (USNA, 1926), who while on the <u>Converse</u> was the first to establish a fighter director group in the Pacific and with another Burke captain, Henry Jacques "Heine" Armstrong (USNA, 1927), created a CIC for destroyers.

I. GUADALCANAL AND PAPUA SECURED.

    1. <u>Guadalcanal Secured</u>. Major General Alexander M. Patch, USA, with 50,000 troops, took over the defense of Guadalcanal early in January 1943. The Japanese had an equal number of troops at Rabaul, but American PT boats and aircraft rendered the Tokyo Express inoperative and Tokyo finally concluded to abandon Guadalcanal. Though the Japanese struck by air, Patch managed to squeeze the remaining Japanese on the island into a pocket. However, the Tokyo Express went into reverse and evacuated the last 12,000 troops to end the Guadalcanal campaign. These troops and fresh ones served to consolidate airfields and bases on islands to the northwest. Moreover, land-based and carrier-based air was sent to restock Rabaul and forward airfields were built on New Georgia and Kolombangara.

    2. <u>Papua Secured</u>. A thousand miles west of Guadalcanal, the Allies had been experiencing similar success. Allied planes had raided the Japanese trail from Lae-Salamaua to Port Moresby and reduced the Japanese to starvation. MacArthur's Americans and Australians had then launched a counterattack and also obtained a position southeast of the Japanese at Buna. While PT boats cut into Japanese attempts to evacuate troops in Buna by sea, MacArthur's troops moved forward with supplies dropped by airlift. Late in January 1943, Buna was in Allied hands. Two roads toward Rabaul, one from Papua, one from Guadalcanal, were now open.

    III. THE CENTRAL SOLOMONS AND HUON PENINSULA

A. STRATEGY IN THE PACIFIC.

1. <u>The New Fleet System</u>. In March 1943, Admiral King inaugurated a numbered fleet system. Halsey, now wearing four stars, was put in direct command of the U.S. Third Fleet and Turner of the Third Amphibious Force. MacArthur's naval forces were designated the Seventh Fleet with Kinkaid soon in command, and with Rear Admiral Daniel E. Barbey in command of the Seventh Amphibious Force. The Central Pacific Force at Pearl Harbor, became the Fifth Fleet, under Admiral Spruance. In July, Turner left the South Pacific to organize a new Fifth Amphibious Force in the Central Pacific area.

2. <u>Central Solomons Planning</u>. Also in March 1943, King issued his task for Phase II in the Pacific War. MacArthur would control Huon Gulf and Peninsula and invade New Britain while Halsey would invade Bougainville and establish airfields thereon for the aerial pounding of Rabaul. To acquire the necessary forward bomber fields, MacArthur would occupy Kiriwina and Woodlark Islands and Halsey would invade the Central Solomons. Halsey would be operating at times in MacArthur's area of responsibility, but since Halsey answered to Nimitz, there was no supreme commander for the campaign against Rabaul. King, moreover, questioned the need of capturing Rabaul. Why not neutralize it, bypass it, break the Bismarcks barrier, and capture the Admiralties beyond?

3. <u>The Central Pacific Drive</u>. The Joint Chiefs' planners rejected MacArthur's plan for a one-track drive along the Papua-western New Guinea-Palau-Philippines line in favor of a dual thrust. A simultaneous northern drive through the Central Pacific would protect MacArthur's right flank, perhaps provoke the Japanese into a fleet engagement, speed up the cutting of Japan's communications with the Southern Resources Area, and place the Americans in position for an early attack on Japan itself. The Combined Chiefs approved both thrusts in May. The advantages of a dual approach lay in keeping Japan off balance and constantly under pressure, driven to divide its forces, and in doubt as to the point of the next attack. Furthermore, concentration could be effected: one force would hold while the other hit.

B. THE DEVELOPMENT OF SURFACE ATTACK DOCTRINE. Strategy involving the use of exterior lines of position was made possible by adequate American shipbuilding, aircraft, and training programs. In addition, a tactical revolution made it possible for American naval forces to successfully counter Japanese night tactics. The leaders in this revolution were men like Frederick Moosbrugger, Arleigh Burke, and Stanton Merrill, who studied <u>Battle Experience</u> reports written after each engagement with the Japanese. Also important was the effective training of personnel in the use of radar, now installed as standard equipment and a vital part of the new Combat Intelligence Center. Convinced that radar and C.I.C. permitted them to control divided forces at night, the Moosbrugger-Burke-Merrill school trained their forces in night tactics and perfected the employment of quasi-independent destroyer tactics. Destroyers would attack the flanks of enemy columns, fire torpedoes, and turn away outboard while cruisers capped the "T." Gunfire would commence simultaneously on all ships once the torpedoes hit. The procedure would be repeated as long as necessary.

C. INVADING THE CENTRAL SOLOMONS. The first step in implementing Phase II was the occupation of the Russell Islands, 65 miles northwest of Guadalcanal. From new airstrips, bombers could reach the Japanese fields on Munda Point, New Georgia Island, and Vila Field, Kolombangara Island. Surface and air bombardment of these fields by Army, Navy, and Marine Corps planes continued while Japanese communications were complicated by air attacks on their shipping and submarines in the Bismarcks area, and the mining of waters about New Georgia and Bougainville. By 1 April, moreover, Allied air forces, reorganized as Air Command Solomons (Airsols), operated from new bomber and fighter bases on Guadalcanal. With General George C. Kenney's Fifth Army Air Force from New Guinea, Airsols in a few months won command of the air over the whole eastern New Guinea-Solomons-Bismarcks area.

Allied expansion into the Central Solomons forced the Japanese to withdraw Rabaul's defenses to the Salamaua-Munda airfield line. Defense of the Central and Upper Solomons was entrusted to Vice Admiral Jinichi Kusaka. Kusaka's night-running Tokyo Express from Rabaul was now exposed to the open sea in daylight to Kenney's air force. When a convoy of eight transports screened by eight destroyers was lost to Kenney's planes in early March (Battle of the Bismarck Sea), the Japanese abandoned troop convoys and resorted to the use of barges or submarines from the Cape Gloucester area. Yamamoto, alarmed, proceeded to Rabaul to direct an all-out air offensive. He knocked out several Allied ships and planes at the cost of many first line pilots and rendered the Imperial Fleet even less battle-worthy than before, and he himself was shot down by Airsols P-38s when he undertook a tour of the defenses of the Upper Solomons. His successor, Admiral Mineichi Koga, further depleted pilot strength by inept raids against the Allies.

1. Munda Airfield, 30 June 1943. Possession of Munda Airfield would enable the Allies to remove a major threat both to Guadalcanal and to an advance westward, and place them in closer bombing distance of Vila Field, Kolombangara, and of Rabaul. After taking Rendova Island, Turner's Third Amphibious Force placed guns on the island, turned them on Munda, and so covered the march of troops on the airfield itself. Japanese troops holed up in strong defenses stretched a four-day campaign into one lasting six weeks, and another six weeks were spent in mopping up.

Nevertheless, the Allied "island hopping" program got underway by bypassing reinforced Kolombangara and striking instead at lightly held Vella Lavella on 15 August. Here Rear Admiral Theodore Wilkinson, who had succeeded Turner, chose to land on an undefended beach, construct a defensive perimeter about an airstrip, and send his troops out to drive the enemy away. Wilkinson's end-run, by rendering Kolombangara impotent and threatening Bougainville, caused the Japanese to refuse to commit more troops to the defense of the Central Solomons. They evacuated nine-tenths of their 10,000 man force from Kolombangara but ran into trouble when they tried to evacuate their 600 men from Vella Lavella.

2. Battles of Kula Gulf, 5-6 July, and of Kolombangara, 12-13 July 1943. In twice attempting to thwart the resurrected Tokyo Express, Admiral Walden L. Ainsworth used the customary night-time disposition, cruisers in center and destroyers in van and rear, and the Kinkaid tactical plan. He failed because he had radar but came in close, into visual range; he withheld fire too long and permitted the Japanese to aim torpedoes carefully at the point where his cruisers would reverse course; his radar operators concentrated on the largest and nearest targets instead of effectively distributing their fire; and he was not alert against counterattack,

not knowing that the Japanese had a torpedo reloading device aboard. In two battles, Ainsworth got only one Japanese cruiser and one destroyer and lost one cruiser and one destroyer, and suffered damage to three cruisers, but he had proved the value of the new night surface tactics.

3. <u>Battle of Vella Gulf, 6-7 August and of Vella Lavella, 6-7 October 1943</u>. In early August, Admiral Wilkinson ordered Commander Moosbrugger's destroyer division to stop the Tokyo Express to Vila. Using Kinkaid-Burke tactics, Moosbrugger achieved a little classic. Approaching four Japanese destroyers on reverse course, he sent one division ahead to fire torpedoes and his second to cross the "T." When the torpedoes struck, both divisions opened fire, with the result that three of the enemy destroyers exploded. Because the torpedo under it failed to explode, the fourth got away. The Japanese lost three destroyers and 1,800 men; Moosbrugger's force was unhurt and Burke applauded the "beautiful attack."

Two months later, Captain Frank R. Walker, with three destroyers, ran across six Japanese destroyers attempting to evacuate Kolombangara. He sank the <u>Yugumo</u> but lost one destroyer and had another damaged. The Japanese succeeded in evacuating Vella Lavella, but they had won their last battle of World War II. Their victory, however, did not conceal the fact that the Allies now controlled the Central Solomons. Indeed, between June and October the Japanese lost about 700 planes and crews in daylight action. Their subsequent resort to night bombing and torpedo attacks proved ineffective. Conversely, Airsols launched 3,259 sorties during October with only 26 plane losses.

D. HUON PENINSULA. While Kenney's Air Force pounded Salamaua, Lae, and Finschhafen, MacArthur moved into Kiriwina and Woodlark Islands and into Nassau Bay. Hopping at night by sea, Admiral Daniel E. Barbey's amphibious forces joined with MacArthur's Americans and Australians near Salamaua. The Japanese pleased MacArthur by reinforcing Salamaua from Lae, for Barbey placed 8,000 Australians between Salamaua and Lae. When the Allies closed in on Lae, the Japanese abandoned Salamaua and sought to hold Lae. Finding this impossible, they moved northward along the Huon Peninsula. Barbey thereupon landed troops ahead of them at

Finschhafen and pushed the Japanese inland. MacArthur was now in control of northeast New Guinea from Milne Bay to Vitiaz Strait, his rapid advance made possible in great part by a touch of sea power that enabled him to land troops where there would be no Japanese resistance. While he took Finschhafen and consolidated his position during the summer, Barbey's destroyers hunted submarines in and about Huon Gulf and Kenney's Air Force reduced Japanese air power on fields now brought within striking distance.

IV. RABAUL NEUTRALIZED AND BYPASSED

A. CHANGES IN PHASE III STRATEGY. The strategic picture in the South Pacific changed abruptly when the decision was made to neutralize and bypass Rabaul instead of capturing it. Phase III would proceed in three steps: 1) MacArthur's Fifth Air Force would launch a series of heavy attacks on Rabaul; 2) Halsey would invade Bougainville in order to establish airfields closer to Rabaul, and 3) Cape Gloucester would be captured in order to secure the eastern side of Vitiaz Strait.

B. BOUGAINVILLE.

   1. *Planning the One-Two Punch*. On 2 October, Wilkinson, Merrill, Frederick C. Sherman, Burke, and others met at Koli Point, Purvis Bay, where Halsey briefed them on the impending campaign to rout the Japanese out of Bougainville. Merrill and Burke would cover assault forces landed in Empress Augusta Bay. Burke's ships, now in DesRon23, were identified by the insignia of an Indian boy with bow, arrow, quiver, and a phallic symbol of huge proportions--and henceforth were known as the Little Beavers. They were to bombard enemy installations, repel the expected Japanese surface attack, and then cover the withdrawal of transports. Burke explained his "one-two punch" destroyer doctrine to Merrill. His DesDiv 45 would launch a torpedo attack and turn away while DesDiv 46 covered. After he turned away, he would open fire and distract the enemy so that DesDiv 46 could attack. He wanted to close to 6,000 yards before launching torpedoes and requested Merrill's permission to operate independently of his cruisers. Merrill granted permission because his cruisers were outmatched by the Japanese and Burke's torpedoes were the only weapons which could reach them.

2. The Landings, 1 November 1943. Most of the 60,000 Japanese on Bougainville were at Buin and Kahili, at the southern tip of the island, and in Buka and Bonis, at the northern end. As in the Vella Lavella operation, Halsey decided to land where the Japanese were not, in this case at Cape Torokina in Empress Augusta Bay. There the invaders would build air strips, construct a defensive perimeter about them, and await the enemy. In mid-October, Airsols strikes rendered Bougainville's airfield unusable. On the 27th, Merrill's Task Force 39 hit Buka and Bonis. While it raced to smash at the Shortlands, Sherman's Saratoga and Princeton group took over on Buka and Bonis. New Zealanders took the Treasury Islands while 700 Marines landed on Choiseul as a diversion. With the Japanese diverted, Wilkinson's amphibious forces entered Empress Augusta Bay on 1 November. Only one percent of the Americans was killed of the 7,000 who landed first, partly because Airsols fighters chased almost all Japanese aircraft away. By nightfall, 14,000 troops and 6,000 tons of supplies were on the beach. The transports pulled out, leaving four minelayers to lay a minefield north of Cape Torokina.

3. The Battle of Empress Augusta Bay, 2 November 1943. The Japanese reacted immediately by sending two heavy and two light cruisers and six destroyers under Rear Admiral Sentaro Omori to smash the landings on Bougainville and also destroy Merrill's cruisers.

Just before midnight, 1-2 November, Merrill's four cruisers entered Kula Gulf, Burke in the van, Commander Bernard "Count" Austin astern. Contact was made at 30,000 yards at 0227 on 2 November. Merrill's plan was to block the entrance to Empress Augusta Bay with his cruisers while his destroyers attacked the enemy's flanks. Omori approached his objective, the American minelaying group erroneously reported to him as a cruiser-destroyers group, in three columns, heavy cruisers in the center, a light cruiser in each of the other columns. A fine deployment for attacking transports, it was poor for opposing a cruiser task force. According to plan, Burke sought Omori's left flank and Austin his right flank. Burke told Merrill "I'm heading in" and fired 25 torpedoes at 5,600 yards. They missed because Omori changed course to the south. Knowing that he had been sighted, Merrill opened fire. Two of the Japanese destroyers collided, and the cruiser

Sendai was set aflame. But Burke now became separated and did not rejoin for an hour, and the Foote, also separated, was torpedoed aft. Merrill kept up his fire and for 30 minutes successfully avoided Omori's shells and torpedoes. Now Omori fired flares and robbed Merrill of his radar advantage. Sighting Merrill, Omori fired torpedoes and shells. Merrill made chemical and funnel smoke and at 1337 Omori turned away for reasons best known to himself. Austin's destroyers, meantime, failed to damage the enemy because of a series of breakdowns in communications and in recognition procedure. Burke, rejoining, sent the Sendai down and helped sink a destroyer. Merrill retired and fought off an awaited air attack that was dissipated only after the arrival of Airsols planes.

American performance in this battle was poor in respect to the accuracy and distribution of radar-controlled gunfire and recognition practice. However, Merrill had repulsed Omori from the beachhead and had demonstrated the soundness of the tactical doctrine and practice begun by Kinkaid.

C. KNOCKING OUT RABAUL.

1. *Carriers against Rabaul.* Incensed, Koga relieved Omori of his command and sent Vice Admiral Takeo Kurita from Truk with a strong cruiser-destroyer force that confronted Halsey with the most desperate emergency he faced as Commander South Pacific. But Kurita stopped to refuel in Rabaul, and Halsey rushed the Saratoga-Princeton group northward to Empress Augusta Bay and ordered Airsols to give it full support. While Airsols provided CAP for the carriers, these launched nearly a hundred planes against Rabaul. At the cost of only ten planes, the Americans put Kurita out of business by damaging 5 heavy cruisers, 1 light cruiser, and 2 destroyers. Elated, Halsey borrowed three large carriers from the 5th Fleet and struck with almost 200 planes. A 120-plane counter-attack obtained the Japanese nothing at a cost of a third of their planes. All the American carriers then left to take part in the opening of the Central Pacific drive.

2. "31-knot Burke." Burke discussed improvements in destroyer doctrine with his captains and desired to operate without cruiser protection. He

was therefore happy when Halsey directed him on 15 November to operate independently, indeed outside of air cover, and destroy any enemy units encountered or targets of opportunity near Buka, Bougainville. That task accomplished, on 24 November Burke began making passage with only five of his Little Beavers. Because of boiler trouble on the <u>Spence</u>, he set squadron speed at 31 knots instead of 35--a corrective to those who believe he obtained the nickname because he got 31 knots out of destroyers designed for 30. Burke was to prevent the Japanese from landing troops at Buka and embarking air personnel. While near the Treasury Islands he received a message from Halsey addressed to "31-knot Burke," saying, "Get athwart the Buka-Rabaul evacuation line about 35 miles west of Buka.... If enemy contact you know what to do." Burke directed that both his divisions remain on the same side of the enemy in order to avoid a melee such as that at Empress Augusta Bay.

At Buka, Captain Kiyoto Kagawa had transferred his troops. He had 5 destroyers faster and in better material condition than Burke's and 3 fast destroyer transports. Burke found him at 0140, swung to collision course, fired torpedoes at 4,500 yards, and turned away toward additional targets astern, leaving Austin to finish off the two Japanese destroyers he had hit. Unable to catch up with the three remaining fast destroyers and fire his torpedoes, Burke used his guns and did not turn back until he was within 60 miles of Cape St. George, around which lies Rabaul. He had fought the nearest thing to a perfect battle: 3 Japanese ships sunk, one damaged, and personnel losses of 1500, and no American lives lost. Soon thereafter Burke was attached to Fast Carrier Task Force 38 as chief of staff to Admiral Marc Mitscher.

    3. <u>Bougainville Secured</u>. Airsols and the Third Fleet protected Bougainville from the Tokyo Express and air attacks while Vandegrift's marines enclosed a 36 square mile defense perimeter about Cape Torokina. When the Japanese on the island finally attacked, January 1944, they did so in vain. Bougainville with its fighter and two bomber strips was secure.

    4. <u>The Score</u>. In the Solomons operation, the Japanese lost 50 warships and suffered damage to numerous others, and almost 3,000 aircraft and crews.

The loss of pilots was vitally important because U.S. pressure prevented their being trained. In contrast, by December 1943, new construction caused American carriers to outnumber Japanese by two to one and American pilots to have over a year of training.

D. MACARTHUR BREAKS THROUGH THE BISMARCKS. Airsols from Bougainville and the Fifth Air Force kept the enemy at Rabaul busy while MacArthur planned to secure the right flank of Vitiaz Strait. Not knowing that the whole Bismarcks defense system had cracked, MacArthur ordered marines onto Cape Gloucester on 1 December 1943. In less than a week the Japanese lost their airfield. As they were being chased back to Rabaul, other MacArthur groups crashed through the Bismarcks barrier by land and sea. On New Guinea, meanwhile, Australians were rolling the Japanese ever westward from Finschhafen. Using Barbey's amphibious forces, MacArthur leap-frogged to Saidor (2 January 1944), forced the Japanese to abandon Sio, and chased them as far as Madang. With Halsey sending a thousand planes a week against Rabaul and ships of the Third Fleet blasting its shore installations almost at will, Rabaul was finished.

To insure that Rabaul was through, MacArthur took the Green Islands and built a fighter strip within 115 miles of Rabaul and within range of Kavieng and Truk. With the capture of the Emirau Islands (March 1944), Rabaul was completely boxed in. Meanwhile MacArthur had captured the Admiralties, with the excellent anchorage at Manus, and was planning a giant leap-frog to Hollandia, whence he would jump to the Philippines. By March 1944, the South Pacific Area was left behind to garrison status.

E. SUMMARY. The 20-month campaign against Rabaul reduced Japanese air power to the point where it would no longer be a serious threat and gave the United States time to build and train for the Central Pacific drive of 1944. Japan lost 1,000 planes in defending New Guinea and 3,000 more in defending the Upper Solomons and Rabaul. The Japanese could still produce 1,700 planes a month, but they could not furnish enough replacement crews. Curtailed training meant increasing losses; loss of air power had left Japan's South Pacific defenses vulnerable. Having drained his carriers of most of their air strength, Koga was forced to withdraw his fleet from the Pacific. He had six months in which to train new crews to repel the American Central Pacific drive. Meanwhile the Americans had established their new timetable. MacArthur would invade Hollandia in April, Mindanao in November 1944, and Luzon in February 1945. Central Pacific forces would invade the Marianas in June, the Palaus in September 1944, and Formosa in February 1945.

CHAPTER 21

WORLD WAR II IN THE PACIFIC:

THE DUAL ADVANCE AND
THE END OF THE JAPANESE EMPIRE

I. THE UNITED STATES REGAINS THE ALEUTIANS

For more than a year American strategy demanded action against the Southern Resources Area supply line to Japan rather than against the Aleutians. However, the Aleutians were needed as bases for ferrying aircraft to Siberia once Russia entered the war, and in March 1943, the United States decided to clear out the Japanese. On 27 March 1943, Rear Admiral Charles H. McMorris, with two cruisers and four destroyers, intercepted Vice Admiral Moshiro Hosagaya, who had two transports screened by four cruisers and four destroyers. In the resulting Battle of the Komandorskis, Hosogaya bent McMorris away for about three hours. However, fear of attack by torpedoes and by Army bombers caused him to retire. On 11 May, a force commanded by Rear Admiral Francis W. Rockwell landed troops which blasted the Japanese out of the hills of Attu by the end of the month. On Kiska, however, an even more powerful force that landed in mid-August found no Japanese, for these had been evacuated by submarine three weeks earlier.

II. STRATEGY OF THE CENTRAL PACIFIC DRIVE

Naval leaders regarded MacArthur's plan to use the navy as an adjunct to an Army advance from New Guinea to the Philippines as wasteful of carrier air power. Freed from mere Army support, carriers could be used continuously to gain command of the sea over ever-increasing areas. Although advance through the Central Pacific meant the acquisition of islands by assault of heavily defended beaches, such advance would open new lines of communications and bring the war more speedily into Japanese waters. Ordered by the Joint Chiefs to plan an invasion of the Marshall Islands, Nimitz suggested the taking of the Gilberts first. The latter would provide bases for the air photographing of the Marshalls, permit land-based air support for the Marshalls operation, and open a line of communications between the Central Pacific and the

South Pacific and Southwest Pacific areas. The Joint Chiefs thereupon ordered the Gilberts to be invaded in November 1943, and the Marshalls in early 1944.

III. THE RECONQUEST OF THE GILBERTS

A. THE FIFTH FLEET: FORCES AND COMMAND RELATIONSHIPS. Power for the new drive was to be provided by Admiral Spruance's Fifth Fleet, which included six heavy, five light, and eight escort carriers, five new and seven old battleships, nine heavy and eight light cruisers, 56 destroyers, 29 transports, and ample numbers of landing craft. The new Fast Carrier Task Force, the greatest concentration of power in naval history, would raid the island target, isolate the beachhead, and provide tactical support for the assault troops by intercepting hostile air and surface forces.

For the Gilberts operation, code name Galvanic, Rear Admiral Charles A. Pownall was in command of the Fast Carriers. Major General Holland M. "Howlin' Mad" Smith, USMC, commanded the V Amphibious Corps, and Rear Admiral John H. Hoover the Fifth Fleet's land-based Air Force (army, navy and marines). Rear Admiral Richmond Kelly Turner, in command of the Fifth Amphibious Force, would control the assault troops, their vessels, and their supporting ships. To provide the Fleet with necessary logistic mobility, a completely mobile supply and maintenance squadron under Vice Admiral William L. Calhoun would set up shop in forward areas, thus freeing the combatant vessels from return to rearward fixed bases.

B. THE ASSAULT. Alerted by American carrier warmup strikes against Marcus, the Gilberts, and Wake in the late summer and fall of 1943, Admiral Koga took his Combined Fleet from Truk to the Marshalls. Deciding that the strikes were a false alarm, he retired to Truk and sent most of his carrier aircraft to defend Rabaul. Halsey chewed these up, rendering Koga's carrier fleet powerless to attack.

1. <u>Makin and Abemama, November 1943</u>. The major American objectives in the Gilberts were the atolls of Makin, Tarawa, and Abemama. Makin, hit heavily on 1 November, held out until the 24th and revealed that Army troops had not been trained realistically in the marine-style of warfare. Abemama fell to a marine

company carried by the submarine Nautilus, which also provided the gunfire support. Tarawa, however, proved tough. It furnished the testing ground for techniques that eventually carried Americans to the shores of Japan.

2. "That Real Toughie": Tarawa, 21-24 November 1943. Betio, the only fortified island in the Tarawa atoll, had 4,800 defenders dug in deeply behind and below concrete-coconut log-and sand fortifications. A coral shelf about its beaches was laced with obstacles that forced the invaders into narrow channels covered by enfilading artillery, and a four-foot barricade enclosed the airfield. In addition to about 100 machine guns, the Japanese had sited 4 heavy anti-air, 6 small coast defense, and 8 large (4 8-inch and 4 5.5-inch) coastal defense guns.

A series of errors aggravated the difficulty encountered in the form of an unwarranted neap tide which forced the invaders to leave their small craft on a coral reef and advance under murderous fire. Carrier planes arrived over target half an hour late and left early to unmask Rear Admiral Harry Hill's naval bombardment. Hill, while spectacular, used a flat instead of plunging trajectory and delivered area rather than point fire, and because smoke interfered and he did not know that the landing troops were 15 minutes late, he raised fire 15 minutes before the troops landed. Half of the Japanese were killed by his bombardment, but a third of the 5,000 Americans who reached Betio or the reef were casualties. On the next day, 22 November, carrier aircraft and call fire from ships was remarkably accurate, and on 24 November Betio was secure.

The slowness of the invasion permitted Japanese submarines to reach the Gilberts and hit the light carrier Independence and sink the escort carrier Liscombe Bay, but air attacks by planes staged to the Marshalls from Truk and Rabaul were skillfully repulsed.

3. Results. Although General H. M. Smith later said that "Tarawa was a mistake," the Gilberts operation, while costly, in a few days won control over a large area, shortened the resupply route from Pearl Harbor to the Solomons and Australia, provided land-

based air sites for reconnaissance and bombing of the Marshalls, cracked the Japanese defense perimeter, and permitted an all-out offensive along the Central Pacific axis. It also shocked the Navy into revolutionizing its support tactics and materials. Surface and air support methods were overhauled to obtain greater precision, the famous Underwater Demolition Program was inaugurated, tide tables were included in hydrographic intelligence estimates, and new types of amphibious craft were made available for assault landings: Alligator--tracked (LVT) landing vehicle; Water Buffalo--a 5-ton amphibious truck; and a DUKW--a 2.5-ton amphibious truck. The Allies would encounter no more Tarawas on their long trek westward, Iwo Jima perhaps excepted.

IV. THE RECONQUEST OF THE MARSHALLS

A. "THE PERFECT ONE": THE KWAJALEIN ATOLL. Lessons learned at Tarawa were applied with good effect in the "almost perfect" invasion of the Marshalls, code name Flintlock. Land-based and carrier-based aircraft destroyed all enemy planes on Kwajalein in a single stroke. For three days, battleships bombarded by night and planes and ships by day. Meticulous study of Tarawa paid off. Four times the bombs and shells used at Betio hit Roi-Namur; aircraft bombed precise targets; ships fired in both low and high trajectories and used both high-capacity and armor-piercing shells; and there was no confusion between point and area fire. On 1 February artillery was sited to cover the landing beaches, and the main assault, on 2 February, drove in with ample numbers of tracked vehicles and was well covered by specially fitted gun-and-rocket boats. Air observers lifted bombardment when the first wave was within 500 yards of the beach. There was, therefore, no opposition at the beach on Roi-Namur. Rapidly advancing marines secured Roi by nightfall, 2 February, and Namur by noon of 3 February.

To the south, on Kwajalein, an almost flawless landing was made, and the island was secured by the end of 5 February. The American casualty rate for Tarawa was 17 percent, for the Marshalls less than 5 percent. The fleet itself was barely scratched.

B. THE ENIWETOK ATOLL. The Eniwetok Atoll, desired by Admiral Spruance as a logistic base to support his next westward move, was only 1,000 miles from Saipan, 700 from Truk, and 600 from Ponape. These latter bases must be neutralized before Eniwetok itself could be invaded.

Task Force 58 divided into four groups; one supported Hill at Eniwetok while three headed for Truk and bombers from Tarawa took the fight out of Ponape. Eniwetok was isolated, and the neutralization of Rabaul was complete. Two groups of Task Force 58 then set out for the Marianas, where on 23 February they wiped out about 150 torpedo bombers before fighters from Japan could arrive to protect them, and photographed airfields and also beaches suitable for assault. Meanwhile Hill occupied the three defended islands of the Eniwetok Atoll with the methods perfected at Kwajalein.

C. SUMMARY. From Kwajalein and Roi-Namur the Americans cleared the Marshalls except for the eastern islands, which were left to wither on the vine. The invasion of the Marshalls extended the reach of the Fifth Fleet far across the Pacific and forced the enemy to retire behind a restricted perimeter. In Spruance-Turner-Smith-Mitscher the Americans found a truly professional team of leaders.

V. THE DUAL ADVANCE TO THE PHILIPPINES

A. TASK FORCE 58 SUPPORTS MACARTHUR BY NEUTRALIZING THE PALAUS. Once MacArthur secured the Admiralties, about 1 April 1944, he planned to use Manus Island as a base for his Seventh Fleet and proceed to liberate the Philippines. Nimitz preferred to bypass the Philippines and invade Formosa or the Chinese mainland. Nimitz flew to Washington to confer with President Roosevelt and the JCS. At that conference, and at a meeting held with President Roosevelt at Pearl Harbor, a compromise was reached: the Navy would invade Saipan, in the Marianas, in June and Formosa in February 1945 while MacArthur secured New Guinea, moved into the southern Philippines late in 1944 and onto Luzon in February 1945. With the Solomons campaign ended, King and Nimitz divided command of the Pacific Fleet between Spruance (Fifth Fleet) and Halsey (Third Fleet) so that one could operate and the other plan the next operation, using the same ships. Until Spruance was ready for Saipan, with D-day set for 15 June, Halsey would occupy the western Carolines, thereby isolating the eastern and central Carolines including Truk. Early in September, Mitscher's TF 38 hit Iwo Jima, the Palaus, and also Mindoro, Leyte, Cebu, and Negros islands in the Philippines. The strikes so weakened Japanese surface and air power that it was decided to scrap both the Yap and Mindanao operations and instead hit Leyte on 20 October and Luzon on 20 December. On 15 September, the First Marine Division landed on Peleliu, and had to dig the Japanese out from well-prepared positions behind the beaches. In contrast, the occupation of Ulithi, a fine anchorage useful as a forward logistic base, was bloodless. The western Carolines having been neutralized, the Fifth Fleet could now support MacArthur in his 400-mile jump west to Hollandia in Western New Guinea, a jump that placed him beyond the range of Fifth Air Force fighters and exposed his flank to attack from the Carolines. Admiral Koga had ordered his aircraft and surface forces to prepare to repel the Americans, but he was killed in a plane crash without learning that TF 58 had neutralized his forces in the western Carolines.

B. SUPPORTING THE HOLLANDIA OPERATION.

    1. *Protecting the Flanks*. In mid-April, TF 58 directly supported the Hollandia landings. Upon its return, it gave Truk a pounding so severe that bombers from Eniwetok and the Admiralties could keep it neutralized henceforth, and also struck Satawan and Ponape.

    2. *Hollandia Secured*. With CVEs on loan from the Fifth Fleet in support, Barbey's Seventh Amphibious Force set two groups ashore within 20 miles of each other in the Hollandia area while Seventh Fleet cruisers and destroyers bombarded the enemy's inshore supply line, causing the expected Japanese attack to collapse. The three enemy airfields behind the Cyclops Mountains were taken and used to obtain forward bomber fields at Sarmi and Wake Island, from which MacArthur could cover his invasion of Mindanao.

C. BIAK. The anticipated Japanese reaction came when MacArthur invaded Biak Island, Geelvink Bay, New Guinea. The Japanese activated their KON operation, in which they concentrated their planes on New Guinea from Japan, the Marianas, and the Carolines, and also set the Tokyo Express running again, from Tawitawi to reinforce Biak.

But their pilots from Japan and the Marianas rapidly succumbed to malaria and jungle fever, and Crutchley's cruiser-destroyer force derailed the Express. Then from Admiral Ozawa's First Mobile Fleet at Tawitawi came a superbattleship-cruiser-destroyer force, under Vice Admiral Matome Ugaki, bent on saving Biak and destroying the Seventh Fleet.

Just as Ugaki prepared to strike, however, Spruance lashed at the Marianas, whence bombers could reach Japan itself. Biak was perforce left to its fate, and the KON plan gave away to the "A" plan, an attack on the Fifth Fleet. Ozawa, from Tawitawi, joined Ugaki to give battle to Spruance in the Philippine Sea. Spruance won, took the Marianas, and relieved the pressure from MacArthur. Shortly thereafter MacArthur advanced to Cape Sansapor. Only the Moluccas and the Talaud Islands stood between him and the Philippines.

VI. THE BATTLE OF THE PHILIPPINE SEA, 19-21 JUNE 1944

A. THE INVASION OF THE MARIANAS. On 6 June TF 58 departed Majuro for the Marianas, followed by 535 ships carrying 127,000 assault troops. Mitscher's planes struck the southern Marianas and the Carolines, reducing Japanese air strength; Willis A. Lee's battleships began to soften up Saipan and Tinian; and Joseph J. "Jocko" Clark's two carrier groups raided Iwo Jima and Chichi Jima to cut communications between Japan and the Marianas. On 14 June the invasion of Saipan began. On 15 June, upon receiving a report that a Japanese fleet was approaching, Spruance postponed the invasion of Guam. The southern half of Saipan was secure as the fleets joined in the Battle of the Philippine Sea to the west on 19 June.

B. THE JAPANESE ESTIMATE OF THE SITUATION AND DISPOSITION. Seeking a decisive battle like that of Tsushima, Admiral Soema Toyoda stationed his now carrier-centered First Mobile Fleet at Tawitawi under Vice Admiral Jisaburo Ozawa and ordered him to join Ugaki's surface units in the Philippine Sea and "attack the enemy in the Marianas area and annihilate the invasion force." Ozawa knew that TF 58 was twice as strong in surface ships and more than twice as strong in the air, and he was well aware of the inadequate training of his pilots. But he would be heading into an easterly wind that would permit him to launch and recover planes while advancing; he would have the aid of land-based planes from Rota, Guam, and Yap; his planes had a hundred mile range advantage over the Americans'; and he believed that the cautious Spruance could not be lured away from the Saipan beachhead. Thus his own planes could strike TF 58, go to Guam for servicing, and strike TF 58 again on the return to their carriers.

On 18 June Ozawa disposed his ships for battle. Vice Admiral Takeo Kurita's Van Force of three single light carrier groups advanced to within 300 miles of TF 58. His own Main Body, two groups containing five heavy and one light carrier in all, remained 100 miles astern. Kurita, with most of the heavy surface ships, would absorb most of Spruance's air attack. Ozawa's plans were defective, however, because the bunkers of many of his ships were full of volatile Tawitawi oil, his pilots were not well trained, his carrier screens were weak, his forces were too dispersed to effect mutual support, he did not know that Spruance had already isolated the Marianas and rendered Guam's airfields unusable, and the great range of his planes was obtained at the expense of armor and self-sealing gas tanks.

C. SPRUANCE'S ESTIMATE OF THE SITUATION AND DISPOSITION. On 14 June, as the invasion of Saipan began and the Guam assault force stood by, two of the groups of TF 58 stood to the west of Saipan while two under Clark were 500 miles to the north neutralizing the Jimas. Ozawa might have succeeded had he struck that day, but coast-watchers' and submarines' reports to Spruance revealed Ozawa's course and disposition and permitted Spruance to strengthen his screen from the Saipan Attack Force and to allow Clark to strike the Jimas and yet return in time for battle. When Clark rejoined on the morning of 18 June, Spruance put Lee in charge of 7 fast battleships, 4 heavy cruisers, and 14 destroyers and placed this battle line to the west of the four carrier groups. Lee would shield the carriers from air attack and/or enter a surface engagement if the opportunity offered. Until Ozawa was pinpointed, however, Spruance meant to steam west by day and east by night, always covering the Saipan beachhead and always close enough to Saipan to prevent end runs by the Japanese. Moreover, he sent Turner's transports 200 miles east of Guam and left Jesse Oldendorf to guard the beachhead with a battle line of 7 old battleships and 8 cruisers and an inshore line of 8 escort carriers and some destroyers and landing craft.

D. RELATIVE COMBAT POWER FOR THE BATTLE OF THE PHILIPPINE SEA.

    1. Surface Forces.

	CV	CVL	BB	CA	CL	DD
Japan	5	4	5	11	2	28
United States	7	8	7	8	13	69

    2. Aircraft.

	Fighters	Dive Bombers	Torpedo Planes	Total Carrier Planes	Floats	Total
Japan	222	113	95	430	43	473
United States	475	232	184	891	65	956

E. THE BATTLE OF THE PHILIPPINE SEA.

    1. First Contacts, 15-18 June. Rear Admiral Charles A. Lockwood's excellent disposition of submarines resulted in contact reports that kept Spruance informed of Ozawa's advance. On the 16th Spruance issued his orders: knock out the carriers, slow the battleships and cruisers, then mop up on the cripples. On the 17th Lee negatived Mitscher's suggestion to steer west for a night action; on the 18th Spruance negatived his suggestion that he steam west for an air strike at dawn on the 19th.

    2. The Marianas Turkey Shoot--19 June. 19 June was a clear day, with visibility unlimited. American radar operated well, picking up targets 150 miles distant. Mitscher started launching at 0530 and shot down planes over Guam and planes coming to Guam from unknown bases. At 1000, with many bogies 150 miles west, Mitscher launched a full strike. Excellent fighter direction and good shooting downed 42 of the 69 Japanese planes in the first wave, which approached TF 58 in uncoordinated fashion. Interception by F6Fs at 60 miles from TF 58 resulted in downing 97 of the 128 planes in the second strike. Of 47 planes in Strike III, 40 returned, but 73 out of 82 of Strike IV were downed, half of them when they tried to land on

Guam. Ozawa had shot his bolt and lost half of his planes. All in all, the Japanese lost 315 planes and the Americans 29 from all causes on 19 June.

3. <u>Sinking of the TAIHO and SKOKAKU</u>. Early on the 19th, the submarine <u>Albacore</u> put a torpedo into the <u>Taiho</u>, Japan's super 33,000 ton carrier. Bad damage control resulted in a great explosion at 1532, when she went down. Within half an hour the <u>Shokaku</u>, hit earlier by three torpedoes from the submarine <u>Cavalla</u>, also blew up and sank.

4. <u>Moving Westward--Night of 19-20 June</u>. When only 20 miles north of Guam at 1500 on 19 June Spruance ordered a chase to the west. Leaving one of his four carrier groups to pound Rota and Guam while it was refueling, Mitscher turned west at 2000 at 24 knots, with Lee in advance. But Ozawa, at 18 knots, had turned NW at 1808, and American search planes launched at 0500 on the 20th missed him by 75 miles. Perhaps Mitscher should have used his 24 night fighters for search. At any rate, Ozawa had to refuel and therefore postponed engaging until the 20th.

5. <u>The Twilight Battle--20 June</u>. When Ozawa encountered difficulty in fueling and then learned that only 100 of his planes were operational, he postponed an engagement until the 21st. With TF 58 closing, he ordered course NW at 24 knots, but an <u>Enterprise</u> pilot spotted him at 1540. With sunset at 1900, Mitscher nevertheless accepted the risk of a full strike and a night recovery. His eleven carriers put 215 planes into the air at 1630. American pilots spotted the Japanese forces, widely scattered, at 1840. Of the 76 planes Ozawa managed to launch, two thirds were knocked down at the cost of 20 American planes. Moreover, <u>Hiyo</u> was sunk and three other carriers were damaged. Ozawa's original 430 planes had dwindled to 35. Spruance negatived Mitscher's suggestion that Lee mop up on Ozawa, and Mitscher was soon busy recovering his planes. He turned all lights on at 2045 and during the night of 20-21 June and on the 21st, while on the course taken by his returning planes, recovered all but 16 pilots and 33 crewmen.

6. <u>Stern Chase--20-22 June</u>. Ozawa retired rapidly while Mitscher had to proceed slowly to recover his downed airmen. Spruance's searches on the

21st finally found Ozawa 360 miles to the northwest, beyond reach. Spruance pushed on for another day but turned back when Ozawa was only 300 miles from Okinawa. "Jocko" Clark gave the Jimas another plastering on his return to join the other groups of TF 58 at Eniwetok.

7. <u>Results</u>. Those who comment about putting a non-aviator, Spruance, in charge of carrier forces should recall that Spruance was responsible for the Marianas operation as well as for the Fifth Fleet, while Mitscher was responsible only for TF 58. Spruance's mission was to cover the Saipan beachhead. With Tsushima in mind and fearful of a Japanese end run, he was justifiably cautious. It has been argued that he was a formalist, hence used his carriers defensively instead of offensively in the meleeist tradition. As it was, he crippled Japan's air arm so that the six carriers left were useful only as decoys, and his victory in the Philippine Sea won him the command of the air and sea that made the Marianas campaign a success. Carrier and land-based aircraft search could have been better, but the loss of only 30 planes in action while downing 243 Japanese planes on 19 June bespeaks the quality of American pilot and plane performance. Lockwood's submarines performed well in sinking both the <u>Taiho</u> and the <u>Shokaku</u>. With the United States in possession of the Marianas, victory over Japan appeared inevitable. The United States now sat athwart Japan's inner defense perimeter. It possessed a staging point and logistic base for new operations and denied the Japanese a submarine base and a staging area for planes from Japan to the South. Most important, B-29s were now within striking range of Tokyo itself.

F. NEW STRATEGIC DECISIONS. Tinian was declared secure on 1 August and Guam, invaded on 21 July, on 10 August. B-29s from the Marianas began winging their way over Japan by November. While the Tojo government fell and the Emperor made known to his new cabinet his desire for peace, the military would not end hostilities, and the "unconditional surrender" goal of the Allies precluded the proffering of terms by them at this time.

Nimitz now ordered Halsey to push back the Carolines salient preparatory to a combined Halsey-

MacArthur push on the Philippines. Halsey's demurrer against taking all of the western Carolines resulted in the decision to bypass many islands and to seize those with air fields, from which the remaining islands could be covered and protection given to MacArthur's right flank. In September, it may be recalled, Halsey took Pelelieu and Angaur and MacArthur took Morotai. The bloodless seizure of Ulithi which followed gave the Pacific Fleet an excellent anchorage and forward logistic base. Meanwhile Halsey relieved Spruance, and TF 58 became TF 38 and the Fifth, the Third Fleet.

Convinced that the Japanese hold on the Philippines was weak, Halsey recommended the bypassing of Yap, the Palaus, and Mindanao, and the invading of the Central Philippine island of Leyte at the earliest date. MacArthur concurred, and the Joint Chiefs set 24 October 1944, as the date for the invasion. All of Halsey's Third Fleet except TF 38 went to MacArthur for the assault.

VII. THE BATTLE FOR LEYTE GULF

A. PRELIMINARIES: HALSEY PAVES THE WAY WITH THE BATTLE OFF FORMOSA. After destroying hundreds of aircraft and sinking numerous vessels in carrier strikes against the central and northern Philippines, TF 38 lashed at Okinawa and then turned its attention to Formosa. In anticipation of Halsey's visit, Vice Admiral Shigeru Fukudome concentrated fighter planes on Formosa and a night-operating torpedo bomber force (Typhoon Attack Force) in southern Japan. He would destroy Halsey's fighters over Formosa, then use the bombers to destroy his carriers, thereby securing part of Japan's inner defense line and staving off Japan's defeat. His ill-trained pilots, however, were no match for Halsey's experienced ones. On 21 and 22 September, TF 38 liquidated Japanese air and naval surface power in Southern Luzon and the Central Philippines. On 10-13 October, that force hit Okinawa, Luzon, then Okinawa again, wiping out Japanese air and numerous small surface craft before wrecking Japan's air power on Formosa. Halsey's strikes cost him 45 planes and damage to the cruisers <u>Canberra</u> and <u>Houston</u> while Fukudome lost 800 planes and 9 freighters and 6 tankers.

B. SUPPORTING THE INVASION OF LEYTE. Leaving Major General Claire L. Chennault's China-based Fourteenth Air Force to neutralize Formosa as a staging base, Halsey took station off Leyte to support the invasion of the Philippines. The dual lines of transpacific advance had finally merged. Although Halsey, MacArthur, and Kinkaid conferred on plans for three days, no overall commander for the invasion was provided. Nimitz operated "by agreement" with his equal, MacArthur, and Kinkaid uncomplainingly commanded "MacArthur's Navy" even though he was denied the publicity given both the General and Halsey. Kinkaid's Seventh Fleet, with more than 700 ships, transported and supported Lt. General Walter Krueger's Sixth Army (200,000 American troops) while Halsey's Third Fleet, stripped to TF 38, provided strategic support and call strikes. Before the end of the day of the invasion, 20 October, Leyte Gulf's beachheads and Tacloban airstrip were in Allied hands. On the beach, MacArthur told the Filipinos that he had kept his promise to return.

C. THE SHO (VICTORY) PLANS. Japanese last-ditch defense plans included the protection of those vital areas the Americans might seek to obtain. The defense of the Philippines, Formosa, and the Ryukyus was imperative, for behind them sailed the tanker fleet bearing life-giving sustenance to the Japanese war machine. U.S. submarines had so cut into this inshore pipeline, however, that Admiral Soemu Toyoda was forced to split his fleet. He kept the carriers at home and recalled Vice Admiral Kiyohide Shima's small surface force from the Kuriles to protect them, and sent Vice Admiral Takeo Kurita's major surface force to the Singapore area, where oil was plentiful. Rather than seeking the enemy, Toyoda would let the Americans come to him. He would strike first by air and then seek a decision with his concentrated fleet. He would activate Sho Plan 1 for the defense of the Philippines; Sho 2 for Formosa, the Ryukyus, and Southern Japan; Sho 3 for Kyushu, Shikoku, and Honshu; and Sho 4 for Hokkaido. Each plan was based on the improbable hope that concentrated air and sea power could turn the tide of war by a new Tsushima and depended upon trained pilots that were not forthcoming and upon mistakes which the Americans did not make.

D. FORCES AND DISPOSITIONS.

1. <u>Sho I: Japanese Forces and Plans</u>. To implement the <u>Sho</u> I plan, the Japanese had the following forces:

<u>Main (Northern) Force</u> (Inland Sea)--Vice Admiral Jisaburo Ozawa
    1 heavy and 3 light carriers
    2 converted battleships with flight decks aft
    a light secreen of cruisers and destroyers
    116 aircraft
<u>First (Center) Striking Force</u> (Lingga Roads)-- Vice Admiral Takeo Kurita
    3 battleship sections totalling 7 battleships, and screen
<u>Second (Southern) Striking Force</u> (Ryukyus)-- Vice Admiral Kiyohide Shima
    3 cruisers and 7 destroyers

Kurita would depart Lingga Roads, fuel at Brunei Bay, Borneo, transit San Bernardino Strait dividing Luzon and Samar with 5 battleships, 12 cruisers, and 15 destroyers and strike Leyte Gulf from the north while Vice Admiral Shoji Nishimura, with 2 battleships, 1 cruiser and 4 destroyers would transit Surigao Strait and hit Leyte Gulf from the south. Shima would depart Amami, stay west of Formosa, and come down to help Nishimura, with the manner and degree of cooperation between their forces left unsettled. Ozawa's carriers would depart the Inland Sea, take position off northern Luzon, and decoy Halsey away from the Leyte beachhead.

The success of an operation involving such forces as Ozawa's, Kurita's, and Nishimura-Shima's depended largely upon good radio communications, timing, and cooperation. Ozawa's radio transmitter failed to put out, but he never realized that he was not being heard by his widely scattered forces, and Shima and Nishimura failed to cooperate.

2. <u>Allied Forces and Disposition</u>. Between 20 and 24 October, the Allied naval forces were disposed off the Leyte beachhead in three layers. Inside Leyte Gulf was the greater part of the Seventh Fleet, its two amphibious forces protected by Rear Admiral Jesse B. Oldendorf's six old battleships (OBBs) and a cruiser-destroyer screen. At the southern end of

Surigao Strait Kinkaid placed 39 PT boats. Just outside the Gulf to the east three Seventh Fleet escort carrier groups commanded by Rear Admiral Thomas L. Sprague were on antisubmarine, antiaircraft, and ground support patrol. Halsey's TF 38, under the command of Vice Admiral Mitscher, lay to the east of Luzon. Vice Admiral John S. McCain and Rear Admirals Gerald F. Bogan, Frederick C. Sherman, and Ralph E. Davison commanded its four task groups, which averaged 23 ships each (2 CVA, 2 CVL, 2 new BBs, 3 cruisers, and 14 destroyers).

E. OPENING ACTIONS, 23 OCTOBER. On his way from Brunei Bay to Surigao Strait, Kurita was attacked off Palawan by the submarines Darter and Dace. Kurita's flagship, the heavy cruiser Atago, sank in 20 minutes; the damaged heavy cruiser Takao was obliged to retire; and the heavy cruiser Maya blew apart and sank in four minutes. Kurita transferred to the superbattleship Yamato and on the 24th passed south of Mindoro into the Sibuyan Sea. Both he and Nishimura-Shima, 200 miles south, were coming within the range of Halsey's planes.

Just as Halsey sent the first of his groups, McCain's, to fuel at Ulithi, he received word of Kurita's approach. He permitted McCain to proceed but called the three remaining groups together for fueling from oilers. By daylight the newly-fueled groups had reached station 125 miles apart--Sherman's off Luzon, Bogan's off San Bernardino Strait, and Davison's off Leyte Gulf. All three groups launched search planes north, west, and south, before 0630.

F. THE BATTLE OF THE SIBUYAN SEA

    1. Halsey Strikes Kurita. Discovering the Nishimura-Shima force in the Sulu Sea, Davison's pilots inflicted some damage but failed to slow its advance. Then Bogan's flyers discovered Kurita about to enter the Sibuyan Sea. Leaving Nishimura-Shima to Kinkaid, Halsey ordered his three groups to concentrate upon Kurita with full strikes and directed McCain to reverse course, fuel at sea, and stand by for further orders.

As he plowed across the Sibuyan Sea virtually without air cover, Kurita suffered five air strikes.

By midafternoon all of his five battleships had been hit. One of them, the superbattleship <u>Musashi</u>, was sunk, and the heavy cruiser <u>Myoka</u> was put out of action. His request for air cover refused, he reversed course and steered west.

2. <u>Fukudome Strikes Halsey</u>. Fukudome's task in carrying out the <u>Sho</u> operation was to strike Halsey's carriers while the latter's planes were attacking Ozawa. Fukudome joined the remnants of his Formosa air force to the hundred-odd planes on Luzon. When a scout sighted Sherman's carriers, he launched every plane he had against what he thought was the entire Third Fleet. During the air battle, not a single Japanese plane got close enough to attack Sherman's carriers. However, a lone bomber later dived out of a cloud and bombed the light carrier <u>Princeton</u>, which eventually had to be abandoned. Sherman moved his other carriers away and launched one of the most successful of the day's strikes against Kurita. But by this time Ozawa had also spotted Sherman and at 1145 sent 76 planes, almost all the operational planes left, against him. Three of his planes returned to their carriers, 30 got to Luzon, and 43 were shot down.

3. <u>Halsey Leaves the Beachhead</u>.

a. <u>Command Confusion</u>. In his operation plan Nimitz had specifically directed Halsey to cooperate with Kinkaid. In September, Halsey had conferred with Kinkaid and MacArthur, but he and Kinkaid had evidently never settled the exact degree of area of responsibility each was to assume. There was no doubt that Kinkaid would furnish close support for the Leyte assault, but who would "cover"? Kinkaid had a "Close Covering Group" which performed support and covering functions, but Nimitz had directed Halsey "to cover and support" MacArthur's forces engaged in seizing objectives in the central Philippines. Moreover, Kinkaid was not prepared to fight a naval battle. Believing that Halsey would cover, he had armed his surface ships and escort carriers with anti-personnel ordnance rather than with armor-piercing shells, heavy bombs, or torpedoes. Yet Nimitz had also approved Halsey's option to destroy a "major portion" of an enemy fleet as a "primary task." Halsey therefore interpreted his mission as offensive rather than defensive. He thus changed Pacific Fleet doctrine, which heretofore had been to protect and assist amphibious forces. Unlike Spruance, who had defended the landings at Saipan, Halsey would defend the invaders at Leyte by destroying the enemy fleet.

      b. <u>Tactical Confusion: Task Force 34</u>. On 24 October Halsey struck at Kurita, assuming that Kinkaid could take care of Nishimura-Shima. Kinkaid guarded Surigao Strait and assumed that Halsey would block Kurita's passage through San Bernardino Strait. At 1512, however, Kurita had turned eastward and proceeded at a speed that would carry him through San Bernardino Strait in the dark. Halsey sent his subordinate commanders a radio message: "Four battleships, 2 heavy cruisers, 3 light cruisers and 14 destroyers will be formed as TF 34" under Vice Admiral Willis A. Lee. Halsey intended it to be understood that <u>if a surface engagement offered</u> he would form TF 34 from TF 38 and send TF 34 ahead as a battle line. Two hours later Halsey elucidated--"If the enemy sorties [through San Bernardino] TF 34 will be formed when directed by me." Kinkaid and Mitscher, among others, assumed that TF 34 had already been formed and did not hear Halsey's TBS (short range radio) elucidation.

    4. <u>Choice of Battles and Choice of Plans</u>. Word finally came, late in the day, that Ozawa was only 190 miles to the NNE. Halsey put the pieces of the jigsaw puzzle together and clearly saw three Japanese forces bent on a rendezvous near Leyte Gulf for an attack on the transports therein. He must thwart their joining.

    Halsey felt that he could overlook Nishimura-Shima and leave them to Kinkaid. Kurita, hurt, had reversed course and was retreating westward and could also be left to Kinkaid. That left Ozawa's undamaged carriers. Practically all Allied commanders at the time believed carriers the principal threat in any naval operation. Halsey was one of them. When his staff offered the options of defending San Bernardino Strait, divide the carrier forces, or strike Ozawa, he chose the last because he could thus preserve his fleet's integrity, leave him the initiative, and also promise him the advantage of surprise. Even if Kurita did reach Leyte Gulf, thought Halsey, he could merely hit and run since he had no logistic support with him. "It's not my job to protect the Seventh Fleet. My job is offensive, to strike with the Third Fleet," he said. His decision reached, he ordered his fleet north at 2000 and radioed Kinkaid that he was going after Ozawa "with three groups." Kinkaid interpreted this to mean that TF 34 was off San Bernardino and that Halsey was going north with three carrier groups. Kinkaid had sent most of his combatant ships against Nishimura-Shima; he was so sure that TF 34 was blocking San Bernardino that he did not send air searches to check on Kurita's movements. But Kurita had again reversed course and was now heading east. All that stood between him and the transports in Leyte Gulf were Rear Admiral T. L. Sprague's escort carriers!

G. THE BATTLE OF SURIGAO STRAIT

1. Oldendorf's Trap. On the afternoon of 24 October Kinkaid alerted the PT boats at the southern end of Surigao Strait and directed Rear Admiral Oldendorf to prepare for a night engagement. Oldendorf decided to let the Japanese come into a neat trap. He placed his six OBBs to cruise at five knots across the northern mouth of the Strait, with cruisers obliquely on their extended left and right flanks, and alerted three destroyer squadrons to be ready to launch torpedoes at the enemy's flanks as he advanced.

2. Nishimura is Defeated. Nishimura entered Surigao Strait ahead of schedule, with Shima 30 miles astern. An hour after midnight Nishimura successfully fought his way past the PT boats. Soon Oldendorf released his destroyers. These drew abreast, fired torpedoes, and reversed course. The battleship Yamashiro blew apart as her magazines exploded; one destroyer went down; and all the other destroyers were put out of action. Battleship Fuso and cruiser Mogami pushed on into range of Oldendorf's Battle Line. Six battleships and eight cruisers soon sent the Fuso down and the Mogami out of control. The American destroyer that got into the middle of the Strait and was put out of action by friend and foe was the only American casualty.

3. Shima is Destroyed. Shima, meanwhile, had the cruiser Abukuma put out of action by PT boats as he entered the Strait. At 0420, when he turned to

fire torpedoes at targets to the north, his flagship rammed the retreating <u>Mogami</u> and he turned south. Of all the Japanese forces that entered the Strait, only 4 cruisers and 5 destroyers, some badly crippled, fought their way by the PT boats and regained the Mindanao Sea. Soon planes from the escort carriers sank the <u>Mogami</u> and army bombers sank the <u>Abukuma</u>. Oldendorf had never even seen Shima, and the threat to Leyte Gulf was removed by dawn of 25 October. News then came that Kurita was attacking an escort carrier group off Samar. Leyte Gulf was now threatened from the north! Three of Halsey's commanders--Admirals Gerald F. Bogan, Mitscher, and Willis A. Lee--thought about protesting to Halsey, as Mitscher's Chief of Staff, Arleigh Burke, advised, then changed their minds.

H. THE BATTLE OFF CAPE ENGAÑO

    1. <u>Halsey Engages Ozawa</u>. At 0200 on 25 October Halsey's search planes sighted Ozawa's advance guard and main body; they were heading for a 0600 rendezvous. Halsey now formed TF 34 and sent it ahead to sink cripples and stragglers left by Mitscher's planes. A 180-plane strike reached Ozawa at 0800, and a second strike at 1000. Bombs sent a destroyer down and hit all three carriers, and torpedoes found the cruiser <u>Tama</u> and the heavy carrier <u>Zuikaku</u>. The light carrier <u>Chitose</u> soon went down, while the light carrier <u>Chiyoda</u> lay dead in the water, afire and listing.

    2. "<u>The Whole World Wants to Know</u>." Now strange messages began to reach Halsey. At 0410 Kinkaid radioed that he was engaging in Surigao Strait and asked whether TF 34 was guarding San Bernardino Strait. Halsey did not receive the message until 0648; he answered that TF 34 was with his carriers. Kinkaid, dumbfounded, was then handed a cry for help from Rear Admiral C.A.F. Sprauge, whose escort carrier unit off Leyte Gulf was being attacked by Kurita. At 0820, 20 minutes after learning that Nishimura-Shima had retired, Halsey knew that Kurita had penetrated San Bernardino. But he figured that the planes from 18 escort carriers and Oldendorf could take care of Kurita. Just as he prepared to attack Ozawa's cripples and stragglers, Kinkaid flashed his need for fast battleships in Leyte Gulf. Halsey thereupon

directed Lee to close Ozawa, to the north, and radioed McCain to help Sprague. Another message from Kinkaid told Halsey that the Seventh Fleet was low on ammunition and in no condition to defend the Gulf. Halsey, 350 miles away and still going north, was finally startled (as was Kurita) by Kinkaid's 1000 plain language message, "Send Lee," and Nimitz's "Where is Task Force 34?" which by a quirk in communication procedure reached him as "The whole world wants to know where is Task Force 34?"

3. <u>Halsey Returns to Leyte Gulf</u>. With two of Ozawa's crippled carriers just 42 miles ahead, Halsey had to turn from due north to due south, his dream of a carrier battle shattered. Task Force 34 followed and was merged with TF 38, but two carrier groups continued to the north to launch the day's last strikes. Soon the <u>Zuikaku</u> and the <u>Zuiho</u> went down and the fourth carrier was in serious trouble. Mitscher sent a surface force to finish off cripples. The last carrier went down but the ten remaining ships outsped their pursuers. Ozawa lost four carriers and seven ships to Halsey, and a destroyer and a damaged cruiser fell to Lockwood's submarines as they retired to Japan. Ozawa had lured Halsey from the beachhead but had accomplished little, for his words never got through to Kurita.

I. THE BATTLE OFF SAMAR, 25 OCTOBER

1. <u>Kurita's Advance</u>. After retreating westward on the 24th, Kurita's four battleships, eight cruisers, and 11 destroyers wheeled southeast at 0300, 25 October, along the coast of Samar. Kurita learned that Nishimura-Shima had been repulsed and of course heard nothing from Ozawa. After sunrise he detected what he assumed to be Halsey's carrier fleet.

a. <u>Light Carriers in Jeopardy</u>. At 0700, with Halsey 300 miles to the north, he opened fire on C.A.F. Sprague's escort carrier units (six 18-knot escort carriers, three destroyers, and four destroyer escorts). A similar unit, Rear Admiral Felix B. Stump's, was just over the horizon to the southeast, and a third, Rear Admiral T. L. Sprague's, was 120 miles to the southeast. C.A.F. Sprague turned east and launched aircraft as 14- 16- and 18-inch shells began to straddle his carriers. Sprague made smoke, headed into a rain squall, radioed for help in plain language, and turned south. Kurita's battleships were astern; his cruisers were coming down Sprague's left flank; and his destroyers had him boxed in on the right.

    b. <u>American Destroyers Save the Day</u>. Desperate, Sprague ordered his destroyers and destroyer escorts to make a suicide torpedo attack on Kurita's whole fleet. Three of the attackers were sunk and the rest damaged, but torpedoes put a heavy cruiser out of action, caused the Battle Line to scatter and lose ground, and confused the tactical situation for Kurita. Moreover, his destroyers were circling away from attacks by Sprague's planes and the battleship <u>Haruna</u> had taken off for a private war of her own with Stump's unit. Kurita closed in and sank the <u>Gambier Bay</u>, but a well coordinated air attack by Stump crippled two heavy cruisers and torpedo attacks by planes caused his ships to scatter.

    c. <u>Kurita Breaks Off</u>. Out of touch with both friend and foe, Kurita suddenly turned north and ordered his ships to close the <u>Yamato</u>. Japanese ships within point blank range of Sprague's carriers and other vessels obeyed the call, leaving T.L. Sprague's bewildered unit to steam on towards Leyte Gulf, just 25 miles away.

    2. <u>Kurita's Withdrawal</u>. Once Kurita surveyed the tactical situation, he directed a heavily damaged battleship and destroyer to retire but had to sink the cruisers <u>Chokai</u> and <u>Chikuma</u>. A final attack from escort carrier planes then caused the heavy cruiser <u>Suzuya</u> to blow apart. Of ten heavy cruisers, Kurita now had only two effectives. Yet Kurita believed he had sunk three or four carriers, two heavy cruisers, and a number of destroyers, and he was willing to try again for Leyte Gulf. As he steamed south, however, he began to lose enthusiasm; in five days the transports were surely unloaded, perhaps had already withdrawn; he could expect no help from Nishimura-Shima; he was not sure where the rest of the "Third Fleet" he had attacked was; he had heard nothing from Ozawa; and he had the feeling that carrier and Leyte-based air forces were converging upon him. Moreover, he had received an erroneous report that American carriers were northeast of Samar. He chose the latter as his objective and at 1300 again reversed course.

Soon McCain's planes found him and damaged his ships enough to cause them to trail oil. Luzon-based aircraft helped him search for the nonexistent carriers in vain. Low on fuel, and utterly exhausted, Kurita headed for San Bernardino Strait, which he entered at 2130 on 25 October, about an hour ahead of Halsey's advance battleship-cruiser, destroyer force, which sank one destroyer. On the 26th, however, Bogan's and McCain's carrier planes found Kurita in the Sibuyan Sea off Panay and further damaged the Yamato and Kumano and sent a light cruiser and a destroyer down.

J. THE KAMIKAZES. On 25 October the Japanese Kamikaze (Divine Wind) Special (suicide) Attack Corps went into action for the first time when Kurita was advancing toward Leyte Gulf. Organized by Vice Admiral Takajiro Onishi, in the Philippines, and aided by Fukudome, these human missiles sought to emulate Kurita's daring. Rear Admiral T.L. Sprague's escort carrier unit was the first to receive the Kamikazes, most of whom dived at ships directly, almost vertically, their bombs still attached to their planes. Three of T.L. Sprague's carriers were damaged shortly after dawn on 25 October, and Rear Admiral C.A.F. Sprague lost the St. Lo and had the Kitkun Bay damaged shortly after Kurita began his retirement. At about noon on the 26th Kamikazes damaged T.L. Sprague's Suwannee. The escort carriers replied by sinking a cruiser and destroyer, the entire escort of a convoy that had landed Japanese troops on the west coast of Leyte the day before. Theirs was the last attack in the Battle for Leyte Gulf.

K. PROFIT AND LOSS IN LEYTE GULF

  1. The Score. The U.S. Navy and its enormous air power won an overwhelming victory in the Battle for Leyte Gulf. In four days, 23-26 October, 3 Japanese battleships, 4 carriers, 10 cruisers, and 9 destroyers were sunk at the cost of 1 light carrier, 2 escort carriers, 2 destroyers, and 1 destroyer escort. The Japanese lost 305,710 tons of combat shipping, or half of their remaining combat strength, the Americans 36,000 tons. The Imperial Japanese Navy ceased to exist as a fighting team and the U.S. Navy won control of the broad Pacific. No true fleet engagement was fought for the rest of the war in the Pacific. The Japanese, moreover, failed to reach

their objective, the transports in Leyte Gulf.

  2. <u>The Japanese Failure</u>. Why did the Japanese fail? The major cause was their lack of air power, chiefly in the matter of trained pilots, the shortage of which began with the Battle of Midway and was aggravated by succeeding battles. A second reason was the complex disposition of their forces, which made concentration impossible, and, third, their inability to coordinate their naval forces and land-based air power.

  3. <u>American Shortcomings</u>. The U.S. Navy, however, achieved less than it should have. Despite overwhelming power, it let six enemy battleships and numerous supporting vessels escape. Halsey's cruise north and south during the critical hours of battle detracted from the efficiency of the U.S. Navy, which like the Japanese failed to coordinate. Ambiguity in directives issued before and during the battle contributed to uncertainty, and faulty communications and errors in judgment hampered the American performance. Later Halsey told Nimitz that "having two autonomous tactical Fleet Commands supporting the same operation cannot be justified from a naval point of view. Cooperation can never be a substitute for command." Whether an overall commander could have brought order out of the chaos attendant four great battles fought on as many days over an area of 30,000 square miles is a moot point. A sampling of American historians who have written about the Battle of Leyte Gulf shows that four (Bernard Brodie, Samuel E. Morison, Clark E. Reynolds, and C. Van Woodward) are critical of Halsey and that one (Stanley L. Falk) believes he made the right decision.

     VIII. THE LAST CAMPAIGNS:
  THE PHILIPPINES, BORNEO, IWO JIMA, AND OKINAWA

A. HOW TO DEFEAT JAPAN?

  MacArthur, believing the New Guinea approach to the Philippines the principal line of advance, viewed Nimitz's Central Pacific thrust as merely protection for his right flank. Many naval officers, however, saw MacArthur's New Guinea drive useful only because it cleared the left flank of the Central Pacific forces and protected Australia. Service squabbles did not hide the fact, nevertheless, that the two drives had been mutually supporting and that they had so weakened Japan's air power that it could not immediately resist MacArthur's invasion of Leyte. With the Battle of Leyte Gulf, the Navy achieved its primary objective of cutting Japan off from the Southern Resources Area by bringing the Army to the Philippines. Assuming the role of partner rather than of commander, it determined to help the Army and Army Air Corps to obtain their objectives. Before it could add support to the twentieth Air Force's bombing of Japan, however, it must aid MacArthur in securing the Philippines.

B. THE LIBERATION OF THE PHILIPPINES

    1. <u>The Leyte Campaign</u>. While the monsoons of November and December bogged Allied aircraft and mechanized equipment in Leyte's mud, General Tomoyuki Yamashita had the advantage of clear weather over Luzon. Given this condition, Halsey reluctantly agreed to Kinkaid's request that he keep the Third Fleet in Philippine waters for an additional month or two. While Halsey's forces struck at Luzon, destroying about 700 aircraft, 2 cruisers, 17 transports, 50 cargo ships, 10 oilers, and many smaller types, Kamikazes damaged various Third Fleet units including 8 carriers and Yamashita increased his strength on Leyte to 35,000 men. The struggle for Leyte, as for Guadalcanal, became a reinforcement race. The Americans won because Allied submarines and carrier aircraft had reduced Japan's transports to below the needed reinforcement rate while the American naval ferry put 240,000 troops onto Leyte by late December. In the meantime, Halsey's staff concluded that Kamikazes could be deterred if not destroyed by 1) placing picket destroyers ahead of their force; sending Combat Air Patrol planes farther out and further up, and 3) having patrols fly at low altitudes.

    2. <u>Mindoro</u>. Plans for the capture of Manila included the seizure of an island to the west of Luzon that had clear weather and on which airfields could be built. While the Third Fleet stood to the east of Luzon and for three days struck its airfields, a Seventh Fleet amphibious force moved from Leyte via Surigao Strait toward Mindoro. The Japanese reacted vigorously by sending out its Second Striking Force

from Indo-China ports and by attacking with more than 150 Kamikazes. Planes from the escort and fleet carriers successfully covered the Mindoro landings, however, and the invaders went ashore on 15 December without opposition and rapidly began to construct two air strips.

3. <u>Luzon</u>. Meantime MacArthur had directed Admiral Kinkaid and General Walter Krueger to proceed with the invasion of Luzon via the historic route, Lingayen Gulf south to Manila. On 1 January 1945, a mighty force of nearly 700 ships approached Lingayen Gulf. Sighting Oldendorf's Seventh Fleet in the Sulu Sea, the Japanese sent their Kamikazes to the attack. When Oldendorf signaled Kinkaid that he considered the use of additional air power urgent and vital, Halsey brought TF 38 south from Formosan waters and temporarily put the airfields on Luzon out of action. Filipino guerrilla's having already cleared Lingayen Gulf of mines, Oldendorf's fleet proceeded with shore bombardment on the 7th. On the 7th and 8th Kamikaze attacks inflicted additional damage upon a number of ships, but the landings themselves were unopposed, and battleships and aircraft soon silenced Japanese artillery firing down from the nearby hills onto the forward edge of the four mile beachhead secured by the close of 8 January. Extreme vigilance and smart shooting on the part of naval personnel saved ships in the Gulf from damage by powerboats carrying depth charges and by naked Japanese swimmers with demolition charges attached to their backs.

4. <u>Halsey in the China Sea, 12-23 January 1945</u>. After losing three destroyers in a typhoon in mid-December, Halsey hit Formosa, signalled his men to "Keep the bastards dying," and daringly took TF 38 through the strait between Formosa and Luzon into the South China Sea, where only American submarines had operated for three years. In 11 days TF 38 hit the coast of Indo-China, Takao, Formosa, and Hong Kong, wrecking 134 planes, damaging 48 ships, and smashing shore installations. Slipping back into the Pacific, Halsey hit Formosa again and moved northeast for an important photo-reconnaissance mission against Okinawa before retiring to Ulithi and relinquishing command of TF 38 to Spruance.

5. <u>Manila</u>. As the First Army Corps pressed Yamashita south from Lingayen Gulf, the Seventh Fleet

put 35,000 troops ashore north of Subic Bay to prevent him from retreating to Bataan, and troops landed south of the city began their march north. The final drive for Manila that began on 1 February ended after a month of house to house fighting.

6. <u>The Central and Southern Islands</u>. The first step in liberating the rest of the Philippines was to capture and convert to Allied use those air bases and ports that Japan might use against Allied sea lines of communications. The first assault was made against Palawan, in late February 1945, with the result that the Allies could cover the two straits connecting the South China Sea and the Sulu Sea and Palawan Passage. The Central Philippines were isolated by landings on all of its important islands. However, the tedious task of mopping up continued in some places long after the official termination of the war.

C. THE BRITISH FLEET JOINS UP--THE BORNEO CAMPAIGN

1. <u>The Royal Navy in the Indian Ocean and in the Pacific</u>. The British strengthened their Eastern Fleet after the surrender of Italy and the United States lent its commander, Sir James Somerville, the <u>Saratoga</u>. In May and June, 1944, the Eastern Fleet undertook a limited offensive against Japanese bases on and around Sumatra and Java. By the fall of 1944, with the invasion of western Europe completed, the Eastern became the major British fleet and the East Indies Fleet an escort carrier-centered force.

Rather than use the Eastern Fleet to recover the oil refineries of Sumatra and Borneo, thus providing relatively cheap oil for all Allied units in the Pacific, Churchill sent its fastest ships to operate under American command in the main attack against Japan and its slower vessels to rid the Bay of Bengal of all major Japanese warships. British carriers were slower than American ones and were equipped differently for taking on supplies at sea. Their great advantage was their armored flight deck. As one American sailor put it, "When a kamikaze hits a U.S. carrier, it's six months' repair at Pearl. In a Limey carrier, it's 'Sweepers, man your brooms.'"

2. <u>The Borneo Campaign</u>. In May and June the Seventh Fleet put Australian troops ashore on Tarakan

Island in Brunei Bay preliminary to the assault on 1 July of the oil-rich and formidably defended port of Balikpapan. Despite very stiff opposition, the invasion proceeded on schedule and the Australians secured Borneo. Oil for the Seventh Fleet now began to flow from the wells of Tarakan.

D. IWO JIMA--AMPHIBIOUS EPIC

1. <u>Iwo's Strategic Position</u>. Halsey's slapdash methods kept the enemy off balance but befuddled his own commanders. With Spruance came readily comprehensible plans prepared on time. With Halsey there was "concern"; with Spruance, "confidence."

The Spruance-Turner-Smith team that took over from Halsey at the completion of the assault on Luzon proceeded to capture Iwo Jima and Okinawa. Lacking fighter protection, B-29s operating against Japan from the Marianas could not bomb precisely because they were forced to climb to about 30,000 feet, and their long trip, of 3000 miles, cut their bomb load from a possible ten to three tons. Moreover, the Japanese on the Volcano and Bonin Islands gave Tokyo early warning of their approach and sent fighters to attack them en route. While Iwo was too small to serve as a major air base, its capture would eliminate its Japanese air fighters, provide fighter and medium bomber bases within 750 miles of Tokyo, a way station for B-29s in need of fuel, a refuge for damaged bombers, and a base for air-sea rescue. Okinawa could support major installations within 325 miles of Japan.

2. <u>Japanese Defenses</u>. Able Lieutenant General Todamichi Kuribayashi's 23,000 troops had transformed Iwo Jima into a Pacific Gibraltar. High ground to the northeast and southeast of the island permitted him to direct enfilade artillery fire onto the only usable beaches, and the soft lava ash would aid him by bogging down Allied mechanized vehicles. Aircraft bombs did little harm to deeply entrenched defenders who could be dislodged only by deliberate, pinpoint naval gunfire using a variety of shells at different trajectories from various angles.

3. <u>The Assault on Iwo</u>. The assault on Iwo Jima began on 16 February while Spruance's TF 58 distracted

the Japanese with raids on Tokyo. Kuribayashi ordered his men to hold fire until the invasion actually began. Violation of this order revealed unsuspected defenses that responded better to the treatment of 5-inch aircraft rockets than to bombs or to battleship gunfire. On the 17th, TF 58 started south to cover Rear Admiral Harry Hill's Attack Force bringing in Major General Harry Schmidt's V Amphibious Corps.

    a. <u>Invasion Difficulties</u>. On D-day, 19 February, aircraft and naval surface fire covered the approach of nearly 500 landing craft. Soft volcanic ash caused amtracs to sink rather than take hold, and succeeding waves of landing craft were unable to beach themselves; many broached and were wrecked before armored bulldozers cut sloping roads up the coastal ridge for tanks. Troops supported by tanks reached the center of the island and the foot of Mount Suribachi by the evening of 19 February, at heavy cost. Mount Suribachi fell in three days. Call fire and illumination from ships aided the slow troop advance northward, and carrier air support proved particularly effective during the four days TF 58 remained off the island. The cooperation and coordination of the various supporting Allied elements reached a new high, but Kuribayashi's men had to be dug out by infantry with tanks at close range.

    b. <u>The Cost</u>. It took a month instead of the estimated five days to take Iwo, and the cost of taking it was high. Kamikazes hit the <u>Saratoga</u>, which had to retire to the United States for major repairs, and sank the escort carrier <u>Bismarck Sea</u>. All but 200 of the 23,000 Japanese defenders were killed, as were 5,500 Americans, with an additional 15,000 wounded. Iwo Jima proved the acme of both American amphibious assault technique and of Japanese defense technique.

    Iwo was worth the high cost. By mid-March B-29s were leaving the Marianas with full pay loads, picking up fighters over Iwo and winging their way unmolested to bomb Japan with precision at low altitude. Damaged bombers found Iwo a haven, and downed bombers could expect rescue by Iwo-based seaplanes.

E. OKINAWA--THE LAST BATTLE

1. **Preparatory Actions.** Even before Iwo's airfields were usable, the United States stepped up its air war against Japan. TF 58 left Iwo and on 25 February cooperated with 200 B-29s on a raid on Tokyo that burned out two square miles of the capital and destroyed 150 aircraft and gutted two airplane factories. After another photo-reconnaissance mission against Okinawa, which lies 325 miles south of Kyushu, on 1 March TF 58 proceeded to Ulithi to prepare for the invasion of the island. Departing Ulithi in mid-March, TF 58 struck so hard at planes and airfields on Kyushu and at naval units in the Inland Sea that the Japanese were helpless to counterattack for several days after the invasion of Okinawa began. Then Kamikazes began their most sustained assault on TF 58, damaging the Enterprise, Yorktown, and Wasp, and knocking the Franklin and Bunker Hill out of action.

2. **The Assault of Okinawa.** TF 58 began to strike Okinawa on 23 March. On the 24th, Vice Admiral Lee's Battle Line from TF 58 joined Rear Admiral W.H.P. Blandy's Amphibious Support Force in opening the naval bombardment. On the 26th the Kerama Islands were taken for a seaplane base and anchorage. Some 350 explosive-laden powerboats in the islands were also captured.

   a. **The Invasion Forces.** Mounted from Leyte, Saipan, Guadalcanal, Oahu, and Espiritu Santo, San Francisco, and Seattle, Vice Admiral Turner's Expeditionary Force of 318 combatant ships and 1,139 non-combatant ships with 182,000 assault troops converged on Okinawa. Knowledge of the power of the assault directed at Iwo Jima determined Lieutenant General Mitsuru Ushijima not to contest the landings. Instead he prepared a defense in depth across the narrows of Southern Okinawa and sought to delay the invaders while airmen from Japan took their full toll of the supporting naval forces. TF 58 covered the approaches from Japan. The British Pacific Fleet, Sir Bruce Fraser commanding, was constituted as TF 57 and covered the approaches from Formosa and neutralized the intervening islands.

   b. **Reducing Okinawa.** On 1 April, 50,000 Allied troops went ashore unopposed on the western shores of the island. By 3 April they had thrust across to the east coast. The elements that swept north were unopposed until they reached Motobu Peninsula. From Motobu, artillery was sited to aid in the capture of the island of Ie Shima, on which air fields were rapidly built. Troops advancing to the south met no resistance until they ran into Ushijima's first defense line north of Naha. It took 11 weeks of combined land fighting and naval gunfire support to compress Ushijima into the southern tip of the island and destroy him.

    c. <u>The Imperial Navy's Last Stand</u>. Meantime the last Japanese fleet sortied from Japan while 355 Kamikazes prepared to take off from Kyushu. The Imperial Second Fleet, including the mighty <u>Yamato</u>, the cruiser <u>Yahagi</u>, and eight destroyers loaded with the last oil available, started on its suicide mission against Turner's transports on 6 April. It was sighted by planes of TF 58 on 8 April and practically obliterated: the <u>Yamato</u>, the <u>Yahagi</u>, and a destroyer went down, and damage to two other destroyers resulted in their being scuttled. During the two months that the Fifth Fleet remained in close support of land operations on Okinawa, Kamikazes damaged four American and three British fleet carriers. Altogether they sank 36 American ships, none larger than a destroyer, and damaged 368, many beyond repair: included were ten battleships, 13 fleet and escort carriers, five cruisers, and 67 destroyers.

F. SPRUANCE'S STRATEGY. Spruance received some criticism for using TF 58 for static defense. But he regarded the protection of the beachhead as his principal task. He would not leave the area until enough airfields out of the range of enemy fire had been obtained on Okinawa for land-based planes to take over the protection of the troops, and he would not relieve his picket vessels until the army had established an effective radar screen ashore. Once these conditions were fulfilled, he withdrew TF 58. Meanwhile he had taken TF 58 on three raids against Kyushu to reduce the Kamikaze menace. Halsey relieved Spruance on 27 May. Nimitz freed TF 58 of support functions and Halsey proceeded to strike twice at Japan before retiring to Leyte Gulf to prepare for the assault on Japan itself.

Okinawa was declared secure in July. At the cost of some 12,000 men and of at least 90 ships sunk or damaged, the United States had wiped out all but 7,400 of its more than 77,000 defenders and secured a position from which air power could strike at the industrial centers of southern Japan and a base for staging the invasion of the home islands.

G. PREPARATIONS FOR THE INVASION OF JAPAN. After exhaustive discussion of whether Japan should be blockaded into submission or invaded, the Joint Chiefs of Staff decided upon direct assault. MacArthur, newly designated Commander-in-Chief U.S. Army Forces Pacific, would command the invasion of Kyushu and southern Honshu, 1 November 1945, and an advance onto the Tokyo Plain in March 1946. Naval forces engaged in these operations were divided: the amphibious and close support forces became the Fifth Fleet under Admiral Spruance; the combined American-British fast carriers became the Third Fleet commanded by Admiral Halsey.

In preparation for the assault on Kyushu, American and Allied forces tightened the blockade and stepped up the bombardment of Japan. Submarines patrolled in the Sea of Japan; naval fleet air wings and Army bombers attacked ships and convoys; B-29s continued their strategic bombardment of Japanese industry. Halsey joined by striking targets in and around northern Honshu and Hokkaido with his aircraft and Battle Line. On 17 July, the most powerful striking force in history raided the naval bases at Yokosuka and Kure, heavily damaging or sinking the remnants of the Imperial Japanese Fleet. However, on Nimitz's order, Halsey did not hit Hiroshima or Nagasaki. While directing another strike against Tokyo on 15 August Halsey received the word to "cease fire."

H. JAPAN SURRENDERS. Emperor Hirohito suggested to his Supreme War Council on 22 June 1945 that Japan must work out a plan for ending the war. The plan must preserve the imperial system and win over those committed to a war to the finish. Terms submitted by radio via Moscow (Russia was still neutral) were intercepted and decoded by American Intelligence, and on 26 July the Potsdam Proclamation declared that "unconditional surrender" would apply only to the Japanese armed forces. However, Japan would be stripped of all territorial gains and retain only its four home islands, and points in Japan would be occupied until there was created a government acceptable to the Allies. An unfortunate misunderstanding of Japanese language made it appear that the Japanese had contemptuously rejected these terms. Acting on this supposed rejection, the United States directed the dropping of an atomic bomb on Hiroshima, 6 August, and a second on Nagasaki, 8 August, the same day that Russia declared war and the Red Army marched into Manchuria.

The Japanese leaders had long deluded their people with fantastic tales of fictional triumphs. The power and mystery of the atomic bomb and the advance of the Red Army convinced even the diehards to desist. Thus the war could end without creating domestic chaos in Japan. The Allies agreed that the imperial system would remain unimpaired except that during the period of occupation the Emperor would submit to the authority of the Supreme Allied Commander in Japan and that the Japanese people should decide his ultimate status through free election. A cease-fire was issued by both sides on 15 August, and the surrender document was signed aboard the *Missouri* on 2 September. The Third Fleet took Japan into custody and liberated about 20,000 Allied prisoners before MacArthur moved to Tokyo to direct the occupation. In November, Halsey retired from the Navy.

I. NAVAL POWER AND VICTORY IN THE PACIFIC

    1. **Naval Power Versus Land Power**. The United States assumed the defensive in the Pacific until industrial production and European developments permitted assumption of the offensive. Japan's major force was its army, and an army normally has to be defeated on land. Interposed between the United States and Japan were many heavily defended positions scattered over the western half of the Pacific Ocean, beyond American aerial range. The Navy therefore had to win control over the enemy's naval and air power before attack could be launched on the land--a navy had to be used to defeat an army. While the Japanese industrial base was too restricted to recoup naval, air, and shipping losses after 1942, America's productive capacity made possible naval and naval-air superiority that increased rapidly, particularly during the last year of the war. The collapse of

Japan became inevitable when its naval and air forces could neither support the homeland nor its shrinking overseas empire. Thus Allied naval power made it unnecessary to conquer the main Japanese armies.

2. <u>Allied Strategy</u>. One reason for Allied victory in the Pacific lay in the strategy of securing a path to Japan by capturing key bases, neutralizing others, and bypassing still others in a classic example of the application of the principles of economy of force, mobility, and concentration. Without disparagement to the successive advances in the Southwest Pacific Area, the Central Pacific was the paramount drive. In the Central Pacific, the key to success was proof of the soundness of American Navy and Marine Corps amphibious assault doctrine. Amphibious assault, American carrier-based air power, and submarine strength were the three most significant factors in bringing about the defeat of Japan. The <u>balancing</u> of tri-elemental forces--armies, fleets, and aircraft--rather than a single force, produced victory.

3. <u>Submarines</u>. By expanding too far, the Japanese placed a severe strain upon their merchant shipping and increased their burden of logistic support. Their merchant marine proved vulnerable to Allied submarines, major exponents of the Allied policy of unremitting blockade. Submarines and the recapture of the Philippines severed Japan's lifeline to the South Resources Area, strangled the home islands, and destroyed Japanese industrial potential. Allied submarines sank 1,000 major vessels, nearly 5 million tons, or 63 percent of all Japanese merchant shipping destroyed, and damaged an additional 530 ships displacing about 3 million tons. They also sank 91 Japanese warships, seven fewer than the number sunk by surface vessels but seven more than those sunk by aircraft.

American submarines proved effective even though they were at first hampered by conservative doctrine and a defective magnetic torpedo exploder and defective contact exploder as well. Wartime doctrine was to attack any or all enemy vessels. The development of an effective steam-turbine torpedo, however, took two years, when the electric torpedo appeared and was preferred. Yet it was well into 1943 that American submarines carried a torpedo that could match the performance of the Japanese "Long Lance."

Although the primary mission of Allied submarines was to raid enemy communications, they also patrolled lines of enemy approach; ferried VIPs, refugees, and troops; undertook photographic reconnaissance; and engaged in lifesaving, weather reporting, scout missions, and mine laying. Vivid accounts of the actions of individual submarines are readily available in a number of books.[1]

4. <u>The Fast Carrier Task Force</u>. The exercise of naval strength by the United States in the Pacific was novel as well as powerful. Building upon doctrines worked out in the 1920s and 1930s, the United States developed and perfected the Fast Carrier Task Force, the most mighty and speedy naval force the world had yet seen. Possessing great mobility and endurance, the fast carriers spearheaded and supported many offensive assaults, successfully countered enemy naval surface and air and land-based aircraft attack, and overwhelmed enemy outposts. The carriers greatly extended the power of naval aircraft; naval aircraft greatly extended the striking range of surface forces. Instead of superseding naval surface power, aircraft enormously multiplied its power.

5. <u>Amphibious Forces</u>. Developments in amphibious warfare made the sea a highway rather than an impediment to the passage of large military forces. New techniques in the use of naval gun and naval air support backed by many specialized types of ships permitted the Navy to advance its bases from Hawaii to Okinawa, to the doorstep of Japan. Naval power transported, supplied, and supported the Allied amphibious assault troops in their Southwest Pacific and Central Pacific drives to the Philippines and beyond. The extraordinary integration of land power and sea power represented by the amphibious force resulted in the creation of a new power dimension; a synthesis of sailors, naval fliers, and fleet-borne troops occurred. The new naval synthesis was firmly based on an adequate doctrine. The production of new amphibious equipment (tractors, Dukw's, tank landing ships, dock landing ships, infantry landing craft, amphibious headquarters ship, and helicopters) and techniques evolved from actual coordination of

supporting arms, refined that doctrine until it reached the stage of near-perfection.

6. **Logistics**. The evolution of spectacular methods of logistic support was another major contribution to Allied victory in the Pacific. Mobile service squadrons in forward areas released fighting fleets from dependence on rearward bases; in a sense modern naval vessels acquired the most unique characteristic of the old sailing ship--ability to operate afloat for indefinite periods of time. Novel methods of fueling, replenishing, and repairing at sea greatly speeded the progress of Allied forces toward Japan.

7. **Science**. Technical innovations made the Allied navies the most formidable ever to sail the seas. Radio, sonar, radar, specialized ships and aircraft, the VT fuse, rockets, and the atomic bomb were but a few of the ingenious inventions that added great strength to naval power. Not to be overlooked are the planners and experimenters who evolved the operational techniques that adapted them to naval use.

8. **The American People**. In the long run, the American people were responsible for victory in the Pacific. Their political leadership reflected public opinion or led it toward desirable goals; their colossal production program and scientific and managerial skill provided the sinews of war; their military services were ably led and, in general, devoted to the principle of cooperation on the staff level and in the field; their regulars provided a nucleus for the indoctrination of reserves; the reserves swelled the Navy of 1945 to more than ten times its prewar size and set a record for the participation of American people in the naval service unsurpassed since the days of the American Revolution.

CHAPTER 22

THE COLD WAR AND AMERICAN
DEFENSE ORGANIZATION, 1945-1950

I. THE COLD WAR, 1945-1950

A. THE SOVIET POSITION AT WAR'S END.

1. <u>Soviet Objectives</u>. World War II did not bend Soviet leaders from their long-range objective of a Communist-dominated world. The devastation of Europe and China, nationalist stirrings in the lands ringing the eastern Mediterranean and the Indian Ocean, the rapid demobilization of the United States, the deep-seated longing for peace by the Western world, and a growing opposition to the use of atomic weapons provided rich fields which the Soviets adroitly exploited.

2. <u>International Weakness</u>. In 1945, the Soviet Union enjoyed the advantages of an interior line of position. To the west lay Europe, ripe for plucking because of its war damage, economic dislocation, and political instability. To the east lay weakened China, already partially under Communist influence, and ever-attractive Korea. Japan, however, was dominated by the United States; without adequate naval power the Soviets could not readily threaten this island group. The tempting oil-producing states of the Middle East, too, were within reach of the Mediterranean and Red Seas, of the Persian Gulf, and of the Indian Ocean and could not be threatened successfully without adequate naval power.

B. SOVIET EXPANIONIST MOVES. At the end of World War II, Estonia, Latvia, Lithuania, Poland, Hungary, Bulgaria, Rumania, and parts of Austria and Germany were within the "Iron Curtain." Albania was already communist, as was Yugoslavia, and communism was making headway in France and Italy.

1. <u>The Coup in Czechoslovakia</u>. In 1948, a successful <u>coup d'etat</u> resulted in complete Soviet control of the government of Czechoslovakia. Famed munitions works and uranium deposits were among the gains enjoyed by the communists.

2. <u>The Berlin Blockade</u>. Much more disruptive of Western strategic plans than the loss of Czechoslovakia

was the Soviet attempt, beginning in June 1948, to blockade Berlin in order to drive France, Great Britain, and the United States from the city. With all land and water traffic to Berlin blocked, the Western powers had to consider means of meeting the Soviet challenge for supremacy in Germany. They could withdraw, stand firm while deciding to withdraw or to remain, or use all methods short of war to enforce their right to remain and risk war as a consequence. They decided to remain. For 11 months a brilliantly executed airlift supplied Berlin with necessities and permitted the West to achieve its objective without the use of force. After the West sponsored the creation of the Federal Government of Germany (Bonn Government), May 1949, the Soviets lifted the blockade. U.S. Navy and Air Force planes carried about 70 percent of the ten million tons of supplies that saved Berlin, British planes the rest.

C. COMMUNIST EXPANSION IN ASIA.

    1. The Communists Take Over in China. Chinese Communists had expended as much effort during World War II fighting Chiang Kai-shek as the Japanese. Corruption and mismanagement in Chiang's government and demands for land reform gave Mao Tze-tung's propagandists ample munition in appealing to the people. With surrendered Japanese arms and weapons captured from the Nationalist Chinese or supplied by Russia, the Communists fought to control China. The United States buttressed Chiang with money and arms and sent various mediators to settle the civil war but withdrew its marines when Chiang's chances appeared hopeless. By late 1948 the Communists controlled all of Manchuria. In December 1949, the Nationalist Government moved to Formosa; by the end of 1950 the Chinese mainland was in Communist hands. A 30-year pact between Mao and the Soviets (15 February 1950) provided for "friendship, alliance, and mutual assistance." Thus within five years a "bamboo Curtain" was drawn between the West and the more than 500 million Chinese were brought under communist domination.

    Henceforth the People's Republic of China will be referred to simply as China and the government of Formosa as Formosa or Taiwan.

    2. Divided Korea. By agreements at the end of

World War II, Russia occupied Korea to the 38th parallel and the United States the area to the south. The Soviets rapidly organized North Korea into a communist camp in opposition to the Democratic party of Syngman Rhee. In violation of agreements, the Soviets refused inspection of North Korea by the United States and the United Nations and also refused to honor their promise to hold free nationwide elections. The United States withdrew its troops from South Korea by the end of June 1949, a year after Rhee had been elected president of the Republic of Korea, which controlled only South Korea. Meanwhile the North Koreans established their People's Democratic Republic. Russia withdrew, leaving an efficient North Korean army trained for offense to face a weak South Korean force trained and armed solely for defense.

3. <u>Indochina</u>. Japan's occupation of Indochina in 1941 crushed a nascent nationalist movement. France's sympathy with the postwar nationalist drive ended when Communist General Ho Chi Minh's Viet Minh forces moved in to replace the recently displaced Japanese. Civil war commenced when France recognized the anti-Communist Provisional Government of Vietnam in June 1948.

4. <u>Occupied Japan</u>. The Allied command named the United States the occupying power for Japan and by the terms of the surrender agreement committed Japan to a democratic government and free elections. Under the direction of General of the Army Douglas MacArthur as Supreme Commander, Japan adopted a new constitution (effective 3 May 1947) which guaranteed a democratic political, economic, and social system and also renounced the right to wage war. Friction with the Soviets over the Kurile Islands, fishing rights in Siberian waters, and Soviet attempts to organize a Communist party in Japan was firmly handled by MacArthur.

D. WESTERN DEFENSE MEASURES.

1. <u>The Power Vacuum</u>. Despite the requirement for occupation forces, and in violation of the principle that diplomacy unsupported by strength rarely succeeds, the American people demanded rapid demobilization. Within a few months of the end of the war, the fighting forces of the United States were reduced to near

impotence, creating a power vacuum which the alert Soviets promptly filled. Short of using diplomatic protests or atomic bombs, the United States had no power to contest Soviet expansion. With American public opinion adverse to the use of atomic weapons and unwilling to endorse a preventive war, the United States could neither force the Soviets to honor their wartime agreements nor stop their territorial expansion.

2. **The West Faces Reality.** The West enjoyed the advantages of the exterior line of position because it controlled most of the littoral areas of Europe, possessed vast staging areas for war in the Atlantic community, and controlled the Pacific Ocean. In the Pacific, Japan was to the Asiatic mainland what Great Britain was to Europe, and defense arrangements with the major Pacific powers made it appear that Russia could be contained because surrounded. So long as a large segment of Western opinion believed this "encirclement" a threat to Russia's "legitimate" defensive policy or was more concerned with domestic problems than with international affairs, Western governments could not make their peoples realize the gravity of the Soviet threat. Indeed, some governments themselves failed to evaluate the threat correctly and to provide an adequate military posture.

3. **Helping the Free to Remain Free.**

    a. **The Truman Doctrine.** Postwar Russian expansion into the Baltic and Balkan states proceeded while the military might of the United States reached a new low. The United Nations averted trouble over Iran in 1947, but Great Britain jarred the free world by stating that it could no longer grant full-scale economic support to Greece. Since Turkey and the eastern Mediterranean might fall into Soviet hands if Greece were not bolstered, President Truman proclaimed that the United States would help free peoples everywhere "against aggressive movements that seek to impose upon them totalitarian regimes" and would support "free peoples who are resisting attempted subjugation by armed minorities or by outside pressures."

Greece was already in the throes of a civil war in which the rebels were receiving aid from Yugoslavia, then a Soviet puppet government. The Truman Doctrine served notice on the Soviets that the United States would support Greece against the Communists and Turkey against Soviet demands for control of the Dardanelles. American supplies, munitions, and military advisers aided the Greek government, and American naval units began their protracted show of force in the Mediterranean. The Congress adopted a face-saving amendment to the original appropriation to the effect that the United States would lay down this burden whenever the United Nations was willing to pick it up. The Truman Doctrine enabled the United States to take the tactical offensive in the cold war to contain communism.

  b. **The Marshall Plan.** In June 1947, Secretary of State George C. Marshall proposed a plan of economic aid to bolster the reconstruction efforts of the European countries. The Soviets refused, kept their puppets from accepting, created the Communist Information Bureau (Cominform) to promote communism by combating the Marshall Plan, and established the Molotov Plan (economic integration of Russia with its satellites). The European Recovery Program was the agency through which America helped rebuild western Europe and kept Italy, particularly, from communist control. Sixteen countries were aided by a total of $34.6 billions in non-military aid and $12.2 billions in military aid between 1946 and 1954.

  c. **Point Four.** President Harry Truman's fourth recommendation to the Congress in his inaugural address in 1948 envisaged a "Bold New Program" in which American technicians and <u>private</u> investors would build up trade in areas where the masses lived in misery, thereby relieving economic distress and countering communism. Nearly two-score countries in the Near East, Africa, Asia, the Pacific, and Latin America have enjoyed the stimulus of about $140,000,000 annually since 1948.

  d. **NATO.** Soviet expansion and other threats to peace determined the Western nations to band together for mutual defense. It was obvious, however, that American aid was needed for the defense of Europe as well as for its economic recovery. In 1949 the United States and 11 other nations signed the North Atlantic Treaty Pact, the first military alliance concluded by the United States in peacetime.[1] A regional alliance within the scope of the Charter of the United Nations, the North Atlantic Treaty Organization promises the support of all members to a party attacked. Such support may be individual or collective and may or may not mean resort to war. The North Atlantic Council is responsible for drawing up strategic plans; the actual implementation of plans is vested in three commands--Supreme Allied Commander Europe (SACEUR), Supreme Allied Commander Atlantic (SACLANT), and the Canada-United States Regional Planning Group. Despite American underwriting, NATO forces grew with dismaying slowness. Supreme Headquarters Allied Powers Europe (SHAPE) controlled 50 divisions in 1953 as compared with Russia's 190. Yet the 350,000,000 people of the NATO countries felt that they possessed enough strength to discourage if not to defeat aggression.

II. THE UNITED STATES STRATEGIC BOMBING SURVEY

In the fall of 1944, President Roosevelt established a United States Strategic Bombing Survey to evaluate the effects of strategic bombing in Europe. Involved were some 1,700 military and civilian researchers and analysts. On 15 August 1945, Truman invited the Survey to include the Pacific theater also, covering the Navy and the atomic bomb as well as the Army. To represent the Navy, Secretary of the Navy Forrestal appointed the widely-experienced naval aviator Rear Admiral Ralph A. Ofstie, who immediately angered Major General Orvil A. Anderson, who demanded that the Air Force control everything that flew in an area of operations, by noting that the Navy had made it possible for the Army Air Force to come within range of striking Japan. The report showed that of Japanese merchant shipping sunk, submarines accounted for 54.7 percent, Navy and Marine air for 20.6 percent, and Army air for only 10.2 percent. In Europe, because other demands siphoned off its planes, the strategic bombing campaign lasted only from September 1944 to VE day, 8 May 1945, and in the Pacific only from November 1944 to VJ-Day, 2 September 1945. In Europe, strategic bombing was 14 percent effective, with 1 bomb in 12 striking near enough to damage a target. In the Pacific, although strategic bombing started in November 1944, Japan was not hurt until after 15 May 1945, when LeMay began using incendiaries. The report showed that strategic bombing was effective in Europe only when it was repeated, sustained, and heavy. Also, only after the Navy had defeated the Japanese Navy and air force and strangled its shipping and then brought B-29s within range of Japan was strategic bombing effective.

III. THE ARMED FORCES OF THE UNITED STATES, 1945-1950

A. THE UNIFICATION BATTLE. In his report on the Navy's wartime operations Admiral Ernest J. King noted that the Navy had operated on land and in the air as well as on and under the water. What kind of doctrine the Navy should follow in the postwar world of demobilization fever and financial pinch was therefore a subject of great importance. While devising methods of protecting its sea forces from atomic attack, it also had to devise means of bringing force to bear against Russia, whose huge land mass is situated in the heart of Eurasia and is guarded by large submarine forces. Influenced by its use of tactical air and Marines in the Pacific in World War II, the Navy wished to prepare for conventional as well as atomic war--meaning that it must gain and keep control of the seas in its tridimensional aspects, transport and supply troops overseas and provide them with tactical air support; seize and defend overseas bases; and improve the power and mobility of carriers. It denied that strategic air war would reduce the will of an enemy. While the Navy was wedded to the task force concept in which air, surface, submarine, and Marine Corps elements could be arranged as needed to perform a task, it saw the need of better integrating foreign, economic, and military policy and planning in top government echelons and of more effectively integrating all service elements in the field--all at an acceptable cost.

The Army, influenced by mass war in Europe and strategic bombing, preferred to have a single chief of staff in a single department of defense and wished to take over the combatant functions of the Marine Corps.

Army Air Forces wanted to win independence from the War Department and to control all air not directly germane to the missions of the Army and Navy. Like the Army, it preferred a single chief of staff. Because it had long-range bombers and atomic bombs, it would use strategic bombing as the best weapon system and desired to take over naval air.

Air Force spokesmen, first to generate the ideas of massive deterrence and massive retaliation, saw atomic-laden bombers as serving as a deterrent to war on the part of the Soviets and also as capable of destroying Russia if war came. Given the huge size of "the bomb"--5 tons--the Air Force alone could deliver it. The AF denied the need for an army or navy because an atomic war would be over in the matter of days and declared that bombers made navies obsolete. They thus overlooked the need for troops to occupy an enemy country and for a navy to provide these troops with tactical and logistic support and to protect shipping. The Navy countered that total reliance upon strategic bombing precluded the provision of balanced forces that could handle sub-atomic (conventional or limited) situations. If all troops went into the army and all aviation into the air force, nothing would be left to it except the missions of antisubmarine warfare and transportation. It intended some day to be able to deliver atomic bombs by carrier-based planes and would not hand over naval air--about 30 percent of the Navy--to the Air Force. Last, surface fleets built about carriers were not obsolete.

President Franklin D. Roosevelt took a step forward in the matter of integration when he created the Joint Chiefs of Staff in 1942, for the chiefs advised him on strategic matters and provided the necessary interservice integration of strategy and operations while the civilian service secretaries obtained the men and materials needed for military operations. The Army's chief of staff, General George C. Marshall, took another step by reorganizing the Army (28 February 1942) so that it contained three major commands: Ground Forces, Air Forces, and Services of Supply, with General Henry H. Arnold, although merely the commander of the Army Air Corps, sitting with the JCS. There were troubles in the JCS, of course, as over whether the Army or Navy should control aircraft engaged in antisubmarine warfare and whether Nimitz, MacArthur, and General Curtis LeMay of the Twentieth Air Force were not fighting individual wars against Japan. The system worked nevertheless because, in general, the Navy granted the Army supremacy in Europe and the Army granted supremacy to the Navy in the Pacific. Once the war ended in Europe, however, the basis for and the need for interservice cooperation disappeared. It was time to reorganize.

Between 1924 and 1945, some 55 bills on unification were introduced in Congress and a dozen studies were made of the subject. The JCS made a contribution by separating operational planning from strategic policy problems and appointing committees that would insure unification in military operations. However, when the Army suggested (January 1943) a departmental reorganization in which a general staff would supervise everything, the Navy responded with a call for a redefinition of the missions and roles of the services including their weapons. The JCS thereupon instructed the Joint Strategic Survey Committee to investigate the issue of a single department of war. In October 1943, the Army Service Forces suggested a single department with unified command and combined staffs in which there would be four operating divisions: army, navy, air, and supply. While General Marshall ordered further studies, a special House Committee on Postwar Military Policy under Clifton A. Woodrum held hearings on the possibility of unification (April-May 1944). When Secretary of the Navy Frank Knox, who said he favored a single military department, died, he was succeeded by James V. Forrestal (19 May 1944), who postponed the issue. Forrestal did not say "No" to unification but argued for more study because he insisted that defense was a government-wide function that could not be undertaken by merely a military department. There must be a supradepartmental organization yet not a monolithic structure under a single chief of staff, such as the Army and Army Air Corps wanted, lest the Navy not be "merged" but "submerged." While the chief of staff system demanded by the Army and Army Air Corps would provide unity of command, it might also strip the Navy of its aviation and Marine Corps.

Although the Army did not oppose independence for its Air Corps--which saw unification as the only way to achieve independence from the Army--it did not wish the latter's appropriations to come out of its own. Hence budget considerations must be taken into account when reorganizing the national security structure. Forrestal agreed but went beyond merely finances, saying that such a reorganization must include in addition foreign policy, domestic economic mobilization policy, application of science and engineering to the creation of new weapons, and maximum exploitation of intelligence data available from <u>all</u> government agencies. To

insure that diplomacy did not go one way and the
military in another, he revived the State-War-Navy
Coordinating Committee (SWNCC, or SWINC) and provided
it with a secretariat to coordinate political and
military policies at the cabinet level. He then
appointed two naval officers to work with two Army
officers on unification plans. This committee, headed
by Admiral James O. Richardson, interviewed 56 top-
ranking American officers and reported to the JCS in
April 1945 that there should be a civilian secretary
of a defense department, a military head to serve as
chief of staff to the President and commander of the
armed forces under the civilian secretary, a JCS
organization to advise the President, an Air Force
man to coordinate with the Army and Navy, and an under
secretary who would direct the business side of the
department. The Army was pleased because the JCS
would have command authority, the Navy because the
civil side of the department would be run by civilians. A plan drafted by General Joseph McNarney of
the Air Corps was quite similar. Forrestal asked
Ferdinand Eberstadt to study the unification question. Eberstadt's report, made in September, was
submitted to the Senate Military Affairs Committee
when it opened hearings on unification in October
1945. With minor changes, Eberstadt's plan was adopted
because it provided three coordinate services, each
headed by a secretary of cabinet rank, but also a
number of coordinating civil-military agencies. Truman,
however, preferred the Army's (General J. Lawton
Collins) plan, which called for a single chief of
staff, and Congress in 1946 showed that it favored
dealing with one rather than three military organizations by merging the military and naval affairs committees and the military and naval appropriations
committees into an Armed Services Committee for each
chamber. Compromise was evident when the Senate Committee approved a merger of the Eberstadt and Collins
plans with the provision that the chief of staff would
have no command authority. The Committee said nothing,
however, about service roles and missions. But the
Senate Naval Affairs Committee upheld the Forrestal-
Eberstadt plan.

    Forrestal and the Secretary of War, Robert Pat-
terson, still disagreed on a single department of
defense and the status of three coordinate military
departments, the Marine Corps, and naval aviation.

Although compromises on these issues were worked out by staff members including Major General Lauris Norstand, USAF, and Vice Admiral Forrest Sherman, Truman sent his own administration bill to Congress. Based largely on the Forrestal-Eberstadt plan, it passed Congress and he signed it on 27 July 1947.

B. THE NATIONAL SECURITY ACT OF 1947. The National Security Act provided for a National Security Council and a National Security Resources Board that would be put into the Executive Office of the White House, and a Central Intelligence Agency that would report to the National Security Council. Second, it provided a new executive department known as the National Military Establishment comprised of three military departments, an Army, Air Force, and Navy. Its head, a secretary of defense, would coordinate and unify their administration. Each time the Navy was mentioned in the act there followed the words "(including naval aviation and the U. S. Marine Corps)," thus preserving these forces by law, and the Secretary of Defense was enjoined not to "merge" the services. The secretary of defense, a cabinet member, was to be the principal assistant to the President in all matters relating to the national security and over defense budgets and expenditures. However, after informing him, a service secretary could present to the President or to the Director of the Budget any report or recommendation he deemed necessary.

While the secretary of defense was not permitted to have a general staff, he would be advised by three special civilian assistants, a War Council (comprised of the four military service heads), the JCS and their Joint Staff, a Munitions Board, and a Research and Development Board. Last, at the request of the Navy, Truman spelled out service roles and missions by executive order, with the Navy to have control over naval aviation and the Marine Corps. Paradoxically, because he objected to the Truman, Army, and Air Corps plans for defense reorganization, Truman appointed Forrestal the first secretary of defense, in consequence of which Forrestal assumed office on 17 September.

C. DOLLARS DETERMINE STRATEGY. Rather than letting Forrestal tell him what funding the department of defense needed to support national interests, Truman set military budget ceilings to which he must accommodate.

Moreover, it took time for the Joint Chiefs to produce a national rather than single service budgets. Forrestal sought forces that would be "balanced" not in their funding but in capabilities. However, between 1946 and 1950 an almost equal sharing of the budget by the services kept capabilities balanced. During these years, the Navy won approval for the building of a 60,000-ton supercarrier, for the modernization of Essex-class carriers so that they could handle jet if not atomic bombers, and for the building of a nuclear-powered submarine. At the same time, the Air Force launched a mighty publicity campaign that asserted that ships were vulnerable to atomic bombs, that neither the army or navy would be needed in a short atomic air war, that strategic air provided an economical and quick victory, that no other power had a large navy, and that since carriers duplicated Air Force power they were costly and wasteful. The Navy replied that the Air Force lacked a truly intercontinental bomber, and could not depend on overseas bases, defend the United States from atomic attack, or provide its own logistic support. It was doing little to prepare for a conventional war. Moreover, its aircraft could not show the flag as ships did or effectively carry on antisubmarine warfare or mount amphibious invasions. Last, reliance on a single weapon and single weapon system would cause stagnation of weapons developments in the other services.

With the end of the war, defense budgets plummeted from $45 billion in FY 1946 to $14.5 in FY 1947, $11.25 billion in FY 1948, $14.25 in FY 1949, and $14.4 billion in FY 1950. Two commissions, one presidential (Thomas K. Finletter) and one congressional (Brewster-Hinshaw) one looking forward from 1948 to 1953, the other from 1948 to 1955, agreed that "the military establishment must be built around the air arm." The Finletter report recommended an Air Force of 70 groups (12,400 planes) and a naval air force of 14,500 planes. The Brewster-Hinshaw report recommended 20,541 planes for the Air Force and commensurate numbers of naval aircraft to be serviced by carriers. Although slower to introduce expensive jets into its inventory, by 21 July 1946, the Navy had jets on a carrier and established its first jet carrier squadron on 5 May 1948. The last report also spoke of the triplification instead of unification that marked the department of defense and that the JCS were as yet unable to provide a unified budget. The argument continued between the Air Force, which wanted to take over naval air, and the Army, which would take over the Marine Corps, while the Navy pointed out that increases in the Air Force meant increases also in the Army and Navy, for these had to support the Air Force. With the Joint Chiefs recommending a military budget of $30 billion for FY 1950 and Truman allotting only $14.4 billion, it was clear that rather than having strategic considerations determine the size of the military budget, that budget determined that quickly usable air-atomic power provided the best strategy.

D. ROLES AND MISSIONS. The definition of service roles and missions in the National Security Act failed to satisfy either the services or Forrestal. The Army, jealous of the Marine Corps particularly because each of its divisions had tactical air wings, wished to command all naval and air forces assigned to an Army mission, and the Air Force insisted that it control everything that flew through the air including atomic weapons and guided missile development. Because roles and missions must be determined before a joint budget for the services could be drafted, Forrestal had the Joint Chiefs meet with him at Key West on 11-14 March 1948, to discuss general principles, command functions of the armed forces, functions of the Joint Chiefs, and the functions of each military service. It was decided to coordinate rather than merge the armed forces and to assign each service primary and also collateral functions. The Air Force, e.g., would have strategic air and continental air defense as primary missions. As a collateral function, the Navy would use whatever air power it had left over from its primary function to support the Air Force, and the Army would contribute anti-aircraft artillery units and defend the United States. While the Navy's primary function was to organize, train, and equip Navy and Marine Corps forces for combat operations at sea, the Air Force's collateral duties included antisubmarine warfare, aerial mine laying, and the protection of shipping. The Joint Chiefs would prepare strategic and logistic plans and formulate policies; annually furnish the secretary of defense a coordinated budget; and in strategic areas establish unified commands in which one of their number would serve as their "executive agent." Strive as Forrestal and the Joint Chiefs did, they still did not make some items completely clear. While air defense was made a primary function of all the services, army aviation and guided missiles were not discussed. Nor was a clear line drawn between the Air Force and Navy on use of strategic and tactical air. In consequence, the Navy was permitted to "attack any targets, inland or otherwise, which appear necessary for the accomplishment of its mission"—a red flag to the Air Force. Included in the Key West agreement was approval by the Joint Chiefs of the building of a supercarrier and use of atomic bombs--another red flag to the Air Force. In August, at Newport, Forrestal and the Joint Chiefs further refined roles and missions.

E. MILITARY DEVELOPMENTS.

1. <u>Naval Progress</u>. Logic dictated that the war plans and military developments of the free nations be made with Russia in mind as a potential enemy. With a vastly superior navy, the United States need not fear Russian naval power on the surface. However, Russia could launch a formidable attack upon seaborne commerce and opposing naval forces with her large number of fleet submarines. Moreover, the Russians were rapidly building their surface fleet into the world's second largest navy.

Faced with growing Soviet strength, the United States wisely provided for a strong ship reserve and a large reserve of trained personnel. "Mothballing" methods were devised to preserve ships, and the Organized and Volunteer Reserve programs kept reservists abreast of latest developments and methods. Meanwhile, fleets operating in Mediterranean or Far Eastern waters, including Fleet Marine Force, followed prescribed training programs, and logistic support forces trained by doing. Joint maneuvers with NATO forces occurred periodically.

Antisubmarine operations and developments in naval aircraft design and operation were given high priority in naval development. Submarines were to be ferreted out by "hunter-killer" groups, and increasingly heavy jet fighters and bombers provoked the radical "canted" deck design for aircraft carriers. Emphasis was also placed upon the provision of atomic propulsion not only for submarines but for surface craft and aircraft as well.

Changes and improvements also occurred in munitions. Redesigned and ahead-thrown weapons reduced the sinking time and augmented the effectiveness of depth charges. Automatic batteries were provided for cruisers. Rocket weapons reached all the services, and experimentation continued on guided missiles, including the intercontinental type.

Using as a model the German V-2, in the summer of 1945 the Bureau of Ordnance began work on a shipborne missile. While a V-2 was launched from the <u>Midway</u> in 1946 as a publicity stunt, the National Research Laboratory provided a high altitude research rocket, and both the Navy and the Army began work on short-range nuclear missiles. In the Army's Operation Paperclip, Wernher von Braun, the German-born space scientist who produced the V-2, headed a team of 120 people that worked on rocketry. Despite opposition from the Air Force, which said that missiles interfered with intercontinental bombers, by 1954 the Army and Navy began to cooperate in producing a 1,500-mile Intermediate Range Ballistic Missile (IRBM) and the Navy to solve problems associated with firing a missile from a submarine.

One of the latest developments, the helicopter, revolutionized tactics both on land and sea. Capable of operating from land or ship, it performs well as spotter, scout, mailman, plane guard, and rescue craft. It can be used for "vertical envelopment," carrying amphibious operations into a new element, as well as for logistic support.

2. <u>Nuclear Weapons</u>. To further evaluate the capabilities of atomic bombs and to learn methods of defense against them, the Army and Navy conducted tests at Bikini Atoll, Marshall Islands, in July 1946. Valuable conclusions on blast damage and radiation contamination were obtained. An underwater blast furnished additional data, particularly on radioactivity. Later tests with thermonuclear weapons were also conducted, the results of which indicated that a hydrogen bomb, e.g., can thoroughly pulverize an area of 10 mile radius, cause extensive damage within an area of 30 mile radius, and that radiation contamination ("fallout") can prove dangerous up to 130 miles from the scene of the blast.

The American monopoly on atomic bombs lasted until 1949. Russia's production of atomic and then of thermonuclear bombs naturally caused the United States to overhaul its strategic conceptions.

F. THE NATIONAL SECURITY ACT AMENDMENTS OF 1949. Within a year of the passage of the National Security Act, suggestions for improving it included the greater centralization of authority in the office of the secretary of defense; the devising of new political, strategic, and budget policies in consequence of technological change (e.g., the atomic bomb, a projected supercarrier and nuclear submarine, and guided missiles); greater integration of the military services; and more economy, the last stressed by the Hoover Commission that looked into the reorganization of the executive branch of the government in 1948. In his first annual report, Forrestal recommended that he be provided a deputy, that the word "general" be removed from the act so that he would have specific "direction, authority, and control" over the military departments; that a nonvoting chairman be added to the JCS and that the number serving on the Joint Staff be increased; and that the secretary of defense alone and not the service secretaries sit on the National Security Council.

The amendments changed the name of the National Military Establishment to Department of Defense; deleted the service secretaries from the National Security Council; gave the secretary of defense "direction, authority, and control" over three military rather than executive departments and aid in the form of a deputy; provided a nonvoting chairman for the JCS and increased the Joint Staff from 100 to 210 men; and assigned one of the assistant secretaries of defense the task of "providing uniform budget and fiscal procedures and organizations."

G. THE REVOLT OF THE ADMIRALS.

1. Supercarrier vs B-36. John L. Sullivan, former Assistant Secretary of the Navy for Air and Under Secretary, succeeded Forrestal as Secretary on 18 September 1947. He scrutinized and finally approved funding a 60,000-ton supercarrier needed to determine doctrine for the employment of heavier aircraft, including jets, but not necessarily to serve strategic bombers. As already noted, both the Con-

gressional Aviation Policy Board and the President's Air Policy Commission (1948) approved the use of carriers for both defense and offense. Their conclusions sat badly with General Carl Spaatz, the Air Force Chief of Staff, who held that the Air Force must be the predominant service because it alone was capable of massive retaliation. The Navy should therefore give up its air arm to the Air Force and exist merely as an auxiliary force conducting antisubmarine warfare and providing sea transportation.

Such naval leaders as Sullivan and the CNO, Fleet Admiral Chester W. Nimitz, who retired on 15 December 1947, and his successor, Admiral Louis E. Denfeld, believed that a fast-moving fleet would be an unprofitable target for atomic bombs and opposed a strategy based upon a single weapon and single delivery system because such a strategy would stifle the development of new weapons and techniques. While the Navy had a defensive role, it could also occupy advanced bases, destroy enemy air power and communications, and even bomb the interior of Russia if necessary with carrier aircraft. As Forrestal saw it, a balanced strategy made good sense when the United States had few atomic bombs and the longest-range Air Force bomber could not come within 2,000 miles of Moscow.

With funds short, Sullivan delayed his 1948 building program until 1949, stopped much conversion work, and built only prototype ships; he was thus able to transfer some funds to the building of a super-carrier. Controversy then heightened when the Air Force urged the Ferdinand Eberstadt Committee of the Hoover Commission, which was investigating national security, to merge naval aviation with the Air Force, and the Army wished to relegate the Navy to the role of escorting convoys. The Navy declared that it had greater capability for strategic bombing than the Air Force, which lacked a bomber that could reach targets in the Soviet Union. The Air Force declined a challenge to a simulated battle between a B-36 and a Navy Banshee fighter. Basing his remarks to the Hoover Commission largely upon position papers drafted by Arleigh Burke, head of the Organizational Policy and Research Division of the Office of CNO (OP-23), Vice Admiral Arthur Radford, Commander-in-Chief Pacific Fleet, opposed "pushbutton warfare" and a single weapon concept. The B-36, said Radford, was "not worth developing," and "the heavy bomber is the Maginot Line weapon that lulls us into defense lethargy." Moreover, the Navy could drop atomic bombs upon naval targets as a normal part of its primary function, as required by the National Security Act, and could do so better than the Air Force. Last, heavy bombers might be made obsolescent by guided missiles, and the Air Force could not be sure that it could have overseas bases to operate from.

3. <u>Enter Louis A. Johnson</u>. Literally driven mad while trying to manage the new department of defense, Forrestal resigned on 1 March 1949 at Truman's direction. His successor was Louis A. Johnson, who was experienced both in the military field and in the Washington bureaucracy. He was also air minded and politically ambitious. According to his naval aide, he "viewed the military establishment in general and the Navy in particular as his personal and deadly enemy" and planned "to merge the Air Force and Naval Aviation" under the Air Force and put the Marines into the Army. He built up a large staff to direct the military services and meant to "crack heads" together to hasten unification and enlarge the Air Force. If he could save from $1 billion to $1.5 billion per year in defense spending, he would have a fine platform on which to run for president in 1952.

Armed with a two-to-one vote of the JCS against the building of the supercarrier, named the <u>United States</u>, on 23 April 1949, Johnson cancelled her construction. Thoroughly infuriated, Sullivan resigned, saying that Johnson's next step would be "to abolish the Marine Corps and to transfer all naval and marine aviation elsewhere." While the Air Force modernized B-36s to give them greater range, it objected even to the modernizing of <u>Essex</u>-class carriers to enable them to operate improved planes.

When it was resolved to investigate Johnson's connection with the procurement of the B-36--he had been a director of its manufacturing company--Chairman Carl Vinson of the House Armed Service Committee undertook the task. Meanwhile Truman chose Francis Patrick Matthews, an attorney, banker, and businessman of Omaha, to be the new Secretary of the Navy. His knowledge of the Navy, he confessed, lay in once having rowed a boat.

Although Russia exploded an atomic bomb in August 1949, Johnson decided to "economize" by not spending $2.5 billion from the FY 1950 and FY 1951 budgets. He thus fueled debate among the services as to their cut of the budget pie. Given Johnson's cut of 50 percent for naval air in FY 1951, the Navy could not support offensive air operations. Strategy therefore continued to be determined not by a review of military requirements but by imposed financial controls.

4. <u>The Vinson Hearings</u>. The National Security Act Amendments of 1949, effective 10 August, increased Johnson's authority over the military departments and added a chairman to the JCS. Johnson emerged clean from his investigation by Vinson, but new charges were made against him, the Air Force, and unification that Vinson determined to investigate. At extensive hearings Matthews revealed his ignorance of naval matters, dissociated himself from his officers, and supported Johnson while Radford refurbished his argument against a single weapon and delivery system. He called the B-36 an Air Force "billion dollar blunder." Most senior naval officers agreed with Radford that unification could not proceed without mutual trust and unified planning within JCS and without permitting each service to bring an experimental weapon like a supercarrier through development, test, and evaluation stages. By siding with the "reformers," mostly aviators, Admiral Denfeld assured the end of his career and Arleigh Burke almost missed being promoted to rear admiral. According to Robert Dennison, Truman's naval aide, "this revolt of the admirals, it wasn't a revolt and it wasn't just the admirals. The whole Navy was questioning what the future held, what were the policies. Why? So it was a disturbing time."

As expected, Symington stood by the B-36 and his strategic bombing mission, and General Omar N. Bradley, Chairman of the Joint Chiefs, mistakenly averred that large-scale amphibious operations would never occur and that the Navy included "fancy Dans' who instead of being team players would not play unless they could call the signals.

Without the test of war, the Navy could not prove that strategic bombing could not provide adequate national security. With its budget for FY 1951 cut 11 percent below that of FY 1950, it had to drop men, stop operating ships including heavy and light carriers, and undertake no new construction or conversion work. However, the Vinson Committee report, issued on 1 March 1950, noted the Navy's demand for mobile and flexible forces tailored to perform given tasks and recommended that a supercarrier be built when funds were available. The report also found the Air Force unbalanced in favor of strategic power and that Johnson had violated law by changing congressional appropriations and cancelling the building of the United States.

H. NSC-68. By May 1950, Bradley and Vinson among others agreed with a National Security Council paper numbered 68. Its authors considered four possible courses of action to follow during the next five years that would provide the United States with security against the Soviets: maintain the status quo with the slow-paced defense programs at hand; the Fortress America concept, or isolationism; preventive war designed to preclude the Soviets from building a nuclear arsenal; and political, psychological, economic, and military programs to reach, "if possible, a tolerable state of order among nations without war and of preparing to defend ourselves in the event that the free world is attacked." The paper called for increasing annual defense spending from the approximately 6 percent of the national income in 1949 to 20 percent by 1954, or from $17-18 billion up to a level of $35-50 billion. Truman ordered the National Security Council to estimate the forces needed to implement NSC-68 and what it would cost and on 10 December suggested that the time frame be moved back to 1952. On 25 June 1950, North Korea invaded South Korea and the costing of NSC-68 shriveled in face of actual military expenditures. Incidentally, with the funding of the first Forrestal-class carriers in 1952, the Navy verged upon breaking the Air Force monopoly on strategic air power.

I. THE PRICE OF UNITY. The acid test for unification was provided by the Korean War, which caught the National Security Council and the armed forces unprepared, thus showing the dire need of improving intelligence of bringing civilian foreign policy makers and military leaders closer together, and of upgrading conventional forces. Those who had recommended a steady rearmament program were proved right in the field. The Strategic Air Command, which could destroy large areas of the Soviet Union, had not deterred the attack on South Korea from the north, and the United States was short such conventional components as carriers that the Air Force denigrated and the Marines Bradley said were unnecessary. Complete reliance on strategic air power was shown to be as false as the need for conventional forces was proved right, for nuclear stalemate predicated the fighting of limited wars only. If by 1952 the Navy had won its battle for more carriers and Marines, it and its sister services had lost the war against unification. The price of unity was paid in the form of a burgeoning office of the secretary of defense authorized to demand service unification.

CHAPTER 23

KOREA AND CONTINUED COMMUNIST CONTAINMENT, 1950-1961

I. HOT WAR--KOREA

A. THE ATTACK. On 25 June 1950, without warning, the Russian-equipped, Russian-trained, and perhaps Russian-inspired North Korean army lunged across the 38th parallel into South Korea. On 25 September 1947 the JCS; in 1949 General Douglas MacArthur, Commander Far Eastern Command; and on 12 January 1950 Secretary of State Dean Acheson had publicly stated that Korea was not within the "defensive perimeter" of the United States. Moreover, Secretary of Defense Louis A. Johnson divorced military from foreign policy matters, thereby making it difficult to correlate foreign, domestic, military, and economic policy. The Russians proved willing to test the West's determination to resist aggression while they sought to fill the gap in their Asiatic holdings and point a dagger at the heart of Japan. The American policy of containment, supported for 5 years by diplomatic and economic measures, suddenly changed from the abstract to the concrete.

B. RELATIVE STRENGTHS. The North Koreans attacked with 110,000 men supported by 1,400 artillery pieces, 126 Soviet T-34 tanks, and 100 tactical aircraft. The South Korean Army had 98,000 men, no heavy guns, no tanks, no tactical aircraft. Well trained in conventional infantry tactics and night operations, the North Koreans enjoyed the advantage of logistic support adapted to Korean geography. They could live off the land and readily conceal themselves. In contrast, the physical aspects of Korea presented almost insurmountable difficulties to mechanized armies and to forces dependent for logistic support on sea and air power. Moreover, the 1,500 mile-long Korean coastline offered few places suitable for amphibious landings. It rapidly became apparent that South Korean ground forces and Allied naval and air forces alone could not stop the advance of the North Korean armies.

C. THE UNITED NATIONS TO THE RESCUE. On the day following the Red attack, the United Nations Security Council condemned the North Korean move as a "breach of world peace," urged a case-fire and ordered military sanctions to be directed by the United States, which had no war plans for Korea and no time to prepare any. Korea was to give the Department of Defense its first combat role as a new organization and provide an acid test for the unification of the services. It would also uphold the contentions of the Navy "reformers," of General Omar N. Bradley, chairman of the JCS, and of the authors of NSC-68 for a continuing program of military preparedness during the cold war. Johnson's economizing, e.g., had reduced the Navy's 610 amphibious ships in 1945 to 362 in 1950, and cut enlisted Marine Corps strength from 78,715 to 67,025 and the Fleet Marine Force from 35,086 to 23,952 officers and men in FY 1950. American strategic air power had not deterred an attack on South Korea; nor could it be used in a limited ground war in which there were only 18 large industrial targets. MacArthur estimated that his forces in Japan were only 50 percent effective and confessed that they were not trained for amphibious operations. Air Force F-80 jets based in Japan had a combat radius of 100 miles and could remain over a Korean target for perhaps 15 minutes, and their pilots were not trained to support ground troops. All Admiral C. Turner Joy had in Japan were a light cruiser, 4 destroyers, 5 small amphibious ships, and 6 minesweepers--and no air--and cuts in forces available to the Pacific Fleet for FY 1950 meant that it could have only 2 of the then 8 carriers, not enough to keep one constantly operating. While the Fleet was assigned 3 of the 7 escort carriers, it had no light carriers (CVLs) and its single cruiser and Fleet Marine Force were slated for retirement in the spring. Truman nevertheless told Acheson that "We've got to stop the sons of bitches no matter what," and Acheson rather than Johnson proposed courses of action Truman adopted.

The direction of UN forces fell to MacArthur, who would command American naval as well as ground forces. To insure that this "police action" would not spread into World War III, President Truman ordered that Formosa be neutralized in order that the communists could not attack Chiang Kai-shek and the latter could not attack the China mainland, and declined Chiang's offer of two divisions to fight in Korea. On 27 June, the UN Security Council formally called upon all members of the UN for military assistance. Nineteen nations eventually sent detachments. The United States furnished the great bulk of the naval and air forces, supplies, and money, and except for the Republic of South Korea, of the men. Almost a million Americans, including many reservists involuntarily recalled to active duty, served in Korea.

D. MILITARY SEESAW.

1. **Early Naval Operations.** Early UN naval operations included the evacuation of American civilians from Korea, escort of merchant and supply shipping, shore bombardment, action against small North Korean naval units, and the ferrying of troops from Japan and later from the United States to Korea. While Vice Admiral A.D. Struble from Okinawa established a neutrality patrol in Formosa Strait, naval and Marine pilots launched interdiction and close support strikes from aircraft carriers sent to Korea.

Lest Korea be a ruse to draw American power away from Europe where the Soviets might launch a major thrust, General Hoyt Vandenberg, Chief of Staff of the Air Force, tripled the strength of the Strategic Air Command (SAC) in England and increased its strength in Guam, Newfoundland, and Labrador as well as in Korea. In addition, a second carrier force was sent to the Mediterranean; the production of guided missiles and of nuclear weapons was accelerated; a North American Defense Command was created to provide air defense for Canada and the United States; negotiations were begun for airfields for SAC in French Morocco and Greenland and for both air and naval bases in Spain; and Truman despatched four divisions to bolster NATO, to which Greece and Turkey were admitted in September 1951; and the CNO, Forrest Sherman, accepted the offer of Marines and of 30 aviation squadrons made by Commandant Clifton B. Cates.

2. **The Surge of the Red Tide.** Smashing past Suwon, the Reds pushed back both the South Koreans and the newly arrived American 24th Infantry Division. Stubborn opposition caused them to overestimate American strength, and instead of pushing south to Pusan they deployed across the country. However, they

soon drove to within thirty miles of Pusan before meeting the determined resistance of the 24th, which dug in and held its Pusan perimeter.

3. <u>UN Reinforcements</u>. Convinced that Korea could not be held without speedy reinforcements, MacArthur requested a Marine Combat Team from the United States and then a full Marine Division. Meantime a new carrier task force arrived in Korean waters. The success of the UN depended upon the timely arrival of the Marines. These debarked at Pusan on 2 August and were employed as a mobile reserve to stop any Red breakthrough in the Pusan Perimeter. Meanwhile Far Eastern Air Forces committed one medium and one light bomber wing and 8 fighter squadrons to Korea and Truman ordered a close naval blockade of the entire Korean peninsula, 5,400 miles long. Naval and Marine Corps carrier aircraft proved especially effective, be they the old propeller-driven, bent-wing F4U Corsairs, F9F Panther jets, and the newer F2H Banshee jets--with jets being used for the first time in combat from aircraft carriers. These planes could remain over a target for almost two hours, and their pilots were trained to support ground troops. Marines flying from escort carriers also used the single-engine prop plane, the AD Skyraider, that could carry more bombs than a B-17; and land-based P2V-5 and PBM-1 planes flew antisubmarine and surface patrol. At the same time the Military Sea Transportation Service and escort carriers bridged 7,000 miles of ocean with ships that funnelled supplies and replacement aircraft and spare parts to ports in Japan, Okinawa, and Korea. To keep the war limited, however, on 27 July Truman said he would not permit the use of atomic bombs. By thus alerting China that he would not use his most powerful weapon, he changed the course of the war in Korea and may have changed the course of history in Southeast Asia.

4. <u>Operation Chromite</u>. On 4 July, when MacArthur wished to test the feasibility of an amphibious landing at Inchon, the port of Seoul, that would make possible pinching off the Red forces to the south of Seoul, the Chairman of the JCS, Omar N. Bradley, strongly opposed because he believed amphibious operations to be obsolete. The Army's General J. Lawton Collins also opposed the use of Marines in such an operation, but Forrest Sherman backed the

5000-to-1 gamble all the way and approval from Washington arrived on 28 August. On 23 August MacArthur conferred with top naval leaders and learned that a tortuous channel, emplaced fortifications, and a tidal range from 29 to 36 feet presented almost insurmountable difficulties. Moreover, proper tide conditions were available for only three days of each lunar month. With the setting of the date of 15 September, only three weeks were left for planning. Weakening of the Pusan perimeter was nevertheless risked to gain an objective obtainable through the mobility of sea power.

Two days of cruiser-destroyer attacks and air strikes softened up the fortress of Wolmi-do, which fell to the Marines by 0800 on 15 September. Sowolmido fell shortly thereafter; and the main landing, in the very heart of a large city, was effected. Heavy equipment could be landed only in downtown Inchon. The Reds could estimate the time of the landing by the time of the tide, and high sea walls had to be breached or knocked down to create a beach. Aided by deep support, interdiction, and close support air strikes, the Marines breached the walls, secured the harbor, cleared the city of defenders, and seized control of the rail line to Seoul. Superb teamwork and complete control of the air and sea had spelled success.

Despite Truman's desire to keep the Korean war limited, Secretary of the Navy Francis P. Matthews on 25 August demanded a preventive war against the Soviets and thus ended his usefulness to the administration. On 12 September, moreover, Truman obtained the resignation of Secretary of Defense Johnson less because he privately talked about a preventive war than because he had supported Truman's call for economy in defense in 1949 and 1950, his political ambition, and his unbelievably crude manner in working with Acheson and other officials. Johnson's successor, General George C. Marshall, who worked well with Acheson, rapidly restored efficiency and morale in the department of defense. As Marshall's deputy Truman named Robert A. Lovett, a naval aviator in World War I who then served as Assistant Secretary of War for Air in World War II and also as Assistant Secretary of State under Marshall. Truman also approved a bill to build a 60,000-ton supercarrier to be named after the first Secretary of Defense, James

V. Forrestal.

5. **Pusan Breakout.** Almost simultaneously with the landings at Inchon, Lieutenant General Walter H. Walker led his Eighth Army north. With forces to the north firing on the Seoul-Taejon road and Allied naval gunfire blasting the east coast road, the Reds were cut off from their supplies. Attacked front and rear, they were truly surprised, in the military sense. The juncture of the UN forces denied the North Koreans their supply lines and their hope of victory.

6. **The Drive North.** Advancing northward, ROKs up the east coast, US troops toward Pyongyang, the UN drive approached the Pyongyang-Hungnam line before political questions interfered with military operations. Were the UN forces merely to liberate South Korea? Were they to proceed north to punish the aggressor? Should they occupy all of North Korea at the risk of Red Chinese intervention?

Truman had originally intervened in Korea in order to restore South Korea to its antebellum status. On 11 September 1950, however, he decided to attempt the political unification of the entire peninsula by conquering the north and authorized MacArthur on 27 September to operate north as well as south of the 38th parallel. Although his order was approved by the General Assembly of the UN on 7 October, the possibility of Soviet or Red Chinese intervention caused him to limit MacArthur: he must not cross the Manchurian borders of Russia and China, use non-Korean troops near the Russo-Manchurian border, or conduct air and naval action against Manchuria or Soviet territory, and he must submit future operation plans for approval by the JCS.

While UN naval and air operations had disregarded the 38th parallel as a dividing line, the decision to send ground forces across the line warranted serious consideration. Most non-communist UN nations would drive North Korean troops far enough north to insure South Korea against future attack. Russia and her satellites naturally denied that UN forces had the right to cross the surveyor's line, and India opposed a crossing because then the UN would be the aggressor and China if not Russia might enter the war. The UN decided to cross the line in order to frustrate

North Korean regroupment for renewed attack.

So important did Truman consider the situation that in mid-October he flew to Wake Island, where MacArthur told him that North Korean resistance should end by Thanksgiving and that his troops would be withdrawn to Japan by Christmas. Would the Chinese or Russians intervene? Truman asked. MacArthur replied negatively even though Chou En-lai, China's foreign minister, had already stated three times that China would enter the war if Americans crossed the 38th parallel. His troops began to cross from Manchuria into North Korea on 27 October.

7. <u>The Chinese "Volunteers" Intervene</u>. Despite Cho En-lai's warnings that China would not stand idly by if North Korea was invaded, MacArthur's Intelligence Officer estimated that the Chinese would not enter the war in significant numbers. Taking his advice, MacArthur sent his forces north from Pyongyang and Hungnam. Eighty miles of mountainous territory divided his forces. Into this gap plunged Chinese armies. The Eighth Army fell back to a new line across Korea south of Seoul, leaving elements of the First Marine Division in the excruciatingly difficult task of extricating themselves from the Chinese surrounding them in the Chosin Reservoir area. With skillful carrier aircraft support they hacked their way through eight Chinese armies to Hamhung and Hungnam (December 1950), brought most of their equipment out, and inflicted many more casualties than they received. Their evacuation from Hungnam, which lasted for two weeks, was masterfully executed; supplies and heavy equipment as well as troops and many civilian refugees were saved. The operation ended with the destruction of the port facilities of Hungnam harbor.

8. <u>Blasting the Yalu Bridges and Pouring Water Over the Dam</u>. While UN naval forces bombarded coastal roads and interdicted other communications lines, forcing the Reds to move mostly at night, air forces performed the spectacular feat of destroying several of the bridges that spanned the Yalu River. Despite Chinese intervention, MacArthur was ordered to refrain from violating Manchurian territory. Thus even UN aircraft in "hot pursuit" could not follow enemy planes into their Manchurian "sanctuary."

MacArthur originally made the southern bank of the Yalu his northern operating limit, but to leave the Yalu bridges for Chinese troops to cross seemed to invite disaster. To destroy the bridges and yet not violate his orders, he moved his line to the center of the river. Navy pilots defied Red MIG-15 jets and antiaircraft batteries on the north bank of the Yalu and blasted the southern ends of three of the seven bridges. The problem of how to destroy the Hwachon Dam in order to knock out Manchurian hydroelectric plants was solved simply by the use of Navy torpedo bombers.

9. <u>The Dismissal of MacArthur</u>. With Chinese intervention, MacArthur had to fight "a new war" for which he believed his directives inadequate. When President Truman reinforced old directives and insisted that the Manchurian sanctuary be respected, MacArthur had to give up his principle of fighting to win in favor of "Operation Killer," which aimed to inflict maximum damage on the enemy but not to capture or recapture territory. Lieutenant General Mathew B. Ridgway, now in command of the Eighth Army, pushed forward just enough to stabilize his line somewhat north of Seoul. MacArthur wanted the right to cross the Yalu when in "hot pursuit," to drop 25 to 30 atomic bombs on Red supply bases and airfields in Manchuria, to lay a radio-active belt of nuclear material across the northern neck of the peninsula, to blockade the China coast, and to use Chiang Kai-shek's 500,000 troops in Korea or on the China mainland in order to take the pressure off Korea. A letter to Joseph W. Martin, Jr., minority leader of the House, containing MacArthur's views, appeared to Truman a violation of presidential directives and as possibly productive of 1) war with Russia if MacArthur used atomic bombs; 2) full Chinese war in Korea if MacArthur bombed Manchuria; and 3) the reopening of the Chinese civil war if MacArthur used Chiang's troops in China. Believing that MacArthur was challenging civil supremacy and making foreign policy in the field instead of leaving the matter to Washington, Truman on 11 April 1951 relieved him of all duties in the Far East. At hearings held before a joint meeting of the Senate Armed Services and Foreign Relations committees (3 May-17 August), it was agreed that the President had a right to remove the general but that the method of removal was unwise. Moreover, the general had not violated directives

and was not in disagreement with the JCS. The committee also found that the Secretary of State had assumed military functions and that nations other than the United States had been remiss in supporting the UN war effort. A cease-fire on the 38th parallel was regarded as equivalent to a victory for aggression. As MacArthur pointed out, "There is no substitute for victory." Secretary of Defense Marshall disagreed with MacArthur, and General Omar Bradley counseled that war with China would be "the wrong war, at the wrong place, at the wrong time, with the wrong enemy."

10. <u>Peace Talks</u>. Upon accepting Russia's proposal that armistice talks be held (June 1951) the UN appointed Vice Admiral C. Turner Joy, USN, to head the delegation opposed to that of North Korean General Nam-Il. Two years of haggling over a demarkation line ensued. The visit to Korea by General Dwight D. Eisenhower, newly elected president of the United States, may have helped break the diplomatic deadlock, but an armistice was not signed until 27 July 1953. This provided for a cease-fire, a buffer zone, and limitations on armaments which the Reds promptly violated. The third largest war in American history ended in a stalemate acceptable to both sides because both sides found continued war unprofitable. Unhappy South Korea was somewhat mollified by a mutual security pact with the United States, 1 October 1953.

11. <u>Casting the Accounts</u>. A truce is not a peace treaty. Nonetheless, the United States had nobly supported its responsibilities to the UN. For the first time in history an international organization had intervened effectively with force; for the first time in the cold war the communists had been stopped cold. China's emergence from the war with a large air force and a huge army trained in modern tactics placed her in position to exert force elsewhere in Asia, but her intervention in Korea served to stiffen the American determination not to recognize her or to allow her to replace Nationalist China in the UN.

The needs of global defense caused American military appropriations to quintuple, from $13 billion in 1950 to $60 billion in 1952. Experience was gained about guerrilla warfare. Underlined was the need for the National Security Council to better mesh foreign and military policy and for the nation to balance its military power not on a service-to-service basis but in view of its global responsibilities, to replace "economizing" with a realistic, long-range preparedness program, and, most important, to insure the tradition of civilian control over the military.

Korea also revealed the inefficacy of the UN as an agency that by punishing aggression could maintain world peace and the divergence of American opinion over the meaning of peace. To MacArthur, Truman's way meant appeasement; to Truman, MacArthur's way spelled World War III. But by not punishing the main instigator of aggression, Russia, Truman accepted the status quo and a defensive posture. He robbed the United States of the initiative and pulled the teeth of his greatest deterrent and striking force, strategic air power. He thus lessened the credibility and prestige of the United States and caused communists to believe that they could continue their aggression by proxy and that if it fought at all the United States would fight only limited wars.

Additional lessons were learned in the field. Three of the four JCS in the days of Korea were from West Point. Hence what was often called "joint" operations merely covered undertakings in which the Nary and Marine Corps contributed much more than did the Army and Air Force. For example, although an Army general lacking amphibious experience, Edward M. Almond, commanded the Inchon landing, that landing was carried out by the Navy and Marine Corps including Marine air less the Army's 7th Infantry Division and some Korean Marines. Although called joint, Joint Task Force 7 was nothing more than elements of the Seventh Fleet commanded by Admiral Struble. In gross violation of at least Marine Corps doctrine, Almond did not assume command ashore until a full six days had followed the landings. Unification therefore had been irrelevant at Inchon, indeed in the Inchon-Seoul campaign. Again, although called the Tactical Air Command, X Corps, and headed by a Marine Corps brigadier general, that command consisted of Marine Air Group 33 and headquarters and service units from the First Marine Air Wing. No Army there, nor in Marine Aircraft Group 12, which operated from the jeep carriers <u>Badoeng Strait</u> and <u>Sicily</u>.

Similarly, the Navy declined the demand of the Air Force that the latter assume operational control over all naval aircraft. At Inchon, naval and Marine pilots supported the landings while the Air Force carried out a deception operation at Kunsan. Moreover, because Far East Headquarters failed to assign areas of responsibility for the air interdiction campaign, the Navy took over the eastern half and the Air Force the western half of Korea. In its half, the Navy coordinated the use of naval surface and air power. Its pilots quickly responded to calls for ground support and were directed by pilots acting as ground observers whereas all requests for help from the Air Force, which preferred bombing to ground support, had to go through a Joint Operations Center, which often sent pilots out too late. No wonder X Corps adopted the Navy-Marine Corps air support system. Last, when the Marine Air Groups were assigned by MacArthur to the Fifth Air Force for employment in support of the Eighth Army as a whole, the Air Force gave Marine Air Groups many tasks that did not call for their specialty. In the field, unification thus separated rather than integrated ground and air.

American air power was vitally important in Korea. It quickly gained command of the air, furnished support to ground troops and transportation for men and supplies, destroyed large quantities of enemy equipment and numbers of troops, and may have deterred communist air strikes for fear of retaliation upon Russia and China. But the Air Force could not exploit its strategic and tactical power to the full because the logistic base of the enemy lay in the privileged sanctuary, Manchuria. The Air Force flew more missions than the Navy and Marine Corps, and the F-86 hammered MIGs into the rice paddies of Korea for a kill ratio of about 7 to 1. Lack of F86s in numbers was made up by naval and Marine air units, yet the much touted Air Force interdiction campaign, Operation Strangle, did not strangle, and some Air Force leaders saw that their operations depended upon what happened on the ground and even that air power had limitations. Obviously, a balance had to be struck between strategic and tactical air and between the Air Force and the other services. Illustrative is the fact that the USAF increase from 48 combat wings on 30 June 1950 to 30 June 1951 provided only 4 additional strategic (B-36) wings but 27 tactical (especially fighter-bomber) wings. During the same year, the Navy added 105 combatant ships--including 5 attack and 6 escort carriers, 2 cruisers, and 73 destroyers--370 mine, patrol, and amphibious craft, and, 1,292 aircraft to its inventory.

Korea also stimulated a reorganization of the department of defense. When Deputy Secretary of Defense Lovett asked the services for recommendations for improvement, the Navy said its organization was adequate but that it would become more "cost conscious." Dead to the lessons of Korea, the Air Force demanded that all air less that performing naval missions be centralized and commanded through an air commander and wished to be relieved of furnishing ground support so that it could operate directly against enemy forces. Nor would it let the Army acquire aircraft lest its services be duplicated. When it wished to expand to 150 groups, or wings, however, Secretary of the Navy Dan A. Kimball, who relieved Matthews on 31 July 1951, objected and Congress suggested augmenting both the Air Force and naval air power: the Air Force could grow to 137 wings while the Navy got two additional supercarriers.

Meanwhile Lovett, who succeeded George C. Marshall as Secretary of Defense on 12 September 1951, early in October asked for an independent evaluation of the force structure recommended by the JCS. As approved, this structure included 20 Army divisions, 409 combatant ships, a Marine Corps of three divisions and three air wings, and a 143-wing Air Force. To be added to the Navy's inventory would be an atomic-powered submarine (the <u>Nautilus</u>), a guided missile cruiser, a supercarrier (the <u>Saratoga</u>) capable of handling strategic bombers, and helicopters for anti-submarine warfare and many other purposes.

In his semiannual report dated 6 December 1952, Lovett said that he expected a reduction in military funding but stressed that the services should not be funded on a "feast or famine" basis. Moreover, he wanted a review of the National Security Act as amended. The act should be changed so that the secretary of defense would have more control over the statutory agencies--JCS, Munitions Board, Research and Development Board. The secretary of defense, not

the JCS, should be the chief military adviser to the
President; the provision that the military services
"be separately administered" should be stricken out
of the act. He would divorce the JCS from administrative and operational duties and restrict them to
preparing and reviewing strategic and logistic plans
and weapons systems. Last, the secretary of defense
should have a staff responsible to him alone.

II. THE "NEW LOOK" AND THE COLD WAR, 1953-1961

A. DOD REORGANIZATION PLAN NO. 6. In his State of
the Union message, 2 February 1953, President Dwight
D. Eisenhower invited the secretary of defense to
propose "plans to give our Nation maximum safety at
minimum cost." Using Lovett's recommendations,
Secretary of Defense Charles E. Wilson charged a committee to recommend improvements in DOD within 60
days and said he interpreted the National Security
Act as giving him complete authority to direct his
department even though the act specified that each
service would be "separately administered." Meanwhile Eisenhower made a clear sweep of the leading
civilian and military defense leaders. The JCS
would include Admiral Arthur W. Radford, chairman,
Admiral Robert B. Carney, CNO, Matthew B. Ridgway,
chief of staff of the Army, and Nathan F. Twining,
chief of staff of the Air Force. Eisenhower ordered
these men to abide by administration policies and
offer no public dissent to them. He would accept no
"split papers" from them, and they must put a price
tag on their recommendations.

Upon reviewing American defense strategy, Eisenhower found that each service was preparing to conduct atomic as well as sub-atomic war, an overlapping
and very expensive process. Determined to obtain
"security with solvency," he asked Congress to grant
more power and staff support to the secretary of defense. Authorized by Congress to reorganize the
executive branch of government, he established a
President's (Nelson Rockefeller) Advisory Committee
on Government Organization. In great contrast to
the unification hearings of 1949, the services said
little about the impending increase in authority for
the secretary of defense and the JCS proved amenable
to reforming their procedures.

The Rockefeller Committee recommended that the secretary of defense be given complete control over his department but hedged that control with various limitations. He could not merge the services, deprive their secretaries of their legal rights to administer their departments, or establish a single military commander-in-chief or general military staff, for example. Second, rather than a bilineal chain of command, service secretaries would have a single chain and thus control both military and civilian elements. The secretary of defense, not the JCS, would have authority to assign executive responsibility for unified commands. The JCS would transfer their administrative duties to deputies and thus be able to concentrate upon joint planning. The functions of the Munitions Board and Research and Development Board would be undertaken by assistant secretaries of defense. To strengthen his administrative staff, the secretary of defense would be given six additional assistant secretaries, making a total of nine. These recommendations Eisenhower sent to Congress as his Reorganization Plan No. 6. At hearings, military men objected because the plan would weaken the autonomy of the services, concentrate power in the secretary of defense, and enable the JCS to operate a Prussian-like general staff that would destroy the liberties of the people. Congress adopted the plan nevertheless, and on 1 October Wilson issued a revision of the Key West Agreement that conformed with it. No changes were made in the roles and missions of the services, but the JCS were removed from the chain of command. Now the secretary of defense, on the advice of the JCS, would appoint a military department to be the executive agent for a particular task. The secretary of that department would then avoid making military decisions by authorizing his chief of staff to act for his department. As predicted particularly by Twining, the door was open to create a superstructure between the secretary of defense and the services. The former secretary of the Air Force, Thomas K. Finletter, spoke of multiplication leading to quadruplication. "It is civilian control gone mad. The 'layering' process has endangered . . . to a high degree our military effectiveness," added the military analyst Hanson Baldwin. Nevertheless, instead of argument, the services complied and the act went into effect on 30 June 1953. Instead of the horizontally organized, federated structure Forrestal envisaged, the secretary of defense was now the prime decision maker and was armed with a staff of assistants to see that his decisions were carried out. Interservice conflict was discouraged by a vertical-unitary structure in which decisions of the secretary of defense could be challenged only by the President. In consequence, while the service secretary still had a vital role as a member of the defense management team, he was reduced in prestige and authority and served mainly as an operational manager.

B. DOD REORGANIZATION PLAN OF 1958. The second Hoover Commission on department of defense reorganization (1955) recommended further increasing the authority of the secretary of defense and eliminating the large number of assistant secretaries and concentrating their duties under four--logistics, research and development, personnel, and financial management--an organization similar to that adopted by the Navy. Close upon the Hoover report came the Rockefeller Brothers Fund Study on International Security, which looked at problems that might face the United States in the decade 1958-1968. Its report emphasized that the armed services were too competitive, that resulting plans and programs were too often mere compromises, and recommended eliminating the service departments from the operational chain of command and the assignment of all forces to unified or specified commands. These commands would receive their orders from the President through the secretary of defense and the Joint Staff, the last of which should be enlarged and strengthened; the service secretaries would be left only the functions of providing logistic support. Although Burke and others who spoke for the Navy had "misgivings" and "apprehensions" about the plan, Eisenhower pressed it upon Congress, which approved. The reorganization act established DOD as a unitary, not federalized, organization. Operating through the JCS, the secretary of defense had responsibility for operations as well as for policy. The planning and conduct of war was vested in functional unified commands using whatever elements of the services they deemed appropriate. The service departments existed only to provide, train, and equip forces for the unified commands. However, directives from the assistant secretaries of defense to the service departments must be authorized by the secretary of defense. After reviewing the department's organization, Secretary of the Navy Thomas Gates concluded that the bilinear structure would continue to serve well, and a meeting of top defense leaders in June 1957 made no change in the Navy's roles and missions.

C. THE "NEW LOOK" IN DEFENSE. In a campaign speech of 24 October 1952, Eisenhower said he would visit Korea and try to end the war. In December, in visiting Korea, he spoke with Admiral Arthur W. Radford, Commander-in-Chief Pacific Fleet (the <u>Helena</u> Conference), liked what Radford said about defense, and determined that he would be the new chairman of the JCS. Radford, sometimes called "The Patton of the Pentagon," had led the "revolt of the admirals" in 1949 because he opposed reliance upon a single strategic concept and single weapon system. As chairman of the JCS, however, he emphasized that air power, both Air Force and Navy, would play a major role. He saw the United States engaged in uncoordinated holding operations in Asia but lacking an effective, long-term, comprehensive strategic plan. It was overextended, with too many forces committed in areas where communists could pin them down. He would concentrate power in a strategic reserve in or near North America, depend upon friendly powers along communist countries to hold front lines, and keep the mobile power of the United States poised to strike at strategic enemy positions in case of war. Radford's ideas pleased Secretary of State John Foster Dulles because they supported his foreign policy of "massive retaliation." Because it was American policy not to deliver a "first strike," estimates put the loss of Americans to a Soviet first strike at 100 million before an American "second strike" would kill a similar number of Russians.

Radford's ideas were upheld by Operation Solarium, a meeting in the sun room at the White House in which defense specialists considered three options: continue the containment policy of the Truman administration; extend containment about the world and threaten the Soviets with severe reprisals for any aggression; and a "liberation" policy that would push back Soviet boundaries by psychological, political, and economic warfare. In NSC-162, the conferees chose course No. 1 and warned that economizing on defense in the light of Soviet air capability would be dangerous. Broad strategic conclusions followed in the *Sequoia* paper written by the JCS early in August 1953 on the yacht of the secretary of the Navy.

The new look, which continued the Europe-first policy, envisaged the "instant" use of "massive" weapons in retaliation to the source of aggression rather than the use of conventional arms; a military establishment reduced in numbers but improved in power; international atomic disarmament; less spending for unproven missile research and pure research; extension of the defense alliance system; ferreting out communism at home and crushing it elsewhere in the Americas; and continued aid to free peoples that they might remain free. Despite the claims of its creators to the contrary, it proved inapplicable to almost all the problems of the Eisenhower years from Berlin to Cuba and made it appear that the United States was paralyzed by the enormity of its own weapons technology. Nuclear weapons did give "more bang for the buck," but in the absence of conventional forces any confrontation would result either in a backdown or in general war.

Eisenhower saw two threats--the external one of Soviet military power, the internal one of bankrupting the nation in order to meet Soviet military power as it nibbled at the edges of the free world. He wanted strength sufficient to defend the free world yet would also end budget deficits and balance the budget. To avoid bankruptcy via maintaining full mobilization, to 1954, the "D-day" of NSC-68, he replaced a fixed D-day with a "floating M-day" whose forces could be paid for without staggering the economy and could be borne for an indefinite period of years. Critics pointed out that he would be unable to stop a Soviet attack on Western Europe or on the United States and that he underestimated Soviet technological capability. The Soviets not only had the atomic bomb (1949) but a fusion (hydrogen) bomb (1953), and in 1954 produced twin-jet Badger bombers somewhat like the B-47. By 1956, moreover, they had both the large turboprop Bear and the pure jet Bison bomber. Nevertheless, Eisenhower had his way with Congress. In part because of reduced defense spending following the truce in Korea, he was able to provide a balanced budget in 1956.

Budget austerity, however, meant major reliance on nuclear weapons.

The impact of the new look upon the military services is quickly revealed by the size of the defense budget and its division. Rather than the annual $50 billion to $60 billion the JCS believed necessary, Eisenhower kept the budget below $40 billion. Throughout his tenure, the defense budget was divided among the services as services rather than on the basis of operating function, with 46 percent for the Air Force, 28 percent for the Navy and Marine Corps, and 23 percent for the Army. With a fixed budget, the JCS became rivals for dollars with which to support largely single service strategies and weapons and hence could not cooperate in a thorough strategic reappraisal of defense needs. Through his control of the budget, the secretary of defense rather than the JCS determined national strategy. The Eisenhower, like the Truman administration, thus let the defense budget determine strategy rather than let national security requirements determine the defense budget. In the end, although the United States had sufficient conventional forces to handle the Taiwan and Lebanon crises, it erred in underestimating Soviet capabilities and in assuming that there would be no more local wars, that the situation in Indochina would be stabilized, that Russia would be quiescent, and that satisfactory progress would be made in EDC and in the rearming of Japan. By adhering to an arbitrary strategy useful for only a short period of time and only for objectives worth the price of a nuclear war, the new look strategy denigrated conventional forces that would be required in the 1960s and 1970s. Both the United States and the Soviets provided their forces with tactical nuclear weapons in the mid-1950s. These, however, offered the options of acquiescing to local defeat or escalating into general war.

D. THE NUCLEAR ARMS RACE. In a dramatic speech on 8 December 1953, Eisenhower proposed that the world pool its atomic power for peaceful purposes. The free world rejoiced but the Kremlin blocked all attempts of the UN to provide an effective system of international control of atomic energy. The free world proceeded with a modified "atoms for peace" program largely subsidized by the United States.

After he learned that the Soviets had exploded a hydrogen bomb (12 August 1953), Eisenhower concentrated upon "such armaments as can deter attack." In March 1954, the United States exploded two hydrogen bombs (equivalent to 40 million tons of TNT each) in the Pacific. H-bombs made global war less likely, with outbreaks localized because of the mutual terror of thermonuclear war even if "termite wars" of subversion continued. With nuclear bombs becoming conventional, however, Eisenhower saw the need for more air power and less conventional power. In June 1956 he suggested cutting military strength from 3.2 million to 2.85 million men, with most of the cut coming from the Army. For security he would rely upon strategic air power, large carriers, guided missiles, atomic-powered submarines, some of them capable of launching atom-laden guided missiles, and ships constructed to withstand the ravages of an atomic war. To insure efficiency and economy, in 1958 he concentrated all DOD antimissile and satellite research and primary development into one organization, the Advanced Research Projects Agency (ARPA). Moreover, the DOD Reorganization Act of 1958 created the new post of Director of Defense Research and Engineering (DDR&E) to advise the secretary of defense on scientific and technical matters and also oversee all DOD-related research and engineering activities.

In 1957, first Britain and then Russia exploded "dirty" hydrogen bombs--and the nuclear race got hot again. Moreover, the Soviets also test-fired the first ICBM--the United States as yet had only 1,500 to 3,000-mile IRBMs--and then shocked the entire world by putting a satellite into orbit in outer space. Their 4-pound satellite of 4 October was followed by a 187-pound payload including a live dog on 3 November. In consequence of this Soviet "scientific Pearl Harbor," which lessened the advantage of the United States in manned bombers and showed that the United States trailed in missile development, Eisenhower called for a NATO summit conference in December and promised to supply IRBMs to NATO partners while on the other hand seeking further negotiations on disarmament with the Soviets.

The American space program stressed safety as well as science. The United States soon orbited a succession of small space vehicles (the first, Explorer I, weighed 30.8 pounds) that were significant for scientific purposes. Khrushchev nevertheless jeered that "You send up oranges and we send up tons." Just after Eisenhower left office, in April 1961, the Soviets made another "first" by orbiting a man about the earth and bringing him back alive-- a feat the United States duplicated a year later. With the Navy's development of "Project Tepee," moreover, monitoring radios could detect missile launchings anywhere in the world.

Sputnik greatly accelerated American scientific research. When Congress established the National Science Foundation in 1950 it funded it at $15 million per year; in 1959, Eisenhower asked for $140 million for it. Yet during Eisenhower's second term, of each Federal research and development dollar 60¢ went for development, 32¢ for applied research, and only 8¢ for pure research. Of the almost $4 billion private industry spent, only 4 percent went for basic research.

E. ATLANTIC AND PACIFIC SECURITY FRAMEWORKS.

    1. Europe.

        a. EDC. Postwar West Germany made a remarkable economic and political recovery. If rearmed, it could enhance the power of the West in dealing with the Soviet menace. In 1950 France suggested the European Defense Community, in which six nations (France, Italy, Belgium, the Netherlands, Luxembourg, and West Germany) would contribute quotas of men. Germany would not be allowed an army of her own but would contribute 12 divisions to EDC. EDC would supersede the existing NATO forces of each of the six countries. In May 1952, the Western Allies virtually restored freedom to West Germany. Thereupon Germany signed EDC and in turn received guarantees which for all practical purposes made her a NATO country. Still fearful of Germany, France delayed action on EDC for two years, then scuttled it. Britain's rapid decision to maintain 4 divisions and a tactical air force on the continent led to a conference (October 1954) which provided that the fourteen NATO countries would bring a rearmed West Germany into NATO under the supervision of the countries in the Western European Union. Thus the West welcomed West Germany as an ally in the common cause against communism. In addition to contributing 200,000 men to NATO in 1957, Germany made plans for a 1,500 plane and 80,000 man air force by 1960. With nuclear weapons as a shield, NATO's conventional forces served as the sword.

  b. **Spain**. Because of the strategic and economic importance of Spain, the Allies carefully nurtured Spanish neutrality throughout World War II. Spain gradually adopted an attitude of benevolent neutrality toward the Allies. At the end of the war a Russian-sponsored anti-Fascist resolution kept Spain out of the UN, and many nations, including the United States, recalled their ambassadors from Madrid. Then the free world evaluated Spain an anti-communist bastion worth cultivating. In 1950 the United States sent its first ambassador to Madrid since 1945, and pleasant diplomatic relations for the future were assured. On 20 September 1955, an executive agreement provided $226,000,000 in economic and military aid in return for the use of key air and naval bases in Spain. The treaty has been renewed several times, always at increased cost to the United States. Despite Soviet objections, Spain was admitted to the UN in 1955.

  c. **Yugoslavia**. While Tito's break with Moscow in 1948 did not make him acceptable in all American eyes, he was anti-Moscow and therefore deserving of American economic and military aid. From 1949 to 1953 Tito received $100 million in loans, food, and military supplies.

  d. **Latin America**. Many Latin Americans saw little difference between the menace of Russian communism and American interventionism, and Latin American hostility to the United States was revealed at the Tenth Inter-American conference held in Caracas, Venezuela, in March 1954. It took a good deal of pressure to obtain a resolution branding communist infiltration of the Americas a "threat." Although the Monroe Doctrine had been multilateralized in 1940, the United States could not let any communist-tinged government exist within easy bombing range of the Panama Canal. Therefore when a Polish ship brought a cargo of Czechoslovakian arms to Guatemala, Secretary of State Dulles branded the move as a Russian violation of the Monroe Doctrine and began to airlift munitions to Guatemala's neighbors. Exiles from Guatemala then banded together to invade their own country and overthrow the communist-infiltrated regime. A communist-tinged government had been overthrown, but such problems as land reform, redistribution of income, and dictatorship that stimulated communism remained. In April 1958, when he visited Latin America, Vice President Richard Nixon was mobbed in Lima and had the windows of his limousine beaten in with iron pipes in Caracas. Eisenhower ordered paratroopers to prepare a rescue mission while Latin America feared another round of American intervention. Galling to the Latins was the small amount of economic aid the United States gave them compared with Europe and Asia; galling in turn to Americans was criticism by those few Latin American nations that adopted democratic forms that the United States was too friendly to despots and not friendly enough to rebels like Fidel Castro.

2. The Pacific.

a. Japan. Faced with rising communism in the Far East, American strategic concepts were overhauled to include the arming of Japan. In the fall of 1951 a 52-nation conference at San Francisco approved a peace treaty with Japan which the Communist-bloc nations refused to accept, and at the same time the United States concluded a bilateral treaty with Japan that permitted American troops to be stationed in Japan. On 28 February 1952, a new pact authorized the United States to keep bases in Japan for defense purposes.

b. The Philippines. The long-deferred independence of the Philippines became a reality on 4 July 1946. In return for tariff preferences and payment of war damages, the United States received 99 year leases on 23 military and naval bases.

c. ANZUS. On 1 September 1951, defense pacts were signed between the United States and New Zealand and Australia. In keeping with a provision for periodic consultation for defensive purposes, several meetings have been held.

d. SEATO. The Asia counterpart of NATO was

formed at Manila in September 1954. By the terms of the South East Asia Treaty Organization, the United States, Britain, France, Australia, New Zealand, the Philippines, Thailand, and Pakistan pledged themselves to consult together for defense purposes whenever threatened by (communist?) aggression or subversion. The Pacific Charter also adopted pledged these nations to promote self-government as an answer to the communist charge of "colonialism." While more a moral commitment to consult than a fast military alliance, SEATO provided for undertaking joint training exercises by military forces.

3. <u>Southeast Asia</u>. Following Korea, communist pressure built up in Indochina, where Vietminh rebels, increasingly aided by China, had been fighting the French-led Vietnam loyalists since 1946. The peninsula was important to the free world because its fertile and well-watered land made it Asia's rice bowl and its fall to communism, as Eisenhower explained it, might cause the fall of nearby countries --the domino theory. American aid to the French in Indochina began with the outbreak of the Korean War. On 29 June 1950, 8 C-47s were delivered in Saigon, and on 3 August a Military Advisory Aid Group (MAAG) arrived, its Navy section consisting of 7 officers and men. American aid reached the sum of $3 billion in 1953, but in a poll taken in September Americans opposed sending troops there by 10 to 1. The Indochina problem was a difficult one to deal with because while France was conducting the war and the United States was looked upon as the world leader against communism and colonialism, by 1954 the United States was paying about 70 percent of the cost of French operations and supplying material and technical aid.

In September 1953, Eisenhower approved General Henri Navarre's "Atlante" plan to increase French forces somewhat, greatly increase the Vietnamese army, and augment American aid in arms and money. With mobile combat teams for offensive operations, Dulles hoped the French could smash the organized body of communists by the end of 1955 and overcome ensuing guerrilla actions by 1956. Whether the United States should intervene militarily in Indochina as it had in Korea was discussed at the White House by Eisenhower, Dulles, and Radford on 4 April 1954.

They decided that the United States would intervene if the "whole free community" did so and Congress also approved, but Eisenhower hoped that intervention could be avoided. The French position deteriorated badly early in 1954. By March, 50,000 communist forces besieged a French army of 12,000 at the frontier fortress named Dienbienphu, 8 miles from the Laos border. While Radford took under advisement limited American intervention from a carrier task force he positioned south of Hainan Island, he and the other Joint Chiefs opposed unilateral American intervention. When the French asked for an air strike at Dienbienphu, Dulles opposed, as did Eisenhower. Dienbienphu fell on 7 May. Both the East (Australia, New Zealand, Thailand, and the Philippines) and the West (the United States, Britain, and France) opposed communism, but none came to the aid of the French.

To settle the Indochina problem, 19 nations conferred at Geneva in April 1954, with 16 nations that had fought the communists in Korea facing 3 that had supported them. The communists held the high cards--military victory. Eisenhower considered sending atomic-laden carrier-based aircraft to help the French if the French and British would cooperate fully. The British followed a policy of appeasement and the French, drained after almost 8 years of war, wanted to get out of Indochina on honorable terms. On 21 July, when the conferees agreed to a partition of Indochina along the 17th parallel and to the holding of general elections, the U.S. Navy as a humanitarian gesture providing passage to the south for those who wished and were able to flee from the north. Operation "Passage to Freedom" used APAs, AKAs, LSDs, LSTs, and MSTS ships to relocate 800,000 people and also removed mountains of military cargo between August 1954 and May 1955.

Although the communists did not obtain control of the entire peninsula, the terms of Geneva gave them a signal victory in the cold war (a Far Eastern Munich) and freedom to strike again at a time of their own choosing. The United States did not participate in the final declaration of the conference but said it would show "grave concern" over the renewal of aggression. One result of Geneva, already mentioned, was the creation of SEATO; a second,

American support for South Vietnam's Ngo Dinh Diem; a third, the Formosa Resolution. Fearing that Formosa might get the United States into an undesirable war with China, which early in 1955 struck at the Tachen Islands, Eisenhower requested Congress for authority to use American forces overseas. In the Formosa Resolution of 24 January 1955, Congress in effect gave him a blank check to defend Formosa. Dulles, however, gave Chiang Kai-shek to understand that the United States was not committed to the defense of the islands of Quemoy and Matsu even though Radford and certain others wanted a showdown war with China. China quieted down after 1958 and the crisis passed as China turned her attention to seizing Tibet and several ill-defined frontier areas in India and supporting the subversion of Laos.

F. PEACEFUL COEXISTENCE. Following the death of Stalin, in 1953, premier N.A. Bulganin and the secretary of the Communist Party, Nikita S. Khrushchev, announced a policy of "coexistence and competition" and of the settlement of differences with the West by peaceful means. Eisenhower welcomed the gesture but desired an earnest Soviet intent of achieving peace (an armistice in Korea, end Soviet aid to communists in Indochina and Malaya, agreement to a free and united Germany, liberation of the European satellites) and urged disarmament and the international control of atomic energy under an inspection system of the UN. Following the freeing of Austria, Eisenhower agreed to a Big Four Conference (U.S., Britain, France, USSR) at Geneva, in July 1955. Eisenhower offered an open skies inspection plan—the U.S. and the USSR to exchange blueprints of their military establishments and permit mutual aerial inspections and thus quiet fears on both sides that one was building against the other. No tangible result followed except perhaps a relaxation of American-Soviet animosity.

Russia moved closer to Tito and spoke about "other roads" than the Russian one to Socialism. Mistaking Soviet meaning and also the meaning of Dulles's policy of "liberation," in 1956 freedom seekers in Poland and Hungary rose up against communist-imposed conditions. Poland won some concessions but the Soviets squashed Hungary and reinstituted a puppet regime. The Iron Curtain continued to imprison Soviet satellites.

G. METO, SUEZ, AND THE EISENHOWER DOCTRINE. To "close the ring" about Russia, the United States sponsored the Middle East Treaty Organization, with Turkey, Iraq, Iran, Pakistan, and Britain joining the Baghdad Pact (1955) and the United States a member of several of its committees.

Meanwhile, Britain sought to mollify Egypt, which quarreled over the Sudan and British bases along the Suez Canal and agreed to remove its bases in 1954. When Egypt's president, Gamal Abdel Nasser, pledged cotton for Czech munitions, he cooled American ardor for helping him build a mile-high Aswan Dam on the upper Nile which would have added about 25 percent to Egypt's arable land. Upon hearing that Nasser might turn to the Soviets and use Soviet arms to destroy Israel and his Middle East security framework, Dulles on 19 July 1956 rescinded his offer of aid. A week later Nasser seized the Suez Canal, which controlled the oil pipe line from the Middle East to Europe, and said he would use its revenues to build the dam. Although the UN Charter forbade the use of force against Nasser, and Dulles tried to restrain the British and French from military measures, the British and French descended on Suez on 31 October 1956. Bereft of most of its amphibious forces, Britain inserted her troops piecemeal in a very poor operation, thereby giving Nasser time to block the canal. Much more effective were the Israelis, who on the 29th had reacted to Egyptian raids with an all out attack. No nation involved bothered to inform the United States, and the timing of the attacks made collusion at least suspect. The Anglo-French action dealt a blow at NATO, yet Eisenhower supported the UN in getting the British and French out of Egypt, in November, and by getting Israel also to withdraw won acclaim from the Arab nations and opponents of interventionism and colonialism. Moreover, he obtained congressional approval for the Eisenhower Doctrine--the United States would provide economic aid and armed support to any nation in the Middle East threatened by communism that asked for it--and $200 million for economic-military aid for the Middle East.

When Egypt and Syria combined to form the United Arab Republic and a pro-Nasser clique took over Iraq

(July 1958), it seemed that Jordan and Lebanon might also come under Nasser's domination. The first test of the Eisenhower Doctrine came when a coup probably engineered by Nasser threatened King Hussein of Jordan. Eisenhower sent the Sixth Fleet to the eastern Mediterranean and gave Hussein $10 million-- enough to save Jordan. When President Chamoun of Lebanon asked for aid, Eisenhower ordered American marines to land. Eventually 14,000 landed, unopposed, and remained until August when tensions eased and they were removed. The United States had proved its willingness and ability to restore order, and by removing its troops it disproved communist charges of "imperialist aggression." With the Baghdad Pact weakened, in August 1959 the Central Treaty Organization (CENTO) was formed. Its members were Britain, Iran, Pakistan, and Turkey. Although the United States did not join, Eisenhower by executive agreement assured Iran, Pakistan, and Turkey military support in critical contingencies.

III. THE AIR FORCE AND THE NEW LOOK

The new look changed no service traditions. The Air Force was happy with its offensive and deterrent strategic roles. Moreover, it gained an Air Force Academy, had Twining as chairman of the JCS from 1957 to 1960, a SAC brought to the acme of effectiveness by Curtis LeMay, B-52 bomber wings, and the F-105 tactical (atomic) fighter. However, it was uninterested in providing air lift or tactical support to the Army and opposed the Army's acquisition of organic aviation or determination of its own air doctrine. The Air Force, which planned to use tactical nuclear weapons in local wars, also fought against the use of strategic aircraft and Polaris missiles by the Navy.

IV. THE ARMY AND FLEXIBLE RESPONSE

Resentful of being a hitchhiker on the Air Force and Navy, the Army wanted organic aviation and would cut the Navy down to a sealift and ASW force and objected to the use of the Marine Corps as a land army. Dependent as it was upon the airman and sailor for tactical air and logistic support, it demanded close cooperation from its sister services. Though a soldier, Eisenhower downplayed the role of the Army in defense policy in favor of expensive air-atomic power. Army chief of staff Matthew B. Ridgway, to June 1955, and Maxwell D. Taylor, to 1961, allied themselves with the Navy in countering an Air Force buildup, opposed Army reductions on purely financial grounds, and argued that tactical atomic war required more rather than fewer troops. Yet for FY 1955 Eisenhower cut the Army by 10 percent, with further cuts that reduced it from 1.5 million to 1 million men. Between FY 1953 and FY 1956, Army funding was halved. Taking a leaf from the "revolt of the admirals," Taylor opposed a single strategic concept and single weapons system on the ground that an enemy would not play to American strength and offered a "National Military Program" including a new strategy he called "Flexible Response" that provided a range of options. Flexible response meant returning to a balanced security system ready to respond with conventional forces to challenges in which nuclear activity would be ineffective or represent an irrational overreaction. It meant more Army forces and funds, and Taylor would have to wait the coming of the Kennedy administration before receiving a welcome for his idea. Meanwhile, however, he restructured army divisions along "pentomic" lines and worked the atomic cannon perfected in 1954 into them.

V. NAVAL ADMINISTRATION, 1951-1961

A. TRUMAN'S LAST NAVAL SECRETARY, DAN ABLE KIMBALL. Kimball had served in the Navy Department for 28 months before he became its head for a tour that lasted from 21 July 1951 to 3 February 1953. A man who had a fine knack for getting along with everyone including Hyman Rickover, he led in the rebuilding of the Navy in consequence of the Korean War even though defense appropriations diminished after the war ended. A contract to build the first supercarrier, the _Forrestal_, was let on 12 July 1951 and a contract for the nuclear-powered submarine _Nautilus_ on the 13th. On 14 June 1952, Kimball introduced President Truman to a large crowd that attended the keel laying ceremonies of the _Nautilus_. He wanted greater speed built into naval ships and all carriers to be able to service aircraft carrying atomic bombs, yet he also wanted adequate antisubmarine and amphibious forces. The first Helicopter Antisubmarine Squadron (HW-1) became operational during the winter of 1951, as did the Hunter-Killer Force

Atlantic Fleet. When the Secretary of Defense, Robert A. Lovett, increased the role of the service secretaries in policy making, Kimball had his say about new force levels in which the Navy got 409 active combatant ships, among them the reconstructed heavy cruisers Boston and Canberra into the fleet's first guided missile cruisers, and the Marines were allowed three divisions and their air wings. In the FY 1952 budget Kimball got a second Forrestal-class carrier, funds to continue modernizing the Essex-class, and the largest appropriation to date for the acquisition of guided missiles. Moreover, by projecting the Navy's needs for carriers against the old Essexes, he tried to assure the Navy a new large carrier each year for the next decade, that some of the new ones would be nuclear powered, and that the Navy would have a total of 12 operating carriers. He fared well again in the budget for FY 1953 and obtained another supercarrier, additional carrier air groups, more Essex conversions, more missiles, and an increase in both naval and Marine personnel strength, but he had to cut back on some low priority ships in order to obtain the new carrier.

Early in 1952, after the Atomic Energy Commission endorsed a carrier nuclear power plant, Kimball asked Westinghouse to develop the engines. He was so pleased with the steam catapult developed by the British that he had one installed in the Hancock while she was being modernized. Greater safety and the possibility of using heavier planes followed with his adoption of the British angled, or canted deck, which obtained its first test on the Antietam in January 1953. If few military men witnessed the laying of the keel of the Nautilus, the Air Force was conspicuous by its absence when the keel of the Forrestal was laid at Newport News on 14 July 1952.

A "lame duck" after the elections of 1952, Kimball fought hard to acquire a third Forrestal carrier in the FY 1954 budget even though the incoming Eisenhower administration might disagree. Lovett approved, but the Bureau of the Budget did not, and it took a meeting at the White House to obtain it. As he left office, Kimball was admittedly dreaming as he spoke of having eight new, nuclear-powered carriers among a future atomic-powered and guided missile fleet.

B. EISENHOWER'S SECRETARIES OF THE NAVY. Despite the new look, the Navy reaffirmed its functional (task) organization and insisted upon operating in the air, on the sea, below the sea and, with the Marine Corps, on land. It revealed little interest in contributing to continental air defense or providing air and sea lift to the Army. Moreover, since research and development was still service oriented, each service tended to stress the utility of the new weapons it produced.

Four naval secretaries served during the Eisenhower years: Robert B. Anderson 4 February 1953-2 May 1954; Charles S. Thomas, 3 May 1954-31 March 1957; Thomas S. Gates, 1 April 1957-7 June 1959; and William B. Franke, 8 June 1959-20 January 1961.

1. <u>Anderson</u>. A Texan trained in the law, Anderson served as a civilian advisor to the secretary of war during World War II and also engaged in business. Important to Eisenhower was that he had been a "Democrat for Eisenhower" in the campaign of 1952 and had the full support of Senator Lyndon B. Johnson. Easily confirmed by the Senate, Anderson brought in as his Under Secretary Charles S. Thomas, a California merchant who frequently advised the Navy Department.

Among Anderson's first tasks was to handle the Hyman G. Rickover case. Having been passed over for a promotion to rear admiral a second time in the summer of 1952, Rickover would be required to retire in July 1953 and thus perhaps endanger progress in the nuclear submarine program. Rickover got his promotion. A second task was to try to fend off budget cuts that imperiled the building of the third <u>Forrestal</u>-class carrier and personnel and aircraft strength. The carrier was saved, but it was given conventional rather than nuclear power, and a reduction of $2 billion from the Truman FY 1954 budget forced some reduction in personnel and in shipbuilding and conversion programs. Anderson had no objection to Eisenhower's Reorganization Plan No. 6, and when it went into effect he was placed in the chain of command from which service secretaries had been excluded in the Key West Agreement. For the rest of his short tour he concentrated upon rationalizing the Navy to its peacetime budget and, though he countered administration policy, called for more conventional rather than atomic power. He also pointed to the rapid aging of the fleet, most of which was built in World War II and would expend its useful life before 1965, and recommended the provision of a fourth large carrier and more destroyers. Among other items, in the FY 1955 budget he acquired the fourth <u>Forrestal</u> carrier and additional <u>Essex</u>-class modernizations. Given the new look stress upon air-atomic power, he urged further development of atomic air capability for carriers and ballistic missiles for submarines. On 8 July 1953, he designated 5 of the older, unmodernized carriers as CVS (Antisubmarine Support Aircraft Carrier). Recognized as a production expert, on 1 May 1953 he succeeded Roger Kyes as Deputy Secretary of Defense.

    2. <u>Thomas</u>. A naval aviator in World War I, Thomas had been a valued adviser to Forrestal and also Under Secretary of the Navy and Assistant Secretary of Defense for Supply and Logistics before becoming Secretary of the Navy. His major problems were to keep the fleet modernized and to acquire technically qualified career personnel. He was helped in solving these problems by Arleigh Burke, whom he chose to succeed Robert B. Carney as CNO in July 1955. To modernize the fleet, light cruisers were given surface to air missiles; to permit vertical assaults, the Marines were given helicopters; to augment ASW capability, a number of ASW ships were given to the navies of the free world and in early 1954 2 carriers were joined to the 5 other CVSs. Like Anderson, Thomas spoke of the need of conventional forces that provided options other than general nuclear warfare. He pushed the redesigning of H-bombs so that they could be carried by carrier aircraft and replaced the Sidewinder with the Sparrow on the latter. By going beyond Regulus with Talos, Terrier, and Tartar missiles, he earned the ire of the Air Force. In December 1956, Secretary Wilson directed that the Air Force would be responsible for missiles with a range of over 200 miles, the Army for those with short range, and gave the Navy all ship-based missile development. Thomas cooperated with the joint Continental Defense Command by providing 36 radar picket destroyer escorts, 16 converted Liberty ships, and radar-equipped Constellations to extend the Distant Early Warning (DEW) line a thousand miles to seaward along the east and west coasts.

For submarines, Thomas wanted a ballistic missile not subject to counterattack. When Burke could not interest the Air Force, he got the Army to agree to work jointly on the solid state Jupiter project. In September 1955 Thomas organized a Special Projects Office as an entity separate from the bureaus, funded it out of regular naval appropriations, and directed its head, Rear Admiral William F. "Red" Raborn, to produce a shipborne long-range missile. Following Sputnik, work on the new weapon, named Polaris, was speeded up, and in late 1959 the first ballistic missile submarine, the <u>George Washington</u>, was ready for sea. If Thomas was unable to obtain nuclear power for the sixth <u>Forrestal</u>-class carrier, the <u>Constellation</u>, he did obtain approval for the first nuclear surface ships, the missile cruiser <u>Long Beach</u> and carrier <u>Enterprise</u> (1958). Meanwhile the <u>Nautilus</u>, commissioned in September 1954, proved herself at sea and forecast a revolution in submarine warfare. Soon Thomas had 21 nuclear submarines authorized or under construction, three of them of the new fleet ballistic missile (FBM) type. For the detection of intruding submarines, he had work begun on Project Caesar, sonar listening stations along both the Atlantic and Pacific coasts. He had to acknowledge several failures--of an atomic airplane, of the large and fast P6M Seamaster seaplane--and the fact that few new destroyers, auxiliaries, or amphibious ships had been added to the Navy. A step forward was taken with a new amphibious assault ship (LPH) planned in 1955. It began operations in 1961. In the interim, 3 converted <u>Essex</u>-class carriers and one jeep carrier served as LPHs. What to some appeared as a step backward occurred with the mothballing of the last four battleships in commission.

3. <u>Gates</u>. Gates commanded aircraft carriers in World War II as a reserve captain and in October 1953 became Under Secretary of the Navy, in which guise he had helped along the Special Projects (Polaris) Office and became well aware of the twin problems of fleet modernization and retention of qualified personnel. One of his first moves after assuming the naval secretaryship on 1 April 1957 was to recommend a second tour as CNO for Arleigh Burke, a second to consider how to meet the challenge of a rising Soviet sea power. The Soviets had new submarines, cruisers, and destroyers while American surface ships were old

and tired. (Given an obsolescence rate of .7 per year, the fleet was 12.4 years old in 1959.) Nevertheless, during his two-year tour the Navy's combatant ships were reduced from 967, of which 409 were combatants, to 860, and his personnel from 677,000 to 626,000. Moreover, in addition to operating the Sixth and Seventh Fleets while the First and Second conducted training exercises, the Navy conducted extensive deployments to the Middle East because of the blocking of the Suez Canal and the 1956 war, sent its annual <u>Unitas</u> cruise to South America, took midshipmen on their summer cruises, and operated in Antarctica. In 1958 there came the Marine landings at Beirut, Lebanon, and the Formosa Straits crisis. By strengthening the Sixth Fleet from the Second and shifting the carrier <u>Essex</u> from the Sixth Fleet to the Seventh, the Navy was able to contain the crises and also show how quickly it could transfer its striking power to wherever it was needed. Gates was in office when two new <u>Forrestal</u>-class carriers, the <u>Ranger</u> and <u>Independence</u>, became operational and the remaining <u>Essexes</u> were modernized. Now all attack carriers could handle the new jet attack and fighter aircraft including the heavy attack A3D Skywarrior and F8U Corsair. Meanwhile specialized hunter killer groups Alpha and Baker concentrated on improving ASW training and techniques and the <u>Seawolf</u>, <u>Skate</u>, and other nuclear boats joined the fleet. With the <u>Skipjack</u>, commissioned on 15 April 1959, came the teardrop-shaped hull of the experimental submarine <u>Albacore</u>, forerunner of the American submarine force of the 1970s. At great cost, Gates also kept ships and planes extending the DEW line, and by reducing the range of the Polaris missile to 1,200 miles he got his first Polaris submarine on station in December 1960 instead of the spring of 1963. Gates's tour was a period of great technological innovation during which missiles replaced guns, nuclear replaced some conventional power, jets largely replaced propeller planes, space was at least pierced, and the first operational Polaris shot occurred from a submarine, on 20 July 1960. The problem with providing a new nuclear-powered carrier each year was the tremendous cost involved; the problem of fitting missiles to old destroyers was evaded by putting them on new frigates instead; and ASW was taken care of in part by producing both high-speed attack submarines and the Polaris type and speeding up production of the latter, doctrine established from the operations of

Task forces Alpha and Bravo, and the provision of Asroc and Subroc ASW weapons, improved sonars, and airborne submarine detection systems. Gates killed an Air Force attempt to put Polaris submarines and their target selection under control of SAC but agreed to integrate strategic targeting under the Joint Target-Strategic Planning Staff and in the latter's SIOP (Single Integrated Operation Plan). He also jealously guarded the Marine Corps from decimation, absorption by the Army, and loss of its air wings to the Air Force while it perfected its vertical assault techniques. In addition to LPHs, the Marines received a new multipurpose ship, the amphibious dock landing ship LPD. The LPH and the LPD would be the backbone of the 20-knot amphibious squadrons of the 1970s.

When Eisenhower prevailed upon Gates to serve as deputy secretary of defense--and after 1 December 1959 as secretary--he elevated Under Secretary William B. Franke to secretary of the Navy.

4. *Franke*. Franke served as Assistant Secretary of the Navy for Financial Management and Comptroller and as Under Secretary. He assumed his new office on 8 June 1959. The loss of an American U-2 over Russia on 1 May 1960 signalled the beginning of a tense summer for DOD. While the Soviets made the Berlin issue bubble, trouble broke out in the Congo and the carrier *Wasp* was sent to stand by off the West Coast of Africa. For the FY 1956 budget Franke proposed a fifth *Forrestal*-class carrier, and for 1957 a sixth even though carriers consumed most of the funds allotted to shipbuilding. To obtain nuclear power for these carriers proved impossible, but for 1958 Franke talked a CVAN up to the Secretary of Defense level while Arleigh Burke argued for it in the JCS. These men would have to wait nine more years before a second CVAN was authorized. To preserve ships, Franke initiated the FRAM (Fleet Rehabilitation and Modernization) program which added from 5 to 8 years to the lives of older ships. To bolster American strength in the Mediterranean and the Pacific, he added a carrier to both the Sixth and Seventh fleets. While the *Triton* circumnavigated the globe under water, the *Sargo* reached the North Pole under the ice, thus proving that the Arctic route could be used in any season, and the tender

Proteus arrived at Holy Loch, Scotland, to establish a Polaris-boat base in the Eastern Atlantic. While Operation Deep Freeze continued in the Antarctic, the first naval Assistant Secretary for Research and Development, James H. Wakelin, began making significant contributions in oceanography and antisubmarine warfare, and Franke merged the Bureau of Aeronautics and Bureau of Ordnance into a new Bureau of Weapons, a precursor step, it turned out, to the merger of all the material bureaus under a Chief of Naval Material in 1963.

The personnel retention problem continued to challenge Franke, for reenlistment rates for first-term sailors averaged but 21 percent and those in technical ratings even lower. Another challenge was that of the Soviet submarine-launched ballistic missile. Franke sought a solution to the ASW problem by establishing the Atlantic Undersea Test and Evaluation Range at Anders Island in the Bahamas. To enhance the quality of the train, he obtained a new class of fast replenishment ship, the Fast Combat Support Ships (AOE) and of Combat Stores Ship (AFS) and helicopters to provide vertical replenishment from these ships at sea. Like his predecessors, Franke fended off dilution of the Marine Corps, which numbered 200,000 men and comprised a quarter of the Navy Department's personnel. He kept one battalion landing team with the Sixth Fleet, one with the Seventh Fleet, and one in the Caribbean where Castro was giving concern to the United States. To prevent Castro from exporting revolution, he sent the <u>Franklin D. Roosevelt</u> to Guantánamo for "routine training" and established a barrier patrol about Cuba. He bequeathed Castro and many other problems to the new President, John F. Kennedy and his own successor as secretary of the Navy, John B. Connally.

VI. CUBA'S CASTRO

Although Cuba's dictator, Fulgencio Batista, kept order and enjoyed American support, his island was ready for revolution because of the ravages of outside exploitive capital, poverty, and unemployment. When Fidel Castro began an insurrection against him, the United States embargoed arms to Batista, who went into exile on 1 January 1959. While not declaring his communist beliefs, Castro's actions revealed them, for he expropriated American property worth $1 billion and permitted no elections or free speech. As thousands of refugees sought refuge in Florida and elsewhere, Castro exported his revolution to Latin American and on 2 December 1961 confessed he was a communist. What were America's options? The United States cut off subsidized Cuban sugar imports in reprisal for the expropriation of its property and embargoed the export of everything but medicine and food to Cuba. Meanwhile the Soviets signed a trade pact to buy Cuban sugar, sent technicians, oil, and arms to Cuba, threatened a missile attack on the United States if it intervened, and sneered at the Monroe Doctrine. As a member of the UN and of the OAS, the United States was forbidden forcible intervention in Cuba, and it found it difficult to overcome Latin American hostility and win a censure of Castro. A meeting of the foreign ministers of the American States of August 1960 condemned "extracontinental intervention in the Americas" but made no mention of Cuba. However, when Castro demanded among other things the return of Guantánamo and on 48 hours' notice reduced the American embassy staff from 87 to 11, Eisenhower established a naval patrol to prevent an invasion of Guatemala or Nicaragua, looked the other way as Americans trained Cuban anti-Castro forces in Guatemala, and severed diplomatic relations on 3 January 1961, only 17 days before John F. Kennedy became President.

CHAPTER 24

KENNEDY, JOHNSON, AND SEA POWER IN THE SIXTIES

I. KENNEDY AND THE NEW FRONTIER

A. THE ELECTION OF 1960. How to prevent the cold war from becoming a hot one was the prime issue in foreign affairs in the election of 1960. Eisenhower backed his vice president, Richard M. Nixon, who was experienced in foreign affairs and took a hard line toward the Soviets. The Democrats chose a 43-year old charismatic Catholic, John F. Kennedy. Kennedy served three terms in the House, 1947-1953, when he was elected to the Senate. He had no experience in foreign affairs outside of serving for a time on the Senate Committee on Foreign Relations. On the other hand, he had traveled abroad extensively, served in the Navy in World War II, and was conscious of the sweep of history. Saying that he would "get the country moving again," he centered upon the donothingism and standpattism of the Eisenhower years and the failure of the United States to keep up with the Soviets in missile development and rate of economic growth. There was no real clash between Nixon and Kennedy on foreign affairs. Nixon, however, had to defend Eisenhower's middle-of-the-road position, Dulles's "brinkmanship," and dependence upon nuclear power that had become suspect abroad. He did not appear well in four televised debates with Kennedy, and although correct in denying that there was a missile gap lost the election by only .02 percent of the popular vote. Especially during his last two years in office, with Dulles ill and then gone, Eisenhower was his own secretary of state. If the Soviets forged ahead and grew stronger, he stood up to them. He "lost" Cuba in the same sense that Truman "lost" China. NATO, cracked by Suez, still functioned. The cold war rather than peace marked Soviet-American relations, but Eisenhower could say that no American soldier had died from enemy fire during his 8 years and that the United States was still the strongest economic and military power in the world and the leader of the earth's free nations. He had almost stopped an inflationary spiral and the American people enjoyed the highest standard of living in their history even if they did so at the cost of becoming a "have not" nation with respect to such natural resources as copper, lead, zinc, and good iron ore.

B. THE KENNEDY ENTOURAGE. Rather than merely rich Democrats for his cabinet Kennedy chose two Republicans to serve him, one as secretary of the treasury, the other, Robert S. McNamara, as secretary of defense. McNamara (Phi Beta Kappa, University of California) had been a "whiz kid" in the supply branch of the Army Air Force in World War II, then president of the Ford Motor Company. Dean Rusk became secretary of state; Adlai Stevenson, ambassador to the United Nations; Dean Acheson, ambassador to NATO; Kennedy's 35-year old brother, Robert F., who had managed his campaign, the attorney general. For Kennedy to prod Congress into action on his New Frontier program including health care for the aged, housing and community development, highway construction, federal aid for schools, and civil rights, however, proved difficult because the Democrats, although in the majority, included many who were conservative and frequently voted with the Republicans.

C. THE McNAMARA "REVOLUTION." The adoption of Flexible Response is considered one McNamara revolution, his use of "cost effective" procedures for reaching strategic decisions another. Unlike Forrestal, who had followed a passive role, McNamara took an active role in defense management. Rather than letting the services administer DOD, he himself managed the business side of his department.

    1. <u>Ninety-nine Trombones</u>. In 1961, DOD spent half the federal budget, or 10 percent of the GNP. Determined to master his sprawling establishment, McNamara adopted ideas offered by his comptroller, Charles J. Hitch, and recruited young men who used computers and cost- and systems-analysis techniques to plot policy changes. He thereby earned the criticism that he overlooked military judgment and professional experience. One of the first conclusions reached by the "whiz kids" was that the Soviets rather than the United States suffered from a missile gap. Although both the United States and the Soviets had ample nuclear overkill capability, Kennedy ruled that the United States must remain ahead in nuclear and missile development. While nuclear-armed missiles were placed in underground sites and Polaris submarines patroled the seas, McNamara ordered a series of studies known as the "Ninety-nine Trombones," which eventually totaled 131. Among subjects for study were the status and needs of

strategic and continental air defense forces, requirements for limited wars, the status of major research and development projects, and whether some military installations could not be reduced or closed.

For general war, McNamara considered minimum deterrence, full counterforce, and flexible response. The first, often called finite deterrence, involved a strike on Soviet cities; the second, also called optimum mix (of bombers and of land-based and Polaris missiles), called for a strike on Soviet military sites as well as on cities; the third involved forces tailored to meet a particular contingency if deterrence failed. The last, which Kennedy chose, meant increasing the production of missiles (as of the Air Force's Minuteman and Titan and additional Polaris boats), counterinsurgency forces,[1] air and sea lift, an enlarged Marine Corps, and improving SAC's airborne capability while reducing the vulnerability of American strategic weapons systems.

2. <u>Growth of the Office of Secretary of Defense</u>. To obtain his goals, McNamara intruded into areas subordinates believed were their legal responsibilities. In point were the unification of service intelligence, supply, procurement, and communications functions; the planning for force structures and budgets on a five-year rather than annual basis; and a cost-effective programming-planning-budgeting-system (PPBS) based on resource categories rather than departments, that improved single-manager control. Instead of grouping by departments, PPBS presented defense costs in terms of personnel; operation and maintenance; procurement; research, development, test, and evaluation; construction; management funds; and military aid. In consequence, McNamara saw little need for the service secretaries, particularly for activists like John Connally of the Navy who might compete with him for service loyalty. Although he rejected Senator W. Stuart Symington's suggestion of 5 December 1960 that all military staff organizations and the budget process be unified under the secretary of defense and that the service secretaries be eliminated, the growth in the number of assistant secretaries of defense provided him a general staff numbering 1,600 military men and civilians. As a result, the authority of the service secretaries waned and civilian overshadowed military input into military planning and operations of the 8 unified commands.

Kennedy's directing that the services not be given sums they could spend as they liked but that the secretary of defense decide what proportion of the total defense budget to allot to them gave McNamara a huge club to drive the services to cooperate. It also meant that decisions made by civilians in McNamara's office might counter the professional judgment of military leaders. Kennedy thereupon reverted to the fixed budget ceiling and McNamara decided to strengthen the power of the service secretaries in the decision-making process.

D. SEEKING OPTIONS. While seeking détente with Russia, Kennedy questioned placing full reliance upon nuclear power. While the latter created a "balance of terror" that made general war unlikely, it could neither stop the progress of Soviet technology nor the simmering of revolutionary forces in the Third World. He opted for special forces and additional conventional forces that could be deployed "with the speed, discrimination, and versatility which may well be needed" to keep limited wars limited--the Flexible Response General Maxwell D. Taylor had long pleaded for. Over a million Americans --regulars, reservists, and civilians--were trained in counterinsurgency. In addition, private firms were authorized to sell arms to overseas purchasers. The prime answer, however, lay in increasing conventional forces. To this end, in September 1961, the Strategic Army Corps and the Tactical Air Command were reorganized into a new unified command called United States Strike Command. Moreover, by 1963 the number of army combat divisions was increased from 11 to 16 and Air Force tactical wings from 16 to 21--and the defense budget increased from $45.6 billion in 1960 to $52.7 billion in 1963. Although McNamara considered reducing the attack carrier force from 16 with 16 airwings to 13 carriers and 13 airwings in 1965, in 1968 he recommended 15 carriers but 12 air wings, with planes to be flown to the carriers as the situation required. By retiring the older Essex-class carriers (42,000 tons), he planned for the mid-1970 carrier force to consist of 4 nuclear-powered carriers of the Enterprise class (86,000 tons), 8 Forrestal- (78,000 tons) and 3 Midway-class carriers (63,000 tons). Because he considered submarines, destroyers, land-based patrol craft, and other means more effective than CVSs, McNamara planned to retire the last with the end of the Vietnam war.

E. RACING TO THE MOON. The American rocket of 1963 had a thrust of 36,000 pounds, a Russian, of 800,000 pounds. But it would take a rocket 50 feet in diameter and 300 feet long with a boost of 7.5 million pounds to land a man on the moon and return him to earth. In May 1961 Kennedy challenged Congress to meet this highest-priority goal by 1970. Congress responded with Project Apollo, which would cost $20 billion and test America's scientific capability. In February 1962, John Glenn launched the United States into the space race with a three-day orbital flight; in May 1962, Alan Shepherd followed suit; on 20 July 1969, Neil A. Armstrong and Edwin E. Aldrin landed their Apollo spacecraft on the moon.

F. THE ALLIANCE FOR PROGRESS. Kennedy converted Eisenhower's "Operation Pan America," designed to provide economic aid to Latin American nations susceptible to "Fidelismo," into the Alliance for Progress. Somewhat like the Marshall Plan, the Alliance was a ten-year plan involving an American contribution of $10 billion for educational and medical aid but also for land and tax reforms. The plan was executed slowly and faced insurmountable obstacles even though Kennedy termed Latin America "the most critical area in the world." Much more effective was the Peace Corps he created in 1961. Under this program, volunteers paid a pittance transferred their knowledge to increase the standard of living in underdeveloped countries.

G. THE BAY OF PIGS. Dedicated to the proposition that "Communist domination in this hemisphere can never be negotiated," Kennedy had to decide whether the 1,200 anti-Castro Cubans trained by the CIA in Guatemala should invade Cuba or be disbanded. He approved the invasion--which was supported by the CIA, JCS, and McNamara--but withheld American air support. About 1,500 men landed in the <u>Bahía de Cochinos</u> (Bay of Pigs) on 17 April 1961. The anticipated uprising against Castro failed to occur and in two days 1,200 men were made prisoners. Condemnation of the United States was almost worldwide, Castro moved closer to the Kremlin, and Khrushchev took a hard line when he talked with Kennedy in Vienna in June and then put pressure on Berlin that might erupt into nuclear war.

H. BERLIN, 1961. Khrushchev set a deadline of 15 June for settling the Berlin issue. Were a peace treaty with Germany not written, he would sign a treaty with East Germany, which would then control the access routes to West Berlin. Khrushchev was irked by the "showcase of democracy" that West Berlin represented and by the 3 million East Germans who had escaped to the West. In August, construction began on the "Berlin Wall," that still separates eastern and western Europe. On 13 August Kennedy sent 1,500 men to Berlin and ordered a partial mobilization including the callup of some reservists and increases in both general purposes and conventional forces. While the Navy took ships out of reserve and the Air Force moved 16 tactical fighter squadrons to Europe, the Army went from 875,000 to 1 million men, of whom 40,000 were sent to Europe. When Kennedy assured Berlin of support, deadlock with Khrushchev ensued.

I. THE CUBAN MISSILE CRISIS. Between July and October 1962, more than 175 Soviet ships delivered equipment, 6,000 technicians and instructors, and missile-laden patrol boats, fighter planes, and surface-to-air missiles to Cuba. Soviet foreign minister Andrei Gromyko assured Kennedy that Soviet aid to Cuba was "solely defensive." Photographic reconnaissance assured Kennedy of that fact, as he admitted on 4 September. "Were it otherwise the gravest issues would arise," he added. When Cuban refugees spoke of offensive missiles being emplaced, however, he ordered high altitude photographic reconnaissance. For a month nothing novel appeared. On 10 October, however, Senator Kenneth B. Keating, of New York, publicized the threat, photographs taken by a U-2 plane on 14 October solidly confirmed it, and photographs taken on succeeding days revealed that work on missile sites was proceeding at startling speed. Moreover, two missile types were discovered: one could reach along the arc of a circle from Washington, D.C., to the Panama Canal (1,000 miles); the other from Hudson's Bay to Lima, Peru (2,000 miles).

Soviet objectives worried Kennedy. Was Khrushchev trying to redress his imbalance in missiles? He had 50 to 75 ICBMs on Russian soil while the United States had 130 ICBMs, 140 Polaris missiles in submarines, and 1,500 strategic bombers. If the United States did nothing, Khrushchev would have 200 to 300 missiles in place 90 miles from America's shore. Instead of the 15-minute warning if missiles were launched from Russia, the United States would have only 2 or 3 minutes for those launched from Cuba. Khrushchev could thus launch a preemptive strike, knock out a large proportion of American retaliatory forces, and kill an estimated 80 million Americans. He would have additional bargaining power in discussing the Berlin and other issues when he paid an expected visit to the United States in November, and possibly draw Latin America into the Soviet orbit.

What organizational machinery did Kennedy have to help him decide what to do? And what options did he have? After the war in Korea began, Truman relied for advice upon the National Security Council, which had a staff directed by an Executive Secretary. Eisenhower added a Special Assistant for National Security Affairs to oversee the work of the Executive Secretary and his staff. When Kennedy retained the organization but preferred to deal with his Special Assistant for International Security Affairs, the latter became an extremely important person in the decision-making process. However, for the Cuban crisis he created an Executive Committee (EXCOMM) of the NSC comprised of Attorney General Robert F. Kennedy, Secretary of State Dean Rusk, Secretary of Defense Robert McNamara; Director of the Central Intelligence Agency John McCrone; Secretary of the Treasury Douglas Dillon; the Special Advisor on National Security Affairs McGeorge Bundy; the Chairman of the JCS, Maxwell Taylor; and a number of others from State, Defense, and other agencies. From 16 to 28 October, the EXCOMM considered options: a quarantine or blockade, or a military strike.

McNamara and Robert Kennedy strongly supported a blockade, arguing that a blockade, although limited in pressure, could be increased if necessary and leave the initiative with the United States. Robert Kennedy opposed a "surgical" air strike--one on the missile sites alone--because military action must include all military sites in Cuba and end with invasion and because American tradition opposed striking a preemptive blow. Hitting such a small country as Cuba would lower America's prestige throughout the world.

Proponents of a military strike, especially the JCS, argued that a blockade would not remove the missiles or stop work on the sites. Rather it would bring about a confrontation with Russia when we stopped their ships and provoke the Soviets to reciprocate, as by blockading Berlin or demanding that the United States remove her missiles surrounding Russia as the price for removing the missiles from Cuba. They were pleased when McNamara directed them to deploy forces for an air strike of 500 sorties on 23 October if such was deemed necessary.

The EXCOMM reported to Kennedy that its majority favored a blockade. Kennedy asked for scenarios, i.e., written expositions of what might happen for each possible course of action, and for a draft of a speech he would deliver to the nation. Advocates of blockade provided their recommendations, those of military action, theirs. Each group advised notifying the UN, the Organization of American States (OAS), and Khrushchev of the president's decision. Kennedy opted for the blockade. With agents prepared to notify the UN, call the OAS into session, Dean Acheson on his way to inform France and Germany, and Britain alerted, Kennedy on 22 October addressed the nation even as four tactical aircraft squadrons were placed on the alert, 156 ICBM crews and a fleet of Polaris submarines were at the ready, troops in the southeastern United States stood by, naval and Marine strength at Guantánamo was strengthened, 180 ships including 8 carriers formed into TF 136 established a 2,100-mile-long ring about Cuba, and SAC B-52s loaded with atomic weapons orbited over various civilian landing fields. Involved were 300,000 men, 2,000 air sorties, 90,000 Marines and paratroopers, and more than 100 amphibious ships. After briefing his cabinet and congressional leaders, Kennedy told the nation he was taking an initial step with the blockade but that the Pentagon was prepared for military action.

On 23 October, when the OAS unanimously supported him, Kennedy wrote Khrushchev a letter in which he asked him to abide by the blockade and not give him reason to fire on Soviet ships. He also directed that if a Soviet ship refused to stop at the blockade line, the Navy was to disable it by shooting at its propellers and rudders rather than sinking it and causing loss of life. Ships that stopped were to be boarded and examined, and the Navy was to take care of Soviet submarines known to be approaching Cuba.

The Navy had established the blockade line 800

miles from Cuba, outside of MIG fighter range. When the British ambassador to the United States told Kennedy that this meant interception within a very few hours after the blockade went into effect on the morning of 23 October, Kennedy ordered it shortened to 500 miles. A story has it that McNamara entered Navy Flag Plot and lectured the CNO, George Anderson, saying that his task was not to shoot Russians but to get a political message across from the President to Khrushchev. Rather than pushing Khrushchev hard and perhaps causing him to retaliate, he was to leave a door open for him to save face as he pulled back. Although Anderson denied it, witnesses reported that in essence he told McNamara not to interfere in naval matters and that he should go back to his office and let the Navy run the blockade. Whatever the reasons, Anderson was not given the customary second term as CNO.[2]

Soviet ships approached the 500-mile line on the 27th. Would they stop or must the Navy stop them? The first two ships to reach the line had a submarine between them. Instead of having a cruiser make the interception, the carrier *Essex*, bearing sonar-equipped helicopters, signalled the submarine to surface and identify itself on penalty of being depth charged. Kennedy sweated until a message arrived stating that the Soviet ships had either stopped at the barrier or turned around. He then ordered the *Essex* to leave the ships alone. Relieved, Robert Kennedy said, "for a moment the world had stood still, and now it was going around again. . . ."

Kennedy wished to give Khrushchev both time to think and an avenue of saving face. While the Navy forced six Soviet submarines to the surface, photographic reconnaissance by Navy P-8U planes showed that the missile sites were almost ready and that IL-28 bombers were being unloaded and assembled. The Navy boarded Soviet ships making passage for Cuba and let pass those that carried no weapons while Kennedy increased the pressure on Khrushchev by sending low-level flights over Cuba every two hours instead of just twice a day, using night flights to take pictures of missile sites with flares, adding oil and lubricants to the embargo list, even preparing a military government for Cuba should he have to invade.

At 1800 on 26 October, Khrushchev cabled Kennedy

that his missiles had been placed in Cuba only to discourage an American invasion. He would withdraw them if Kennedy would lift the blockade and promise not to invade. In a second letter, however, he demanded that Kennedy remove American missiles from Turkey. Kennedy was embarrassed because the decision to remove the obsolete missiles had already been made but their removal would appear to be yielding to Khrushchev's demand. He was also pressured by the JCS to permit the launching of an air strike on Monday, 24 October, because the missiles in Cuba were operative, as revealed when they shot down a U-2 aircraft. Kennedy ordered a review of all possible courses of action, had all nuclear weapons defused so that they could be used only by his direct order, and decided against a strike, yet he told Khrushchev that he would not remove the missiles from Turkey and would make no "trade." Upon the advice of Brother Robert and others, Kennedy told Khrushchev he agreed to the terms contained in his first letter: Russia would take her missiles out of Cuba under UN verification and the United States would not invade. Robert Kennedy meanwhile told the Soviet ambassador that the United States would shoot back if SAMs shot at American U-2 planes, a step that might lead to an untenable escalation of conflict, and that Russia had publicly and privately denied placing missiles in Cuba, a fact that could not be denied. If Khrushchev did not offer a favorable reply on the morrow, the United States would destroy the missile sites. He sweetened the pill by adding that the United States had already decided to remove its missiles from Turkey and from Italy as well. Khrushchev buckled. His failure in Cuba and the Sino-Soviet split caused his removal from the top Soviet leadership in October 1964.

Had Kennedy stretched the meaning of blockade in international law by using it when belligerency did not exist? Khrushchev deemed the blockade illegal, and it remains an aberration to those who see international law as an accretion of norms and principles that are fixed. Much like the British when it suited them to use their sea power, Kennedy used his Navy to support national policy. He is upheld by those who see international law as subject to growth and development and applaud his using it not as a guide to action but as a tool. Moreover, his legal status was firm, for he acted only after receiving approval from the OAS and the major nations in NATO.

Castro remained, but Khrushchev removed the missiles, and a "hot line" was installed between Washington and Moscow for use during emergencies.

J. AIDING INDIA AGAINST CHINA. While Kennedy handled the Cuban missile crisis, China pushed Indian troops back along the Himalayan frontier, thus violating a nonaggression pact signed in 1954. China's motives may have been to lower Indian prestige in southeast Asia, counter Soviet economic aid to India, and hurt India, which was friendly toward even if unaligned with the West. Kennedy authorized military aid in the form of Air Force transports, and China ceased her intrusion. Factors other than a few "flying boxcars" undoubtedly influenced China, which continued supporting communist guerrillas in South Vietnam, Laos,[3] and Thailand.

K. VIVE LA FRANCE. In great part because of the Marshall Plan, Western Europe by the time Kennedy took office had not only become prosperous; the annual growth of some countries was greater than that of the United States. No longer needing American economic aid, these countries might strive to end American hegemony. Stating that the Atlantic community must be maintained, Kennedy got Congress to cut tariffs and improved American relations with the European Common Market. Perhaps because he had grandiose plans for rebuilding the French Empire, de Gaulle vetoed British admission to the Common Market, opposed a plan to create a multilateral force (MLF) in which sailors from all NATO countries would serve in ships, and said he would create his own "force de frappe," or nuclear power. De Gaulle knew that he would remain under the American nuclear umbrella but believed that by building his own nuclear weapons he could gain an independent if not leading voice in European affairs. France, China, and Cuba were the only three out of more than a hundred countries that did not adhere to the Kennedy Test Ban Treaty of 5 August 1963 that applied to atmospheric but not underground testing.

II. THE GREAT SOCIETY AND VIETNAM

A. "LET US CONTINUE." Two hours after Kennedy's death, Vice President Lyndon Johnson was sworn in as President. He kept Kennedy's cabinet, promised to fight for the programs of the New Frontier, indeed to create a Great Society that would eradicate want and racial discrimination. With the passage of most of the necessary legislation, the Great Society almost appeared in view, only to be thwarted by the longest, most frustrating, and most unpopular war in American history.

B. PANAMA AND THE DOMINICAN REPUBLIC. Three months of negotiations ended in April 1964 when the United States and Panama agreed to a new treaty effective September 1965. Instead of retaining the perpetual rights and full control over the Canal Zone as provided in 1963, the United States recognized Panamanian sovereignty over the Zone but kept troops there to defend it. Latin America applauded Johnson's restraint in not resorting to military intervention and occupation --until Johnson sent troops to the Dominican Republic in April 1965.

After the murder of Raphael Trujillo and the end of his brutal regime, Kennedy had the Navy protect a provisional government and used economic aid to make the republic a showcase in his Alliance for Progress. When fighting broke out between liberals and conservatives, Johnson ordered troops sent to Santo Domingo ostensibly to protect American lives and property but really to prevent the establishment of a Castro-style government. On 27 April, a Navy amphibious task force including the LPH Boxer prepared to evacuate Americans and Marines at Camp Lejeune and the 82d Airborne Division were alerted. As helicopters from the Boxer evacuated Americans from Santo Domingo, Johnson's order to intervene went via McNamara and General Earle Wheeler, Chairman of the JCS, to the Navy. At 1910 on the 28th, the Boxer began landing Marines by helicopter. Late on the 29th, advance elements of the 82d Airborne Division were landed and with Marines created an International Security Zone from which refugees could be evacuated in safety. Within six days, the amphibious task force landed more than 8,000 men of the Fourth Marine Expeditionary Brigade. Soon 22,000 troops were on the island even though the war was escalating in Vietnam. While he spoke of a threatened communist seizure of power, Johnson violated the nonintervention clause of the Charter of the OAS and earned bitter criticism from throughout Latin America. Although he said that "The O.A.S. couldn't pour piss out of a boot if the instructions were written on the heel," he soon persuaded the O.A.S. to provide a peace-keeping force to take over control from American troops. He subsequently backed a government acceptable to both conservatives and liberals, and on 3 September his intervention ended. The Kennedy-McNamara flexible response worked well for Johnson, and he kept the intervention limited in time, cost, and number of troops, but he cracked the concensus he had earned at home, a concensus soon shattered by his escalation of the war in Vietnam.

C. FRENCH LESSONS. The United States had aided France to crush Ho Chi Minh's rebels in Vietnam from 1946 to 1954. Among lessons that the United States should have learned from the French experience were that: 1) mobility that does not result in concentration for battle is useless; 2) air support is of little value in underdeveloped countries; 3) atomic war is useless when an enemy advances single file and is supported by porters bringing ammunition stored in caves; 4) before a population will provide a fighting army and its equipment, the local government must win its loyalty through honest and efficient administration, public health programs, agrarian reforms, and the like. Indeed, Eisenhower estimated that an election held in 1954 would have upheld Ho Chi Minh by 80 percent, in great part because Ho could "deliver the vote" of his 15 million people.

D. THE SECOND VIETNAM WAR

1. Supporting Diem. After the French left Vietnam, the United States supported the authoritarian Catholic prime minister Ngo Dinh Diem against increasingly active Vietcong guerrillas (Charlie) who killed off local chiefs in large numbers in part because Diem reestablished his authority over the national government only. When he refused to undertake social reforms, he was visited in May 1961 by Vice President Johnson, who recommended American economic aid but not military intervention. He also told Kennedy that South Vietnam was a major American commitment and that American failure to support it would be like telling the world "that we don't live up to our treaties and don't stand by our friends." Kennedy adopted Eisenhower's domino theory but said that Diem would lose the war unless he won the loyalty of his people. Although the JCS said it would take 40,000 troops to clean out

Charlie, Kennedy sent only 400 Special Forces (Green Berets). In October, General Maxwell Taylor and his special military adviser, Walt Rostow, also visited Diem. They recommended sending more military advisers, 10,000 men for defensive combat operations, and pursuing a "flexible policy" if infiltration from North Vietnam could not be stopped. Kennedy sent more advisers but otherwise refused to escalate the conflict. By supporting Diem and permitting American advisers to take part in combat operations, he nevertheless started the second Vietnam war. The 1,364 American advisers in Vietnam in 1961 grew to 9,865 by the end of 1962; American aid of about $300 million a year to 1963 increased to about $550 million in 1963. A cut in aid caused Diem to adopt some constructive measures, but in November 1963 he was deposed by a generals' coup and killed. By the time of Kennedy's assassination, 22 November 1963, 16,732 advisers were in Vietnam, 60 American soldiers had been killed, and the Malayan-type strategic hamlet program started by Kennedy in 1962 had failed. Despite the use of every counter-insurgency trick devised--the defoliation of vegetation under which Charlie hid, high-speed automatic weapons, amphibious armed personnel carriers, and rocket-armed helicopters--Charlie persisted and more Americans died.

2. <u>The Tonkin Gulf Resolution</u>. The first permanent U. S. naval presence in Vietnam came in August 1950, when a Navy Section of the Military Advisory Aid Group was formed in Saigon with 8 officers and men. Its tasks were to build up river and coastal forces and establish repair and logistic facilities to help the French Navy in Vietnam. This pattern was followed for the next 15 years, but as late as 1963 there were only 742 American naval officers and men in Vietnam.

In the presidential campaign of 1964, which pitted Johnson against the hawkish Barry Goldwater, Johnson resisted clamor for escalating the Vietnam War. When he was told that on 2 and 4 August 1964 three North Vietnamese Soviet-built torpedo boats had attacked American destroyers in international waters in the Gulf of Tonkin, he ordered retaliatory air strikes against North Vietnam torpedo boat bases and oil storage facilities, asked Congress for full authority to "resist aggression," and notified Khrushchev that American ships in international waters must not be molested. The Tonkin Gulf resolution easily passed Congress, and

Johnson was able to escalate by using the conventional forces Kennedy had provided. By doubling the draft, he did not have to call up reservists. But he was destined to pay the price for containment. As Walter Lippmann put it, the United States was between "unattainable victory and unacceptable defeat."

3. <u>From Counterinsurgency to Conventional War</u>. American escalation proceeded with a buildup to 23,000 naval officers and men at the end of 1964 and systematic air strikes against North Vietnam early in 1965 from up to 5 carriers on Yankee Station, in the Gulf of Tonkin, and from land bases. Air Force and Marine flyers provided close support to American and ARVN (Army of the Republic of Viet Nam) forces, and B-52s from Guam joined in striking North Vietnam targets selected at luncheon meetings of Johnson and the JCS. Meanwhile the number of American troops increased from 23,000 late in 1964 to 250,000 a year later, and to 550,000 in 1968. Counterinsurgency had given way to conventional warfare, and rumors had it that Ho Chi Minh's peace feelers were rejected because the United States was in the midst of a presidential campaign and his terms neither permitted the United States to save face nor guaranteed the safety of South Vietnam.

4. <u>Johnson Bows Out</u>. As in Korea so in Vietnam, air strikes only slightly impeded infiltration of men and supplies from the north to the south, few strategic targets were available, the arsenal of Ho Chi Minh lay outside of his borders in Russia and China, mechanized troops did not fare well against guerrillas who when outnumbered could retreat to a sanctuary in Laos or Cambodia. As in Korea, the United States fought in Vietnam always with an eye on the hard-line Chinese, who might intervene if Hanoi appeared to be defeated. American air bombing of North Vietnam aroused particular opposition at home and overseas and made the war a moral issue. The Air Force claim that it would obtain a favorable response from Hanoi in a matter of weeks was quickly disproved, and Johnson limited the war by not bombing the cities of North Vietnam, invading the north, or blocking Haiphong Harbor in which Soviet and Chinese ships regularly unloaded supplies. Tight tactical restrictions on bombing, and strikes ordered from Washington for political purposes did not fit the tactical situation in the field. Moreover, in late March 1968 Johnson permitted bombing only south of the 20th parallel, subsequently declared bombing halts

to give Hanoi time to think things over, and in October ordered a "bombing pause" and agreed to peace talks in Paris. Meanwhile his repeated cry that the war was almost over earned the same credibility as that of "wolf, wolf."

Despite all his management logic, McNamara learned that Vietnam refused to be systems-analyzed. Unlike Korea, the United States did not obtain the support of any major ally and got bogged down in a land war in Asia even if it did not try to "liberate" North Vietnam as it had North Korea. The war was so expensive--$6 billion in 1965-1966, about $30 billion in 1967-1968 or $35,111 for each Charlie killed or captured--that the Great Society was gravely threatened: inflation reached a 4.7 percent level in 1968, and pacifists, liberals, academics, Negroes, and students in often explosive campus revolts demanded an end to the war and that America provide the world with moral leadership and stop trying to become an empire by following the policy of containment. Eugene McCarthy's winning of 42 percent of the Democratic primary vote in March 1968; Robert Kennedy's entry into the presidential race; McNamara's leaving the cabinet because he opposed bombing, as did his successor Clark Clifford; and the great drop in his popularity due to the Vietnam war determined Johnson not to seek the presidency again.

5. <u>Nixon Pulls Out</u>. The new President, Richard M. Nixon, supported by his secretary of defense, Melvin Laird, sought to "Vietnamize" the war. He would let a rearmed ARVN fight with American air and naval aid, pull American troops out, and so win support for the war at home. In the winter of 1970, when he sent American and ARVN troops to clear out the communist sanctuaries in Laos and Cambodia, great unrest surged on many campuses. By mid-1971, American troop strength was cut in half and naval strength was reduced proportionately. Some 248 naval craft worth $68 million were transferred beginning 1 February 1969 to the government of Nguyen Van Thieu, and 25 percent of the American sailors came home in 1969 and another 25 percent in 1970. In April 1972, Hanoi launched its largest assault since the Tet offensive in 1968 in order to discredit Thieu's regime and embarrass Nixon politically. Nixon kept his troop withdrawal on schedule, increased the number of carriers on Yankee Station

from 4 to 5 and their planes from 250 to 700 in one week, and authorized the bombing of any North Vietnam target because Hanoi had violated the "understanding" of 1968 in which Johnson stopped the bombing. In May, he ordered the mining of Haiphong and of six other North Vietnam harbors and the bombing of hitherto immune power plants in the Haiphong area while causing a 25-mile "bomb line" to be respected along the China border. As long as Hanoi would not agree to terms, the bombing continued, with 15 B-52s lost to Soviet-made SAMs. In 1972, Nixon visited China and Russia and arranged a détente. In a radio and television address on 23 January 1973 he announced the end of the war, effective 27 January, and the bringing of "peace with honor" to Vietnam. In 1975, South Vietnam fell to the Communists, whereupon the world questioned American credibility and the United States pulled its forward position back from Vietnam and Thailand to Guam. The U.S. Navy transported thousands of Vietnamese refugees to safety and in its last action removed the mines in Haiphong harbor by using helicopters towing special sleds.

  6. <u>The Navy in Vietnam</u>. The U.S. Navy provided sealift, warships, aircraft, Marines, and logistic support for the Vietnam War. About 98 percent of the materials sent to Vietnam went by sea in a variety of ships operated by MSTS--with 304 dry-cargo ships alone at sea on any day in 1967 and the tonnage sent to Vietnam approximately equal to all other American exports. Except for priority items, everything went by sea, for the cost of sending one ton by plane from Dover, Delaware, cost $709, the same ton by ship, $73.50. While ammunition ships ran independently and Fast Deployment Logistic ships (FDL) were added to MSTS ships, the lack of warehousing in Vietnam stimulated the use of container and of roll-on, roll-off (Ro/Ro) ships.

  a. <u>Combatant ships</u>. Every conceivable type of ship was used in Vietnam; large and jeep carriers, the battleship <u>New Jersey</u>, cruisers, destroyers, landing ships, supply and ammunition ships, mine craft, repair ships, tenders, patrol boats, river boats, Coast Guard cutters, even air cushioned vehicles and LPHs. In addition to engaging in surveillance, small ships engaged in interdiction and blockade operations. For example, LSMs, LCPLs, AKAs, Swift boats, and Coast Guard cutters were used in Operation Jackstay, 1967, which sought to clear Charlie out of the Mekong Delta.

Since about half of Charlie's cargo moved on internal waterways, naval aircraft mined a number of river mouths in North Vietnam but not its three main deep water ports. Beginning in 1965, the first large-scale American operation, Market Time, tried to stop the infiltration of supplies by small boats into South Vietnam. The destroyers and destroyer escorts of TF71 patrolled a line 12 miles off the coast and 1,000 miles long from the 17th parallel to the Cambodian border. Involved were a Sea Force (PC, PCE, PGM, MSC, LSIL, LSSL types) and a Coastal Force of sailing or motor junks. To more effectively investigate the estimated 50,000 passenger and freight junks in the area, recourse was had to 22-knot Swift boats (PCF) and the 82-foot, 17-knot Coast Guard cutter (WPB). Because of Market Time, the communists shifted their logistic supply lines inland through neutral Cambodia and Laos. The United States in consequence shifted to riverine warfare in Operation Game Warden.

b. <u>Riverine Warfare</u>. TF116, the River Patrol Force, engaged in riverine warfare not new to the United States because it had used it in Florida, in the Civil War, in the Philippines, and in Nicaragua and along the Yangtse as well. In Operation Game Warden, the Navy's River Assault Flotilla transported and supported Army troops even though armed helicopters were faster in catching Charlie. Included were Monitors (MON), Command and Control Boats (CCB), Assault Support Patrol Boats (ASPP), River Minesweepers (MSM), Armored Troops Carriers (mechanized LCSMs known as ATCs), River Patrol Boats (PBR), Fast Patrol Boats (PCF), and the aforementioned Patrol Air Cushioned Vehicle (PACU). In September 1968, when Vice Admiral Elmo Zumwalt assumed command of riverine forces, the U.S. Navy had 38,386 men in Vietnam.

c. <u>Aircraft</u>. Naval aircraft of various types were used: the light but long-range A-4 Sky Hawk for close ground support and interdiction; the A-6 Intruder for all weather attack; the A-7 Corsair II which replaced the A-4 and which the Air Force also adopted after using F-4Cs, F-100s, and F-105s, and the twin turbo-prop E-2A Hawkeye, an early-warning plane that could tie into a carrier's Naval Tactical Data System. Most accurate was the Walleye, a TV guided air-to-surface glide bomb introduced in March 1967. Carriers launched attack and fighter interdiction strikes to 1965 and engaged in systematic bombing until 1968 and intermittently thereafter. Operation Sea Dragon involved the cooperation of aircraft and Seventh Fleet cruisers and destroyers in hitting targets along North Vietnam's coast. To avoid interference, Air Force and Navy aircraft were assigned six different geographical areas ("route passages"). At least the <u>Bon Homme Richard</u>, <u>Ranger</u>, <u>Kitty Hawk</u>, <u>Independence</u>, <u>Forrestal</u>, <u>Intrepid</u>, <u>Ticonderoga</u>, <u>Hancock</u>, <u>Constellation</u>, <u>Oriskany</u>, <u>Coral Sea</u>, and the <u>Enterprise</u> served off Vietnam, the last for 2 tours. In 37 months of operations, the Navy had 300 planes destroyed over North Korea, 1,000 more damaged, and lost 83 pilots and crewmen, with 200 others missing.

    d. <u>The Marine Corps</u>. The Marine Corps provided the first ground forces for Vietnam when they landed 2 battalions (3,500 men) at Danang, 300 miles north of Saigon, in March 1965. By June there were 20,000 American troops in Vietnam, of whom 75 percent were Marines and, as noted earlier, 555,000 men by the end of 1967. At its peak strength in 1968, the Marine Amphibious Force had 85,755 men in Vietnam.

    e. <u>Service Force</u>. Nimitz's saying that the Service Force was "our greatest secret weapon in World War II" could also be said of the Service Force that served Vietnam. To transfer supplies brought 7,000 miles from home and funneled through Japan, Okinawa, Guam, and the Philippines, 5 deep draft ports and 5 lesser ports for LSTs and facilities for jet and other aircraft were built in Vietnam. By mid-1967, the Service Force included Mobile Logistic Support Groups and 26 shore activities employing 69,000 Americans and foreign nationals. It operated advance support bases, built air bases and ports, and provided resupply, survey, salvage, and medical support. It used 120 ships of 24 types, 284 small craft of 37 types, and 8,400 Seabees in 11 battalions. It transferred more fuel and ammunition at sea than was accomplished in World War II and set new records in so doing. In 1945, AE-3 transferred 342 tons in 3 days; in 1967, AE-16 transferred 416 tons in 56 minutes. In 1945, tanker pumping rates were 100,000 gallons per hour; in 1967, 273,000 gallons.

f. **Lessons Learned.** Although damage to North Vietnam was extensive, the air bombing campaign drew Hanoi to the peace table but did not stop its aggression against South Vietnam. Despite President Johnson's saying that the United States would "never grow tired" in supporting South Vietnam, Ho Chi Minh outlasted the United States. Interdiction strikes were not only spasmodic but were tightly controlled from Washington. Haiphong and other targets were declared off limits even though 85 percent of the war supplies used by North Vietnam came through that port. Interdiction might have been effective had it been persistent and as effective by night as by day. While carriers were extremely useful, they were employed as static airfields subject to air and submarine attack rather than as mobile striking forces. Washington's policy of "gradualism," of increasing the pressure in small doses, proved to be ineffective. Tactically, the Vietnam war drove the propeller drive plane from the battlefield and introduced modern electronic and missile warfare. "Civilian control was complete, unquestioned, ubiquitous, and detailed, not merely at the higher levels of strategy and political decisions, but also--very importantly--at the lower levels of operations and tactics," Vice Admiral Malcolm Cagle has written, thereby implying that civilians rather than the military lost the war in Vietnam.

III. THE NAVY AND McNAMARA

A. JOHN B. CONNALLY. A Texas lawyer and orator, Connally joined the Navy as a Reserve ensign in June 1941. He served in the office of Under Secretary of the Navy Forrestal and helped plan the invasion of Italy as a staff member to General Eisenhower before acting as a fighter director in the *Essex* for two years, August 1943 to August 1945. As president of KVET, Austin, Texas, 1946 to 1949, he met Senator Lyndon B. Johnson, whom he served as administrative assistant for a time until he turned to practicing law. A conservative Democrat, he supported Eisenhower for President in 1952, when he managed Lyndon Johnson's primary campaign against Kennedy. When Kennedy suggested Franklin D. Roosevelt, also a naval veteran of World War II, as Secretary of the Navy, McNamara said he preferred Connally, perhaps because he thought Connally would not challenge his leadership in the defense department.

Connally inherited from William B. Franke a navy comprised of 817 (383 combatant) ships, 6,800 aircraft, and slightly over 1.2 million people almost equally divided between military and civilians. The two greatest problems Connally faced were to fix the role of carriers in defense and the building of the TFX fighter plane. While McNamara questioned the value of aircraft carriers per se, Connally said he planned to build no nuclear-powered ones like the <u>Enterprise</u>, which joined the other 14 attack carriers on 3 January 1962 because they were too costly compared to conventionally-powered ones. McNamara thereupon scrapped the building of a second nuclear carrier but called for the funding of a conventional one (CVA-67) in the FY 1962 budget.

McNamara, who equated controversy from the services as challenges to his authority, wanted a plane designed to serve all three services. But how could one plane accommodate the Army and Marines, who wanted a simple, inexpensive, close-support aircraft and also the Air Force and the Navy, who wanted a high-performance plane but disagreed on its characteristics. The long-range, fast, sturdy, and low-flying Air Force version was too large and too heavy to operate from carriers and could not remain long on CAP at high altitudes. It seemed logical to provide two planes, one for the Army and Marines, one for the Navy and Air Force. McNamara directed that one plane be designed by the Air Force and Navy. When Connally spurned the new design and requested permission to let the Navy design its own plane, McNamara directed the Air Force, which would use most of the planes, to design one plane. Of 8 bids, those by General Dynamics and Boeing proved most suitable.

Without support from Kennedy and differing with McNamara, Connally resigned effective 20 December 1960 to run for the governorship of Texas. While in that office he was wounded at the same time Kennedy was killed in that fateful day in Dallas, 22 November 1963.

B. FRED KORTH. Korth was a Texas lawyer and banker who served in the personnel section of the Army Air Corps during World War II, as legal counsel for the Secretary of the Army, as Assistant Secretary of the Army (Manpower), and as civilian aide to the Secretary of the Army. Upon becoming Secretary of the Navy, on

4 January 1962, he inherited Connally's problems: the carrier issue, TFX, and fitting the Navy into McNamara's revolution in management procedures. To the latter end, in May he ordered a review of naval management procedures by his administrative assistant, the capable John H. Dillon, who completed work in December. From Dillon's report came a limited reorganization of the Navy Department in which the bilinear form was retained but all "producer," or logistic, bureaus were placed under a Chief of Naval Material who would be directly responsible to the Secretary. The department also integrated its PPBS with that of the Department of Defense.

Admiral George Anderson, who succeeded Arleigh Burke as CNO, objected to the TFX and wanted the Navy to design its own plane. Both Korth and the Army's secretary, Eugene Zuckert, however, suggested giving General Dynamics and Boeing additional time to design a plane to suit the Navy. McNamara agreed. All leading military men opted for Boeing's design but McNamara chose General Dynamics, with Korth and Zuckert supporting him and Anderson and the Chief of Staff of the Air Force opposing. Korth felt compromised because he was still active in a Fort Worth bank which had lent money to General Dynamics, which would build the F-111-A for the Navy and F-111-B for the Air Force. and because he countered Anderson's professional judgment. Although a senate investigation cleared Korth of conflict of interest, Attorney General Robert F. Kennedy suggested that he resign.

McNamara favored the use of carriers and in his first budget, for FY 1963, recommended building a non-nuclear attack type (CVA-67). Korth supported him, most likely on the ground of economy, as did Anderson on the same ground and also because a conventionally-powered could be built more quickly than a nuclear-powered version. When the *Enterprise* showed her worth during the Cuban missile crisis, however, Korth recommended nuclear power for CVA-67. McNamara said he would withhold judgment until Korth made a comprehensive quantitative study of a conventional vs nuclear ship. On 4 April 1963, Korth recommended not only that CVA-67 be nuclear-powered but that "all major warships [8,000 tons and over] should be nuclear-powered." Unsatisfied with his quantification of nuclear- vs conventional-powered ships, McNamara directed Korth to make another study. Korth's conclusion was that nuclear-powered forces were about 3 percent more effective than conventional-powered forces. McNamara disagreed, directed that CVA-67 have conventional power, and questioned a JCS recommendation of a 15 carrier force level, whereupon Korth resigned.

C. PAUL H. NITZE. A Wall Street prodigy, Nitze served as Forrestal's assistant when the latter was Under Secretary of the Navy and in a variety of economic and planning positions in the Department of State, as vice chairman of the U.S. Strategic Bombing Survey, as an adviser to President Eisenhower, and as McNamara's Assistant Secretary of Defense for International Security Affairs until Lyndon Johnson appointed him Secretary of the Navy just one week after Kennedy's assassination. Into the office next to his he placed the new CNO, Admiral David L. McDonald.

Nitze stressed a "War at Sea" program designed to defend the United States and its allies in a limited war against Soviet or Soviet-inspired forces. The program included missiles, mining and patroling Soviet submarine routes, deploying Marines in 20-knot assault ships and by vertical envelopment, carrier strike forces, and new naval and merchant ship construction to replace a fleet and merchant marine still largely of World War II date. Although the Enterprise, cruiser Long Beach, and destroyer Bainbridge, all nuclear-powered, circumnavigated the world late in 1964 at a speed of advance of 22 knots and without logistics support, and the Enterprise and Bainbridge subsequently served as the first nuclear-powered ships in combat, off Vietnam, neither Congress or McNamara was sufficiently impressed by these occurrences to recommend the augmentation of nuclear-powered ships.

It may be recalled that McNamara directed that the CVA-67 be given conventional power and looked askance at a 15-carrier force level. When Nitze opted for 15 carriers, McNamara said he intended to reduce carrier strength to 13 by the early 1970s and took carriers out of the Strategic Integrated Operations Plan. While President Johnson gave the name of John F. Kennedy to CVA-67, Nitze requested funds to build a nuclear-powered carrier to be named the Nimitz and questioned the conclusions on nuclear carriers McNamara reached by operations analyses. Although no carrier was provided in the FY 1966 budget, advance procurements funds were made available for the CVAN-69, the _Eisenhower_. By this time, however, both McNamara and Nitze were out of office, with Nitze becoming Deputy Secretary of Defense and then, under Nixon, the senior DOD representative of the Strategic Arms Limitation Talks (SALT) until Watergate caused him to resign, on 14 June 1974.

Before he left office, Nitze supervised a major reorganization of the Navy Department that went into effect on 1 May 1966. In this reorganization the familiar bilinear structure was abandoned in favor of a unilinear, functional structure. The Naval Material Support Establishment, which included the bureaus of Ships, Yards and Docks, Naval Weapons, Supplies and Accounts, and Special Projects, was expanded into a command comprised of six systems commands: Air, Ship, Electronic, Ordnance, Supply, and Facilities Engineering. In addition to commanding the operating forces, the CNO was given command not only over the Chief of Naval Material but over the Chief of Naval Personnel and Chief of the Bureau of Medicine and Surgery. Knowing the needs of his operating forces, the CNO could now better obtain the logistic support they required.

CHAPTER 25

THE CHALLENGE OF THE SOVIET NAVY

I. NIGGARDLY NATURE

Nature designed Russia to be large land mass, not a large sea power. Yet Russia today has the largest number of naval ships in the world. The Soviets can reach warm water via the Barents, Baltic, and Black Seas, but the exits of these can be blocked by foreign powers. Although icebreakers can keep the Arctic Sea route open for part of the year and reduce the distance from London to Yokohama by 4,000 miles, this run is treacherous and expensive and entices little foreign shipping. However, it is vital for getting out products that flow down Russian rivers, almost all of which flow northward. Following the disappearance of the nuclear-powered icebreaker Lenin, the Soviets used diesel-electric types until late 1974, when the latter were joined by the huge nuclear-powered Arktika (500 feet long with a 100 foot beam).

Russia's largest shipbuilding center, Leningrad, is located on the tideless and shallow Baltic Sea. That sea is designed like a trap, for it is ringed by NATO airfields, its waters can be mined easily, and it is excellent for torpedo boat operations. With the Polish and East German navies, the USSR has a 4 to 1 naval superiority in the Baltic, where emphasis is placed upon mine warfare and the use of Osa- and Komar-class MTBs (Osa: 200 tons, 38 knots, 4 SSM launchers; Komar: 100 tons, 40 knots, 2 SSM launchers). Odessa is the major Soviet Black Sea merchant fleet port, and Sevastopol the major naval port in the Black Sea, the last of great interest because it provides the squadron that confronts the U.S. Sixth Fleet in the Mediterranean. However, by the Montreaux Convention of 1936 Turkey defends the Straits and decides what warships may pass through them. To the East, Vladivostok is the terminal of the Transiberian Railroad and home of the Soviet Navy's Pacific Fleet even though pack ice infests it for several months a year. To exit from the Sea of Japan, the safest route is northward, toward Saghalin, for Japan and South Korea guard the straits to the south. In sum, surface ships of the four Soviet fleets (Arctic, Baltic, Black, and Pacific) can either be sealed off at straits or, if they manage to reach an ocean, can hardly operate beyond the reach of shorebased air cover, say 1,500 to 2,000 miles, thereby still leaving Polaris submarines ample sea from in which to launch their missiles at Russia.

Conversely, the Soviet land mass is difficult to attack from the oceans and the internal waterway communications system is excellent. Major canals connect the Black with the Caspian, Baltic, and White Seas and work continues on directly joining the Baltic and Black. Hence specialized river-sea craft of about 5,000 tons and small naval vessels with less than a 12-foot draft can crisscross the country without going into international waters. The system is vulnerable, however, as the Nazi's showed when they bombed the locks of the Baltic-White Canal in June 1941.

II. THE SOVIET MERCHANT MARINE

Most Soviet trade is with other communist countries (12 percent in 1968), then with industrially developed countries (4 percent), last with developing nations (2 percent). Whereas the Soviets in 1972 carried almost half their own trade, the United States carried less than 6 percent of its own trade. If the United States does not improve the status of its merchant marine, which now equals the Soviet in carrying capacity, it is probable that it must rely upon Soviet ships to handle its international trade, with clear implications for Western security and self-sufficiency.

The Soviets decided about 1950 to build their own merchant marine in order to stop a drain on their currency and also to earn currency, and for political and psychological reasons, particularly to influence Third World countries. Between 1952 and 1972, that merchant marine increased from 471 to 2,059 ships, or from 12th to 6th in world ship tonnage, while the American merchant marine decreased from 3,464 to 1,372 ships. While the average age of the Soviet merchant ship in 1972 was 10 years, that of the American was 22 years. Current five-year plans call for building 1 million tons annually until 1980, when 23 million deadweight tons will be in service.

Unusual increases in Soviet foreign trade began with Cuba starting in 1962, with North Vietnam to 1975, with Egypt from 1955 to 1972, and also with about half of the number of African countries. Students of the

Soviet merchant marine find that it is more important
in the Soviet campaign to seek world influence and
control than the Soviet Navy because it can challenge
the acquisition by the United States of overseas strategic materials which the USSR has within its large
land mass, support the Navy at war, gather intelligence. As Khrushchev put it, "merchant ships can
carry ideas as well as cargo to the far corners of the
world." Since most Soviet merchant ships are smaller
than American ones, they can visit small ports if
nuclear war makes large ones untenable.

III. SCIENCE SUPPORTS WARFARE AND FISHING

Since the International Geophysical Year of 1957-
1958, the Soviets have sponsored a larger oceanographic
program than has any other nation. Their huge oceanographic ships make acoustic studies useful for submarine and antisubmarine warfare, geological studies
helpful in offshore oil drilling and metal ore harvesting, for research and recovery, and for finding
schools of fish. While the American and British fishing industries remain static (the impact on American
fishing by the extension of the seaward boundary of the
United States to 200 miles in 1976 awaits evaluation),
the Soviets, with 4,000 ocean-going fishing ships,
rank only behind Japan and Peru as the world's greatest
fishermen. Meanwhile some 50 fishing trawlers (AGIs)
are often used as intelligence collectors or spy ships,
especially off Loch Ness, Scotland; Rota, Spain; Guam;
off Cape Kennedy; and also to dog NATO exercises.
(The United States stopped using spy ships after the
Pueblo and Liberty incidents.) The Soviets also use
radars and satellites to acquire target and other
intelligence and for long-range communications.

IV. THE SOVIET NAVY

A. STEPS IN DEVELOPMENT. The modern Soviet Navy has
been affected by four major developments: 1) the paucity
of funding from the days of the Revolution and of the
Kranstadt mutiny of 1921, which discredited the Navy
in the eyes of the Soviet political leaders until about
the 1930s; 2) political interference by such leaders as
Stalin and Khrushchev through the commissar system;
3) the primacy given the Army rather than the Navy; and
4) challenges posed by Western technology especially in
the form of the aircraft carrier, the Polaris submarine,

and SAC.

The first modern fleet was created by Stalin, who between 1926 and 1941 built 53 warships: 3 battleships, 8 cruisers, 85 destroyers and torpedo boats, 100 minesweepers and minelayers, 300 motor torpedo boats or motor gunboats, and about 250 submarines. These were not only divided between the Arctic, Baltic, Black, and Pacific fleets but as late as World War II were built without much of the technological information known to the West. The Soviets' underwater detecting apparatus was poor and they lacked knowledge of degaussing and of sweeping magnetic and acoustic mines. Moreover, Stalin's fleet was designed to serve as a "fortress fleet" that would operate with other forces in passive defense against amphibious invasion. A balanced carrier-centered fleet must await postwar reconstruction, an improved financial situation, and the acquisition of technical competence. Furthermore, the "old school" strategists who supported the fortress fleet concept were challenged by a "young school" who believed that the submarine and aircraft made the battleship obsolete.

B. WORLD WAR II AND THE KUZNETSOV ERA. While Admiral Nikolai G. Kuznetsov served as the Navy's Commander-in-Chief, the Soviet Navy accomplished little. The Baltic Fleet provided escort of convoys of some 4,000 ships but not for the Murmansk run. Trapped in the Baltic, Soviet sailors fought on land. Mines laid in the Black Sea proved to be unnecessary because the Germans never reached it, and the Pacific Fleet operated against Japan for only a very short time. Because the Navy was kept subordinate to the Army and relegated to Army support and a coastal defense role, its World War II experience, according to Kuznetsov's successor, Sergei G. Gorshkov, was "unhappy," the result of "stagnation" in technological progress due to Army and Party leaders. Gorshkov was understandably happy, therefore, when Stalin in 1950 approved a ten-year plan for building a large surface fleet which would provide a carrier for each of the four Soviet fleets, heavy cruisers of the <u>Stalingrad</u> class, light cruisers of the <u>Chapayev</u> and <u>Sverdlov</u> classes, destroyers of the <u>Skoryi</u> class, and submarines of the W class.

C. KHRUSHCHEV AND GORSHKOV. Shortly after the death of Stalin, in 1953, Khrushchev assumed power. In 1955, when he was but 45 years of age, a fellow Ukranian and wartime comrade named Sergei G. Gorshkov became Commander-in-Chief of the Soviet Navy and began to change it from a defensive to a defensive-offensive one. In 1955, the Soviet Navy ranked fourth in the world, following the United States, British, and French navies. The 23 20,000-ton <u>Sverdlov</u>-class light cruisers, which revealed German and Italian influence, and large fleet of medium-sized (W-class) submarines were considered defensive, as shown by the assignment of almost half of the submarine forces to the Northern (Atlantic) Fleet to counter NATO. Seeing heavy cruisers and aircraft carriers (the latter Khrushchev's "floating coffins") as inordinately expensive, Khrushchev turned to submarines instead of surface ships and to missiles rather than guns. In Gorshkov he found a politically reliable missile enthusiast.

Gorshkov's navy, served by 500,000 men, was allotted 15 percent of the Soviet military budget. He has been credited with saving eight of the cruisers Khrushchev wished to scrap, preventing the Navy from being subjugated to the Army, and for placing emphasis upon ships built for offense, especially submarines, and upon naval aircraft armed with nuclear missiles. The first Soviet nuclear-powered submarine and first Soviet ships armed with surface-to-surface (air breathing) missiles appeared in 1958. Impressed though he was by U.S. aircraft carrier operations during the Korean War, the mobility of British and French seapower at the time of Suez, the U.S. Sixth Fleet during the Lebanon crisis, and American carriers during the Cuban missile crisis, he did not seek a balanced fleet, i.e., one that contained carriers that would provide cover for surface ships. On the other hand, the failure of missiles to save Cuba from Kennedy's blockade turned his attention to the value of general purpose forces. In any event, the decision not to build carriers, approved by the Twentieth Party Congress held in 1956, may well rest upon the fact that Soviet aircraft can cover most of the Mediterranean and North Africa from bases in southern Russia while planes from Vladivostok can cover the Japan and China Seas. Gorshkov's strategy, apparently, was to interdict his enemy's carrier-centered fleets (or possibly his merchant fleet in the unlikely case of a long war) with torpedoes and missiles launched by aircraft, surface ships, and nuclear- or diesel-powered submarines.

In 1958 there appeared the Kildin-class DDG, in 1959 the high speed patrol boat (Komar), both carrying SSMs; in 1960 the Kynda-class cruiser carrying both SSMs (Shaddock) and SAMs; and in 1961 the Krupny-class destroyer (SSMs and SAMs); and also a series of nuclear-powered submarines. (The Hotel, Echo, and November submarine classes have a speed of about 20 knots and carry both torpedoes and varying numbers of SSMs.) In 1964 came about 40 submarines carrying ballistic missiles, another 40, antiship cruise missiles, the last giving a submarine a standoff weapon that frees it from sonar detection by surface escorts. (The United States has belatedly entered the cruise missile field.) Older Soviet cruisers, which are comparable to World War II American and British models, are most useful for defense, supporting amphibious operations, or as staff and communications ships. Much more powerful are the three new classes of guided missile cruisers (Kresta I and II and Kynda) and Kashin-class missile frigates. The Krestas and Kyndas, however, have no target acquisition capabilities and must rely for this information upon other sources. The larger Kara-class cruisers (1972; 9,000 tons vs. 6,000 tons) are much better sea boats. The first of these, the Nikolaev, was seen as she transited the Turkish Straits to the Mediterranean on 1 March 1973. The largest Soviet warship propelled by an entirely gas turbine plant, she displaces 10,750 tons when fully loaded and, in the fashion of Soviet naval thinking, is overarmed to fit into a strike fleet concept, for she is equipped for a short, sharp, overwhelming encounter. Unlike the American California (10,150 tons) class, she has dual systems for almost every weapon but is cramped, provides her crew poor habitability, and probably could not defend herself after launching a first strike. Soviet destroyers of the Kotlin and Skoryi classes, built between 1949 and 1957, are like American general purpose destroyers, and the Riga and Elbing-class destroyers compare with American destroyer escorts. Many of these and large numbers of motor torpedo boats and missile corvettes lack antiair defense but carry Styx and other SSMs. In the Yom Kippur War, 1973, however, Israeli Saar-class boats with Gabriel missiles destroyed several Osa and Komar boats without suffering a casualty.

Given the constraints of operating in the shallow waters of the Baltic and Black Seas, the Q- and W-class submarines assigned there are quite small. The W-class (Whiskey to NATO), a diesel-powered follow-on of the German Type XXI, displaces less than 1,600 tons. Built between 1950 and 1957, this class is being retired. Larger are the fleet K-class. Of the approximately 400 modern submarines, perhaps 100 are nuclear-powered. Some have antiship weapons (SSN); some ballistic missiles useful for hitting land targets (SSBN). None is as quiet as an American SSN or SSBN, and Soviet ASW technology most probably lags the American. Nonetheless, between 1949 and 1972 the Soviets produced 24 new classes of warships. Given a production rate of 15 to 16 nuclear-powered submarines a year, by 1980 the USSR will have 280 SSNs and SSBNs. To use other words, although half the size of the 1958 submarine fleet, 75 percent of the 1980 fleet will be nuclear-powered and contain much more powerful armament than in 1958.

In 1972, the average Soviet fleet ship averaged 9 years in age, the American, 16, and the Soviet fleet numbered 568 major surface combatant ships and submarines compared to 378 for the United States. Modern Soviet ships can operate outside of protective air cover and do influence particularly Third World nations. However, the absence of air cover, the small size of many fleet elements, the restricted naval train, and the undependability of foreign bases will make it difficult for Soviet forces to exist in a hostile environment far from home waters.

D. SOVIET NAVAL AIR. The Soviet Air Force is an independent entity of vast proportions—some 20,000 planes including perhaps 4,000 jet aircraft and 70,000 men. It provides squadrons of about 100 planes for each of the four fleets. Since 1951, however, the Soviet Navy has controlled its own air, which plays a tactical role with reconnaissance, bomber, and helicopter types, and in 1972 included about 1,200 aircraft. Soviet types fairly match American ones, indeed in some cases are copies, as the Tu-4 is a copy of the B-29 and the Beriev-6 of the Martin PBM Marlin. Examples are, in NATO language, the Beagle, a light jet bomber; Bison, a long range reconnaissance bomber; Bounder, long range jet bomber; Bosun, jet bomber; Badger, heavy jet bomber being replaced by the partially variable-geometry strategic bomber Backfire; and Bear, long range bomber. The Bison has a range of about 9,000 miles. In addition there are flying boats and transports.

While a few helicopters fly from cruisers and destroyers, most Soviet naval aircraft are land-based. Best estimates of the Soviet "carrier" *Kiev* give it a displacement of 25,000 to 40,000 tons and an angled flight deck 600 feet long, adequate for V/STOL but not for fixed wing planes. On the other hand, Soviet naval air has a long reach, as revealed when two reconnaissance Bears in April 1970 flew nonstop from Murmansk down the Norwegian Sea, across the Atlantic, and landed in Cuba. Similar aircraft periodically fly reconnaissance missions along the U.S. Atlantic coast while the South Atlantic is covered by aircraft flying out of Conakry, Guinea.[1]

E. SOVIET AMPHIBIOUS FORCES. Sadly neglected earlier, since 1963 the Soviets have built up their amphibious forces with naval infantry ("black berets"), tank landing ships (LST, LSMR, and LCT types), and naval auxiliaries (supply, oiler, and repair ships). Some 6,000 black berets appeared in a celebration held in Red Square in October 1967. Their number in 1973 was said to be between 15,000 and 19,000, when they were reported to be using 102 amphibious ships, 131 landing craft, and 6 air cushion vehicles. Soviet overseas force projection nevertheless compares very unfavorably with that of the United States and would be extremely difficult to implement beyond the range of covering aircraft.

V. A DEFENSIVE OR OFFENSIVE NAVY?

The forward surge of the Soviet Navy can be accounted for in part because of its qualitative improvement, in part because of the decrease in Western force levels. The most obvious missions of the Soviet Navy are: 1) nuclear strike deterrence, 2) sea denial, 3) control of sea frontiers, 4) presence, and 5) seaborne projection.

Given twice the number of submarines than the United States and Great Britain and some 200 fleet submarines, the Soviets evidently plan to use submarines not only to deter or blunt an attack but also to challenge the West's control of the sea, especially by destroying his aircraft carriers. This conclusion is supported by the fact that though the United States stopped building Polaris submarines when No. 41 was completed in 1974, Admiral Rickover at that time predicted a Soviet submarine fleet of 165 SSN and SSBN boats compared with the American 106-109. Both the U.S. and the U.S.S.R. have also increased the range of their submarine missiles, with Polaris going from A-1 (1,400 miles) to A-2 (1,700 miles), and to A-3 (almost 3,000 miles), and the Soviets from 1,300 to about 4,000 miles, meaning that they can hit the United States when still 1,200 to 1,500 miles out at sea with the 760 missiles expected to be at sea in mid-1975. Conversely, American submarine-launched missiles can reach the major political, military, and industrial centers of Russia from the Arctic, Irish Sea, Bay of Biscay, the Mediterranean, and from off the coast of sub-Sahara Africa. Moreover, the Poseidon can launch MIRVs. Ten Tridents, approved late in 1973 and expected in 1978, will have a 10,000 km range that will increase the range now covered by twentyfold. Larger (540 feet long) quieter, and faster than Polaris, Trident will carry 24 nuclear missiles with a range of almost 7,000 miles.

Carrier aircraft such as the A-3D Skywarrior, with a range of 2,000 miles, could reach Soviet targets 600 to 700 miles inland, and follow-on planes can do even better. The Soviets therefore must risk attack from U.S. aircraft if they wish to close a carrier task force to effective gun range. In the late 1950s, the Soviets began providing first SAMs and then SSMs to their ships. In consequence of the danger to carriers, the United States released them for service with general purposes and relied instead upon Polaris submarines. Unable to defend itself against Polaris, the Soviets built their own SSBNs as a mutual strategic deterrent. Moreover, cruise missiles on 20 Soviet surface ships, 66 submarines, and 300 aircraft pose a serious challenge to any Western concentration of naval forces while the Moskva, Kiev, and long range patrol planes extend somewhat the Soviet ASW capability.

Since 1962 the Soviets have developed a blue water fleet. Ships are sent to sea for exercises or to visit farflung ports, and their presence at times of international crisis (the 1967 Arab-Israeli war, the 1970 Jordanian civil war, the 1971 Indo-Pakistani war, the October-November 1973 Middle East crisis [Yom Kippur war of Egypt, Israel, and Syria]) must give the West some pause for thought prior to intervening unilaterally in such crises even if the United States did so in the Lebanon crisis of 1958.

Item 1. **The North Atlantic**. In 1962, Soviet naval exercises in the North Atlantic Ocean and Norwegian Sea included 4 surface ships, 20 submarines, and some land-based patrol planes.

Item 2. **East of Suez**. In 1965, Soviet warships began "making calls" at Indian Ocean ports. Directly following the Arab-Israeli War of 1967, a pro-Soviet South Yemen government was established which asked the British to withdraw from their naval and air base at Aden. Several days later a small Soviet naval force (a cruiser, missile destroyer, and ASW ship) from the Soviet Pacific Fleet began a four-month tour of the Indian Ocean and Persian Gulf. It called at ports in India, Pakistan, Iran, Iraq, Ceylon, Somalia, and South Yemen. Since 1969, Aden has since supported from 10 to 30 Soviet warships cruising in the Indian Ocean, and the Soviets have aircraft landing rights and trawler facilities on the island of Mauritius and the possibility of using the seaport of Chittagong in Bangladesh. In sum, Soviet has replaced British seapower East of Suez.

Even if the Soviet naval presence in the Indian ocean is not aggressive, it does exert political, economic, and ideological as well as military power in an area important because it guards one end of the Middle East oil line and also serves as a counter to Chinese influence in the area. On the other hand, U.S. submarines in the Arabian Sea could reach the Soviet heartland (and China as well) with their missiles. The Soviets have a well-balanced force in the Indian Ocean including missile cruisers and destroyers, nuclear submarines, oceanographic ships, and fishing vessels which occasionally visit ports in India, Ceylon, Tanzania, Mozambique, Yemen, and Barbera, Somalia, in the last of which Soviet fuel farms and SAM sites have been established. This force can quite readily be reinforced by ships from the Mediterranean using the Suez canal, which was reopened by American, British and Egyptian personnel in June 1974. They could thus threaten an American investment of over $4 billion in the Persian Gulf area alone and the oil that is so desperately needed by Europe, Japan, and the United States. Therefore the United States occasionally augments its normal Indian Ocean Middle Eastern Force, (two destroyers and one amphibious ship), with aircraft carriers or nuclear frigates.[1] More important is the American request from the British for permission to use the island of Diego Garcia (an island 14 miles long and 5 miles wide located roughly in the middle of the Indian Ocean) for airfields, improve the harbor, and install naval and air supply facilities. In this way Soviet naval power in the Indian Ocean would not only be balanced but its survivability would be questionable if the United States used carriers in a limited war.

Item 3. **The Permanent Soviet Mediterranean Fleet.** The Soviet Mediterranean Fleet, created in 1963 and made permanent at the time of the Arab-Israeli war, 1967, started with 5 ships and since then at times has been larger (up to 70 ships) than the American Sixth Fleet. In 1965, Soviet ship days in the eastern Mediterranean were 4,000; in 1974, more than 15,000. Until President Nixon's **Incidents at Sea Agreement** with Russia of 25 May 1972, some of these ships engaged in harassment ("game of chicken") that caused collisions and sometimes loss of life.

Item 4. **Ships Mean Influence.** In 1962, when he introduced missiles into Cuba, Khrushchev had some submarines but no surface fleet to escort his merchant ships. Since then, Soviet ships exercise at sea and have shown the flag throughout the world. Moreover, the sale or barter of about 700 Soviet ships to other communist states and to underdeveloped countries creates a need for Soviet technicians in the host country, reliance on the Soviets for spare parts, and visits to Russia for ship overhauls.

Item 5. **Soviet Task Forces in the Gulf of Mexico and Caribbean Sea.** In 1967 and 1970, three Soviet task forces sailed into the Gulf and Caribbean. The first, comprised of 7 ships including surface types, SSBNs, a tender, and a tanker, penetrated the Gulf to within 300 miles of New Orleans and came within 35 miles of the Florida coastline. Some ships visited Havana, then joined another SSBN for ASW exercises. These ships obtained oceanographic information as they traversed rich fishing grounds and acquired intelligence

about the major ship routes to New Orleans and the
Panama Canal. They had as much right of course to be
in these international waters as the U.S. Navy has in
sending 2 destroyers annually through the Turkish
Straits to visit the Black Sea, but the challenge to
the Monroe Doctrine is obvious.

Item 6. OKEAN. In 1970, Operation Okean involved
about 150 surface ships, 50 submarines, and several
hundred aircraft--all controlled from Moscow. The
worldwide exercise ranged through the Baltic, Norwegian, Barents, Black, Philippine, Mediterranean, and
Japan Seas and the Atlantic, Pacific, and Indian Oceans.
Some of the ships visited Cienfuegos, Cuba, and a second
visit to the same port led the United States to believe that the Soviets were building a submarine base
there, a notion the Soviets discounted. Nevertheless,
the Soviets had penetrated America's middle seas--
with ominous implications for the security and trade
of the United States--in the same way that the United
States since 1947 has established a presence in
Europe's middle sea.

OKEAN 1975. In the last week of April 1975, in
exercises the Soviets called "Spring" but the West
nicknamed Okean 1975, at least 200 surface ships, 100
submarines, and many land-based aircraft were sighted
in all oceans and in many seas. In the Mediterranean
at least, the Sixth Fleet did the "dogging" rather
than vice versa.[2]

Item 7. Hawaii. In 1971, 10 Soviet ships including a
light cruiser, 2 destroyers, 3 submarines, and support
craft left Vladivostok, made passage along the Aleutians, sailed between the Hawaiian Islands to within
25 miles of Diamond Head, and returned home.

Item 8. BUT-- Some limitations on Soviet power projection have been eased. The use of icebreakers and
covered building and repair ways at northern shipyards
reduce the severe impact of Russian weather. The
overseas deployment of surface ships armed with SSMs;
the basing of aircraft in Cuba, Egypt (until 1972),
Guinea, and Syria makes up for the lack of protective
air cover; the Moskva, Leningrad, and Kiev provide
helicopter ASW and V/STOL aircraft; and open-ocean
replenishment is undertaken by the use of merchant
ships. Seagoing ships are kept out of the Baltic and

Black Seas and are deployed in forward areas where they are provided logistic support. Still to be overcome is the charge that the Soviet is a "one-shot" Navy optimized for strong initial striking power but with relatively limited weapon reloads. In addition, in the words of former Secretary of Defense Elliot Richardson in 1973: "The Soviets must contend with a paucity of all-weather ports, a lack of air cover when the surface fleet operates far from the Soviet homeland, and insufficient open-ocean replenishment. Consequently, Soviet surface units and some submarines have significantly less combat and sustaining capability when operated far from the Soviet homeland. Further, the surface units are dispersed among four widely separated fleets." In addition to the internal problem of keeping its peoples captive, the Soviets have no allies, only satellites, and their options are narrowed because they must simultaneously guard their huge borders, compete with the United States, negotiate with the West, contain China when polycentrism has replaced Moscow's once monolithic control over party dogma, and extend their power by imperialistic methods that United States, Britain, France, Holland, and Belgium renounced a generation ago; pay for costly aid programs to underdeveloped countries; and counter the détente initiated by President Nixon with such nations as Rumania and China and accommodation with Castro impending with the Carter administration.

VI. SALT AND NAVIES

The relative positions of the United States and the Soviet Union have changed greatly since the Strategic Arms Limitation Talks began in 1967. Statistics show:

	1967 US	1967 USSR	1973 US	1973 USSR
ICBM launchers	1,054	720	1,054	1,618
SLBM launchers	656	30	656	740
Heavy Bombers	697	155	400	195

While the American inventory of ICBMs and SLBMs remained static during these years and the number of bombers decreased, the Soviet inventory of SLBMs increased over 20 times and the number of bombers increased slightly. To the last, however, should be added the Backfire bomber. In MIRVs (multiple independently targetable reentry vehicles), the United States still has a lead, but one that cannot be guaranteed. Moreover, in 1971 Secretary of Defense Melvin Laird estimated the number of Soviet land-based ICBMs to be 1,520, with another 100 building and, as of July 1972, 805 SLBMs. While the older Golf and Hotel diesel-electric submarines carry only 3 SLBMs, the Yankee class (1967) carries 16 and the newer Delta-class can accommodate 12 Sawfly missiles which have a range of 4,000 miles.

The interim SALT Agreement of 26 May 1972 fixed the Soviet limits at 62 SSBN and 740 SLBMs, the latter of which, however, can be replaced by more modern models.

VII. U.S. NAVAL ADMINISTRATION, 1967-1972

A. PAUL ROBERT IGNATIUS, 1 September 1967-1 January 1969. As already noted, the years 1962-1972 were particularly lean for the U.S. Navy. Little that either Secretary of the Navy Paul Robert Ignatius or his successor, John Hubbard Chafee, did sufficed to reverse this trend.

A Phi Beta Kappa who specialized in economics, Ignatius was a management consultant until World War II, when he joined the naval officer corps and served with an air group on a jeep carrier in the invasion at Leyte Gulf and subsequent strikes against Okinawa and operations off Japan. He obtained an M.B.A. from Harvard Business School in 1946 and taught at Harvard for three years before joining several others in founding a management consulting firm that specialized in defense logistics. In 1961 he entered the Pentagon as Assistant Secretary of the Army for Installations and Logistics. After a year he became Under Secretary of the Army. After only another year, on 21 December 1964 Secretary of Defense Robert S. McNamara drafted him to be the Assistant Secretary of Defense for Installations and Logistics, a vital billet at a time when the Vietnam War was heating up. As chairman of the Vietnam Steering Group, his task was to monitor the supply requirements for the armed forces and match them with production and delivery schedules, transport availability, and port cargo capacities.

In the summer of 1967, Vance retired and was

succeeded by Paul Nitze. To replace Nitze as Secretary of the Navy, McNamara chose John T. McNaughton. When the latter was killed in an air crash on 19 July, McNamara recommended Ignatius to President Lyndon Johnson. Johnson agreed; Senate confirmation was unanimous. He entered office just when the administration was considering winding down the Vietnam War, thus forecasting reduced naval budgets and programs in the years ahead.

Among others with whom Ignatius worked was Admiral Thomas D. Moorer, CNO; Marine Corps commandants Wallace M. Greene and Leonard Chapman; and a young rear admiral named Elmo R. Zumwalt. Zumwalt, who headed the systems analysis group for the CNO, left in August 1968 to command U.S. Naval Forces Vietnam as a vice admiral (and would return as CNO in 1970). Another officer who impressed Ignatius was Captain Worth H. Bagley, his executive assistant and aide who became a vice admiral at the age of forty-eight years.

While McNamara kept a firm administrative grip on the military services, Ignatius had to serve as his assistant but also as naval advocate, with the two tasks sometimes conflicting. It was he who briefed McNamara on the <u>Pueblo</u> and Arnheiter affairs, on the increase of Soviet naval power to a global force and the Soviet production of SSBNs, helicopter carriers, and cruise missile boats. Even if the Soviets spent less than half of what the United States did on its Navy, their Navy was the second largest in the world by 1968, and their building program contrasted sharply with the American, which was allotted only 4 percent of the FY1968 budget ($800 million). The American program suffered from the rising costs of the Vietnam War and from the aging of its World War II ships. In 1968, the United States had 337 ships equipped for ASW, AAW and other tasks, but the Soviets had 230 cruiser-destroyer-escort ships fitted with surface-to-surface and surface-to-air missiles. In aircraft carriers, amphibious lift, and mobile logistic support systems, however, the United States ranked far ahead of the Soviets.

Because of his own training in management and great need for them, Ignatius selected for promotion officers who combined military professionalism with proficiency in management techniques. On the other hand, with popular and professional opposition to the Vietnam War rising, many young officers were resigning, especially from the nuclear submarine force. Industry was luring well-trained enlisted specialists away, and domestic airlines beckoned alluringly to naval pilots. His answer was to shorten overseas deployments, increase pilot training, provide additional education for enlisted men, reduce demands on manpower by shipboard automation, and greatly augment the number of black naval and Marine officers through recruiting at predominantly Negro colleges and obtaining more black candidates for the Naval Academy until the number of minority officers was proportional to their percentages in the population. Despite the fact that his budget, of about $21.5 billions for FY1967/68/69 remained static, Ignatius was able to win an increase of from 663,000 officers and men in 1963 to 765,000 in 1968, of midshipmen from 4,000 to 4,500, and a Marine Corps buildup of from 190,000 to 307,000.

The battle of nuclear-powered vs. conventional ships continued under Ignatius, with McNamara and his systems analysis staff opposed to additional nuclear ships, the Navy in general and its congressional supporters favoring them, but Ignatius opposed, because of their high cost--he preferred to obtain more ships for less money. So did the battle over the F-111 (McNamara's hope for one plane embodying enough commonality to serve all three services), with Ignatius and Moorer holding out for the F-111B, the Navy version. In the FY1969 defense budget the F-111B program was scrapped in favor of the VFX, later called the F-14.

As Ignatius prepared to leave office, Representative Porter Hardy, a member of the House Armed Services Committee, reported that the Sixth Fleet suffered from "a marginal state of readiness" attributable to a condition of overall degradation and accelerated deterioration of equipment--a condition largely caused by the shifting of skilled personnel to the Seventh Fleet. Well aware of the situation, Ignatius noted that the shipbuilding program must be increased, particularly for ASW types including 110 nuclear- and conventionally-powered submarines. He regretted the inactivation of the Randolph, a CVS that fell victim to the cost of the Vietnam War and applauded both the modernization of 31 of the 41 SSBNs with Poseidon missiles and plans for building specially configured submarines armed with advanced long-range ballistic missiles (ULMS). The latter later became known as Trident. He recommended a level of four nuclear-powered attack carriers, two of which were funded through the FY1968 and FY1969 budget. While he thought the extant 77 ocean escorts were sufficient, he demanded a multiyear replacement program for the old general purpose destroyers of World War II vintage. The Navy had no funds, however, to build more than two nuclear-powered frigates. And he had high praise for the new general purpose amphibious assault ship (LHA).

B. JOHN CHAFEE, 31 January 1969-4 April 1972. Chafee took office at a time when a number of perjorative changes were occurring in the Navy: a relatively poorer position vis-a-vis the Soviet Navy, novel ship designs, and minority group problems. A "liberal" Republican recently defeated in his bid for the governorship of Rhode Island, Chafee could be expected to try to help those whom he considered underprivileged. Indeed, he was asked to fill the naval secretaryship by more conservative Republicans who saw the need to place key "liberal" East Coast Republicans in office as a demonstration of party unity. In 1968, he had supported George Romney, then Nelson Rockefeller, and opposed Richard Nixon and Spiro Agnew. As President, however, Nixon told Secretary of Defense Melvin Laird to choose his own staff. Supported by his Deputy Secretary, David Packard, Laird chose Chafee for the Navy even though Chafee looked upon his post as a temporary billet until he could return to active Rhode Island politics.

While a sophomore at Yale, Chafee volunteered for the Marine Corps following Pearl Harbor and served in some of the hottest fighting in the Solomons. Recommended for officer training, he attended officer candidate school and served as staff intelligence officer at Guam and at Okinawa before helping American forces accept the surrender of Japanese troops in North China at the end of the war. Following the war he obtained a law degree at Harvard and was practicing law when he was recalled to active duty with the First Marine Division in Korea and then in the legal office of the Fleet Marine Force. He spent six years in uniform before returning to the law. Elected to the state legislature in 1956, he was reelected in 1958 and 1960 and went on to serve two terms as governor, 1962-1966, meanwhile gaining national notice as a supporter of civil rights and other "liberal" causes.

McNamara relied heavily upon his systems analysts for advice on military matters. Following Nixon's demand for an "open" administration, Laird offered the service secretaries a larger voice in the planning of force levels and the formulation of personnel polities, relaxed the centralized control exercised by McNamara, and used the systems analysis group in an advisory rather than a reviewing role. Now systems analysis would confirm professional military judgments rather than determine them. Like McNamara, however, Laird made it clear that Chafee "rode two horses," i.e., administered the Navy yet was responsible to the Secretary of Defense.

For his under secretary, Chafee chose John Warner, like him a veteran of World War II and Korea and also a lawyer, and worked closely with Admiral Thomas Moorer, who gained a second two-year term as CNO.

Chafee's main task was to build a fleet in keeping with the Nixon (or Guam) Doctrine announced 25 July 1969: the United States would keep its treaty commitments, provide a nuclear shield, and furnish assistance to allies when needed, but would not get involved in overseas wars. The Doctrine thus signalled a greater emphasis on sea-based forces, forces which should be able to provide both a strategic deterrent (e.g., SSBNs) and general purpose units capable of projecting force and insuring control of the seas. Chafee faced the awesome task for providing such forces while his budget was reduced. In consequence on 21 August 1969 he ordered 100 ships deactivated--leaving 786 ships--and a 10 percent reduction in personnel amounting to 72,000 men. With the cost of Vietnam rising from $5 billion in 1967 to $20 billion in 1968 and 1969, he explained, he had to lay up old ships and use his reduced budget to acquire smaller numbers of modern ships, planes, and weapons capable of challenging the Soviet fleet in the 1970s and 1980s.

Given a national mood exhibiting symptoms of fatigue and disillusionment with the Vietnam War that showed themselves in civic unrest, racial confrontations, rebellion against authority, and popular unhappiness with large cost overruns in several defense contracts, Chafee--and Moorer--were greatly concerned with the reenlistment rate, which for first-term sailors dropped from 17 percent in 1968 to 14 percent in 1970 when the Navy needed 31 percent. Moreover, instead of keeping 55 percent of its naval aviators, the Navy was keeping only 31 percent. As in the days of Ignatius, industry siphoned off trained naval personnel and graduate education appealed to many younger officers, but Chafee noted the deleterious effect of long ship employment schedules and the great demand for shipborne maintenance that wore down both officers and crews being squeezed into poorer quarters by the accretion of more and more technical equipment. With an all-volunteer force scheduled to go into effect in July 1973, Chafee wondered whether the Navy could obtain its quota of qualified men. His answer was to provide more family housing, motels at naval bases, sea pay, better shipboard habitability, faster petty officer promotion, and large housing allowances. Nevertheless, he came up with 63,000 instead of the 73,000 men he needed in FY1972.

Chafee had to review the court martial held on Lloyd M. Bucher for "permitting his ship to be seized while he had the power to resist." Because the men on the *Pueblo* had endured eleven months of cruel treatment in a North Korean prison camp, Chafee decided that they had suffered enough and declared the incident closed. Laird then ordered decommissioned the other two special intelligence-gathering ships. Chafee also had to deal with the Soviet practice of harassing NATO ships ("chicken of the sea game"), a practice that resulted in occasional tragedy, and the challenge posed by its ability to operate its warships on a global basis, as revealed in OKEAN, April 1970. Instead of obtaining more funds to build up the Navy, however, Chafee was forced to reduce the service by 189 ships and 264,000 men between July 1969 and July 1971. The laying up of an attack carrier, 3 ASW carriers, 4 cruisers, 51 destroyer types, 54 amphibious ships, and 32 auxiliaries represented a 20 percent cut. To put it another way, while the Soviets from 1963 to 1971 added forty major combatants to their fleet, the United States cut 100 of these types from its fleet. In 1971, the Soviets had about 250 attack submarines; the United States, 90. To rebuild his fleet, Chafee told Congress in 1969, required $3.5 billion rather than the $2 billion it was getting each year for the next ten years. When Congress instead cut almost $1 billion from his budget, he had little choice but to deactivate additional ships and air squadrons; postpone budget planning for the proposed fourth nuclear carrier, CVN-70, to 1972; deactivate the Fifth Marine Division, and close 83 shore facilities.

With the aid of Mendel Rivers, chairman of the House Armed Services Committee, Chafee in 1969 contracted for nine LHAs and 16 *Spruance* (DD-963) destroyers with Litton Industries. Rivers's warning of the danger of costly overruns shortly proved true. When the LHAs ran 16 months behind schedule, Chafee cut their number from nine to five. Similar problems marred the F-14 contract with the Grumman Aerospace Corporation, for again an agreed-upon price for a "total package" contract soared out of sight. With unit cost rising from $11.5 million to $16.8 million per copy between 1969 and 1973, Chafee cut the number to be produced from 463 to 313. In any event, the first F-14 Tomcat squadrons, commissioned in October 1972, proved for the first time in naval history that a plane could launch multiple missiles against multiple air targets.

Chafee enthusiastically pushed fuller participation of minorities in all sectors of government. As Assistant Secretary of the Navy for Manpower and Reserve Affairs, John E. Johnson became the highest ranking black official in DOD, and during Chafee's term Samuel L. Gravely was the first black selected for flag rank. Warned by Laird that the races needed to be taught to communicate, Chafee had various naval and Marine officers trained as race relations instructors. However, his attempt to increase the number of minority midshipmen by lowering admission standards was resisted by the Academy superintendent, James Calvert, and by such spokesmen for the Naval Academy Alumni Association as former CNO George Anderson. Nevertheless, the 23 minority candidates who entered the Academy in 1969 (19 blacks) increased to 94 (73 blacks) in 1972. The lowering of enlistment standards however, resulted in the enrollment of some recruits whose background failed to enable them to qualify for training schools. Their detail to the deck force, ships' laundries, or galley made them prime targets for militants.

In his quest for younger flag officers, Chafee reduced such requirements as command at sea in a senior billet. He also violated naval mores by sending a non aviator, Isaac Kidd, to command the Sixth Fleet, and an aviator, Dick Guinn, to head the Bureau of Naval Personnel. Furthermore, when Moorer in 1970 was appointed Chairman of the Joint Chiefs of Staff, Chafee replaced him with Elmo R. Zumwalt, who at 49 years of age was junior to all but 21 of the Navy's 302 admirals. Although Zumwalt served imaginatively as Commander Naval Forces Vietnam, he lacked experience in senior billets or familiarity with JCS operations. Determined that "personnel management and some personnel procedures must be altered to conform to changing social attitudes," Zumwalt issued a flurry of "Z-grams" designed to please naval personnel without relaxing standards of good order and discipline. Men could now grow mustache, beards, and wear their hair long; they wore new uniforms; and they could wear their working uniforms to and from home (Rumor had it that midshipmen donned long-hair wigs once they got beyond the Academy walls.) Certain elements, however, either mistook Zumwalt's objective of having naval men "conform to changing social attitudes" by seeking to erode discipline. Cases in point are the riots that occurred on board the carriers <u>Constellation</u> and <u>Kitty Hawk</u> and the oiler <u>Hassayampa</u>. While the Marines kept rigorous standards that made them an elite force, Chafee applauded Zumwalt while certain older officers of great experience criticized him for permitting the undermining of the discipline necessary in a military service.

As Chafee prepared to leave office early in 1972, he warned Congress of the relative growth and power of the Soviet Navy, showed how he had sponsored improved fleet readiness, and noted that he had successfully completed the naval part of the "Vietnamization" program, as in turning over to South Vietnam 685 combat craft and 290 other ship types. He also warned of the dire need of better technically qualified personnel. If 108 new ships had entered the inventory during his tenure, more than that number had been retired, making it more difficult for the United States to support its worldwide commitments. His record shows that while he consistently sought to improve the quality of the service environment, he presided at a time when large cutbacks occurred in men and ships, with the 926 ships he had inherited down to 594 when he left. Among his new acquisitions, however, must be listed the F-14, CVAN-70, the 688-class SSN, and the *Trident* missile submarine, the last a naval alternative to the B-1 bomber. To his credit also are the maintenance of a 16 carrier force; nuclear frigates, the LHA and the *Spruance*-class destroyers, and surface effects ships; and the smooth transition the Navy made in retiring from Vietnam. The greatest criticism of him was that he (and Zumwalt) had relaxed too far the standards of discipline needed in the service. To his great credit, he had opposed congressional measures that reduced the Navy to a 600-ship force, one that might not be able to support American national interests in the light of the now global Soviet Navy.

Appendix A. SOVIET NAVY ORDER OF BATTLE
(Active Ships as of January 1975)

Submarines--Nuclear Propelled
- SSBN Ballistic Missile Submarines (12/16 tubes) .... 40+
- SSBN Ballistic Missile Submarines (3 tubes)............................ 9
- SSGN Cruise Missile Submarines............... 40
- SSN   Attack Submarines 35

Submarines--Diesel Propelled
- SSB   Ballistic Missile Submarines (3 tubes) 22
- SSG   Cruise Missile Submarines 25
- SS   Attack Submarines .... (about) 150

Helicopter Carriers 2

Cruisers
- CLG   Guided Missile Cruisers, SAM/SSM* 18
- CLG   Guided Missile Cruisers SAM 1
- CLC   Command Cruisers SAM 2
- CA   Heavy Cruisers 1
- CL   Light Cruisers 9

Frigates--Destroyers
- DLG   Frigates SAM (some SSM) 19
- DDG   Destroyers SAM/SSM 8
- DDG   Destroyers SAM 33
- DDG   Destroyers SSM 4
- DD   Destroyers 37

Escort Ships 109

Small Combat Craft
- Missile Craft 135
- Patrol/ASW/Torpedo/Craft 445
- Minesweepers 270

* SAM: Surface-to-Air Missile
  SSM: Surface-to-Surface Missile

Amphibious Ships
    LST   Tank Landing Ship
              (ALLIGATOR) 12
    LSM   Medium Landing Ships
              (POLNOCNY) 62
    LSM   Miscellaneous Landing Ships ǂ 22

Auxiliary Ships 750

ǂ Over 200 feet in length.

Source: **Understanding Soviet Naval Developments** (Washington: Office of the Chief of Naval Operations, April 1975).

CHAPTER 26

SEA POWER FOR THE 1980s

I. THE NAVY: ARMY SUPPORTER AND AIR FORCE PARTNER

In the decade following the end of World War II and the onset of the cold war, the Soviets established naval control over the Baltic and Black seas while the American Sixth Fleet remained unchallenged in the Mediterranean, NATO forces guarded the North Atlantic, and mostly American forces fought the communists to a draw in Korea. In 1949, the strategic situation became stabilized when the Soviets exploded their first atomic bomb; nuclear deterrence became nuclear stalemate. However, on the basis that war was not declared, the United States denied itself the right to control the seas by the use of a naval blockade in either Korea or Vietnam, thereby serving merely as an adjunct to the Army in these wars and a partner to the Air Force in a nuclear strategy.

A. THE AMERICAN DEFENSE PROGRAM, FY 1970-1974. Beginning with Robert S. McNamara, the Annual Posture Statement issued by the Secretary of Defense sets forth the general situation and the rationale for the defense budget. Between FY 1970 and 1975, that budget, heavily devoted to meeting the needs of the Vietnam war, stretched out or deferred less essential projects and activities. It also involved reducing the Navy by 425 ships including 11 carriers and 105 open sea escorts. Between 1962 and 1972, while the USSR built 911 warships of all classes, the United States built only 263. The total obligational authority of the DOD nevertheless increased from $50.5 billion, or 7.3 percent of the gross national product, in FY1965, to $83 billion, or 8.3 percent of the gross national product, in FY1970. That sum could be reduced if two conditions were met--the end of the war in Vietnam in consequence of peace talks beginning 13 May 1968 in Paris, and agreement with the Soviets upon the limitation of strategic nuclear weapons. In June 1968, when they had about 1,000 hardened, land-based ICBMs but lagged behind the United States in strategic aircraft and SSBNs, the Soviets agreed to strategic arms limitations talks.

US vs Soviet Intercontinental Nuclear Forces

	1 Sept. 1968	
	US	USSR
ICBM launchers	1,054	900
SLBM launchers	656	45
Total	1,710	945
Intercontinental bombers	646	150
Approximate number of warheads	4,200	1,200

In August 1968, however, their invasion of Czechoslovakia showed that the Soviets would submit to no challenge to their brand of orthodoxy and confirmed the NATO nations not only of the continued need of unity and firmness of purpose but of concrete improvement in their force posture including flexible response. Continued Soviet sales of arms to Third World nations and their sending warships to call at ports in the Indian Ocean following Britain's exodus east of Suez clearly revealed their opportunistic foreign policy.

1. <u>Manned Bombers and Missiles</u>. Changes in the American manned bomber program through FY1974 including cutting back the FB-111 from 210 to 112 planes and retaining the B-58 force beyond a phase-out date of FY1971 and also retaining rather than retiring the last of the B-52C force. To enable bombers better to penetrate Soviet defenses they would be provided with Short-Range Attack Missiles (SRAM) and Subsonic Cruise Armed Decoy (SCAD). The missile program, however, would continue as planned and provide 1,000 Minuteman and 496 Poseidon by the end of FY1974, with 54 Titan IIs in addition by the end of FY1973. The Poseidon refit program, involving 31 SSBNs, would be completed by FY1975, with work also being undertaken on an Undersea Long-Range Missile System (ULMS).

2. <u>Tactical Air Forces</u>. Tactical air forces planned for FY1974 included 5,000 active fighter/attack aircraft in 23 mixed A-7, F-4, and F-111 Air Force and Navy wings. Except for substituting the F-14A for the F-111B, the Navy air inventory would remain unchanged: 1,650 aircraft with 16 attack carriers through the end of the Vietnam war, when the force would be reduced to 1,350 aircraft and 15 carriers. The Marine Corps' three wings (of A-4, A-6,

and F-4 squadrons) would remain unchanged. The F-15 (twin engines, one pilot), optimized for combating enemy fighters, would carry the long range Phoenix missile; the F-14A, also carrying the Phoenix, would provide air superiority and fleet defense.

3. <u>Sea Forces</u>. Improvements were planned for all the Navy's Sea Forces (other than tactical air), involving ASW forces, the Amphibious Assault fleet, submarines, and carriers and their escorts. In FY1970, carrier forces included one nuclear-powered carrier, the <u>Enterprise</u>; 8 conventionally powered <u>Forrestals</u>; 3 <u>Midways</u>; 3 <u>Essexes</u>; and the <u>Shangri-La</u>, the last slated to become a CVS at the end of the Vietnam war. By the end of FY 1976, plans called for having 4 nuclear powered carriers (<u>Enterprise</u>, <u>Chester W. Nimitz</u>, <u>Carl Vinson</u>, <u>Eisenhower</u>), 8 <u>Forrestals</u>, and 3 <u>Midways</u>, with the others being transferred to the CVS force.

The questionable utility of CVSs against newer Soviet submarines led to a program to modernize them and provide them with VSX aircraft. Each carries in addition ASW helicopters, A-4s for defense, and E-1s for airborne warning and control mission. Continued also was the ASW patrol aircraft program of P-3C and P3A/B carrying DIFAR sonor buoys and the Mark 46 torpedo.

4. <u>Escorts and Sea Lift</u>. The high costs of escort ships (47 nuclear, 58 conventional DX, DXG) to bring the escort force to the 239 ships considered necessary resulted in fewer nuclear-powered escorts than planned, so that this type is provided for only two of the CVAN task groups. The goal for the amphibious forces is to provide sufficient 20-knot ships to move 1 2/3rds Marine Expeditionary Force in the Pacific and 2/3rds of one in the Atlantic. The mainstay of this force is the large general purpose assault ship (LHA).

5. <u>Logistic Support</u>. Planned for the end of FY1974 were 204 logistic support ships—Underway Replenishment, Fleet Support (tenders, salvage tugs), Special Combat, and Small Patrol vessels. The number of UNREP ships would be reduced with the end of the Vietnam war. Although DOD is very short of sea lift forces, especially of the RO/RO type, Congress has declined to fund the 30 FDL (fast deployment logistic

ships) requested, with the result that the Navy has had to rely upon MSTS ships which have about half the capacity of an FDL and lack some of the latter's special features such as helicopter-carrying capability.

6. The Costs of DOD. The total obligational authority granted DOD increased from $50.5 billion in FY1965 to $83 billion in FY1970. In the same years, sums for the Army went from $12.4 billion to $26.4 billion; for the Air Force, $19.5 billion to $26.2 billion; and for the Navy, $14.7 billion to $24.4 billion. To be subtracted is an inflation rate of 15 percent for these years.[1] Notable changes in expenditures included an increase of from $6.9 billion for strategic forces to $9.6 billion but an increase of from $19 billion to $32.1 billion for general purpose forces, while airlift and sealift increased only from $1.3 billion to $2 billion.

Useful in itself and for comparison with later statistics is a table showing the numbers and types of American naval ships as of 1 January 1970:

Type	Active	Reserve	Total	Building
Aircraft carriers	21	4	28	2
Submarines	154	19	192	23
Amphibious ships	109	51	160	36
Battleships		4	4	
Cruisers	11	24	35	3
Frigates	30	3	33	3
Destroyers	170	121	314	8
Escort ships	44	143	196	42
Patrol vessels	39		45	
Mine warfare vessels	73	42	131	
Auxiliary ships	373	89	462	26
Totals (not including ships used for Naval Reserve Training)	1,025	504	1,602	146

(Adapted from Naval Review, 1970, p. 459.)

B. THE AMERICAN DEFENSE PROGRAM, FY1974-1977. In testifying before the Senate Armed Services Committee on 19 March 1969 in support of a supplemental and FY1970 DOD budget, Melvin R. Laird noted that significant distortions in American general purpose forces could not be eradicated until the Vietnam war ended and that the rapid buildup of Soviet strategic forces required a reassessment of the American strategic forces program. This reassessment included the building of the Sentinel ABM system at a cost of between $6 billion and $7 billion, reduction of the F-111 program, and building of an advanced strategic bomber (AMSA). Laird also noted that the Navy Shipbuilding Program "is in urgent need of a much more comprehensive review than we have thus far had time to give it." Because serious cost overruns endangered the building and modernization programs, he recommended slowing down the SSN-668 building program and eliminating construction of a number of ships and aircraft. President Ford's FY1978 budget called for the expenditure of $440 billion and a deficit of $47 billion. The Carter administration recommended instead $459 billion and a deficit of $57.4 billion. Ford wanted to increase funds for DOD by $11 billion to $124.3 billion. Carter suggests $3 billion less.[1]

C. THE AMERICAN NAVY OF THE EARLY 1980s. As already noted, the Navy's slice of the defense budget for 1970 was $24.9 billion. Since that time, calls for rebuilding the Navy to 600 ships so that it can meet the challenge of the growing Soviet Navy includes a budget request of $40.3 billion for new construction alone for FY1978. The 156 ships to be built in the five year program ending in FY 1982 are:

Trident SSBN	8	AO	14
SSN 688	2	AOE	1
CVV	2	AD	2
CSGN	2	AR	2
DDG-47	10	T-AGOS	12
FFG-7	56	T-ATF	7
MCM	19	T-ARC	2
FFGX	2	T-ASR	4
LX (LSD-41)	6		

The FY1978 budget called for building small aircraft carriers carrying V/STOL aircraft instead of a fifth nuclear-powered carrier and a service life extension program (SLEP) for existing carriers which in a two-year overhaul will add 15 years of useful life.

II. HIGH-LOW

Admiral Elmo R. Zumwalt retired from the Navy in 1974 after serving four years as CNO. In 1976 he published his memoirs, On Watch. Included is a chapter entitled "High-Low." The idea of "high-low" came to him, he said, in 1962:

> 'High' was short for high-performance ships and weapons systems that also were so high-cost that the country could afford to build only a few of them at a time; there are some missions the Navy cannot perform without the great flexibility and versatility of such ships. 'Low' was short for moderate-cost, moderate-performance ships and systems that could be turned out in relatively large numbers; they would ensure that the Navy could be in enough places at the same time to get its job done.

Given the rapid obsolescence of the U.S. Navy since the end of World War II as opposed to the growth and modernization of the Soviet Navy at the same time, Zumwalt advised Secretary of the Navy John Chafee in 1970 to abandon older ships and shift funds from them to more effective ships and systems both strategic and conventional. Three decisions were needed: 1) how to reduce current capability while building new ships yet not tempt the Soviets into rash action; 2) how to balance the number of high and low ships built; and 3) how to provide expensive strategic forces yet not let conventional forces reach so low a point that a conventional threat could be countered only by nuclear war. Unlike the Soviets, who are quite self-sufficient and need only defensive naval forces, the United States must trade overseas. Hence its navy must not only maintain "sea control"--keep the sea lanes open --but be ready for "projection"--to apply its military power overseas, with the second dependent on the first. Following Korea, however, except for submarines, the United States let its control forces wither, and Zumwalt charged that part of the withering was caused by Admiral Rickover, whose excellent relations with Congress enabled him to siphon naval funds into nuclear propulsion. While nuclear propulsion is excellent for submarines "and a limited number of big carriers and their escorts," he said, the size and weight of the plant is such that it requires large ships which are bigger and in some cases five times more expensive than conventionally-powered ships that fight almost as well. Therefore a larger number of small aircraft-carrying ships would be better than a single supership.

For example, a FY1971-1979 high program could provide 36 ships including 2 CVAN, 4 DLGN, and 30 DD-963 for $5.3 billion, or $150 million per copy, while a low program could provide 89 ships including 1 carrier, 8 DCS, 50 PF, and 30 PHM for $4.8 billion, or $55 million per copy. The cost of building and operating a nuclear-powered ship over its life span is 3 percent greater than that of a conventional ship--a percentage that may change if nuclear power remains relatively cheap but oil becomes more costly --but overhaul costs are triple those of the latter. Debate therefore centers on whether the tactical advantages of nuclear power are worth the increased cost. These advantages include virtually unlimited endurance at high speed; increased on-station time; freedom from bases or mobile logistic replenishment, a particularly important factor when operating in high threat areas; and a cleaner ship because of the absence of funnel smoke. Compared with a conventional carrier, a nuclear carrier has 70 percent more aviation fuel and 50 percent more aviation ammunition stowage capacity, 4 catapults rather than 2, facilities to house double the number of air wing personnel, and ability to handle heavy aircraft--e.g., the A-6, F-14, E-2, and RA-5--that cannot be handled by smaller carriers and of course not by SCSs. Furthermore, the cost of escorts for small carriers is the same if not greater than that for escorts for large ones.

To "reoptimize" the Navy, Zumwalt asked Captain Stansfield Turner and then Rear Admiral Worth Bagley to head "Project 60." Since the U.S. Navy already had ample "high" in the SSN-668 class ($300 million a copy), the $133 million LHA, the $100 million DD-963 <u>Spruance</u> class, the CVANs 68 (<u>Nimitz</u>) and 69 (<u>Eisenhower</u>), and five nuclear-powered DLGNs, Zumwalt favored "low." At the time, however, there were no "low" ships on the drawing boards. Project 60 came up with four new sea control ship classes. First, the speedy, missile-armed hydrofoil patrol boat (PHM) for striking enemy surface vessels. Second, a patrol frigate (formerly PF, now FFG-7) displacing 3,400 tons, carrying two Harpoon missiles and two helicopters, speed of about 28 knots, and costing "only" $50 million. Third, an "air capable" or "sea control" ship--17,000 tons, 600 feet long, gas turbine propulsion, 25 knots, carrying 14 SH-3 helicopters and 3 Harrier V/STOL aircraft--to cost $100 million--one-eighth the cost of a nuclear carrier. The function of this ship will be to show the flag in dangerous waters while the big carriers withdraw out of reach of an enemy first strike and, being ready to deliver a strike, to deter a first strike. In time of war, the role of the small and large carriers would be reversed. Last, the "surface-effect ship," a 4,000-5,000-ton ship that would skim over the surface of the water at 80 to 100 knots and carry aircraft or troops or be devoted to antisubmarine, antiair, and many other uses. All CVA and CVS, meanwhile, would become dual purpose carriers merely by changing the kinds of aircraft embarked, with preference given to the F-4 and the improved SH-2 helicopter known as LAMPS (light airborne multipurpose system). In addition, Zumwalt would use helicopters rather than minesweepers to sweep mines, develop cruise missiles in a crash program, push Captor (a mine that fires a Mark 46 torpedo when it senses a submarine), and improve fleet electronics and communications, the last especially with submarines.

Argument over Zumwalt's account of "High-Low," particularly for his saying there were self-centered submarine, aviation, and surface "unions" in the Navy, continues. It has been said that he provided "more fiction than fact," had no postgraduate education, was short of operating experience because his only sea command was that of a destroyer, and that he waited until retiring before criticizing others rather than putting his career on the line while on active duty. Some doubt the need of sea control ships when wars will be so short that there will be no convoys to protect. (Add to this point that submarines armed with antiship missiles with a 100-mile range and wire-guided terminal homing torpedoes with a 10-mile range will make it extremely difficult if not impossible to protect convoys with traditional ASW tactics.) Others say that his low is so low that it cannot compete with the enemy; it is not the propulsion system but the weapons on a ship that count; he was biased towards the surface navy and critical of the "wing" and "dolphin" unions; he tried to fit planes to ships rather than building ships to fit planes; he overlooked the "low" provided by allied navies; and that a balanced mix of forces does not mean "equal" between "high" and "low."

In the end, Congress determines what the Navy will have. In 1975, it disapproved construction of SCS and requested new designs. Three designs were provided: 1) SCS; 2) a 25 percent larger and faster SCS carrying helicopters and V/STOL aircraft and armed with Harpoon; and 3) a SCS able to handle S-3 aircraft.

To maintain a 600-ship fleet--the smallest believed necessary to enable the Navy to meet its peacetime and wartime missions--means building 20 new ships a year given a 30-year life or 24 ships given a 25 year life. Between 1968 and 1975 only 12 ships a year were built. Congress authorized 22 ships for FY1975 and 23 for FY1976. The Navy's request for FY1977 was 29.

III. PROSPECTS FOR THE 1980s

A. SEA POWER AND THE GUAM DOCTRINE. The 1975-1976 edition of <u>Jane's Fighting Ships</u> defines sea power as "That strength in naval ships, associated aircraft and training which enables a country to promote the political and trading interests of itself and its allies in peacetime and their supremacy over the enemy in war." It may well be argued that the United States should be a naval rather than a land power and that this objective requires a major reshaping of its defense establishment. More than 60 percent of its boundaries are shorelines; more than 70 percent of its trade goes overseas; and it faces no threat from its land neighbors. In 1974, 34,732 foreign flag ships entered U.S. ports, its foreign trade was worth $142 billion, and American investments overseas reached about $119 billion. Vital raw materials for American industries are imported: 98 percent of the manganese, 91 percent of the chromium, 72 percent of the nickel, 37 percent of the oil--with reliance upon foreign supplies ever increasing.[2] On 8 July 1977, in the first meeting of top officials on Presidential Review Memorandum No. 10, stress was placed upon Soviet advantage in being close to Persian Gulf oil and the U.S. Navy's concern that the Soviets could shut off much of NATO's oil by controlling the few straits used by tankers.

The Guam Doctrine, adopted by the Nixon administration following the Vietnam war, asserts that the United States not be considered a source of ground troops in its alliances except during an obvious threat directed against the homeland. Because it is cheaper to provide foreign than American troops, the United States must operate primarily as an air and sea power in support of the ground troops of its allies, thus giving vent to its technological and industrial superiority. Hence the great importance of investing capital in research and development and in the procurement of weapons systems. In FY1976, although the U.S. Army, with 1,645,000 men, was the third largest in the world (785,000 Army, 197,000 Marines, 225,000 Army Reserve, 33,000 Marine Corps Reserve, and 405,000 National Guard, with 8,930 tanks, 5,000 artillery pieces, and more aircraft [11,000] than the Air Force [9,400]) only about half of its 19 active divisions were so armored, mechanized, or airborne that they could operate in a high-intensity conflict. This is not to denigrate the symbolic value of the 198,000 American troops in West Germany facing Warsaw Pact forces or the 33,000 in Korea who President Carter intends to withdraw in due course. In FY1977, the Army and Marine Corps cost about $31 billion; the Navy minus the Marine Corps, about $34 billion. Out of each dollar for the Army, 64 percent goes to meet manpower costs; out of each naval dollar, 30 percent. In 1975 the Soviets spent about $103.8 billion for defense (11 percent of the GNP); the United States $92.8 billion (6 percent of the GNP). The Soviets spend only 25 percent of their total budget for manpower; the United States, 55 percent. Therefore the Soviets can spend almost double for research and development and for procurement than does the United States.[3] While seaborne forces on the high seas pose a lesser threat than do predisposed and precommitted land forces "on the line" in close proximity to a potential enemy, these forces can as quickly engage as disengage, depending upon decisions made by the civilian policy makers.

Even before the end of World War II, shifts in the world balance of power could be foreseen following the defeat of the totalitarian states. With the UN unable to maintain world peace and the United States adverse to reaching political wartime agreements with the Soviets and its call for an end to colonialism, Churchill's vision of an "iron curtain" came true. Nazi Germany and Fascist Italy no longer separated the western Democracies from the Soviet Union; to the East, Communist China replaced a China that had been friendly to the West, while defeated Japan sided with the West and provided a bulwark to the eastward expansion of communism. Because of her central location, man-power, resources, ideological unity, and determined leadership Russia acquired a monolithic predominance in the heart of Europe. The sea powers therefore sought a new balance by cooperating against her. A bipolar world had been created. That balance, made precarious by the relative weakness of Britain and France, the pluralism of the Western World, and NATO's lack of maritime power, places most of the burden for redressing it upon the United States. The situation is thus an aggravated form of contest in which the sea powers are aligned against the strongest land power the world has ever seen, one aided by the great mobility of its land, air, and now sea forces and awesome armaments.

Since the West will not use a preventive war, the Soviets under the umbrella of mutual terror can use graded degrees of political subversion that do not warrant the use of nuclear weapons or call for nuclear punishment.

The role of sea power thus remains to move enough military strength into the enemy's territory to defeat his forces, neutralize his attack sites, and occupy his land. The key is still the ability of the West to sail ships across the seas and project its armed might against an enemy enjoying interior lines of communications in the face of his long-range missiles and "dirty" atomic bombs, while simultaneously operating from railheads and ports that are not radioactively contaminated.

B. A REVIEW OF THE SOVIET NAVAL CHALLENGE. Because the United States is export and import oriented, it must provide "sea control" in order to freely use the sea at all times. The more self-sufficient Soviet Union is much less dependent upon the sea. Her merchant marine, which may be considered a convenience and a psychological weapon rather than a necessity, is designed to deny control of the sea to those who depend upon it. "Sea denial" is easier than "sea control." To deny the sea, one destroys his opponents' ships; to enjoy sea control, one must protect his own and his allies' ships and also destroy hostile forces. Food for thought is provided in Jane's for 1975-1976: the Soviets have 2,290 ships, of which 1,512 are warships; the United States has 479 naval vessels in commission, of which 361 are combatants. The United States (13 aircraft carriers, 2 building, and 7 helicopter carriers) leads the Soviets in sea-based aircraft (2 helicopter carriers and 2 carriers for fixed wing V/STOL aircraft and another building). Soviet superiority in other classes of warships is shown by the following table, true as of January 1976.

	US	USSR
Missile cruisers	27	21
Gun cruisers	..	10
Missile destroyers	39	50
Gun destroyers	30	45
Ocean escorts/frigates	65	110
Missile craft	5	130
Patrol-Torpedo-ASW craft	2	440
Mine countermeasures craft	3	285
Amphibious ships (over 200 feet)	55	87

Later figures show that the Soviets have 75 nuclear-powered SSNs, 40 of which carry antiship missiles, and the United States 65, none of which carries missiles. The Soviets have about 185 diesel attack submarines, the United States 65 nuclear-powered and 8 diesels. The configuration of missiles carried by Soviet submarines is vitally important with respect to countermeasures. A cruise missile, e.g., has a comparatively long flight time and a fairly horizontal posture that permits its countering by aircraft and shipborne antiair weapons. A tactical ballistic missile, however, can cover a 400-mile range in 3 to 4 minutes and has a high attack angle that makes its detection and countering almost impossible. If the Soviets succeed in making their SS-N-13 a ballistic antiship missile, they will have made a breakthrough by providing the first ballistic missile with a homing capability. Unless the guidance system of a ballistic missile is highly accurate, it cannot use a conventional warhead. An SS-N-13 with a nuclear warhead, however, could be used either as an antiship or antisubmarine weapon if the Soviets wished to escalate a crisis to the tactical nuclear level. Not to be overlooked are the large numbers of naval aircraft the Soviets are sending to sea in aviation ships.

More important than numbers alone is the capability of Soviet submarines to knock out American carriers and NATO shipping. Experience of World War II showed that for each U-boat there were 25 Allied warships and 100 aircraft but that the Allies almost lost the Battle of the Atlantic. The current American ratio of ASW ships to Soviet nuclear-powered submarines is 1:1. Because American surface ships are designed as antisubmarine and antiair escorts for carriers and for merchant shipping, by far the greatest amount of striking power is contained in carrier aircraft. Because this is so, the Soviets have eschewed building carriers and concentrated upon ships carrying antiship missiles with ranges of between 23 and 350 miles. They have more than 100 missiles for each carrier without reloading. Moreover, a carrier operating in a crisis situation near Soviet antimissile ships and air bases could lead to a confrontation in which the Soviet option to "fire first" might lead the carrier to withdraw and allow the Soviets to gain their political objective. This accounts for the great appeal of using ships we can afford to lose in high crisis areas and saving the carriers for lower threat areas as a second strike force. Decisions in favor of low-mix of course would greatly change our shipbuilding program and place emphasis upon building sea control ships carrying V/STOL (VSS aircraft such as the Rockwell VSV-12 or the Grumman Nutcracker/Seacat) and missile boats; providing antiship and antiair missiles to the nuclear-powered frigates and DD-963 _Spruances_, which lack them; and expanding the use of Surface Effect Ship (SES) and of the Hydrofoil Ocean Combatant (HOC) as antisubmarine systems and of amphibious fire support ships (LFS). The cost of such a program is admittedly high--about $50 billion additional during the 1980s.

C. SALT. The meeting at Vladivostok in 1974, where the outlines of a SALT II accord were reached, was probably the high point of U.S.-Soviet ties in the Nixon-Ford years. Relations soured almost immediately thereafter, however, in part because of Soviet irritation over restrictions placed by Congress on credits and Soviet emigration policies, in part because differing definitions of detente. To the Soviets, detente apparently means the possibility of achieving limited disarmament and engaging in scholarly, scientific, cultural, and commercial exchanges without implementing social reforms or expanding the freedom of Soviet citizens.[2] Secretary of State Henry Kissinger's attempt to reach an accord on SALT in January 1976 failed because of Soviet support for Cuban forces in Angola. Would the Carter administration be interested in breaking the stalemate? No sooner had Carter called in his inaugural address for the elimination of "all nuclear weapons from this earth" than the Army recommended deploying nuclear cannon artillery along the NATO front.

Both the United States and the Soviet Union have enough H-bombs to destroy each other regardless of who strikes first. Delivery systems are varied so that all of them will not be destroyed in a first strike. Some are below ground under concrete, some in bombers, still others in submarine missiles. On 4 August 1970, the United States proposed limiting the number of ICBMs and heavy bombers to about 1900 on each side. This proposal became the basis for an interim five-year agreement of 3 October 1972 to limit nuclear weapons. Such a temporary agreement was reached at Vladivostok in 1974 between President Gerald Ford and Leonid I. Brezhnev. Each side would have no more than 2,400 ICBM launchers and bombers, and no more than 1,320 weapons could carry MIRVs. These numbers gave the United States between 11,930 and 13,230 atomic warheads and bombers and the Soviets between 5,518 and 7,218--a two to one American advantage that disappears in light of the heavier Soviet weapons throw weight. Cruise missiles and improved SLBMs were not covered.

The American objective since Vladivostok has been to obtain "deep cuts" in the number of first strike weapons, thereby reducing the threat of a surprise nuclear attack, and to desist from deploying large and more accurate ICBMs like the American MX and the Soviet SS-18. Both the United States and USSR are also gravely concerned about the spread of nuclear weapons. The Soviets rely more on land-based ICBMs, the United States upon a triad of land-based, airborne, and seaborne forces, with greatest emphasis upon the last. Were the United States to get the Soviets to reduce their land forces and take to the sea, the difficulty of detecting submarines would reduce the temptation to try a first strike.

The SALT agreement of 1972 expires on 3 October 1977. Early in 1976, Secretary of State Kissinger was blocked by the Pentagon and Senate "hawks" in negotiating a 10 percent cut in the Vladivostok figures on the basis of a cruise missile-Backfire compromise. On 24 February 1977, Secretary of Defense Harold Brown told Congress that American and Soviet nuclear forces were in balance and that the United States could keep the balance "without excessive effort," adding that only $10.6 billion of the $120.3 billion defense budget goes for long-range missiles, bombers, and submarines. (DOD got 23 percent of the $394 billion federal budget in FY1976.) Late in March, Carter sent Secretary of State Cyrus R. Vance to Moscow on what the American press called "mission impossible." One suggestion was to reduce by 25 percent the figures agreed upon at Vladivostok, thereby leaving the Soviets stronger in ICBMs but the United States ahead in bombers and warheads. The Soviets objected because the new figures did not accord with those of Vladivostok, which they preferred, and covered neither some 500 planes on U.S. carriers or nuclear weapons possessed by America's allies. Moreover, the suggestion did not control the American cruise missile which, they said, both Nixon and Ford had promised not to deploy and they wanted limited to a 600 km (372 miles) range. On the other hand, controls were to be placed on the Backfire, which the Soviets said was a medium bomber, not an intercontinental weapon. When Carter proposed swapping his long range (1,550-mile) cruise missile for the Backfire, he distressed both his Navy and Air Force, the Navy because it needs such missiles to use against enemy targets in wartime and was seeking to perfect its 2,000-mile and very accurate Tomahawk missile, the AF because it needs a standoff weapon. He also distressed the NATO nations, especially West Germany, which is very interested in acquiring the weapon.[3] Carter then suggested employing American cruise missiles but keeping the Backfire limited to its 3,100-miles range--still enough to let it bomb the United States and reach Cuba. The Soviets said "nyet." However, American and Soviet "working groups" given no deadlines were established to deal with such subjects as curbing the spread of nuclear weapons, reducing arms sales, halting all nuclear weapons tests and reducing the number of missile tests, banning new types of mass destruction weapons, and demilitarizing the Indian Ocean, the last soon reduced to "keeping a military balance" therein.

The American objective is to obtain a SALT II agreement based on the Vladivostok figures to last until 1985; a three-year protocol covering such unresolved issues as the U.S. cruise missile and Soviet Backfire bomber; and a statement of principles to govern the conditions of a third SALT agreement to follow. A possible compromise mentioned in late May 1977 was that the United States could continue to develop a long-range air-launched cruise missile but put a three-year moratorium on testing sea-launched and ground-launched versions, and the Soviets would restrict the range of the Backfire bomber and agree to some cuts in nuclear weapons below the Vladivostok figures.

President Carter said in May 1977 that he had no intention of speeding up the development of the cruise missile, B-1 bomber,[4] the mobile MX missile,[5] or the far more potent Mark 12A warhead for Minuteman III fixed-site missiles. Despite what may be considered Soviet intransigeance and Pentagon insistence that the B-1 is the best option for upholding the air leg of the American strategic triad, on 30 June Carter decided to put cruise missiles on B-52s rather than have the B-1 produced, although tests and research would continue with the 3 B-1 models built and with the one in production. He also said he would decide before 1 October, the deadline for the FY1978 budget, whether to proceed further with the enhanced neutron "cookie cutter" tactical bomb which is to be deployed in 1979. This bomb, carried by the 56-foot Lance missile, will kill people by radiation rather than destroy installations and equipment by heat and blast. On 21 June, both Armed Services committees directed the Pentagon to develop a non-nuclear warhead for use by NATO against Warsaw Pact forces. A land-based version of the Navy's Tomahawk, whose guidance system includes a computerized map in its mechanic brain to check the flight path on the ground, would be operated by the Air Force while similar "killer" shells would be provided for some 2,000 nuclear artillery pieces in Europe (8-inch and 155mm howitzers). Funding in the FY1978 budget also provides for a naval antiship version of the Tomahawk, for perfecting the AF's ACLM A (airplane cruise missile with a 700-mile range) and ACLM B (2,000-mile range). The Senate appropriations committee approved the funds on 22 June and the full Senate the next day. Effects of these developments upon SALT remain to be seen. There may be enough hard-line hawks in the Senate to block passage of an arms reduction treaty, which requires a two-thirds vote for approval if such a treaty does not provide for equality of power. Moreover, agreement upon such a treaty is made difficult by the destabilizing influence of technology, for each side feels impelled to match the other and develop a new weapons system not covered by agreement.

D. HUMAN RIGHTS. A document signed in Moscow in May 1972 by Nixon and Brezhnev pledged both sides to "noninterference in internal affairs" of the other. In 1974, Congress asked Secretary of State Kissinger if he could report on the condition of human rights in countries that receive U.S. aid. When Kissinger replied that the idea was impractical, Congress made the report mandatory. The first report, submitted in mid-March 1977, showed that human rights were violated in 59 of the 82 countries to which the United States gives aid. The Soviets hoped that the Carter administration would be easier to deal with than was the Ford-Kissinger team. Early in his administration, however, Carter called for a broadening of American foreign policy beyond narrow alliances rooted in anticommunism and said he would be "unswerving" in embracing the thirst for social justice in a "politically awakening world." While his concern for winning respect for human rights, which all UN members have agreed to support, is cheered where such rights are respected, indeed cherished, it is opposed in such countries as South Africa and of course by the Soviets, who have charged that the United States denies civil liberties to Indians, blacks, Communists, and antiwar activists. Even if the new policy attempts to correct Kissinger's supposed lack of concern for humane considerations, it is difficult to see how the issue can be applied to such friendly countries as South Korea, a veritable police state but one with which the United States has security arrangements, or in Russia. Seeing

the issue as a declaration of ideological war, the
Soviets launched the severest crackdown on dissidents
in a decade, noted that the policy would endanger
arms control negotiations, and charged that it equated
with interference in the internal affairs of social-
ist countries and would be counterproductive. Evidently the Soviet need to protect its ideology against
what it calls criminals and "scum" is more important
than bettering relations with the United States, with
these relations in mid-1977 reaching a low point in
the detent era that began in 1972. That the administration is serious in the matter is revealed in its
request that cuts in military aid be made for Argen-
tina, Ethiopia, and Uruguay because these nations
violate the human rights of their citizens. At least
five Latin American countries have rejected such aid
because angered by American criticism, yet on 15 June
1977, the United States explicitly tied its trade and
aid with Latin America to the observance of human
rights. The same issue rendered very difficult the
reaching of agreement at the 35-nation Belgrade conference of the summer of 1977 that sought to assess
the results of the 1975 Helsinki summit accord on
European security and cooperation,[6] and also settlement of the Arab-Israeli conflict.

E. THE FUNCTIONS OF THE U.S. NAVY. Given the current
international situation and knowledge of the military
forces available to the West and to the Soviets, a
rewarding exercise is to determine what kind of a
Navy the United States should have in order to carry
out its functions, the last defined as follows in
DOD Directive 5100.1:

> To organize, train, and equip Navy . . .
> forces for the conduct of prompt and sustained
> combat operations at sea, including operations
> of sea-based aircraft and land-based naval air
> components--specifically, forces to seek out and
> destroy enemy naval forces and to suppress enemy
> sea commerce, to gain and maintain general naval
> supremacy, to control vital sea areas and to
> protect vital sea lines of communication, to
> establish and maintain local superiority (in-
> cluding air) in an area of naval operations,
> to seize and defend advanced naval bases, and
> to conduct such land and air operations as may
> be essential to the prosecution of a naval cam-
> paign.

Include in your discussion:
Antiair warfare; antisubmarine warfare; anti-surface ship warfare; strike warfare (nuclear and conventional); amphibious warfare (vertical assault, over the beach, close support); mine warfare; special warfare (e.g., riverine warfare, coastal and beach reconnaissance); supporting tasks (intelligence, surveillance); command, control, and communications; electronic warfare; logistics.

Finally, recommend how naval forces can be used to:

1. assist those suffering from natural disasters or accidents;

2. enforce domestic and international laws;

3. contribute to civil works at home and abroad;

4. show the flag to reassure friendly governments threatened by internal or external aggression;

5. show the flag to deter an aggressor nation contemplating acquisitive military action;

6. gain or increase access to new countries;

7. deter an attack upon the homeland and upon friendly countries;

8. defend the homeland or the lands of friendly countries from attack;

9. project force in guerrilla wars, limited wars, and interventions;

10. obtain command of the sea in a conventional or nuclear war;

11. exercise command of the sea in a conventional or nuclear war;

12. obtain the political, economic, and military intelligence necessary to implement each of the above.

CHAPTER 1

NOTES

1. John M. Collins, <u>Grand Strategy: Principles and Practices</u> (Annapolis, Md.: Naval Institute Press, 1973), p. 14.

2. <u>Ibid.</u>, p. 19.

3. Moltke and Liddell Hart cited in <u>ibid.</u>, p. 335.

BIBLIOGRAPHY

VA454 A67	Archibald, E.H.H. <u>The Wooden Fighting Ship</u> (New York: ARCO, 1968).
U162 .B413	Beaufre, André. <u>An Introduction to Strategy</u>. Trans. R.H. Barry. (New York: Praeger, 1965).
U102 .C65	Clausewitz, Carl von. <u>On War</u>. Ed. and trans. by Michael Howard and Peter Paret (Princeton, N.J.: Princeton University Press, 1976).
U162 .C64	Collins, John M. <u>Grand Strategy: Principles and Practices</u> (Annapolis, Md.: Naval Institute Press, 1973).
DA70 .A1	Corbett, Sir Julian Stafford, ed. <u>Fighting Instructions, 1530-1816</u> (London: Naval Records Society, 1905).
V163 .C7	_____. <u>Some Principles of Maritime Strategy</u> (London: Longmans, Green, 1911).
V169 .C7	Creswell, John. <u>British Admirals of the Eighteenth Century: Tactics in Battle</u> (Hamden, Conn.: Archon Books, 1972).
V108 .C74	_____. <u>Naval Warfare</u>, 2d rev. ed. (Brooklyn, N.Y.: Chemical Publishing Co., 1942).
D27 .E6	<u>Sea Warfare: The Encyclopedia of Sea Warfare</u> (New York: Thomas Y. Crowell, 1975).

CHAPTER 2

BIBLIOGRAPHY

VM139 .B55	Blake, George. __British Ships and Shipbuilders__ (London: Collins, 1946).
DA447 .P4B91	Bryant, Sir Arthur. __Samuel Pepys__, new ed. (London: Collins, 1948).
DA445 .B85	_____. __King Charles II__ (London: Longmans, Green, 1949).
PA447 .P4B8	Casson, Lionel. __Ships and Seamanship in the Ancient World__ (Princeton, N.J.: Princeton University Press, 1971).
DA70 .C68	Clowes, Sir William L. __The Royal Navy__, 7 vols. (London: Sampson Low, Marston, 1897-1903).
HC275 .C63	Cole, Charles W. __Colbert and a Century of French Mercantilism__, 2 vols. (Hamden, Conn.: Archon Books, 1964).
HF3508 .S7C6	Connell-Smith, Gordon. __Forerunners of Drake__ (London: Longmans, Green, 1954).
DA70 .A1	Corbett, Sir Julian, ed. __Fighting Instructions, 1530-1816__ (London: Naval Records Society, 1905).
DA70 .A1 vo. 35	_____, ed. __Signals and Instructions, 1776-1794__ (London: Naval Records Society, 1908).
V169 C7	Creswell, John. __British Admirals of the Eighteenth Century: Tactics in Battle__, rpt. (Hamden, Conn.: Shoestring Press, 1972).
	Greenhill, Basil et al. __Archaeology of the Boat: A New Introductory Study__ (Middletown, Conn.: Wesleyan University Press, 1976).
V27 .H3	Hannay, David. __The Navy and Sea Power__ (New York: Holt, 1913).

HE587 .G7H3	Harper, Lawrence A. *The English Navigation Laws* (New York: Columbia University Press, 1939).
VA503 .J46	Jenkins, Ernest Harold. *A History of the French Navy from Its Beginnings to the Present Day* (London: Macdonald, Macdonald, and Jane, 1973).
VA454 .L595	Lewis, Michael A. *The Navy of Britain* (London: George Allen & Unwin, 1948).
VB315 .G7L4	_____. *England's Sea-Officers: The Story of the Naval Profession* (London: Allen & Unwin, 1939).
DA360 .L67	_____. *The Spanish Armada* (London: B.T. Batsford, 1960).
D27 .M21	Mahan, Alfred Thayer. *The Influence of Sea Power on History, 1660-1783* (Boston: Little, Brown, 1890).
VA454 .M32	Marcus, Geoffrey J. *A Naval History of England*, 3 vols. (London: Longmans, Green, 1961). Vol. 1. *The Formative Centuries*.
DA86 .P37	Penn, Christopher D. *The Navy Under the Early Stuarts* (London: Hogg, 1920).
DA86.1 .B6P68	Powell, John R. *Robert Blake: General-at-Sea* (New York: Crane, Russak, 1972).
V27 .R59	Robertson, Frederick Leslie. *The Evolution of Naval Armament* (London: H.T. Storey, 1968).
V167 .R6	Robison, Samuel S. *A History of Naval Tactics from 1530 to 1930* (Annapolis, Md.: U.S. Naval Institute, 1942).
DE61 .N3R6	Rodgers, William L. *Greek and Roman Naval Warfare* (Annapolis, Md.: U.S. Naval Institute, 1937).
V43 .R6	_____. *Naval Warfare Under Oars* (Annapolis, Md.: U.S. Naval Institute, 1939).

DA86　　Tanner, Joseph R. *Pepys Memoirs of the Royal*
.P45　　*Navy, 1679-1688* (Oxford: Clarendon Press, 1906).

DA86　　Tedder, Arthur W. *The Navy of the Restoration*
.T3　　 (Cambridge: University Press, 1916).

DA495　 Trevelyan, George M. *England Under Queen*
.T7　　　*Anne*, 3 vols. (London: Longmans, Green, 1930-
　　　　 1934).

V103　　Southworth, John Van Duyn. *War At Sea.* 3
.S64　　vols. (New York: Twayne, 1968-1972). Vol. 1.
　　　　 The Ancient Fleets.

CHAPTER 3

BIBLIOGRAPHY

JV1011　Beer, George L. *Origins of the Old Colonial*
.B3　　　*System, 1578-1660* (New York: Macmillan, 1908).

HF3025　_____. *The Commercial Policy of England*
.B43　　 *Toward The American Colonies* (New York: Columbia University Press, 1893).

E178　　Bourne, Edward G. *Spain in America, 1450-1580*
.A54　　(New York: Harper, 1905).

JV2511　Boxer, Charles R. *The Dutch Seaborne Empire,*
.D67　　*1600-1800* (New York: Knopf, 1965).

E101　　Brebner, John B. *Explorers of North America,*
.B83　　*1492-1806* (Garden City, N.Y.: Doubleday, 1955).

D6. R5　Cheyney, Edward P. *The Dawn of a New Era,*
Vol. 1　*1250-1453* (New York: Harper, 1936).

HE823　 Burwash, Dorothy. *English Merchant Shipping,*
.B86　　 *1460-1550* (Toronto: University of Toronto
　　　　 Press, 1947).

UF565　 Cipolla, Carlo M. *Guns, Sails, and Empires*
.E9C5　 (New York: Pantheon Books, 1966).

DA70　　Corbett, Sir Julian. *Papers Relating to the*
.A1　　 *Navy during the Spanish War, 1585-1587* (London:
Vol.11　Naval Records Society, 1898).

DA86.22.C75	_____. *Drake and the Tudor Navy*, 2 vols. (London: Longmans, Green, 1917).
DP162.D3	Davies, Reginald T. *The Golden Century of Spain, 1501-1621* (London: Macmillan, 1937).
DA47.3.E4	Edmundson, George. *Anglo-Dutch Rivalry during the First Half of the Seventeenth Century* (Oxford: Clarendon Press, 1911).
DJ109.G43	Geyl, Pieter. *The Revolt of the Netherlands, 1555-1609* (London: Williams and Norgate, 1932).
V45.G84	Guilmartin, John Francis. *Gunpowder and Galleys* (New York: Cambridge University Press, 1974).
G20 H142 1589a	Haklyut, Richard. *Principal Navigations . . . of the English Nation*, 2 vols. (Cambridge: University Press, 1965).
F1410.H25	Haring, Clarence H. *Spanish Empire in America* (New York: Oxford University Press, 1947).
F1411.K57	Kirkpatrick, Frederick A. *Spanish Conquistadores* (London: Black, 1934).
DA360.L67	Lewis, Michael A. *The Spanish Armada* (London: B.T. Batsford, 1959).
VA454.M32	Marcus, Geoffrey J. *A Naval History of England*, 3 vols. (Boston: Little, Brown, 1962), vol. 1. *The Formative Years*.
DP588.O6	Martins, Joaquim P. Oliveira. *Golden Age of Prince Henry the Navigator* (New York: Dutton, 1914).
DA360.M3	Mattingly, Garrett. *The Armada* (Boston: Houghton Mifflin, 1959).
E111.M86	Morison, Samuel E. *Admiral of the Ocean Sea: A Life of Christopher Columbus* (Boston: Little, Brown, 1942).
E178.P94	Priestly, Herbert T. *The Coming of the White Man, 1492-1848* (New York: Macmillan, 1929).

JV1811 .P73	_____. France Overseas Through the Old Regime (New York: Macmillan, 1939).
E188 .R895	Rowse, Alfred L. Elizabethans and America (New York: Harper, 1959).
E169. 1.S27	Savelle, Max. Seeds of Empire (New York: Knopf, 1948).
E18 .S33	_____. Empires to Nations: Expansion in America, 1713-1824 (Minneapolis: University of Minnesota Press, 1974).
E188 .T95	Tyler, Lyon G. England in America, 1580-1652 (New York: Harper, 1904; Greenwood, 1969).
	Peterson, Charles W. "English and Danish Naval Strategy in the Seventeenth Century," (PH. D. diss., University of Maine, 1975).

CHAPTER 4

NOTES

1. Geoffrey J. Marcus, A Naval History of England, 3 vols. (London: Longmans, Green, 1961), 1: 252.

2. Sir Herbert Richmond, The Navy in the War of 1739-1748, 3 vols. (Cambridge: University Press, 1920), 2: 56.

3. Ibid., 1: xi.

4. Catherine Drinker Bowen, John Adams and the American Revolution (Boston: Little, Brown, 1950), p. 42.

BIBLIOGRAPHY

D286 .A5	Anderson, Matthew S. Europe in the Eighteenth Century, 1713-1783 (London: Longmans, 1961).
DA87.1 .A646	Anson, W. V. The Life of Admiral Lord Anson: The Father of the British Navy (London: Murray, 1912).

DA87.1   Burrow, Montagu. *The Life of Admiral Lord*
.H3B8   *Hawke* (London: Allen, 1883).

DA30   *Cambridge History of the British Empire*,
.C3   Vol. 1.

DJ201   Carter, Alice Clare. *The Dutch Republic in*
.C35   *Europe in the Seven Years' War* (New York:
1971b   American University Press, 1971).

DA435   Clark, George N. *The Later Stuarts, 1660-1714*
.C55   (Oxford: Clarendon Press, 1934).

DA86   Corbett, Sir Julian. *England in the Mediter-*
.C7   *ranean . . . 1603-1713* (London: Longmans,
          1904).

DA87   _____. *England in the Seven Years' War*,
.C7   2 vols. (London: Longmans, 1907).

U39   Creswell, John. *Generals and Admirals: The*
.C74   *Story of Amphibious Command* (London: Longmans,
          1952).

DS462   Dodwell, Henry H. *Dupleix and Clive* (London:
.D6   F. Cass, 1967).

DA87.1   Hartman, Cyril Hughes. *The Angry Admiral*
V5H3   [Vernon] (London, Heinemenn, 1953).

DA480   Jarrett, Derek. *Britain 1688-1815* (New York:
.J35   St. Martin, 1965).

          Kopperman, Paul E. *Braddock at the Mononga-*
          hela (Pittsburgh: University of Pittsburgh
          Press, 1976).

E188   Lawson, Don. *The Colonial Wars: Prelude to*
.L37   *the American Revolution . . . 1689-1763* (New
          York: Abelard-Schuman, 1972).

DA47   Lord, Walter F. *England and France in the*
.1L7   *Mediterranean, 1669-1830* (London: Low, Marston,
          1901).

DA87.5   Marcus, Geoffrey J. Quiberon Bay (London:
.1759   Hollis and Carter, 1960).
.M5

HF3505   Minchinton, W. F. ed., The Growth of English
.4.M48   Overseas Trade in the Seventeenth and Eight-
          eenth Centuries (London: Methuen, 1969).

DA87   Owen, John H. The War at Sea Under Queen
.C8   Anne (Cambridge: University Press, 1938).

DA87.1   Pack, S.W.C. Admiral Lord Anson: The Story
.A6P3   of Anson's Voyages and Naval Events of the
          Day (London: Cassell, 1960).

F1621   Pares, R. War and Trade in the West Indies,
.P32   1739-1763 (Oxford: Clarendon Press, 1936).

JX5261   _____. Colonial Blockade and Neutral
.G7P3   Rights, 1739-1763 (Oxford: Clarendon Press,
          1938).

JV165   Parry, John H. Trade and Dominion: The Euro-
.P35   pean Overseas Empires in the Eighteenth Cen-
          tury (New York: Praeger, 1971).

DA87.1   Pope, Dudley. At Twelve Mr. Byng Was Shot
.B896   (Philadelphia: Lippincott, 1962).

DA301   Plumb, John H. Sir Robert Walpole, 2 vols.
.W2P73   (Boston: Houghton Mifflin, 1960).

D279   Powley, Edward B. The Naval Side of King
.5.P69   William's War (Hamden, Conn.: Shoestring
          Press, 1974).

DA67.1   Reilly, Robin. The Rest to Fortune: The Life
.W8R4   of Major General James Wolfe (London: Cassel,
          1960).

DA87   Richmond, Sir Herbert. The Navy in the War
.R5   of 1739-1748, 3 vols. (Cambridge: University
          Press, 1920).

DA483   Sherrard, Owen A. Lord Chatham: Pitt and the
.P6S53   Seven Years' War (London: Bodley Head, 1955).

513

E199 .S78	Stacey, Charles P. *Quebec, 1759: The Siege and the Battle* (New York: St. Martin, 1959).
DA495 .T7	Trevelyan, George M. *England Under Queen Anne*, 3 vols. (London: Longman, 1930-1934).
DA505 .W38	Watson, John Steven. *The Reign of George III 1760-1815. Oxford History of England*, v. 12 (Oxford: Clarendon Press, 1960).
F1030 .W95	Wrong, George M. *The Rise and Fall of New France*, 2 vols. (New York: Macmillan, 1928).
D286 .W5	White, R.J. *Europe in the Eighteenth Century* New York: St. Martin, 1965).
E199 .W62	Whitton, Frederick E. *Wolfe and North America* (Boston: Little, Brown, 1929).
	Morgan, Robert J. "Louisbourg: Key to a Continent," *Journal of the Commonwealth and Comparative Politics* (Summer 1976): 3-14.

CHAPTER 5

NOTES

1. Robert G. Albion, *Forests and Sea Power* (Cambridge: Harvard University Press, 1926), p. 232.

2. *Ibid.*, p. 248.

3. *Ibid.*, pp. 250, 251.

4. *Ibid.*, p. 232. For colonial warships, see Joseph A. Goldenberg, *Shipbuilding in Colonial America* (Charlottesville: University Press of Virginia, 1976), pp. 108-16.

5. Albion, *Forests and Sea Power*, pp. 244-46; Goldenberg, *Shipbuilding in Colonial America*, p. 53.

BIBLIOGRAPHY

VA454 .A6	Albion, Robert G. *Forests and Sea Power* (Cambridge: Harvard University Press, 1926).

JV1016　Basye, Arthur H. *The Lords Commissioners of*
.B3　*Trade and Plantations, 1748-1782* (New Haven: Yale University Press, 1925).

JK128　Becker, Carl. L. *The Declaration of Independ-*
.B4　*ence: A Study in the History of Political Ideas* (New York: Knopf, 1942).

HD9515　Bining, Arthur C. *British Regulation of the*
.B5　*Colonial Iron Industry* (Philadelphia: University of Pennsylvania Press, 1933).

HB91　Buck, Philip N. *The Politics of Mercantilism*
.B8　(New York: Octogon Books, 1964).

E306　Burnett, Edmund C. *The Continental Congress*
.B96　(New York: Macmillan, 1941).

　　　Crowshurst, R.P. *British Oceanic Convoys in the Seven Years' War, 1756-1763* (London: University of London, 1970).

E215　Dickerson, Oliver M. *The Navigation Acts and*
.1.D53　*the American Revolution* (Philadelphia: University of Pennsylvania Press, 1951).

　　　Flood, Charles Bracelen. *Rise and Fight Again: Perilous Times Along the Road to Independence* (New York: Dodd, Mead, 1976).

VM23　Goldenberg, Joseph A. *Shipbuilding in Colonial*
.G64　*America* (Charlottesville: University Press of Virginia, 1976).

HE587　Harper, Lawrence A. *The English Navigation*
.G7H3　*Laws* (New York: Columbia University Press, 1939).

JV1016　Henretta, James A. *"Salutary Neglect": Colo-*
.H45　*nial Administration under the Duke of Newcastle* (Princeton, N.J.: Princeton University Press, 1972).

DA512　Hoffman, Ross J.S. *The Marquis. A Study of*
.R6H63　*Lord Rockingham, 1730-1782* (New York: Fordham University Press, 1973).

E209 .J33	Jameson, J. Franklin. *The American Revolution Considered as a Social Movement* (Princeton, N.J.: Princeton University Press, 1926).
E210 .K65	Knollenberg, Bernhard. *Origin of the American Revolution, 1759-1766* (New York: Macmillan, 1960).
JK54 .L3	Labaree, Leonard W. *Royal Government in America* (New Haven: Yale University Press, 1930).
E332 .M25	Malone, Dumas. *Jefferson the Virginian* (Boston: Little, Brown, 1948).
E302.6 .A2M56	Miller, John C. *Sam Adams: Pioneer in Propaganda* (Stanford: Stanford University Press, 1936, 1960).
E210 .M5	_____. *Origins of the American Revolution* (Boston: Little, Brown, 1943).
E208 .M55	Mitchell, Broadus. *The Price of Independence: A Realistic View of the American Revolution* (New Brunswick, N.J.: Rutgers University Press).
PS3535 .O176 N67	Roberts, Kenneth L. *Northwest Passage* (Garden City, N.Y.: Doubleday, 1937).
PS3535 .O176 .O45	_____. *Oliver Wiswell* (Garden City, N.Y.: Doubleday, 1940).
PS3535 .O176 R32	_____. *Rabble in Arms* (Garden City, N.Y.: Doubleday, 1933).
JK31 .R6	Rossiter, Clinton L. *Seedtime of the Republic* (New York: Harcourt, Brace, 1953).
KF361 .R88 1976	Russell, Elmer Beecher. *The Review of American Colonial Legislation by the King in Council* (New York: Octogon Books, 1976, c1915).
HF3025 .S3	Schlesinger, Arthur M. *The Colonial Merchants and the American Revolution, 1773-1776* (New York: Ungar, 1918, 1957).

HF3025 .S717   Shepherd, James F. and Gary M. Walton. Shipping, Maritime Trade, and the Economic Development of Colonial North America (Cambridge: Cambridge University Press, 1972).

E179.5 .T95   Turner, Frederick J. The Frontier in American History (New York: Holt, 1920).

E216 .U22   Ubbelohde, Carl. The Vice-Admiralty Courts and the American Revolution (Chapel Hill: University of North Carolina Press, 1960).

E302.6 .F8V32   Van Doren, Carl C. Benjamin Franklin (New York: Viking, 1938).

CHAPTER 6

BIBLIOGRAPHY

E271 .A42   Allen, Gardner Weld. A Naval History of the American Revolution, 2 vols. (Boston: Houghton Mifflin, 1913).

E208 .A35   Alden, John Richard. The American Revolution, 1775-1783 (New York: Harper, 1954).

E267 .A34   Anderson, Troyer Steele. The Command of the Howe Brothers During the American Revolution (New York: Oxford University Press, 1936).

HJ1013 .B155   Baker, Norman. Government and Contractors: The British Treasury and War Supplies, 1775-1783 (London: Athlone, 1971).

E231 .B5   Bird, Harrison. Attack on Quebec: The American Invasion of Canada, 1775 (New York: Oxford University Press, 1968).

E267 .B68   Bowler, R. Arthur. Logistics and the Failure of the British Army in America, 1775-1783 (Princeton, N.J.: Princeton University Press, 1975).

DA506 .A2B75   Brooke, John. King George III (New York: McGraw-Hill, 1972).

Browning, Reed. The Duke of Newcastle (New Haven: Yale University Press, 1975).

E230 .C32	Carrington, Henry B. <u>Battles of the American Revolution, 1775-1781</u> (New York: Barnes, 1876).
E237 .C43	Chadwick, French Ensor. <u>The Graves Papers and other Documents Relating to the Naval Operations of the Yorktown Campaign July to October 1781</u> (New York: Printed for the Naval History Society by the DeVinne Press, 1916).
VA56 .C5	Chapelle, Howard I. <u>The American Sailing Navy</u> (New York: Norton, 1949).
E207 .B2C5	Clark, William Bell. <u>Gallant John Barry, 1745-1803</u> (New York: Macmillan, 1938).
E207 .B48C6	_____. <u>Captain Dauntless: The Story of Nicholas Biddle of the Continental Navy</u> (Baton Rouge: Louisiana State University Press, 1949) [LSUP].
E302.6 .F8C55	_____. <u>Ben Franklin's Privateers: A Naval Epic of the American Revolution</u> (Baton Rouge: LSUP, 1956).
E207 .W63C7	_____. <u>Lambert Wickes: Sea Raider and Diplomat</u> (New Haven: Yale University Press, 1932).
E271 .C57	_____. <u>George Washington's Navy</u> (Baton Rouge: LSUP, 1960).
E271 .U583	_____, and William James Morgan, eds. <u>Naval Documents of the American Revolution</u>, 7 vols. (Washington: GPO, 1964-).
E230 .C62	Coakley, Robert W. and Stetson Conn. <u>The War of the American Revolution</u> (Washington: GPO, 1975).
E265 .D85	Dull, Jonathan R. <u>The French Navy and American Independence: A Study of Arms and Diplomacy, 1774-1787</u> (Princeton, N.J.: Princeton University Press, 1976).
E241 .Y6E32	Eckenrode, Hamilton James. <u>The Story of the Campaign and Siege of Yorktown</u> (Washington: GPO, 1931).

E271   Fowler, William M., Jr. Rebels Under Sail:
.F68   The American Navy during the Revolution (New York: Scribner, 1976).

E312   Freeman, Douglas S. George Washington: A
.F82   Biography, 7 vols. (New York: Scribner, 1948-1957), esp. vols. 4 and 5.

E267   Gruber, Ira D. The Howe Brothers and the
.H63   American Revolution (New York: Atheneum, 1972).

E210   Higginbotham, Don. The War of American Inde-
.H63   pendence: Military Attitudes, Policies, and Practice, 1763-1789 (New York: Macmillan, 1971).

E241   Hough, Franklin B., ed. The Siege of Savannah
.C4H8   by the Combined American and French Forces, under the Command of General Lincoln and the Count D'Estaing, in the Autumn of 1779 (Albany, N.Y.: J. Munsell, 1867).

E271   Jackson, John W. The Pennsylvania Navy, 1775-
.J26   1781: The Defense of the Delaware (New Brunswick, N.J.: Rutgers University Press, 1974).

E271   James, William M. The British Navy in Adver-
.J28   sity (London: Longmans, 1926).

DA47.1   Jarrett, Derek. The Begetters of Revolution:
J37   England's Involvement with France, 1759-1789 (Totowa, N.J.: Rowan and Littlefield, 1973).

E195   Jensen, Merrill. The Founding of a Nation:
.J4   A History of the American Revolution, 1763-1776 (New York: Oxford University Press, 1968).

E241   Johnston, Henry P. The Yorktown Campaign and
.Y657   the Surrender of Cornwallis, 1781 (New York: Harper, 1881).

E312   Knox, Dudley W. The Naval Genius of George
.25.K67   Washington (Boston: Houghton Mifflin, 1932).

E265   Lewis, Charles Lee. Admiral De Grasse and
.L45   American Independence (Annapolis, Md.: U.S. Naval Institute, 1945).

VA454 .L595	Lewis, Michael A. *The Navy of Britain* (London: Allen & Unwin, 1948).
VA454 .L59	_____. *The History of the British Navy* (Fairlawn, N.J.: Essential Books, 1954).
E208 .M14	Mackesy, Piers. *The War for America, 1775-1783* (Cambridge: Harvard University Press, 1964).
D295 .M23	Madariaga, Isabel de. *Britain, Russia, and the Armed Neutrality of 1780* (New Haven: Yale University Press, 1962).
E271 .M22	Mahan, Alfred Thayer. *The Major Operations of the Navies in the War of American Independence* (Boston: Little, Brown, 1913).
E271 .M52	Miller, Nathan. *Sea of Glory: The Continental Navy Fights for Independence, 1775-1783* (New York: McKay, 1974).
E320 .6.M7M5	Mintz, Max M. *Gouverneur Morris and the American Revolution* (Norman: University of Oklahoma Press, 1970).
E230 .M5	Mitchell, Joseph B. *Decisive Battles of the American Revolution* (New York: Putnam, 1962).
E303 .M82	Montross, Lynn. *The Reluctant Rebels: The Story of the Continental Congress, 1774-1789* (New York: Harper, 1970).
E255 .M66	_____. *Rag, Tag, and Bobtail: The Story of the Continental Army, 1775-1783* (New York: Harper, 1952).
E271 .M67	Morgan, William James. *Captains to the Northward: The New England Captains in the Continental Navy* (Barre, Mass.: Barre Gazette, 1959).
E207 .J7M6	Morison, Samuel Eliot. *John Pual Jones: A Sailor's Biography* (Boston: Little, Brown, 1959).
E271 .C77	Neeser, Robert Wilden. *Letters and Papers Relating to the Cruises of Gustavus Conyngham* (New York: De Vinne Press, 1915).

E271 .R76	*Letter Books and Order Book of George, Lord Rodney, Admiral of the White Squadron, 1780-1782*, 2 vols. (New York Historical Society Collections, 1932, 1933, published by the University of Virginia Press).
E230 .P24	Palmer, Dave Richard. *The Way of the Fox: American Strategy in the War for America, 1775-1783* (Westport, Conn.: Greenwood, 1975).
E271 .P298	Paullin, Charles O. *The Navy of the American Revolution*, 2 vols. (Chicago: Burrows, 1906).
DA70 .R52	Richmond, Admiral Sir Herbert. *Statesmen and Sea Power* (Oxford: Clarendon Press, 1946).
DA510 .R5	Ritcheson, C.R. *British Politics and the American Revolution* (Norman: University of Oklahoma Press, 1954).
E208 .R6	Robson, Eric. *The American Revolution in its Political and Military Aspects, 1763-1783* (London: Batchworth Press, 1955).
E259 .R67	Rossie, Jonathan Gregory. *The Politics of Command in the American Revolution* (Syracuse: Syracuse University Press, 1975).
	Selby, John. *The Road to Yorktown* (New York: St. Martin, 1976).
E271 .O61	Shea, John D.G., ed. *The Operations of the French Fleet Under the Count De Grasse in 1781-1782* (New York: Da Capo Press [1864] 1971).
E230 .P43	Shy, John. *A People Numerous and Armed: Reflections on the Military Struggle for American Independence* (New York: Oxford University Press, 1976).
DA87.1 .R6S8	Spinney, D. *Rodney* (London: Allen & Unwin, 1969).

E216   Stout, Neil R. *The Royal Navy in America,*
.S76   *1760-1775: A Study of Enforcement of British*
           Colonial Policy in the Era of the American
           Revolution (Annapolis, Md., U.S. Naval Institute, 1973).

E237   Thayer, Theodore. *Yorktown: Campaign of*
.T47   *Strategic Options* (Philadelphia: Lippincott, 1975).

E271   Tornquist, Karl G.   Trans. Amandus Johnson.
.T6   *The Naval Campaigns of Count de Grasse during*
           the American Revolution, 1781-1783 (Philadelphia: Swedish Colonial Society, 1942).

E302.6   Ver Steeg, Clarence. *Robert Morris: Revolu-*
.M8V4   *tionary Financier* (Philadelphia: University of Pennsylvania Press, 1954).

E230   Ward, Christopher. *War of the American Revo-*
.W34   *lution,* 2 vols. (New York: Macmillan, 1952).

E267   Wickwire, Franklin and May. *Cornwallis: An*
.W48   *Adventure* (Boston: Houghton Mifflin, 1976).

           Wickwire, Mary Botts. "Lord Sandwich and the King's Ships: British Naval Administration, 1771-1782" (Ph. D. diss., Yale University, 1963).

CHAPTER 7

BIBLIOGRAPHY

E322   Adams, John. *Diary and Autobiography.* Ed.
.A3   by L.H. Butterfield (Cambridge: Belknap Press of Harvard University Press, 1961).

E335   Allen, George W. *Our Navy and the Barbary*
.A42   *Corsairs* (Boston: Houghton Mifflin, 1905).

E323   _____. *Our Naval War with France* (Bos-
.A42   ton: Houghton Mifflin, 1909).

E314   Bemis, Samuel Flagg. *Jay's Treaty* (New York:
.B45   Macmillan, 1923).

E162 .B5	Bird, Harrison. <u>Navies in the Mountains: The Battles on Water of Lake Champlain and Lake George, 1609-1814</u> (New York: Oxford University Press, 1962).
E310 .B57	_____. <u>War for the West, 1790-1813</u> (New York: Oxford University Press, 1971).
E183.8 .F8B5	Bowman, Albert Hall. <u>The Struggle for Neutrality: Franco-American Diplomacy during the Federalist Era</u> (Knoxville: University of Tennessee Press, 1974).
E342 .B72	Brant, Irving. <u>The Fourth President: A Life of James Madison</u> (Indianapolis: Bobbs-Merrill, 1970).
E321 .B84	Brown, Ralph A. <u>The Presidency of John Adams</u> (Lawrence: University Press of Kansas, 1975).
E357 .B86	Brown, Roger H. <u>The Republic in Peril: 1812</u> (New York: Columbia University Press, 1964).
E360.6 .S575	Byron, Gilbert. <u>The War of 1812 on Chesapeake Bay</u> (Baltimore: Maryland Historical Society, 1964).
E323 .D4	De Conde, Alexander. <u>The Quasi War: The Politics and Diplomacy of the Undeclared War with France, 1797-1801</u> (New York: Scribner, 1966).
VB23 .E34	Eckert, Edward K. <u>The Navy Department in the War of 1812</u> (Gainesville: University of Florida Press, 1973).
DA87 .E3	Ekins, Sir Charles. <u>Naval Battles from 1744 to the Peace of 1814</u> (London: Baldwin, Cradock, 1824).
E182 .T7F43	Ferguson, Eugene S. <u>Truxton of the Constellation</u> (Baltimore: Johns Hopkins Press, 1956).
E182 .F81	Frost, Holloway. <u>We Build a Navy</u> (Annapolis, Md.: U.S. Naval Institute, 1929).

DA68   Glover, Richard. <u>Britain at Bay: Defence</u>
.G55   <u>Against Bonaparte, 1803-1814</u> (New York:
          Barnes and Noble, 1973).

E355   Hitsman, J. Mackay. <u>The Incredible War of</u>
.H5   <u>1812: A Military History</u> (Toronto: University
          of Toronto Press, 1965).

E353.1   Hoyt, Edwin Palmer. <u>The Tragic Commodore</u>:
.P4H6   <u>The Story of Oliver Hazard Perry</u> (New York:
          Abelard-Schuman, 1966).

JK131   Jensen, Merrell. <u>The Articles of Confedera-</u>
.J4   <u>tion</u> (Madison: University of Wisconsin Press,
          1940).

E183.8   Jones, Wilbur D. <u>The American Problem in</u>
.G7J66   <u>British Diplomacy</u> (Athens: University of
          Georgia Press, 1974).

E335   Knox, Dudley W., ed. <u>Naval Documents Related</u>
.A35   <u>to the United States Wars with the Barbary</u>
          <u>Powers</u>, 7 vols. (Washington: GPO, 1939-1945).

E323   _____, ed. <u>Naval Documents Related to</u>
.U75   <u>the Quasi-War Between the United States and</u>
          <u>France</u>, 7 vols. (Washington: GPO, 1935-1938).

UA23   Kohn, Richard H. <u>Eagle and Sword: The Feder-</u>
.K737   <u>alists and the Creation of the Military</u>
          <u>Establishment in America, 1783-1811</u> (Riverside,
          N.J.: Free Press, 1975).

E382   James Marquis. <u>Andrew Jackson: Portrait of</u>
.J27   <u>a President</u> (Indianapolis: Bobbs-Merrill,
          1937).

E353.1   Lewis, Charles Lee. <u>The Romantic Decatur</u>
.D29L5   (Philadelphia: University of Pennsylvania
          Press, 1937).

E354   Lloyd, Alan. <u>The Scorching of Washington: The</u>
.L55   <u>War of 1812</u> (Washington: Robert B. Luce, 1974).

E354   Lord, Walter. <u>The Dawn's Early Light</u> (New
.L85   York: Norton, 1972).

E182 .P88 M32 McKee, Christopher. *Edward Preble: A Naval Biography, 1761-1807* (Annapolis, Md.: Naval Institute Press, 1972).

E354 .M212 Mahan, A.T. *Sea Power in Its Relation to the War of 1812* (Boston: Little, Brown, 1905).

E355 .M33 Mahon, John K. *The War of 1812* (Gainesville: University of Florida Press, 1972).

E353.1 .D29N5 Nicolay, Helen. *Decatur of the Old Navy* (New York: Appleton-Century, 1942).

E353.1 .R7P28 Paullin, Charles O. *Commodore John Rodgers, Captain, Commodore, and Senior Officer of the American Navy, 1773-1838: A Biography* (Cleveland: Clark, 1910).

E357 .P9 Pratt, Julius. *Expansionists of 1812* (New York: Macmillan, 1925).

E355 .R42 Reilly, Robin. *The British at the Gates: The New Orleans Campaign in the War of 1812* (New York: Putnam, 1974).

E313 .R5 Ritcheson, Charles R. *Aftermath of the Revolution: British Policy toward the United States, 1783-1795* (Dallas: Southern Methodist University Press, 1969).

E360 .R86 Roosevelt, Theodore. *The Naval War of 1812* (New York: Putnam, 1882).

E336.5 .S42 Sears, Louis Martin. *Jefferson and the Embargo* (Durham: Duke University Press, 1927).

E182 .S57 Smelser, Marshall. *The Congress Founds the Navy, 1787-1798* (Notre Dame, Ind.: University of Notre Dame Press, 1959).

E182. .S78 Sprout, Harold and Margaret. *The Rise of American Naval Power, 1776-1918* (Princeton, N.J.: Princeton University Press, 1939).

E302.6 .G16W3 Walters, Raymond, Jr. *Albert Gallatin: Jeffersonian Financier and Diplomat* (New York: Macmillan, 1957).

E335   Watson, Paul Barron. *The Tragic Career of*
.B256   *Commodore James Barron, U.S.N.* (New York:
          Coward-McCann, 1942).

E183.7   White, Patrick C.T. *The Critical Years:*
.W65   *American Foreign Policy, 1793-1823* (New York:
          Wiley, 1970).

E183.8   Wright, J. Leitch, Jr. *Britain and the Ameri-*
.G7W94   *can Frontier, 1783-1815* (Athens: University
          of Georgia Press, 1975).

CHAPTER 8

NOTES

1. The eight were: Thomas Y. Mason, 10 Sept. 1846 to 7 Mar. 1849; William B. Preston, 8 Mar. 1849 to 22 July 1850; William A. Graham, 2 Aug. 1850 to 25 July 1852; John P. Kennedy, 26 July 1852 to 7 Mar. 1853; James C. Dobbin, 8 Mar. 1853 to 6 Mar. 1857; and Isaac Toucey, 7 Mar. 1857 to 6 Mar. 1861.

BIBLIOGRAPHY

F2161   Allen, George W. *Our Navy and the West Indies*
.A48   *Pirates* (Salem, Mass.: Essex Institute, 1929).

E404   Bauer, K. Jack. *The Mexican War, 1846-1848*
.B37   (New York: Macmillan, 1974).

E410   _____. *Surfboats and Horse Marines:*
.B38   *U.S. Naval Operations in the Mexican War,*
          1846-1848 (Annapolis, Md.: U.S. Naval Institute, 1969).

E403   Bayard, Samuel John. *The Life of Commodore*
.1S8B3   *Robert F. Stockton* (New York: Derby and
          Jackson, 1856).

DS740.5   Costin, W.C. *Great Britain and China, 1833-*
.G5C65   *1860* (Oxford: Clarendon Press, 1937, 1968).

JN216   Gash, Norman, comp. *The Age of Peel* [1815-
.G37   1848] (London: Edward Arnold, 1968).

E183.8　　Jones, Wilbur Devereux. *The American Problem*
.G7J66　　*in British Diplomacy, 1841-1861* (Athens:
　　　　　University of Georgia Press, 1974).

GC30　　　Lewis, Charles Lee. *Matthew Fontaine Maury:*
.M4L4　　 *The Pathfinder of the Seas* (Annapolis, Md.:
　　　　　U.S. Naval Institute, 1927).

E353　　　Long, David F. *Nothing Too Daring: A Biography*
.1.P7L6　*of Commodore David Porter, 1780-1843* (Annapolis,
　　　　　Md.: Naval Institute Press, 1970).

E182　　　Meade, Rebecca Paulding. *Life of Hiram Pauld-*
.P32　　　*ing, Rear Admiral, U.S.N.* (New York: Baker &
　　　　　Taylor, 1910).

E182　　　Morison, Samuel E. *"Old Bruin": Commodore*
.P466　　*Matthew C. Perry, 1794-1858* (Boston: Little,
　　　　　Brown, 1967).

E407　　　Rappaport, Armin, ed. *The War with Mexico:*
.R2　　　 *Why Did it Happen*? (Chicago: Rand McNally,
　　　　　1964).

DS755　　 Selby, John Miller. *The Paper Dragon: An*
.S4　　　 *Account of the China Wars, 1840-1900* (New
　　　　　York: Praeger, 1968).

CHAPTER 9

BIBLIOGRAPHY

E591　　　Knox, Dudley W., ed. *Official Records of the*
.U58　　　*Union and Confederate Navies in the War of the*
　　　　　Rebellion. Series I, 27 vols.; Series II, 4
　　　　　vols. (Washington: GPO, 1894-1927).

E469　　　Adams, Ephraim D. *Great Britain and the*
.A25　　　*American Civil War*, 2 vols. (London: Longmans,
　　　　　1925).

E182　　　Ammen, Daniel. *The Old Navy and the New*
.A51　　　(Philadelphia: J.B. Lippincott, 1891).

JX5261 .U6B46	Bernath, Stuart L. <u>Squall Across the Atlantic: American Civil War Prize Cases and Diplomacy</u> (Berkeley: University of California Press, 1970).	

E469
.B57
1968
Bigelow, John. <u>France and the Confederate Navy, 1862-1868</u> (New York: [1888] Bergman Publishers, 1968).

E183
.G7B68
1967b
Bourne, Kenneth. <u>Britain and the Balance of Power in North America, 1815-1908</u> (London: Longmans, 1967).

E470.6
S.B87
Burton, E. Milby. <u>The Siege of Charleston, 1861-1865</u> (Columbia: University of South Carolina Press, 1970).

T40
.E8C6
Church, William C. <u>The Life of John Ericcson</u>, 2 vols. (New York: Scribner, 1890).

E468
.C3
Catton, Bruce. <u>This Hallowed Ground: The Story of the Union Side of the Civil War</u> (Garden City, N.Y.: Doubleday, 1956).

E468
.C29
_____. <u>The Centennial History of the Civil War</u>, 3 vols. (Garden City, N.Y.: Doubleday, 1961-1965).

E672
.C295
_____. <u>Grant Takes Command</u> (Boston: Little, Brown, 1969).

E468
.C293
_____. <u>The Civil War</u> (New York: American Heritage Press, 1971).

E458
C.3
_____, and William Catton, <u>Two Roads to Sumter</u> (New York: McGraw-Hill, 1963).

E487
.C83
Coulter, Ellis Merton. <u>The Confederate States of America, 1861-1865</u> (Baton Rouge: Louisiana State University Press, 1950).

Cullen, Joseph P. <u>The Peninsula Campaign 1862</u> (New York: Bonanza Books, 1973).

E473
.2.D3
Daly, Robert W. <u>How the Merrimac Won</u> (New York: Crowell, 1957).

E467.1 D24D2	Davis, C.H. <u>Life of Charles Henry Davis, Rear Admiral, 1807-1877</u> (Boston: Houghton Mifflin, 1899).
E470 .D4	Deaderick, Barron. <u>Strategy in the Civil War</u> (Harrisburg, Pa.: Military Service Publishing Service, 1946).
E468 .D65	Donald, David. ed. <u>Why the North Won the Civil War</u> (Baton Rouge: Louisiana State University Press, 1960).
E467.I A2D8	Duberman, Martin B. <u>Charles Francis Adams, 1807-1886</u> (Boston: Houghton Mifflin, 1961).
E182 .E92	Evans, Robley D. <u>A Sailor's Log</u> (New York: D. Appleton, 1901).
E591 .G67	Gosnell, Harpur Allen. <u>Guns on the Western Waters: The Story of River Gunboats in the Civil War</u> (Baton Rouge: Louisiana State University Press, 1949).
E591 .D9 1967	Hayes, John D., ed. <u>Samuel Francis Du Pont: A Selection from His Civil War Letters</u>, 3 vols. (Ithaca: Cornell University Press, 1969).
E467.1 .F68H7	Hoppin, James Mason. <u>Life of Andrew Hull Foote</u> (New York: Harper, 1874).
E470 .B329	Johnson, Robert U. and C.C. Buell, eds. <u>Battles and Leaders of the Civil War</u>, 4 vols. (New York: Century Co., 1887-1888).
E591 .J6	Jones, Virgil Carrington. <u>The Civil War at Sea</u>, 3 vols. (New York: Holt, Rinehart, Winston, 1960-1962).
E467.1 .F23L48	Lewis, Charles Lee. <u>David Glasgow Farragut: Our First Admiral</u> (Annapolis, Md.: U.S. Naval Institute, 1943).
E591 .M32	Mahan, Alfred T. <u>The Gulf and Inland Waters</u> (New York: Scribner, 1883).
E467.1 F23M2	_____. <u>Admiral Farragut</u> (New York: Appleton, 1892).

E591   Merrill, James M. *The Rebel Shore: The Story*
.M48   *of Union Sea Power in the Civil War* (Boston: Little, Brown, 1957).

E470   _____. *Battle Flags South: The Story of*
.8.M46   *the Civil War Navies on Western Waters* (Rutherford, N.J.: Fairleigh Dickinson University Press, 1970).

E470   Mitchell, Joseph B. *Decisive Battles of the*
.M69   *Civil War* (New York: Putnam, 1955).

E415   Nevins, Allan. *The Ordeal of the Union*,
.7.N4   2 vols. (New York: Scribner, 1947).

E415   _____. *The Emergence of Lincoln*, 2 vols.
.7.N38   (New York: Scribner, 1950).

E468   _____. *The War for the Union*, 4 vols.
.N43   (New York: Scribner, 1959-1971).

E488   Owsley, Frank L., Harriet Owsley, ed., 2d ed.
.O85   *King Cotton Diplomacy* (Chicago: University of
1959   Chicago Press, 1959).

V820   Owsley, Frank L., Jr. *The C.S.S. Florida: Her*
.O9   *Building and Operations* (Philadelphia: University of Pennsylvania Press, 1965).

E467   Niven, John. *Gideon Welles: Lincoln's Secre-*
.1W46N5 *tary of the Navy* (New York: Oxford University Press, 1973).

E476   Parker, Foxhall A. *The Battle of Mobile Bay*
.85.P24   *and the Capture of Forts Powell, Gaines, and Morgan* (Boston: Williams, 1878).

E591   Porter, David D. *Naval History of the Civil*
.P84   *War* (New York: Sherman Publishing Co., 1886).

E601   _____. *Incidents and Anecdotes of the*
.P74   *Civil War* (New York: Appleton, 1885).

E591   Pratt, Fletcher. *Civil War on Western Waters*
.P87   (New York: Holt, 1956).

E473   _____. *The Monitor and the Merrimac*
.2.P7   (New York: Random House, 1951).

E468 .R26	Randall, James G. *The Civil War and Reconstruction* (Boston: Heath, 1937).
E457 .R2	——————. *Lincoln the President*, 4 vols. (New York: Dodd, Mead, 1945—1955).
E468 .R47	Rhodes, James Ford. *History of the Civil War, 1861-1865* (New York: Macmillan, 1917).
E596 .R65	Robinson, William M. *The Confederate Privateers* (New Haven: Yale University Press, 1928).
E596 .S31	Scharf, J. Thomas. *History of the Confederate States Navy* (New York: Rogers and Isherwood, 1887).
E599 .A3S64	Semmes, Raphael. *Memoirs of Service Afloat During the War Between the States* (New York: Rogers and Isherwood, 1887).
V63 .I8S5	Sloan, Edward William. *Benjamin Franklin Isherwood, Naval Engineer: The Years as Engineer-in-Chief* (Annapolis, Md.: U.S. Naval Institute, 1965).
E591 .N32	Soley, James R. *The Blockade and the Cruisers* (New York: Scribner, 1883).
E182 .S78	Sprout, Harold and Margaret. *The Rise of American Sea Power, 1776-1918* (Princeton, N.J.: Princeton University Press, 1939).
E471 .IS9	Swanberg, W.A. *First Blood: The Story of Fort Sumter* (New York: Scribner, 1957).
E591 .F79	Thompson, Robert Means and Richard Wainwright, eds. *Confidential Correspondence of Gustavus Vasa Fox*, 2 vols. (New York: DeVinne Press, 1920).
E459 .T7	Trefouse, Hans L., comp. *The Causes of the Civil War: Institutional Failure or Human Blunder* (New York: Holt, Rinehart, & Winston, 1971).
E415 .9S4V3	Van Deusen, Glyndon G. *William Henry Seward* (New York: Oxford University Press, 1967).

E600 .V3   Vandiver, Frank E. *Confederate Blockade Running Through Bermuda, 1861-1865* (Austin: University of Texas Press, 1947).

E468 .W44   Welles, Gideon. *The Diary of Gideon Welles*, 3 vols. (Boston: Houghton Mifflin, 1911).

E467 .1P78W4   West, Richard S. *The Second Admiral: A Life of David Dixon Porter* (New York: Coward-McCann, 1937).

E467.1 .W46W4   _____. *Lincoln's Navy Department* (Indianapolis: Bobbs-Merrill, 1943).

E591 .W44   _____. *Mr. Lincoln's Navy* (New York: Longmans, 1957).

E605 .W8   Wise, John S. *The End of an Era* (Boston: Houghton Mifflin, 1899).

Baxter, James P. "The British Government and Neutral Rights, 1861-1865," *American Historical Review* 34 (Oct. 1928): 9-29.

Bearss, Edwin C. "The Ironclads at Fort Donelson: The Ironclads Sail for the Cumberland (Part I)," *Register of the Kentucky Historical Society* (Jan. 1976): 1-9; "The Confederates Prepare for the Ironclads (Part II)," ibid. (Apr. 1976): 73-84; and "The Ironclads Fail (Part III)," ibid. (July 1976): 167-91.

Melvin, Philip. "Stephen Russell Mallory, Southern Naval Statesman," *Journal of Southern History* 10 (1944): 137-60.

CHAPTER 10

BIBLIOGRAPHY

VA454 .A66   Archibald, E.H.H. *The Metal Fighting Ship in the Royal Navy 1860-1970* (New York: ARCO, 1971).

VM20 .B3   Barnaby, K.C. *100 Years of Specialized Shipbuilding and Engineering* (London: Hutchinson, 1964).

V5V .B26	Barnaby, Sir Nathaniel. <u>Naval Development of the Century</u> (London: W. & R. Chambers, 1904).
V799 .B3	Baxter, James P. <u>The Introduction of the Ironclad Warship</u> (Cambridge: Harvard University Press, 1933).
VA55 .B48	Bennett, Frank M. <u>The Steam Navy of the United States: A History of the Growth of the Steam Vessel of War in the U.S. Navy, and of the Naval Engineer Corps</u> (Pittsburg: W.T. Nicholson, 1896).
V25 .B7	Brodie, Bernard. <u>Sea Power in the Machine Age</u> (Princeton, N.J.: Princeton University Press, 1941).
E664 .T72C66	Cooling, Benjamin Franklin. <u>Benjamin Franklin Tracy: Father of the Modern American Fighting Navy</u> (Hamden, Conn.: Archon Books, 1973).
V63 .E85A3	Evans, Holden A. <u>One Man's Fight for a Better Navy</u> (New York: Dodd, Mead, 1940).
E182 .E92	Evans, Robley D. <u>A Sailor's Log: Recollections of Forty Years of Naval Life</u> (New York: Appleton, 1901).
E182 .E934	Falk, Edwin A. <u>Fighting Bob Evans</u> (New York: Cape and Smith, 1931).
E182 .F54	Fiske, Bradley A. <u>From Midshipman to Rear-Admiral</u> (New York: Century, 1919).
E182 .L92	Gleaves, Albert. <u>Life and Letters of Rear-Admiral Stephen B. Luce, U.S. Navy: Founder of the Naval War College</u> (New York: Putnam, 1925).
V855 .W5G7 1975	Gray, Edwyn. <u>The Devil's Device: The Story of Robert Whitehead, Inventor of the Torpedo</u> (London: Seeley, Service, 1975).
E182 .H15	Hagan, Kenneth J. <u>American Gunboat Diplomacy and the Old Navy, 1877-1899</u> (Westport, Conn.: Greenwood, 1973).

Q11   Hammett, Hugh B. *Hilary Abner Herbert: A*
.P612   *Southerner Returns to the Union* (Philadelphia:
vol.110   American Philosophical Society, 1976).

E182   Hayes, John Daniel and John B. Hattendorf.
.L92H39   *The Writings of Stephen B. Luce* (Newport:
          Naval War College, 1975).

V765   Hovgaard, George William. *Modern History of*
.H6   *Warships* (London: E. & F. Spon, 1920).

E182   Herrick, Walter R. *The American Naval Revo-*
.H46   *lution* (Baton Rouge: LSUP, 1967).

E664   Hirsch, Mark D. *William C. Whitney: Modern*
.W613H5   *Warwick* (New York: Dodd, Mead, 1948).

E727   Long, John D. *The New American Navy*, 2 vols.
.L84   (New York: Outlook Co., 1903).

DA881   Marder, Arthur. *The Anatomy of British Sea*
.M3   *Power; A History of British Naval Policy in*
          the Pre-Dreadnought Era, 1880-1905 (New York:
          Knopf, 1940).

E697   Nevins, Allan. *Grover Cleveland: A Study in*
.N465   *Courage* (New York: Dodd, Mead, 1931).

E467.1   Niven, John. *Gideon Welles: Lincoln's Secre-*
.W46N5   *tary of the Navy* (New York: Oxford University
          Press, 1973).

V65.533   Padfield, Peter. *Aim Straight: A Biography of*
.P3   *Admiral Sir Percy Scott* (London: Hodder and
          Stoughton, 1966).

E182   Puleston, William D. *Mahan, The Life and Work*
.M256   *of Captain Alfred Thayer Mahan* (New Haven:
          Yale University Press, 1939).

E664   Richardson, Leon B. *William E. Chandler:*
.C38R5   *Republican* (New York: Dodd, Mead, 1940).

E182   Seager, Robert II and Doris D. Maguire, eds.
.M24   *The Letters and Papers of Alfred Thayer Mahan*
          (Annapolis, Md.: Naval Institute Press, 1975).

              Seager, Robert II. <u>Alfred Thayer Mahan: The Man and His Letters</u> (Annapolis, Md.: Naval Institute Press, 1977).

V63 .I8S5   Sloan, Edward William. <u>Benjamin Franklin Isherwood, Naval Engineer: The Years as Engineer-in-Chief, 1861-1869</u> (Annapolis, Md.: Naval Institute Press, 1975).

E182 .S78   Sprout, Harold and Margaret. <u>The Rise of American Naval Power, 1776-1918</u> (Princeton, N.J.: Princeton University Press, 1939).

VM140 .R6S9   Swann, Leonard Alexander. <u>John Roach, Maritime Entrepreneur: The Years as Naval Constructor, 1882-1886</u> (Annapolis, Md.: U.S. Naval Institute, 1965).

              Symonds, Craig L., ed. <u>Charleston Blockade: The Journals of John B. Marchand, U.S. Navy, 1861-1862</u> (Newport: Naval War College, 1976).

E467.1 .P78W4   West, Richard S. <u>The Second Admiral: A Life of David Dixon Porter, 1813-1891</u> (New York: Coward-McCann, 1937).

E467.1 .W46W4   _____. <u>Gideon Welles: Lincoln's Navy Department</u> (Indianapolis: Bobbs-Merrill, 1943).

              Buhl, Lance Crowther. "The Smooth Water Navy: American Naval Policy and Politics, 1865-1876: (Ph. D. diss., Harvard University, 1968).

              Spector, Ronald. "Professors of War: The Naval War College and the Modern American Navy" (Ph. D. diss. Yale University, 1967).

              Allard, Dean C. "The Influence of the U.S. Navy upon the American Steel Industry, 1880-1900" (M.A. thesis, Georgetown University, 1959).

CHAPTER 11

BIBLIOGRAPHY

E715 .A51   _____. American-Spanish War. A History by the War Leaders (Norwich, Conn.: Charles C. Haskell and Son, 1899).

E723 .B47   Benton, Elbert Jay. International Law and Diplomacy of the Spanish-American War (Baltimore: Johns Hopkins Press, 1908).

E182 .B73   Braisted, William R. The U.S. Navy in the Pacific, 1897-1909 (Austin: University of Texas Press, 1958).

E183.8 .S7C4   Chadwick, French Ensor. The Relations of the United States and Spain: Diplomacy (New York: Scribner's, 1909).

E715 .C43   _____. The Relations of the United States and Spain: The Spanish-American War, 2 vols. (New York: Scribner's, 1911).

E182 .C57   Clark, Charles E. My Fifty Years in the Navy (Boston: Little, Brown, 1917).

E725.3 .C6   Cosmas, Graham A. An Army for Empire: The United States Army in the Spanish-American War (Columbia: University of Missouri Press, 1971).

E182 .W138C8   Cummings, Damon E. Admiral Richard Wainwright and the United States Fleet (Washington: Navy Department, 1962).

E714.6 .D51D52   Dewey, George. Autobiography of George Dewey: Admiral of the Navy (New York: Scribner's, 1913).

E182 .E92   Evans, Robley D. A Sailor's Log: Recollections of Forty Years of Naval Life (New York: Appleton, 1901).

E182 .F54   Fiske, Bradley A. From Midshipman to Rear Admiral (New York: Century, 1919).

DS679 .F5   _____. Wartime in Manila (Boston: Gorham Press, 1913).

E727 .G73	Graham, George Edward. <u>Schley and Santiago</u> (Chicago: Conkey, 1902).
E661.7 .G7	Grenville, John A.S., and George B. Young, <u>Politics, Strategy, and American Diplomacy</u> (New Haven: Yale University Press, 1966).
E727 .H68	Hobson, Richmond Pearson. <u>The Sinking of the Merrimac</u> (New York: Century Co., 1899).
E743 .H632	Hofstadter, Richard. "Cuba, the Philippines, and Manifest Destiny," <u>The Paranoid Style in American Politics and Other Essays</u> (New York: Knopf, 1965).
E711.6 .L4	Leech, Margaret. <u>In the Days of McKinley</u> (New York: Harper, 1959).
E715 .L82	Lodge, Henry Cabot. <u>The War with Spain</u> (New York: Harper, 1899).
E727 .L84	Long, John D. <u>The New American Navy</u>, 2 vols. (New York: Outlook Co., 1903).
E664 .L84A3	Long, Margaret, ed. <u>The Journal of John D. Long</u> (Rindge, NH: R. Smith, 1956).
E182 .M21	Maclay, Edgar Stanton. <u>A History of the United States Navy from 1775 to 1900</u>. New and enl. ed., 3 vols. (New York: Appleton, 1901).
E727 .M21	Mahan, A.T. <u>Lessons of the War with Spain and Other Articles</u> (Boston: Little, Brown, 1899).
E715 .M76	Millis, Walter. <u>The Martial Spirit: A Study of Our War With Spain</u> (Boston: Houghton, Mifflin, 1931).
E711.6 .M7	Morgan, H. Wayne. <u>William McKinley and His America</u> (Syracuse: Syracuse University Press, 1963).
E715 .M85	_____. <u>America's Road to Empire: The War with Spain and Overseas Expansion</u> (New York: Wiley, 1965).

E727 .P25	Parker, James. <u>Rear-Admirals Schley, Sampson, and Cervera</u> (New York: McNeale Publishing Co., 1910).
E713 .P895	Pratt, Julius W. <u>Expansionists of 1898</u> (Baltimore: Johns Hopkins Press, 1936).
E7216 .R5	Rickover, H. G. <u>How the Battleship Maine Was Destroyed</u> (Washington: Department of the Navy, Naval History Division, 1976).
E182 .S34	Schley, Winfield Scott. <u>Forty-five Years Under the Flag</u> (New York: Appleton, 1904).
V63 .S4A3	Schroeder, Seaton. <u>A Half Century of Naval Service</u> (New York: Appleton, 1923).
E714.6 .D51568	Spector, Ronald. <u>Admiral of the New Empire: The Life and Career of George Dewey</u> (Baton Rougle: Louisiana State University Press, 1974).
E727 .S739	Spears, John Randolph. <u>Our Navy in the War with Spain</u> (New York: Scribner's, 1898).
E721 .6W.4	Weems, John Edward. <u>The Fate of the Maine</u> (New York: Holt, 1958).
E714.5 .W4	West, Richard S. <u>Admirals of American Empire: The Combined Story of George Dewey, Alfred Thayer Mahan, Winfield Scott Schley, and William Thomas Sampson</u> (Indianapolis: Bobbs-Merrill, 1948).
E727 .W74	Wilson, Herbert W. <u>The Downfall of Spain: Naval History of the Spanish-American War</u> (Boston: Little, Brown, 1900).
E727 .S315	<u>Record of Proceedings of a Court of Inquiry in the Case of Rear-Admiral Winfield S. Schley, U.S. Navy, Convened at the Navy-Yard, Washington, D.C., September 12, 1901</u>, 2 vols. (Washington: GPO, 1902).

CHAPTER 12

BIBLIOGRAPHY

E757 .B4   Beale, Howard K. *Theodore Roosevelt and the Rise of America to World Power* (Baltimore: Johns Hopkins Press, 1956).

E182 .B73   Braisted, William R. *The United States Navy in the Pacific, 1897-1909* (Austin: University of Texas Press, 1958).

V25 .B7 1943   Brodie, Bernard. *Sea Power in the Machine Age*, 2d ed. (Princeton, N.J.: Princeton University Press, 1943).

F1418 .C22   Callcott, William H. *The Caribbean Policy of the United States, 1890-1920* (Baltimore: Johns Hopkins Press, 1942).

E183 .8G7 C28   Campbell, Charles S. *Anglo-American Understanding, 1898-1903* (Baltimore: Johns Hopkins Press, 1957).

E182 .W138 C8   Cummings, Damon. *Richard Wainwright and the United States Fleet* (Washington: Navy Department, 1962).

E664 .H41D3   Dennett, Tyler, *John Hay* (New York: Dodd, Mead, 1933).

E183.8 .J3E8   Esthus, Raymond A. *Theodore Roosevelt and Japan* (Seattle: University of Washington Press, 1966).

E182 .E91   Evans, Robley D. *A Sailor's Log* (New York: D. Appleton, 1901).

E182 E.172   _____. *An Admiral's Log* (New York: D. Appleton, 1910).

E182 .E934   Falk, Edwin R. *Fighting Bob Evans* (New York: Cape and Smith, 1931).

E182 .F54   Fiske, Bradley A. *From Midshipman to Rear-Admiral* (New York: Century Co., 1919).

V103 .F4	_____.	*The Navy as a Fighting Machine* (New York: Scribner's, 1916).

V103　　　　　_____. *The Navy as a Fighting Machine*
.F4　　　　　(New York: Scribner's, 1916).

V750　　　　Fletcher, R. A. *Warships and Their Story*
.F6　　　　　(London: Cassell, 1911).

D5518　　　Griswold, A. Whitney. *The Far Eastern Policy*
.8G75　　　*of the United States* (New York: Harcourt, Brace, 1938).

E757　　　　Harbaugh, William H. *Power and Responsibility*:
.H28　　　　*The Life and Times of Theodore Roosevelt* (New York: Farrar, Straus and Cudahy, 1961).

E183.8　　Herwig, Holger H. *Politics of Frustration*:
.G3H44　　*The United States in German Naval Planning, 1889-1941* (Boston: Little, Brown, 1976).

E756　　　　Hill, Howard C. *Roosevelt and the Caribbean*
.H65　　　　(Chicago: University of Chicago Press, 1927).

V765　　　　Hovgaard, George W. *Modern History of Warships*
.H6　　　　　(London: E. and F.N. Spon, 1920).

E664　　　　Howe, Mark A. De Wolfe. *George von Lengerke*
.M573H5　*Meyer: His Life and Public Services* (New York: Dodd, Mead, 1919).

TA140　　　Hughes, Thomas Parke. *Elmer A. Sperry: Inventor*
.S68H79　*and Engineer* (Baltimore: Johns Hopkins Press, 1971).

E664　　　　Leopold, Richard W. *Elihu Root and the Con-*
.R7L4　　　*servative Tradition* (Boston: Little, Brown, 1954).

E727　　　　Long, John D. *The New American Navy*, 2 vols.
.L84　　　　(New York: Outlook Co., 1903).

DA88　　　　Marder, Arthur. *The Anatomy of British Sea*
.M3　　　　　*Power: A History of British Naval Policy in the Pre-dreadnought Era, 1880-1905* (New York: Knopf, 1940).

E756　　　　Mowry, George E. *The Era of Theodore Roose-*
.M85　　　　*velt, 1900-1912* (New York: Harper, 1958).

E664 W594 N52   Nevins, Allan. <u>Henry White: Thirty Years of American Diplomacy</u> (New York: Harper, 1930).

E182 .O34   O'Gara, Gordon C. <u>Theodore Roosevelt and the Rise of the Modern Navy</u> (Princeton, N.J.: Princeton University Press, 1943).

Patterson, David S. <u>Toward a Warless World: The Travail of the American Peace Movement, 1887-1914</u> (Bloomington: Indiana University Press, 1976).

E183.8 .G7P42   Perkins, Bradford. <u>The Great Rapprochement: England and the United States, 1895-1914</u> (New York: Atheneum, 1968).

E757 .P96   Pringle, Henry F. <u>Theodore Roosevelt: A Biography</u> (New York: Harcourt, Brace, 1931).

DA88 .1.S3A5   Scott, Percy. <u>Fifty Years in the Royal Navy</u> (London: J. Murray, 1919).

E714.6 .D51568   Spector, Ronald. <u>Admiral of the New Empire: The Life and Career of George Dewey</u> (Baton Rouge: Louisiana State University Press, 1974).

E182 .S78   Sprout, Harold and Margaret. <u>The Rise of American Naval Power, 1776-1918</u> (Princeton, N.J.: Princeton University Press, 1939).

V63 .S75 A3   Stirling, Yates. <u>Sea Duty: The Memoirs of a Fighting Admiral</u> (New York: Putnam's, 1939).

D511 .W657   Williamson, Samuel R. <u>The Politics of Grand Strategy: Britain and France Prepare for War, 1904-1914</u> (Cambridge, Mass.: Harvard University Press, 1969).

Costello, Daniel J. "Planning for War: A History of the General Board of the Navy, 1900-1914" (Ph. D. diss., Fletcher School of Diplomacy, 1958).

Kelly, Patrick J. "The Naval Policy of Imperial Germany" (Ph. D. diss., Georgetown University, 1970).

U420　　　Spector, Ronald. "Professors of War: The
.L1　　　　Naval War College and the Modern American
S64　　　　Navy" (Ph. D. diss., Yale University, 1967).

　　　　　Coletta, Paolo E. "The Perils of Invention:
　　　　　Bradley A. Fiske and the Torpedo Plane,"
　　　　　American Neptune 37 (June 1977): 111-27.

　　　　　Hattendorf, John. "Technology and Strategy:
　　　　　A Study in the Professional Thought of the
　　　　　U.S. Navy, 1900-1916," U.S. Naval War College
　　　　　Review 24 (Nov. 1971): 25-48.

　　　　　Little, William McCarty. "The Strategic Naval
　　　　　War Game or Chart Maneuvers," U.S. Naval
　　　　　Institute Proceedings 38 (Dec. 1912): 1213-34.

E664　　　Wiegand, Wayne August. "Patrician in the Pro-
.M573　　　gressive Era: A Biography of George von
W54　　　　Lengerke Meyer" (Ph. D. diss., Carbondale:
　　　　　Southern Illinois University, 1974).

CHAPTER 13

BIBLIOGRAPHY

D568　　　Ashmead-Bartless, Ellis. The Uncensored
.3A75　　　Dardanelles (London: Hutchinson, 1928).

D581　　　Bacon, Admiral Sir Reginald. The Dover Patrol,
.B2　　　　1915-1917, 2 vols. (New York: George H. Doran,
　　　　　1919).

G21　　　　Baldwin, Hanson W. World War I: An Outline
.B24　　　History (New York: Harper & Row, 1962).

D582　　　Bennett, Geoffrey M. Coronel and the Falk-
.F2B4　　　lands (New York: Macmillan, 1962).

D772　　　_____. Battle of the River Plate (London:
.G7B45　　Allen, 1972).

D580　　　_____. Naval Battles of the First World
.B4　　　　War (New York: Scribner, 1968).

D582　　　_____. The Battle of Jutland (London:
J8B53　　　Batsford, 1964).

D568 .3.B87	Bush, Eric W. Gallipoli (New York: St. Martin, 1975).
D522 .A52	By the Editors of American Heritage. Narrative by S.L.A. Marshall. The American Heritage History of World War I (New York: American Heritage Pub. Co., 1964).
D568 .3C3	Callwell, Sir Charles E. The Dardanelles, 2d ed. (Boston: Houghton Mifflin, 1924).
DA89.1 B4C5	Chalmers, William S. Life and Letters of David, Earl Beatty (London: Hodder & Stoughton, 1951).
D581 .C45	Chatterton, Edward Kemble. The Auxiliary Patrol (London: Sidgwick & Jackson, 1923).
D27 .C5	_____. Battles by Sea (London: Sidgwick & Jackson, 1925).
D581 .C5	_____. Q Ships and Their Story (London: Sidgwick & Jackson, 1922).
D581 .C53	_____. The Sea Raiders (London: Hurst & Blackett, 1931).
D581 .C46	_____. The Big Blockade (London: Hurst & Blackett, 1932).
D521 .C5	Churchill, Winston. The World Crisis, 4 vols. (New York: Scribner, 1927-1930).
D580 .C75	Corbett, Sir Julian and Henry Newbolt. History of the Great War, Based on Official Documents, 5 vols. (London: Longmans, 1920-1931).
D581 .F3	Fayle, C. Ernest. Seaborne Trade, 3 vols. (London: J. Murray, 1920-1924).
VA454 .F4	Ferraby, H.C. The Grand Fleet (London: Jenkins, 1917).
D580 .F75	Frothingham, Thomas G. The Naval History of the World War, 3 vols. (Cambridge: Harvard University Press, 1924-1926).

D591   Gibson, Richard H. and Maurice Prendergast.
.G5   The German Submarine War, 1914-1918 (London:
         Constable and Co., 1931).

D582   Gibson, Langhorne, and J.E.T. Harper. The
.J8G35   Riddle of Jutland (New York: Coward-McCann,
         1934).

D593   Gray, Edwyn. The Underwater War: Submarines
.G7   1914-1918 (New York: Scribner, 1971).

D593   _____. A Damned Un-English Weapon: The
.G7   Story of British Submarine Warfare, 1914-1918
         (London: Seely, Service, 1971).

D591   _____. The Killing Time: The U-boat War
.G68   1914-1918 (New York: Scribner, 1972).

D580   Guichard, Louis. The Naval Blockade, 1914-
.G98   1918. Trans. and ed. by Christopher R. Turner.
         (New York: Appleton-Century-Crofts, 1930).

D568   Hamilton, Ian S.M. Gallipoli Diary, 2 vols.
.3.H25   (New York: George H. Doran, 1920).

D521   Hayes, Grace P. World War I: A Compact History
.H353   (New York: Hawthorn Books, 1972).

D568   Higgins, Trumbull. Winston Churchill and the
3.H5   Dardanelles (New York: Macmillan, 1963).

         Hoyt, Edwin Palmer. The Karlsruhe Affair
         (London: Arthur Baker, 1976).

D568   James, Robert. Gallipoli (London: Batsford,
.3J3   1965).

D581   Jellicoe, Lord John R. The Crisis of the
.J36   Naval War (London: Cassell, 1920).

D581   _____. The Grand Fleet 1914-1916 (New
.J4   York: George H. Doran, 1919).

D581   Keyes, Lord Roger J.B. The Naval Memoirs of
.K382   Admiral of the Fleet Sir Roger Keyes; Scapa
         Flow to Dover Straits (New York: Dutton, 1935).

D532 .G7K63	Kopp, George. *Two Lone Ships: Goeben and Breslau* (London: Hutchinson, 1931).
D511 .L19	Lafore, Laurence D. *The Long Fuse: An Interpretation of the Origins of World War I* (Philadelphia: Lippincott, 1965).
D397 .L28	Langer, William L. *European Alliances and Alignments, 1871-1890* (New York: Knopf, 1966).
D397 .L282	_____. *The Diplomacy of Imperialism, 1890-1902* (New York: Knopf, 1935).
D570 .45A5	McClellan, Edwin N. *The U.S. Marine Corps in the World War* (Washington: GPO, 1920, 1968).
D582 .G7M3	McLaughlin, Redmond. *The Escape of the GOEBEN: Prelude to Gallipoli* (New York: Scribner, 1974).
VA454 .M35	Marder, Arthur J. *From Dreadnought to Scapa Flow: The Royal Navy in the Fisher Era*, 3 vols. (New York: Oxford University Press, 1961-1966).
VA454 .M345	_____. *From the Dardanelles to Oran: Studies of the Royal Navy in War and Peace, 1915-1940* (New York: Oxford University Press, 1974).
D568 .3M3	Masefield, John. *Gallipoli* (New York: Macmillan, 1916).
D521 .M46	Maurice, Sir Frederick. *Lessons of Allied Cooperation: Naval Military and Air, 1914-1918* (New York: Oxford University Press, 1942).
D568 .3M59	Moorehead, Alan. *Gallipoli* (New York: Harper, 1956).
DD101 .5.R553	Ritter, Gerhard. *The Schlieffen Plan: Critique of a Myth* (London: World, 1958).
D582 .F257	Rothwell, Victor Howard. *British War Aims and Peace Diplomacy, 1914-1918* (Oxford: Clarendon Press, 1971).

D581 .S25   Scheer, Reinhard. *Germany's High Seas Fleet in the World War* (London: Cassell, 1920).

D581 .S33   Schubert, Paul. and Langhorne Gibson. *The Death of a Fleet* (New York: Coward-McCann, 1952).

V163 .S3   Schurman, Donald M. *The Education of a Navy: British Naval Strategic Thought, 1867-1914* (London: Cassell, 1965).

DA88 .1.S3   Scott, Sir Percy. *Fifty Years in the Royal Navy* (New York: George H. Doran, 1919).

D581 .S5   Siney, Marion C. *The Allied Blockade of Germany, 1914-1916* (Ann Arbor, Mich.: University of Michigan Press, 1957).

D522 .T3   Taylor, A.J.P. *Illustrated History of the First World War* (New York: Putnam, 1964).

DD231 .T5A5   Tirpitz, Alfred von. *My Memoirs*, 2 vols. (New York: Dodd, Mead, 1919).

DA47.2 .W6   Woodward, Ernest L. *Great Britain and the German Navy* (Oxford: Clarendon Press, 1935).

CHAPTER 14

BIBLIOGRAPHY

D619 .B25   Bailey, Thomas A. *The United States and the Neutrals, 1917-1918* (Baltimore: Johns Hopkins Press, 1942).

E767 .B16   Baker, Ray Stannard. *Woodrow Wilson: Life and Letters*, 8 vols. (Garden City, N.Y.: Doubleday, Doran, 1927-1939).

D590 .B4   Belknap, Reginald R. *The Yankee Mining Squadron: Or Laying the North Sea Mine Barrage* (Annapolis, Md., U.S. Naval Institute, 1920).

E766 .B95   Buehrig, Edward H. *Woodrow Wilson and the Balance of Power* (Bloomington: Indiana University Press, 1955).

HC106 .2.C67	Clarkson, Grosvenor. *Industrial America in the World War* (Boston: Houghton-Mifflin, 1923).
VC553 .C6	Clephane, Lewis P. *History of the Naval Overseas Transport Service in World War I* (Washington: Naval History Division, 1969).
D619 .C63	Cohen, Warren I., ed. *Intervention, 1917: Why America Fought* (Lexington, Mass.: Heath, 1966).
E664 .B87C55	Coletta, Paolo E. *William Jennings Bryan: Progressive Politician and Moral Statesman, 1909-1915* (Lincoln: University of Nebraska Press, 1969).
E766 .D29	Cronon, E. David, ed. *The Cabinet Diaries of Josephus Daniels, 1913-1921* (Lincoln: University of Nebraska Press, 1963).
D570 .75C7	Crowell, Benedict and Robert F. Wilson. *The Armies of Industry*, 5 vols. (New Haven: Yale University Press, 1921).
E766 .D3	Daniels, Josephus. *The Wilson Era: Years of Peace, 1910-1917* (Chapel Hill: University of North Carolina Press, 1944).
E766 .D33	_____. *The Wilson Era: Years of War and After, 1917-1923* (Chapel Hill: University of North Carolina Press, 1946).
E182 .F54	Fiske, Bradley A. *From Midshipman to Rear-Admiral* (New York: Century, 1919).
E664 .P15H4	Hendrick, Burton J. *The Life and Letters of Walter H. Page*, 3 vols. (Garden City, N.Y.: Doubleday, Page, 1922-1925).
D644 .H7	House, Edward M. and Harris Seymour, eds. *What Really Happened at Paris* (New York: Scribner, 1921).
VM23 .H8	Hurley, Edward N. *The Bridge to France* (Philadelphia and London: J.B. Lippincott Co., 1927).

D589 .U6K6	Kittredge, Tracy. *Naval Lessons of the Great War* (New York: Doubleday, Page, 1921).
D589 .U6L4	Leighton, John L. *SIMSADUS: London: The American Navy in Europe* (New York: Holt, 1920).
E766 .L5	Link, Arthur S. *Woodrow Wilson and the Progressive Era, 1910-1917* (New York: Harper, 1954).
E767 .L65 vol.3	_____. *Wilson: The Struggle for Neutrality, 1914-1915* (Princeton, N.J.: Princeton University Press, 1960).
E767 .L65 vol.4	_____. *Wilson: Confusions and Crises, 1915-1916* (Princeton, N.J.: Princeton University Press, 1964).
E767 .L65 vol.5	_____. *Wilson: Campaigns for Progressivism and Peace, 1916-1917* (Princeton, N.J.: Princeton University Press, 1965).
D642 .M36	Maurice, Sir Frederick B. *The Armistice of 1918* (New York: Oxford University Press, 1943).
D619 .M383	May, Ernest. *The World War and American Isolation, 1914-1917* (Cambridge, Mass.: Harvard University Press, 1959).
D619 .M47	Millis, Walter. *Road to War: America, 1914-1917* (Boston: Houghton Mifflin, 1935).
E748 .S52M6	Morison, Elting E. *Admiral Sims and the Modern American Navy* (Boston: Houghton Mifflin, 1942).
D619 .M64	Morrisey, Alice M. *The American Defense of Neutral Rights, 1914-1917* (Cambridge: Harvard University Press, 1939).
D570 .P32	Palmer, Frederick. *Newton D. Baker: America at War* (New York: Dodd, Mead, 1931).
D619 .S435	Seymour, Charles. *American Neutrality, 1914-1917* (New Haven: Yale University Press, 1935).

| E766 .H85 | _____, ed., The Intimate Papers of Colonel House, 4 vols. (Boston: Houghton Mifflin, 1926-1928). |

| D589 U656 | Sims, William S. and Burton J. Hendrick. The Victory at Sea (New York: Doubleday, Page, 1920). |

| E741 .S63 | Slosson, Preston William. The Great Crusade and After, 1914-1928 (New York: Macmillan, 1930). |

| E768 .S62 | _____. The Great Departure: The United States and World War I (New York: Wiley, 1965). |

| D619 .T32 | Tansill, Charles C. America Goes to War (Boston: Little, Brown, 1938). |

| D544 .T7 | Trask, David F. The United States in the Supreme War Council: American War Aims and Inter-Allied Strategy, 1917-1918 (Middletown, Conn.: Wesleyan University Press, 1961). |

| D611 .T73 | _____. Captains and Cabinets: Anglo-American Naval Relations, 1917-1918 (Columbia: University of Missouri Press, 1972). |

| D511 .T77 | Tuchman, Barbara. The Zimmermann Telegram (New York: Viking, 1958). |

| D530 .T8 | _____. The Guns of August (New York: Macmillan, 1962). |

| D589 .U5A4 No.2 | U.S. Office of Naval Records. The North Barrage and Other Mining Activities (Washington: GPO, 1920). |

U.S. Navy Department, Office of Naval Intelligence (Historical Section). The American Naval Planning Section, London (Washington: GPO, 1923).

| VF23 .A6 1918 | U.S. Bureau of Ordnance. Navy Ordnance Activities, World War 1917-1918 (Washington: GPO, 1920). |

Lundeberg, Philip K. "The German Naval Critique of the U-boat Campaign, 1915-1918," *Military Affairs* 27 (1963): 109-13.

_____. "Undersea Warfare and Allied Strategy in World War I: Part 1: To 1916," *The Smithsonian Journal of History* 1 (Autumn 1966): 1-30, and "Part II. 1916-1918," ibid. (Winter 1966): 49-72.

Smith, Daniel M. "National Interest and American Intervention, 1917: An Historiographical Appraisal," *Journal of American History* 52 (June 1965): 5-24.

CHAPTER 15

BIBLIOGRAPHY

D770 .A23	Abbazia, Patrick. *Mr. Roosevelt's Navy: The Private War of the U.S. Atlantic Fleet, 1939-1942* (Annapolis, Md.: Naval Institute Press, 1975).
E746 .M6A7	Arpee, Edward. *From Frigates to Flat-Tops [Life of William A. Moffett]* (Lake Forest, Ill.: 1953).
D741 .A75	Aster, Sidney. *1939: The Making of the Second World War* (New York: Simon and Schuster, 1973).
D643 .A7B5	Birdsall, Paul. *Versailles Twenty Years After* (New York: Reynal and Hitchcock, 1941).
E785 .B8	Buckley, Thomas H. *The United States and the Washington Conference, 1921-1922* (Knoxville, University of Tennessee Press, 1970).
E807 .B835	Burns, James McGregor. *Roosevelt: The Lion and the Fox* (New York: Harcourt, Brace, 1956).
VA50 .B87	Bywater, Hector C. *Sea-Power in the Pacific: A Study of the American-Japanese Naval Problem*, 2d ed. (London: Constable and Co., 1934).
DD120 .R8C3	Carr, Edward H. *German-Soviet Relations Between the Two World Wars, 1919-1939* (Baltimore: Johns Hopkins Press, 1951).

JX1974   Dingman, Roger. Power in the Pacific: The
.D465   Origins of Naval Arms Limitation, 1914-1922
           (Chicago: University of Chicago Press, 1976).

DS77   Dorn, Frank. The Sino-Japanese War, 1937-1941:
.55.D67 From Marco Polo Bridge to Pearl Harbor (New
           York: Macmillan, 1974).

E801   Emerson, E. Hoover and His Times (Saxton,
.E75   Pa.: Brandywine Books, 1932).

E801   Ferrell, Robert H. American Diplomacy in the
.F4   Great Depression: Hoover-Stimson Foreign Policy,
           1929-1933 (New Haven: Yale University Press,
           1957).

E807   Freidel, Frank Burt. Franklin D. Roosevelt:
.F74   The Ordeal (Boston: Houghton Mifflin, 1954).

E183.8   Fry, Michael C. Illusions of Security: North
.G7F7   Atlantic Diplomacy, 1918-1922 (Toronto: Uni-
           versity of Toronto Press, 1972).

E183.8   Herzog, James H. Closing the Open Door:
.J3H47   American-Japanese Negotiations, 1936-1941
           Annapolis, Md.: Naval Institute Press, 1973).

E784   Hicks, John D. Republican Ascendancy, 1921-
.H5   1933 (New York: Harper and Brothers, 1960).

E802   Hoover, Herbert. The Memoirs of Herbert
.H7   Hoover: The Cabinet and the Presidency, 3 vols.
           (New York: Macmillan, 1952).

DA70   Howarth, David A. Sovereign of the Seas: The
.H73   Story of Britain and the Sea [to World War II]
           (New York: Atheneum, 1974).

UG633   Hurley, Alfred F. Billy Mitchell: Crusader
.M45H8   for Air Power (Bloomington: Indiana University
           Press, 1975).

DS888   Kasai, Jiuji George. The United States and
.5K355   Japan in the Pacific [in the 1930s] (New York:
           Arno Press, 1970).

E182 .K53	King, Ernest Joseph and Walter Muir Whitehead. *Fleet Admiral King: A Naval Record* (New York: Norton, 1952).
JX1974 .5.K6	Knox, Dudley W. *The Eclipse of American Sea Power* (New York: American Army and Navy Journal, 1922).
D753 .L27	Lash, Joseph P. *Roosevelt and Churchill 1939-1941* (New York: Norton, 1976).
D757 .L38	Leach, Harry A. *German Strategy Against Russia, 1939-1941* (Oxford: Clarendon Press, 1973).
DS518.4 .L43	Lee, Bradford A. *Britain and the Sino-Japanese War, 1937-1939* (Stanford: Stanford University Press, 1973).
E792 .M117	McCoy, Donald R. *Calvin Coolidge: The Quiet President* (New York: Macmillan, 1967).
E748 .W79M32	McFarland, Keith D. *Secretary of War Harry H. Woodring and the Problems of Readiness, Rearmament, and Neutrality, 1936-1940* (Lawrence: University of Kansas Press, 1975).
V874 .3.M44	Melhorn, Charles M. *Two-Block Fox: The Rise of the Aircraft Carrier, 1911-1929* (Annapolis, Md.: U.S. Naval Institute, 1974).
DA47.2 .M53	Middlemas, Robert Keith. *The Strategy of Appeasement: The British Government and Germany, 1937-1939* (Chicago: Quadrangle Books, 1972).
VA50 .M6	Moore, F. *America's Naval Challenge* (Saxton, Pa.: Brandywine Books, 1929).
E748 .S883M6	Morison, Elting E. *Turmoil and Tradition: A Study of the Life and Times of Henry L. Stimson* (Boston: Houghton Mifflin, 1960).
D773 .M6	Morison, Samuel Eliot. *History of United States Naval Operations in World War II*, 15 vols. (Boston: Little, Brown, 1947-1972), vol. 1, *The Battle of the Atlantic, September 1939-May 1943* (1964).

DA578 .M67	Mowat, Charles Loch. <u>Britain Between the Wars, 1918-1940</u> (Chicago: University of Chicago Press, 1955).
E785 .N6	Noggle, Burl. <u>Teapot Dome: Oil and Politics in the 1920s</u> (Baton Rouge: Louisiana State University Press, 1962).
JX1974 .L6	O'Connor, Raymond Gish. <u>Perilous Equilibrium: The United States and the London Naval Conference of 1930</u> (Lawrence: University of Kansas Press, 1962).
D742 .J3P44	Pelz, Stephen. <u>Race to Pearl Harbor</u> (Cambridge, Mass.: Harvard University Press, 1974).
V874 .P6	Polmar, Norman. <u>Aircraft Carriers</u> (Garden City, New York: Doubleday, 1969).
KF8745 .H8P8	Pusey, Merlo J. <u>Charles Evans Hughes</u>, 2 vols. (New York: Macmillan, 1951).
V874 .R4	Reynolds, Clark G. <u>The Fast Carriers: The Forging of an Air Navy</u> (New York: McGraw-Hill, 1968).
DU19 .R6	Roosevelt, Nicholas. <u>The Restless Pacific</u> (New York: Scribner's, 1928)
D436 .R68	Roskill, Stephen. <u>Naval Policy Between the Wars: The Period of Anglo-American Antagonism, 1919-1929</u> (New York: Walker and Co., 1968).
D436 .R68	_____. <u>Naval Policy Between the Wars: The Period of Reluctant Rearmament, 1930-1939</u> (Annapolis, Md.: Naval Institute Press, 1976).
UG630 .S5	Sherman, W.C. <u>Air Warfare</u> (New York: Ronald, 1926).
TL659 .A456	Smith, Richard K. <u>The Airships Akron and Macon: Flying Aircraft Carriers of the United States Navy</u> (Annapolis, Md.: U.S. Naval Institute, 1965).
E182 .S79	Sprout, Harold and Margaret. <u>Toward a New Order of Sea Power, 1918-1922</u> (Princeton, N.J.: Princeton University Press, 1940).

JX1974 Tate, Merze. *The United States and Armaments*
.T32   (Cambridge, Mass.: Harvard University Press, 1948).

DS783   Thorne, Christopher G. *The Limits of Foreign*
.7T48   *Policy: The West, the League, and the Far Eastern Crisis of 1931-1933* (New York: Putnam, 1972).

D742   Trefousse, Hans. *Germany and American Neu-*
.U5T66 *trality, 1939-1941* (rpt. New York: Octogon Books, 1951)

D774   Tuleja, Thaddeus, *Climax at Midway* (New York:
.M5T8   Norton, 1960).

VG93   Turnbull, Archibald D. and Clifford L. Lord,
.T8   *History of United States Naval Aviation* (New Haven: Yale University Press, 1949).

E746   Wheeler, Gerald E. *Prelude to Pearl Harbor:*
.W5   *The United States Navy and the Far East, 1921-1931* (Columbia: University of Missouri Press, 1963).

V63.P7 _____. *Admiral William Veazie Pratt,*
W45   *U.S. Navy: A Sailor's Life* (Washington: Department of the Navy, Naval History Division, 1974).

E792   White, William Allen. *A Puritan in Babylon:*
.W577   *The Story of Calvin Coolidge* (New York: Macmillan, 1938).

VG93   Wilson, Eugene E. *Slipstream: The Autobiography*
.W47   *of an Air Craftsman* (New York: Whittesey House, 1950).

Andrade, Ernest. "United States Naval Policy in the Disarmament Era, 1921-1937" (Ph. D. diss. Michigan State University, 1966).

Fagan, George V. "Anglo-American Naval Relations, 1927-1937" (PH. D. diss., University of Pennsylvania, 1954).

VA50 .T83	Tuleja, Thaddeus V. "U.S. Naval Policy in the Pacific, 1930-1941" (Ph. D. diss., Fordham University, 1961).
	Wilson, John R.M. "Herbert Hoover and the Armed Forces: A Study of Presidential Attitudes and Policy (Ph. D. diss., Northwestern University, 1971).
	O'Connor, Raymond G. "The 'Yardstick' and Naval Disarmament in the 1920s," *Mississippi Valley Historical Review* 45 (Dec. 1958): 441-463.
	Wheeler, Gerald E. "The United States Navy and the Japanese 'Enemy,'" *Military Affairs* 21 (Summer 1957): 61-74.

CHAPTER 16

BIBLIOGRAPHY

D770 .A238	Abbazia, Patrick. *Mr. Roosevelt's Navy: The Private War of the U.S. Atlantic Fleet, 1939-1942* (Annapolis, Md.: Naval Institute Press, 1975).
D755 .A3	Adams, Henry H. *Years of Deadly Peril: The Coming of the War, 1939-1941* (New York: McKay, 1969).
E744 .A26	Adler, Selig. *The Isolationist Impulse: Its Twentieth Century Reaction* (New York: Abelard-Schuman, 1957).
D511 .A77	Aster, Sidney. *1939: The Making of the Second World War* (New York: Simon and Schuster, 1973).
DG568 .5B37	Barclay, Glen. *The Rise and Fall of the New Roman Empire: Italy's Bid for World Power, 1890-1943* (New York: St. Martin, 1973).
D643 .A7B5	Birdsall, Paul. *Versailles Twenty Years After* (New York: Raynal and Hitchcock, 1941).

DS518 .8.B5	Bisson, Thomas A. <u>American Policy in the Far East, 1931-1940</u> (New York: Institute of Pacific Relations, 1940).
HJ257 .B6	Blum, John, ed. <u>From the Morgenthau Diaries: Years of Urgency, 1938-1941</u> (Boston: Houghton Mifflin, 1965).
DS784 .B65	Borg, Dorothy. <u>The United States and the Far Eastern Crisis of 1933-1938</u> (Cambridge: Harvard University Press, 1964).
DS890 .T57B8	Butow, Robert J.C. <u>Tojo and the Coming of the War</u> (Princeton, N.J.: Princeton University Press, 1961).
D743 .C47	Churchill, Winston. <u>The Second World War</u>, 6 vols. (Boston: Houghton Mifflin, 1948-1953). Vol. 1. <u>The Gathering Storm</u>, 1948).
DD247 .H5C58	Compton, James V. <u>The Swastika and the Eagle: Hitler, the United States and the Origins of World War II</u> (Boston: Houghton Mifflin, 1965).
D753 .D57	Divine, Robert A. <u>The Reluctant Belligerent: American Entry into World War II</u> (New York: Wiley, 1965).
E806 .D58	_____. <u>The Illusion of Neutrality</u> (Chicago: University of Chicago Press, 1962).
DS777 .55D67	Dorn, Frank. <u>The Sino-Japanese War, 1937-1941: From Marco Polo Bridge to Pearl Harbor</u> (New York: Macmillan, 1974).
E806 .D7	Drummond, Donald F. <u>The Passing of American Neutrality, 1937-1941</u> (Ann Arbor, Mich.: University of Michigan Press, 1951).
D742 .U5F3	Farago, Ladislas. <u>The Broken Seal: The Story of "Operation Magic" and the Pearl Harbor Disaster</u> (New York: Random House, 1967).
E806 .F33	Fehrenbach, T.R. <u>F.D.R.'s Undeclared War, 1939 to 1941</u> (New York: McKay, 1967).

D753 .F4	Feis, Herbert. *The Road to Pearl Harbor: The Coming of the War Between the United States and Japan* (Princeton, N.J.: Princeton University Press, 1950).
	Gibbs, N.H. *Grand Strategy. Vol. 1. Rearmament Policy.* United Kingdom Military Series. *History of the Second World War.* (London: HMSO, 1976).
DS849 .U6G7	Grew, Joseph C. *Ten Years in Japan* (New York: Simon and Schuster, 1944).
DT387 .8.H35	Harris, Brice. *The United States and the Italo-Ethiopian Crisis* (Stanford: Stanford University Press, 1964).
E183.8 .J3H47	Herzog, James H. *Closing the Open Door 1936-1941* (Annapolis, Md.: Naval Institute Press, 1973).
D741 .H3	Hoffman, Ross J.S. and C. Grove Haines. *The Origins and Background of the Second World War* (New York: Oxford University Press, 1943).
E748 .H93A3	Hull, Cordell. *The Memoirs of Cordell Hull*, 2 vols. (New York: Macmillan, 1948).
E744 .J667	Jonas, Manfred. *Isolationism in America, 1935-1951* (Ithaca, N.Y.: Cornell University Press, 1966).
DS845 .J6	Jones, Francis C. *Japan's New Order in East Asia* (London: Oxford University Press, 1954).
D773 .K3	Karig, Walter. *Battle Report*, 6 vols. (New York: Rinehart, 1944-1952).
DK63 .3.K38	Kennan, George Frost. *Russia and the West Under Lenin and Stalin* (Boston: Little, Brown, 1960).
E748.K 374A3	_____. *Memoirs, 1925-1950* (Boston: Little, Brown, 1967).
D753 .K5	Kimball, Warren F. *The Most Unsordid Act: Lend-Lease, 1939-1941* (Baltimore: Johns Hopkins Press, 1969).

D843   Knapp, Wilfrid. *A History of War and Peace,*
.K554   *1939-1965* (New York: Oxford University Press,
          1967).

E183.8   Koginos, Manny. *The Panay Incident: Prelude*
.J3K56   *to War* (Lafayette, Ind.: Purdue University
          Studies, 1967).

D744   Langer, William L. and S. Everett Gleason.
.L3   *The Challenge to Isolation, 1937-1940* (New
          York: Harper, 1953).

D748   _____. *The Undeclared War, 1940-1941*
.L3   New York: Harper, 1953).

D757   Leach, Harry A. *German Strategy Against*
.L38   *Russia, 1939-1941* (Oxford: Clarendon Press,
          1973).

D767   Lord, Walter. *Day of Infamy* [Pearl Harbor]
.92L6   (New York: Holt, 1957).

DA47   Middlemas, Robert K. *The Strategy of Appease-*
.2.M53   *ment: The British Government and Germany,*
          1937-1939 (Chicago: Quadrangle Books, 1972).

D748   Millis, Walter. *This Is Pearl! The United*
.M5   *States and Japan*--1941 (New York: Morrow,
          1947).

E748   Morison, Elting E. *Turmoil and Tradition*:
.S883   *A Study of the Life and Times of Henry L.*
M6   *Stimson* (Boston: Houghton Mifflin, 1960).

D773   Morison, Samuel E. *History of United States*
.M6   *Naval Operations in World War II*, 15 vols.
          Vol. 1. *The Battle of the Atlantic, September*
          1939-May 1943 (1947).

D741   Mosley, Leonard. *On Borrowed Time: How World*
.M65   *War II Began* (New York: Random House, 1969).

E744   Murphy, Robert Daniel. *Diplomat Among War-*
.M87   *riors* (Garden City, N.Y.: Doubleday, 1964).

E183.8   Neumann, William L. *America Encounters Japan*:
.J3N39   *From Perry to MacArthur* (Baltimore: Johns
          Hopkins Press, 1963).

E173 .C555   Nevins, Allan. *The United States in a Chaotic World: A Chronicle of International Affairs, 1918-1933* (New Haven: Yale University Press, 1950).

E745 .M37P6   Pogue, Forrest. *George C. Marshall: The Education of a General, 1880-1939* (New York: Viking, 1963).

E183.7 B46 Vol.12-13   Pratt, Julius. *Cordell Hull*, 2 vols. (New York: Cooper Square Publishers, 1964).

E183.8 .J3R3   Rappaport, Armin. *Henry L. Stimson and Japan, 1931-1933* (Chicago: University of Chicago Press, 1963).

E807 .R3   Rauch, Basil. *Roosevelt: From Munich to Pearl Harbor* (New York: Creative Age Press, 1950).

D741 .R62   Robertson, Esmonde M., ed. *The Origins of the Second World War: Historical Interpretations* (London: Macmillan, 1971).

D742 .J3S38   Schroeder, Paul W. *The Axis Alliance and Japanese-American Relations, 1941* (Ithaca: Cornell University Press, 1948).

E807 .S45   Sherwood, Robert E. *Roosevelt and Hopkins* (New York: Harper, 1948).

DS783 .7L45   Smith, Sara R. *The Manchurian Crisis, 1931-1932* (New York: Columbia University Press, 1948).

E806 .T8   Tansill, Charles C. *Back Door to War: The Roosevelt Foreign Policy, 1933-1941* (Chicago: Henry Regnery, 1952).

DS783 .7.T48   Thorne, Christopher. *The Limits of Foreign Policy: The West, the League, and the Far Eastern Crisis of 1931-1933* (New York: Putnam, 1972).

D742 .U5T66   Trefouse, Hans L. *Germany and American Neutrality, 1939-1941* (New York: Bookman Associates, 1951).

E746 .T8 Tuleja, Thaddeus V. *Statesmen and Admirals: Quest for a Far Eastern Naval Policy* (New York: Norton, 1963).

E744 .W52 Welles, Sumner. *Time for Decision* (New York: Harper, 1944).

E746 .W5 Wheeler, Gerald E. *Prelude to Pearl Harbor: The United States Navy and the Far East, 1921-1931* (Columbia: University of Missouri Press, 1963).

D767 .92W6 Wohlstetter, Barbara. *Pearl Harbor: Warning and Decision* (Stanford: Stanford University Press, 1962).

F1418 .W683 Wood, Bryce. *The Making of the Good Neighbor Policy* (New York: Columbia University Press, 1964).

Cole, Wayne C. "American Entry into World War II: A Historiographical Appraisal," *Mississippi Valley Historical Review* 43 (March 1957): 595-617.

Ferrell, Henry C. Jr. "Claude A. Swanson of Virginia" (Ph. D. diss. University of Virginia, 1964).

V859 .G353 Saville, Allison W. "The Development of the German U-boat Arm, 1919-1935" (Ph. D. diss., Seattle: University of Washington, 1963).

CHAPTER 17

BIBLIOGRAPHY

In addition to the works of Barclay; Churchill; Karig, Morison, S.E.; Pratt, Sherwood; Tuleja; and Wood, see:

D755 .4A4 Adams, Henry H. *1942: The Year that Doomed the Axis* (New York: McKay, 1967).

D771 .A746 Ansel, Walter. *Hitler Confronts England* (Durham: Duke University Press, 1960).

560

D779.F7 .A823	Auphan, G.A.J.P. and Jacques Mordal. <u>The French Navy in World War II</u> (Annapolis, Md.: U.S. Naval Institute, 1957).
	Bagnasco, Erminio. <u>Submarines of World War II</u> (Annapolis, Md.: Naval Institute Press, 1977).
	Baker, Elisabeth. <u>British Policy in Southeast Europe in the Second World War</u> (New York: Barnes & Noble, 1976).
D756 .B27	Baldwin, Hanson W. <u>The Crucial Years, 1939-1941: The World at War</u> (New York: Harper & Row, 1976).
D755.1 .B3813	Beaufre, André. <u>1940: The Fall of France</u>. Trans. Desmonde Flower. (London: Cassell, 1967).
D771 .B38813	Bekker, Cajus. <u>Hitler's Naval War</u>. Trans. and ed. by Frank Zeigler (Garden City, N.Y.: Doubleday, 1974).
D580 .B4	Bennett, Geoffrey M. <u>Naval Battles of the First World War</u> (New York: Scribner, 1969).
D772 .B5B84	Berthold, Will. <u>The Sinking of the BISMARCK</u>. Trans. Michael Bullock. (London: Longmans, 1958).
D756 .B7	Bradley, Omar Nelson. <u>A Soldier's Story</u> (New York: Holt, 1951).
HJ257 .B6	Blum, John M. <u>From the Morgenthau Diaries: Years of War, 1941-1945</u> (Boston: Houghton Mifflin, 1967).
D775 .B683	Bragadin, Marc' Antonio. <u>The Italian Navy in World War II</u>. Trans. Gale Hoffman. (Annapolis, Md.: U.S. Naval Institute, 1957).
	Brown, David. <u>TIRPITZ: Floating Fortress</u> (Annapolis, Md.: Naval Institute Press, 1977).

D743   Bryant, Sir Arthur. <u>Triumph in the War: A</u>
.B73   <u>History of the War Years Based on the Diaries</u>
           <u>of Field-Marshal Lord Alanbrook, Chief of the</u>
           <u>Imperial Staff</u> (Garden City, N.Y.: Doubleday,
           1959).

DA69.3   Chalfont, Arthur G.J. <u>Montgomery of Alamein</u>
.M56C45   (New York: Atheneum, 1976).

D743   Churchill, Winston. <u>The Second World War</u>,
.C47   6 vols. (Boston: Houghton Mifflin, 1948-1953).
           Vol. 1. <u>The Gathering Storm</u>, and Vol. 2.
           <u>Their Finest Hour</u>.

D770   Creswell, John. <u>Sea Warfare, 1939-1945</u> (New
.C7   York: Longmans, 1950).

DA89.1   Cunningham, Andrew B. <u>A Sailor's Odyssey</u>
.C8A3   (New York: Dutton, 1951).

D753.2   Dawson, Raymond H. <u>The Decision to Aid</u>
.R9D3   <u>Russia, 1941: Foreign Policy and Domestic</u>
           <u>Politics</u> (Chapel Hill: University of North
           Carolina Press, 1959).

D761   De Gaulle, Charles. <u>The War Memoirs of</u>
.G3733   <u>Charles de Gaulle</u>, 3 vols. (New York: Simon
           & Schuster, 1955-1960).

D763   Derry, T.K. <u>The Campaign in Norway</u> (London:
.N6D47   H.M.S.O., 1952).

D763   Dickens, Peter. <u>Narvik: Battles in the</u>
.N6D52   <u>Fjords</u> (Annapolis, Md.: Naval Institute Press,
           1974).

D756.5   Divine, David. <u>The Nine Days of Dunkirk</u> (New
.D8D5   York: Ballentine Books, 1959).

D781   Dönitz, Karl. <u>Ten Years and Twenty Days</u> (New
.D613   York: World Pub. Co., 1959).
1959

TL540   Dupre, Flint O. <u>Hap Arnold: Architect of</u>
.A69   <u>American Air Power</u> (New York: Macmillan, 1972).
D896

D810　　　Farago, Ladislas. *The Game of the Foxes: The*
.8S7F33　*Untold Story of German Espionage in the*
　　　　　United States and Great Britain During World
　　　　　War II (New York: David McKay, 1971).

E745　　　_____. *Patton: Ordeal and Triumph* (New
.P3F3　　York: Obolensky, 1964).

D783　　　_____. *The Tenth Fleet* (New York:
.F3　　　Obolensky, 1962).

U162　　　_____. *Axis Grand Strategy* (New York:
.F36　　　Farrar & Rinehart, 1942).

D765　　　Falk, Stanley L. *Seventy Days to Singapore*
.5.F34　(New York: Putnam, 1975).

D786　　　Fleming, Peter. *Operation Sea Lion* (New York:
.F56　　　Simon and Schuster, 1957).

D772　　　Frank, Wolfgang and Bernhard Rogge. *German*
.A74R59　*Raider ATLANTIS* (New York: Ballentine Books,
　　　　　1956).

D751　　　Friedlaender Saul. *Prelude to Downfall. Hitler*
.F713　　*and the United States, 1939-1941* (New York:
　　　　　Knopf, 1967).

D763　　　Gerárd, Francis. *Malta Magnificent* (New York:
.M3G4　　Whittlesey House, 1943).

D772　　　Grenfell, Russell. *The Bismarck Episode* (New
.B5G7　　York: Macmillan, 1949).

D770　　　_____. *Main Fleet to Singapore* (New
.G73　　　York: Macmillan, 1952).

D763　　　Hay, Ian [John Hay Beith]. *Malta Epic* (New
.M3B4　　York: Appleton-Century, 1943).

D763　　　Higgins, Trumbull. *Soft Underbelly: The Anglo-*
.I8H53　*American Controversy over the Italian Campaign,*
　　　　　1939-1945 (New York: Macmillan, 1968).

D744　　　_____. *Winston Churchill and the Second*
.H5　　　*Front, 1940-1943* (New York: Oxford University
　　　　　Press, 1957).

D771 Kemp, Peter. <u>Key to Victory: The Triumph of
.K38 British Sea Power in World War II</u> (Boston:
1957a Little Brown, 1957).

D772 _____. <u>Escape of the SCHARNHORST and
.S35K45 GNEISNAU</u> (Annapolis, Md.: Naval Institute
   Press, 1975).

D787 Lee, Asher. <u>The German Air Force</u> (London:
.14 Duckworth, 1946).

UG635 _____. <u>The Soviet Air Force</u> (London:
.R9L43 Duckworth, 1950).

UG635 _____. <u>The Soviet Air and Rocket Forces</u>
.R9L42 (New York: Praeger, 1959).

D655 Lukacs, John. <u>The Last European War, Septem-
.L84 ber 1939-December 1941</u> (Garden City, N.Y.:
   Doubleday, 1976).

D766.99 Marder, Arthur. <u>Operation "Menace": The
.S4M37 Dakar Expedition and the Dudley North Affair</u>
   (London: Oxford University Press, 1976).

D771 Macintyre, Donald. <u>The Naval War Against
.M276 Hitler</u> (New York: Scribner, 1971).

D810 Masterman, John C. <u>The Double-Cross System
.S7M28 in the War of 1939 to 1945</u> (New Haven: Yale
   University Press, 1972).

D756 Morgan, Frederick. <u>Overture to Overlord</u>
.M64 (Garden City, N.Y.: Doubleday, 1950).

D773 Morison, Samuel E. <u>History of United States
.M6 Naval Operations in World War II</u>, 15 vols.
   (Boston: Little, Brown, 1947-1962), vol. 1.
   <u>The Battle of the Atlantic, September 1939-
   May 1943</u> (1947).

D773 _____. <u>The Two Ocean War: A Short History
.M62 of the United States Navy in the Second World
   War</u> (Boston: Little Brown, 1963).

D775.5 .M3P3	Pack, S.W.C. The Battle of Matapan (New York: Macmillan, 1961).
D766.7 .C7P24	_____. The Battle for Crete (Annapolis, Md.: Naval Institute Press, 1973).
V65.C85 .P3	_____. Cunningham the Commander (London: Batsford, 1974).
D27 .P2	_____. Sea Power in the Mediterranean (London: A. Barker, 1971).
D766 .P6	Playfair, Ian S.O. The Mediterranean and Middle East (London: H.M.S.O., 1954).
E745 .M37P6	Pogue, Forrest. George D. Marshall: Ordeal and Hope, 1939-1942 (New York: Viking, 1966).
D772 .G7P6	Pope, Dudley. The Battle of the River Plate (London: William Kimber, 1956).
	_____. Graf Spee: The Life and Death of a Raider (Philadelphia: Lippincott, 1956).
DD256 .5R54	Robertson, E.M. Hitler's Prewar Policy and Military Plans, 1937-1939 (London: Longmans, 1963).
D771 .R69	Roskill, Stephen W. The Navy at War, 1939-1945 (London: Collins, 1960).
D770 .R833	Ruge, Frederich. Der Seekrieg: The German Navy's Story, 1939-1945 (Annapolis, Md.: U.S. Naval Institute, 1957).
D748 .S57	Snell, John L. Illusion and Necessity: The Diplomacy of Global War (Boston: Houghton Mifflin, 1963).
D734 .C7	_____. The Meaning of Yalta (Baton Rouge: Louisiana State University Press, 1956, 1965).
	Stoler, Mark A. The Politics of the Second Front: American Military Planning and Diplomacy in Coalition Warfare, 1941-1943 (Westport, Conn.: Greenwood, 1976).

D766.7 Thompson, Laurence. *1940* (New York: William
.C7S734 Morrow, 1966).

D771   Von der Porten, Edward P. The German Navy
.V65   in World War II (New York: Ballentine Books,
       1969).

D772   Watts, Anthony J. Loss of the SCHARNHORST
.S35W3 (London: Allan, 1970).

VA653 _____. The Imperial Japanese Navy
.W32   (London: Macdonald, 1971).

D771   Wheatley Roland. Operation Sea Lion (Oxford:
.W38   Clarendon Press, 1958).

D743   Wilmot, Chester. The Struggle for Europe
.W53   [1939-1945] (London: Collins, 1952).

CHAPTER 18

NOTES

1. Forrestal's work in 1946 and until he became Secretary of Defense in September 1947 is covered in chapter 22.

BIBLIOGRAPHY

D755   Adams, Henry H. 1942: The Year that Doomed
.4.A4 the Axis (New York: McKay, 1969).

D755   _____. Years to Victory (New York:
.6A3   McKay, 1973).

D755   _____. Years of Expectation: Guadalcanal
.5A3   to Normandy (New York: McKay, 1973).

V825.3 Alden, John D. Flush Decks and Four Pipes
.A7   (Annapolis, Md.: U.S. Naval Institute, 1965).

D771   Ansel, Walter. Hitler Confronts England (Dur-
.A746 ham: Duke University Press, 1960).

D766   _____. Hitler and the Middle Sea (Dur-
.A65   ham: Duke University Press, 1972).

D743 .B34   Baldwin, Hanson W. *Battles Lost and Won: Great Campaigns of World War II*. (New York: Harper & Row, 1966).

Q127 .U6B3   Baxter, James P. *Scientists Against Time* Boston: Little, Brown, 1948).

D777 .B37   Bennett, Geoffrey M. *The Loss of the Prince of Wales and Repulse* (Annapolis, Md.: U.S. Naval Institute, 1973).

D770 .B456   _____. *Naval Battles of World War II* (London: Batsford, 1975).

D775 .B683   Bragadin, Marc' Antonio. *The Italian Navy in World War II* (Annapolis, Md.: U.S. Naval Institute, 1957).

V765 .B6813   Breyer, Siegfried. *Battleships and Battle Cruisers, 1905-1970*. Trans. from the German by Alfred Kurti (Garden City, N.Y.: Doubleday, 1973).

D780 .G72   [British] Admiralty, *The Battle of the Atlantic: The Official Account of the Fight Against the U-boats, 1939-1945* (London: HMSO, 1946).

D769 .B8   Buchanan, Albert Russell. *The United States and World War II*, 2 vols. (New York: Harper & Row, 1964).

D781 .C49   Chatterton, Edward Kemble. *Commerce Raiders* (London: Hurst & Blackett, 1943).

D756.5 .D8C5   _____. *The Epic of Dunkirk* (London: Hurst & Blackett, 1940).

D590 .C49   _____. *Fighting the U-boats* (London: Hurst & Blackett, 1942).

D73 .C47   Churchill, Winston. *The Second World War*. Vol. 3, *The Grand Alliance* (1950); vol. 4, *The Hinge of Fate* (1950); Vol. 5, *Closing the Ring* (1951).

D773 .C6   Coale, Griffith B. *North Atlantic Patrol* (New York: Farrar and Rinehart, 1942).

VC263 .C65	Connery, Robert H. *The Navy and the Industrial Mobilization in World War II* (Princeton, N.J.: Princeton University Press, 1951).
D790 .A47	Craven, Wesley F. and John L. Cate. *The Army Air Forces in World War II*, 7 vols. (Chicago: University of Chicago Press, 1948-19).
D743 .E35	Eisenhower, Dwight D. *Crusade in Europe* (Garden City, N.Y.: Doubleday, 1948).
D756.5 .N6D35	Eisenhower Foundation. *D-Day: The Normandy Invasion in Retrospect* (Lawrence: University Press of Kansas, 1971).
D756 .E39	Ellis, Lionel F. and others. *Victory in the West: The Battle of Normandy*. vol. 1 of *History of the Second World War* (London: HMSO, 1962).
D783 .F3	Farago, Ladislas. *The Tenth Fleet* (New York: Obolensky, 1962).
D781 .F742	Frank, Wolfgang. *The Sea Wolves: The Story of German U-boats at War* (New York: Rinehart, 1955).
D25 .D43	Frankland, Noble and Christopher Dowling, eds. *Decisive Battles of the Twentieth Century: Land, Sea, Air* (New York: McKay, 1976).
VB23 .F8	Furer, Julius Augustus. *Administration of the Navy Department in World War II* (Washington: GPO, 1959).
D782 U18G5	Gallery, Daniel V. *Twenty Million Tons under the Sea* (Chicago: Henry Regnery, 1956).
D774 .G8G3	_____. *Clear the Decks!* (New York: Morrow, 1951).
TL540 .D62 G55	Glines, Carroll V. *Jimmy Doolittle: Daredevil Aviator and Scientist* (New York: Macmillan, 1972).
D743 U44	Greenfield, Kent R., ed. *Command Decisions* New York: Harcourt, Brace, 1959).

D769 .A533 v.3	Harrison, Gordon A.	*Cross-Channel Attack* (Washington: GPO, 1951).
D769 .A523 v.11	Howe, George F.	*Northwest Africa: Seizing the Initiative in the West* (Washington: OCMH, 1957).
QC773 .A1I69	Irving, David J.C.	*The German Atomic Bomb* (New York: Simon & Schuster, 1967).
D773 .K3	Karig, Walter.	*Battle Report: Atlantic War* (New York: Rinehart, 1946).
E182 .K53	King, Ernest J. and Walter Muir Whitehill.	*Fleet Admiral King: A Naval Record* (New York: Norton, 1952).
D753 .L25	Langer, William L.	*Our Vichy Gamble* (New York: Norton, 1947).
D769 .L4	Leahy, William D.	*I Was There* (New York: McGraw-Hill, 1950).
D743 .L514	Liddell Hart, B.M.	*History of the Second World War* (London: Cassell, 1970).
E836 .L96	Lyon, Peter.	*Eisenhower: Portrait of the Hero* (Boston: Little, Brown, 1974).
D771 .M3	Martienssen, Anthony.	*Hitler and His Admirals* (London: Secker and Warburg, 1948).
D769 .A533 v.4	Matloff, Maurice.	*Strategic Planning for Coalition Warfare, 1943-1944* (Washington: OCMH, 1959).
D769 .A533 v.2	Matloff, Maurice and Edwin M. Snell.	*Strategic Planning for Coalition Warfare, 1941-1942* Washington: GPO, 1953).
D756 .M48	Michie, Allan A.	*The Invasion of Europe: The Story Behind D-Day* (New York: Dodd, Mead, 1964).
D770 .M5	Middlebrook, Martin.	*Convoy* (New York: Morrow, 1977).

E813 .F6	Millis, Walter, ed. The Forrestal Diaries (New York: Viking, 1951).
D756 .M58	Montgomery, Field Marshal. Normandy to the Baltic (Germany: British Army of the Rhine, 1946).
DA69.3 .M56A3	_____. Memoirs (Cleveland: World Publishing Co., 1958).
D773 .M6	Morison, Samuel E. History of United States Naval Operations in World War Two (Boston: Houghton Mifflin, 1947-1962). Vols. 1. The Battle of the Atlantic, Sept. 1939-May 1943 (1947); 2. Operations in North African Waters, Oct. 1942-June 1943 (1947). 9. Sicily, Salerno, Anzio, Jan. 1943-June 1944 (1954). 10. The Atlantic Battle Won, May 1943-May 1945 (1956).
E744 .M87	Murphy, Robert D. Diplomat Among Warriors (Garden City, N.Y.: Doubleday, 1964).
D770 .N6	Norman, Albert. Operation Overlord, Design and Reality: The Allied Invasion of Western Europe (Harrisburg, Pa: Military Service Pub. Co., 1952).
E835 .P3	Parmet, Herbert S. Eisenhower and the American Crusades (New York: Macmillan, 1972).
D761 .P393	Perrault, Gilles. The Secret of D-Day (Boston: Little, Brown, 1957).
D769 .A533 v.3	Pogue, Forrest. The Supreme Command: U.S. Army in World War II (Washington: GPO, 1954).
D771 .P6	Pope, Dudley. '73 North: The Battle of the Barents Sea (London: Weidenfeld & Nicholson, 1958).
D773 .R6	Roscoe, Theodore. United States Destroyer Operations in World War II (Annapolis, Md.: U.S. Naval Institute, 1953).
D773 ..R6	_____. United States Submarine Operations in World War II (Annapolis, Md.: U.S. Naval Institute, 1955).

D771 .R68	Roskill, Stephen W. *The War at Sea*, 3 vols. in 4 (London: HMSO, 1954-1961).
	Rowher, Jurgen. *Critical Convoy Battles of World War II* (Annapolis, Md. U.S. Naval Institute, 1977).
D756 .5N6R9	Ryan, Cornelius. *The Longest Day: June 6, 1944* (New York: Simon and Schuster, 1959).
	Schofield, Brian B. *Operation Neptune* [The Naval Side of "Overlord"] (Annapolis, Md.: Naval Institute Press, 1974).
VA454 .S27	———. *British Sea Power: Naval Policy in the Twentieth Century* (London: Balsford, 1967).
D786 .S365	———. *The Attack on Taranto* (Annapolis, Md.: Naval Institute Press, 1973).
VA58 .S58	Silverstone, Paul H. *U.S. Warships of World War II* (Garden City, N.Y.: Doubleday, 1966).
DA585 .S58A3	Slessor, Sir John C. *The Central Blue: Recollections and Reflections* (London: Cassell, 1956).
D763. .M3S58	Smith, Peter Charles. *Battles of the Malta Striking Forces* (Annapolis, Md.: U.S. Naval Institute, 1974).
DA69 .3T35A3	Tedder, Arthur. *With Prejudice* (Boston: Little Brown, 1966).
D769 .A533 v.4	Watson, Mark. *Chief of Staff: Prewar Plans and Preparations* (Washington: OCMH, 1950).
D743 .W53	Wilmot, Chester. *The Struggle for Europe* [1939-1945] (London: Collins, 1952).
D771 .W42	Winton, John. *Air Power at Sea, 1939-1945* (New York: Crowell, 1976).
D785 .U63	*United States Strategic Bombing Survey* (Washington: GPO, 1945-1947).

D772   Woodward, David. The TIRPITZ and the Battle
.T5W6   for the North Atlantic (New York: Norton,
          1954).

D771   _____. The Secret Raiders: The Story of
.W58   the Armed Merchant Raiders in the Second World
          War (New York: Norton, 1955).

CHAPTER 19

BIBLIOGRAPHY

D783   Blair, Clay, Jr. Silent Victory: The United
.B58   States Submarine War Against Japan (Phila-
          delphia: Lippincott, 1975).

          Brown, David. Carrier Operations in World
          War II: The Royal Navy (London: Ian Allen,
          1974).

V63   Buell, Thomas B. The Quiet Warrior: A Biog-
.S68B3   raphy of Admiral Raymond A. Spruance (Boston:
          Little, Brown, 1974).

          Dull, Paul S. A Battle History of the Imper-
          ial Japanese Navy, 1941-1945 (Annapolis, Md.:
          Naval Institute Press, 1977).

D767   Dyer, George C. The Amphibians Came to Con-
.D9   quer: The Story of Admiral Richmond Kelly
          Turner (Washington: Department of the Navy,
          1972).

D767   Forrestel, Emmet P. Admiral Raymond A.
.F6   Spruance, USN: A Study in Command (Washington:
          GPO, 1966).

D774   Frank, Pat and Joseph D. Harrington. Rendez-
.M5F7   vous at Midway: U.S.S. Yorktown and the
          Japanese Carrier Fleet (New York: John Day,
          1967).

D774   Fuchida, Mitsuo and Masatake Okumiya. Midway:
.M5   The Battle That Doomed Japan (Annapolis, Md.:
F814   U.S. Naval Institute, 1955).

E746 .H3A3	Halsey, William F. and J. Bryan III. <u>Admiral</u> <u>Halsey's Story</u> (New York: McGraw-Hill, 1947)
D767.99 .W3U5	Heinl, Robert D. <u>The Defense of Wake</u> (Washington: HQ, USMC, 1947).
D769 .369 .U53	Hough, Frank O., Verle E. Ludwig, and Henry I. Shaw. <u>Pearl Harbor to Guadalcanal</u> (Washington: HQ, USMC, Historical Branch, G-3, 1958).
D774 .C63H69	Hoyt, Edwin Palmer. <u>Blue Skies and Blood:</u> <u>The Battle of the Coral Sea</u> (New York: S. Eriksson, 1975).
D769 .25I7	Isely, Jeter A. and Philip A. Crowl. <u>The U.S.</u> <u>Marines and Amphibious War</u> (Princeton: Princeton University Press, 1951).
E745 .M353	James, Dorris C. <u>The Years of MacArthur</u> (Boston: Houghton Mifflin, 1970).
D774 .L456	Johnston, Stanley. <u>Queen of the Flattops:</u> <u>the U.S.S. Lexington and the Coral Sea Battle</u> (New York: Dutton, 1942).
D811 .K42	Kenney, George C. <u>General Kenney Reports:</u> <u>A Personal History of the Pacific War</u> (New York: Duell, Sloan and Pearce, 1949).
D767.92 .K54	Kimmel, Husband E. <u>Admiral Kimmel's Story</u> (Chicago: Henry Regnery, 1955).
E182 .K53	King, Ernest J. and Walter Muir Whitehill. <u>Fleet Admiral King: A Naval Record</u> (New York: Norton, 1952).
D774 .M5L6	Lord, Walter. <u>Incredible Victory</u> [Battle of Midway] (New York: Harper & Row, 1967).
E745 .M3A34	MacArthur, Douglas. <u>Reminiscences</u> (New York: McGraw-Hill, 1964).
D769 .A533 v.4	Matloff, Maurice and E. M. Snell. <u>Strategic</u> <u>Planning for Coalition Warfare, 1941-1942</u> (Washington: OCMH, 1953).

V63   Merrill, James M. *A Sailor's Admiral: A*
.H34M7   *Biography of William F. Halsey* (New York:
             Crowell, 1976).

D748   Millis Walter. *This Is Pearl, The United*
.M5   *States and Japan - 1941* (New York: Morrow,
             1947).

D774   Millot, Bernard. *The Battle of the Coral*
.C63   *Sea* (Annapolis, Md.: Naval Institute Press,
.M5413   1974).

D774   Newcomb, Richard F. *Savo: The Incredible*
.S318N4   *Naval Debacle Off Guadalcanal* (New York:
             Holt, Rinehart & Winston, 1961).

             Oosten, F. C. van. *The Battle of the Java*
             Sea (Annapolis, Md.: Naval Institute Press,
             1977).

V63   Potter, Elmer. *Nimitz* (Annapolis, Md.: Naval
.N55P67   Institute Press, 1976).

E746   Clark, Joseph and Clark G. Reynolds. *Carrier*
.C55A3   *Admiral* (New York: McKay, 1967).

V874   Reynolds, Clark G. *The Fast Carriers: The*
.R4   *Forging of an Air Navy* (New York: McGraw-
             Hill, 1968).

TL540   Reynolds, Quentin. *The Amazing Mr. Doolittle*
.D62R4   (New York: Appleton-Century-Crofts, 1953).

D773   Sherman, Frederick C. *Combat Command: The*
.S52   *American Aircraft Carriers in the Pacific*
             War (New York: E.P. Dutton, 1950).

D767   Sherrod, Robert. *Tarawa: The Story of a*
.917.S5   *Battle* (New York: Duell, Sloan and Pearce,
             1944).

D790   _____. *History of Marine Corps Aviation*
.S495   *in World War II* (Washington: Combat Forces
             Press, 1952)

D774   Smith, Chester Leo. *Midway 4 June 1942*
.M556   (London: Regency, 1962).

D769 .369 .S58	Smith, Holland M. and Percy Finch. <u>Coral and Brass</u> (New York: Scribner's, 1949).
E746 .M58T3	Taylor, Theodore. <u>The Magnificent Mitscher</u> (New York: Norton, 1954).
D767 .98.T7	Tregaskis, Richard W. <u>Guadalcanal Diary</u> (New York: Random House, 1943).
VG93 .T8	Turnbull, Archibald D. and Clifford L. Lord. <u>History of United States Naval Aviation</u> (New Haven: Yale University Press, 1949).
E746 .V3	Vandegrift, Alexander Archer. <u>Once a Marine: The Memoirs of General A.A. Vandegrift, USMC</u> (New York: Norton, 1964).
E745 .M3W5	Willoughby, Charles A. and John Chamerlain. <u>MacArthur, 1941-1951</u> (New York: McGraw-Hill, 1954).
D774 .M5A5	U.S. Office of Naval Intelligence. <u>The Japanese Story of the Battle of Midway</u> (Washington: GPO, 1947).
	Borsodi, Marion S., comp. <u>Fleet Admiral Chester William Nimitz, USN: A Selected Bibliography from the Collection of the Nimitz Library</u> (Annapolis, Md.: U.S. Naval Academy, 1973).

CHAPTER 20

BIBLIOGRAPHY

In addition to works already cited, see:

Brown, David. <u>Carrier Operations in World War II: The Pacific Navies</u> (London: Ian Allan, 1974).

E745 .C35A3	Chennault, Clair L. <u>Way of a Fighter: The Memoirs of Claire Lee Chennault</u> (New York: Putnam, 1949).

D774 .M5A8	Heinl, Robert D. <u>Marines at Midway</u> (Washington: HQ, USMC, 1948).
D749 .345 .H87	Huston, James A. <u>Out of the Blue: U.S. Army Airborne Operations in World War II</u> (West Lafayette, Ind.: Purdue University Press, 1972).
D773 .K3	Karig, Walter. <u>Battle Report: Pacific War, Middle Phase</u> (New York: Rinehart, 1946).
D767 .98L4	Leckie, Robert. <u>Challenge for the Pacific: Guadalcanal, the Turning Point of the War</u> (Garden City, N.Y.: Doubleday, 1965).
	Lundstrom, John B. <u>The First South Pacific Campaign: Pacific Fleet Strategy, December 1941-June 1942</u> (Annapolis, Md.: Naval Institute Press, 1976).
D767.99 .M3M3	Marshall, S.L.A.M. <u>Island Victory: The Battle of Kwajelein Atoll</u> (Washington: Infantry Journal, 1945).
D769 .A533 v.2	Miller, John, Jr. <u>CARTWHEEL: The Reduction of Rabaul</u> (Washington, OCMH, 1959).
D767.6 .P43	Peers, William R. and Dean Brelis. <u>Behind the Burma Road</u> (New York: Avon, 1963)
D774 .M5T8	Tuleja, Thaddeus V. <u>Climax at Midway</u> (New York: Norton, 1960).

CHAPTER 21

BIBLIOGRAPHY

In addition to the works cited for chapters 19 and 20, see:

D773 .B34	Ballentine, Duncan S. <u>U.S. Naval Logistics in the Second World War</u> (Princeton, N.J.: Princeton University Press, 1947).

D769.52 Barbey, Daniel E. MacArthur's Amphibious Navy
.A45B3 (Annapolis, Md.: U.S. Naval Institute, 1969).

D773 Bulkley, Robert J. At Close Quarters: PT Boats
.B8 in the United States Navy (Washington, D.C.:
Naval History Division, 1962).

D821 Butow, Robert J.C. Japan's Decision to
.J3B8 Surrender (Stanford: Stanford University
Press, 1954).

D773 Cant, Gilbert. America's Navy in World War II
.C27 (New York: John Day, 1943).

D769. Carter, Worrall Reed. Beans, Bullets and
.537 Black Oil (Washington: GPO, 1953).
10th
.C3

D773 _____ and Elmer Ellsworth Duvall. Ships,
.C33 Salvage, and Sinews of War (Washington: GPO,
1954).

D743 Churchill, Winston. The Second World War.
.C47 Vol. 6. Triumphant Tragedy (1953).

D767 Driscoll, Joseph. Pacific Victory, 1945
.D7 Philadelphia: Lippincott, 1944).

D767 Dyer, George C. The Amphibians Came to Con-
.D9 quer: The Story of Admiral Richmond Kelly
Turner, 2 vols. (Washington: Department of
the Navy, 1971).

D767.4 Falk, Stanley L. Decision at Leyte (New York:
.F3 Norton, 1966).

V162 Farago, Ladislas, comp. and ed. The Axis
.F36 Grand Strategy (New York: Farrar and Rinehart, 1942).

D810 _____. The Game of the Foxes: The Untold
.S7F33 Story of German Espionage in the United States
and Great Britain During World War II (New
York: McKay, 1971).

E745   _____. Patton: Ordeal and Triumph (New
.P3F3   York: Obolensky, 1964).

D783   _____. The Tenth Fleet (New York:
.F3   Obolensky, 1962).

D767   Feis, Herbert. The Atomic Bomb and the End
.2.F4   of World War II, rev. ed. (Princeton, N.J.:
        Princeton University Press, 1966).

E183.8   _____. The China Tangle: The American
.C5F4   Effort in China from Pearl Harbor to the
        Marshall Mission (New York: Atheneum, 19).

D802   _____. Contest Over Japan (New York:
.J3F45 Norton, 1967).

D843   _____. From Trust to Terror: The Onset
.F387   of the Cold War (New York: Norton, 1970).

D777   Field, James A. The Japanese at Leyte Gulf
.F5   (Princeton, N.J.: Princeton University Press,
        1947).

VB23   Forrestal, James V. et al. The Navy: A Study
.P8   in Administration (Chicago: Public Administra-
        tion Service, 1946).

VB23   Furer, Julius Augustus. Administration of
.F8   the Navy Department in World War II (Washing-
        ton: Department of the Navy, Naval History
        Division, 1959).

E746   Halsey, William F. and J. Bryan III. Admiral
.H3A3   Halsey's Story (New York: McGraw-Hill, 1947).

D767.99 Heinl, Robert D. and John A. Crown. The Mar-
.M3U52 shalls: Increasing the Tempo (Washington: HQ,
        USMC, 1954).

D783   Holmes, W.J. Undersea Victory: The Influence
.H6   of Submarine Operations on the War in the
        Pacific (Garden City, N.Y.: Doubleday, 1966).

V864   Hoyt, Edwin Palmer. The Glorious Flattops
.H6   (Boston: Little, Brown, 1965).

D767 .H65	_____. How They Won the War in the Pacific: Nimitz and His Admirals (New York: Weybright and Talley, 1970).
D774 .P4H69	_____. The Battle for Leyte Gulf: The Death Knell of the Japanese Fleet (New York: Weybright and Talley, 1972).
D792.J3 I513 1958	Inoguchi, Rikihei, Tadshi Nakajima, and Roger Pineau. The Divine Wind: Japan's Kamikaze Force in World War II (Annapolis, Md.: U.S. Naval Institute, 1958).
VA503 .J46	Jenkins, Ernest Harold. A History of the French Navy From Its Beginnings to the Present Day (London: Macdonald, Macdonald and Jane's, 1973).
E182 .B96 J6	Jones, Ken and Hubert Kelly. Admiral Arleigh [31 knot] Burke: The Story of a Fighting Sailor (Philadelphia: Chilton, 1962).
D773 .K3	Karig, Walter. Battle Report: End of an Empire (New York: Rinehart, 1948).
D773 .A5 1945	King, Ernest J. U.S. Navy at War, 1941-1945: Official Reports to the Secretary of the Navy by Fleet Admiral Ernest J. King, USN (Washington: Navy Department, 1946).
E745 .L4A3	Le May, Curtis, with Mackinlay Cantor. Mission with Le May: My Story (Garden City, N.Y.: Doubleday, 1965).
D773 .L57	Lockwood, Charles A. and Hans Christian Adamson. Battles of the Philippine Sea (New York: Crowell, 1967).
D785 .U575 .M3	McIsaac, David. Strategic Bombing in World War Two: The Story of the United States Strategic Bombing Survey (New York: Garland Publishing, 1976).
V63 .H34 M47	Merrill, James M. A Sailor's Admiral: A Biography of William F. Halsey (New York: Crowell, 1976).

D773   Morison, Samuel E. <u>History of United States</u>
.M6   <u>Naval Operations in World War II</u>: Vol. 8.
          <u>New Guinea and the Marianas, March 1944-</u>
          <u>Aug. 1944</u> (1953); Vol. 12. <u>Leyte Gulf, June</u>
          <u>1944-January 1945</u> (1958); Vol. 13. <u>The Libera-</u>
          <u>tion of the Philippines: Luzon, Mindanao,</u>
          <u>the Visayas, 1944-1945</u> (1959); Vol. 14. <u>Vic-</u>
          <u>tory in the Pacific, 1945</u> (1960).

D773   Pratt, Fletcher. <u>Fleet Against Japan</u> (New
.P68   York: Harper, 1946).

D767   _____. <u>The Marine's War: An Account of</u>
.P7   <u>the Struggle for the Pacific from both Ameri-</u>
          <u>can and Japanese Sources</u> (New York: W. Sloane
          Associates, 1948).

UF23   Rowland, Buford, and William B. Boyd. <u>U.S.</u>
.A62   <u>Navy Bureau of Ordnance in World War II</u>
          (Washington: GPO, 1953).

D734   Stettinius, Edward Reilly. <u>Roosevelt and the</u>
.C7S8   <u>Russians: The Yalta Conference</u>, Walter Johnson,
          ed. (Garden City, N.Y.: Doubleday, 1949).

D767   Winton, John. <u>The Forgotten Fleet: The British</u>
.W52   <u>Navy in the Pacific, 1944-1945</u> (New York:
          Crown-McCann, 1970).

D773   Woodward, C. Vann. <u>The Battle for Leyte Gulf</u>
.W6   (New York: Macmillan, 1947).

          Transcripts of oral interviews of Richard L.
          Conolly, Ferald F. Bogan, Arleigh Burke,
          Thomas C. Kinkaid, and Hanson W. Baldwin,
          Annapolis, Md.: U.S. Naval Academy Library,
          Special Collections.

CHAPTER 22

BIBLIOGRAPHY

E748   Albion, Robert G. and Hobert H. Connery. <u>For-</u>
.F68A6   <u>restal and the Navy</u> (New York: Columbia Univer-
          sity Press, 1962).

580

E744 .A477   Ambrose, Stephen E. <u>Rise to Globalism: American Foreign Policy Since 1938</u>, rev. ed. (Baltimore: Penguin Books, 1976).

DT107 .83.B 413   Beaufré, Andre. <u>The Suez Expedition 1956</u>. Trans. from the French by Richard Barry (New York: Praeger, 1969).

VA65 .N3B4   Blair, Clay. <u>The Atomic Submarine and Admiral Rickover</u> (New York: Holt, 1954).

UA236 .B6   Borklund, Carl W. <u>Men of the Pentagon: From Forrestal to McNamara</u> (New York: Praeger, 1966).

UA236 .B58   _____. <u>The Department of Defense</u> (New York: Praeger, 1968).

UA11 .B7   Brodie, Bernard. <u>Strategy in the Missile Age</u> (Princeton, N.J.: Princeton University Press, 1959).

UA23 .C24   Caraley, Demetrious. <u>The Politics of Military Unification: A Study of Conflict and the Policy Process</u> (New York: Columbia University Press, 1966).

UA646 .3C54   Cleveland, Harlan. <u>NATO: The Transatlantic Bargain</u> (New York: Harper & Row, 1970).

V63.R54 D37   David, Heather M. <u>Admiral Rickover and the Nuclear Navy</u> (New York: Putnam, 1970).

VA50 .D34   Davis, Vincent. <u>Postwar Defense Policy and the U.S. Navy, 1943-1946</u> (Chapel Hill: University of North Carolina Press, 1962).

VA23 .D29   _____. <u>The Admirals Lobby</u> (Chapel Hill: University of North Carolina Press, 1967).

VF347 .D3   _____. <u>The Politics of Innovation: Patterns in Navy Cases</u> (Denver: University of Denver, 1967).

DD881 .D3   Davison, William P. <u>The Berlin Blockade: A Study in Cold War Politics</u> (Princeton, N.J.: Princeton University Press, 1958).

D443 .D642	Donnelly, Desmond. *Struggle for the World: The Cold War, 1917-1965* (New York: St. Martin, 1965).
TL789 .E45	Emme, Eugene M. *A History of Space Flight* (New York: Holt, Rinehart & Winston, 1965).
E835 .D85F5	Finer, Herman. *Dulles Over Suez* (Chicago: Quadrangle Books, 1964).
D421 .F613	Fontaine, André. *A History of the Cold War: From the Korean War to the Present*, 2 vols. (New York: Pantheon, 1969).
E744 .G25	Gaddis, John L. *The United States and the Origins of the Cold War, 1941-1947* (New York: Columbia University Press, 1972).
UG633 .G6	Goldberg, Alfred, ed. *A History of the United States Air Force, 1907-1957* (Princeton, N.J.: Van Nostrand Reinhold, 1957).
E744 .G69	Graebner, Norman A. *Cold War Diplomacy: American Foreign Policy, 1945-1960* (Princeton, N.J.: Van Nostrand, 1962).
D743 .G666	Greenfield, Kent Roberts. *American Strategy in World War II: A Reconsideration* (Baltimore: Johns Hopkins Press, 1963).
UB .23.H3	Hammond, Paul Y. *Organizing for Defense: The American Military Establishment in the Twentieth Century* (Princeton, N.J.: Princeton University Press, 1961).
E813 .H42	Haynes, Richard F. *The Awesome Power: Harry S. Truman as Commander in Chief* (Baton Rouge: Louisiana State University Press, 1973).
VM317 .H48	Hewlett, Richard G. and Francis Duncan. *Nuclear Navy, 1949-1962* (Chicago: University of Chicago Press, 1974).
VE23 .H4	Heinl, Robert Debs. *Soldiers of the Sea: The United States Marine Corps, 1775-1962* (Annapolis, Md.: U.S. Naval Institute, 1962).

VA25 .H88	Huzar, Elias. *The Purse and the Sword: Control of the Army Through Military Appropriations, 1933-1950* (Ithaca: Cornell University Press, 1950).
UA646 .3.A55	Ismay, Lord Hastings L.I. *NATO: The First Five Years* (Paris?: 1954?).
E744 .K17	Kaplan, Lawrence. *Recent American Foreign Policy: Conflicting Interpretations*, rev. ed. Homewood, Ill.: Dorsey Press, 1972).
UA646 .3.K36	_____. *NATO and the Policy of Containment* (Boston: Heath, 1968).
E182 .B9656	Jones, Ken and Hubert Kelley, Jr. *Admiral Arleigh (31-Knot) Burke: The Story of a Fighting Sailor* (Philadelphia: Chilton, 1962).
D773 .K3	Karig, Walter. *Battle Report: The War in Korea* (New York: Rinehart, 1951).
D811 .K42	Kenney, George C. *General Kenney Reports: A Personal History of the Pacific War* (New York: Duell, Sloane & Pearce, 1949).
UA646 .3K5	Knorr, Klaus, E., ed. *NATO and American Security* (Princeton, N.J.: Princeton University Press, 1959).
E744 .LU2	Lederer, William J. *A Nation of Sheep* (New York: Norton, 1961).
PS3562 .E3U45	_____ and Eugene Burdick. *The Ugly American* (New York: Norton, 1958).
E183.8 .R9L26	LaFeber, Walter. *America, Russia, and the Cold War, 1945-1966* (New York: Wiley, 1967).
E745 .L4A3	LeMay, Curtis E., with MacKinlay Cantor. *Mission with LeMay: My Story* (Garden City, N.Y.: Doubleday, 1965).
D840 .L8	Lukacs, John. *A History of the Cold War* (Garden City, N.Y.: Anchor Books, 1962).

D785   MacIsaac, David. Strategic Bombing in World
.U573   War Two: The Story of the United States Stra-
.M3   tegic Bombing Survey (New York: Garland, 1976).

E748   McLellan, Davis S. Dean Acheson: The State
.A15M32   Department Years (New York: Dodd, Mead, 1976).

E813   Millis, Walter, with Eugene S. Duffield, ed.
.F6   The Forrestal Diaries (New York: Viking, 1951).

UA646   Osgood, Robert E. NATO: The Entangling Alli-
.3.O8   ance (Chicago: University of Chicago Press,
           1962).

E840   _____ and others. America and the World:
.A615   From the Truman Doctrine to Vietnam (Baltimore:
           Johns Hopkins Press, 1970).

V858   Polmar, Norman. Atomic Submarines (Princeton,
.P6   N.J.: Van Nostrand, 1963).

UA646   Richardson, James L. Germany and the Atlantic
.3.R48   Alliance (Cambridge: Harvard University Press,
           1966).

VA23   Ries, John C. The Management of Defense:
.R495   Organization and Control of the U.S. Armed
           Forces (Baltimore: Johns Hopkins Press, 1964).

UA23   Schilling, Warner R., Paul Y. Hammond, and
.S33   Glenn H. Snyder. Strategy, Politics, and De-
           fense Budgets (New York: Columbia University
           Press, 1962).

UA23   Stanley, Timothy W. American Defense and Na-
.S675   tional Security (Washington: Public Affairs
           Press, 1956).

D849   _____ and Darnell M. Whitt. Detente
.S7   Diplomacy: United States and European Security
           in the 1970's (Cambridge, Mass.: University
           Press of Cambridge, 1970).

D845   _____. NATO in Transition: The Future of
.2.S8   the Atlantic Alliance (New York: Praeger, 1965).

E814   Truman, Harry S. *Memoirs by Harry S. Truman,*
.T75   2 vols. (Garden City, N.Y.: Doubleday, 1955-
          1956).

D785   Webster, Charles and Noble Frankland. *The*
.W38   *Strategic Air Offensive Against Germany, 1939-*
          1945, 4 vols., in J.R.M. Butler, ed. United
          Kingdom Military Series, *History of the Second*
          World War (London: H.M.S.O., 1961).

E183   Whitaker, Arthur P. *Spain and the Defense of*
.8.S7W5   *the West: Ally and Liability* (New York:

          Yergin, Daniel. *Shattered Peace: The Origins*
          of the Cold War and the National Security State
          (Boston: Houghton Mifflin, 1977).

UG1282   York, Herbert F. *The Advisors: Oppenheimer,*
.A8Y67   *Teller, & the Superbomb* (San Francisco: W.H.
          Freeman, 1976).

          Annual and Semiannual Reports of the Secretary
          of Defense, 1945-1953 (Washington: GPO).

          U.S. President's Air Policy Commission. *Sur-*
          vival in the Air Age: A Report (Washington:
          GPO, 1948).

          U.S. House Committee on Armed Services. *Na-*
          tional Defense Program, Hearings Before the
          Committee 81st Cong., 1st Sess. Oct. 6-21,
          1948 (Washington: GPO, 1949).

          Report of the Congressional Aviation Policy
          Board. *Naval Aviation Policy* (Sen. Report 949,
          81st Cong., 2d Sess. (Washington: GPO, 1948).

          U.S. House Committee on Armed Services.
          National Defense Program: Unification and
          Strategy, Hearings Before the Committee, 81st
          Cong., 1st Sess. (Washington: GPO, 1949).

          USSBS. *Overall Report (European War)*, Septem-
          ber 30, 1945 (Washington: 1945).

_____. Summary Report (Pacific War) 1 July 1946 (Washington, 1946).

Transcripts of oral interview of the following men in Annapolis, Md. U.S. Naval Academy Library, Special Collections: Hanson W. Baldwin, Gerald F. Bogan, Arleigh Burke; Richard L. Conolly, Daniel V. Gallery, Charles D. Griffin, Fitzhugh Lee, and Herbert D. Riley.

Cagle, Malcolm W. "Task Force 77 in Action off Vietnam," U.S. Naval Institute Proceedings, Naval Review, 1972.

Hammond, Paul Y. "Super Carriers and B-36 Bombers: Appropriations, Strategy and Politics," in Harold Stein, ed. American Civil-Military Decisions (Birmingham: The University of Alabama Press, 1962), pp. 465-567.

Herring, George C. "The Truman Administration and the Restoration of French Sovereignty in Indochina," Diplomatic History 1 (Spring 1977): 97-117.

CHAPTER 23

BIBLIOGRAPHY

E744 Acheson, Dean. Present at the Creation: My
.A2174 Years in the State Department (New York: Norton, 1969).

DS918 _____. The Korean War (New York: Norton,
.A59 1971).

E835 Adams, Sherman. First Hand Report: The Story
.A3 of the Eisenhower Administration (New York: Harper, 1961).

E835 Alexander, Charles C. Holding the Line: The
.A645 Eisenhower Era, 1952-1961 (Bloomington: University of Indiana Press, 1973).

VA23 Aliano, Richard A. American Defense Policy
.A57 from Eisenhower to Kennedy: The Politics of Changing Military Requirements, 1957-1961 (Columbus: Ohio University Press, 1975).

VB230   Ambrister, Trevor. *A Matter of Accountabil-*
.A75   *ity: The True Story of the Pueblo Affair* (New York: Coward-McCann, 1970).

VA23   Art, Robert J. *The TFX Decision: McNamara and*
.A73   *the Military* (Boston: Little, Brown, 1968).

VA646   Beaupre, Andre. *NATO and Europe.* Trans. Joseph
.3.B383   Green (New York: Knopf, 1966).

JX1974   Bechhoefer, Bernhard G. *Postwar Negotiations*
.B35   *for Arms Control* (Washington: Burns and Mac-Eachern, 1961).

Z3319   Blanchard, Carroll H., Jr. *Korean War Bibliog-*
.K6B5   *raphy and Maps of Korea* (Albany: Korean Conflict Research Foundation, 1964).

VA23   Bottome, Edgar M. *The Missile Gap: A Study of*
.B728   *the Formulation of Military and Political Policy* [1958-1961] (Rutherford, N.J.: Fairleigh-Dickinson University Press, 1971).

VA23   Borklund, Carl W. *Men of the Pentagon: For-*
.6B6   *restal to McNamara* (New York: Praeger, 1966).

VB230   Brandt, Edward. *The Last Voyage of the USS*
.B7   *Pueblo* (New York: Norton, 1969).

VA11   Brodie, Bernard. *Strategy in the Missile Age*
.B7   (Princeton, N.J.: Princeton University Press, 1959)

JX1391   _____. *War and Politics* (New York: Mac-
.B68   millan, 1973).

E744   Brown, Seyom. *The Faces of Power: Constance*
.B78   *and Change in U.S. Foreign Policy from Truman to Eisenhower* (New York: Columbia University Press, 1968).

VB230   Bucher, Lloyd M. *Bucher: My Story* (Garden
.B7999   City, N.J.: Doubleday, 1970).

DS920   Cagle, Malcolm and Frank A. Manson. *The Sea*
.A2C3   *War in Korea* (Annapolis, Md.: U.S. Naval Institute, 1957).

E743 .C248	Caridi, Ronald H. *The Korean War and American Politics* (Philadelphia: University of Pennsylvania Press, 1968).
DS918 .C55	Clark, General Mark W. *From the Danube to the Yalu* (New York: Harper, 1954).
UA26 .K6C56	Clough, Ralph N. *Deterrence and Defense in Korea: The Role of U.S. Forces* (Washington: Brookings, 1976).
DS918 .C62	Collins, J.P. Lawton. *War in Peacetime: The History and Lessons of Korea* (Boston: Houghton Mifflin, 1969).
DS557 .A6C6	Corson, William R. *The Betrayal* (New York: Norton, 1968).
VA230 .C7	Crawford, Don. *Pueblo Intrigue* (Wheaton, Md.: Tyndale House, 1969).
E835 .D6	Donovan, Robert J. *Eisenhower: The Inside Story* (New York: Harper, 1956).
E743 .D77	Druks, Herbert. *From Truman Through Johnson: A Documentary History*, 2 vols. (New York: R. Speller, 1971).
E835 .E33	Eisenhower, Dwight D. *Mandate for Change: The White House Years, 1953-1957* (Garden City, N.Y.: Doubleday, 1963).
E835 .E47	_____. *Waging Peace: The White House Years, 1957-1961* (Garden City, N.Y.: Doubleday, 1965).
UG630 .E5	Emme, Eugene M., ed. *The Impact of Air Power: National Security and World Politics* (Princeton, N.J.: D. Van Nostrand, 1959).
DS550 .F28	Fall, Bernard B. *Hell in a Very Small Place: The Siege of Dienbienphu* (Philadelphia: Lippincott, 1966).
DS550 .F3	_____. *Street Without Joy*, 4th ed. (Harrisburg, Pa.: Stackpole, 1964).

DS557   _____. The Two Vietnams: A Political and
.A5F34   Military Analysis (New York: Praeger, 1963).

DS557   _____. Vietnam Witness, 1953-1956 (New
.A5F35   York: Praeger, 1966).

E183   Ferrell, Robert H. George C. Marshall (New
.7.B462 York: Cooper Square Publishers, 1966).

DS920   Field, James A. History of United States Naval
.A2F5   Operations: Korea (Washington: Department of
         the Navy, 1962).

E835   Finer, Herman. Dulles Over Suez (Chicago:
.D85F5   Quadrangle Books, 1964).

E835   Finletter, Thomas K. Power and Policy: United
.F5   States Foreign Policy and Military Power in the
         Hydrogen Age (New York: Harcourt, Brace, 1954).

DS920   Futrell, Robert Frank, Lawson S. Moseley, and
.2.U5F8 Albert F. Simpson. The United States Air Force
         in Korea, 1950-1952 (New York: Duell, Sloan &
         Pearce, 1961).

VB230   Gallery, Daniel V. The Pueblo Incident (Garden
.G3   City, N.Y.: Doubleday, 1970).

E744   Gavin, James M. Crisis Now (New York: Random
.G35   House, 1968).

DS919   Guttmann, Allan, ed. Korea and the Theory of
.G8   Limited War (Lexington, Mass.: Heath, 1967).

UA11   Halperin, Morton H. Limited War in the Nuclear
.H34   Age (New York: Wiley, 1963).

VE23   Heinl, Robert D. Soldiers of the Sea: The
.H4   United States Marine Corps, 1775-1962 (Annapo-
         lis, Md.: U.S. Naval Institute, 1962).

DS918   _____. Victory at High Tide: The Inchon-
.2.I5H4 Seoul Campaign (Philadelphia: Lippincott, 1969).

DS918   Higgins, Trumbull. Korea and the Fall of Mac-
.H515   Arthur: A Precis on Limited War (New York:
         Oxford Press, 1960).

DS557   Hoopes, Townsend. *The Limits of Intervention*
.A63H6   (New York: McKay, 1969).

D773   Karig, Walter. *Battle Report: The War in Korea*
.K3   (New York: Rinehart, 1952).

UA23   Kaufman, William W. *The McNamara Strategy* (New
.K37   York: Harper, 1964).

UA23   Kintner, William R. and others. *Forging a New*
.3.K5   *Sword: A Study of the Department of Defense*
           (New York: Harper, 1958).

UA23   Kissinger, Henry. *Nuclear Weapons and Foreign*
.K49   *Policy* (New York: Harper, 1957).

DK275   *Khrushchev Remembers*. Edited by Edward Cran-
.K5A326   shaw. (Boston: Little, Brown, 1970).

UB223   Korb, Lawrence J. *The JCS: The First Twenty-*
.K67   *five Years* (Bloomington: Indiana University
           Press, 1976).

E183.8   LaFeber, Walter. *America, Russia, and the Cold*
.R9L26   *War, 1945-1966* (New York: Wiley, 1967).

DS918   Leckie, Robert. *Conflict: The Story of the*
.L36   *Korean War, 1950-1953* (New York: Putnam's,
           1962).

D773   Lott, Arnold S. *Most Dangerous Sea: A History*
.L6   *of Mine Warfare and an Account of U.S. Navy*
           Mine Warfare Operations in World War II and
           Korea (Annapolis, Md.: U.S. Naval Institute,
           1959).

E745   MacArthur, Douglas. *Reminiscences* (New York:
.M3.A34   McGraw-Hill, 1964).

DA566.9   Macmillan, Harold. *Riding the Storm, 1956-*
.M33A27   *1959* (New York: Harper & Row, 1971).

DA566.9   _____. *At the End of the Day, 1961-1963*
.M33   (New York: Harper & Row, 1973).
A254

VA23   McNamara, Robert S. *The Essence of Security*
.M25   (New York: Harper and Row, 1968).

DS918.2.C4M3	Marshall, Samuel Lyman Atwood. *The River and the Gauntlet: Defeat of the Eighth Army by the Chinese Communist Forces, November, 1950, in the Battle of the Chongchon River, Korea* (New York: Morrow, 1953).
UA23.M9	Murdock, Clark A. *Defense Policy Formulation: A Comparative Analysis of the McNamara Era* (Albany: SUNY Press, 1974).
VB230.M87	Murphy, Edward R. Jr. *Second in Command* [The *Pueblo* Affair] (New York: Holt, Rinehart and Winston, 1971).
D792.J3N 2513	Nagatsuka, Ryuji. *I was a Kamikaze* (New York: Macmillan, 1974).
E856.A25	Nixon, Richard. *Six Crises* (Garden City, N.Y.: Doubleday, 1962).
DS918.O25 1969b	O'Ballance, Edgar. *Korea: 1950-1953* (Hamden, Conn.: Archon Books, 1969).
Z6835.U5M3 No.6 1970	O'Quinlivan, Michael. *Annotated Bibliography of the United States Marines in the Korean War* (Washington: HQ, USMC, 1962).
UA23.O8	Osgood, Robert E. *Limited War: The Challenge to American Strategy* (Chicago: University of Chicago Press, 1957).
DS919.P33	Paige, Glenn D. *The Korean Decision, June 24-30, 1950* (New York: Free Press, 1968).
UA23.O47	Quester, George. *Nuclear Diplomacy: The First Twenty-five Years* (New York: Dunellen, 2d ed., 1973).
DS913.R43	Rees, David. *Korea: The Limited War* (Baltimore: Penguin Books, 1970).
E745.R5A35	Ridgway, General Matthew B., as told to Harold H. Martin. *Soldier: The Memoirs of Matthew B. Ridgway* (New York: Harper, 1956).

UA23 .R495	Ries, John C. The Management of Defense (Baltimore: Johns Hopkins Press, 1964).
UA23 .R6	Rockefeller Brothers Fund Study. International Security, The Military Aspect: Report of Panel II of the Special Studies Project (Garden City, N.Y.: Doubleday, 1958).
E841 .S3	Schlesinger, Arthur M. A Thousand Days (Boston: Houghton Mifflin, 1965).
V25 .S6	Sokol, Anthony E. Seapower in the Nuclear Age (Washington: Public Affairs Press, 1961).
E744 .S8	Spanier, John W. The Truman-MacArthur Controversy and the Korean War (New York: Norton, 1965).
F1408 .S9	Szulc, Tad. Latin America (New York: Atheneum, 1966).
E744 .T3	Tarr, David W. American Strategy in the Nuclear Age (New York: Macmillan, 1966).
UA23 .T33	Taylor, Maxwell D. The Uncertain Trumpet (New York: Harper, 1959).
E745 T317 1972	_____. Swords and Plowshares (New York: Norton, 1972).
	Thomas, Gordon and Max Morgan Witts. Enola Gay (Garden City, N.Y.: Doubleday, 1977).
JK468 .I6T8	Tully, Andrew. CIA: The Inside Story (New York: William Morrow, 1962).
UA23 .T88	Twining, Nathan F. Neither Liberty nor Safety: A Hard Look at United States Military Policy and Strategy (New York: Holt, Rinehart and Winston, 1966).
DS919 .A516	U.S. Marine Corps Operations in Korea, 1950-1953, 5 vols. (Washington: HQ, USMC, Historical Branch, G-3, 1955-1972).

VG93 .A79	United States Naval Aviation, 1910-1970 (Washington: Department of the Navy, 1971).
AS36 .R3R356	Whiting, Allen S. China Crosses the Yalu: The Decision to Enter the Korean War (New York: Macmillan, 1960).
E745 .M3W48	Whitney, Courtney. MacArthur: His Rendezvous with History (New York: Knopf, 1956).
E745 .M3W5	Willoughby, Charles A. and John Chamberlain. MacArthur 1941-1951 (New York: McGraw-Hill, 1954).
DK68.7 .C5Z3	Zagoria, Donald S. The Sino-Soviet Conflict, 1956-1961 (New York: Atheneum, 1967).
	U.S. Congress. House Committee on Armed Services. Military Posture Hearings, 87th Cong., 2d Sess. (Washington: GPO, 1962).
	U.S. Senate Permanent Subcommittee on Investigations, Committee on Government Operations. The TFX Contract Investigation: Hearings, 88th Cong., 1st Sess., 1963 (Washington: GPO, 1963).
DS918 .U55	U.S. Senate Committee on Foreign Relations and Senate Committee on Armed Services. Hearings on the Military Situation in the Far East, 82nd Cong., 1st Sess. (Washington: GPO, 1951).
	Semiannual Report of the Secretary of Defense, 1953-1961.
	The United States Air Force Policy on Doctrine and Procedures for the Air Defense of the United States (Washington: Department of the Air Force, 30 June 1949).
	United States Air Force Operations in the Korean Conflict, 3 vols. (Maxwell Air Force Base: Historical Division, 1952-1956).
	The Progressive Development of the Strategic Air Command, 1947-1970 (Offut Air Force Base: SAC, 1970).

Major Changes in the Organization of the Joint Chiefs of Staff, 1942-1969 (Washington: U.S. Joint Chiefs of Staff, Historical Division, 1969).

United States Marine Operations in Korea, 1950-1952, 5 vols. (Washington: HQ, USMC, Historical Branch, G-3, 1954-1972).

Comfort, Kenneth L. "Nuclear Security Policy and the Development of Tactical Nuclear Forces, 1948-1958" (Ph. D. diss, Columbia University, 1970).

Dart, Robert C. "Flexible Response: A Case Study of the Policy Process for National Security" (Ph. D. diss., University of Virginia, 1973).

McGeehan, Robert J. "American Diplomacy and the German Rearmament Question, 1950-1953" (Columbia University, 1969).

Moulton, Harland B. American Strategic Power: Two Decades of Nuclear Strategy and Weapons Systems, 1945-1965 (Ph. D. diss., University of Minnesota, 1969).

Schneider, Mark B. "Nuclear Weapons and American Strategy," (Ph. D. diss., University of Southern California, 1974).

Schratz, Paul R. "The United States Defense Establishment: Trends in Organizational Structures, Functions, and Interrelationships, 1958-1970" (Ph. D. diss., Ohio State University, 1972).

Weaver, James Devers. "The Commander-in-Chief, Civilian Supremacy, Command and Control: Civil-Military Relations in the Eisenhower Presidency" (Ph. D. diss., New York University, 1972).

DS919 .F59 Flint, Roy K. "The Tragic Flaw: MacArthur, the Joint Chiefs of Staff and the Korean War" (Ph. D. diss., Duke University, 1975).

Cagle, Malcolm. "Errors of the Korean War," U.S. Naval Institute Proceedings 84 (Oct. 1958): 31-35.

Korth, The Honorable Fred. "The Challenge of Navy Management: A Report from the Secretary of the Navy," U.S. Naval Institute Proceedings 89 (Aug. 1963): 26-31.

MacDonald, Scot. "How the Decisions Were Made: Exclusive Inside Story of Naval Reorganization," Armed Forces Management 12 (May 1966): 74-82.

Schratz, Paul R. "The Nuclear Carrier and Modern War," U.S. Naval Institute Proceedings 98 (Aug. 1972): 18-25.

Admiral Arleigh A. Burke, USN (RET), "The Lebanon Crisis," Proceedings Naval History Symposium (Annapolis, Md.: U.S. Naval Academy, April 27-28, 1973), pp. 70-80.

Admiral George W. Anderson, Jr., USN (RET), "The Cuban Missile Crisis," ibid., pp. 81-86.

Wilson, Larman C. "The Dominican Policy of the United States," World Affairs 128 (July-Sept. 1965): 93-101.

_____. "International Law and the United States Quarantine of 1962," Journal of Inter-American Studies 7 (Oct. 1965): 485-92.

Transcripts of oral interviews of the following men in Annapolis, Md., U.S. Naval Academy Library, Special Collections: Hanson W. Baldwin, Arleigh A. Burke, Daniel V. Gallery, Paul D. Stroop, and John S. Thach.

CHAPTER 24

NOTES

1. The solid-fueled Minuteman, introduced in 1963, was programmed at a level of 1,000 for the years 1967 and 1968, the liquid-fueled Titan at 54 through 1971. The 6 Polaris boats of 1961 were increased to 41 in 1967, some carrying the Polaris A-2 missile with a range of 1,500 miles, some the A-3, with a range of 2,500 miles. In 1967, McNamara decided to produce Poseidon as the successor to Polaris for the 1970s.

2. The blockade was directed by a CINCLANTFLT Quarantine Center established in consequence of Kennedy's speech of the 22nd and instructions from the JCS. CINCLANTFLT designated Commander SECOND Fleet Quarantine Force Commander and Commander TF 136. As CINCLANTFLT was also COMASWFORLANT and Commander Task Forces 81-83, he was directed to conduct air surveilliance as requested by the Commander Quarantine Force. Commander SECOND Fleet (VADM Alfred G. Ward), divided TF136 into three task groups. CTG 136.1 (RADM John W. Ailes) had a cruiser-destroyer force: CTG 136.2 (RADM Ernest E. Christensen), had the *Essex* and her screen; and CTG 136.3 (Captain W.O. Spears), commanded 3 oilers and an ammunition ship and their destroyer screen. On 24 October, all information and displays with respect to the blockade were placed in one room known as the OPCON Center (Special Quarantine Plot), in which some 30 persons worked. Naval aircraft and 6 Air Force RB-47s during the first week provided more than 200 sightings of Cuba-bound ships, the 46 blockading ships only about 50. A constantly monitored Remington Rand Univac sea surveillance computer system kept track of all contacts, thus providing information for launching sea or air searches. Information about the blockade was disseminated in Quarantine Plot's SITSUMS (situation summaries). Special Quarantine Plot personnel were disbanded on 26 November. Since then the plot is maintained by COMASWFORLANT to plot merchant ships going to and from Cuba.

3. The communist Pathet Laos, presumably supported by Russia, were waging a vigorous offensive against

the government supported by the United States, and Vietcong trained in North Vietnam were infiltrating through Laos into South Vietnam. To bolster Laos, in May 1962 Kennedy sent the Seventh Fleet to the South China Sea and 5,000 troops to Thailand. In June, a neutralist government of a neutralized Laos was recognized by 19 nations.

BIBLIOGRAPHY

E841 .A2   Abel, Elie. *The Missile Crisis* (Philadelphia: Lippincott, 1966).

E744 .A2174   Acheson, Dean G. *Present at the Creation: My Years in the State Department* (New York: Norton, 1969).

UA646 .3.A75   Amme, Carl H. *NATO without France* (Stanford: Hoover Institution on War, Revolution, and Peace, 1967).

E183.8 .V5B3   Bator, Victor. *Vietnam: A Diplomatic Tragedy: The Origins of United States Involvement* (Dobbs Ferry, N.Y.: Oceana Publications, 1965).

D1065 .U5B4   Beloff, Max. *The United States and the Unity of Europe* (New York: Random House, 1963).

F1414 .B49   Berle, A.A. *Latin America: Diplomacy and Reality* (New York: Harper & Row, 1962).

Brown, Weldon A. *The Last Chopper: The Denouement of the American Role in Vietnam, 1963-1975*, 2 vols. (Port Washington, N.Y.: Kennikat Press, 1976).

D5557 .A5B83   Buttinger, Joseph. *Vietnam: A Dragon Embattled*, 2 vols. (New York: Praeger, 1967).

D5559 .5.C36   Caputo, Philip. *A Rumor of War* [Vietnam] (New York: Holt, Rinehart, and Winston, 1977).

E841 .C48   Chayes, Abram. *The Cuban Missile Crisis* (New York: Oxford University Press, 1974).

DS518 .8.C57   Clubb, O.E., Jr. *The United States and the Sino-Soviet Bloc in Southeast Asia* (Washington: Brookings Institution, 1962).

DS550 .C6	Cole, Allan B. <u>Conflict in Indochina and International Repercussion: A Documentary History 1945-1955</u> (Ithaca: Cornell University Press, 1956).
DS557 .A6C6	Corson, William R. <u>The Betrayal</u> (New York: Norton, 1968).
UA2 .D43	Deitchman, Seymour J. <u>Limited War and American Defense Policy</u> (Cambridge: N.I.T. Press, 1964).
E841 .D45	Dinerstein, Herbert S. <u>The Making of a Missile Crisis: October 1962</u> (Baltimore: Johns Hopkins Press, 1976).
E841 .D5	Divine, Robert A., ed. <u>The Cuban Missile Crisis</u> (Chicago: Quadrangle Books, 1971).
D5550 .D6	Dooley, Thomas A. <u>Deliver Us from Evil: The Story of Viet Nam's Flight to Freedom</u> (New York: Farrar, Straus, and Cudahy, 1956).
E847 .E9	Evans, Rowland and Robert Novak. <u>Lyndon B. Johnson: The Exercise of Power</u> (New York: New American Library, 1966).
UA23 .F3R	Falk, Stanley L. <u>The National Security Structure</u> (Washington: ICAF, 1967).
DS557 .A5F34	Fall, Bernard. <u>The Two Vietnams: A Political and Military Analysis</u>, rev. ed. (New York: Praeger, 1965).
DS557 A5F35	_____. <u>Viet-Nam Witness</u> (New York: Praeger, 1966).
DS550 .F3	_____. <u>Street Without Joy</u> (Harrisburg, Pa.: Stackpole, 1964).
DS550 .F28	_____. <u>Hell in a Very Small Place: The Siege of Dien Bien Phu</u> (New York: Lippincott, 1967).
DS557 .A7 H533	_____, ed. <u>Ho Chi Minh on Revolution</u> (New York: Praeger, 1967).

E744 .F886	Fulbright, William J. The Arrogance of Power (New York: Random House, 1967).
E744 .G25	Gaddis, John L. The United States and the Origins of the Cold War, 1941-1947 (New York: Columbia University Press, 1972).
U240 .G3	Galula, David. Counterinsurgency Warfare: Theory and Practice (New York: Praeger, 1962).
UA770 .G29	Garthoff, Raymond L. Soviet Image of Future War (Washington: Public Affairs Press, 1959)
UA23 .G53	Gavin, James. War and Peace in the Space Age (New York: Harper & Row, 1958).
E847 .G6	Goldman, Eric F. The Tragedy of Lyndon Johnson (New York: Knopf, 1969).
UA23 .G77	Goulding, Phil G. Confirm or Deny (New York: Harper and Row, 1970).
U240 .G833	Guevara, Ernesto. Che Guevara on Guerrilla Warfare (New York: Praeger, 1961).
DS557 .A6H3	Halberstam, David. The Making of a Quagmire (New York: Praeger, 1961).
E841 .H25	_____. The Best and the Brightest (New York: Random House, 1972).
DS557 .A5H25	Hammer, Ellen. Vietnam Yesterday and Today (New York: Holt, Rinehart & Winston, 1966).
UG633 .H3785	Harvey, Frank. Strike Command (New York: Duell, Sloan & Pearce, 1962).
E839 .H42	Heath, Jim F. Decade of Disillusionment: The Kennedy-Johnson Years (Bloomington: University of Indiana Press, 1975).
E840 .H5	Hilsman, Roger. To Move a Nation: The Politics of Foreign Policy in the Administration of John F. Kennedy (Garden City, N.Y.: Doubleday, 1967).
UA23 .H52	Hitch, Charles J. Decision-Making in Defense (Berkeley: University of California Press, 1965).

TL789.8 Holmes, Jay. *America on the Moon* (Philadel-
.U5H6   phia: Lippincott, 1962).

DS557   Hooper, Edwin B. *Mobility, Support, Endurance:*
.A645   *A Story of Naval Operational Logistics in the*
H66   *Vietnam War, 1965-1968* (Washington: GPO, 1972).

DS557   _____, Dean C. Allard, and Oscar P. Fitz-
.A645H7 gerald. *The United States Navy and the Viet-*
        nam Conflict. Vol. I. The Setting of the Stage
        to 1959 (Washington: Department of the Navy,
        Naval History Division, 1976).

F841   Hubbell, J.G. *Strike in the West: The Com-*
.D3   *plete Story of the Cuban Missile Crisis* (New
        York: Holt, Rinehart, Winston, 1963).

F1788   Johnson, Haynes. *The Bay of Pigs* (New York:
.J6   Norton, 1964).

DS557   Kahin, George and John Lewis. *The United*
.A6K28 *States in Vietnam*, rev. ed. (New York: Dell
        Pub. Co., 1969).

UF767   Kahn, Herman. *On Thermonuclear War* (Princeton,
.K25   N.J.: Princeton University Press, 1961).

UA23   Kaufman, William W. *The McNamara Strategy* (New
.K37   York: Harper & Row, 1964).

E847   Kearns, Doris. *Lyndon Johnson and the Ameri-*
.K4   *can Dream* (New York: Harper & Row, 1976).

E183   Kennedy, Robert F. *Thirteen Days: A Memoir of*
.8.R9   *the Cuban Missile Crisis* (New York: Norton,
K42   1969).

E835   Kissinger, Henry. *The Necessity for Choice:*
.K5   *Prospects of American Foreign Policy* (New York:
        Harper, 1961).

F1938   Martin, John Bartlow. *Overtaken by Events:*
.55M34 *The Dominican Crisis from the Fall of Trujillo*
        to the Civil War (New York: Doubleday, 1966).

DS557   Mecklin, J. *Mission in Torment: An Intimate*
.A6M4   *Account of the U.S. Role in Vietnam* (Garden
        City, N.Y.: Doubleday, 1965).

UG633 .M325	Medaris, John B., with Arthur Gordon. <u>Countdown for Decision</u> (New York: Putnam, 1960).
F1788 .M45 1962	Meyer, K.E. and Tad Szulc. <u>The Cuban Invasion</u> (New York: Ballantine Books, 1962).
DS557 .A6M5	Moore, Robin. <u>The Green Berets</u> (New York: Crown, 1968).
UA23 .M29	Murdock, Clark A. <u>Defense Policy Formation: A Comparative Analysis of the McNamara Era</u> (Albany: SUNY Press, 1974).
U55 .G505	O'Neill, Robert J. <u>General Giap: Politician and Strategist</u> (New York: Praeger, 1969).
U240 .P3	Paret, Peter and John W. Shy. <u>Guerrillas in the 1960s</u> (New York: Praeger, 1962).
V874 .P6	Polmar, Norman. <u>Aircraft Carriers: A Graphic History of Carrier Aviation and Its Influence on World Events</u> (Garden City, N.Y.: Doubleday, 1967).
UA23 .A4122	Posvar, Wesley W. and others. <u>American Defense Policy</u> (Baltimore: Johns Hopkins Press, 1965).
V162 .6.Q4	Quester, George H. <u>Deterrence before Hiroshima: The Background of Modern Strategy</u> (New York: Wiley, 1966).
E183 .8K5R3	Rankin, Karl Lott. <u>China Assignment 1949-1959</u> (Seattle: University of Washington Press, 1964)
UA23 .6.R3	Raymond, Jack. <u>Power at the Pentagon</u> (New York: Harper & Row, 1964).
UA23 .R6	Rockefeller Brothers Fund. <u>Prospect for America: The Rockefeller Panel Reports</u> (New York: Doubleday, 1961).
E741 .R67	Rostow, Walt W. <u>The United States in the World Arena</u> (New York: Harper, 1960).
D535 .S35	Scalapino, Robert A., ed. <u>The Communist Revolution in Asia</u> (Englewood Cliffs, N.J.: Prentice-Hall, 1965).

Schandler, Herbert Y. <u>The Unmaking of a President: Lyndon Johnson and Vietnam</u> (Princeton, N.J.: Princeton University Press, 1977).

F183
.8.C9
S56
Smith, Earl E. <u>The Fourth Floor: An Account of the Castro Communist Revolution</u> (New York: Random House, 1962).

E841
.S6
Sorenson, Theodore C. <u>Kennedy</u> (New York: Harper & Row, 1965).

DK63
.3.S86
Strausz-Hupe, Robert and others. <u>Protracted Conflict</u> (New York: Harper, 1963).

F1938
.55.S95
Szulc, Tad. <u>Dominican Diary</u> (New York: Delacorte, 1965).

DK274
.T3613
Tatu, Michel. <u>Power in the Kremlin</u> (New York: Viking, 1969).

UA23
.T33
Taylor, Maxwell D. <u>The Uncertain Trumpet</u> (New York: Harper, 1960).

UA23
.T34
_____. <u>Responsibility and Response</u> (New York: Harper & Row, 1967).

DT107
.83.T42
Thomas, Hugh. <u>Suez</u> (New York: Harper & Row, 1967).

Thompson, W. Scott and Donaldson D. Firzzel. <u>The Lessons of Vietnam</u> (New York: Crane & Russak, 1977).

Tucker, Samuel A., ed. <u>A Modern Design for Defense Decision: A McNamara-Hitch-Enthoven Anthology</u> (Washington: ICAF, 1966).

DK266
.U49
Ulam, Adam. <u>Expansion and Coexistence: The History of Soviet Foreign Policy, 1917-1967</u> (New York: Praeger, 1968).

UA23
.Y68
Yoshpe, Harry and others. <u>Defense Organization and Management</u> (Washington: ICAF, 1967).

U.S. Senate Permanent Subcommittee on Investigations, Committee on Government Operations. <u>The TFX Contract Investigation: Hearings</u>, 6 vols., 88th Cong., 1st Sess. (Washington: GPO, 1963).

U.S. Joint Chiefs of Staff. <u>Organization and Functions of the Joint Chiefs of Staff</u>. JCS Pub. 4, rev. (Washington: 1 October 1966).

U.S. Defense Department Study. <u>United States-Vietnam Relations, 1945-1971</u> (Washington: GPO, 1971 [12 books commonly known as the Pentagon Papers]).

Kirkpatrick, Prof. Lyman G., Jr. "Paramilitary Case Study--The Bay of Pigs," USNWCR 25 (Nov.-Dec. 1972): 32-43.

Michaelis, ADM Frederick H., USN. "Material for Naval Combat," <u>National Defense</u> (May-June 1977): 449-52.

Simmons, BGEN Edwin H., USMC (RET). "Marine Corps Operations in Vietnam, 1965-1966," <u>USNIP Naval Review 1968</u>. The years 1969-1972 are covered in <u>ibid</u>. for May 1973, **pp.** 198-223.

Spitz, Prof. Allan W. "Conventional versus Nuclear Power for CVA-67: A Study of Defense Management," USNWCR 24 (Apr. 1972): 3-14.

CHAPTER 25

NOTES

1. The helicopter carriers <u>Moskva</u> and <u>Leningrad</u> displace 15,000 tons. The Montreaux Convention of 1936 prohibits passage of ships bearing offensive weapons through the Bosporous. When the <u>Kiev</u> transited the strait, on 18 July 1976, she carried Yak-36 V/STOL aircraft similar to the British Harrier, a clearly offensive weapons system. The Soviets, however, called the ship a "submarine intercepting cruiser" that was allowed passage. A sister ship to the <u>Kiev</u>, the <u>Minsk</u>, is building at a Black Sea yard, and another large carrier at Leningrad. In mid-May 1977, the United States sent a four-ship force headed by a guided missile cruiser to the Indian Ocean, its leaders saying they would continue visiting until the Soviets stopped doing so. In June, a similar Soviet force visited the Gulf of Mexico.

2. Although the Soviets normally keep 77 submarines in the Atlantic, in April 1977 they deployed 89. Forty of these operated south of Iceland, where American troopships must pass on their way to Europe in the event of war. With them were many surface ships and the <u>Kiev</u>, covered by land-based planes out of Murmansk. While NATO submarines tracked the Soviet SSBNs, its surface and air surveillance system was stretched to the utmost.

   The McNamara strategy of being able to fight $2\frac{1}{2}$ wars--1 in the Atlantic, 1 in the Pacific, and a small one somewhere else--was revised in 1969 by Secretary of Defense Melvin Laird to a $1\frac{1}{2}$ war, with the 1 pointing to the Atlantic since the end of the Vietnam war in 1975. To prove that NATO can hold either the northern or southern flank in Europe, 8,000 U.S. Marines landed in Norway in 1976. In September 1977, in Operation "Display Determination," 6,000 Marines and their air exploited their speed and maneuverability in landings in Turkey.

   Since 1974, acrimony between Greece and Turkey over Cyprus damaged NATO in the Eastern Mediterranean. It also hurt Greece's chances of entering the European Common Market. On 30 July, the U.S. and Greece initialed a new 4-year accord that enables the U.S. to use 2 Greek naval bases, Souda Bay on Crete, and Hellenikon airport outside of Athens in return for $700 million in aid. Although Greece is not a member of NATO, its participation in NATO maneuvers held in August 1977 normalized its relations with the U.S. and the new accord will help the U.S. to monitor Soviet naval forces in the Mediterranean.

3. The members of SEATO, created in 1954, lowered their flags at Bangkok for the last time on 28 June 1977. Never a viable military organization, France and Pakistan had withdrawn from it before President Nixon sought detente with China and pulled out of Vietnam. Citing "new realities of the region," the Philippines and Thailand particularly have sought new diplomatic arrangements with China. Since the collective defense treaty (Manila Pact) remains in force, the member nations are still committed to aid the Philippines and Thailand in the event of

external aggression. Meanwhile both Australia and Japan have offered financial support to ASEAN (1967: Thailand, Malaysia, Singapore, Indonesia, and the Philippines), the organization of the 5 non-communist nations in Southeast Asia committed to resist Communist aggression.

BIBLIOGRAPHY

G680 .A7   Armstrong, Terence E. *The Northern Sea Route: Soviet Exploitation of the Northeast Passage* (Cambridge: Harvard University Press, 1952).

VA573 .B55   Blechman, Barry M. *The Changing Soviet Navy* (Washington: Brookings, 1973).

VA573 .B713   Breyer, Siegfried. *Guide to the Soviet Navy* (Annapolis, Md.: U.S. Naval Institute, 1970).

VA573 .G46   The Center for Strategic and International Studies. *Soviet Sea Power*. Special Report Series, No. 10, June 1, 1969 (Washington: Georgetown University, 1970).

HC336 .2C7   Cressy, George B. *Soviet Potentials: A Geographical Appraisal* (Syracuse: Syracuse University Press, 1962).

VA573 .E43   Eller, Ernest McNeill. *The Soviet Sea Challenge* (Chicago: Cowles, 1971).

VA50 .E4   Eliot, George Fielding. *Victory without War, 1958-1961* (Annapolis, Md.: U.S. Naval Institute, 1958).

UF767 .H2   _____. *The H Bomb* (New York: Didier, 1950).

VA573 .F35   Fairhall, David F. *Russian Sea Power* (Boston: Gambit, 1971).

UA770 .G295   Garthoff, Raymond L. *Soviet Military Policy* (New York: Praeger, 1966).

DS740 .5.R8G3	_____, ed. Sino-Soviet Military Relations (New York: Praeger, 1966).
DK59 .G67	Gorshkov, Sergei G. Red Star Rising at Sea (Annapolis, Md.: Naval Institute Press, 1974).
REF TL526 .R9G7	Green, William and Gordon Swanborough, comps. The Observer's Soviet Aircraft Directory (London: Frederick Warne and Co., 1975).
Q127 .R9H37	Harvey, Mose L. Leon Goure, and Vladimir Prokofieff. Science and Technology as an Instrument of Soviet Policy (Coral Gables: University of Miami, 1972).
VA570 .H4	Herrick, Robert Waring. Soviet Naval Strategy: Fifty Years of Theory and Practice (Annapolis, Md.: U.S. Naval Institute, 1968).
VA40 .F523	Jane's Fighting Ships (New York: ARCO). Annual, 1929—).
TL501 .J3	Jane's All the World's Aircraft (London: S. Low, Marston, 1909—).
DK274 .S68	Kohler, Foy D. et al. Soviet Strategy for the Seventies: From Cold War to Peaceful Coexistence (Coral Gables: University of Miami, 1973).
VA573 .M32	McCGwire, Michael, Ken Booth, and John McConnell, eds. Soviet Naval Policy: Objectives and Constraints (New York: Praeger, 1975).
U162 .A3 No. 58	Mackintosh, John M. The Evaluation of the Warsaw Pact (London: Institute for Strategic Studies, 1969).
DK633 .M23	_____. Strategy and Tactics of Soviet Foreign Policy (London: Oxford University Press, 1962).
VA573 .P6	Polmar, Norman. Soviet Naval Power in the 1970s, 2d ed. (New York: Crane, Russak, 1974).
	_____. Soviet Air Power. An Audio-Visual Presentation (Springfield, Va.: Creative Technologies).

UA23   Quanbeck, Alton H. and Barry M. Blechman.
.Q35   Strategic Forces: Issues for the Mid-Seventies
           (Washington: Brookings, 1973).

VA23   Quester, George H. Nuclear Diplomacy: The
.Q42   First 25 Years, 2d ed. (New York: Dunellen,
           1973).

JX1974   _____. The Politics of Nuclear Prolif-
.7Q47   eration (Baltimore: Johns Hopkins Press, 1973).

VA573   Saunders, Malcolm G., ed. The Soviet Navy (New
.S3   York: Praeger, 1958).

VA573   Theberge, James D., ed. Soviet Seapower in
.S59   the Caribbean: Political and Strategic Impli-
           cations (New York: Praeger, 1972).

VA573   Wegener, Edward. The Soviet Naval Offensive.
.W413   Trans. from the German by Henning Wegener
           (Annapolis, Md.: Naval Institute Press, 1974).

A536   Weinland, Robert G. The Changing Mission
.C466   Structure of the Soviet Navy (Arlington, Va.:
No. 80   Center for Naval Analyses, 1971).

E744   Wolf, Charles. United States Policy and the
.W575   Third World (Boston: Houghton Mifflin, 1967).

DK67   Wolfe, Thomas W. Soviet Power and Europe,
.W6   1945-1970 (Baltimore: Johns Hopkins Press,
           1970).

A536   _____. The Global Strategic Perspective
.R28   from Moscow (Santa Monica, CA: Rand Corp,
           1973).

AS36   _____. Soviet Naval Interaction with the
.R28   United States and its Influence on Soviet
No.4913   Naval Development (Santa Monica, CA: Rand
           Corp., 1972).

DK56   Woodward, David. The Russians at Sea: A
.W6   History of the Russian Navy (New York: Praeger,
           1966).

U.S. House Committee on Armed Services. <u>The Changing Strategic Naval Balance: U.S.S.R. vs. U.S.A.</u> (Washington: GPO, 1968).

U.S. Navy. Chief of Naval Operations. <u>Understanding Soviet Naval Development</u>, 2d ed. (Washington: Navy Department, April 1975).

VA573 .A53   Ackley, Richard Thomas. "Soviet Maritime Power: An Appraisal of the Development, Capabilities, and International Influence of the Soviet Navy, Fishing Fleet, and Merchant Marine" (Ph. D. diss., University of Southern California, 1974).

VA573 .B3   Bates, CDR Sheldon S., USN. "Why Soviet Naval Power? The Role of the Soviet Navy in General War" (Maxwell Air Force Base: Air University War College, April 1960).

CHAPTER 26

NOTES

1. Carter's revision of Ford's last budget deleted funds for a fourth <u>Nimitz</u>-class carrier, 8 nuclear-powered strike cruisers, and forced the closing or consolidation of 11 bases or facilities. In May 1977, an historic era ended when Congress declined to fund a nuclear carrier and spoke favorably of medium carriers of 40,000-50,000 tons and of "mini" (or "midi") carriers of half that size. Thus far Congress has denied requests by top naval leaders for funds with which to develop V/STOL aircraft to serve on mini-carriers.

2. Disaster for the United States would result if nations rich in natural resources aped the Arab oil squeeze. For example, the U.S. imports 98% of its cobalt from Zaire and more than a third of its manganese ore from Gabon. Rocks containing manganese, cobalt, copper, and nickel abound on the ocean floor. Although the U.S. has the technological capacity to mine this floor, failure has attended year-long attempts to reach international agreement on the ownership of these resources.

3. The best intelligence available in January 1977 was that American military research had virtually stopped because of the shrinking of the dollar by inflation, exorbitant costs of the all-volunteer force, and competition from the non-defense sector, with a constant congressional critic of DOD adding that payments of military pensions alone equal the costs of the Navy. A study by John Hughes, deputy director of the Defense Intelligence Agency, concluded that the Soviets spend between 13 and 16 percent of their GNP on arms; the U.S., 5.4 percent--or that Soviet expenditures are 140 percent greater than American.

4. As already noted, in June 1977 Carter stopped the production of the B-1.

5. The MX missile will travel along tunnels up to 20 miles long. When fired it will push its way through its concrete cover and deliver its warhead with unerring accuracy. The Air Force plans to build such tunnels in a Western desert area on an experimental basis during the fall of 1977.

BIBLIOGRAPHY

Booth, Ken. <u>Navies and Foreign Policy</u> (New York: Crane & Russak, 1977).

Breyer, Siegfried and Norman Polmar. <u>Guide to the Soviet Navy</u>, 2d ed. (Annapolis, Md.: Naval Institute Press, 1977).

U162.6 .B413 Beaufré, Andre. <u>Deterrence and Strategy</u>. Trans. R. H. Barry (New York: Praeger, 1966).

UA23 .C235 Canan, James W. <u>The Superwarriors: The Fantastic World of the Pentagon Superweapons</u> (New York: Weybright and Talley, 1975).

<u>CNO Report: A Report by Admiral James L. Holloway III, U.S. Navy, Chief of Naval Operations, on the Posture of the U.S. Navy, April 1977</u> Washington, Chinfo).

HC110 .D4W34	Cooling, Benjamin Franklin, ed. War, Business and American Society: Historical Perspectives on the Military-Industrial Complex (Port Washington, N.Y.: Kennikat Press, 1977).
	Couhat, Jean Labayle, ed. Combat Fleets of the World 1976-77: Their Ships, Aircraft, and Armament (Annapolis, Md.: Naval Institute Press, 1976).
	Davis, Jacqueline K. and others. SALT II and the Search for Strategic Equivalence (Philadelphia: Foreign Policy Research Institute, 1975).
	Defending America: Toward a New Role in the Post-Detente World (San Francisco, CA: Institute for Contemporary Studies, 1977).
JD9743 .U6F7	Fox, J. Ronald. Arming America (Cambridge: Harvard University Press, 1977).
VG76 .H489	Hezlet, Sir Arthur. Electronics and Sea Power (New York: Stein & Day, 1975).
	International Defense Review (Interavia: Cointrin-Geneva, Switzerland).
UA23 .K28	Kahan, Jerome H. Security in the Nuclear Age: Developing U.S. Strategic Arms Policy (Washington: Brookings, 1975).
HD9698 .G42K44	Kelleher, Catherine McArdle. Germany and the Politics of Nuclear Weapons (New York: Columbia University Press, 1975).
	Lens, Sidney. The Day Before Doomsday: An Anatomy of the Nuclear Arms Race (New York: Stein & Day, 1977).
	Lowenthal, Abraham F., ed. Armies and Politics in Latin America (New York: Homes and Meier, 1976).
UA23 .S38	National Strategic Information Center. Arms, Men and Military Budgets: Issues for FY 1978. Ed. by Francis P. Hoeber and William Schneider, Jr. (New York: Crane, Russak, 1977).

JX1974 .7.P49	Pfaltzgraff, Robert L. and Jacquelin K. Davis. *Salt II: Promise or Precipice?* (Washington: University of Miami Center for Advanced International Studies, 1976).
	Pechman, Joseph A., ed. *Setting National Priorities: The 1978 Budget* (Washington: Brookings, 1977).
U162 .P6	Polmar, Norman. *Strategic Weapons: An Introduction* (New York: Crane & Rssak, 1975).
	Risitzke, Harry, comp. and ed. *The Intelligence Community: History, Organization, and Issues* (New York: Bowker, 1977).
	Rosencrance, Richard, ed. *America as an Ordinary Country: U.S. Foreign Policy and the Future* (Ithaca: Cornell University Press, 1976).
UA23 .S23	Sanders, Ralph. *The Politics of Defense Analysis* (New York: Dunellen, 1973).
	Stoessinger, John G. *Henry Kissinger: The Anguish of Power* (New York: Norton, 1976).
VG632 .T38	Taylor, Michael J.H. and John R.W. Taylor. *Missiles of the World* (New York: Scribner, 1972).
D1065 .U5T73	Trezise, Philip H. *The Atlantic Connection: Prospects, Problems, and Policies* (Washington: Brookings, 1975).
TL781 .V59	Von Braun, Wernher, and Fred I. Ordway. *The Rockets' Red Glare* (Garden City, N.Y.: Anchor Press, 1976) [A history of rocketry in lay language.]
U162 .W35	Walters, Robert E. *Sea Power and the Nuclear Fallacy: A Re-evaluation of Global Strategy* (New York: Holmes and Meier, 1975).
	Wolfe, Thomas W. *The SALT Experience: Its Impact on U.S. and Soviet Strategic Policy and Decisionmaking* (Santa Monica, CA: Rand, 1976).

ABBREVIATIONS USED IN THE INDEX

<u>Nationalities</u>: Aust Australian; Br British; Du Dutch; Fr French; Ger German; It Italian; Jap Japanese; Ru Russian; Sp Spanish; US United States.

<u>Naval grades:</u>		<u>Air Force, Army, and Marine Corps grades:</u>	
ADM	admiral		
VADM	vice admiral	GEN	general
RA	rear admiral	LGEN	lieutenant general
COMMO	commodore	MGEN	major general
CAPT	captain	BGEN	brigadier general
CDR	commander	COL	colonel
LCDR	lieutenant commander	LCOL	lieutenant colonel
LT	lieutenant	MAJ	major
LTJG	junior lieutenant	CAPT	captain
ENS	ensign	LT	lieutenant

C/S	chief of staff
DOD	Department of Defense
Mar	Marshal
ONI	Office of Naval Intelligence
OSD	Office of the Secretary of Defense
SECA	Secretary of the Army
SECAF	Secretary of the Air Force
SECNAV	Secretary of the Navy
USA	United States Army
USAF	United States Air Force
USN	United States Navy
USSBS	United States Strategic Bombing Survey
WWI	World War I
WWII	World War II

INDEX

"ABCDs," 142, 143
ABC-1 Staff Agreement, 283
ABDA forces, 307-08
Acheson, Dean, 402, 443
Adams, Charles F. (US SECNAV), 242-44
Adams, John, 76, 79-81
Additional Fighting Instructions, 50
Aguinaldo, Emilio, 161
Ainsworth, Walden L., (US ADM), 336-37
Aircraft: early developments, 160; American contributions of, WWI, 202
(US) Aircraft carriers: take aviation to sea, 232; and the Morrow Board, 232; and the task force concept, 232-33; absent from Pearl Harbor, 7 Dec. 1941, 305
Algiers, 78, 84
Allan Ethan, 63
Allied Naval Council, 207-211
Almond, Edward M. (US GEN), 411
Amherst, Lord Jeffrey (Br GEN), 45, 46
Amphibious doctrine: ix-x; in the American Civil War, 119-20, 122, 124-26; in the Dardanelles campaign; 189-90; and the USMC, 235-36
Anderson, George (US ADM), 446, 459
Anderson, Robert B. (US SECNAV), 431-32
Anson, George (Br ADM), 38, 51, 57
Anzio, 291
ANZUS, 423
Arnold, Benedict (US GEN), 63, 68
Arnold, Henry H. (US AAC GEN), 387
Articles of Confederation, 75
Asiento, the, 35, 36
Atomic Weapons, 375, 378, 383
Austin, Bernard (US ADM), 339-40
Austria-Hungary, 179
B-1 bomber, 501, 609
Badger, George E. (US SECNAV), 102
Badoglio, Pietro (It MAR), 290
Bainbridge, William (US CAPT), 85, 88
Baldwin, Hanson W., 415
Bancroft, George (US SECNAV), 108-09
Barbary Powers, 74, 76, 77, 84-86, 94-95
Barbey, Daniel E. (US ADM), 335, 338-39
Barron, James (US COMMO), 75
Battle (of, for, off): Beachy Head, 19, 25, 34; Bismarck Sea, 335; Blenheim, 35; Borneo, 369-70; Bougainville, 338-40; Boyne, 34; Cape Engaño, 362-63; Cape Esperance, 328; Cape Matapan, 279-80; Cape St. George, 333; Caporetto, 209; Central Solomons, 333-40; Coral Sea, 311-14; 324; Coronel, 180-81; Dardanelles, 186-90; Dogger Bank, 182-83; Eastern Solomons, 327-28; Empress Augusta Bay, 333, 339-40; Falkland Islands, 180-81; Formosa, 355; Gabbard, 17; Gallipoli--see Dardanelles; Gilbert

613

Islands, 345-48; Guadalcanal, 325-33; Hampton Roads, 128-29; Hollandia, 350; Heligoland Bight, 181-82; Iwo Jima, 345-46; Java Sea, 308; Jutland, 182-85; Kolombangara, 336-37; Kula Gulf, 336-37; Lagos, 43-44; Lake Champlain, 89-90; Lake Erie, 89; Lepanto, 26; Leyte Gulf, 355-66; Malta, 280-81, 296-97; Manila Bay, 156-57; Marianas, 351-54; Marshall Islands, 347-48; Midway, 314-23, 324; Mobile Bay, 123-24; Moonlight, 59; Munda, 313; New Orleans, (1815), 90-91; (1862), 122-23; Okinawa, 371-74; Quebec, 50-51; Philippine Sea, 350-54; Port Royal, 112; Rabaul, 290; Saint's, 62; Salerno, 290; Samar, 363-64; Santa Cruz, Islands, 329-30; Santiago Bay, 158; Saratoga, 68-69; Savo Island, 326; Shilo, 132-33; Sibuyan Sea, 358-59; Spanish Armada, 29; Surigao Strait, 361-62; Tassafaronga, 331-32; Tarawa, 346-47; Texel, 19; Toulon, 19-20; Ushant, 69; Valcour Island, 68; Vella Gulf, 337; Vella Lavella, 337; Virginia Capes, 71-72

Beatty, David (Br ADM), 1 182-86

Belleisle, Louis, Duc de, 41

Benson, William S. (US ADM), 197, 203, 211

Berlin blockade, 380-81

Bibliographical aids, 1

Blockade runners, Civil War, 129-30

Board of Naval Commissioners, viii, 91, 95

Board on Construction, 145

Bogan, Gerald R. (US ADM), 358, 362

Bonaparte, Charles J. (US SECNAV), 175-76

Borah, William, 220

Borie, Adolph (US SECNAV), 140

Boscawen, Edward (Br. ADM), 44, 45

Braddock, Edward (Br. GEN), 39, 58

Bradley, Omar N. (US GEN), 398, 403, 405

Branch, John (US SECNAV), 99

Braun, Wernher von, 394

British colonizing methods, 30-32

Brown, Wilson (US ADM), 309

Bryan, William J., 163

Buchanan, Franklin (USN& CSN, 109, 121, 129

Buchanan, James, 111, 115

Bucher, Lloyd M. (US CDR), 480

Burgoyne, John (Br GEN), 68-69

Burke, Arleigh A. (US ADM): 332, 363; and destroyer doctrine, 333-35, 340-41; and the Battle of Empress Augusta Bay, 339-40; and the Battle of Cape St. George, 340; and OP23, 396, 398; and CNO, 432, 434, 435

Bureau system: viii, 102-03; revised during Civil War, 138; revised 1940, 298; revised 1966, 461

Butler, B.F. (MGEN,USA), 122, 123, 125-26
Byng, John (Br. ADM), 41-42
Cabot, John, 26
Calhoun, William L. (US ADM), 345
Callaghan, Daniel J. (US ADM), 330
Campioni, Angelo (It ADM), 276-77
Campos, Martinez (Sp GEN), 150
Cannon, naval, 8
Carden, S.H. (Br ADM), 187-88
Carleton, Guy (Br GEN), 68
Carney, Robert B. (US ADM), 414
Carter, Jimmie, 501-03
Castro, Fidel: seizes Cuba, 436-37; exports revolution, 437; and the Bay of Pigs, 442; and the Cuban missile crisis, 443-48
Cates, Clifton B. (USMC GEN), 404
Cervera, Pasqual (Sp ADM), 157, 138-59
Chadwick, French Ensor (US ADM), 174: first naval attaché, 143; and the Yorktown, 145; and the Bureau of Equipment, 148; and the Spanish-American War, 159-60
Chafee, John (US SECNAV), 478-83
Chandler, William E. (US SECNAV), 142
Chauncey, Isaac (US CAPT), 89
Chauvenet, William, 106, 109
Chennault, Claire L. (US GEN), 357
Chiang Kai-shek, 404

Chief of Naval Operations, ix, 197
China, "loss of," 381
Choiseul, Duc of, 43, 44
Chou En-lai, 408
Churchill, John. See Duke of Marlborough
Churchill, Winston, 187-90, 269
Civil War (US), 116-37
Clark, Joseph J. (US ADM), 350-54
Clark, Mark (US GEN), 290
Cleveland, Grover, 151
Clinton, John (Br GEN), 68, 69
Clive, Robert, 49
Colbert, John Baptiste, 224-25
Collins, J. Lawton (US GEN), 389, 405
Columbus, Christopher, 26
Command of the sea, 4-5, 92
Concentration, defined, 3
Conflans, Hubert (Fr ADM), 48
Connally, John (US SECNAV), 436, 457-58
Conner, David (US COMMO), 108, 110-111
Continental Navy, 66
Coontz, Robert E. (US ADM), 236
Crace, J.C. (Aust ADM), 312
Cradock, Christopher (Br. ADM), 181
Crutchley, V.A.C. (Br ADM), 326, 350
Crowninshield, Benjamin (US SECNAV), 91, 97
Cuba: in the Spanish American War, 150-65
Cuban missile crisis, 443-48
Cunningham, Andrew B.C. (Br.

ADM), 275, 277, 279, 287-88, 289
Cushing, William B. (USN LT), 129
Dahlgren, John A. (US ADM), 101, 107, 113, 125
Daniels, Josephus (US SECNAV): opposes preparedness for World War I, 196-97; directs naval effort in World War I, 199-203; and relations with the Allies, 203-11; and Sims's "Certain Naval Lessons of the War," 211-15
Darlan, Jean Francois (Fr. ADM), 261, 287
Davis, Charles Henry (US ADM), 133
Davis, Jefferson, 126
Davison, Ralph E. (US ADM), 358
D'Ache, Comte de (Fr ADM), 47-48
D'Estaing, Comte de (Fr ADM), 69
De Gaulle, Charles (Fr GEN and president), 269, 448
De Grasse, Comte (Fr ADM), 70-72
De la Clue, Sabran (Fr ADM), 44
De Langara, Don Juan (Sp ADM), 69
Decatur, Stephen (US COMMO), 85
De Lome, Dupuy, 153
Denby, Edwin C. (US SECNAV), 236-39
Denfeld, Louis E. (US ADM), 396
Destroyer deal, 1940, 264
Devereaux, James P.S. (USMC COL), 306
Dewey, George (US ADM), 156-57, 161, 173-74
Dickerson, Mahlon (US SECNAV), 99-100

Diem, Ngo Dinh, 450-51
Disarmament, nuclear. See Strategic Arms Limitation Tasks.
DOD: Reorganization Plan No. 6, 421; Reorganization Plan of 1958, 416-17, 420; and its budget, 1965-1970, 476-77; and its budget 1970-1974, 479-81
Doenitz, Karl (Ger ADM), 272, 273, 284, 291, 292
Doolittle, James (USAF GEN), 309, 310
Doorman, Karel (Du ADM), 308
Downes, John (USN CAPT), 96, 99
Duke de Choiseul, 43
Duke of Marlborough, 35
Dulles, John Foster, 423-27
Dunkirk evacuation, 267-68
DuPont, Charles (US ADM), 109, 122, 125
Eberstadt, Ferdinand, 389
Edison, Charles (US SECNAV), 244, 247-48
Edison, Thomas A., 198
Eisenhower, Dwight David, 410: and World War II in Europe, 286-95; and the New Look, 414-19; and Indochina, 424-25; and the Formosa Resolution, 426; and the Eisenhower Doctrine, 427-28
Ericsson, John, 119
European Defense Community, 421-22
Farragut, David G. (US ADM), 98: and the capture of New Orleans, 122-23; and the Mobile Bay campaign, 123-24;

and the Mississippi River campaign, 133-35
Faxon, William, 117
<u>Fighting Instructions</u>, 14-15, 18-21, 50, 72, 73; and the Formal and Melee Schools, 17-18
Finletter, Thomas K., 391, 415
First Continental Congress, 62
Fisher, John (Br ADM), 187-90
Fiske, Bradley A. (US ADM), 148, 157, 168-69, 172, 174, 176, 197, 241
Fitch, Aubrey (US ADM), 311
Fletcher, Frank Jack (US ADM), 306, 309, 311-14, 316-23, 325-26
Foote, Andrew Hull (US ADM), 131-32
Formosa Resolution, 426
Forests and sea power, 54-56
Forrestal, James V. (US SECNAV AND SECDEF), 301, 388-89, 391, 395, 396, 406-07
Forts: Barrancas, 116; Clinch, 116; Donaldson, 131; Duquesne, 43; Fisher, 124, 125-26; Gaines, 123-24; Henry, 131; Jackson, 116, 123; Morgan, 116, 123-24; Moultrie, 117, 125; Philip, 116, 123; Pickens, 117, 125; Pillow, 123; Pinckney, 115; Powell, 124; Pulaski, 116; Sumter, 115, 117-118, 125; Wagner, 125
Fox, Gustavus Vasa, 117, 125
Franke, William B. (US SECNAV), 435-36
Frederick the Great, 40, 50
Fremont, John (USA CAPT), 111, 115

Fukudome, Shigeru (Jap ADM), 355, 359
Fullam, William F., 174
Galissionere, Marquis de (Fr ADM), 41
Galley warfare, 6-7
Gates, Artemus, 244, 298
Gates, Thomas S. (US SECNAV), 433-35
General Board of the Navy, 173
Geneva Naval Conference, 1927, 226-27
Gensoul, Marcel (Fr ADM), 268
Germany (chronologically): and the Morocco crisis of 1905, 158; and the Morocco crisis of 1911, 158; and World War I, 165-202; admitted to the League of Nations, 235; and her Anticomintern Pact with Japan, 240, 246; and World War II, 250-283; admitted to NATO, 394-95
Ghormley, Robert L. (US ADM), 282-83, 324, 325
Gillis, James M. (USN LT), 114
Gilmer, Thomas (USN SECNAV), 106-07
Goering, Hermann (Ger Mar), 269, 270
Goldsborough, Louis M. (US ADM), 97, 122, 139
Gomez, Maximo, 150
Goodrich, Caspar F. (US ADM), 142
Gorshkov, Sergie G. (Ru ADM), 465-67
Graves, Sir Thomas (Br ADM), 70-72
Great Britain (chronologically): as a colonizer, 30, 34-36; and her weaknesses during the

War of the American Revolution, 57-58; issues Orders in Council during the Wars of the French Revolution, 68-69, 76-77; and her neutrality during the American Civil War, 116-17; and beginning of World War I, 166-75; and World War II, 235-65
Grenville, George, 60
Guadalcanal campaign, 325-33
Guam: seized by the US, 1898, 157; seized by Japan, 1941, 306. See Marianas Campaign.
Guam Doctrine. See Nixon Doctrine.
Halsey, William F. (US ADM): 309, 314, 329, 374: as Commander Third Fleet, 334; and the Battle of Formosa, 355; and the Battle of Leyte Gulf, 355-66; and the Battle of Cape Engaño, 362-63; in the China Sea, 374
Hamberger, DeWitt C.E. (USN officer), 333
Hamilton, Alexander, 76, 79
Hamilton, Ian (Br GEN), 189-90
Hamilton, Paul (US SECNAV), 87
Hara, Tadaichi (Jap ADM), 312
Hart, Liddle, 2
Hart, Thomas (US ADM), 300, 306, 308
Haswell, Charles H., 108
Hawke, Edward (Br ADM), 44, 48
Helfrich, Conrad (Du ADM), 308
Henshaw, David (US SECNAV), 106-07
Herbert, Hilary A. (US SECNAV), 147-48
Hewitt, H. Kent (US ADM), and the North African campaign, 287-88; and the Sicilian campaign; 289-90; and Operation Dragoon, 295-96
High-low, 491-94
Hill, Harry (US ADM), 346-48
Hipper, Franz (Ger ADM), 182-84
Hitler: 248, 250; seizes Austria, 250; seizes Czechoslovakia, 251; and the Munich Conference, 250; and the Rome-Berlin Axis, 251; and World War II, 251
Hobson, Richmond Pearson (US CAPT), 158, 197
Hofstadter, Richard, 155
Holtzendorf, Hennings von (Ger GEN), 193
Hood, Sir Samuel (Br ADM), 70
Hoover, John M. (US ADM), 345
Hosogaya, Moshiro (Jap ADM), 316-23, 344
House, Edward M., 211
Howe, Richard (Br ADM), 42, 43, 70
Hughes, Charles Evans, 221-24
Hull, Isaac (USN CAPT), 97
Humphreys, Joshua, 78
Hunt, William Henry (US SECNAV), 141-42
Iachino, Angelo (It ADM), 279
Ignatius, Paul R. (US SECNAV), 475-78
Indochina: occupied by Japan, 382; reoccupied by France, 382; and the Geneva Conference,

1954, 425. See Vietnam War.
Invasion of Italy, 290-91
Isherwood, Benjamin F., 118, 139
Island No. 10, 132
Italy: and World War I, 178-217; and World War II, 250-281
Jackson, Andrew, 98, 99
Jahncke, Ernest L., 242
Japan: and World War I, 220; and Manchuria, 229, 255; and the German-Japanese Anticomintern Pact, 256; and World War II, 304-379; occupied by the US, 375-76; treaty with the US, 1951, 423
Jefferson, Thomas, 76; and his naval plans, 82-86
Jellicoe, John (Br ADM), 183-86, 204-05
Johnson, Louis A. (US SECDEF), 397-399, 402, 406
Johnson, Lyndon B.: and the Great Society, 448-49; and the Treaty with Panama, 449; and intervenes in the Dominican Republic, 449-50; and the Second Vietnam War, 450-52; and the election of 1964, 452-53; declines to run in 1968, 453
Jones, Thomas ap Catesby (USN officer), 105, 109
Jones, William (US SECNAV), 91, 92-93
Jordan crisis, 1958, 428
Joy, C. Turner (US ADM), 403, 410
Kagawa, Kiyoto (Jap CAPT), 342
Kamikazes, 365
Kearney, Lawrence (US COMMO), 101, 105
Kennedy, John F., 436, 437: and the election of 1960, 438; and war options, 441; and the race to the moon, 442; and the Alliance for Progress, 442; and the Bay of Pigs, 442; and the Berlin crisis, 1961, 442-43; and the Cuban missile crisis, 443-48; and Indochina, 448
Kennedy, Robert F., 439, 446, 453
Kenney, George C. (USAAC GEN), 335
Kesselring, Albert (Ger GEN), 290
Key, Albert L. (USN officer), 176
Keyes, Sir Roger (Br ADM), 188
Key West Agreement on roles and missions, 392-93, 415
Khrushchev, Nikita: and the space race, 420-21; and "peaceful coexistence," 426-27; and the Berlin crisis, 1961, 442-43; and the Cuban missile crisis, 443-48; and the Soviet Navy, 465-67
Kimball, Dan Able (US SECNAV), 429-31
Kimmel, Husband (US ADM), 300, 306
Kinkaid, Thomas C. (US ADM): 335, and the Battle of the Santa Cruz Islands, 329-30; and destroyer doctrine, 331; and the Battle for Leyte Gulf, 354-66
King, Ernest J. (US ADM), 241, 284, 300, 301, 302, 306, 324, 334, 348, 386
King, James W. (USN

engineer), 141
Kirk, Allan G. (US ADM), 293-94
Kitchener, Horatio (Br GEN), 187, 189-90
Knox, Frank (US SECNAV), 297-301, 388
Koga, Mineichi (Jap ADM), 336, 346, 350
Kondo, Nobutake (Jap ADM), 316-23, 327, 329, 330
Korean War, 381-82, 402-13
Korth, Fred (US SECNAV), 458-60
Kuribayshi, Todamichi (Jap GEN), 370-71
Kurita, Takeo (Jap ADM), 309, 350 66
Kusaka, Kinichi (Jap ADM), 335
Kuznetsov, Nikolai G. (Ru ADM), 465
Kwajelein, 347-48
Laird, Melvin (US SECDEF), 489-90
Lansing, Robert, 200
Lavalette, E.A.F. (USN CAPT), 109
League of Nations, 216
League of Nations Disarmament Conference, 226
Leahy, William D. (US ADM), 286
Lebanon crisis, 1958, 428
Lee, Fitzhugh, 153
Lee, Willis A. (US ADM), 331, 350-54
LeMay, Curtis (USAF GEN), 385, 428
Lend-Lease Act, 264-65
Lenthall, John, 119, 139
Lincoln, Abraham, 116, 117, 118, 119
Lloyd George, David, 208-10, 221
Lockwood, Charles A. (US ADM), 352
Logistics, defined, 3

London Naval Conference, 1930, 227-28
London Naval Conference, 1935-36, 236-37
Long, John D. (US SECNAV), 154, 157, 173
Louisbourg, 39, 45
Lovett, Robert A. (US SECDEF), 406, 413, 430
Lowry, Frank J. (US ADM), 291
Luce, Stephen B. (US ADM), 140, 143, 174
Lynch, William F. (USN officer), 112, 114
MacArthur, Arthur (US GEN): and World War II, 306-378; and the Korean War, 402-13
McCalla, Bowman H. (US ADM), 158, 170
McCain, John S. (US ADM), 358
McCauley, (US COMMO), 118
Macdonough, Thomas (USN officer), 90
Mackenzie, Alexander S. (US CDR), 101, 105
McKinley, William, 151-64
McLean, Ridley (US ADM), 174, 176
McMorris, Charles H. (US ADM), 344
McNamara, Robert S. (US SECDEF), 439; and the managerial revolution in in DOD, 439-40; and growth of OSD, 440-41; and the Bay of Pigs, 442; and the Cuban missile crisis, 443-48; and the TFX, 457-60; and nuclear powered ships, 457-64
McNarney, Joseph (USAF GEN), 389
Madison, James, 87
Mahan, Alfred Thayer (US

ADM), 140, 143, 156
Mallory, Stephen, 111, 119, 128
Marlborough, Duke of, 42
Marshall, George (US GEN), 387, 388, 406
Mason, John Y. (US SECNAV), 107-08, 112
Mathews, Thomas (Br ADM), 37
Matthews, Francis P. (US SECNAV), 397-99, 406
Maury, Matthew F. (USN officer), 114
Mayo, Henry (US ADM), 204, 209
Mercantilism, 32-33
Merrill, Aaron S. (US ADM), 335, 338, 339-40
Metcalf, Victor H. (US SECNAV), 176-77
Meyer, George L. (US SECNAV), 169
Mikawa, Gunichi (Jap ADM), 326, 330-31
Mitchell, William (US GEN), 238
Mitscher, Marc A. (US ADM), 241, 349; and the Battle for Leyte Gulf, 350-66
Moffett, William A. (US ADM), 238, 241
Moltke, Helmuth von, 1
Montcalm, Marquis de (Fr GEN), 45
Montgomery, Bernard (Br Mar), 289-90, 293-96
Montgomery, Richard, 68
Montojo, Patricio (Sp ADM), 157
Moody, William H. (US SECNAV), 173
Moosbrugger, Frederick (US CAPT), 335, 337
Morrow Board, 232, 241
Morton, Paul (US SECNAV), 174-75
Mulberries, 294-95

Murphy, Robert, 286-87
Mussolini, 278: and the Rome-Berlin Axis, 261; enters World War II, 260; deposed, 290
Nagumo, Chuichi (Jap ADM), 309, 315-23
Nasser, Gamal Abdel, 427
National military policy, 1
National Security Act, 1947, 390, 391
National Security Act Amendments of 1949, 395
NATO. See North Atlantic Treaty Organization.
Naval disarmament conferences. See by name.
Naval Reserve Officers Training Corps, 242
Naval Strategy Board, 1898, 155, 173
Newberry, Truman H. (US SECNAV), 175, 177
Neutrality Patrol, 247, 264
Newcastle, Duke of, 40
"New Look" in diplomacy and defense, 414-19
Nimitz, Chester W. (US ADM), 248, 300, 306, 307, 348, 396; and the Battle of Midway, 314-23; and the Rabaul campaign, 324-43; and the battle for Leyte Gulf, 355-66
Nishimura, Shoji (Jap ADM), 308
Nitze, Paul H. (US SECNAV), 460-61
Nixon, Richard M., 424: and the election of 1960, 438; and the Vietnamization of the war, 453; and pulls out of Vietnam, 452-53; and the Nixon (Guam) Doctrine, 495

621

Norstadt, Lauris (USAF GEN), 39
North American Treaty Organization, 384-85, 404, 421-22
North African campaign, 286
North Sea Mine Barrage, 206-07, 211-12
NSC-68, 399, 403, 418
NSC-162, 417-18
Nuclear arms race, 420-21
ONI, 143
Ofstie, Ralph A. (US ADM), 383
Oldendorf, Jesse (US ADM), 351-52, 357, 361-62
Omori Sentaro (Jap ADM), 339-40
Onishi, Takajiro (Jap ADM), 365
Operation Anvil. See Dragoon.
Operation Avalanche. See invasion of Italy.
Operation Bolero, 286, 289
Operation Chromite, 405-06
Operation Dragoon, 295-96
Operation Dynamo, 267-68
Operation Flintlock. See Marshalls campaign.
Operation Game Warden, 455
Operation Galvanic. See Gilbert Islands campaign.
Operation Husky. See Sicilian campaign.
Operation Gymnast, 286
Operation Jackstay, 454-55
Operation Magic, 288
Operation Market Time, 455
Operation Menace (Dakar), 269
Operation Overlord, 291, 293
Operation Roundup. See Operation Overlord.
Operation Paperclip, 394
Operation Sea Lion, 285, 260, 269
Operation Sledgehammer, 286
Operation Solarium, 417
Operation Strangle. See Korean War.
Operation Torch. See North African campaign.
Operation Watchtower. See Guadalcanal campaign.
Ozawa, Jisaburo (Jap ADM): and the battle of the Java Sea, 308; and the Battle of Philippine Sea, 350-54; and the Battle of Leyte Gulf, 350-66
Panama and the canal, 449
Patch, Alexander M. (US GEN), 295, 333
Patton, George (US GEN), 287, 289
Paulding, Hiram (USN COMMO), 118
Paulding, James K. (US SEC-NAV), 97, 100-02
Pearl Harbor, 257, 304-05
Pepys, Samuel, 22-24
Perry, Matthew C. (US COMMO), 100, 101, 102, 105, 109, 110, 114
Perry, Oliver H. (USN officer), 89
Petain, Philippe (Fr. Mar), 286
Pierce, Franklin, 96
Pitt, William, the Elder, 40, 43, 45, 48, 49
Pocock, George (Br ADM), 49
Point Four, 384
Polaris, 433
Polk, James K., 108, 110
Porter, David D. (US ADM), 97, 123, 125-26, 134-35, 140-41
Potsdam Declaration, 374
Pownall, Charles A. (US ADM), 345
Pratt, William Veazie (US ADM), 204, 245
Preble, Edward (US COMMO),

622

Prince Henry the Navigator, 26
Privateers: in the War of the American Revolution, 67; in the War of 1812, 88, 92; in the American Civil War, 120, 127-28. See also Commerce raiders.
Proclamation Line of 1763, 59
Pueblo affair, 480
Raborn, William F. (US ADM), 433
Radford, Arthur W. (US ADM): and the "revolt of the admirals," 395-400; and the New Look in defense, 414-19
Raeder, Erich (Ger ADM), 269, 272
Ramsay, Bertram (Br ADM), 289-90, 294-95
Reuterdahl, Henry, 176
Richardson, James O. (US ADM), 300, 389
Richelieu, Cardinal of, 24-25
Rickover, Hyman G. (US ADM), 429, 431
Ridgway, Mathew B. (US GEN), 409, 414, 429
Roberts, Edmund, 99
Robeson, George M. (USN SECNAV), 140
Revel, Count Paolo Thaon de (It ADM), 207-10
Roach, John, 142
Robeck, John de (Br ADM), 189
Rochambeau, Count de, 71
Rockefeller Committee on Government Organization, 414-16
Rodgers, John (USN COMMO), 97, 100
Rodgers, John (US ADM), 141-42
Rodney, George B. (Br ADM), 85
69, 70, 72
Roosevelt, F.D.: 244-48, 293: and neutrality legislation, 1935-1939, 253; and Pan Americanism, 253-54; and the Casablanca Conference, 289
Roosevelt, Henry Latrobe, 244
Roosevelt, Theodore: 156, 158, 167, 176-77; and the Monroe Doctrine, 170; and the cruise of the Great White Fleet, 170-71, 176
Roosevelt, Theodore, Jr., 236
Rule of 1756, 79
Rusk, Dean, 439
Russia: and World War I, 179, 190, 250; and the Berlin Nonaggression Pact, 251; and the Berlin Blockade, 380-81; withdraws from North Korea, 381-82; obtains atomic weapons, 398; and builds a modern navy, 462-85; and SALT, 474-75, 486, 498-502
SALT. See Strategic Arms Limitation Talks.
Sampson, William T. (US ADM), 147, 153-54, 156, 157-60
Sanders, Otto Liman von, (Ger GEN), 188-89
Saunders, Charles (Br ADM), 46-47
Scheer, Reinhard (Ger ADM), 183-85
Schley, Winfield Scott (US ADM), 156, 159-60
Scott, Norman (US ADM), 328, 330
Sea, command of, 4-5
Sea power, influence of,

vii-viii, 73
Second Continental Congress, 63, 66
Semmes, Raphael (CSA), 121, 128
Seward, William H., 117
Shafter, William (US GEN), 158-61
Sherman, Forrest (US ADM), 390, 404, 405
Sherman, Frederick C. (US ADM), 338, 358
Shima, Kiyohide (Jap ADM), 357
Ships: round, sailing, 7-8; sailing characteristics of, 9; classification of, 10; nomenclature, 10-11; rigs, 11-12; of the line, 8-9, 12-14
Ships (by nationality).
AUSTRALIAN: Australia, 296; Hobart, 296; Sydney, 277

BRITISH: Amphion, 182; Ark Royal, 271; Barham, 279, 285; Canopus, 181; Devastation, 140; Dorsetshire, 271; Dreadnought, 162; Duke of York, 278; Eagle, 277; Exeter, 168; Formidable, 270-71, 280; Glasgow, 181; Good Hope, 181; Great Harry, 10; Hood, 270-71; 280; Illustrious, 276, 279; Invincible, 184; Irresistible, 189; Jamaica, 278; King George V, 271; Lusitania, 192-98; Malaya, 270; Monmouth, 181; Nelson, 294; Norfolk, 270; Ocean, 189; Otranto, 168; Prince of Wales, 271, 306; Queen Elizabeth, 274; Ramillies, 270; Renown, 271, 307; Rodney, 271, 294; Southampton, 279; Suffolk, 270, 271; Sydney, 261; Valiant, 274; 279, 290; Victorious, 270; Warspite, 279, 290, 294

CONFEDERATE STATES OF AMERICA: Alabama, 128, 129; Albemarle, 129; Arkansas, 133; Atlanta, 129; Chicora, 125; Florida, 128; Hunley, 129; Louisiana, 123; Manassas, 123; Merrimack, 119, 128; Mississippi, 123; Palmetto State, 125; Shenandoah, 128; Sumter, 128; Tennessee, 124; Virginia (see Merrimack).

FRENCH: Bearn, 261; Bretagne, 268; Dunkerque, 261, 268; Insurgente, 81; Jean Bart, 268, 288; Provence, 268; Richelieu, 272; Strasbourg, 261, 268; Sussex, 193, 200; Vengeance, 81

GERMAN: Admiral Scheer, 259, 254; Bismarck, 259; Blucher, 182, 266; Breslau, 180; Deutschland, 259, 265; Dresden, 181; Emden, 180; Gneisenau (1914), 181, (1939), 259, 266, 267, 270; Goeben, 180; Graf Spee, 259, 265-66; Hipper, 267, 270, 254; Karlsruhe, 180, 266, 251; Konigsberg, 266, 251; Leipzig, 181; Lutzow, 184, 296; Nurnberg, 181; Panther, 158; Prince Eugen, 270, 271; Scharnhorst (1914), 181, (1939), 259, 266, 270, 292; Scheer, 270,

624

296; *Seydlitz*, 182; *Tirpitz*, 259, 292-93

ITALIAN: *Calleoni*, 277; *Cavour*, 277; *Duilio*, 277; *Fiume*, 279; *Littorio*, 261; *Vittorio Veneto*, 279; *Zara*, 279

JAPANESE: *Abukuma*, 361, 362; *Akagi*, 315, 320; *Atago*, 358; *Chikuma*, 329, 364; *Chitose*, 362; *Chiyoda*, 362; *Chokai*, 364; *Fuso*, 364; *Hiei*, 307; *Hiryu*, 316, 320; *Kaga*, 315, 320; *Kirishima*, 331; *Kumano*, 365; *Maya*, 364; *Mikuma*, 321, 322; *Mogami*, 321, 322, 361, 362; *Musashi*, 359; *Myoka*, 373; *Ryujo*, 327; *Sendai*, 340; *Shoho*, 312, 313; *Shokaku*, 313, 314, 326, 329; *Soryu*, 316, 320; *Suzuya*, 360; *Taiho*, 353; *Takanami*, 332; *Takao*, 358; *Tama*, 362; *Yahagi*, 373; *Yamashiro*, 361; *Yamato*, 358, 364, 365; *Zuiho*, 329, 363; *Zuikaku*, 313, 326, 362, 363

RUSSIAN: *Arktika*, 465; *Kiev*, 470, 473; *Komar* boats, 462; *Lenin*, 465; *Leningrad*, 473; *Moskva*, 470-473; *Osa* boats, 465

SPANISH: *Maria Teresa*, 159; *Reina Mercedes*, 159

UNITED STATES: *Alabama*, 147; *Albacore*, 353,434; *Antietam*, 431; *Arkansas*, 222, 237, 294; *Astoria*, 326; *Atlanta* (1883), 142, 143, 145, 148; (CL-104) 330; *Badoeng Strait*, 411; *Bainbridge*, 460; *Baltimore* (1798), 88; (1886), 144 145; *Bismarck Sea*, 371; *Blue*, 326; *Boise*, 328; *Bon Homme Richard*, 456; *Boston* (1883), 142, 132, 145, 157 (CAG), 430; *Boxer*, 449; *Brooklyn* (1863), 124 (1892), 146, 148, 159; *Bunker Hill*, 347; *California*, 470; *Canberra* (CAG), 355; *Carolina*, 90; *Caroline*, 101; *Carondelet*, 132; *Cavalla*, 353; *Charleston*, 140, 144, 157; *Chesapeake*, 86, 88; *Chester*, 328; *Chicago* (1883), 140, 143, 145 (CA-136), 326; *Columbia*, 146; *Concord*, 157; *Congress*, 129; *Constellation* (1798), 81; (CVA) 433, 456, 482; *Constitution*, 78; *Converse*, 333; *Coral Sea*, 456; *Cumberland*, 129; *Dace*, 358; *Darter*, 358; *Delaware*, 175; *Dolphin*, 142; *Eisenhower*, 460, 488; *Enterprise* (CV), 234, 309, 314, 315 (CVAN), 433, 456, 458, 460, 488; *Essex*, 446, 458; *Florida*, 237; *Foote*, 340; *Forrestal*, 429, 455; *Franklin*, 372; *Fulton I*, 100; *Fulton II*, 100; *Galena*, 125; *Greer*, 255; *Gulflight*, 198; *Hancock* (CV), 430, 456; *Hartford*, 124; *Hasayampa*, 422; *Hornet* (CV), 234, 309, 328, 329; *Housatonic*, 129; *Houston*, 355; *Illinois*, 147; *Independence* (CV), 434, 456; *Indiana*, 146, 159;

Intrepid, 456; Iowa, (1890), 147, 148, 159; Itasca, 123; James, Reuben, 255, 283, 297; Juneau, 330; Jupiter, 232; Kearsarge (1864), 128; (1900), 147; Kennedy, John F., 461; Kentucky, 147; Kitkun Bay, 365; Kitty Hawk (1961), 456, 482; Langley, 236, 308; Lexington (CV), 232, 309, 312-14; Liscombe Bay, 323; Long Beach, 433, 461; Louisiana, 91, 125; Maine (1886), 144, 152-53, Massachusetts (1890), 135, 145 (1921), 272-288; Merrimack, 118; Michigan (1839), 104; Midway, 394; Minneapolis, 146; Mississippi (1839), 104, 112; Missouri (1839), 104; (1944), 350; Monitor, 119, 128-29; Nashville, 157; Nautilus (1944), 346; (SSN), 413, 429; Neosho, 311, 312; Nevada, 294; New Ironsides, 128; Newark, 143, 170; New York (CA), 144, 148, 159 (BB), 172, 460; Nimitz, Chester W., 460, 461; Northampton, 315; North Carolina, 234, (BB), 328; O'Brien, 328; Octarora, 124; Olympia, 144, 156; Oregon, 146, 159, 213; Oriskany, 456; Panay, 256; Pennsylvania (1816), 95; Petrel, 157, 158; Philadelphia (1798), 75; (1887), 144; Pinola, 123; Pittsburgh, 132; Powhatan, 112, 117; Princeton (1843), 104, 106, 107, (CV), 339, 340, 359; President, 80; Pueblo, 480; Quincy, 326; Raleigh, 157; Randolph (CV), 477; Ranger (CV), 234, 288, 434, 456; Roosevelt, F.D., 436; San Diego, 205; San Francisco (1887), 143; Saratoga (CV), 232, 234, 327, 339, 340, 369, 371, 413; San Jacinto, 112; Saranac, 112; Sargo, 435; Seagull, 98; Seawolf, 434; Shangri La, 461; Sicily, 411; Sims, 312, 313; Skate, 434; Skipjack, 434; Somers, 105, 109; South Dakota, 331; Spence, 341; Star of the West, 117; Susquehanna, 112; Suwanee, 365; Talbot, Ralph, 326; Tecumseh, 124; Texas (1886), 144, 159 (1910), 172, 294; Ticonderoga, 456; Trent, 117; Trenton, 140; Triton, 435; Union, 104; Utah, 237; Vincennes, 326; Vinson, Carl, 488; Wampanoag, 139; Washington (BB), 328, 329, 331 (SSBN), 406; Wasp (CV), 234, 328; Weehawken, 125, 129; West Virginia, 234, Wisconsin, 147, 294; Wyoming, 237; Yorktown (CV), 234, 309, 311-14, 322-23

Shufeldt, Robert W. (US ADM), 142
Sicard, Montgomery (US ADM), 153, 156
Sicilian campaign, 289-90
Sigsbee, Charles (US ADM), 154
Sims, William S. (US ADM), 172, 174, 176, 203-15
Slidell, John, 110

Sloat, John D. (US COMMO), 108, 111
Smith, Holland M. (USMC GEN): and the Gilberts campaign, 345-47; and Iwo Jima, 370-71
Smith, Robert (US SECNAV), 84
Soley, James R., 143, 147
Somers mutiny, 105
Somerville, James (Br ADM), 268, 369
Southard, Samuel L. (US SECNAV), 98-99, 101
Soviet amphibious forces, 470
Soviet merchant marine, 463-64
Soviet naval air, 468-69
Soviet Navy, 462-75
Spaatz, Carl (USAAC GEN), 396
Spain: as a colonizer, 26; and her Golden Century, 28-29; keeps the Mississippi closed, 74; and war with the US, 1898, 150-65; and air and naval bases for the US, 422
Spee, Count Graf von (Ger ADM), 181
Spencer, Philip, 109
Sperry, Elmer, 168-69
Sprague, C.A.F. (US ADM), 358, 362, 365
Sprague, Thomas L. (US ADM), 358, 365
Spruance, Raymond (US ADM), 354: and the Battle of Midway, 311-23; and the Gilberts, 345-47; and the Marshalls, 347-48; and the Battle of the Philippine Sea, 350-54; and Iwo Jima, 371-72; and Okinawa, 371-74; and the invasion of Japan, 374
Standley, William H. (US ADM), 246
Stark, Harold R. (US ADM), 284, 300
State navies, 66-67
Stevenson, Adlai, 439
Stimson, Henry L., 248, 297
Stockton, Robert F. (US COMMO), 101, 108, 111
Stoddert, Benjamin (US SECNAV), viii, 80
Strategic Arms Limitation Talks, 474-75, 486, 498-502
Strategy, defined, 1
Stringham, Silas (US COMMO), 117, 122
Struble, Arthur D. (US ADM), 404
Suez crisis, 1956, 437-48
Swanson, Claude (US SECNAV), 244-47
Symington, W. Stuart (US SECAF, 398, 440
Tactics, defined, 2-3
Tanaka, Raizo (Jap ADM), 327, 330, 331-32
Taylor, Henry C. (US ADM), 173
Taylor, Maxwell D. (US GEN), 429, 441, 443, 451
Taylor, Zachary (US GEN), 108; and President, 110
Tedder, A.W. (Br. Air Chief Mar), 289
Tenth Fleet, 285
TFX, 457-60
Theobald, Robert A. (US ADM), 318
Thomas, Charles S. (US SECNAV), 97-98
Tirpitz, Alfred von (Ger ADM), 192, 193
Tonkin Gulf resolution, 451-52
Toucey, Isaac (US SECNAV), 111, 115

Tovey, John (Br ADM), 270-71
Toyoda, Soema (Jap ADM), 350-54, 356
Tracy, Benjamin F. (US SEC-NAV), 144-45
Treaties (agreements, alliances, conventions): Aix la Chapelle, 43; Algeciras, 158; Amity and Commerce (Fr-Am, 1778), 69; ANZUS, 423; Casablanca, 289; Central Treaty (CENTO), 401; Five Power Naval Treaty, 223-24; Four Power, 222, 226; Franco-American Alliance (1778-1800), 71-72; Guadalupe-Hidalgo, 112; Geneva, 1954, 399, Ghent, 91; Jay's, 69; Kellogg-Briand, 239; London, Treaty of, 1916, 193, 195; London Naval Treaty, 1930, 214-15; London Naval Treaty, 1936, 216-17; Middle East Treaty, 427; Montreaux Convention, 435; Munich, 1938, 234; Nine Power Treaty, 222-23, 225, 255; Paris, 1763, 60; Paris, 1783, 74; Paris, 1898, 149-51; Pinckney Treaty, 79; Root-Takahira, 171; Rush-Bagot, 81; Ryswick, 38; SEATO, 423-24, 425; Taft-Katsura, 171; Tripartite Pact, 261; United States-Japan, 1951, 423; United States-Panama, 1965, 423; Utrecht, 40; Versailles, 216, 250-51
Trent affair, 127
Trident conference, 290
Tripoli, 84-85, 94
Truman, Harry S.: 301, 302, and the Truman Doctrine, 383-84; and the Marshall Plan, 384; and Point Four, 384; and the USSBS, 385-86; and the Korean War, 402-13
Truman Doctrine, 383-84
Truxton, Thomas (USN CAPT), 81
Tunis, 84, 94
Turkey, 180, 186-90, 383, 404, 428, 462
Turner, Richmond Kelly (US ADM), 300, 334; and the Guadalcanal campaign, 325-33; and the Gilberts campaign, 345-47; and the the Marshalls campaign, 347-49; and the Marianas campaign, 350-54; and Iwo Jima, 370-71; and Okinawa, 371-74
Turpitz, Alfred (Ger ADM), 192
Twining, Nathan F. (USAF GEN), 414, 428
Tyler, John, 105, 107, 108
Ugaki, Matome (Jap ADM), 350
Unification of the Armed forces, 386-400. See also National Security Act, 1947; National Security Act Amendments; "revolt of the admirals"
United Kingdom. See Great Britain.
Upshur, Abel P. (US SEC-NAV), 102-06
USA and the New Look, 417-18
USAF: and the unification of the armed services, and the New Look, 386-400, 417-18
US naval aviation: goes to sea, 169, 173, 232-33; and the Morrow Board, 232; and Moffett's Five Year Plan, 232;

628

and the Korean War, 411-14; and the Vietnam War, 455-56
US Marine Corps: doctrine devised following WWI, 235-36; in the Korean War, 394, 404-12; land in Lebanon, 1958, 428; in Vietnam, 456
US merchant marine, 463
US Naval Academy, 109
US Naval Institute, 142-43
USNROTC, 242
US Naval War College, 142-43
US Navy, functions of, 503-504
US Navy, ships, table of organization of, 1970, 491
USSBS, 385-86
Usedom, Guido von (Ger GEN), 188
Ushijima, Mitsuru (Jap GEN), 372
Van Buren, Martin, 100, 101
Vandegrift, Alexander A. (USMC GEN): and the Guadalcanal campaign, 325-33
Vandenberg, Hoyt T. (USAF GEN), 404
<u>Virginius</u> affair, 138, 140
Vinson, Carl, 245, 397-400
Vinson-Trammel Act, 245
Wainwright, Richard (US ADM), 143
Wake Island, 306
Walker, Frank R. (US ADM), 336
Walker, John G. (US ADM), 145
Walpole, Sir Robert, 36
War: American Civil, 106-26; American Revolution, 56-63; Austrian Succession, 34, 36-40; Barbary, 74-76; English Succession, 34; France (undeclared, 1798-1800), 70-72; of the Pacific, 130; of 1812, 76-83; King George's, 43-44, 58; King William's, 58; Korea, 402-14; Queen Anne's, 58; Seven Years', 39-51; Spanish-American, 138-52; Spanish Succession, 34, 35-36; Vietnam, 424-26, 448, 450-57; World War I, 178-217; World War II, 250-379

Washington, George, 39, 58, 63, 71, 76, 79
Washington Naval Disarmament Conference, 219-24
Watson, Charles (Br ADM), 49
Welles, Gideon (US SECNAV), 112, 116-38
Weygand-Murphy accord, 287
Weyler, Valeriano (Sp GEN), 150-51
Whitney, William C. (US SECNAV), 143-44
Wilbur, Curtis C. (US SECNAV), 239-42
Wilkes, Charles (USN CAPT), 96, 100, 114
Wilkinson, Theodore (US ADM), 336, 337, 338
Wilson, Charles E. (US SECDEF), 414, 416, 432
Wilson, Woodrow: opposes preparedness for WWI, 196; orders preparedness for WWI; 198-99; enters WWI, 200-01
Woodbury, Levi (US SECNAV), 99
Wolfe, James (Br GEN), 42, 46-47
Worden, John L. (US ADM), 129
Wright, Carleton (US ADM), 331-32
XYZ Affair, 79

Yamamoto, Isoroku (Jap ADM), 304, 310; 331; and the Battle of Midway, 315-23, 336

Zumwalt, Elmo R. (US ADM): and "Z-grams," 482; and high-low, 491-94

LIBRARY OF DAVIDSON COLLEGE

Books on regular loan may be checked out for **two weeks.** Books must be presented at the Circulation Desk in order to be renewed.

A fine is charged after date due.

Special books are subject to special regulations at the discretion of the library staff.

MAY 21, 1986